DEATH IN LIFE | *Survivors of Hiroshima*

BOOKS BY ROBERT JAY LIFTON

Death in Life: Survivors of Hiroshima
History and Human Survival
Boundaries: Psychological Man in Revolution
Revolutionary Immortality:
  Mao Tse-tung and the Chinese Cultural Revolution
Thought Reform and the Psychology of Totalism
Birds
Crimes of War (editor, with Richard Falk and Gabriel Kolko)
America and the Asian Revolutions (editor)
The Woman in America (editor)
Home From the War
Living and Dying (with Eric Olson)
Explorations in Psychohistory (editor, with Eric Olson)

SURVIVORS OF HIROSHIMA

DEATH IN LIFE

BY ROBERT JAY LIFTON

Basic Books, Inc., Publishers

NEW YORK

The author wishes to thank the following for permission to reprint material appearing in this book:

University of North Carolina Press—for a selection from *Hiroshima Diary* by Michihiko Hachiya, edited by Warner Wells.

Duell, Sloan and Pearce, an affiliate of Meredith Press—for a selection from *We of Nagasaki* by Takashi Nagai. Copyright, 1951, 1958 by Duell, Sloan and Pearce.

Harcourt, Brace & World—for selections from *Blood From the Sky* by Piotr Rawicz and from *Children of the Ashes* by Robert Jungk, translated from the Japanese by Constantine Fitzgibbon.

Grove Press, Inc.—for a selection from *The Long Voyage* by Jorge Semprun, translated from the French by Richard Seaver. © Copyright 1964 by Grove Press, Inc.

Hill and Wang, Inc.—for a selection from *Night* by Elie Wiesel.

Kawade Shobo Co., Ltd.—for a selection from *Shikabane No Machi* by Yoko Ota, © Copyright 1955.

Orion Press—for a selection from *Survivor in Auschwitz* by Primo Levi.

The Hokuseido Press—for a selection from *Devil's Heritage* by Hiroyuki Agawa.

Shincho-sha Co.—for selections from *Kuroi Ame* by Masuji Ibuse; and the *Japan Quarterly* for the use of a translation of *Kuroi Ame* appearing in the April–June, 1967, issue, parts of which I incorporated in my own translation.

Printed in the United States of America
10 9 8 7 6 5 4 3 2 1

To the memory of my father and the world of my children

CONTENTS

    DILEMMAS   451

XII THE SURVIVOR   479

    APPENDIX   543

    NOTES   557

    INDEX   577

    LIST OF SURVIVORS QUOTED   593

INTRODUCTION

Could it be that now, in 1982, we are finally beginning to confront what happened in Hiroshima? If so, why has it taken so long?

One of my most vivid memories of Hiroshima is of a particular moment in the commemoration ceremonies held on the evening of August 6, 1962—children of the Folded Crane Club (formed in response to the death from leukemia of Sadako Sasaki, the Anne Frank of Hiroshima), marching solemnly through the Hiroshima streets, chanting the words of the Hiroshima poet Sankichi Toge: "Give back my father, give back my mother,/give grandpa back, grandma back/Give our sons and daughters back!/Give me back myself, give mankind back. . . ." The children then stopped at a riverbank where, carrying out the evening's custom, they floated paper lanterns, each bearing the name of a person killed in the atomic bomb—in their case, the name of a child victim (see page 285).

Just a few weeks ago I encountered a similar scene, as recorded in a sensitive British documentary film shown widely on American television. In many other ways as well Hiroshima seems nearer to us than at any time in the past.

At meetings on the subject of nuclear war one regularly encounters pictures of Hiroshima victims.

August 6 and August 9 (the day of the bombing of Nagasaki) are increasingly commemorated in this country. An important new study of the physical, medical, and social consequences of the atomic bombings (*Hiroshima and Nagasaki: The Physical, Medical, and Social Effects of the Atomic Bombings*, Basic Books, 1981) has been produced by a Japanese group commissioned especially for that purpose. At the rally on June 12, 1982, at the time of the United Nations Special Session on Disarmament, it was the voices of the Hiroshima survivors that made the greatest impact on the 700,000 assembled.

Our new awareness of Hiroshima has been part of a striking increase of awareness with respect to nuclear weapons in general.

How important does Hiroshima remain for us? We know that the atomic bomb dropped on it was a tiny weapon compared to contemporary nuclear devices that are more than one thousand times its explosive power and of equivalent radiation effects. Yet we sense that Hiroshima has a special significance for us nonetheless. In the terrible narrative of nuclear weapons it is a source event, the abyss into which we can look. It is a form of what the Greeks called *kairos*, an early event which is decisive for the outcome of actual and potential future events.

"Tiny" as that first bomb was, the human impact was staggering, both because of the weapon's destructive power and of the endlessly delayed radiation effect. Only Hiroshima and Nagasaki can give awesomely concrete substance to our abstract nuclear terror.

Yet I reintroduce this description of Hiroshima in a spirit of new hope. That hope is founded on our evolving capacity to acknowledge Hiroshima and to make proper use of it. The June 12, 1982, New York City rally was another historical event—another form of *kairos* —suggesting that we possess the human power to prevail over the menace we have created, that the lesson of Hiroshima has not been lost.

But that process, too, has only just begun. Nor has the lesson yet been fully understood. We still have a very great deal to learn from Hiroshima and, above all, from its aging survivors. That knowledge, as much as any, can save us.

NOTE FROM THE AUTHOR

I have kept the book in its original form, rather than try to bring it up to date in terms of such things as further discoveries of cancers caused by the bomb or additional manifestations of social dislocations. I felt that the message was there.

It should also be noted that a film adaptation of this book was made in 1975 by Robert Vas for the BBC, with my collaboration, entitled: *To Die, To Live: Survivors of Hiroshima* (distributed in this country by Films, Inc., of Wilmette, Illinois).

DEATH IN LIFE | *Survivors of Hiroshima*

INTRODUCTION:
RESEARCH AND RESEARCHER

Research is a form of re-creation. I have tried to record the most important psychological consequences of exposure to the atomic bomb in Hiroshima. In order to relate the atomic survivor to general human experience, I extended the inquiry to include a wider concept of "the survivor" as an entity highly relevant to our times. These concerns in turn led to a study of death symbolism and the overall impact of nuclear weapons, which will be published later as a separate volume entitled *The Sense of Immortality*.

Hiroshima stimulates ready resistance within the would-be researcher. It does so partly because of its specific association with massive death and mutilation, and partly because of the general reluctance of those in the human sciences to risk professional confrontation with great historical events which do not lend themselves to established approaches or categories. In any case, I have little doubt of my own resistance to Hiroshima; I had lived and worked in Japan for a total of more than four years, over a ten-year period, before I finally visited the city in early April of 1962.

At that time I was completing two years of research on Japanese youth, as part of a long-standing interest in the interplay between individual psychology and historical change, or in "psychohistorical process." In Kyoto, where I was working, I thought only occasionally about the world's first atomic bombed city, which lay about two hundred miles to the southwest. Nor was Hiroshima mentioned particularly frequently by the young men and women, mostly university undergraduates, whom I was interviewing daily—except by those who happened to have grown up in its general area. The great majority had either no memory of the war at all or only the most meager recollections of it. But what became clear when I explored with them their sense of themselves and their world was the enormous significance for them, however indirectly expressed, of the fact that Japan alone had been exposed to atomic bombs. This historical "fact" had much to do with the power of the peace symbol for all Japanese. It played a very important part in the anti-war sentiment of the mass demonstrations of 1960, an extraordinary spectacle which I was able to observe closely and to discuss with militant young participants when they could free themselves for a few moments from their demanding activities on the streets. And it was a matter to contend with even in the "Revival Boom" which followed—the reawakened interest in war films, military music, and the literature of military strategy.

These seemingly opposite tendencies can be understood as related parts of a general struggle to cope with an unmastered past and a threatening future, a struggle in which Hiroshima faces both ways. The atomic bombings were experienced, even by Japanese born after they took place, as both an annihilatory culmination of a disastrous period of home-grown fascism and militarism, and a sudden infliction of a new and equally unfortunate historical destiny—a destiny which could, moreover, be repeated, and which was open to everyone. What I am saying is that nuclear weapons left a powerful imprint upon the Japanese which continues to be transmitted, historically and psychologically, through the generations. But I could not begin to understand the complexities of this imprint until I embarked upon my work with Hiroshima victims themselves.

One effect the atomic bombings had upon the Japanese, I soon discovered, was to create an intensity of feeling which could interfere with evaluating their human impact. When I began to look into the matter during two preliminary visits to Hiroshima, I discovered that despite the seventeen years that had passed since the bomb, no Japanese individual or group had carried out a detailed or systematic study of its general psychological and social effects. The few scholars who had initiated such studies had cut them short, and had either reported their findings in fragmentary, exaggeratedly technical form, or else had been so struck by the human suffering encountered that they ceased their research and dedicated themselves to programs of much-needed social welfare. Nor had anything more than preliminary surveys been attempted by Americans, despite their extensive involvement in studies of physical aftereffects. Here too it appeared that there were important emotional impediments.*[1]

The complexities of the research were to impress themselves upon me soon enough, but before discussing them it is well to say a word about factors contributing to my own involvement in the work. With a problem of this kind it is particularly mischievous to pretend that the investigator undertakes his study as a tabula rasa or an uncontaminated "instrument," totally free of bias or preconception. In my case there were at least three important influences upon both my decision to attempt the research and my way of going about it: a professional and personal interest in East Asian culture responsible for my being in Japan at the time; a central intellectual commitment to the study of the extreme historical situations characteristic of our era, and to the evolution of a suitable psychological approach to them; and concern with nuclear weapons and with psychological factors influencing war and peace. I had had enough experience to recognize the vicissitudes of work in these broad areas, the importance of a disciplined receptivity to truths built of unusual combinations, and the need to accept limitations in what one could expect to grasp and explain.

I was also aware of the significance of the investigator's relationship to the environment in which he has chosen to work. And I felt drawn to this glitteringly rebuilt, carefully planned city—its new roadways almost too wide and too even for its older atmosphere to encompass, its odd juxtapositions of contemporary tourist hotels and equally contemporary atomic bomb monuments, its attractive entertainment district, the mixed charm and plainness of its streets and of flat terrain that would be undistinguished were it not softened by the many interlacing branches of the Ōta River and set off by mountains in the distance.

But the issue for me in Hiroshima was the atomic bomb. During these first visits I sought out people who could tell me about the bomb's impact upon the city: scholars, writers, artists, doctors and administrators of medical programs, political and religious officials, and leaders of survivor organizations and peace movements. Almost all of these

---

* Numbered Notes are listed at the back of the book, beginning on page 557.

people had themselves experienced the bomb and then emerged as spokesmen, usually controversial ones, for some segment of the more than ninety thousand survivors in Hiroshima. I also talked to Europeans and Americans, some of them long-term residents of the city, others there on briefer professional and public missions. I heard complicated mixtures of personal experience and public response, and what emerged was less a clear picture than a psychological kaleidoscope of an extraordinary immersion in death, lasting imagery of fear surrounding the possibility of radiation aftereffects, and lifelong struggle to integrate the event and its elaborate web of psychic consequences. Hiroshima struck me as the only place in Japan where people were still, vividly and articulately, aware of World War II—but in a manner so special as to transcend the war itself. The most consistent impression of all was that there was much to be learned in Hiroshima.

I made the decision to extend my stay in Japan and devote six months to a systematic study of atomic bomb survivors. For most of that April, I commuted from Kyoto to Hiroshima; in early May, I moved there and remained until mid-September; and then spent a few additional weeks in Tokyo on atomic bomb issues that could best be pursued there. I conducted the research mainly through individual interviews with two groups of survivors: one consisting of thirty-three chosen at random from the lists kept at the Hiroshima University Research Institute for Nuclear Medicine and Biology* as a representative cross-section of responses; and the second consisting of forty-two survivors especially selected because of their general articulateness and particular prominence in atomic bomb problems—mostly the scholars, writers, physicians, and leaders mentioned before. It turned out that the two groups did not differ significantly in their basic psychological responses; rather, the contrasts in their manner of expression threw varying shades of illumination on common themes.

I have spoken so far of "atomic bomb survivors," but there is more to be said about the question of names. The Japanese use the term *hibakusha*,† as I shall throughout this book, to delimit those who have experienced the bomb. *Hibakusha* is a coined word whose literal meaning, "explosion-affected person(s)," suggests a little more than

---

* Names were selected at intervals of five hundred.

† Pronounced hi-bak'-sha. The Romanization system of the 1954 edition of Kenkyūsha's *New Japanese-English Dictionary* is used throughout the book. Japanese surnames are placed last, following Western rather than Japanese practice, both because they are rendered this way in many medical references cited, and as a means of emphasizing the general relevance of the Japanese experiences described.

merely having encountered the bomb and a little less than having experienced definite injury from it. The category of *hibakusha*, according to official definition, includes four groups of people considered to have had possible exposure to significant amounts of radiation: those who at the time of the bomb were within the city limits of Hiroshima as then defined (an area extending from the hypocenter—the place above which the bomb is thought to have exploded—to a distance of four thousand, and in some places five thousand, meters); those who came into the city within fourteen days and entered a designated area extending to about two thousand meters from the hypocenter; those who came into physical contact with bomb victims, through various forms of aid or disposal of bodies; and those who were *in utero* at the time, and whose mothers fit into any of the first three groups.*

But informally, the word *higaisha*, which means victim or injured party, and definitely conveys the idea of suffering, is used almost as frequently as *hibakusha*; and the Japanese word for survivor, *seizonsha*, is rarely employed by anyone other than scientific investigators, and not too frequently even by them. I was told that Japanese avoid *seizonsha* because it emphasizes the idea of being alive—with the implication that this emphasis is unfair to the less fortunate people who were killed. Thus, simply from the choice of terms, we begin to get a sense of the importance of the pattern of "guilt over survival priority," which we shall see to be a major theme of the experience, and also of the strength of the residual sense of victimization. Americans, on the other hand, generally use the word survivor, even as a rendering of *hibakusha* or *higaisha*. While this usage may be attributed to conventions surrounding the English word and to the need for a relatively neutral term, it may also reflect American tendencies toward "detoxifying" the experience.

In making arrangements for the interviews, I was aware of my delicate—even Kafkaesque—position as an American psychiatrist approaching people about their feelings concerning the bomb. From the beginning I relied heavily upon introductions—first from Tokyo and Hiroshima colleagues and friends to various individuals and groups in the city (particularly at the university, the medical school, and the City Office), and then from the latter to actual research subjects. In the case

---

* The exact distance from the hypocenter has great significance for the question of physical aftereffects. It also has importance for psychological responses, but we shall see that these do not lend themselves to the same precise correlation between distance and impact.[2]

of the randomly selected group, ordinary Japanese who would have been extremely dubious about a direct approach from a psychiatrist or an American, I first made a personal visit to the home, together with a Japanese social worker from the Hiroshima University Research Institute for Nuclear Medicine and Biology. He and I, in fact, spent many exhausting hours that spring and summer on the hot Hiroshima streets, tracking down these dwelling places. He would first present his card to the *hibakusha*, or if he or she were not home, to a family member, explain who I was, and introduce me. I would in turn present my card (which made clear my academic affiliation) and then exchange a few words with the survivor or family member, including a simple explanation of my purposes in undertaking the study. We would then either arrange for an interview appointment (usually in the small office I had rented near the center of the city, but sometimes, particularly in the case of elderly or ill *hibakusha*, right there in the home); or we would set a time for an assistant to return (or else telephone) to make interview arrangements, and frequently to pick up the *hibakusha* and accompany him to my office.

My previous experience in Japan, including the ability to speak a certain amount of Japanese, was helpful in eliciting the many forms of cooperation so crucial to the work. But perhaps of even greater importance was my being able to convey to both colleagues and research subjects my sense of the ethical as well as scientific issues involved: the conviction that it was important to understand people's reactions to exposure to nuclear weapons, and that rather than loose impressions and half-truths, systematic research was needed; and the hope that such research might make some contribution to the mastery of these weapons and the avoidance of their use, as well as to our general knowledge of man.

The community's willingness to trust these motivations was enhanced by a partly (but by no means entirely) fortuitous event—the publication, in the *Asahi Journal* (something like the *New York Times Magazine*) of a Japanese translation of an article I had written six months before on the Japanese peace symbol.[3] The article discussed the symbol's psychological ramifications, and while noting various manipulative abuses, argued that if preserved and deepened, it could have universal value. Many Hiroshima intellectuals and officials, including a number of those in my "special group" of research subjects, turned out to have read the article; and whether or not they agreed with everything it said, it enabled them to overcome whatever suspicion they might have had that I was simply trying to gather militarily useful information for the United States government. For precisely this suspicion had been held in relationship to other American research scientists working in Hiroshima on studies of physical aftereffects, as we shall discuss later.

In all, I was able to obtain excellent cooperation from *hibakusha*. Only on one or two occasions was I unable to arrange at least one detailed interview with people whom I contacted. Involved in this willingness to participate were, I believe, such factors as the response to an authoritative request (from a person or group of considerable standing in the city) that they meet and talk openly with me; the anticipation of finding an outlet for emotions and ideas about the bomb, either in the sense of spreading one's message to the world or of achieving therapeutic relief, or both; and a generally affirmative (though, as we shall see, by no means entirely unambivalent) feeling about my work.

The interviews, usually about two hours in length, were conducted in Japanese with the help of a research assistant trained to interpret in a way that allowed for maximum ease of communication. I tried to see each *hibakusha* twice, though I saw some three or four times and others just once. Throughout all interviews I encouraged spontaneous expressions of thoughts and feelings of any kind. But my questions were focused upon three general dimensions of the problem: recollection of the original experience and exploration of its meaning seventeen years later; residual concerns and fears of all kinds, particularly those surrounding delayed radiation effects; and the survivor's inner "formulation" of his experience, his struggles with mastery and with the overall *hibakusha* identity. I tape-recorded all sessions with research subjects in the randomly selected group, and many of those with the special group as well, always with the individual *hibakusha*'s consent, and had typescripts prepared in romanized Japanese (*rōmaji*) and English, thereby providing me with permanent voice and written records of the original Japanese.

I knew it was inevitable that after seventeen years elements of selectivity and distortion would appear concerning the original experience. I tried to evaluate these, in ways I shall later suggest, as having importance in themselves. But what impressed me throughout the work was the vividness of recall, the sense conveyed that the bomb was falling right there in my office—a vividness which seems to reflect both the indelible imprint of the event and its endlessly reverberating psychological repercussions.*

There was one other valuable source of "data"—my own reactions during the first few days of intensive interviewing, reactions which gave me new sympathy for the abortive and erratic nature of Japanese research on the problem. Prior to this I had held informal meetings during which matters far from pleasant were discussed, but on the whole at a general interpretive level. But now, instead of dealing with "the atomic bomb problem," I was confronted with the brutal details of actual experiences of human beings who sat before me. Despite considerable previous research experience with people subjected to "extreme situations," and a certain amount of beginning knowledge (from earlier informal talks and from reading) of the atomic bomb exposure, I was not prepared for the things that I heard. I found that the completion of each of these early interviews left me profoundly shocked and emotionally spent. I did not consider abandoning the enterprise, though I did feel some longing for the relatively relaxed atmosphere of my interviews with university students in Tokyo and Kyoto. But very soon—within a few days, in fact—I noticed that my reactions were changing. I was listening to descriptions of the same horrors, but their effect upon me lessened. I concentrated upon recurrent patterns I was beginning to detect in these responses, that is, upon my scientific function, and while I by no means became insensitive to the suffering described, a more comfortable operating distance between *hibakusha* and myself quickly developed. This distance was necessary, I came to realize, not only to the intellectual but the emotional demands of the work. The experience was an unforgettable demonstration of the "psychic closing-off" we shall see to be characteristic of all aspects of atomic bomb exposure, even of this kind of "exposure to the exposed." It also taught me the importance of "making sense" of the event, of calling upon one's personal and professional resources to give it form, as a means of coping with it.

What follows is a composite statement of what I consider to be the major responses to atomic bomb exposure, immediate and long-range. My emphasis is upon shared psychological and historical themes, but these themes express themselves through, and are inseparable from, individual psychological experience. In themselves they are neither

---

* These descriptions, moreover, were not only consistent with one another in their general emotional themes, but also with earlier published accounts, Japanese and American, insofar as the latter touched upon psychological patterns.[4]

pathological nor "normal." Rather, they are consistent human adaptations to nuclear weapons exposure. They both resemble and differ from themes encountered in other disasters, and in other kinds of survivors, as we shall discuss in the final chapter. They take shape within the psychological contours of Japanese culture, but are distinctly universal in nature.* And while their composite description includes more than any individual person could have experienced, nothing in it is alien to any *hibakusha*.

:

My work stems from the psychoanalytic tradition. But in evolving a modified psychoanalytic approach, I have been moving toward the kind of symbolic and thematic emphasis now prominent in much scientific thought which focuses upon form and configuration. The analytic component remains important, though not in the nineteenth-century sense of attributing all observations to ultimate explanatory mechanisms. Rather, the stress is upon the development of psychic forms, or upon a "psychoformative" perspective. I shall take up these general theoretical issues in my next volume, but this perspective will be evident as we confront Hiroshima's vast patterns of disintegration as well as its efforts at psychic rebuilding or "formulation."

I have learned much over the years from exchanges with Erik Erikson; he and I took the initiative in forming the Group for the Study of Psychohistorical Process, to whom parts of the final chapter of the book were first presented. David Riesman and Kenneth Keniston shared generously in the complex explorations of the study. Frederick C. Redlich, formerly Chairman of the Department of Psychiatry and now Dean of the School of Medicine at Yale, did much to make it possible. All four made helpful suggestions concerning the manuscript, as did Howard Hibbett, who was kind enough to make a careful final reading. L. Takeo Doi contributed much during our by now traditional dialogues in Tokyo and New Haven. Kiyoshi Shimizu and Shōji Watanabe of Hiroshima University provided invaluable help with research arrangements; and Lawrence Freedman of the Department of Medicine at Yale

---

* The principle involved here is the three-way interplay I have elsewhere suggested to be applicable to all group behavior: psychological tendencies common to all mankind, those given special emphasis within a particular (in this case, Japanese) cultural tradition, and those stimulated by contemporary historical forces. Under extreme conditions, universal patterns become especially manifest. But while in this study I stress psychological universality and specific (atomic bomb) historical experience, I refer to cultural emphases as well, and try to avoid an "either-or" or "nothing-but" position.[5]

counseled on physical effects of the bomb. All conclusions are of course my own.

Since my knowledge of spoken Japanese is limited and I do not read the language, I depended greatly upon the skillful research assistance of Kyōko Ishikure and Kaoru Ogura, as well as upon the bilingual transcriptions of Yaeko Sato. Mrs. Lily B. Finn prepared the manuscript with her usual dedication and care. John J. Simon and Rachel Whitebook of Random House gave sensitive editorial advice.

The various kinds of help contributed by my wife, Betty Jean Lifton, extended from the moment of our arrival in Hiroshima (and before that) to the last revision.

Finally, I am extremely grateful to the many people of Hiroshima who gave so much of themselves, both as "research subjects" and as fellow observers of a problem demanding attention.

HIROSHIMA

one

The Name of a City

One hears the word and wants to know more, but one also wants to forget it. One has heard both too much and not enough about Hiroshima. For the city evokes our entire nuclear nightmare, and any study of it must begin with this symbolic evocation.

Its literal meaning, "broad island," suggests little more than the city's relationship to rivers and to the sea. Does one care about the literal meaning of Carthage, Troy, Sparta, Ch'ang An, Lidice, or Coventry? What Hiroshima does convey to us—indeed press upon us—is the realization that it actually happened and the implication that it could happen again. The mythological metaphors usually employed to suggest this idea—the genie let out of the bottle or Pandora's box opened—do not seem adequate for the phenomenon. That of man threatened by his Frankenstein comes closer, but this more recent myth, though technologically based, humanizes and keeps finite its monster. We need new myths to grasp our relationship to the cool, ahuman, *completely* technological deity which began its destructive reign with Hiroshima.

It has often been pointed out that statistics of the power of the blast, or even of the number of people killed in Hiroshima, convey no sense of the brutalized human being, because "statistics don't bleed." The statement is true, and I shall have much to say about the phenomenon of "psychic numbing" which it illustrates. But it can also be somewhat misleading. For when we hear reports about the Hiroshima bomb, our emotions are not exactly the same as when confronted with equivalent evidence of bomb destruction in London, Amsterdam, Hamburg, Dresden, or Tokyo. These cities, to be sure, convey their own messages of man's capacity and inclination to assault himself. But with Hiroshima (and her neglected historical sister, Nagasaki) something more is involved: a dimension of totality, a sense of ultimate annihilation—of cities, nations, the world.

The feeling may be vague, but it is of the greatest psychological importance. What I am suggesting is that our perceptions of Hiroshima are the beginnings of new dimensions of thought about death and life. These perceptions, of course, are strongly affected by what we psychically bring to Hiroshima, by deep need for its wisdom no less than debts of guilt. But our need and guilt are ultimately bound to what actually happened there. And what did happen—what people in Hiroshima experienced and felt—seems to be precisely what we have thought least about. I am genuinely uncertain as to how adequately my study of Hiroshima survivors can fill this strange gap in our knowledge, or even whether a complete grasp of the bomb's human effects could influence our fortunes in our current struggles with the new deity. But I am thoroughly convinced that the encounter of people in Hiroshima with the atomic bomb has specific bearing upon all nuclear age existence. It follows that a better understanding of what lies behind this word, this name of a city, might enable us to take a small step forward in coming to terms with that existence.

THE ATOMIC BOMB EXPERIENCE

two

1) Anticipation

Anticipation is prior imagination, and the extent of one's capacity to imagine a profound event has important bearing upon the way in which one responds. In the case of Hiroshima's encounter with the atomic bomb, the predominant general tone was that of extreme surprise and unpreparedness. Neither past experience nor immediate perceptions—the two sources of prior imagination—could encompass what was about to occur.[1]

People did, of course, expect conventional bombing. They knew that Japanese cities were being attacked from the air, and they could observe the destructive power of American raids in the devastation of the nearby naval base of Kure. Though wartime censorship kept them from full knowledge of Japan's desperate plight, such things as diminishing food rations and the lull in military activity in their own city were indications that the situation was serious. They also noted the large-scale demolition work underway in Hiroshima, for which thousands of schoolchildren had been recruited, in the effort to create fire lanes to control anticipated conflagration. They wondered when Hiroshima's turn would come.

They were puzzled that virtually no bombs had been dropped on their city, despite its obvious strategic significance as a major staging area for Japan's military operations in China and Southeast Asia, its large military population, and its war industries. There had been frequent air-raid warnings when planes passed over Hiroshima on the way to other targets, and when single planes dropped relatively innocuous bombs on what turned out to be practice runs for the atomic bomb mission. Gradually realizing that Hiroshima was one of the few major Japanese cities not yet badly bombed, people sought to comprehend this strange state of affairs through various rumors which began to circulate.

Some of these rumors were strongly wishful, such as the very common one emphasizing the fact that sizable numbers of people from the area had emigrated to America. As an elderly widow recalled:

> Hiroshima was so related to America. . . . So many people had relatives in America, and therefore America would show sympathy toward Hiroshima—there were many in our neighborhood who had relatives in America, and believed this.

Equally wishful was the idea that both Hirsohima and Kyoto were being spared because they were "so beautiful that Americans might build their villas there [after occupying Japan]. . . ."* Other rumors minimized Hiroshima's military significance: "There were not too many big factories in Hiroshima . . . so we thought it would not be bombed until all of the really big cities had been bombed." There was also a rumor that Americans were holding back because of the presence of "important foreigners" in Hiroshima, and a German priest who, with his missionary colleagues, made up virtually the entire foreign population, told me how in those days Japanese officials would sometimes, with half-humorous seriousness, comment appreciatively to him that things were all right "thanks to you."† In a somewhat similar vein was the even more far-fetched rumor that a relative of President Truman—"perhaps his mother"—was in the area. The underlying element of denial in these rumors is suggested by another expression of anxious humor· "We

---

* Sometimes mentioned in support of this rumor was the proximity to Hiroshima of the island of Miyajima, a place of considerable beauty as well as religious significance. For Kyoto the rumor turned out to be partly true—the city was given a last-minute reprieve from atomic bombing, not because of any plan to build American villas there, but because of its unique cultural importance and concern about the consequences should it be annihilated.[2]

† The Japanese phrase, *okagesama de*, is more vague in its connotation. Literally "under your shadow," it is used to convey one's actual or ostensible gratitude toward another, usually of superior status, for his beneficent influence. There were also rumors, apparently never confirmed, that American prisoners of war were in Hiroshima. One *hibakusha* insisted to me that he saw, in a Japanese military area soon after the bomb fell, a severely wounded and moribund GI.

thought that perhaps the city of Hiroshima was not on the American maps."

But there was also the opposite kind of rumor—"the Americans must be preparing something unusually big" for the city—which turned out to be true. Some discussed this possibility in terms of a "special bomb"; and there was an occasional skeptical reference among scientists to an actual atomic bomb. As one mathematician put it, "I doubted that such a bomb could be made. . . . We simply discussed the possibility."*

Many used the Japanese word *bukimi*, meaning weird, ghastly, or unearthly, to describe Hiroshima's uneasy combination of continued good fortune and expectation of catastrophe. People remembered saying to one another, "Will it be tomorrow or the day after tomorrow?" One man described how, each night he was on air-raid watch, "I trembled with fear. . . . I would think, 'Tonight it will be Hiroshima.'" These "premonitions" were partly attempts at psychic preparation, partly a form of "imagining the worst" as a magical way of warding off disaster.

Leaflets were dropped on Hiroshima from American planes on July 27, threatening Hiroshima (and other major cities on which they were dropped) with total destruction if Japan did not surrender immediately, but they made no mention of the atomic bomb or of any other special weapon. Nor did the leaflets appear to have reached many people—only a single person among those I interviewed, then a child, remembered picking one of them up, and when he brought it back to his elders, they scoffed at it, whether out of genuine disbelief or, more likely, a sense of how one was supposed to react to such a threat. In any case, the people of Hiroshima received no warning about the atomic bomb; American policymakers, for various strategic reasons, had decided against any prior notice.†

Still another factor added to the surprise. After two air-raid alerts during the night the sirens had sounded a third time in Hiroshima at 7:10 A.M. because of planes sighted over southern Japan. Some time later a single B-29 approaching the city (which turned out to be the atomic bomb mission's weather plane) was seen, but since it quickly

---

* Scientists throughout the world shared enough information about nuclear chain reactions to know that an atomic bomb was theoretically feasible, but few considered it at all likely that one could actually be made at that time.

† A number of American scientists and a few political and military leaders favored some form of warning or demonstration prior to any use of the bomb on a populated area. But they were overruled because the alternatives they suggested "were judged impractical, ineffective, or risky."[3] The debate on this issue still continues in this country.

departed, the all-clear was sounded at 7:32 A.M. Shortly after 8 A.M., air-defense spotters observed two or three additional B-29s (the planes which carried out the atomic bombing) heading for Hiroshima, but no additional alert was sounded; a radio broadcast mentioned the planes, urging that people take shelter should the planes appear over the city, and then adding the reassuring note that they seemed to be only on a reconnaissance mission.[4]

This reassurance might have been one of the reasons why most of those I interviewed in Hiroshima had the impression that the all-clear had sounded "just a few minutes" before the bomb fell. In any case, with alerts so frequent and the city remaining untouched, few bothered to take shelter, and those who did emerged. But the combination of the alert and the all-clear created the psychological sense that the danger had already approached and receded—that one had already "been through it."

Since people began their days early during the wartime summer, many were already at work or en route to their jobs by foot or public conveyances. Housewives were completing after-breakfast chores with the charcoal in their *hibachi* (small braziers) still burning (a factor thought to contribute to the fires that sprang up when the bomb fell). The general atmosphere of the city was apparently one of early-morning wartime routine—Hiroshima's equivalent of a "rush hour." But in retrospect it was to seem idyllic, as we sense from a description written later by a history professor:

The sky was serene, the air was flooded with glittering morning light. My steps were slow along the dry, dusty road. I was in a state of absent-mindedness. The sirens and also the radio had just given the all-clear signal. I had reached the foot of a bridge, where I halted, and was turning my eyes toward the water. . . .

People were unprepared for the atomic bomb on many psychological dimensions: the immediate relaxation induced by the all-clear signal, the feeling of being in some way specially protected, the general sense of invulnerability which all people in some measure possess even (or especially) in the face of danger, and the *total inability to conceive of the unprecedented dimensions of the weapon about to strike them.* As one man put it: "We thought something would happen, but we never imagined anything like the atomic bomb."

2) *Immersion in Death*

Only those at some distance from the explosion could clearly distinguish the sequence of the great flash of light accompanied by the lacerating heat of the fireball, then the sound and force of the blast, and finally the impressive multicolored cloud rising high above the city. This awesome spectacle was not without beauty—as recorded by the same history professor, who witnessed it from a suburb five thousand meters (a little more than three miles) away:

A blinding . . . flash cut sharply across the sky. . . . I threw myself onto the ground . . . in a reflex movement. At the same moment as the flash, the skin over my body felt a burning heat. . . . [Then there was] a blank in time . . . dead silence . . . probably a few seconds . . . and then a . . . huge "boom" . . . like the rumbling of distant thunder. At the same time a violent rush of air pressed down my entire body. . . . Again there were some moments of blankness . . . then a complicated series of shattering noises. . . . I raised my head, facing the center of Hiroshima to the west. . . . [There I saw] an enormous mass of clouds . . . [which] spread and climbed rapidly . . . into the sky. Then its summit broke open and hung over horizontally. It took on the shape of . . . a monstrous mushroom with the lower part as its stem—it would be more accurate to call it the tail of a tornado. Beneath it more and more boiling clouds erupted and unfolded sideways. . . . The shape . . . the color . . . the light . . . were continuously shifting and changing. . . .

Even at that distance, he and others experienced what is called the "illusion of centrality," as is succinctly suggested by a later poem originally written in the classical tanka style:

Thinking a bomb must have fallen close to me, I looked up, but it was a pillar of fire five kilometers ahead.*

* No attempt has been made to retain in translation the classical form of the Japanese—*i.e.*, thirty-one syllables in five lines of, respectively, five, seven, five, seven, and seven syllables.[5]

This illusion, usually attributed to the sudden loss of a sense of invulnerability, is actually an early perception of death encounter, a perception which the atomic bomb engendered at enormous distances.

The bomb was completely on target and exploded, with a force equivalent to twenty thousand tons of TNT, eighteen hundred feet in the air near the center of a flat city built mainly of wood. It created an area of total destruction (including residential, commercial, industrial, and military structures) extending three thousand meters (about two miles) in all directions; and destroyed sixty thousand of ninety thousand buildings within five thousand meters (over three miles), an area roughly encompassing the city limits. Flash burns from the heat generated by the release of an enormous amount of radiant energy occurred at distances of more than four thousand meters (two and a half miles), depending upon the type and amount of clothing worn and the shielding afforded by immediate surroundings. Injuries from the blast, and from splintered glass and falling debris, occurred throughout the city and beyond.

The number of deaths, immediately and over a period of time, will probably never be fully known. Variously estimated from 63,000 to 240,000 or more, the official figure is usually given as 78,000, but the city of Hiroshima estimates 200,000—the total encompassing between 25 and 50 per cent of the city's then daytime population (also a disputed figure, varying from 227,000 to over 400,000). The enormous disparity is related to the extreme confusion which then existed, to differing methods of calculation, and to underlying emotional influences, quite apart from mathematical considerations, which have at times affected the estimators. An accurate estimate may never be possible, but what can be said is that *all of Hiroshima immediately became involved in the atomic disaster.**

Two thousand meters (1.2 miles) is generally considered to be a crucial radius for susceptibility to radiation effects, and for high mortality in general—from blast, heat, or radiation—though many were killed outside of this radius. Within it, at points close to the hypocenter, heat was so extreme that metal and stone melted, and human beings were literally incinerated. The area was enveloped by fires fanned by a violent "firewind"; these broke out almost immediately within a radius

---

* The aiming point was a central area adjacent to an Army Headquarters, but so congested were nearby commercial and residential districts that 60 per cent of the population was within 1.2 miles of the hypocenter. The accuracy of the drop was said to be such that the bomb exploded within two hundred yards of the aiming point.[6]

of more than three thousand meters (up to two miles). The inundation with death of the area closest to the hypocenter was such that if a man survived within a thousand meters (.6 miles) and was out of doors (that is, without benefit of shielding from heat or radiation), more than nine tenths of the people around him were fatalities; if he was unshielded at two thousand meters, more than eight of ten people around him were killed. Mortality indoors was lower, but even then to have a 50-per-cent chance of escaping both death or injury, one had to be about twenty-two hundred meters (1.3 miles) from the hypocenter.

Those closest to the hypocenter could usually recall a sudden flash, an intense sensation of heat, being knocked down or thrown some distance, and finding themselves pinned under debris or simply awakening from an indeterminate period of unconsciousness. *The most striking psychological feature of this immediate experience was the sense of a sudden and absolute shift from normal existence to an overwhelming encounter with death.* This is described by a shopkeeper's assistant, who was thirteen years old at the time of the bomb and fourteen hundred meters from the hypocenter:

I was a little ill . . . so I stayed at home that day. . . . There had been an air-raid warning and then an all-clear. I felt relieved and lay down on the bed with my younger brother. . . . Then it happened. It came very suddenly. . . . It felt something like an electric short—a bluish sparkling light. . . . There was a noise, and I felt great heat—even inside of the house. When I came to, I was underneath the destroyed house. . . . I didn't know anything about the atomic bomb so I thought that some bomb had fallen directly upon me. . . . And then when I felt that our house had been directly hit, I became furious. . . . There were roof tiles and walls—everything black—entirely covering me. So I screamed for help. . . . And from all around I heard moans and screaming, and then I felt a kind of danger to myself. . . . I thought that I too was going to die in that way. I felt this way at that moment because I was absolutely unable to do anything at all by my own power. . . . I didn't know where I was or what I was under. . . . I couldn't hear voices of my family. I didn't know how I could be rescued. I felt I was going to suffocate and then die, without knowing exactly what had happened to me. This was the kind of expectation I had. . . .

Characteristic here is the way in which the dominant theme of individual and group death encompasses all other emotions—including those of confusion, helplessness, and abandonment, prominent in adults as well as in children.

Many others (perhaps with retrospective reconstruction, but not without significance in any case) recalled initial feelings related to death and dying, such as "This is the end for me"; "My first feeling was, 'I think I will die' "; and, in the case of a psychologist, then a university student, who found himself pinned under the heavy beams of a collapsed house at two thousand meters, and abandoned by two friends who had unsuccessfully attempted to pull him out:

> I began to see my mother's image before me. . . . I regretted that I was going to die. I thought I was young, and had just been successful in very difficult [academic] competition. . . . I wanted to study more in the life ahead of me. . . . And I was dying without seeing my parents.

This kind of maternal image was reminiscent of reports about Japanese soldiers in World War II: trained to go to their deaths with the phrase "Long live the Emperor" on their lips, they instead called out, "Mother!" Both cases suggest an effort to reassert the ultimate human relationship in the face of death's severance, along with (as the psychologist made clear) a protest against what is perceived as premature death.

Beyond these feelings was the sense that *the whole world was dying*. A physicist, covered by falling debris, found himself temporarily blinded:

> My body seemed all black, everything seemed dark, dark all over. . . . Then I thought, "The world is ending."

A Protestant minister, himself uninjured, but responding to the evidence of mutilation and destruction he saw everywhere around him during extensive wanderings throughout the city, experienced his end-of-the-world imagery in an apocalyptic Christian idiom:

> The feeling I had was that everyone was dead. The whole city was destroyed. . . . I thought all of my family must be dead—it doesn't matter if I die. . . . I thought this was the end of Hiroshima—of Japan—of humankind. . . . This was God's judgment on man. . . .

And a woman writer, Yōko Ōta:

> I just could not understand why our surroundings had changed so greatly in one instant. . . . I thought it might have been something

which had nothing to do with the war, the collapse of the earth which it was said would take place at the end of the world, and which I had read about as a child. . . .[7]

This sense of world-collapse could also be expressed symbolically, as in the immediate thought of a devoutly religious domestic worker: "There is no God, no Buddha."

For many, immersion in death was epitomized by olfactory imagery— by memories of "the constant smell of dead bodies," and the lasting nature of those memories: "I can feel the smell of those dead bodies in my nostrils even now." The survivor originally experienced this "smell of death" not only from corpses around him but from the general odor of mass open cremations soon carried out by authorities (both for the prevention of disease and in accordance with Japanese custom); however derived, it became psychologically interwoven with the entire atomic bomb experience.

These cremations could even give rise to a certain amount of "atomic bomb gallows humor," as in the case of a professional cremator who, despite severe burns, managed to make his way back to his home (adjoining the crematorium), and said he then felt relieved because "I thought I would die soon, and it would be convenient to have the crematorium so close by."

DEATH IN LIFE

Beyond death imagery per se, there was a widespread sense that life and death were out of phase with one another, no longer properly distinguishable—which lent an aura of weirdness and unreality to the entire city. This aura was often conveyed by those who had been on the outskirts of the city and entered it after the explosion, as was true of an electrician, then in his mid-forties, working at a railroad junction five thousand meters from the hypocenter.

I was setting up a pole . . . near a switch in the railroad tracks. . . . There was a flash . . . a kind of flash I had never seen before, which I can't describe. . . . My face felt hot and I put my hands over my eyes and rushed under a locomotive that was nearby. I crawled in between the wheels, and then there was an enormous boom and the locomotive shook. I was frightened, so I crawled out. . . . I couldn't tell what happened. . . . For about five minutes I saw nobody, and then I saw someone coming out from an air-raid shelter who told me that the youngest one of our workers had been injured by falling piles . . . so I put the injured man on the back of my bicycle and tried to take him to the dispensary. Then I saw that almost all of the people in that area were crowded into the dispensary, and since there was also a hospital nearby, I went there. But that too was already full. . . . So the only thing to do was to go into [the center of] Hiroshima. But I couldn't move my bicycle because of all the people coming out from Hiroshima and blocking the way. . . . I saw that they were all naked and I wondered what was the matter with them. . . . When we spoke to people they said that they had been hit by something they didn't understand. . . . We were desperately looking for a doctor or a hospital but we couldn't seem to have any success. . . . We walked toward Hiroshima, still carrying our tools. . . . Then in Hiroshima there was no place either—it had become an empty field—so I carried him to a place near our company office where injured people were lying inside, asking for water. But there was no water and there was no way to help them and I didn't know what kind of treatment I should give to this man or to the others. I had to let them die right before my eyes. . . . By then we were cut off from escape, because the fire was beginning to spread out and we couldn't move—we were together with the dead people in the building—only we were not really inside of the building because the building itself had been destroyed, so that we were really outdoors, and we spent the night there. . . .

This rote and essentially ineffectual behavior was characteristic of many during the first few hours in those situations where any attempt at all could be made to maintain a group cooperative effort. People were generally more effective in helping members of their immediate families or in saving themselves. This same electrician, an unusually conscientious man, kept at his post at the railroad over a period of several weeks, leaving only for brief periods to take care of his family. Again his description of the scene of death and near-death takes on a dreamlike quality:

There were dead bodies everywhere. . . . There was practically no room for me to put my feet on the floor. . . . At that time I couldn't figure out the reason why all these people were suffering, or what illness it was that had struck them down. . . . I was the only person taking care of the place as all of the rest of the people had gone. . . . Other people came in looking for food or to use the toilet. . . . There was no one to sell tickets in the station, nothing . . . and since trains weren't running, I didn't have much work to do. . . . There was no light at all, and we were just like sleepwalkers. . . .

Part of this aura was the "deathly silence" consistently reported by survivors. Rather than wild panic, most described a ghastly stillness and a sense (whether or not literally true) of slow-motion: low moans from those incapacitated, the rest fleeing from the destruction, but usually not rapidly, toward the rivers, toward where they thought their family members might be, or toward where they hoped to find authorities or medical personnel, or simply toward accumulations of other people, in many cases merely moving along with a gathering human mass and with no clear destination. Some jumped into the rivers to escape heat and fire, others were pushed into the water by the pressure of crowds at the river banks; a considerable number drowned. Many seemed to be attracted to the disaster center, overcoming numerous obstacles—such as spreading fire and, later on, guards posted at various points to prevent any influx of people—and made their way through the debris, often losing sight of their ostensible rescue missions in their aimless wandering.

As Dr. Hachiya described the scene in his classic, *Hiroshima Diary:*

Those who were able walked silently toward the suburbs in the distant hills, their spirits broken, their initiative gone. When asked whence they had come, they pointed to the city and said, "That way": and when asked where they were going, pointed away from the city and said, "This way." They were so broken and confused that they moved and behaved like automatons.

Their reactions had astonished outsiders who reported with amazement the spectacle of long files of people holding stolidly to a narrow, rough path when close by was a smooth, easy road going in the same direction. The outsiders could not grasp the fact that they were witnessing the exodus of a people who walked in the realm of dreams.[8]

One of these "automatons" walking in the "realm of dreams," a watch repairman, at the time of the bomb in his twenties and three thousand meters from the hypocenter, describes his own mindless merging with a group of victims:

All the people were going in that direction and so I suppose I was taken into this movement and went with them. . . . I couldn't make any clear decision in a specific way . . . so I followed the other people. . . . I lost myself and was carried away. . . .

The phrase he and others used, *muga-muchū*, literally "without self, without a center," suggests an obliteration of the boundaries of self. The physical state of many greatly contributed to this obliteration: complete or near-nakedness (partly because of clothes blown off by the blast and partly through being caught in an early-morning state of undress), various injuries and forms of bleeding, faces disfigured and bloated from burns, arms held awkwardly away from the body to prevent friction with other burned areas. Fellow survivors characterized such people (and by implication, themselves) as being "like so many beggars," or "like so many red *Jizō** standing on the sides of the road," implying that their identity as living human beings had been virtually destroyed.

Indeed, a few *hibakusha* described being rendered literally unrecognizable: one girl of thirteen, whose face was so disfigured by burns that when she returned home, her parents did not know who she was—until she began to cry; and another, one year older, was not only similarly disfigured but also unable, probably on a psychological basis, to see or speak:

My mother and I were taken to [a nearby] island. . . . I couldn't see and couldn't say anything—that is what I heard later. . . . My eyes were not injured. I think I closed my eyes when the bomb fell. My face was so distorted and changed that people couldn't tell who I was. After a while I could call others' names but they couldn't recognize me. . . . We were considered the very worst kind of patients. . . . Of the thirty-five people put on this island, only two survived.

Dr. Hachiya also noted the "uncanny stillness" permeating the hospital where he was, for a time, both director and patient:

An old woman lay near me with an expression of suffering on her face; but she made no sound. Indeed one thing was common to everyone I saw—complete silence. . . . Miss Kado [a nurse] set about examining my wounds without speaking a word. No one spoke. . . . Why was everyone so quiet? . . . It was as though I walked through a gloomy, silent motion picture. . . .⁹

Yōko Ōta referred to this silence right after her description of the "end of the world," and more explicitly equated it with a general aura of death:

---

* A Buddhist deity, whose images in natural stone can be found along roads and paths.

It was quiet around us . . . in fact there was a fearful silence which made one feel that all people and all trees and vegetation were dead. . . .[10]

And a grocer, himself severely burned, conveyed in his description this profound sense of *death in life*, of ultimate death-life disruption:

The appearance of people was . . . well, they all had skin blackened by burns. . . . They had no hair because their hair was burned, and at a glance you couldn't tell whether you were looking at them from in front or in back. . . . They held their arms bent [forward] like this [he proceeded to demonstrate their position] . . . and their skin—not only on their hands, but on their faces and bodies too— hung down. . . . If there had been only one or two such people . . . perhaps I would not have had such a strong impression. But wherever I walked I met these people. . . . Many of them died along the road—I can still picture them in my mind—like walking ghosts. . . . They didn't look like people of this world. . . . They had a special way of walking—very slowly. . . . I myself was one of them.

The other-worldly grotesqueness of the scene, the image of neither-dead-nor-alive human figures with whom the survivor closely identifies himself, is typical. One man put the feeling more directly: "I was not really alive."

"UNNATURAL ORDER"

Related to the sense of death in life was a total disruption of individual and social order—of rules governing what is expected of one and whom one can depend on. Thus, the severely burned thirteen-year-old girl mentioned before (later to become a hospital worker) was assigned with her classmates to do "voluntary labor" on the fire lanes sixteen hundred meters from the hypocenter, and was as much disturbed by the sudden breakdown of teachers' standards of responsibility for their pupils as she was by her own injuries:

I felt my body to be so hot that I thought I would jump into the river. . . . I couldn't tell what was going on, but everything seemed strange. . . . The teacher from another class, a man whose shirt was burning, jumped in. And when I was about to jump, our own class teacher came down and she suddenly jumped into the river. . . . The river was filled with people and I could not swim very well, so I was afraid of jumping. . . . At that time we felt quite lost. . . .

Since we had always looked up to our teachers, we wanted to ask them for help. But the teachers themselves had been wounded and were suffering the same pain we were.

Such disruption reaches deeply into psychic experience, and can produce strange and desperate behavior—as it did in a young non-commissioned officer stationed in the center of Hiroshima, but on leave in the suburbs ten thousand meters away when the bomb fell:

We were under military order to return to our unit immediately in case of any attack or emergency, so I returned almost without thinking. . . . At first I couldn't get through . . . so in the evening I started out again. This time I didn't try to help anyone but just walked through them. I was worried about the Army camp because according to what . . . people told me, it had simply gone up in flames and disappeared. I was also a bit ashamed of having taken such a long time to return. But when I finally got back to the camp, just about everyone was dead—so there was no one to scold me. . . . The first thing I did was to give water to three people lying on the ground who were badly hurt—but a high-ranking officer came and told me not to give water to wounded people if they were suffering from burns. . . . Next thing I did was to look for the ashes of the military code book—since we had a military order to look for this book even if it were burned, as it was a secret code which had to be protected. Finally I located the ashes of the book, and wrapped them in a *furoshiki** and carried this around with me. I wanted to take it to military headquarters as soon as possible, but when I finally did take it there the next morning, the officer scolded me for doing such a stupid thing. . . . I was fresh from the Military Academy and my head was full of such regulations. . . .

He stuck to military regulations so inappropriately, not only because he was "fresh from the Military Academy" and unusually conscientious (even compulsive), but also because he was inwardly not yet able to accept the full dimensions of what had taken place and was behaving *as if* a familiar form of order still existed.†

* A square piece of cloth of varying size and quality which is used to wrap and carry objects large and small.
† The Japanese cultural stress upon external and internal order encouraged this kind of response, as it might also have influenced the sense of quiet and slow-motion mentioned before. But similar behavior has been noted by Wolfenstein and other observers in American victims of ordinary disasters. One must also keep in mind the extraordinary intensity of the atomic bomb experience and its capacity to impose its own responses, whatever the racial or cultural group involved.

Rather than total disorder, the decimation of the city created an atmosphere so permeated by bizarre evidence of death as to make whatever life remained seem unrelated to a "natural order" and more part of a "supernatural" or "unnatural" one. These impressions emerged in frequently expressed imagery of a Buddhist hell, here described by a young sociologist exposed at twenty-five hundred meters:

> Everything I saw made a deep impression--a park nearby covered with dead bodies waiting to be cremated . . . very badly injured people evacuated in my direction. . . . The most impressive thing I saw was some girls, very young girls, not only with their clothes torn off but with their skin peeled off as well. . . . My immediate thought was that this was like the hell I had always read about. . . . I had never seen anything which resembled it before, but I thought that should there be a hell, this was it—the Buddhist hell, where we were taught that people who could not attain salvation always went. . . . And I imagined that all of these people I was seeing were in the hell I had read about.

Most "unnatural" of all was the sudden nonexistence of the city itself—as described by the history professor:

> I climbed Hijiyama Hill and looked down. I saw that Hiroshima had disappeared. . . . I was shocked by the sight. . . . What I felt then and still feel now I just can't explain with words. Of course I saw many dreadful scenes after that—but that experience, looking down and finding nothing left of Hiroshima—was so shocking that I simply can't express what I felt. I could see Koi [a suburb at the opposite end of the city] and a few buildings standing. . . . But Hiroshima didn't exist—that was mainly what I saw—Hiroshima just didn't exist.

And two days after the bomb Dr. Hachiya groped unsuccessfully for language which could comprehend the unnatural order he observed:

> For the first time, I could understand what my friends had meant when they said Hiroshima was destroyed. . . . For acres and acres the city was like a desert except for scattered piles of brick and roof tile. I had to revise my meaning of the word destruction or choose some other word to describe what I saw. Devastation may be a better word, but really, I know of no word or words to describe the view

from my twisted iron bed in the fire-gutted ward of the Communications Hospital.[11]

Summarizing the psychological significance of this early phase, I would stress the *indelible imprint of death immersion, which forms the basis of what we shall later see to be a permanent encounter with death;* the fear of annihilation of self and of individual identity, along with *the sense of having virtually experienced that annihilation;* destruction of the non-human environment, of the field or context of one's existence, and therefore of one's overall sense of "being-in-the-world";[12] and the *replacement of the natural order of living and dying with an unnatural order of death-dominated life.*

3) "Psychic Closing-off"

Human beings are unable to remain open to experience of this intensity for any length of time. Very quickly—sometimes within minutes or even seconds—*hibakusha* began to undergo a process of "psychic closing-off"; that is, they simply ceased to feel. They had a clear sense of what was happening around them, but their emotional reactions were unconsciously turned off.

For instance, when the noncommissioned officer who had searched so desperately for the military code book was put in charge of a group assigned to carry out mass cremations, he found that he could dispose of the corpses with surprisingly little difficulty:

> After a while they became just like objects or goods that we handled in a very businesslike way. . . . Of course, I didn't regard them simply as pieces of wood—they were dead bodies—but if we had been sentimental we couldn't have done the work. . . . We had no emotions. . . . Because of the succession of experiences I had been through, I was temporarily without feeling. . . . At times I went about the work with great energy, realizing that no one but myself could do it.

His lack of feeling extended even to seemingly supernatural events surrounding death, in sharp contrast to the terror experienced by an "outsider" just entering the disaster area:

> Everything at that time was part of an extraordinary situation. . . . For instance, I remember that on the ninth or tenth of August, it was an extremely dark night. . . . I saw blue phosphorescent flames rising from the dead bodies—and there were plenty of them. These were quite different from the orange flames coming from the burning buildings. . . . These blue phosphorescent flames are what we Japanese look upon as spirits rising from dead bodies—in former days we called them fireballs. And yet, at that time I had no sense of fear, not a bit, but merely thought, "Those dead bodies are still burning." . . . But to people who had just come from the outside, those flames looked very strange. . . . One of those nights I met a soldier

who had just returned to the city, and I walked along with him. . . .
He noticed these unusual fireballs and asked me what they were. I
told him that they were the flames coming from dead bodies. The
soldier suddenly became extremely frightened, fell down on the
ground, and was unable to move. . . . Yet at that time I had a state
of mind in which I feared nothing—though if I were to see those
flames now, I might be quite frightened. . . .

Dr. Hachiya similarly recorded his "changed outlook" in which he
began to "accept death as a matter of course," "ceased to respect its
awfulness," and "considered a family lucky if it had not lost more than
two of its members."[13]

Some made strong efforts to turn away from the disaster, as in the
case of a professor of education, who, despite having devoted great time
and energy to caring for an injured senior colleague, nonetheless insisted
that he "did not see the disaster," and "in fact . . . avoided seeing
it . . . [because] I did not want to see frightening things." Here the
closing-off process is more clearly allied with conscious will.

Others' immersion in larger responsibilities was accompanied by a
more gradual form of closing-off, which may be termed "psychic numbing." A high city official in Nagasaki, for instance, immediately became
deeply involved in the enormous task of re-establishing a city office and
directing various emergency operations. Only late at night, thirteen
hours after the bomb fell, did he return to his home, where he found
the corpses of his wife and two of his children; the following day he
found the corpse of still another child. But he threw himself energetically into his work, and "had no time for personal grief." After his wife
and children had been cremated, he kept their remains with him in his
office, "and did not even have a chance to bury them for two months."

Many *hibakusha* had to defend themselves more directly from grotesque deaths around them by desensitizing themselves to death in
general, as in the case of the grocer mentioned before:

Well . . . the whole situation around me was very special . . . and
my mental condition was very special too. . . . There were these
people lying close to me. . . . Well, today the person next to me
would die, and the day after another person next to me would
die. . . . One of them would be talking to me, and then when I
would call him a few minutes later he was dead. . . . About life and
death. . . . How shall I put it? . . . I just couldn't have any re-

action. . . . I don't think I felt either joy or sadness. . . . My feelings about human death weren't really normal. . . . You might say I became insensitive to human death. . . .

Even the professional cremator, whose occupation ordinarily brought him into regular contact with death, noticed that his feelings were now unusually blunted:

When I burned soldiers' bodies, I usually felt pity for them and for their parents because they died so young. But when I saw people dying from the bomb, I didn't especially feel any pity. I thought, while on my way to my home, that I might die like the others.

Psychic closing-off could be transient or it could extend itself, over days or even months, into more lasting psychic numbing. In the latter case it merged with feelings of depression and despair—as in the case of the physicist, who, after walking among corpses for a full week searching for the bodies of relatives, experienced what he called a "state of emptiness," which he explained with the help of a metaphor:

As I walked along, the horrible things I saw became more and more extreme and more and more intolerable. And at a certain point I must have become more or less saturated, so that I became no longer sensitive, in fact insensitive, to what I saw around me. I think human emotions reach a point beyond which they cannot extend—something like a photographic process. If under certain conditions you expose a photographic plate to light, it becomes black; but if you continue to expose it, then it reaches a point where it turns white. . . . Only later can one recognize having reached this maximum state. . . .

This "maximum state" could take many forms. In the olfactory realm psychic numbing could enable one not only to accept the "smell of death" but even to require it. A novel about the atomic bomb describes such a sequence (apparently based on actual occurrence) in a hospitalized survivor:

They say that the sense of smell quickly becomes dulled. Afterwards when healthy people came in from the outside they would all say that the place simply stank. . . . Toward evening—from where we didn't know—a terrible smell, like broiling sardines, came drifting in. It was so bad that even we couldn't stand it. We wondered what it was, and somebody finally told us that it was the dead being cremated. . . .

But . . . after about a month of this, with the evening meal being brought in each day at just about the time that the smell of death . . . came floating in, I began to have a queer craving for the smell, and my appetite was better than ever. Apparently my appetite had somehow become stimulated by the smell of the burning corpses. . . . My father and I barely survived without giving the others the chance to sniff the same odor from us.[14]

The cryptic final remark, with a touch of atomic bomb gallows humor, again expresses the close relationship between psychic numbing and imagery of one's own death; it also contains another emotion we shall soon discuss: the tainted joy over having survived amid others' deaths.

Yōko Ōta describes first an acute "feeling of paralysis of my mind" from "outside shock," and then goes on to describe more protracted psychic numbing associated with her strong awareness of her writer's identity and task:

My younger sister said to me with a critical tone, "You are certainly good at watching those corpses. . . ." I answered her, "I see them both with the eyes of a person and the eyes of a writer.". . . There was no time for us to experience [the A-bomb] as fearful. . . . It will not become fearful until two or three years from now. But the shadow of death crosses in front of me, comes back and passes through me. Besides the living me, there is another me which has been dead. . . .[15]

Miss Ōta's last sentence suggests some of the complexity of the psychic closing-off process. We have observed its function, as a defense mechanism, to be that of closing oneself off from death itself: the unconscious message is, "If I feel nothing, then death is not taking place." But as Miss Ōta's words suggest (and as we shall discuss in the final section), psychic closing-off is itself a symbolic form of death. Thus, the survivor's frequent use of such terms as "nightmare," "like a dream," "the dream realm," and "like walking ghosts"—his entire sense of a death-saturated "unnatural order"—is part of his closing-off process, a means of creating emotional distance between himself and the intolerable world immediately around him.

Another tanka conveys this and much more:

The flash that covered the city in morning mist was much like an instant dream.[16]

4) Survival Priority

Significant as it was, psychic closing-off could by no means fully protect the survivor from either the threatening stimuli from without or within. The latter took the form of self-condemnation, of guilt and shame. From the moment of atomic bomb exposure, the *hibakusha* experienced a need to justify his own survival in the face of others' deaths, a sense of "guilt over survival priority"* which was to plague him from then on.

Thus, the noncommissioned officer assigned to cremate corpses who had spoken of his attitude toward them as "businesslike" later questioned his own use of the word. He emphasized the pity and sympathy he felt, particularly when handling the remains of men from his own unit, and the pains he took to console family members who came for these remains; he even recalled feeling frightened at night when passing the spot where he worked at cremation by day. He was, in effect, telling me that not only was his psychic closing-off incomplete, but that he was retrospectively appalled—felt ashamed and guilty—at having behaved in a way he now thought callous; at not having experienced emotions (or not strongly enough) he now thought appropriate. For he had indulged in activities which ordinarily, for him, were strongly taboo, and had done so with an energy, perhaps even an enthusiasm, which must have mobilized within him primitive feelings of a frightening nature.

Similarly, after revealing that he "considered a family lucky if it had not lost more than two of its members," Dr. Hachiya immediately added: "How could I hold my head up among the citizens of Hiroshima with thoughts like that in my mind?" Psychic closing-off, in other words, has its own cost in the currency of guilt and shame.

Guilt resulting from the death encounter—what we may broadly call death guilt—in this way both interferes with, and is further stimulated by, psychic closing-off. The psychic vise in which the *hibakusha* finds himself is vividly expressed by the history professor in his account of his walk through the city:

---

* The phenomenon of survivor guilt has been widely recognized, but I use this admittedly more awkward phrase to emphasize issues of sequence and timing in the question of who dies and who survives.

I went to look for my family. Somehow I became a pitiless person, because if I had pity, I would not have been able to walk through the city, to walk over those dead bodies. The most impressive thing was the expression in people's eyes—bodies badly injured which had turned black—their eyes looking for someone to come and help them. They looked at me and knew that I was stronger than they. . . . I was looking for my family and looking carefully at everyone I met to see if he or she was a family member—but the eyes—the emptiness—the helpless expression—were something I will never forget. . . . There were hundreds of people who had seen me. . . . And I often had to go to the same place more than once. I would wish that the same family would not still be there. . . . I saw disappointment in their eyes. They looked at me with great expectation, staring right through me. It was very hard to be stared at by those eyes. . . .

In other words, he felt accused by the eyes of the anonymous dead and dying of wrongdoing and transgression (a sense of guilt), for not helping them, for letting them die, for "selfishly" remaining alive and strong; and "exposed" and "seen through" by the same eyes for these identical failings (a sense of shame). Psychic closing-off was thus broken through by feelings of self-condemnation, by death guilt.* And this "psychic opening-up" exposed him to various forms of delayed guilt over having been so "pitiless" a person while his feelings were numbed.

Sometimes the delayed guilt takes the form of remembered voices of those left to die while one was oneself being rescued—as described by the elderly widow, who was carried to safety in a wheelbarrow by her son and daughter-in-law:

I heard many voices calling for help, voices calling their fathers, voices of women and children. . . . Even now I wonder what has happened to those people. . . . I couldn't move my body very well, and my son had six children to take care of in addition to me, so, well, we just didn't help other people. . . . I felt it was a wrong thing not to help them, but we were so much occupied by running away ourselves that we left them. . . . Even now I still hear their voices. . . .

The unspoken self-accusation here is that her life was saved at the expense of many others'.

---

* I shall use the term "death guilt" throughout the book to encompass all forms of self-condemnation associated with literal or symbolic exposure to death and dying, including those usually linked with the sense of shame. Guilt over survival priority, then, is a form of death guilt. These issues will be pursued further in the final chapter.

The weapon's unknown features and aftereffects made it possible to experience guilt related to a more direct sense of having contributed to others' deaths—as was true for the noncommissioned officer:

> I made one mistake. When I cremated the bodies and did the work of clearing them away, I told everyone to work. But there were some [soldiers] without any external marks or injuries . . . who soon began to say that they felt tired and miserable. . . . Yet I insisted they work and even punished them for not working. . . . Of course, I did not understand then that they were suffering from the effects of the bomb. Later, when I realized this, I sent them home to their families. . . . But I wish I had sent them back a little earlier. If I had—and if I had given them more vegetables to eat—the percentage among them who died might have been lower. . . .

FAILED RESPONSIBILITY

The closer the relationship to a person one failed to help (or later thought one should have helped), the greater one's sense of being responsible for that person's death. A domestic worker described the later repercussions of having, together with her adult daughter, ignored the pleas of a severely injured neighbor, with whom they had been on close terms, to take his nine-year-old son to a hospital:

> His head was covered with blood, and when he saw us he called to us. . . . "Yano [the daughter]," he said, "Yano-san [a more polite form], please take my child with you. Please take him to the hospital over there.". . . The child couldn't seem to move its arms . . . and seeing the fire approaching us so closely, I was afraid that we ourselves would not live. . . . I thought, We have got to escape by hardening ourselves against pity. . . . But as we went on, his cry, "Yano-san, please," stuck in my mind. . . . My daughter and I always talked about how bitter he must have felt toward us for not helping him. . . . I heard later that he survived . . . but that the child died. . . . And when I think of not helping him despite his begging me to help, I can only say that it is a very pitiful thing. . . .

Painful decisions had to be made about whom to help. The physicist, for instance, was torn by feelings of responsibility toward his senior professor, with whom he had a relationship of affection and obligation, and toward the latter's family after his death; toward anonymous victims; and toward another critically injured close colleague:

When I looked around . . . and saw all the incredibly miserable people . . . I thought I should do something for them. But this feeling was replaced by the feeling that I had to notify the professor's family; that was my responsibility. . . . The experience of not being able to extend help to those people I more or less forgot later on. But there was a certain person—a close friend, also on the faculty of the university—who later died. . . . I thought about going to help him during the time that I was walking . . . and knowing that I might have done something to save him—this has caused me great pain. . . .

The Protestant minister who had viewed the atomic holocaust as "God's judgment on man" went on in the same idiom to express guilt over his sense of failed responsibility:

I felt my unconditional surrender to God's judgment. I wanted to kneel down before Him. I thought, What does it mean to lose fifty-six church members and to have a Christian church destroyed—what is the meaning of this loss? I thought, This is the time to die, and I should have died. . . . My inner command was: "Die! Die!" but I couldn't die.

That is, he had "failed" both his parishioners and his God by permitting the former to die and by not himself dying in their stead. And his guilt was compounded by what was clearly a strong urge to live.

Death guilt was, of course, most focused and intense in relationship to family members. Indeed, families often seemed to respond to the disaster as a unit, especially mothers and children. As one mother said, "I thought if I died, it would be together with all the children"; she then went on to suggest that this would be preferable to some family members' dying and others' surviving. Potential guilt over survival priority is so great that total family annihilation may seem less disturbing.*

Children's deaths had particularly strong impact, whatever the circumstances. These aroused in parents a special kind of guilt associated with failure to carry out the most fundamental psychobiological tasks in caring for the young—giving life to them and maintaining it in them.

* Involved here is the Japanese cultural stress upon the inseparability of mother and child. One finds something of a corollary in the not infrequent tendency for suicidal Japanese mothers to kill their small children before killing themselves, so that all die together. But again these are unusually intense expressions of universal psychic tendencies.

Parents' later self-reproaches had more to do with these basic emotions than with the actual details of a child's death, which, in fact, they often reconstructed in a way that made them most culpable. For instance, a middle-aged businessman had returned to Hiroshima from a brief trip during the early-morning hours of August 6. Having been up all night, he was not too responsive when his twelve-year-old son came into his room to ask his father to remove a nail from his shoe. The father, wishing to get the job done quickly, placed a piece of leather above the tip of the nail and promised he would take the whole nail out when the boy returned later that afternoon. As was true of many youngsters sent to factories to do "voluntary labor," the boy's body was never found— and the father, after a desperate but fruitless search for his son throughout the city, was left with the lingering self-accusation that the nail he had failed to remove might have impeded the boy's escape from the fire.

Similar emotions became associated with requests one had denied one's children (or other family members) which turned out to be last requests. Such an experience was described in a poem, which became well known in Hiroshima, telling of a mother whose thirteen-year-old son, before leaving for his work detail, asked if he could have a tomato. She told him it would be better to eat it when he returned. But the boy did not return and his remains were never found. His mother later constructed an altar for her dead son, on which she put a paper box covered by a white cloth, and on top of the cloth a tomato.[17]

Children whose parents were killed also experienced intense and lasting guilt, the theme of which was expressed by a young woman who had become an "A-bomb orphan" at the age of four through the death of her mother (her father had died earlier) and who said to me: "We did nothing bad—and still our parents died." The child invariably interprets a parent's death as a form of punishment for its misbehavior. And since any child, when angry at a parent, may experience and even express the wish that the parent were dead, the parent's actual death— and indeed the entire suffering visited upon a family by the atomic bomb—can be perceived by the child as the product of its own evil wish.

Such patterns of death guilt were strong in situations in which children were unable to rescue their parents, particularly when the parent had first helped the child—as was the experience of the shop-keeper's assistant (then thirteen years old) who had been trapped under the debris of his house:

I kept screaming "Mother!" very loudly, and then I saw my mother
staggering toward me. . . . I think she pulled the debris away from
my body, and then there was a hole I could crawl out through. . . .
We also were able to dig out my baby brother, and my grandmother
carried him away. . . . But my mother was very weak and began to
collapse and fall on her side. So I helped her up and tried to drag her
along. But the road was cluttered with pieces of destroyed houses and
I couldn't move her at all. . . . The fire was all around us so I
thought I had to hurry. . . . I was suffocating from the smoke and
I thought if we stayed like this, then both of us would be killed. I
thought if I could reach the wider road, I could get some help, so
I left my mother there and went off. . . . I found a neighbor . . .
and told him my mother was lying in there and asked him please to
fetch her. . . . He went back for her . . . while I held his child
. . . but after a while he returned and said that he could not get into
that place any more. . . . I was later told by a neighbor that my
mother had been found dead, face down in a water tank . . . very
close to the spot where I left her. . . . If I had been a little older or
stronger I could have rescued her. . . . Even now I still hear my
mother's voice calling me to help her. . . .

The elderly country woman experienced a related form of guilt
through the death from radiation effects of a brother who came into the
city after the bomb and then spent three days looking for her. She spoke
concretely of the issue of survival priority:

My brother's wife told me how lucky I was, since he, who had not
been exposed directly to the bomb, like me, but had merely breathed
the poison air, died, while I could survive. I feel so sorry for him. . . .
His dying like that still gives me very deep emotion . . . because he
had been in the area for such a short time and yet went so many places
. . . to look for me, and because he preceded me in death. . . .

Legends which grew up around the way in which family members
died could themselves be expressions of painful guilt on the part of
survivors. A divorced housewife, just twelve years old at the time of the
bomb, described her father's last words—his question about whether
other family members were all right, and when told that they were, a
final comment: "Then only one of us must die, and I am happy to be
sacrificed for the others." The girl remained convinced that her father's
sacrifice and spiritual influence had enabled the rest of the family to
survive. She did not understand the nature of the guilt she retained, the

part it might have played in embellishing memories of her father's last words (which could well have contained resentment over being "sacrificed"), or the way in which guilt affected her life in general.

Guilt could also become importantly related to the revulsion felt by survivors toward dying family members—a revulsion which was related to severe death anxiety and which prevented a proper farewell. A woman (later to experience eye disease), fourteen years old at the time and with her mother, was told that her father had been taken to a neighbor's house in a severely injured state:

> There was a small room . . . where the three of us could sleep. . . . My father smelled terribly because foul matter came out of his wounds. I remember complaining about the bad smell . . . and my own legs began to swell and pain . . . so I was moved to my mother's family home . . . and a little later I heard that my father died. I was very sad but I was also so frightened that I couldn't go to see him. . . . The appearance of a person injured by the A-bomb was terrible. Even with my father, my own flesh and blood, it gave me a very bad feeling. . . . Now I regret it when I think back on it. . . . Why didn't I go to see my father when he was dying? I think I must have been exhausted then, physically and spiritually.

In all of these instances guilt is magnified by previous resentments one felt toward family members—and the survivor can never be inwardly certain to what degree his "neglect" of a parent, child, or spouse is related to such prior feelings. Lack of foreknowledge about atomic bomb effects could enter into these patterns. The history professor, after locating his wife and finding that "she had some burns but did not look too bad," left her to lend assistance to some of his students:

> I did not give her all the care I should have. . . . She began to show symptoms of A-bomb disease—which we knew nothing about—and at the end she became mentally abnormal and died. It was strange, but when she died, I did not feel extremely sad. Everyone was losing family members and losing just one person did not seem so extreme. . . . Of course, I did not have enough knowledge at the time, but since then I have said to myself constantly: I wish I could have given her more care and attention. . . .

Here ignorance, conflicting responsibilities, psychic closing-off, and ambivalence are inextricably intertwined in their contribution to guilt.

Guilt toward family members could also be expressed more indirectly.

One man, for instance, told me in some detail and with great discomfort of his inability to rescue a nephew killed in the room next to him, and conveyed the strong impression that he inwardly wondered how great an effort he had made. I also heard many stories of children and parents separated from one another, then dramatically reunited, again separated, and so on, in which I could detect unconscious rhythms (in the child or parent describing the event) of guilt-anger-abandonment alternating with those of relief-gratitude-restored nurturance—with the guilt reasserting itself particularly strongly where one of the people involved eventually died. Such conflicts were particularly poignant in a culture which places extraordinary stress upon dependency and mutual responsibility, and which instills with exquisite sensitivity the fear of abandonment.[18]

Guilty conflicts could be greatly alleviated by more or less permanent reunions of family members, and by the reassertion of patterns of care—between husbands and wives or parents and children. But there were cases in which those from whom care was required were emotionally incapable of providing it. Thus one mother, whose divorce just one year before the bomb had left *her* with a sense of abandonment, was suddenly confronted with the responsibility for saving her eight-year-old daughter and her one-year-old son; all three had minor injuries from exposure at two thousand meters, and the children had possible symptoms of irradiation:

> I tried to take some things out of the house but everything was buried . . . and so carrying only the baby's diapers . . . and myself wearing only a panty and slip, the three of us—a mother with two children—what should we do? In what direction should we escape? . . . I had no clear destination but I felt we had to run away. . . . The eight-year-old began to complain that her stomach was hot—and she threw up—a dark liquid like coal-tar . . . and then the baby began to throw up also. . . . I tried to go over a nearby bridge but it was on fire so we couldn't go that way. I was told to escape to Itsukaichi [a suburb] but I knew that with my injury and with the two children, I did not have the strength to go there. . . . A man with his eyes sticking out about two inches called me by name and I felt sick. . . . People's bodies were tremendously swollen—you can't imagine how big a human body can swell up. . . . And then I lost consciousness. . . . It was not so much my bodily injuries [that caused me to faint] but the feeling of helpless desperation . . . the things I saw around me. . . . I didn't know what I could do about

caring for my children, what would happen to us. . . . I lost my self-confidence. . . . I felt lonely and fearful. . . . That was at about nine A.M., and when I awoke it was about four in the afternoon. . . . My older child was looking at me, and the first thing I saw was her face . . . and the baby I think I had been unconsciously holding all the time. . . . Even stronger than thoughts about life and death was this feeling of loneliness and fear . . . of having no home and no family. . . .

Her feelings of abandonment, helplessness, and death anxiety greatly interfered with her capacity for providing maternal care, which in turn resulted in strong feelings of guilt and undoubtedly also of resentment (toward whomever she felt had abandoned her and toward her children for their demands upon her); her loss of consciousness and prolonged sleep probably resulted largely from these conflicts.* Her experience, rather than being unique, epitomized psychological struggles within all who were responsible for nurturing others under conditions that made adequate nurturance impossible. The resulting guilt in many cases was considerably stronger than hers because of the death of the children involved.

I encountered many analogous patterns of behavior, in relationship to family members as well as to more generalized conflict over responsibility. In addition to fainting these patterns included various impairments of mobility, vision, hearing, and speech. Such symptoms had two symbolic functions: they "solved" the conflict over responsibility and abandonment by incapacitating the *hibakusha* so that little more could be demanded of him (though like the abandoned mother, he could continue to provide minimal nurturance while incapacitated); and at the same time they "struck him down" (whether he was rendered still, blind, deaf, or dumb) in the sense of punishing him for remaining alive and rendering him "dead." They were thus a radical form of psychic closing-off in response to extreme death guilt.

CONFIRMATION AND CONDEMNATION

With the survivor burdened by this combination of death guilt and strong feelings of abandonment, the appearance of someone who could

---

* Divorce in Japan, especially prewar Japan, has even greater connotations of abandonment than it does in the West. Usually initiated by the husband or his relatives, it conveys to the wife the sense of being cast out from the family she had made her own through marriage, and her connection with a proper "family line" severed. Children, moreover, were usually kept by the husband or his family, unlike the situation in this case.

evoke a sense of the pre-bomb world meant a great deal. A mathematician who had experienced a serious eye injury described how, upon leaving the hospital to which he had been taken only to be quickly released (because doctors were preoccupied with even more critical injuries), he felt weak, nauseated, "uneasy," and "wondered what was going to happen"—until, while resting under a tree with his eyes closed, he was pleasantly surprised by the voices of several of his students calling "*Sensei*" (the general term used to address a teacher or a superior). The word immediately "gave me a very relaxed feeling." Being so addressed at such a moment can have the significance for the survivor of being "confirmed" in his prior identity, and to a considerable extent "recognized" as one who is, and has a right to be, alive.* Correspondingly, the absence of such confirmation and recognition could cause these issues to remain psychologically in doubt, and leave the survivor abandoned to his sense of guilt and worthlessness.

This was particularly true for a generally downtrodden woman laborer, middle-aged and alone in life when exposed at eighteen hundred meters. Her leg severely injured (eventually leading to permanent deformity), she was taken to an emergency treatment area, where for about a week virtually nothing was done for her. As one accustomed to neglect, she stifled her rage at first and even justified her being ignored, but was soon so overcome by feelings of worthlessness as virtually to reach out for death:

> I thought others should naturally be treated first because their cases were more serious than mine . . . until my leg began to become infested with maggots. . . . I showed them how bad it had gotten, but all they said was, "I'll come back to take care of you later.". . . I felt very lonely and sad, but also resigned since nothing could be done. . . . My being so helpless and unable to move caused so much trouble to others that I thought it would be better if I were dead. . . .

Also greatly contributing to death guilt, and to feelings of worthlessness and abandonment, were survivors' impressions of generalized selfishness, of absence of concern or desire to help. People were too busy coping with their own death anxiety to make available ordinary com-

---

* The term *sensei* can convey acknowledgment of superior position or genuine respect and even affection, though it can also be used ironically. Frequently lost sight of is the strong dependency of the senior person, the "*sensei*," upon his juniors, which is greatly increased under extreme conditions like these. I use "confirmation" in Martin Buber's sense.

passion for others. Many used such phrases as "Every man thought of himself"; "People took care of themselves or sometimes their relatives but not anyone else"; and (in reference to the inevitable looting which followed, even, or perhaps especially, in a disaster of this dimension) "People thought nothing of stealing from one another . . . like hungry demons . . . and an honest man was likely to starve."

The history professor also spoke in these terms, but made it clear that his condemnation was also directed at himself:

> Of course I thought much about my children, but egotism was so great that each person was alone. . . . I felt strongly that human beings were animals—even in the case of parents and children, they still fought with one another to get their food. . . .

He noted that help existed only within families, that there did not exist "a strong tie with a group or a community," and that even the military helped "only because it was ordered to do so, not for humanitarian reasons." He went on to describe an incident in which he urged acceptance of human limitations, but which again reveals the *hibakusha*'s almost automatic preoccupation with his own survival and the resulting death guilt:

> I think that the wish to rescue oneself is always the first thought that comes to the human mind. For example, my second son, who was just seven years old, was at home. My wife's youngest sister was in the next house. When the bomb dropped, my son was buried under our house. . . . Hearing many others screaming for help . . . the boy also called out, "Help, help." My wife's sister told me that she heard his cries and then got others to help her get him out. But she confessed that she first forgot about him and only later, secondarily, did she think of him. I told her not to feel badly, that it is quite natural to think of oneself. . . .

Yōko Ōta is more consistent and more scathing in her attribution of the abandonment of *hibakusha* to historically imposed Japanese character traits:

> Japanese people remained silent without saying anything, without encouraging or comforting one another. No one came to take care of injured people and no one came to tell us how and where we should spend the night. We were simply left alone. . . . Over a long period of time we had lost our autonomy. . . . We had given even our

hearts' function to narrow-minded leaders . . . but after this disaster we received no guidance from anyone. . . . Victims were isolated. There was nothing we could do but observe . . . the inactive traits of Japanese, which became quite clear in these circumstances—their negligent attitude, their utter lack of wisdom and other . . . shallow qualities and human defects. Even after such an extraordinary event, which one is likely to encounter no more than once in his lifetime, the people concerned [bus company employees with a few buses at their disposal] had no definite plan for transporting victims. They confined themselves to their offices as if in hiding, as if feeling that prompt action and quick judgment, or kindness to bombed-out citizens, or enthusiastic, thoughtful help, would only cause them to be criticized later on. . . .*

We may suspect that Miss Ōta's own *hibakusha* feelings of abandonment and death guilt contributed to the intensity of her views; her observations are by no means entirely unwarranted, but they neglect universal psychological tendencies toward psychic closing-off and preoccupation with individual survival in the face of massive death immersion.

An occasional survivor among those I interviewed expressed an opposite feeling, and emphasized the selfless cooperation among atomic bomb victims—something resembling the "post-disaster utopia" that has been described in other holocausts.[20] But in each of these descriptions there was evidence of inner doubt, either in the form of transparent wishfulness or of sufficiently strong qualifications to negate the original claim. The most enthusiastic statement of cooperation, and endorsement of Japanese character in general, was the following:

Everyone helped. . . . This is a very good tradition. . . . They are accustomed to earthquakes and catastrophes, and in such situations the whole town always helps. . . .

But no Japanese made such a claim. These were the words of a European priest, who had been living in Japan for almost thirty years when I met him, and like many missionaries in the long tradition of Christian involvement in East Asia, had become immersed in a pro-

---

* These characteristics of dependent passivity, detachment from those to whom one has no formal tie, and inertia as a means of avoiding responsibility and criticism, are notably strong in Japanese and were undoubtedly prominent at the time. But they can be found elsewhere, and, as I suggest below, were enormously encouraged by the conditions of the atomic bombed environment.[19]

tracted struggle to achieve a sense of belonging within his "mission-land"; his idealization of Japanese behavior was part of his struggle to become "Japanese," and part of a generally unstable post-bomb adjustment.[21]

The professor of education who had "avoided seeing" the disaster first claimed that "people were very cooperative," but almost immediately afterward recited (more convincingly) numerous examples of selfish behavior and general loss of moral standards. His contradictory attitudes reflected patterns of emotional disorder which were later to become manifest. Similarly, a philosopher colleague of his mentioned "the feeling of brotherhood, the desire to cooperate closely with each other," but this seemingly positive stress turned out to be associated with other efforts at denial, and was, moreover, largely abandoned when he corrected himself and spoke of "the egotism of people at the extreme moment."

A few others contrasted the spirit of mutual assistance during and immediately after the disaster with its subsequent absence—suggesting what has been called "the breakdown of the post-disaster utopia." A leftist woman writer, referring partly to her sense of being liberated from the control of Japanese militarists, went so far as to say that people's unselfish help—"rich or poor, strong or weak"—gave her and others "a reason to live," but that soon afterward "something strange happened and some of the weak became strong . . . and stopped offering help." And the noncommissioned officer illustrated this shift by contrasting the ease with which he could flag a passing truck and be picked up during the first month following the disaster with the abrupt cessation of such cooperative gestures thereafter. We may assume that there existed "a rise and fall of post-disaster utopia";[22] but the rise was so slight and wavering that, for many, it went unnoticed, and the fall was often felt, as we shall observe in the next chapter, as merely a continuation of the disintegration that had begun with the bomb itself.

The generally negative imagery about human behavior suggests a fundamental guilt-linked theme, with both social and individual implications. In a disaster of this magnitude, the extreme conditions drastically limit the possibilities of cooperation and mutual aid, and thereby greatly accentuate the awareness of ordinary urges toward self-preservation. The idea that an individual's first and strongest impulse is directed toward his own survival becomes vividly displayed and, in this death-saturated context, totally unacceptable. Even more unacceptable is the inner joy at having survived, whatever the fate of one's fellows. Miss

Ōta described one of the rare situations in which this joy could be expressed:

> When I woke up in the morning and found myself still living, there was nothing I could do but spend the whole day basking in the brightness of having returned from hell, and in the joy of having been brought back from death.[23]

On both counts, the *hibakusha* has further cause to equate his survival with evil. Takashi Nagai, the Catholic physician-hero of Nagasaki, later wrote:

> In general, then, those who survived the atom bomb were the people who ignored their friends crying out *in extremis*; or who shook off wounded neighbors who clung to them, pleading to be saved. . . . In short, those who survived the bomb were, if not merely lucky, in a greater or lesser degree selfish, self-centered, guided by instinct and not civilization . . . and we know it, we who have survived. Knowing it is a dull ache without surcease.[24]

Nagai goes on to condemn himself for having forgotten about his brother (who died) at the time, for taking two days to get back to his house "where my wife lay dead," and for, under the guise of rendering dedicated and unselfish help in directing the rescue of patients at the hospital, having the secret motive of wishing "to win praise from everybody . . . to be called a hero." That is, the *hibakusha* must look upon his motives and urges as evil—because he is part of a disaster which (whatever he did or did not do) defeated cooperative effort to limit its human toll, and because he cannot accept either his urge to survive or the fact of his survival.

THE ULTIMATE HORROR

A type of memory which epitomizes the relationship of death to guilt appears in what I have called the *ultimate horror*—a specific image of the dead or dying with which the survivor strongly identifies himself, and which evokes in him particularly intense feelings of pity and self-condemnation. Thus the noncommissioned officer, who had become an experienced social worker by the time I talked with him, described an event which affected his life even more than did his crematory activities:

> I entered the city . . . [and] walked along the [river] bank near the present Yokogawa Bridge [where] I saw the bodies of a mother and

her child. . . . That is, I thought I saw dead bodies, but the child was still alive—still breathing, though with difficulty. . . . I filled the cover of my lunch box with water and gave it to the child, but it was so weak it could not drink. I knew that people were frequently passing that spot . . . and I hoped that one of these people would take the child—as I had to go back to my own unit. Of course, I helped many people all through that day . . . but the image of this child stayed on my mind and remains as a strong impression even now. . . . Later, when I was again in that same area, I hoped that I might be able to find the child . . . and I looked for it among all the dead children collected at a place nearby. . . . Even before the war I had planned to go into social work but this experience led me to go into my present work with children—as the memory of that mother and child by Yokogawa Bridge has never left me, especially since the child was still alive when I saw it.

Most images of ultimate horror involved women and children, universal symbols of purity and vulnerability, and particularly so in Japanese culture. But they also could consist of the *hibakusha*'s own family members or of anonymous people who came to symbolize for him the entire event. The ultimate horror thus forms the *hibakusha*'s *residual image*—the pictorialization of his central conflict in relationship to the disaster.

A single image could both express these general themes and have specific guilt-stimulating relevance—as in the case of the scene of dead children recalled by the man who had not been able to rescue a nephew of about the same age:

What made the strongest impression on me was [something I saw] three days after the bomb—children of about five or six years old. Well, there was a railway crossing in what is now Yokogawa, and about twenty of them were all lined up to be burned [cremated] and there were some who had stuck their heads in a water tank . . . two children with their heads still sticking in the tank . . . this was an extremely impressive sight and I felt great pity for them. . . .

And the image of corpses of young boys who had tried unsuccessfully to flee recalled by the businessman who had failed to remove the nail from his own son's shoe:

In front of the First Middle School there were . . . many young boys the same age as my son . . . and what moved me most to pity was that there was one dead child lying there and another who seemed to be crawling over him in order to run away, both of them burned to blackness. . . .

What greatly contributed to the emotional power of these scenes of ultimate horror was their giving stark external actuality to the most primitive inner anxieties concerning annihilation and separation—as we observe in the case of one woman, seventeen years old at the time of the bomb, who recalled her search for her parents:

> I walked past Hiroshima Station . . . and saw people with their bowels and brains coming out. . . . I saw an old lady carrying a suckling infant in her arms. . . . I saw many children . . . with dead mothers. . . . I just cannot put into words the horror I felt. . . .

In addition to causing horror, such scenes had elements of fascination. This was true for a technician, at the time employed in a war factory in the suburbs, who came into the city on a confused mission of investigation and relief. His voluble, even enthusiastic, descriptions of females, brutalized and naked, suggested that what he saw attracted as well as repelled him, and that powerful feelings of death guilt can combine with existing psychic inclinations toward perverse sexual and aggressive fantasies:

> I saw women . . . one corpse with the flesh removed from the bones . . . then about one hundred people, mostly women and children, none of them with clothes on, lying on the asphalt pleading for help. . . . When I first saw these victims I was reminded of leprosy patients. . . . And one thing that has never disappeared from my mind, even today, a miserable thing was . . . a girl in the rain of about eighteen or nineteen years old, and she had no clothing on her body except half of her panties, which did not cover her. She took a few steps toward me but as she was ashamed of her situation, she then crouched on the ground and she asked me for help—putting her hands in a position of prayer. And when I looked at her hands I saw the skin was burned off as if she were wearing gloves. Her hair was disheveled and her breast was red from burns. . . . Since she was the first to ask me directly for help, I wanted to do something for her, but she was stark naked . . . and the company order—which was really like a military order—was supreme to me . . . so I was at a loss. . . . I told her she better stay under the eaves of the destroyed house and

that I would come back to help her later . . . but I met the same kind of people one after another . . . and I couldn't do anything at all, so I did not go back. And even now, after seventeen years, I think of the horrible situation of that girl . . . ashamed of being naked,. crouching on the ground, praying with her hands for help from me. . . .

Such psychic inclinations were particularly strong in this man, but they are universal, and that is why it is probably accurate to say that all *hibakusha* were in some degree drawn to these grotesque scenes. Dr. Hachiya confirms this in his description of the impact made by the sudden appearance at his hospital on the day after the bomb of a man who not only recounted in great detail the grotesque scenes he had observed but "repeated himself two or three times":

It seemed to give Mr. Katsutani some relief to pour out his terrifying experiences on us; and there was no one who would have stopped him, so fascinating was his tale of horror. While he was talking, several people came in and stayed to listen.[25]

Much of the survivor's fascination with these horrors has to do with his inner contrast between those experiencing them and himself—in the unconscious reassurance that "they, not I, are being brutalized." But this "reassurance" also evokes within him precisely those fantasies whose aggressive and perverse content has always rendered them unacceptable, so that strong currents of guilt from early life join forces with his immediate death guilt.

One form of ultimate horror was both frequent and particularly significant—the recollection of requests by the dying which could not be carried out, particularly of pleas for a few sips of water. Water was withheld not only because of survivors' preoccupation with saving themselves and their own families, but because authorities spread the word that water would have harmful effects upon the severely injured. Yet *hibakusha* retained particularly troubled feelings about these requests, and usually gave an explanation to the effect that "Since they were to die anyway, I should have given them the water they wanted so badly."

Indeed, it turns out that the request for water by the dying, in addition to reflecting the victims' physical state (their shock and dehydration), has special significance in Japanese cultural tradition. It is related to an ancient belief that water can restore life by bringing back the spirit that has just departed—or is about to depart—from the body,[26] a Japanese version of a universal tendency to equate water and life. Associated with this belief, there has evolved a general custom for water to be requested by and offered to the dying. These pleas by A-bomb victims were therefore as much psychological expressions of old cultural symbolism as they were of physical need; one might well say that they were pleas for life itself. The survivor's failure to acquiesce to them, whatever his reasons, came to have the psychological significance for him of refusing another's request for the privilege of life—while he himself clung so tenaciously to that same privilege.

HATE, CHANCE, AND SELF-HATE

Survivors' guilt was intensified by the meagerness of their hostility. So physically and emotionally overwhelmed were they at the time that they had little capacity for focused anger.

Some did describe, at the moment of the bomb, feelings equivalent to "Damn them!" or "The bastards!" or simply "Damnit." And there was a certain amount of immediate resentment toward the pilots who dropped the bomb or toward "the Americans"; toward Japanese military and civilian authorities for having deceived the people and brought them to ruin, for not having prevented the bomb or even prepared the population for it, and particularly for failing to provide adequate help; as well as toward Japanese scientists and physicians for not having somehow done more sooner. There was also resentment on the part of those severely burned or otherwise injured toward those who were not. And there was said to have been a good deal of general antagonism to "foreigners" (meaning Westerners) right after the bomb fell.[27]

But these hostilities were sporadic and variable, much less prominent than other feelings we have been discussing. As Miss Ōta observed: "We even forgot to resent the A-bomb." Such relative absence of hostility is consistent with the "stunned" condition of victims of any disaster, which has been termed "the disaster syndrome,"[28] and with what I have called psychic closing-off. More than this, the special dimensions of Hiroshima would seem to have created a holocaust too vast and incomprehensible for locating objects of hate. As one psychoanalyst put it after listening to a description of the event: "You can't hate magic."[29] While it would be an oversimplification to claim that hostility was simply "turned inward," one can speak of a vicious circle in which the inability to experience hostility increases tendencies toward guilt, which in turn inhibit the capacity for hostility, and so on.

An indirect manifestation of guilt was the stress upon "accidents of survival"—the "chance" factors that kept one man at home, made another decide to leave for work earlier or later, caused still another to make a last-minute change in a previous plan—which resulted in a person's being at a greater distance from the hypocenter than he otherwise would have been. These "accidents" were often inwardly associated with another's death. The electrician, for instance, when questioned about such chance factors, immediately replied: "I wish you wouldn't ask me that. I lost a child in the bomb." This was his first mention of his loss; the question had triggered off his sense of having survived *instead* of the boy.

These outcomes were attributed to unknowable forces of "destiny," and the good fortune of surviving could be seen as a special kind of "grace" or, in psychological terms, invulnerability, conferred by those unknowable forces. The young sociologist who compared the bomb scene to pictures of Buddhist hell had been required just a few days earlier to move from a boarding house very close to the hypocenter (which was being torn down to make a fire lane) to one much further away:

> If I had been in the first house, I would certainly have been killed by the bomb. . . . I am very lucky that I am still living. I have a feeling about human destiny, which comes to me very strongly and very frequently. . . . In my case I have a good destiny and this is more than just a coincidence. I look upon this kind of destiny as something beyond the personal effort we make—perhaps not exactly the influence of God—but something beyond the personal will, which controls human existence. . . .

The implication is that some kind of personal virtue contributed to this "good fortune" or "special luck" (*ii unmei*)—but that both the virtue and its "reward" were and are precarious. Hence survival may be directly equated with a virtuous decision—as in the case of a professor of English who decided to leave his home in the center of the city the night before, rather than wait for the morning, in order to be on hand at the student dormitory in the suburbs to help with arrangements for the next day's assigned labor:

> I too would have been dead—and we would not be sitting here and talking together—if I had not decided to leave that night. . . . I can't exactly describe my feeling then—perhaps it was a feeling of

duty, or just a feeling that I should go there. . . . Because of this experience I have become a fatalist. . . . It was the Goddess of Fortune that saved me. . . .

In suggesting that he had "earned" this favorable intervention from the "Goddess of Fortune," he gave me the distinct impression that he needed to find justification for having survived.

Such need for justification is even greater where the *hibakusha* inwardly suspects that lack of conscientiousness was connected with the "accident of survival." The abandoned mother, for instance, was keenly aware of her good fortune in being at home that day rather than at the office where she worked, which was much closer to the hypocenter. But in explaining why she was at home, she quickly poured out "three reasons"—to help arrange a farewell party for several men who were enlisting, to help with ration books, and to participate in voluntary labor in the neighborhood—in a way that strongly suggested that none of these "reasons" was inwardly convincing to her as evidence of a "virtuous decision."

Only one *hibakusha* I interviewed, the professor of education, openly attributed his survival to a specific lapse in virtue:

> Usually I was in the habit of getting up much earlier, and would go to the city hall [which was very close to the hypocenter] or other places, taking care of various responsibilities. I am ordinarily very punctual, but that day I was somehow very slow—which turned out to be a very fortunate, a very lucky fate.

But even he had a need to emphasize usual virtue, and there was a good deal of additional evidence of guilt surrounding his survival.

The relationship between guilt and "chance" factors in survival can be complicated, as was true of the seamstress who, then a schoolgirl, had remained at home the day before the bomb instead of reporting to her "voluntary labor" (very close to the hypocenter) because of stomach trouble. She considered staying home the next day as well, partly because her aunt and cousin were visiting, and even offered to cut her cousin's hair. But the two relatives chose to go out on another visit, which in turn led the girl to decide to report to her labor assignment. The cousin and aunt disappeared without a trace, and the seamstress, because of departing five minutes later, was still far enough away to escape death, although she did get severely burned and was eventually left with a disfiguring facial keloid which she has considered to be a blight upon her life:

> I feel that if I had cut her hair, they would still be living today. And every time I experience hardship because of my physical condition, I find myself feeling that if only I had stayed home that day, I wouldn't have these wounds and wouldn't have this hardship. I feel it even more strongly nowadays.

Her feelings about "chance survival" include guilt over survival priority in relationship to the cousin and aunt (accentuated by a feeling of special responsibility for their deaths because of not having detained them by cutting their hair); unexpressed anger toward them for deciding not to stay at home; a sense of "bad fortune" because of the miseries she has endured over the years; a sense of "good fortune" over being alive at all—again in contrast to her aunt and cousin, and in a way, instead of them; and perhaps strongest of all, the wish to "undo"—or relive—this entire destiny, so that it might have a happier outcome.

This wish to undo all or part of the A-bomb experience is central to imagery of chance survival: "If only I had done this, or not done that" often means "If only the dead could be brought back, and the living relieved of their guilt and suffering." But there is a quality of ambivalence even about this "undoing" because the survivor realizes that should the disaster be "rerun," he might be the one to die. This ambivalence is suggested in the emphasis of many upon how thin—"the thickness of one sheet of paper," as the Japanese proverb several people quoted to me has it—was the margin of survival.

Only the professional cremator could bring his usual mocking (and self-mocking) humor to a sweeping wish to "undo" the entire atomic bomb constellation: "If only *this* thing hadn't been dropped, all of *those* things wouldn't have happened."

Whatever his sense of good or bad fortune, whatever his claimed virtue or inner sense of the opposite, the survivor's concern about "accidents of survival" reflect his profound feeling that he was "saved" by an unknowable destiny or fate which he must both constantly propitiate and view with uneasiness—since these same larger forces willed the death of so many others. Survivors feel that they "owe a death" not only to God or Destiny, but to the actual A-bomb dead.

Everything returns the *hibakusha* to his self-accusatory inner question: "Why did I live while they died?" None can satisfactorily answer the question, but some attempt to cope with it by making what amounts to an offer to reverse survival priority. One man, a writer and manufacturer, told me, for instance, how he felt when watching his child dying: "If it were possible, I wanted to sacrifice myself in place of my daughter." The psychological difficulty, as we have seen, is that one both wants to and is relieved that one cannot. To survive—and worse, to want to survive—is perceived as improper, wrong, inexcusable, even hateful.

The professor of English calls upon Dickens and Dante to help him express these sentiments:

> When people go through such experiences, they reach the very root of existence, and at such times their emotions are very simple. It is just a matter of the question: Is it life or is it death? . . . They should have helped their "fellow-passengers among human beings," as Dickens put it, but they . . . could not. . . . I had read Dante before, but now I really understood what this great man was saying. . . . I saw . . . true hellfire for the first time.*

By "true hellfire" he means not only massive death and devastation, but the psychic flames of death guilt.

Yōko Ōta similarly raised the problem of survival priority when she spoke of "the shame of living," of being "bothered by the fact that I was still alive," and even more specifically in the phrase: "I was sorry for the people who died because I was living."[30] *The survivor can never, inwardly, simply conclude that it was logical and right for him, and not others, to survive. Rather, he is bound by an unconscious perception of organic social balance which makes him feel that his survival was made possible by others' deaths: If they had not died, he would have had to; if he had not survived, someone else would have.* Such guilt, as it relates to survival priority, may well be that most fundamental to human existence.

---

* He was speaking to me in English, and his allusion to "hellfire" in Dante probably refers to the latter's idea of the *Inferno*. In any case, it has the same psychological significance.

INVISIBLE CONTAMINATION

three

1) The "Epidemic"

Soon after the bomb fell—sometimes within hours or even minutes, often during the first twenty-four hours or the following days and weeks—survivors began to notice in themselves and others a strange form of illness. It consisted of nausea, vomiting, and loss of appetite; diarrhea with large amounts of blood in the stools; fever and weakness; purple spots on various parts of the body from bleeding into the skin (purpura); inflammation and ulceration of the mouth, throat, and gums (oropharyngeal lesions and gingivitis); bleeding from the mouth, gums, throat, rectum, and urinary tract (hemorrhagic manifestations); loss of hair from the scalp and other parts of the body (epilation); extremely low white blood cell counts when these were taken (leukopenia); and in many cases a progressive course until death.*

These manifestations of toxic radiation effects aroused in the minds of the people of Hiroshima a special terror, *an image of a weapon which not only instantly kills and destroys on a colossal scale but also leaves behind in the bodies of those exposed to it deadly influences which may emerge at any time and strike down their victims.* This image was made

---

* The gastrointestinal symptoms appeared first and the hemorrhagic manifestations and other bone marrow effects some weeks later, so that the overall syndrome only gradually revealed itself.[1]

particularly vivid by the delayed appearance of these symptoms and fatalities—two to four weeks later—in people who had previously seemed to be in perfect health and externally untouched.

The shopkeeper's assistant, whose parents were killed by the bomb, describes his reactions to the death of two additional close family members from these radiation effects, and the general atmosphere of death that prevailed:

My grandmother was taking care of my younger brother on the fourteenth of August when I left; and when I returned on the fifteenth, she had many spots all over her body. Two or three days later she died. . . . My younger brother, who . . . was just a [five-month-old] baby, was without breast milk—so we fed him thin rice gruel. . . . But on the tenth of October he suddenly began to look very ill, though I had not then noticed any spots on his body. . . . Then on the next day he began to look a little better, and I thought he was going to survive. I was very pleased, as he was the only family member I had left, and I took him to a doctor—but on the way to the doctor he died. And at that time we found that there were two large spots on his bottom. . . . I heard it said that all these people would die within three years . . . so I thought, "sooner or later I too will die.". . . I felt very weak and very lonely—with no hope at all . . . and since I had seen so many people's eyebrows falling out, their hair falling out, bleeding from their teeth I found myself always nervously touching my hair like this [he demonstrated by rubbing his head]. . . . I never knew when some sign of the disease would show itself. . . . And living in the countryside then with my relatives, people who came to visit would tell us these things, and then the villagers also talked about them—telling stories of this man or that man who visited us a few days ago, returned to Hiroshima, and died within a week. . . . I couldn't tell whether these stories were true or not, but I believed them then. And I also heard that when the *hibakusha* came to evacuate to the village where I was, they died there one by one. . . . This loneliness, and the fear. . . . The physical fear . . . has been with me always. . . . It is not something temporary . . . I still have it now. . . .

We find here a link between the early sense of ubiquitous death from radiation effects and later anxieties about death and illness. The *hibakusha*'s own sense of impending death is also brought out by Miss Ōta in her belief at the time that "within two or three days I would die. If

not within a few days, then within three months or so I would die.
. . ."²

The writer-manufacturer who expressed his willingness to have died
in his daughter's place describes the impact upon him of her sudden
illness and death:

My daughter was working with her classmates at a place a thousand
meters from the hypocenter. . . . I was able to meet her the next day
at a friend's house. She had no burns and only minor external
wounds, so I took her with me to my country house. She was quite all
right for a while but on the fourth of September she suddenly became
sick. . . . The symptoms of her disease were different from those of a
normal disease. . . . She had spots all over her body. . . . Her hair
began to fall out. She vomited small clumps of blood many times.
Finally she began to bleed all over her mouth. And at times her fever
was very high. I felt this was a very strange and horrible disease. . . .
We didn't know what it was. I thought it was a kind of epidemic—
something like cholera. So I told the rest of my family not to touch
her and to disinfect all utensils and everything she used. . . . We
were all afraid of it, and even the doctor didn't know what it was.
. . . After ten days of agony and torture she died on September
fourteenth. . . . I thought it was very cruel that my daughter, who
had nothing to do with the war, had to be killed in this way. . . .

Survivors were thus affected not only by the fact of people dying around
them but by the way in which they died: a gruesome form of rapid
bodily deterioration which seemed unrelated to more usual and "de-
cent" forms of death.

For many, these deaths had an eerie quality, as suggested by the
electrician on the basis of his vigil at the railroad station:

Those sick people . . . from their outward appearance, didn't seem
to be in pain. Only they couldn't move, and even as we watched them
they seemed to become faint. . . . But their minds were quite clear
. . . not like people who had severe burns or shock or other injuries.
. . . There was one man who asked me for help and everything he
said was clear and normal. . . . He even told me how somebody
robbed him of his wristwatch . . . but in another three hours or so
when I looked at him he was already dead. . . . And even those who
looked as though they would be spared were not spared. . . . People
seemed to inhale something from the air which we could not see.
. . . The way they died was different . . . and strange.

Nor did naming the illness lessen this terror. Rather, as a Buddhist priest explains, the name itself became a symbol of the mysterious and deadly force before which all were helpless:

> We heard the new phrase, "A-bomb disease." The fear in us became strong, especially when we would see certain things with our eyes: a man looking perfectly well as he rode by on a bicycle one morning, suddenly vomiting blood, and then dying. . . . Soon we were all worried about our health, about our own bodies—whether we would live or die. And we heard that if someone did get sick, there was no treatment that could help. We had nothing to rely on, there was nothing to hold us up. . . .

An occasional *hibakusha* made herculean, if desperate, efforts to save dying family members, and when these failed, to give meaning to their deaths—as was true of the Protestant minister with his daughter:

> As for her symptoms, she had fever on the thirtieth [of August]. . . . She had been quite well until then. But the following day she couldn't eat or drink anything. It was difficult to get food but I got some eggs and tomatoes. I tried to nourish her. There was a doctor in the next village and I thought, We have to get him. He said that if these are effects from A-bomb disease then it is very difficult, and that the best thing was a blood transfusion. So I borrowed a syringe from a nurse and I tried to take blood from my wife and put it into my daughter . . . but her condition became worse. She had various symptoms—urine coming out, high temperature, her hair falling out a little. . . . I tried to have a farewell. In our religion the Reverend serves the Lord's Supper. She wouldn't take bread and instead of wine we used tomato juice. . . . We sang hymns of farewell. On the fourth night I showed her the mountain ranges from the window. That night she said, "I hear my name—Yōko—being called. My name is being called." I said, "It is God calling you. Are you prepared?" She said, "Yes." Her mouth opened and she fell back and died. . . . It was rather strange that all of a sudden someone could be taken ill and die. . . . We were told that all A-bomb victims would die within a month . . . so we were waiting for her death—like a death sentence. . . . We waited for our own deaths too. . . .

Whether or not the account of the girl's death was retrospectively idealized to fit the Christian frame, it suggests the sense of the inexorability of the prevailing "death sentence," even among those who fought against it.

Some were intrigued and attracted by the very weirdness of the symptoms, as in the case of a doctor quoted by Miss Ōta:

> An old woman . . . died within a few days after the bomb, showing many spots on her body. Dr. S. [who had attended her] told me: "I know it is terrible to say this, but those spots were beautiful. They were just like stars—red, green-yellow, and black—all over her body, and I was fascinated by them."[3]

We may suspect that underneath this characteristically Japanese aesthetic imagery lay the primitive and perverse emotions mentioned earlier in connection with other kinds of fascination; and that the doctor was also expressing unconscious relief that these striking colors were not present on his own body.

Miss Ōta goes on to tell of impressions created by the impersonality of the deaths, by their lack of relationship even to the war, and particularly by the mystery surrounding them:

> The war is over, but because of the war we are now dying. I find that very strange. . . . An old man said, "I hear that those who went into Hiroshima after the bomb and inhaled poison . . . are gradually dying.". . . Death was reeling before our eyes. We confronted death day and night. Cancer or leprosy patients are put in a large room together. . . . They realize their illness is incurable . . . and every day, without fail, two or three of them know death. . . . We were very much like them but we were not even sick. . . . We were being killed against our will by something completely unknown to us. . . . It is the misery of being thrown into a world of new terror and fear, a world more unknown than that of people sick with cancer. . . .[4]

Even more than did burns or injuries, radiation symptoms profoundly affected human relationships. The relief experienced by those free of such symptoms became associated with guilt, and with *a strong unconscious wish to separate oneself from the afflicted group*. These patterns were particularly evident in the mathematician upon his return to the "contaminated" world of Hiroshima after two months spent in another city for treatment of his eye injury:

> I was surprised to find people . . . walking about the city with little hair on their heads. . . . I was struck by the power of the bomb to

cause these later effects. . . . I was very relieved to realize that although I had been in Hiroshima at the time [of the bomb], I did not have these effects. . . . As time went by, and I learned more about the sickness caused by the bomb . . . I felt extremely sorry for these people. . . .

Dr. Hachiya describes the generalized dread of telltale purple spots:

Everyone had begun to examine one another for these ominous spots until it seemed we were suffering from a "spot phobia." I, too, became afraid. When I got back to my bed, I examined every inch of my body and you can imagine the relief I felt when I found no petechiae. So far, I was all right.[5]

But he does not mention the terrifyingly ambivalent wishes which must have accompanied these mutual examinations, wishes that the spots appear upon other people rather than upon oneself.

The *hibakusha's* urge to protect himself from the "epidemic" and from its dead victims was revealed in attitudes toward corpses, as recalled by the professional cremator:

Some people were very happy to leave dead bodies here because the bodies had such a terrible smell. Therefore they were . . . not sorrowful, but rather pleased that the bodies would be disposed of in this way. There was no medicine at the time, and families found it [care for the moribund] extremely difficult—and were often pleased that people who had suffered so badly finally died. . . .

Those who were afflicted with radiation effects could have a similar sense of grotesque contamination in relationship to their own bodies—as the same man also reveals:

I was all right for three days . . . but then I became sick with fever and bloody diarrhea. . . . After a few days I vomited blood also. . . . There was a very bad burn on my hand, and when I put my hand in water something strange and bluish came out of it, like smoke. After that my body swelled up and worms crawled on the outside of my body. . . .

Even after recovery from these symptoms, such people could retain a feeling that their bodily function has been mysteriously and permanently altered—as was true of a female poet exposed originally at fifteen hundred meters:

> Although it was not the proper time, I had my menses right after that. Also diarrhea. Then my hair began to fall out and I had spots all over my body. . . . I have never recovered. . . .

2) Atomic Bomb Mythology

Such symptoms became readily entangled with atomic bomb mythology —whether this mythology had to do with victims' specific bodily responses, or with more general qualities of the weapon itself—with the "poison" it emitted and its impact upon the environment. As is true of all mythology, the beliefs embraced had a quality of psychic truth, as well as psychic necessity, whatever their logical absurdity.

BODIES AND CORPSES

Bodily mythology frequently centered around which symptoms were dangerous and which protected one from danger. It often included a kind of "law of compensation"—beliefs such as "Those who suffered from severe burns were more healthy than those struck from minor burns"; "People who had burns did not get the spots and those who did not have burns got them"; and "Death approached those who were slightly injured or not injured at all . . . while those who were badly burned survived."[6] These beliefs were not only useful contributions to the psychic closing-off process; they provided desperately needed imagery of life to balance overwhelming death anxiety and death guilt, as well as ordering principles that could be grasped midst otherwise incomprehensible disorder. And such life-enhancing formulations could connect themselves to almost any kind of observable bodily trait—as Miss Ōta suggests:

> Dr. S. said, ". . . all the wounds [I have seen] are horizontal. . . . Yours . . . is the only exception. . . ." So . . . just because my cut was not horizontal but vertical, I thought I might not die. . . .

Central to these mythological ideas was the theme of detoxification, of getting rid of the "poison." One way to get rid of it was through a special kind of hemorrhage, as described by the divorced housewife who had been left with her mother after her father's seemingly sacrificial death:

> My mother began to show the symptoms and her condition seemed hopeless. Her hair fell out so that her head looked as though it were

shaved. She had spots . . . and she had no color in her face and no appetite. She had all of the symptoms people talked about, but hers seemed worse than most. . . . Her feet began to become cold and we thought she wouldn't live. . . . Then the next day she began to bleed. . . . She was at that period of life when a woman's menstruation stops . . . and so we thought she was having this bleeding just before it was ending. . . . But she bled so much that we could not find enough cotton or cloth to use, and it had a terrible odor. . . . This bleeding lasted about one week, which was unusual . . . and we thought it let the poison in her body out, and saved her life. . . .

Vomiting could accomplish the same purpose, as we learn from the abandoned mother:

When the children threw up . . . that dark liquid . . . I was at a loss as to what to do. But later I heard that what they threw up came from the gas, so it was good for them to throw up. I heard this from many people. . . .

The same woman also expressed a different form of mythology, the idea that the A-bomb could literally "strike one dumb," in this case her one-year-old baby:

I don't know whether such a young baby can receive a severe shock, but for about one year, until the following July, he didn't cry, didn't laugh, didn't make any sound with his voice. . . . At the time of the bomb I turned to the child . . . and his eyes opened as wide as possible—I was surprised to see how wide a baby could open its eyes. . . . He held his arms toward me . . . and made the sound "aa aa aa" at that moment, because he was very frightened. . . . And from then on I did not hear his voice. . . .

The rest of her story suggested that she had exaggerated the extent of the child's silence, and that its developmental problems were more a function of her continuing difficulty in providing nurturance than of any single "shock." But the point is that she felt the bomb capable of inflicting upon the child this temporary form of symbolic death.

More powerful mythology surrounded those actually dead. In addition to impressions of how people died, there were beliefs about special characteristics of corpses. I was told that "men floated face downward and women face upward," an imaginary observation which might be related to positions men and women characteristically assume in sexual relations and to that assumed by women when nursing, particularly so since most of these corpses were naked.

The cremator brought his imagination to actual observations:

> The bodies were black in color . . . most of them had a peculiar smell, and everyone thought this was from the bomb. . . . The smell when they burned was caused by the fact that these bodies were decayed, many of them even before being cremated—some of them having their internal organs decay even while the person was living. . . . All of the bodies swelled and had a color like the bluish substance of my burned hand—so maybe there was some kind of poison in the bomb. . . . Also, it was hard to burn those bodies. The ones who died with extremely high blood counts were dry and thin and also very hard to burn. . . . Other people didn't know about these matters—only I did—but about the smell, of course everybody knew about that, because the city was filled with that smell. . . .

Since Hiroshima resembled a vast open-air crematorium, this type of corpse-mythology was widespread. Miss Ōta's comment on the matter was bitterly ironic: "Someone said that the ashes of the dead made good fertilizer. What a cheap fertilizer they were!"[7] But the cremator's further impressions were more grim, extending to survivors in what might be termed a "living-corpse mythology":

> There is some difference, but I can't quite explain it . . . a slight difference in the look in people's eyes and the lines of their faces. . . . Even now if you go to the hospitals you can locate patients suffering from A-bomb disease from the look on their faces. . . .

Even highly educated *hibakusha* called upon mythological imagery from their individual and cultural pasts, as was true of the professor of English in telling of the "blue flames" with which we are already familiar:

> When I was a little boy, I was told that when people died and were cremated, they burned with a blue phosphorescent flame. Of course, I never believed this. But as I was walking along—it was pitch black, I was walking with a friend, and we were returning by a long route to the city because of the fires—we saw many corpses all around us. . . . I tried not to let myself see anything except my friend, but . . . I saw people being burned, and I saw those little phosphorescent flames

all over. Anybody who was in the city that day saw them. So the thing that I had been taught, which I had not believed, was true.

While he does not explicitly connect these blue flames with the original belief that they represent souls departing from the body, we may assume that this association had psychological importance for him and for others. Indeed, he went on to suggest that there were no limits to what survivors believed and did, and he spoke of corpse-mythology in a way that left some doubt as to where he himself stood:

> Whatever you hear about the experience, whatever wild stories—and no matter how unbelievable they seem—they are true. . . . When people were searching in the city for relatives they knew were dead, they believed that when they came close to the corpse of such a relation, it would give them some indication—make some movement, perhaps open its mouth, to indicate to them it was there. . . .

This imagery of communication between corpses and surviving family members is in one sense a form of denial of the relative's death; but it also represents the use of folk belief in the service of a sense of continuity in life and death—as is revealed by the observations of the noncommissioned officer-turned-social worker:

> When parents of dead soldiers would come to look at the large piles of bones in which they thought—but were not sure—their sons' bones were included, they would sometimes talk to these piles of bones. They would say, "Tatsuo," or whatever their son's name was, "if you are there, please move a bit so that I will know you are there, and then I will take you home."

TREES, GRASS, AND FLOWERS

Whatever the integrative aspects of folk belief and corpse-mythology, the terrors of the "epidemic atmosphere" could not be checked. They found expression in three widely circulated rumors about the general Hiroshima environment which dominated the mythological vista.

The first rumor simply held that all who had been exposed to the bomb in the city would be dead within three years. The time sometimes varied, but not the message, which was: None can escape the poison; the epidemic is total; all shall eventually die. This naked death symbolism derived mainly from the impact of radiation effects.

But a second rumor, even more frequently described to me and, I believe, with greater emotion, was that trees, grass, and flowers would never again grow in Hiroshima; from that day on, the city would be unable to sustain vegetation of any kind. The message here was: Nature is drying up altogether; life is being extinguished at its source. *This suggested an ultimate form of desolation, which not only encompassed human death but went beyond it.* In a culture placing such stress upon nature as aesthetically enveloping and energizing all of human life,* such symbolism had great emotional force—as various statements made by *hibakusha* reveal:

> I heard that no trees and flowers would grow. . . . I thought it would be forever. . . . I felt lonely . . . in a way I never had before. . . .

> Without trees and grass you can't live. I was fearful about whether we would die or live. . . .

> . . . An ordinary bomb kills people hit by it and some people within so many meters. . . . But the A-bomb kills not only people but also trees and grass. . . . This makes me extremely afraid. . . .

A third rumor, closely related to the other two, held that for a period of seventy-five (sometimes seventy) years, Hiroshima would be uninhabitable; no one would be able to live there. Here was the sense that the mysterious poison emitted by the weapon had more or less permanently deprived the city of its life-sustaining capacity—had deurbanized, literally devitalized, Hiroshima. At least partial belief in this rumor was reflected by the sudden drop in real estate prices reported to have occurred during the period immediately after the bomb, and by the serious consideration given a plan to rebuild Hiroshima Teachers' College (later Hiroshima University) on a nearby island instead of in the center of Hiroshima, where it had previously stood. While one factor was the existence on the island of several solid buildings at a time when new construction was almost impossible, the sociologist made clear that another was "the feeling that Hiroshima would not be a safe place in which to stay . . . [because] the rumor seemed to make people feel that if they did stay in Hiroshima, they might not live a very long life. . . ."

There were also, immediately after the bomb fell, more transient and

---

* But since variations on this form of nature symbolism are universal, rumors such as these could probably occur among any people subjected to atomic bomb effects.

sporadic rumors to the effect that American planes would return and drop additional weapons of the same or even greater power—rumors consistent with the "fear of recurrence"[8] characteristic for any disaster, and related to death anxiety and to death guilt. People feared new American attacks with "poison gases" or "burning oil" that would further decimate the city. There was also a rumor that having dropped such a dreadful "hot bomb," America would next drop a "cold bomb" (or "ice bomb") which would simply "freeze everything" in a way that "everyone would die"; and another that America would drop "rotten pigs" so that "everything on the earth would decay and go bad." These additional rumors conveyed the sense that the environment had been so fundamentally disturbed, and the individual sense of security (and invulnerability) so threatened, that further devastation of *any imaginable kind* must be anticipated. Beyond the sense experienced in all disasters that "a catastrophic universe has come into being,"[9] there was the feeling that *deadly catastrophe knew no limits*.

To what extent were these rumors believed and acted upon? I found that people varied in the extent of their belief, but no one could entirely dismiss them. Relatively uneducated *hibakusha* often accepted them unquestioningly, while intellectuals had ambivalent and convoluted responses which were more a form of participation in the general atmosphere of death than clear-cut convictions. As the sociologist explained, "these rumors did not say that people would die as soon as they stepped into Hiroshima, but contained a [general] feeling about the future." And the mathematician reveals the conflict between rational doubt and emotional susceptibility even in a scientist who knew something about the overall problem:

> I half believed [the rumor that Hiroshima would be uninhabitable for seventy years], half doubted it. . . . I thought that the effects of radiation would last for some time, and that there could be a greater effect from radiation if people remained in the city—though seventy years did seem very long. I thought perhaps for five years or so, but seventy years was too long. . . .*

And concerning the loss of vegetation, he describes a powerful feeling-tone rather than a precise belief:

---

* The actual danger period from residual radiation is considered, at the very maximum, two or three weeks. But this was not known at the time, and is a matter of dispute even now.[10]

I never really pictured Hiroshima without people or without grass or trees. Instead, my mind was full of the thought that I should leave, that I should go somewhere else. I thought of going to a suburb near the country, though I only thought of this for a short time. . . .

Similar mental processes took place in physicians, as we learn from Dr. Hachiya's description of his reaction to hearing one of these rumors from another doctor at the prefectural office one week after the bomb fell:

"Is something the matter?" I asked, fearful that the news I had been so anxious to get might not be welcome news.

"You've no doubt heard that an 'atom bomb' was dropped on Hiroshima?" Dr. Kitajima answered. "Well, I've learned that no one will be able to live in Hiroshima for the next seventy-five years."

"One of our nurses died suddenly, yesterday," I answered, as if to confirm the ominous import of his words.

After I had spoken, I was annoyed at having given credence to what my mind recognized only as an ugly rumor. . . . Nothing is so unstable as a man's mind, especially when it is fatigued. Regardless of the direction one's thoughts take, the mind is ever active, ever moving, at times slowly, at times with lightning rapidity. My mind was a confusion of strength and weakness, sometimes fused, sometimes separated.[11]

Among those few *hibakusha* who claimed to be totally unaffected by the rumors, there were usually memory lapses and other indications of strong denial and of continuing inability to confront the actual emotional experience—as was true of the philosopher:

Those [rumors] came perhaps one or two months later—but I don't remember, may be two or three weeks later. . . . I started to hear the rumor that Hiroshima would be barren ground—nothing would grow there. That might have been in the newspaper. I don't remember. . . . I felt nothing in particular about them. . . .

The rumors persisted in the face of contrary evidence—green grass still visible in parts of the city and weeds sprouting from the ruins. And again, naming the source of contamination had limited effect; as the sociologist put it, "Ordinary people spoke of poison, the intellectuals spoke of radiation." For the rumors' message of ubiquitous death, and of desolation beyond death, had sufficient symbolic validity to overcome whatever logic could be mustered against them. Like most of the early atomic bomb mythology, their power declined after a few months, particularly as people found themselves able to return to the center of the city and, in one way or another, to resume their lives there. But the rumors remained quite active for more than a year (the length of time it took for real estate prices to show a significant rise), and their psychic remnants, as we shall see later, continue to affect life in Hiroshima.

The origins of the three major rumors—and particularly of the figure of seventy-five years—remain obscure to *hibakusha* even today. One source mentioned by several is a Japanese saying that a rumor stops after seventy-five days. The physicist referred to a substance he came upon, which through nuclear fission is said to have effects for seventy-five years. But of definite psychological interest was the widespread impression that the rumors themselves came "from the outside," "possibly from America," "from scholars," or "from a certain scientist, possibly an American." Here the implication is that America was the source not only of the deadly contamination but of foreknowledge of its nature. And the idea of a scholarly or scientific source conveys authority.*

* Dr. Tsuzuki himself was reported to have approached the first Allied military-scientific team to reach Hiroshima (arriving on September 8) with the dual question of whether the atomic bomb contained some kind of poison gas and whether there was any truth to the "foreign news report" of a claim by "an American expert" to the effect that toxic influences from the bomb would last for seventy-five years. Dr. Tsuzuki added, "I believe [the report] to be entirely wrong," but both his asking the question and his mention of an American source of the rumor are significant. I was unable to obtain in Hiroshima any more specific information about the origins of this quotation from an "American expert." But later, through the help of Austin M. Brues of the Argonne National Laboratory, I learned that such a statement had actually been made within forty-eight hours of the news of the first atomic bombing by Harold F. Jacobson, a chemist and science writer, who had earlier been involved in atomic bomb research in a minor capacity. In an interview with an International News Service representative, Jacobson was reported to have said that radioactivity from the atomic bomb would be fatal to anyone entering Hiroshima for a period of seventy years. Jacobson also said that gamma rays given off when uranium is broken down "destroy the red corpuscles in the blood and eventually cause leukemia." His statements were quickly disseminated throughout the world, so that the first information to reach Japan from America about radiation effects did so accompanied by this extraordinary distortion about duration of contamination. On August 8 there were published denials on the part of the War Department and of J. Robert Oppenheimer, who had headed scientific work on the bomb, as well as a modification (though not a complete retraction) by Jacobson of his original statement. Indeed, when informed by military authorities that he could be imprisoned under the Espionage Act for a period of ten years for what he had said, Jacobson collapsed in his New York office and was described as "too disturbed" to meet with newspaper reporters. Jacobson's statement was merely one expression of the awesome early rumors about the bomb which took hold in America (where they were based upon quasi-scientific speculation) as well as Japan, and included the idea that the bomb would be "lethal beyond the range of bodily injury by consuming all the oxygen in

Whatever the rumors' source, the intense anxiety they contained could well have impaired the capacity of many *hibakusha* to recover from either wounds or radiation effects. Thus, Miss Ōta commented at the time that these beliefs, together with incomplete but frightening medical reports, "sometimes invite victims to a violent death"—by which she meant either that they could expect nothing but their own death or that only suicide was appropriate, or both.[13] Moreover, accurate information did not necessarily dispel the mythology (the medical man who mentioned the rumor of seventy-five-year uninhabitability to Dr. Hachiya also mentioned that an atomic bomb had been used), and could even, because of the actual nature of radiation effects, intensify anxiety. As the history professor put it, "At first our fear was not too great—then, as we got more understanding about the bomb, our fear became extreme."

For atomic bomb mythology was, in essence, a mythology of contamination. Indeed, this entire second stage of death encounter was characterized by the fear of epidemic contamination to the point of bodily deterioration, along with a sense of individual powerlessness in the face of an invisible, all-enveloping, and highly mysterious poison;* the guilt-filled rejection of the afflicted by the unafflicted; and the inner sense that this *total* contamination—seemingly limitless in time and space—must have a supernatural, or at least more-than-natural origin, so that one's survival was likely to be merely a temporary respite from these invincible forces of destruction and toxicity.

THE WEAPON PERCEIVED

The atomic bomb itself, as a weapon, gave rise to additional mythological responses. For from the moment of exposure to it, *hibakusha* felt a strong need to place it within some framework of understanding.

Initial formulations of many reverted to past experience of a more or less "ordinary" wartime nature· "I thought this must be a terrible

---

the air." A possible source of the seventy-five (rather than seventy) -year figure can be found in an early newspaper claim that "Dispatches from Washington said that scientists, piecing together their knowledge, reported that the area where the bomb had struck would be uninhabitable for from five to seventy-five years." But there remains the likelihood that Japanese sources also contributed significantly to the various rumors of contamination.[12]

* Contributing to the force of this imagery was a longstanding Japanese cultural preoccupation with "contamination," as reflected by the stress upon purification in Shinto religious ritual and by analogous emphases in individual-psychological experience.

firebomb"; "I thought perhaps a weapons factory had exploded"; or "I thought an ammunition dump had blown up." Others called forth electrical imagery, either as simile ("It was like an electric short circuit") or as being causally related to what actually happened ("The electric wires were broken and there was a big fire"). Some thought of natural calamity ("It was like an earthquake") and still others of imagery that suggested supernatural alteration of nature ("like purple lightning" or "like thunder from the bottom of the earth"). Most were made quickly and uneasily aware that their imagery was inadequate, that they had no relevant experience on which to base their impressions.

Japanese authorities unwittingly encouraged atomic bomb mythology by refusing to identify the weapon accurately, referring to it simply as a "special weapon" or "special bomb." This was done as a measure of wartime censorship, to avoid frightening the population of Hiroshima and of Japan in general, and to maintain the cherished illusion that nothing—not even this weapon—had been unforeseen by them or was beyond their capacity to deal with. In a way the policy represented a kind of "negative mythology," of a weapon which, however devious, was not sufficiently revolutionary or destructive to defeat Japan's invincible spirit. (Subsequent restriction of information by American authorities, as we shall later discuss, reflected its own form of negative mythology and also perpetuated myths surrounding the weapon.)

Japanese leaders in Tokyo knew almost immediately that Hiroshima had been destroyed by an atomic bomb, having been so informed by President Truman's announcement broadcast by shortwave throughout the world soon after the event. And as early as August 8 the military flew leading physicists and medical authorities on radiation from Tokyo to Hiroshima in order to determine what had happened to the city. Soon afterward physicians came from nearby Okayama University, and in mid-August a team from Kyoto University. But these scientists' findings were of a very preliminary nature, and midst the extreme confusion and military censorship very little accurate information was communicated to the people of Hiroshima or even to the city's own surviving doctors. Most of the latter did not become clear about atomic bomb effects until September 3, when special lectures were given for an assembled medical group by two of the Tokyo consultants.[14]

Meanwhile, the idea that an atomic bomb had been used began to circulate among ordinary people—like the shopkeeper's assistant—as simply another frightening rumor:

At first I heard it was a new type of bomb . . . and then I heard people calling it an atomic bomb. . . . When I heard the words "atomic bomb," I didn't know what "atomic" meant . . . so I just accepted what I heard. But what I did know very well was that it was a horrible thing. . . .

Others greeted information about the weapon with awed incredulity: "It seemed unbelievable that such a weapon as the atomic bomb could exist. . . ." And although intellectuals were quicker to grasp both the fact that an atomic bomb had been used and some of the implications of the weapon, they were not necessarily any less confused. A written recollection by the history professor of a conversation which took place on the day of the bomb, even if altered in retrospect, suggests the strange atmosphere of half-knowledge that came to prevail:

I noticed a young Army officer among the refugees, his appearance and his demeanor suggesting that of a drafted "student-soldier." . . . I said in a somewhat demanding tone, "What has happened, Officer?" . . . He looked at me in dubious silence. . . . In those days the militarists had severe prohibitions against spreading what they called "sensational rumors in the street" . . . so I quickly produced my name card which bore my titles. . . . The officer relaxed somewhat and said: "The fact is, I am also from a university and majored in scientific subjects and I fear it was an atomic bomb." . . . I recalled someone having told me that a small match-box of atoms could blow up all of Mount Fuji . . . or destroy an entire city . . . and I said to myself, "Yes, it must be that." . . . I was one of the first to realize the kind of bomb it was . . . but even so, at that time I could not really understand the A-bomb . . . only afterward.

Intellectuals sought out knowledgeable friends and colleagues, and within a few weeks pamphlets and articles describing the A-bomb were published. But during this early period even scientists themselves—though aware of the theoretical feasibility of an atomic bomb, and now faced by the most extreme external evidence that one had been used—had considerable psychological difficulty coming to this conclusion. The mathematician, for instance, tells how he and his colleagues had to be told what had happened by outside authorities before they could believe what they already had reason to know:

I understood the possibility of making a bomb with so much explosive energy . . . and friends and I had talked about the possibility of the enemy using an atomic bomb, but we doubted whether they could. . . . Then after it fell I wondered if it could have been an atomic bomb. . . . I thought that an atomic bomb must be much bigger . . . of enormous explosive power, even more than whatever had been dropped upon us. . . . But the fact that there was no particular spot where the bomb hit the ground and yet it had such great effects, the large number of people burned by the bomb, the black cloud of dark rain, and the great flash it produced—for all these reasons I thought it might be an atomic bomb. . . . Then I talked with other science professors. . . . We had different opinions among us—but gradually we heard from the outside that it was an atomic bomb. . . . When I heard this, I wondered how they had made the bomb. . . . I thought that America had been very quick to succeed in making such a bomb. . . .

Similarly, the physicist described having been misled by information given him by the Japanese military about a different kind of bomb, also exploded in mid-air, which allegedly caused damage over a cone-shaped area—but his further associations also revealed psychic unreadiness to accept the fact of the atomic bomb:

Of course, as far as theory was concerned, I had knowledge of that since 1939, when the principles of nuclear fission were disclosed. I knew about the potential power of nuclear explosions, but putting this into practice and making technological use of it was another matter, and in fact seemed impossible, especially from where we were in Japan. . . . I felt we had been defeated in the scientific field . . . and that science had a lot to do with this enormous destruction. . . . But about the A-bomb problem and the A-bomb reality, it was hard to say. . . . I couldn't really feel it in a week or in a month . . . or have a true realization of the problem of radiation until two or three years later. . . .

For either man to conclude that an atomic bomb had been used required a complex inner adjustment. Each had to encompass the existence of a technical achievement thought impossible, one reflecting overwhelming American superiority, the use of science for this new dimension of destruction, and the idea of having oneself been victimized and one's life threatened by it. No wonder, then, that Hiroshima scientists required confirmation from informed outsiders. Always strongly dependent upon the latter's authority, this dependency was now magnified by their own sense of helplessness, anxiety, and guilt in relationship to their death encounter. And even after reaching the inevitable conclusion that an atomic bomb had been used, Hiroshima scientists were still, like everyone else, ignorant of the bodily aftereffects of the bomb, and faced formidable psychic barriers to learning about these.

"BACILLARY DYSENTERY" AND "CHANGE IN ATMOSPHERIC PRESSURE"

Surviving physicians knew even less about nuclear energy and its effects. Observing widespread patterns of loss of appetite, nausea, and severe bloody diarrhea, they suspected some form of infectious dysentery and tried, however feebly under the circumstances, to institute isolation procedures to prevent contagion.

Dr. Hachiya's *Diary* frankly reveals the extreme confusion prevalent even in one of the few intact treatment centers where physicians were available. On August 7 he suspects "poison gas or perhaps some deadly germ" thrown off from a new weapon, and that night becomes convinced that "we were dealing with bacillary dysentery." On August 9 the bizarre symptoms he was observing, particularly the various kinds of hemorrhage, make him doubt his original impressions; and recalling that he heard no sound at the time of the bombing, he suspects that "a sudden change in atmospheric pressure" caused both the bleeding and widespread deafness. On August 12 he is told by a Navy captain that an atomic bomb had been used, and that one symptom it caused was a low white blood cell count; but although this strikes a chord in him ("Why, that's the bomb I've heard could blow up Saipan, and with no more than ten grams of hydrogen"), he finds that "the more I thought, the more confused I became." Therefore, when again told on August 13 that an atomic bomb had been used, this time by a more reliable authority (the physician at the Prefectural Office), he combines the two ideas in the assumption that the "sudden change in atmospheric pressure" might have been caused by the bomb. On August 19 he still despairs over his inability to understand why so many patients are dying, but takes up the theory (whether originally his own or someone else's is uncertain) that the gangrenous tonsilitis he observed clinically was causing toxic effects which resulted in a decreased white blood cell count, and that this in turn caused all of the other symptoms. The next day, after obtaining a microscope and confirming the extremely low white blood cell counts, he concludes that things were the other way around: he proudly (and more accurately) announces that "We are dealing with agranulocytosis [absence of white cells] due to an un-known cause and that's what caused the gangrenous tonsilitis!" During the next few days he apparently received additional information from authorities concerning radiation effects, and on the basis of this as well as his own continuing observations, including those made at an autopsy, he publicly posts a "Notice Regarding Radiation Sickness." The notice, which correctly advocated rest for those found to have low white counts, was later criticized for a somewhat over-optimistic tone (it was prepared largely to reassure people and counter their irrational fears), and for advising those who had not been in the center of the city at the time of the bomb, and did not have low white counts, to remain at their jobs. Finally, on September 3, he attends the lectures given by the two outside consultants (Dr. Tsuzuki and Dr. Miyake), finds their con-clusions to be the same as his, is somewhat troubled by the fact that they were the first to make their report, but returns to his hospital determined to complete his own statistical study.[15]

When I discussed these matters with Dr. Hachiya seventeen years later, he explained that he had had a very early impression, based upon his knowledge of x-ray effects, that the bomb's effects could be con-nected with radiation, but that this impression was extremely vague. Moreover, he did not associate these thoughts with an atomic bomb, even after being told by the Navy officer that an atomic bomb had been used. Not until he received further official information from the military (between August 21 and 26) did he become convinced of the connec-tion between the atomic bomb and radiation sickness: "The Army was in charge, so I thought they must be right." And only after Dr. Tsu-zuki's talk on September 3 did he really feel certain, since "Dr. Tsuzuki was a professor at Tokyo University . . . and ranked highly as a military consultant." We again note the *hibakusha*-scientists's need, if he is to accept the new formulation of the atomic bomb and its effects, for a pronouncement from someone who conveys authority and is himself "uncontaminated" by the bomb. But most of all we are struck by the way in which the death-saturated environment interferes with clarity of thought and formulation.

"A BOMB SUCH AS THAT"

The A-bomb's insidious feature made a particularly strong impression on individual *hibakusha*. As one said, "Ordinary bombs just destroy in a visible manner, but the A-bomb destroys people invisibly." This invisibly lethal capacity was sometimes attributed to "oil" or "electricity," but usually to "poison gas" or just "poison." Many held tenaciously to this imagery, even after information about radiation effects had been published in the newspaper—as we learn from Miss Ōta:

> They made no effort to learn scientifically about the cause of their fear of death; they just believed they had inhaled poison. One would say he inhaled poison, and another would say he, too, inhaled poison.[16]

"Poison gas" and "poison" might have been preferable to "radiation effects" because they were at least knowable, elements one could begin to fit into a "theory" of what had occurred. The idea of poison gas or oil was also consistent with another manifestation of the weapon which made an enormous impression upon people at the time of the bomb: the "black rain" which fell from the "big black cloud." This rain actually resulted from vaporization of moisture in the bomb's fireball and condensation in the cloud that formed; but, as the domestic worker tells us, it was often seen as the outpouring of deadly poison:

> Black rain began to fall and I wondered what it was. . . . It gave me a horrible feeling. . . . Facing toward Yokogawa everything looked black and we thought it was something caused by the bomb. . . . Later, people said it might be oil rain. . . . Among my friends we had two opinions. We wondered if it was oil to make fire or to harm people . . . whether they might be planning to kill all of the people by burning them . . . or whether this oil would stick to the skin of all of the people, making everyone die one after the other . . . even those who were exposed to just a very little bit of it. . . .

For others, like the divorced housewife, this "black cloud" symbolized the weapon's ubiquitous embrace. In extending imagery of the "black cloud" to include the entire A-bomb panorama, she may be distorting what she originally saw, but she conveys the *totality* of the weapon's impact:

> My strongest impression when the bomb fell was the clouds . . . one after another . . . which became spread out larger and larger, all black . . . chasing me . . . like a black hand stretched out . . . gradually expanding . . . to envelop everyone in it . . . covering everyone so that I too would inevitably be crushed by it. . . .

The electrician suggests the same kind of perception:

> I had seen a warship destroyed by bombs . . . and also one area of a town . . . but in Hiroshima it was a whole city. . . . I could never imagine a bomb such as that.

And the history professor, in a more literary way:

> Such a weapon has the power to make everything into nothing.
> :

One way to come to terms with the weapon was to give it a name other than its scientific one. Before very long it began to be widely referred to by the nickname *pikadon*, literally "flash-boom," and many *hibakusha* used this term when discussing the bomb with me. Those who experienced its full effects within the central area of the city first called it only *pika*, or "flash," since they heard no sound of the explosion; the *don*, or "boom," was supplied by those who were outside the city at the time but came in later. In any case, the nickname was the survivor's way of taming or domesticating the monster, of making it into something one could deal with through one's accustomed range of emotions. People sometimes mentioned the *pikadon* to me with a touch of humor—even occasionally with a suggestion of that nostalgic affection one permits oneself to feel toward an old enemy. This A-bomb jocularity reached its peak in the word *pikadon-don* ("flash-boom-boom"), used in connection with an early postwar literary movement in Hiroshima (known as "Decadence and Dadaism"), as part of the ridiculing of all awesome social symbols.[17] But by and large the monster has not submitted to taming. However the word *pikadon* may attenuate perceptions, it nonetheless conveys the full constellation of death imagery with which we are familiar.

Another way of dealing with the weapon was to identify oneself with it, or at least with its power. Such identification was present in the *hibakusha*'s urge to retaliate in kind—an A-bomb for an A-bomb— which Dr. Hachiya describes in what is, from the standpoint of general human psychology, one of his *Diary*'s most chilling passages:

> Following the news that Nagasaki had been bombed, a man came in from Fuchu [a nearby town] with the incredible story that Japan had the same mysterious weapon, but until now, had kept it a strict secret and had not used it because it was judged too horrible even to mention. This man went on to say that a special attack squad from

the Navy had now used the bomb on the mainland of America and that his news had come from no less a source than the General Headquarters. The blow had been dealt by a squadron of six-engined, trans-Pacific bombers, two of which failed to return. Those bombers were assumed to have dived right into their targets to make certain of success.

If San Francisco, San Diego, and Los Angeles had been hit like Hiroshima, what chaos there must be in those cities!

At last Japan was retaliating!

The whole atmosphere in the ward changed, and for the first time since Hiroshima was bombed, everyone became cheerful and bright. Those who had been hurt the most were the happiest. Jokes were made, and some began singing the victory song. Prayers were said for the soldiers. Everyone was now convinced that the tide of the war had turned.[18]

What is significant here is the sense of "the dead rising" through a vision of their *own* atomic bomb's making victims of others.

For some, identification with the bomb was related to being in awe of its power. The grocer, for instance, upon hearing the various rumors which circulated during the early months, and seeing enough to make him believe them, remembered feeling

. . . only the greatness of the bomb. "Greatness" is a funny way to put it, but the lasting effects of the bomb . . . toward these I felt great fear.

This combination of awe and fear could sometimes come close to admiration, resembling the psychological defense mechanism of "identification with the aggressor"—that is, of dealing with the power one fears by becoming like it or part of it.

Others were proud of having experienced the world's most advanced weapon. A few (notably the cremator) derived satisfaction from having seen the bomb fall and from recounting the contrast between the object's small size and the vastness of the damage it inflicted.* One or two referred contemptuously to "our foolish spears" (with which the Japanese were actually planning to defend themselves) in comparison to "this great bomb." One scholar, before dying from bomb effects, was quoted as saying, "The Americans are a great people, because anyone

---

* More visible than the bomb itself, and sometimes confused with it, were the three parachutes attached to recording equipment, dropped simultaneously from an accompanying airplane.

who makes such a terrible weapon must have some greatness in them," suggesting a form of identification initiated by the bomb but reaching for some nobility beyond it. Merely being moved by the beauty of the bomb's celestial panorama was a form of identification, as was becoming in any way lastingly absorbed by its effects.

Seeing the bomb as an agent of liberation from a repressive regime, as some did, was still another form of identification; and so was the early tendency of certain *hibakusha* to assume leadership in A-bomb problems. Probably the oddest form of identification was expressed in a rumor which held that Americans made use of a German pilot to drop the A-bomb, and that the Germans had originally developed the weapon and planned to drop it on New York but had had it taken away from them by the Americans. The unspoken assumption here is that this "great weapon" came not from the enemy, but from the nation with which Japan herself was then—militarily, politically, and culturally—most closely identified.*

There was also very early imagery about particular characteristics of the atomic bomb that made it seem a thing apart from ordinary weapons. Some emphasized as its unique feature "all of the people killed instantly"; many focused upon elements of invisible contamination; and many others simply called forth an overall image of "this special thing known as the atomic bomb," in which its uniqueness derived from its entire array of destructive capacities.

Finally, there developed, also rather early, a sense that this new weapon was still in the laboratory stage when it was dropped, and that the people of Hiroshima were thus victims of a vast "experiment." Some, like the divorced housewife, felt that had work on the experiment been more advanced, the outcome would have been worse:

> If the bomb had been perfected at the time it fell, we could not have survived, but as the [development of] bomb had not yet been completed, the situation was no worse than what happened.

Here is a psychological effort to see the bomb's destructiveness as limited, a guilty feeling that one has "cheated death," and the beginnings of imagery of being experimented upon, which we shall later observe to be central to the overall *hibakusha* experience.

* The same rumor, it turned out, spread in other parts of the world, and in fact continues to hold sway. Thus, in 1965, there appeared in *Pueblo,* a Madrid publication, an article entitled "La Bomba Atómica de Hiroshima era Alemana."[19]

3) "Vacuum State"

The sense of loss, on many symbolic levels, had a cumulative impact upon survivors, and brought about a widely shared psychic state. These symbolic losses did not necessarily have to be directly associated with atomic bomb exposure. For many, particularly among the older generation, the Emperor's surrender speech nine days later seemed more shattering than the bomb itself—as an elderly widow tells us:

> Hearing his words . . . I didn't think about the war itself. . . . What I understood well was that we were defeated. This thought was hard to bear. . . . I listened in tears. It is impossible for me to put into words how painful it was. . . . I felt terribly sorry for the Emperor . . . and this feeling remains with me even now when I imagine how he felt then. . . . [Comparing my feelings] when the bomb was dropped and when the Emperor [spoke], well, with the A-bomb, we didn't understand anything about it at the time . . . so I think the Emperor's words were harder to bear. . . .

There were also those among the younger generation who, like the seamstress, then fourteen years old, were totally unable to absorb the realities imposed by the Emperor's speech:

> The doctors had a radio and they told us about the surrender. . . . I was very young and had given up all studying in order to do voluntary labor. . . . Up to then everybody used the phrase, "until we win the victory." . . . So when the grownups around me told me that the end of war had come, my feeling was, This couldn't be so; the end hasn't come yet.

Miss Ōta expresses this sense of total collapse in more evocative literary style:

> I came out of the gate of Dr. S.'s large house [where she had heard the Emperor's speech] and down the stone steps. . . . I felt as if I were thrown into white air . . . it was an indescribable emptiness . . . which almost made me dizzy, as if I were on a high mountain. It was as though I were walking in a mist where there were no other

people, and my legs trembled. My body was so shaky I found it difficult to walk. . . .[20]

Such responses to the Emperor's speech became psychologically inseparable from reactions to the atomic bomb initiated nine days earlier. Indeed, we may speak of a merging of end-of-the-world experiences: the end of the ideological world of Japan's national mystique and of the immediate physical world of the Hiroshima environment. While the first seems more clearly a symbolic loss, both are ultimately experienced on the symbolic level. And it is quite possible that the extreme sense of loss initiated at the time of the bomb intensified *hibakusha* reactions to the Emperor's speech.

Within the actual atomic bomb experience one may delineate two dimensions of loss: the destruction of the human matrix, the group ties and coordinated patterns of existence which constitute what we usually speak of as the social fabric or social structure; and of the non-human environment, the material surroundings within which people conduct their lives. The breakdown of the non-human environment had particular significance in a culture which places such emphasis upon the background or context of life, and which views the individual person as less a separate being than an extension of his surroundings. Thus, within *hibakusha* internal symbolism, the material desolation of Hiroshima as a dwelling place, merged with human annihilation in a common image of disintegration.

This combined imagery dominated post-disaster themes of flight from the contaminated city, homeless wandering, occasional reunions, and further losses. The situation was epitomized by the large numbers of young orphans wandering through the city, violently severed from both human and non-human environments through the death of parents and destruction of homes. These youngsters gathered in various places in Hiroshima, particularly around the old Hiroshima Station, where they formed a nucleus for black-market activities and every other kind of antisocial behavior. Known as *furō-ji*, or homeless waifs, they conveyed to other survivors the sense of total breakdown of society.

The general atmosphere of disintegration is described by the shopkeeper's assistant:

At the place where our house was there was nothing left. . . . Here and there were [bodies of] people burned to blackness . . . everything was burned. We had buried some canned rice under the ground . . . and I tried to dig it out. But I found that the rice was black and couldn't be eaten. . . . The food situation was very bad. . . . The world was in complete chaos. . . .

He was more fortunate than many A-bomb orphans in having relatives and acquaintances to go to; but this did not prevent him from experiencing a profound sense of homelessness which continued even after some of the city's life had been restored:

At the farmer's house . . . they might have felt a bit troubled [by my presence], I think . . . so they told me it would be better for me to go out and learn some kind of skill in order to get a job. . . . I went to Hiroshima . . . and soon afterward my father's younger sister visited me . . . and asked me to come to her place to live, so that I could go to school. But . . . I stubbornly refused to go there. Later, when I was having a very hard time, I decided I would go there, but then the situation reversed itself [and I did not feel accepted] . . . so I quickly left. . . . I felt very lonely . . . as I had no parents . . . and there was no place where I was treated with the warmth of parents. . . .

A similar sense of internal and external disintegration prevented the seamstress from accepting the actuality of the overall disaster:

I didn't know that our house had been destroyed by the fire . . . so I begged the doctors to let me go home . . . but there was no house to return to. . . . We [she and her mother] stayed at the school [a temporary treatment center] until March, the time of my birthday. I was cured by then [she refers to her acute wounds; she was left with severe keloid scars] but we had no place to go . . . and we had great difficulty because we did not have enough money to live on. We went to stay with my aunt in the country, but could only remain there one week. Then my mother's friend . . . invited us to stay with her back in the city. This was my first return to Hiroshima. . . . Although I had been told the name of the bomb that had been dropped, I found it difficult to believe what I saw. . . . I couldn't believe that I had been in the midst of such a great disaster and had received such terrible injuries myself. . . .

And the history professor relates the breakdown of cultural values to the problem of starvation:

Because there was so little food in the city, to live each day without starving became the most important thing. When the Americans gave surplus food to the people, they were very grateful. . . . In Japan, our great moral principle was loyalty. But as soon as the new authority came into the country, people blindly obeyed it. . . . I felt that this blind submission to authority was very sad. . . .

While such unquestioning acceptance of the new authority occurred throughout the country and was a much more complex phenomenon than he suggests, the extremity of disintegration in Hiroshima undoubtedly accentuated the process because it greatly heightened the need for authorities of any kind to pull the world together.

Moreover, the food problem he referred to was very acute. People were desperate for anything edible, and many sustained themselves on a kind of weed known as "railroad grass," so named because it grew near the train tracks on the outskirts of the city, and according to one man, "was said to have originally come from America with the railroad." Some made a kind of dumpling from it, but since the weed was "so strong that the buds sprouted from hard rocks," eating the dumpling was "like chewing on sand." Ingesting too much of this weed caused diarrhea, and the eating of it is generally recalled with a sense of humiliation.

Humiliation, in fact, became a powerful psychological theme, together with the sense of being victimized, as Miss Ōta points out:

Before I realized it, I found myself falling into the sense of being a victim just like the others. When I noticed this, I felt burdened by self-contempt, but there was nothing I could do. . . . When my mother . . . spoke of the "afflicted people" [*risaimin*], I said to her, "Please do not say '*risaimin.*' It sounds miserable and I don't like it. At least say, '*risaisha*' [also "afflicted ones," but suggests a little less of being dissolved into an afflicted mass]." . . . My younger sister said, "I feel humiliated at all of [our family] going [to find shelter at someone else's home] together." . . .*

"CORPSES OF HISTORY"

Miss Ōta also tells of the impact upon her of the loss of Hiroshima's landmarks, of those parts of the non-human environment whose sym-

* Whatever the difference in usage of the two words for "afflicted people," the important thing for Miss Ōta was to avoid the one which conveyed to her the greatest sense of absolute victimization, humiliation, and obliteration of identity.[21]

bolic meaning was strongest. She describes having finally got used to the general destruction, even to the ubiquitous corpses, until

> I reached a bridge and saw that the Hiroshima Castle had been completely leveled to the ground, and my heart shook like a great wave. . . . This destruction of the castle gave me a thought. Even if a new city should be built on this land, the castle would never be built and added to that city. The city of Hiroshima, entirely on flat land, was made three-dimensional by the existence of the white castle, and because of this it could retain a classical flavor. Hiroshima had a history of its own. And when I thought about these things, the grief of stepping over the corpses of history pressed upon my heart. . . .[22]

The "corpses of history" are the ruins of significant symbols, in this case physical structures which enhanced a sense of continuity with the historical past. Miss Ōta's choice of words suggests once more the inseparability of imagery of symbolic and bodily forms of death.* In response to this general pattern of disintegration, *hibakusha* did not seem to develop clear-cut psychiatric syndromes.† To describe the emotional state they did develop they frequently used the term *kyodatsu-jōtai*, which means a state of despondency, abstraction, or emptiness, and may be translated as "state of collapse" or "vacuum state." Also relevant is a related state which Miss Ōta described as so widespread in the early stages as to constitute a medical symptom—that of *muyoku-ganbō*, a listlessness, withdrawn countenance, "expression of wanting nothing more," or what has been called in other contexts "the thousand-mile stare."‡ Conditions like the "vacuum state" or "thousand-mile stare" may be thought of as apathy, but are also profound expressions of despair: a form of severe and prolonged psychic numbing in which the survivor's responses to his environment are reduced to a minimum—

---

* What I am suggesting is that the many levels of disintegration—biological, physical-non-human, social, generally human, ideological (including the most primitive assumptions about the functioning of the universe), and historical—all fuse into a single, inclusive image. Moreover, these various breakdowns of order and life, whether perceived in themselves or in this collective fashion, can be inwardly absorbed only through a form of psychic re-creation characteristic of mental life in general; that is, they are perceived through symbolic transformation.[23]

† There are no accurate records, but my impression concerning the relative absence of full-blown psychiatric disorders has been confirmed by other observers, as I shall discuss in the next chapter.[24]

‡ The term "thousand-mile stare" was informally used to characterize the facial expressions of American prisoners of war repatriated from camps in North Korea in 1953.[25]

often to those necessary to keep him alive—and in which he feels divested of the capacity either to wish or will. Phrases like *kyodatsu-jōtai* and *muyoku-ganbō* eventually took on the secondary function of publicly acknowledged categories; these lent a structure to the period in that they gave form to its structurelessness.

The electrician experienced such a state when, after five weeks of struggling against chaos, he felt that his responsibilities at the railway station were over:

> I had been trying to put everything in order. When I couldn't find documents . . . I made new cards. But when I got everything in order I felt discouraged and despondent . . . tired of it. . . . Until then I had the sense that we were all in a war situation . . . and I had my responsibilities. . . . But then I saw all of the damage . . . and I thought I had been silly [to be so conscientious]. . . . And once I had fulfilled my responsibility, I didn't have any idea of what I should do after that. . . . I felt very lonely. . . .

The vacuum state was perpetuated by such things as delayed news of deaths of family members, but as the grocer reveals in describing his reactions to hearing confused details of his mother's death six weeks after it occurred, the same state interferes with responses to this kind of news:

> I heard [from my uncle] that my mother was killed . . . that she died in the house . . . when the house was burning . . . that she was asphyxiated by the smoke and died. . . . He explained it that way. . . . But I think it was his imagination . . . because my grandfather told us that my mother was out buying things at the store . . . so she must have been killed on the way to the market and not at home . . . somewhere around the center of the city. Well, this too is imagination . . . but since we couldn't find any remnant of her body or bones, we could only imagine. . . . Rather than a feeling of sorrow [what I experienced] was shock, strong shock. . . . It must have been shock that I felt—maybe not exactly at that moment, but anyhow when I heard it—as if all of the blood in my body were frozen. . . . And I heard later that my face at that time was completely pale . . . so I think it was really a shock. . . .

We sense that at the time he felt less "shock" than he now thinks he should have, and that feelings of death guilt prevent *hibakusha* from inwardly accepting the depths of emotional withdrawal they had experienced.

The middle-aged businessman describes the absence of visions of possibility:

> In those days we were in a vacuum state. . . . We lost hope entirely. In prewar times we thought in terms of getting ahead in the world—becoming a rich man, a cabinet minister, a doctor, a high-ranking salaried man. . . . Then suddenly we lost these hopes. . . . And I lost all other kinds of hope as well. . . .

And the abandoned mother tells of the combined impact of personal displacement, invisible contamination, and further victimization by looting:

> In September . . . at the end of the month, I was given permission to live in the street railway car [owned by the company for which she worked]. . . . And then I heard the rumor that for seventy years there would be no trees or grass and there would never be human beings living in Hiroshima. . . . And although all of the things remaining in my house were stolen, I did have some other things which had been taken to the country and I took these back and put them in the car. . . . But from the car too almost everything was stolen. . . . I was surprised to find that among our own Japanese, and even among workers in the same company, there were thieves. . . . But my feeling was, there was no place to go . . . so if I were to die, it was all right, I would die here where the bomb fell. . . . A feeling of not caring—not a feeling based on understanding but just not caring. . . .

The philosopher spoke of "a blank, nihilistic stage," with everyone concerned only with "how to live, how to get wood to burn, how to get food, how to sustain ourselves." The mathematician contrasted the compassion for those with injuries which he encountered in Kyoto (where he had gone for treatment of his eye) with people's incapacity for such compassion in Hiroshima because "everyone had been afflicted." The sociologist told how he and many others "for about one half year after the war's end . . . had no desire to find any job anywhere, or to work for a salary" because "things were very chaotic [and] there was no special rhythm of life to live by."

Adding to the general disintegration, and to the vacuum state, were floods which began on September 17, less than six weeks after the bomb, and took many more lives, including those of most of a team of Kyoto physicians who had come to Hiroshima to offer their help. This was a new form of "contamination," and carried people, if it were possible, even beyond the vacuum state—as is suggested by Shinzō Hamai, long-term Mayor of Hiroshima and a man known to have made extraordinary efforts in the face of the most extreme difficulties:

The city looked like a huge lake. Beneath its waves it was possible to detect tiled roofs and the outline of much else as well. I felt as though this were the final burial! For what reason had the citizens of Hiroshima been condemned to such frightful sufferings? Suppose the flood waters were never to recede, and it [Hiroshima] were all to remain drowned forever? In that case, I thought, so much the better. I said this to myself in all seriousness.* [26]

* Hiroshima's terrain is such that it has always been subject to floods, and *hibakusha* did not express to me the belief that the flood had been caused by the bomb. But they did perceive it as part of the limitless devastation of their environment.

4) *Tainted Rebirth*

The vacuum state could, paradoxically, be a prelude to symbolic rebirth. Psychic numbing and despair could serve as a means of "holding on" prior to taking the first steps toward reintegration. But for this to happen the patterns of disintegration had to be interrupted—the whole city, so to speak, had to be "detoxified." Only then could three fundamental qualities of active existence within the self-process be reasserted: the sense of connection, the sense of life-energy and movement, and the sense of symbolic integrity or meaning. Such reintegrative processes were perforce incomplete—the detoxification could be only partial—hence the rebirth was inevitably tainted by unmastered death imagery.

Human bonds were crucial to this early movement toward rebirth, most prominently within families, but also among friends, acquaintances, and even strangers. The dedicated efforts of a small group of city officials to distribute the available food and clothing not only provided emergency physical replenishment but also helped *hibakusha* to reassert their sense of connection to other human beings and their sense of movement or revitalization, both of great importance in counteracting death anxiety and death guilt.

Even the exchange of "horror stories" about various aspects of the bomb could contribute to these reintegrative tendencies—as is suggested in Dr. Hachiya's description to me of the atmosphere in which these stories were told:

> One would say that "So and so was killed in my family," and the other would say, "Well in my family so and so and so were killed." . . . There seemed to be almost a pride in misery . . . and a desire to blend with one another by sharing similar stories.

Dr. Hachiya went on to tell how, even during those first days after the bomb, some *hibakusha* would resort to the rambling, semi-comical *mandan* or vernacular style of storytelling. Such exchanges of horror provided intense emotional contact, mutual support, and identification around the only subject people were concerned with, and the only one all had in common. They were an immediate outlet for emotions, both joyful and guilty, surrounding survival. And they supplied the crude beginnings of formulations of the disaster—whether through agitated commentary, moments of detachment, or a glimmer of humor suggesting that the entire affair was an absurdity.

The cremator, when discussing these early exchanges with me, was interrupted by his wife who told the kind of story that only a wife could tell:

> He was so concerned with ordinary everyday things. For instance, after the bomb there was a distribution of beer in the city, and he walked all the way to the center of Hiroshima for one glass of beer.

The story may be a bit exaggerated (though its protagonist denied nothing), but it suggests the enormous importance such amenities can have for stimulating the symbolic processes as well as the thirst buds. The availability of a glass of beer could convey the sense that "ordinary everyday" life still existed, that one had awakened—or begun to awake —from the A-bomb nightmare.

Even the black market and related illegalities could be inwardly symbolized as social disintegration in the service of rebirth. The general craving for goods, the extraordinary energy and ingenuity of black-market operators, their thriving business not only in food and clothing but in building materials and roof-tiles, in watches, various metal objects, and in such particularly valued (and by Occupation decree, illegally held) items as old Japanese swords—all this accentuated the sense of a return to life's energy and movement. Youngsters picked up from the central black-market area near Hiroshima Station and put in orphanages would often run away from the orphanages because, as the director of one of them put it at the time, "They just cannot forget the atmosphere of the station and the black market where they have lived in the past."[27] Here is more than simply the "appeal of chaos": it is the sense of being drawn to the most active expressions of the reassertion of life.

This kind of rebirth, however, had to be perceived as tainted. Many items first sold on the black market had been taken from the dead, whether removed directly from corpses or looted from destroyed homes, which created imagery of drawing strength from the dead by means of further violating them. And in a more general sense, participation in the black market (which very few *hibakusha* could totally avoid) took on the psychological significance of "stealing life"—from the dead, the forces of destiny, the immediate authorities, and from one another. In other words, the payment for such life-sustaining experience and imagery took the form of additional death guilt.

SHACKS, MOUNTAINS, AND RIVERS

Nothing was more important to symbolic rebirth than the reclaiming of Hiroshima itself. A first step was the re-establishment of some of the city's transportation facilities—and the operation, three days after the bomb, of one part of a streetcar line, three railroad stations, and a number of charcoal-driven buses graphically conveyed a sense of return of life's motion. But reclaiming Hiroshima as a living area was a more difficult task. A considerable number of people never left the city and (usually because they had no place to go) simply scrounged in the rubble to keep alive. Most fled to outlying districts and towns, where they stayed with relatives, friends, or strangers, and then gradually came back to claim their damaged homes or the leveled sites where their homes had stood. A few returned almost immediately, some not until six months to two years later, but a considerable number within one to three months. One month after the bomb fell the *Chūgoku Shimbun*, Hiroshima's leading newspaper (which had itself made heroic improvisations to resume publication at the end of August), estimated the city's population at 130,000, about one third of its pre-disaster figure. But most of these people lived in the outskirts rather than in the "hollowed center," the last part of the city to be repopulated.

Hibakusha told me that they returned because they became convinced (through public announcements and observations of others) that the city was safe to live in; because they feared losing their property to squatters or having it further damaged by scavengers (who came into the city right after the bomb); because the city administration announced that it would provide some free building materials to those whose houses had been totally demolished; because they wanted to be settled in before the onset of the typhoon season (usually early or mid-September); and because they learned that public services were being resumed, particularly electricity (on September 13). But underlying all of these factors was the profound human tendency to reclaim one's original "territory," to reassert one's earlier relationship between self and dwelling-place, and to conduct the struggle for mastery of a death encounter on what is literally familiar ground, however that ground has been devastated. In Hiroshima there was also evidence that *hibakusha* did not feel they had the right to abandon the dead.

The shopkeeper's assistant describes the contagious impact of the reassertion of life in the city:

> When I came to Hiroshima in December, there were shacks standing here and there. . . . I had heard that . . . there would be no people living in Hiroshima in the future, but within a few months I found these shacks standing . . . with people living in them, and this made me feel that I too had to do something to keep myself going. . . . I began to think that as long as I was alive, I had to go on living. . . . I still had fear but gradually, as time passed by . . . I gained a sort of fighting spirit about life, and when the fear arose in me, I pressed it down. . . .

This developing activity within Hiroshima could become a lure for those forced to remain outside of the city for a long period of time, as the grocer makes clear:

> In those days I should have had nothing to complain about, as my aunt was taking care of me . . . but I still thought about leaving the place to which we had been evacuated. . . . Although I had fears about influences from the bomb, at the same time, as an ordinary child, I wanted to go back to the city . . . back to a lively place. . . . That was more than a year and a half after the bomb. . . . And people who went back to Hiroshima and then returned to the country told me that in Hiroshima there were many houses and markets. . . . From where we were in the countryside, returning to Hiroshima took on strong meaning, like a dream—but we had this dream. And when people left there, saying that they were headed for Hiroshima, . . . I too wanted to go back.

The "dream" was that of life restored in the place where one had known it in the past. And while it is true that an ordinary child craves "a lively place," the craving is greatly intensified by the atmosphere of death produced by an atomic bomb.

Certain attitudes had great importance for sustaining people in those early days. The sociologist, for instance, spoke of a form of "optimistic resignation," which kept him and others going:

> I tend to be optimistic, and I took the view it can't be helped [*shōganai*], things would somehow take care of themselves. The

greatest concern people had was for their everyday life . . . and they did not think about the future. . . .

Even spiritual leaders, like the Buddhist priest, came to share a general focus upon life-sustaining *materials*, for this focus itself was a powerful reassertion of symbolic rebirth:

> *Hibakusha* didn't have the supernatural on their mind but were more concerned with getting solutions for everyday problems, for recovering their health. . . . We thought that if we were to live—and if we had *things*, that is, food, clothing, houses—these might fill up some of the void. But there were no such things . . . so we felt we must find some way to keep on living. . . . I cultivated a field right near here and grew potatoes and vegetables—even though I couldn't work even half a day without feeling extreme fatigue. . . .

He goes on to make clear that eating "railroad grass" came to symbolize not only the humiliation mentioned before but also human endurance and will to life:

> Ordinarily, we wouldn't think this "railroad grass" edible, but we all went to look for it since it was the only thing we could find to eat that still seemed to be strongly growing. . . . You found that you simply had to find something for today, and then for tomorrow—especially for the wounded [his wife had been severely injured] and for the children. . . .

Indeed, this grass that was "strongly growing," and which, as we heard before, was "so strong that the buds sprouted from hard rocks," was perceived as an infusion of strength, and the idea that it came "from America with the railroad" suggests that America was responsible for some of this infusion even as it was responsible for the devastation :

Nature itself also had great prominence in early imagery of rebirth, as expressed in the Japanese saying quoted to me by several *hibakusha*: "The state may collapse, but the mountains and rivers remain." A young writer put similar sentiments in more contemplative language:

> I returned to Hiroshima on September first. When I saw the destruction, I was amazed, but at the same time I felt: This is really the state of man. What man had added to nature has now been destroyed, but nature is there. . . . At the same time that I saw the destruction, I

also saw rivers flowing, clouds in the sky, mountains in the background. Maybe this is an Oriental way of thinking . . . [but] I
found it very aesthetic. . . .

That part of nature which had been destroyed—half-burnt dead trees
throughout the city—made people uncomfortable until removed. A
story is told of how Prince Takamatsu, the Emperor's brother, during a
second visit to Hiroshima in December, 1945, noted with approval that
the burnt trees were no longer visible; as the Prince made his comment,
it is said, he playfully assumed the posture of a Japanese ghost (by
holding his two hands loosely in front of himself). Destroyed nature, in
other words, is ghostlike.

But intact nature outlasts all. And the appearance of the buds,
particularly those of the cherry blossoms, in the first post-bomb spring
(March and April of 1946) conveyed to many a sense of the city's
symbolic detoxification. Mayor Hamai associated the buds wih a simultaneous "flowering" of shacks and other buildings and with "a new
feeling of relief and hope."

But nature's revitalizing force cannot be kept separate from the A-
bomb dead—as a leading *hibakusha* poet explains:

Well, the newspapers and various authorities said there would be no
trees or grass in Hiroshima for seventy years or so. But when I looked
at the rivers and saw how quickly they regained their original beauty,
I didn't believe that the city had been reduced to such sterility. . . .
I wrote about mud and soil and grass and trees. But I felt the soil of
Hiroshima was mixed with the bones of the dead, and the young trees
and grass growing out of the ground were—if I can speak metaphori-
cally—the eyes of the dead, looking at the people who had survived.
. . . When I noticed all of these trees and greens, I began to think
more constructively about my present condition and about my future.
I thought . . . I must live as honestly and truthfully as I could. . . .

The dead are thus perceived to have blended with nature; the blending
provides support and continuity to *hibakusha* but is also a reminder of
death guilt.

SOLUTIONS AND TASKS

Imagery of nature and of reclaiming Hiroshima were, in their special
ways, early formulations of the experience. There were also more
personal formulations in which the bomb was felt to be an agent of

individual death and rebirth. This could be a result of release from misguided ideological convictions, a painful process described by a young company executive:

> I had believed that we ought to work hard for the country's war effort. . . . I tried to enter the Naval Academy . . . because I wanted to get on a warship . . . and when I was unsuccessful, I entered a technical college out of my wish to be involved in work contributing to the manufacture of military weapons. . . . At the age of eighteen I was putting my schoolwork aside and working at the Navy with only one or two days off a month. . . . I had a very cooperative feeling toward the war . . . until that moment when I realized that war created such large numbers of victims who are not involved in fighting. I realized that this was the worst part of war, and was unavoidable. So from that moment . . . although I was incapable of doing any real thinking—just in a state of blankness—I began to have a negative feeling toward war. . . .

Implied here, as in similar sentiments expressed by quite a few, is the *hibakusha*'s self-accusatory sense that his own war enthusiasms played a part in bringing about the atomic holocaust.

Some, like the professor of education, quickly associated the bomb with alleviation of war suffering ("I thought, Now this war must end") and were relieved by the Emperor's speech because "something which should have been done long before was finally being done."

Others felt liberated from military controls, a suppressive regime, and from their own ambivalence or even hypocrisy in relationship to it. The despair that Miss Ōta experienced following the bomb and the Emperor's speech—her "indescribable emptiness" and feeling of "floating in white air"—was mixed with a sense of release and opportunity for personal renewal.

The history professor is more explicit in associating the bomb with personal reintegration and rebirth:

> When the war ended, I felt greatly relieved. This was the feeling shared by many intellectuals who were not content with military rule. . . . During the war I was a hypocrite. I had to work for the government and the war effort—to pretend to be what I was not. . . . We intellectuals had to lead a double life. . . . We couldn't feel any sense of strength as individual persons. . . . I feel that

through the use of the bomb, we found a way to happiness sooner than if the bomb had not been used. . . .

And a leftist woman writer went even further in viewing the bomb as a harbinger of a new life:

> When the war ended as a result of the A-bomb . . . we found something . . . to live for. . . . The disaster was horrible, but through it we felt a new meaning in life. We thought no one would want to repeat it. . . . For us Japanese . . . seeing the death of the military was a very exciting thing in our lives. The anger we felt at the end of the war was not toward the bomb but the Japanese militarists. We greatly enjoyed the fact that we had no longer any military leaders in power.

Both she and the history professor, however, along with the relief they described, also experienced considerable despair and the entire gamut of atomic bomb emotions.

Curiosity about the American victors, sometimes indicating a beginning identification with them, could also be a stimulus to recovery. In the case of the seamstress, for example, who had been severely injured by the bomb and bitterly disillusioned by the surrender speech, the urge to get a glimpse of the newly arrived American troops quite literally inspired her to get back on her feet:

> I couldn't stand up or walk . . . but it was strange . . . that although I was fearful I wanted to see them [the American troops]. I just wanted to see. I was not supposed to stand so the doctors had to help me.

Like others all over Japan, she was disarmed by the easygoing friendliness of these strangers, and struck by their contrast with the monsters she had been led by Japanese wartime propaganda to expect. This contrast was probably even more extreme for *hibakusha* than for other Japanese, since their images of Americans included not only conventional ones of rapers and looters but a new and unprecedented image— "droppers of the atomic bomb," though no one seemed to have a clear picture of what such people would look like. (We shall have much more to say later about the *hibakusha*'s long and complex encounter with Americans.)

Sometimes during these early months there were specific turning points which permitted *hibakusha* a return to significant symbols and a recovery of meaning. This turning point could take the form of a meaningful task, as in the case of the professor of education, who was so immersed, over a considerable period of time, in caring for a senior colleague and his family that "I really couldn't think much about anything else," and at the same time followed this colleague's guidance in contemplating Japan's future to the extent of feeling "inspired . . . to follow a new path in my field." Hearing that scholars in some other parts of Japan were living under even more extreme deprivation than those in Hiroshima, and were in fact close to starvation, he initiated a program in which university students and younger faculty members from Hiroshima would take rice to professors in Tokyo who would in return provide thoughts and suggestions about "how we should carry on . . . how we should learn to stand on our feet." This led to an organized exchange and study group which dedicated itself eclectically to works of Japanese and American humanists considered relevant for the general crisis—the philosophy of Nishida and novels of Sōseki, as well as the writings of John Dewey and William James: "First we had to break with the old tradition, then study certain basic principles, and then develop an approach." He concluded that the turbulence immediately following the bomb had provided valuable experience for him:

> After the A-bomb I felt as though I had been driven into a storm. . . . Without the A-bomb I would not have had the opportunity to comprehend so thoroughly [these] teachings. . . . I was forced to find my own path and to work very hard to do that. . . .

But we shall see later that within his psychological life, the "storm" was not soon to abate.

A related pattern was the restoration of significant human relationships—such as that of teacher and student—with their lifelong patterns of future responsibility and dependency. This was true for the sociologist, who had lost his scholarly ambition and left the city to stay with his family, returning to Hiroshima only at the instigation of his old teacher, who found a job for him there: "It was a kind of *on* which brought me back."* Once back, and rooted in this personal tie and in a new position, he could participate in the early postwar dialogues—efforts at

---

* An *on* is an obligation or debt of gratitude to one's benefactor. The principle is part of the overall system of *giri-ninjō*, the traditional cultural patterning of obligation and dependency.[28]

formulation taking place throughout Japan but particularly poignant in Hiroshima:

> The anger we felt was directed not toward the country which dropped the bomb but toward war itself. People's feeling was that they had had bad fortune, and that since Japan had started the war—as they were now taught—this was understandable punishment. . . . Then . . . students, professors, and intellectuals began to think more about how to reconstruct Japan—not just Hiroshima, but in terms of the whole nation and in relationship to the whole world. They lifted their eyes outside of their small society and developed greater concern about the whole of human destiny. . . .

We shall see later that this redirection of hostility was not quite as clearcut as he suggests, but this atmosphere of ideological search had great importance for early reintegration.

The philosopher similarly tells how the "blank-nihilistic stage" previously mentioned gave way to serious efforts at formulation:

> After two months, when things began to be a little bit restored, we began to ask questions. . . . Why did this war have to take place? How was it brought about? How does war come about? We felt great hatred for war—and along with this we thought about politics, the form of politics in society, and about social organization. We had a strong hatred toward militarism. We had the feeling people had been deceived by the military. And of course our discussions came down to capitalism and socialism—these discussions were limitless, and we always tried to expand them. . . .

For others the important turning point was a suggestion of the possibility of economic recovery, permitting a vision of the future that transcended immediate chaos—as described by the middle-aged businessman:

> I had lost hope . . . until I heard over the radio what Mr. Ichirō Nakayama [a well-known economist] said about Japan's future. He said that if Japan could keep the principle of neutralism, as laid out in the Potsdam Declaration, then Japan would be able to recover before too long. At that time [several months after the bomb] prices were going up and the black marketeers were prosperous, so I thought that if I couldn't find a way to earn a living quickly, all of my family would be in difficulty. . . . And then when I heard Mr. Nakayama's ideas, I

thought that Japan would someday become emancipated . . . and when I began a new business . . . about one year after the war . . . my feeling was even more changed and I began to have hope for the future. . . .

Miss Ōta describes personal struggles, during the first months after the bomb, toward recovery of meaning and creation of a new set of significant symbols:

> The time has come for a revolution against mankind's tragic tendency to be unable to make any progress without being destroyed. . . . I do hope this defeat can be the thing that makes Japan truly peaceful. This is the meaning of my writing this book in the midst of pain. . . . I am happy to begin to feel the flame of the writer's spirit burning in myself. . . . Just as water purified by a filter emerges as drops of clean water, all my grief seems to be separating out from my writer's spirit. . . . Frankly, I was more angry with the ignorant imperialism which attempted to destroy my writer's life than with the fact that Hiroshima was destroyed . . . an anger which included grievous thoughts about my own country. . . . Japan must now take the big step of freeing herself from the hold of tradition. But the fact that Japan lost the war does not mean she was defeated in everything else. To think that she was, is a secondary psychological effect. . . . Now [November, 1945] the farmers are beginning to reap their rice . . . but little joy can be found among them. . . .[29]

We note how pride in her writer's identity combines with sweeping formulations about man as she seeks, even this early, to find profound meaning in what happened in Hiroshima; and we note also her awareness of a residual shadow ("little joy can be found among them").

Fundamental to whatever recovery and rebirth did take place in Hiroshima, tainted or otherwise, was the infusion of energy from the outside. This infusion began with the rescue teams (however inadequate) organized mostly by the Japanese military, followed by a trickle of physicians and supplies, then by the American Occupation, which provided various kinds of help, and finally by a surge of "outsiders" (non*hibakusha*) who quickly repopulated the city. Those who came included Hiroshima natives stationed elsewhere during the war, people deprived of their homes in overseas possessions now taken from Japan, others from the nearby Kansai area and especially from business districts around Osaka, and various fringe elements—scavengers, black-market operators, and criminals—from all of these places. For the "contaminated city" was rapidly transformed into a "boom town" of unlimited opportunity—a social void in whose filling anything was possible. Though it turned out, psychologically speaking, that the contamination was overlaid rather than eliminated, this "frontier atmosphere" contributed to a general sense of renewed life.

Many of these non*hibakusha*, in addition to being physically and emotionally stronger than the survivors, came from more aggressive Japanese subcultures than that of Hiroshima's provincial traditionalism, making them in every way better suited to deal with the chaos and change of the immediate post-bomb period. Inevitably, they aroused considerable resentment among *hibakusha*, who saw them as reaping most of the profits of Hiroshima's recovery without having undergone its special suffering.

But the part played by outsiders' vitality in making possible that recovery could not be denied, as the Buddhist priest tells us:

> The *hibakusha* were activated by people from the outside . . . from China, Manchuria, and the South Seas, and also other outsiders, non*hibakusha* coming from different parts of Japan into Hiroshima. . . . Then they [the *hibakusha*] went to work again. . . . But . . . , it was the outsiders who had to come in and begin the work. The survivors had to be dragged along [*hikizuru*] by the outsiders. . . .

The middle-aged businessman describes how this resentment was accompanied by admiration for their successful, if unscrupulous, approach:

> Those who came back from overseas . . . were extremely active. They didn't hesitate to do business on the black market . . . because they came back to Japan with not even clothes on their backs. . . . I think that they are now the most successful people. In any case, they were extremely active, and I think other people followed them and adopted their ways. . . .

There is a suggestion here, in response to residual guilt, that when *hibakusha* themselves participated in illegalities, they were "merely following" examples set by outsiders. But this does not alter the *inner realization on the part of survivors that their own and their city's recovery, physically and psychologically, would have been impossible without a functioning "outside" as a source of energy and direction.* Precisely this "knowledge," along with the frequent need to deny its truth, was to contribute greatly to later conflicts over weakness and dependency.

Early psychological rebirth, then, was both gradual and periodic, accomplished imperceptibly as well as through conscious effort. It required preliminary struggles toward formulation and called upon costly psychological defenses along with unsuspected resources. It had to take place within Hiroshima survivors themselves but was totally contingent upon outside forces. It was an extraordinary achievement, entailing as it did a measure of mastery over history's greatest single act of manmade devastation, but it was to remain severely tainted by a variety of physical and emotional remnants, all related to an aura of death.

four

"A-BOMB DISEASE"

1) *Impaired Body Substance*

We have observed that physical fears experienced in relationship to early radiation effects could turn into lifetime bodily concerns. During the years that followed, these fears and concerns became greatly magnified by a development which has come to epitomize the *hibakusha*'s third encounter with death: his growing awareness that medical studies were demonstrating an abnormally high rate of leukemia among survivors of the atomic bomb. There has thus arisen the scientifically inaccurate but emotionally charged term "A-bomb disease," which has taken for its medical model this always fatal malignancy of the blood-forming organs.

The increased incidence of leukemia was first noted in 1948, and reached a peak between 1950 and 1952. It has been greatest in *hibakusha* exposed closest to the hypocenter, mainly those who were within two thousand meters; for those within a thousand meters the incidence of leukemia has been between ten and fifty times the normal.[1] Since 1952 the rate has considerably diminished, but it is still higher than in non-exposed populations, and fears remain strong. The symptoms of leukemia, moreover, rather closely resemble those of earlier radiation effects, including the dreaded "purple spots" and other kinds of hemorrhage, various forms of blood abnormalities, fever, progressive weakness, and (inevitably in leukemia, and often enough in acute irradiation) death.*

Psychologically speaking, leukemia—or the threat of leukemia—became an indefinite extension of earlier "invisible contamination"; and individual cases, particularly in children, became a later counterpart of the "ultimate horror" of the first moments of the experience.

One such case of leukemia in a twelve-year-old girl named Sadako Sasaki has, in fact, become Hiroshima's equivalent of an Anne Frank legend. Just two years old at the time of the bomb, she was said to have been exposed at about sixteen hundred meters, but to have shown no ill effects, and even to have been unusually vigorous and athletic, until stricken almost ten years later. Sadako, it is told, struggled to maintain her life by folding paper cranes, in keeping with a Japanese folk belief that since the crane lives a thousand years, the folding of a thousand paper cranes cures one of illness. When she died—still thirty-six short of that number, so the legend goes—her classmates added the missing paper cranes and placed the full thousand in her coffin with her. The same children then played an active part in a national campaign for the construction of a monument to Sadako and all other children who have died because of the atomic bomb. Paper cranes and financial contributions were received from all over Japan, and the monument now stands in the center of Hiroshima's Peace Park. The story has been told and retold in many versions, including a widely distributed film, and has come to symbolize the bomb's recurrent desecration of the pure and vulnerable—of childhood itself.[2]

Just when the incidence of leukemia was recognized as diminishing and approaching the normal, evidence began accumulating that various other forms of cancer were increasing in incidence among survivors—including carcinoma of the stomach, lung, thyroid, ovary, and uterine cervix. Such increases are consistent with the knowledge that these cancers *can* be induced by irradiation, and that the latent period following irradiation is much longer for them than for the leukemias.[3] Moreover, while leukemia is a rare disease (even with its increased incidence, fewer than two hundred cases have been reported among

* The two conditions cause similar symptoms because both affect the blood-forming tissues in the bone marrow. In leukemia the peripheral blood is flooded with immature white corpuscles, and white blood cell counts are characteristically extremely high; but they can also be abnormally low, as in acute irradiation. Severe anemia occurs in both.

Hiroshima's significantly exposed population), cancer is not; should the trend continue, as appears likely, the increase in cancer will undoubtedly give further stimulus to various elaborations of death symbolism, just as some of these were beginning to decline. Even now, aware of the increasing statistical evidence in this direction, survivors tend to see themselves as endlessly susceptible: when one lethal condition begins to show signs of attenuation, another, equally deadly, makes its appearance.

Other medical conditions, with varying amounts of evidence, have been thought to result from delayed radiation effects. There has been a definite increase in cataracts and related eye conditions, most of which appeared within one or two years after exposure. There has been convincing evidence of impairment in the growth and development of exposed children; and although it is difficult to distinguish the part played by radiation from that played by other factors—physical trauma at the time, and later socioeconomic deprivation—this impairment contributes to survivors' sense of being "stunted" and physically inferior. There is also a large group of divergent conditions, which, without clear-cut scientific confirmation, are thought by some physicians (and most *hibakusha*) to result from the bomb: several kinds of anemia, and other blood and liver diseases; endocrine and skin disorders; central nervous system (particularly midbrain) impairment; premature aging; sexual dysfunctions; and, most difficult of all to evaluate, a borderline condition of general weakness and debilitation constantly reported to me by survivors.

Nor are the fears of *hibakusha* limited to their own bodies; they extend to future generations. Survivors are aware of the general controversy about genetic effects of the atomic bomb—a very serious emotional concern anywhere, but particularly so in an East Asian culture which stresses family lineage and the continuity of generations as man's central purpose in life and (at least symbolically) his means of achieving immortality. Again, people in Hiroshima know that radiation *can* produce congenital abnormalities, as has been widely demonstrated in laboratory animals; and abnormalities have frequently been reported among the offspring of survivors—sometimes in lurid journalistic terms, sometimes in more restrained medical reports. Actually, systematic studies of the problem have so far revealed no higher incidence of abnormalities in survivors' offspring than in those of control populations, so that findings in this sense may be said to be negative. There was, however, one uncomfortably positive genetic finding reported in the 1950s regarding disturbances in the sex ratio of offspring: men exposed to a significant degree of radiation tended to have relatively fewer daughters, while exposed women tended to have fewer sons, because, it was thought, of sex-linked lethal mutations involving the X chromosome. But later studies failed to confirm this finding, and suggested that it was of dubious significance. Nonetheless, there are Japanese physicians who believe they have observed evidence of an increase in various forms of internal (and therefore invisible) congenital abnormalities in children of survivors, however inconclusive that evidence may be. Nor can anyone, with absolute scientific certainty, assure *hibakusha* that abnormalities will not eventually appear in their children, their grandchildren, or in still later generations.[4]

Another factor here is the definite damage from radiation experienced by exposure *in utero*, which not only caused many stillbirths and abortions, but resulted in a high incidence of microcephaly with and without mental retardation. This damage occurred almost exclusively in pregnancies that had not advanced beyond four months, and is, of course, a direct effect of radiation upon sensitive, rapidly growing fetal tissues. Scientifically speaking, it has nothing to do with genetic problems. But ordinary people often fail to make the distinction: to them, children born with abnormally small heads and retarded minds seem still another example of the bomb's awesome capacity to inflict a physical curse upon its victims and their offspring.

This sense of impairment has been reinforced by actual discrimination survivors have encountered, not only in occupational areas (which we shall discuss later) but in marital arrangements—the latter, in Japan, usually made by families through a go-between, with fundamental importance attached to the physical health of each of the prospective partners and to his or her capacity to produce robust offspring.

:

The young company executive, in a voice that betrayed considerable anxiety, described the way in which the entire range of bodily and genetic concerns could become incorporated into the psychic life of the survivor:

Even when I have an illness which is not at all serious—as, for instance, when I had very mild liver trouble—I have fears about its cause. Of course, if it is just an ordinary condition, there is nothing to worry about, but if it has a direct connection to radioactivity, then I might not be able to expect to recover. At such times I feel myself very delicate. . . . This happened two or three years ago. I was working very hard and drinking a great deal of saké at night in connection with business appointments, and I also had to make many strenuous trips. So my condition might have been partly related to my using up so much energy in all of these things. . . . The whole thing is not fully clear to me. . . . But the results of statistical study show that those who were exposed to the bomb are more likely to have illnesses—not only of the liver, but various kinds of new growths, such as cancer or blood diseases. My blood was examined several times but no special changes were discovered. . . . When my marriage arrangements were made, we discussed all these things in a direct fashion. Everyone knows that there are some effects, but in my case it was the eleventh year after the bomb, and I discussed my physical condition during all of that time. From that, and also from the fact that I was exposed to the bomb while inside of a building and taken immediately to the suburbs, and then remained quite a while outside of the city—judging from all of these facts, it was concluded that there was very little to fear concerning my condition. . . . But in general there is a great concern that people who were exposed to the bomb might become ill five or ten years later or at any time in the future. . . . Also when my children were born, I found myself worrying about things that ordinary people don't worry about, such as the possibility that they might inherit some terrible disease from me. . . . I heard that the likelihood of our giving birth to deformed children is greater than in the case of ordinary people . . . and at that time my white blood cell count was rather low. . . . I felt fatigue in the summertime and had a blood count done three or four times. . . . I was afraid it could be related to the bomb, and was greatly worried. . . . Then after the child was born, even though he wasn't a deformed child, I still worried that something might happen to him afterward. . . . With the second child, too, I was not entirely free of such worries. . . . I am still not sure what might happen, and I worry that the effects of radioactivity might be lingering in some way. . . .

Here is a man of thirty, carrying on his life quite effectively, essentially healthy, with normal children, and yet continually plagued by underlying anxieties—first about his own general health, then about marriage arrangements, and then in relationship to the birth of each of his children. Each hurdle is surmounted, only to reappear in new form.

The grocer expresses similar feelings in still stronger fashion, and makes clear the way in which bodily fears are related to renewed identification with the dead and the dying:

> Frankly speaking, even now I have fear. . . . Even today people die in the hospitals from A-bomb disease, and I worry that I too might sooner or later have the same thing happen to me. . . . So when I hear about people who die from A-bomb disease, or who have operations because of this illness, then I feel that I am the same kind of person as they. . . .

THE PSYCHOSOMATIC BIND

"A-bomb disease," then, represents for the *hibakusha* a painful psychosomatic bind: he is likely to associate even the mildest everyday injury or sickness with possible radiation effects; and anything he links to radiation effects becomes associated with death. Equated as it is with both earlier invisible contamination and later leukemias, A-bomb disease has the ring of fatality; yet loose usage may cause it to be applied to such innocuous conditions as fatigue, sensitivity to hot weather, borderline anemia, susceptibility to colds or stomach trouble, or general nervousness—all of which are frequent complaints among survivors. The bind is self-perpetuating, part of a vicious circle, which includes the death imagery of continuing invisible contamination, renewed identification with the dead and the dying, association of virtually any kind of ailment with deadly "A-bomb disease," intensified death imagery, etc. And the pattern is intensified, though not created, by strong Japanese cultural focus upon bodily symptoms as means of expressing anxiety and conflict.

The writer-manufacturer reveals to us one of the ways in which the psychosomatic bind perpetuates itself:

> Aftereffects are fatal to many people . . . and once they appear, they show very rapid progress. . . . Two good friends of mine died from these effects approximately ten years after the A-bomb was dropped. The symptoms are easy to identify. First you bleed from the nose, and then spots begin to appear over your body. . . . I myself frequently bleed from my nose. Doctors say it has nothing to do with aftereffects from the A-bomb, but I wonder. . . .

It is possible that the two friends actually died of leukemia related to atomic bomb exposure (though considering the small number of such cases in Hiroshima, this would be an extraordinary coincidence), or from some other form of fatal blood disease associated with radiation effects (even more dubious, given the highly equivocal relationship between the atomic bomb and fatal blood conditions other than leukemia). It is therefore also quite possible that one or both of these friends died of conditions unrelated to atomic bomb exposure, and that we are dealing with a form of later atomic bomb mythology which attributes all death to radiation aftereffects. The one thing we are certain of is the writer-manufacturer's own death anxiety.

At the heart of this later mythology is "A-bomb disease" itself, and a description of that condition by the physicist makes clear that even a scientific education does not protect one from its terrors:

In ordinary sickness you usually either get well or else you die. But with radiation you just don't seem to get well, or if you get well, you become ill again. You may be well, perfectly healthy for a few years, and then it comes back again, and with no apparent cause you suddenly die, the only reason for this death being the original radiation. . . . And if you get ill, there are likely to be complications, so that if one thing heals, there is still something else which doesn't heal and the patient dies. . . . For instance, the wife of a colleague had an operation for a form of woman's disease which seemed to cure her condition. Just as she was about to be released from the hospital, she passed away from radiation disease. . . . And in regard to my personal experience, some time ago I began to feel tired a good part of the time and I thought that perhaps I was just working too hard, using my eyes too much. But then the fatigue seemed to be unusually great, beyond ordinary fatigue, so I had my blood count taken, and it was found that my blood count was not normal. That was the reason for my fatigue. I received early treatment so it was all right. Then, recently, I have had stomach trouble, and I also had an examination of my liver and my blood. I was told that my white blood count and my red blood count were low, and this really concerned me quite a bit, so I decided to take a long vacation. I am not worried about my stomach or my liver, but I must say I am worried about my white blood count and red blood count. Of course, these have not been too bad in my case, but as a physicist I know enough to be careful. If I feel fatigue, I immediately look into it, and if my red blood count or white blood count is down, I rest. . . .

Here we get the general sense of A-bomb disease as a thing apart from ordinary medical problems—more obscure, devious, ubiquitous, in every way deadly. Death anxiety becomes focused upon blood counts, as numerical indicators of the condition, to the point of near-phobia.

Confronted with still limited medical knowledge, with the reality of early deaths from irradiation and later ones from radiation-linked leukemia, and with the generally overwhelming impact of the weapon, survivors are likely to have evoked—years after the bomb no less than at the moment it fell—those primitive layers of the mind which lend themselves to mythological thought.

The sense of impaired body substance is so widespread that no *hibakusha* I met appeared to be entirely free of it. It could be expressed, as in the case of the grocer, through simultaneous admission and negation:

> I have had these fears, and even now have them. But I don't think that my body tires easily, or that when I get a cold, it tends to develop into something worse, or that my body is particularly weak. Up to now I would say that I have had no effects [from the bomb]. . . .

The things he says are *not* happening to him are precisely those he fears and anticipates happening. He goes on to make these fears more explicit when he discusses concerns about his children:

> What I did think about very seriously when I married was what effects my future children might have. No effects have appeared [in my baby] so I feel relieved right now. But I have the feeling that in the future I must be very careful. . . . It is often said that those who were exposed to the bomb might have deformed or handicapped children . . . and other than this, after the baby was born, in addition to its health I worried about its mental ability. . . . I heard that those exposed to the bomb experience harmful effects upon their cells . . . and that these effects might particularly affect the brain cells . . . the cell is destroyed or lacks something it should have—I heard something like this . . . as a rumor. . . . I have no clear source for this opinion . . . but the ratio of abnormal children is higher [among *hibakusha*] than among ordinary people. . . . These are the kind of things [I worry about]. . . .

As with many *hibakusha*, his sense of bodily impairment is reinforced by a conglomeration of partially accurate information (bomb exposure did have harmful effects on bodily cells), controversial claim (of a higher ratio of abnormal children among *hibakusha*), and questionable conclusion (that he is likely to have handicapped or mentally retarded children). Again we get the distinct impression that clarification is resisted (in this case in a man of more than average intelligence), that the death taint which dominates the *hibakusha*'s body image is more real than the "logic" of actual medical findings. And we shall see that these findings are themselves often contradictory and confusing. In other words, the psychosomatic bind is maintained not only by the fear of aftereffects per se, but by the entire sequence of death anxiety and death guilt experienced from the moment of atomic bomb exposure onward.

This bind can become particularly pressing for those hospitalized for diseases of organs often thought to be susceptible to radiation effects—especially when treated in a center dedicated mainly to the management of these effects, and when one has a history of early radiation symptoms from exposure close to the hypocenter. Such was the case of a young laborer, originally exposed at about a thousand meters, whom I interviewed in the Atomic Bomb Hospital, where he seemed to be recovering from infectious hepatitis:

> Of course, I was a little worried. I heard that radiation affects the liver. Now I am not so worried, as the doctors have explained to me that I don't have A-bomb disease. But I had diarrhea for ten days after the A-bomb . . . they gave me herb medicines to remove the poison from my body. I didn't become sick after that until this illness. But I hear every year about victims who die, and I worried that this year I might become one of them. . . .

Nor are those too young to remember their atomic bomb exposure free from the psychosomatic bind—though they may be less consciously preoccupied with it. For instance, a young member of Japan's outcast (or *burakumin*) group, originally exposed as a boy of two, described vague but diffusely persistent bodily concerns:

> Well, the fact of my being exposed to the bomb, this is the big cause of my worry. . . . Something like dizziness—well, I don't actually have it now—but if I do I get nervous . . . or a stomach-ache—and, well, everyone catches cold—but there are many things. It is not any one special thing. . . . Well [what I am afraid of] during my life is that A-bomb disease. . . .

NAGGING DOUBTS AND PERSONAL MYTHS

Pervading these ill-defined psychosomatic concerns is what we may call the *hibakusha*'s "nagging doubt" about possible radiation effects, his sense of himself as being particularly fragile, one who cannot afford to take chances. As the social worker explains:

> I myself have this [fear of A-bomb disease] . . . in my everyday life. For instance, when I find myself staying up late at night because I have work I think I should finish, then I tell myself to be careful and not to overwork. . . . When I am tired or when I am in bed with a cold, and wonder whether I should stay in bed or get up, I tend to decide to stay in bed for one more day, and my wife also urges me to do so. . . .

The nagging doubt can be related to one's general health or bodily integrity, to the suspected origins of a particular organic condition—or it can combine both of these in a sense of a physical turning-point associated with atomic bomb exposure. Some, like the electrician, felt this turning-point to apply not only to themselves but to all exposed members of their families. He had suffered from a severe roundworm infestation, which he knew to be related more to generally deprived living conditions than to radiation effects per se; nonetheless he associated it with a general sense of impairment he shared with his two exposed children:

> When I got sick, I didn't think it was an effect of the bomb. But two of my children [age nineteen and twenty-two] who were exposed to the bomb are still not so healthy . . . and their condition . . . might . . . be slightly related to this exposure. . . . They just don't seem to be fully well. The doctor doesn't diagnose them as being sick from atomic bomb effects—they don't have any specific illness—but the fear I have is that children who were young then might have been slightly affected by the atomic bomb. . . . None of us [in my family] has had any of the actual symptoms of what we call A-bomb disease, but in general we have weak health. . . . But among my children it is only those two [who have difficulty]. My two youngest girls, who were born after the bomb, are perfectly healthy. . . .

The nature of this "weak health" is unclear, as is its relationship to the A-bomb; but his separation of his children into exposed-impaired and non-exposed-healthy categories is clear enough.

The sense of physical turning-point associated with the bomb tends to be greatest among the elderly. One seventy-six-year-old man, originally exposed at seventeen hundred meters, told me, when I visited his home where he had been bedridden for six years, that he had been quite well until experiencing diarrhea and other gastrointestinal symptoms at the time of the bomb, and that since then his "stomach" had never functioned properly. Actually, his complaints were still mainly gastrointestinal, but he had a variety of additional bodily ailments. It is difficult, indeed, to say whether the decline in health of a man then sixty years old was merely coincidental with the atomic bomb, or whether possible radiation effects or the general psychosomatic stress of the experience were important factors. But in any case the nagging doubt itself might well have contributed to his ill health by convincing him that he was a man who could not expect to become well.

Similar patterns could exist in younger people as well. The woman who at fourteen felt too frightened and repulsed by her father's symptoms to attend him during his last hours developed an ophthalmic condition (apparently an unusual form of corneal opacity) about ten years later:

> The doctors say that they cannot find the cause for my condition, and they very vaguely say that it might be inherited. But I think this inherited tendency would not have come out if I had not gone through the bomb, though of course I can't be sure. . . . I am in an unsettled frame of mind about this. I don't think that everything was caused by the A-bomb, and I don't think either that the A-bomb had absolutely no effect. I suffer from this problem. . . .

She implies that her emotional well-being, and possibly an improvement in her eye condition as well, depend upon her coming to some understanding of the nature of that condition. But she also seems to realize that a precise evaluation of the part played by the A-bomb is impossible.

The psychosomatic bind can also take on rather complex convolutions of fear and denial, as we observe in the sequence described by the abandoned mother:

> My daughter is a bit weak and anemic, and I worry about her. But I don't want to think she is an A-bomb patient. I try not to think this way. . . . I do think she should go to the A-Bomb Hospital [for a checkup] but she herself doesn't like to be bound to the word A-bomb, which she dislikes very much. . . . It is not only she, and not only myself, who think this way. Ordinary people among the *hibakusha* all do. Although we do have great physical fears, we feel that if we go for a careful examination and then are told we have to be hospitalized for quite a number of days in order to treat what the doctors find out to be wrong . . . we are faced with living expenses

during hospitalization . . . and our families would be unable to get along. . . . So for this reason . . . people tend to resist careful physical examinations. . . .

The economic problems she mentions can be very real indeed, but the underlying psychological sequence (for her, the daughter, and many others) is this: I fear that the symptoms I have may be those of A-bomb disease; if I go to the hospital, this fear may be confirmed, and I would be doomed; by avoiding a hospital visit, I can therefore avoid this death sentence. In this way many *hibakusha* demonstrate what is usually called "denial of illness," but the illness being denied is likely to be itself essentially a symbolic—that is psychological—product of the overall *hibakusha* experience.

The matter may become even more complicated, as the following vignette suggests. During a brief visit to Nagasaki, I interviewed a group of six people, all of whom were active in *hibakusha* organizations, and most of whom felt themselves in one way or another to be suffering from aftereffects. One of them, a forty-five-year-old engineer, who had lost most of his family in the bomb, had been troubled for many years by gastrointestinal symptoms. These symptoms, plus his and his wife's inability to conceive a child despite the fact that "my family used to be very fertile," caused him to "worry every day" and think that "it must be the A-bomb." After some reluctance, he finally submitted to a complete medical examination, and was relieved to be told that he had a mild stomach ulcer and slight liver dysfunction, probably related to drinking, not to the atomic bomb. An old friend of his among those present, however, then offered an additional interpretation: "They [the symptoms] might be caused by radiation, but he is trying to believe that they are not and that they are his own fault." Here we may say that the engineer's original pattern of fearful denial was interrupted by re-assuring medical opinion. But his friend, out of his own fears and ideological needs (to stress the ubiquitousness of radiation effects), probably restimulated the anxieties that the engineer had, with such difficulty, temporarily stilled. We observe here in microcosm the general patterns of social reinforcement of the psychosomatic bind which we shall see to exist throughout an atomic bombed city.

:

I also encountered various kinds of individual bodily mythology. A young housewife, who had been exposed at fifteen hundred meters at the age of fifteen, told me she seemed to have become healthier as a result. Under treatment in a hospital for severe diarrhea when the bomb fell, her condition not only immediately improved ("something in the bomb seemed to cure me"), but during the years following, she felt herself less prone to illness than she had been before. Yet it turned out that she was unusually anxious about the possibility of giving birth to abnormal children, perhaps more so than anyone else I interviewed. She questioned me about the problem at some length, asked whether many people I interviewed had had abnormal children, and seemed disappointed that I did not conduct physical examinations to evaluate the dangers. While one cannot absolutely rule out the possibility that radiation from the bomb had some beneficial effect upon her body, she left me with the distinct impression that she had evolved this kind of personal mythology in order to compensate for—and magically reverse—her profound physical anxieties.

Such personal mythology could express these anxieties much more directly, as was true of a seventeen-year-old high school student who had been exposed to the bomb when just six weeks old. Dependent mostly upon his parents' descriptions for his knowledge of the A-bomb experience, he was particularly impressed by their telling him that a large amount of glass had become embedded in his head; and during one of our interviews he insisted that whenever he has a haircut he can see small pieces of glass emerge. His psychological associations to these bits of glass (and we may be dubious about their appearing in this way seventeen years later) were a series of recollections and comments about illness and weakness: memories of being frequently sick as a child during the years after the bomb and taking up long-distance running to overcome his fragility; feeling "sick" and "glad I wasn't killed" whenever he saw pictures of the bomb; hearing mass-media reports of A-bomb disease which made him feel that "if I get sick, I won't live long"; and attributing his general opposition to all nuclear weapons to the fact that "I have been sick." The symbolic truth behind his personal bodily mythology was the sense of being involved in a continuous "sickness," ordinarily hidden, but threatening to emerge and become visible (like the glass from his head) at any time.

"A DARK FEELING IS PASSED ON THROUGH THE GENERATIONS"

We have seen fears of genetic impairment to be closely related to the overall sense of bodily taint, but they also take on specific forms of their own. The paradox which surrounds the whole issue—essentially negative findings, but with enough scientific doubt to cause anxiety in an area of ultimate concern—results in paradoxical behavior on everyone's part. Hiroshima and Nagasaki physicians, for instance, are frequently consulted by couples in which one or both are *hibakusha*—or by families of such couples—about the advisability of marriage and the likelihood of abnormal births. Almost invariably the doctors advise them to go ahead with the marriage and assure them that their children will be all right. But these same doctors, in discussing the problem with me, are likely to add such comments as, "Of course, I cannot be absolutely certain that they will not have abnormal children," suggesting doubts about the matter which they probably convey to their patients, whatever their wish to reassure.

But *hibakusha* themselves, despite their fears, do not appear as a group to have avoided marriage and children. The reverse might, in fact, be the case, as there has been some evidence to suggest that *hibakusha* have a greater tendency to marry and have children than do non-exposed people of a comparable age.[*5] If this is so—and there have been similar impressions concerning concentration camp survivors—it probably represents a compensatory effort to reassert imagery of the continuity of life and of symbolic (biological) immortality. Rather than proving the absence of genetic fears, the urge to marry and have children can go hand-in-hand with such fears.

The quality of these fears was conveyed to me by a Nagasaki educator as he described, with some feeling, his unending generational worries— first the difficulty in making marriage arrangements for his daughter (also a *hibakusha*), then his fear that she might have abnormal children, and now, when the children seem to have turned out all right, his concern that *their* future children might be deficient:

I heard from Tokyo scholars that it [harmful atomic bomb effects] could carry over to future generations. When *hibakusha* hear these things, a dark feeling is passed on through the generations. . . . Those who died are dead, and must bear their fate, but the living must live with this dark feeling. . . .

---

* But even if it can be established that *hibakusha* marry and have children at least as frequently as non*hibakusha*, one cannot assume that discrimination concerning marriage has not existed. I have observed a number of cases in which discrimination has been encountered, but marriage eventually arranged; and I have the impression that feeling their "bargaining power" in such arrangements to be weakened, *hibakusha* may sometimes marry into families of lower socioeconomic standing than their own, or else accept certain conditions they would not ordinarily agree to.

The "dark feeling" he refers to suggests an extension of invisible contamination into a lineal infinity, a sense of being "doomed for posterity."

So strong are such emotions that one leading Hiroshima politician, himself a *hibakusha*, expressed to me the strong conviction that *hibakusha* submit to a voluntary program of sterilization:

> I had my wife sterilized because I don't want abnormal children. . . . I think that [for *hibakusha* exposed] up to two thousand meters, sterilization should be done . . . [because of] the tragedy for the family in the future [should there be an abnormal child] along with the social menace. . . . We should set them [*hibakusha*] aside and not mix them with the rest of the population . . . and take very seriously this problem of *hibakusha*. . . . All this is difficult to propose—there would also have to be benefits to accompany it—but I think about it seriously. . . . Scientists don't say whether there will be abnormalities or not—no one can assure you there will not be later effects. . . . What to do—whether there should be a program or not—is a painful question for me. . . .

The symbolic suggestion is that of breaking the chain of bodily impairment. But given the implications of group extinction or even genocide, as well as survivors' particularly strong need to reassert the continuity of life through marriage and children—not to mention the further threat to body image and sexual identity—we can well understand a politician's hesitation to convert these connections into an actual public proposal. Nor is it without significance that he had his wife and not himself sterilized.* Whatever the psychological, scientific, and political complexities surrounding talk of sterilization in Hiroshima, it is another illustration of the strength of the *hibakusha*'s sense of his own bodily taint.

For most survivors, however, these genetic fears are more muted, though ineradicable—as the sociologist describes in characteristically Japanese terms:

> After we were married, I worried about having an abnormal child— since my wife had also been exposed to the bomb. I knew my wife

---

* She was his second wife. The fact that he had three children by his first wife (who had been killed by the bomb) might have influenced his willingness to have his second wife sterilized. And while we know nothing of her feelings about the matter, it is possible that she was beyond an optimal childbearing age.

was worried about it, too . . . but we did not discuss it with each other. We never talked about the matter but we each understood. . . . I thought of the possibility—perhaps I should not say that I had a fear of an abnormal child, but rather that I had a very strong desire to have a normal one. . . . You might say that I worried about one per cent in the corner of my heart. . . . As we say about children in general, if one has an ugly child, then that child will have ugly children. . . .

2) "A-Bomb Neurosis"

Hiroshima doctors have another term, "A-bomb neurosis," which they apply to behavior that appears to be psychically caused, especially to those who become involved in a lifelong preoccupation with "A-bomb disease"—with blood counts and bodily complaints, particularly that of weakness—to the point of greatly restricting their lives or even becoming bedridden.

Studies have shown that *hibakusha* are more generally prone to hypochondriasis than other people, especially those *hibakusha* who experienced symptoms of acute irradiation at the time of the bomb.* And we have already observed their phobic tendencies in their generalized fear of leukemia, cancer, or simply of "A-bomb disease." But as compared to usual hypochondriacal and phobic patterns encountered in psychiatric work, those in *hibakusha* are much more directly related to actual bodily assaults that can result from atomic bomb exposure. While this makes them in one sense more specific, their association with invisible contamination is part of a diffuse involvement with death imagery. The *hibakusha*'s preoccupation with white blood counts becomes not only an effort to "measure" that contamination but also a means of physically localizing it and giving it form. In addition, these hypochondriacal and phobic concerns inevitably become bound up with every kind of ordinary psychological conflict, so that *one may characterize "A-bomb neurosis" as a precarious inner balance between the need for symptoms and the anxious association of these symptoms with death and dying.*

"A-bomb neurosis" can also become a family affair, because of shared original exposure as well as continuous mutual reinforcement. Thus, one middle-aged mother told me of her own fatigue, dizziness, and sensitivity to both heat and cold which she believed particularly marked in those parts of her body where glass had become embedded at the time of the bomb; her son's huskiness of voice ("As one baptized by the A-bomb, I carry this husky voice," was the note which the boy wrote under his picture in a classmate's yearbook at the time of his high school

---

* As detected by the Cornell Medical Index, borderline complaints are consistently more frequent in *hibakusha* than in non*hibakusha*.[6]

graduation) as well as his severe acne, which she, and possibly he, attributed to the A-bomb; and her daughter's generally frail health, which she and the girl thought due to radiation effects. While one cannot exclude the possibility that all three retained some bodily influences from radiation, it seemed clear from the nature of the complaints, and from other details of their life together (the boy's acne, for instance, consistently improved when he was away from home) that various individual and family conflicts had become channeled into the A-bomb symbol. Indeed, her own symptoms are very commonly found among middle-aged Japanese women, and are often related to problems of suppressed anger, and to the family nurturer's own need for nurturance.

MIND AND BODY

The special difficulty in Hiroshima is that no one is ever certain where radiation effects end and psychological manifestations begin.

A case in point is that of the European priest, who complained of chronic exhaustion, dizziness, and general inability to work. Following his original exposure at thirteen hundred meters, he had sustained bodily wounds that were unusually slow to heal, as well as severe symptoms of acute irradiation, including weakness, dizziness, fever, dysentery, and low white blood cell counts. He was hospitalized from October to December and told of having been so ill that one doctor later remarked: "Father, I didn't think we would be able to pull you through." After leaving the hospital, he again began to suffer from dizziness and extreme fatigue—"not the usual kind, but a very exceptional kind"—as well as loss of appetite; and white blood cell counts taken were said to be low. He was repeatedly hospitalized during the next three years and (after a few years on the outside) again during the ensuing years so that, in all, he spent more than one third of the seventeen-year period since the bomb in hospitals, including a full-year's stay in the Atomic Bomb Hospital three years prior to our interview. At that time his physical examination was essentially normal, and the laboratory findings were somewhat equivocal: a slightly low white blood cell count (4,000); a positive serology (test for syphilis), apparently caused by the extensive blood transfusions he had received as the main treatment during his early hospitalizations and not considered a factor in his symptoms; and slightly diminished liver function, also possibly influenced by the transfusions. The syphilitic reaction was successfully treated, but his general weakness, dizziness, diffuse aches and pains, and susceptibility to colds and minor illnesses continued. And during a still later hospitalization, which took place after our interview, both red and white blood counts were normal, but there was evidence of arteriosclerotic heart disease and of arthritic involvement of various joints (he was by then sixty-one years old).

He attributed his difficulties entirely to his atomic bomb exposure and repeated to me a statement made by a doctor during one of his hospitalizations which had impressed him greatly: "We don't have a cure for A-bomb disease." He also described a mottling of the skin of uncertain origin which he associates with abnormalities of the blood, and went on to reveal a terrified sense of shifting vulnerability:

I used to be extremely healthy. . . . Now my resistance is weak. . . . Recently I had pus in my fingers and the condition would not heal. Dr. K. said, "I don't like to cut you." But he did, and the wound healed. . . . They tell me my regeneration is not so good and that is why I need blood transfusions . . . but people [like us] become uneasy, because with no reason these things occur. Then three months after getting one thing, something of a new kind begins. Right now I am not normal. . . . You are always thinking: "What is the next thing that will happen?" . . . I asked the doctor, "What will happen if the blood comes out in my brains?"

He told me that his nervousness and inability to concentrate was such that he could no longer even organize a sermon, and that he had progressively limited his professional activities to the point of avoiding contact with any but his old parishioners. He said he accepted his condition as "God's will," but one could perceive, in addition to his fear, a sense of guilt over the pattern of his life:

Sometimes people say unkind things: "Why doesn't he do more? He looks so well. It must be an escape into disease in order to avoid work." One man said to me, "It is only because you like to be in the hospital that you stay there for so long." And there are some who, without saying it, think the same thing. But if it is another [hibakusha], he understands. . . .

His words conveyed the feeling of inner doubt about the nature of his illness, about his right to remain so helpless. And there was much evidence that earlier doubts and conflicts were at play: conflicts over his general ability and choice of life work (he was a man of modest intellectual attainments in a missionary order noted for its brilliance); and identity struggles, which were both a cause and a consequence of the essentially impossible psychological task of a Westerner's becoming totally absorbed into Japanese life—including conflicts in the sexual sphere. In general, he gave the impression of more than a little quiet despair.

In such a case who can have the temerity to distinguish sharply among such influences as: (1) delayed radiation effects, (2) direct organic injury from the bomb, (3) other indirect consequences of the bomb, (4) treatment procedures themselves, (5) psychological conflicts relating to the bomb, including the sense of being doomed, (6) independent disease processes, and (7) the aging process? What can be said is that a *hibakusha*'s psychic state has important bearing upon his health, and one must assess an overall equilibrium of all aspects of his being—following the general principle that "The broad definition of disease does not confine our attention to any single system of organization of the body" and "does not restrict us to any single ideological concept" but "permits us to conceptualize disturbances or failures at all levels of organization—biochemical, cellular, organic, psychological, interpersonal, or social—and to consider their interrelationships."[7] Thus, psychic conflict directly influences the outcome of whatever radiation effects may be present, and any bodily damage sustained from the bomb influences "A-bomb neurosis." There are few cases as elaborately ambiguous as that of the European priest, but the principles it illuminates so exaggeratedly are applicable to all.

:

There were cases, however, where the psychological component seemed particularly prominent in establishing "A-bomb neurosis" as a way of life—as was true of the female poet. When I visited her home, I found her looking troubled and behaving in a demonstrably weak manner. Although she was expecting me, she was dressed in a disheveled housecoat and appeared generally unkempt. Aware that I am a physician, she had the need to make very clear to me her sense of being an invalid:

Can you tell me how it is possible to put my body back into good health? My doctors advise me to sleep a great deal. If I rest for a while, I feel fine. Then I try to move about a bit and do some work, and I quickly feel an unbearable sense of fatigue. The doctors say my red blood count and white blood count are only one third of normal.

. . . I have been feeling this way ever since the bomb fell seventeen years ago. Before the bomb I was in fine health and would never lie down in the middle of the day. . . .

She spoke of early radiation effects but in a vague manner difficult to evaluate. She seemed to make little distinction between early effects and present symptoms ("Even now I have spots every once in a while on my body. And my hair remained extremely thin until five years ago") and emphasized that "I have never recovered." Her way of describing her symptoms was frequently bizarre, particularly in relationship to her fear of cancer:

> For this condition [A-bomb effects] it is best to have someone else's blood put in my veins, but if this is done, there is danger that I might develop cancer because my blood is very sensitive. . . . What I really suffer from now is liver trouble and trouble with my pancreas . . . and I was told that I had a tendency toward cancer of the uterus. . . .

It turned out that the medical examination in which she claimed to have been told she had this cancerous tendency took place nine years before, and that later gynecological examination revealed no such findings. Her fear was related to the fact that her father had died of cancer believed to have been brought out by radiation effects; and she had closely identified with him, both in regard to atomic bomb exposure ("He had been affected by A-bomb disease in the same way I had") and in a general psychological sense.

She did reveal a certain amount of insight concerning the relationship of her bodily symptoms to marital and family conflicts. Her first husband had died prior to the bomb, and when she married again during the postwar years, she noted that her symptoms disappeared ("During the period right after we married I felt rather good"). But her respite was only temporary. She perceived her husband to be losing interest in her and suspected him of coveting her property; the marriage dissolved within two years. At the time of our interview, moreover, she was involved in painful conflicts with her son and his wife who lived with her. She was convinced that her daughter-in-law did not believe in the genuineness of her illness ("She thinks I am lazy, and there are troubles between us"), and even when the daughter-in-law treated her considerately, she would suspect that, like her former husband, it was only because the girl wished to inherit the property. She would in turn condemn herself for having such thoughts, refer to the "ugliness of my own heart," and attempt to get rid of them through Buddhist devotion. She was thus aware that hostility and suspiciousness had bearing upon her symptoms, as did a general sense of being rejected and unloved:

> I feel that a person in my situation . . . if she only had someone whom she could love and who loved her, this person—that is, I myself—could be rid of these physical problems without any difficulty. But unfortunately, I don't have such a person whom I can love or who loves me, so I have to continue being in my present physical condition. . . . When a person has a weak body and an ugly face, nobody really cares for her. . . .

Also involved were long-standing feelings of abandonment which contributed to her sense of being, even in middle age, an "A-bomb orphan": "I myself lost my mother when I was very young, and then later my father died of cancer—so I have great sympathy even now for those who lost their parents in the A-bomb." And she went on to generalize about the relationship of such matters to "A-bomb disease" or "A-bomb neurosis":

> It looks as though marriage and the normal life one leads with marriage is good for the health. . . . Among A-bomb victims, those who are married and well established with their families have fewer complaints. Of course, even those who are settled in their families remember the incident. But on the whole they are much better off and feel better . . . their attitude is, it can't be helped [shōganai]. "It is useless to look back on old memories," they keep saying. They are simply interested in their immediate problems of marriage and everyday life. They look forward rather than backward. . . . Those without families, on the other hand, keep remembering everything. . . . They curse the whole world—including what happened in the past and what is happening now. Some of them even say, "I hope that atomic bombs will be dropped again, and then the whole world will suffer the same way I am suffering now."

What emerges is an association between lack of fulfillment in any area of life and *hibakusha* symptoms, including hostility to the point of wish for cosmic retaliation (probably experienced by the female poet herself), a form of imagery we shall say more about later on. For her and many other *hibakusha* a negative psychological constellation evolves from a combination of the A-bomb experience and all additional emotional vicissitudes. Fed by lifelong conflicts around love, nurturance, and hate, symptoms are mitigated to the extent that these conflicts find resolution, and worsened by situations in which the conflicts are reactivated. But the special feature of this negative constellation—that is, of "A-bomb neurosis"—is the merging of these conflicts with unusually strong death imagery.

After having written the above, I learned that this same female poet had developed a breast cancer, which was detected one year after our interview and resulted in her death two years later. One is humbled by such news on many levels, among them that of evaluating psychological and physical influences. The emotional factors she herself emphasized, and my own comments upon them, still seem valid to me. But what continues to elude us—in evaluating effects of the atomic bomb as in medicine in general—is a full grasp of the nature of the undoubtedly fundamental unity of psychological and physical factors. We may therefore suspect that not only did radiation effects contribute to her cancer but that her emotional conflicts, particularly her persistent sense of loss and abandonment, did as well*—while at the same time keeping in mind hereditary factors (we know that her father died of cancer) and the host of unknown or half-known causal influences (relating to viruses, chemical substances, hormones, chronic irritation, and cellular defensive reactions). But when she herself wrote to my assistant to tell us of her condition, she described the matter with stark simplicity: "I was told that I have cancer of the breast from A-bomb disease."

PSYCHIATRIC ENTITIES

"A-bomb neurosis" was also used rather generally for various neurotic and even psychotic tendencies less frequently encountered. One of these, known in ordinary psychiatric terminology as "traumatic neurosis," is characterized by lingering fears and phobias specifically related to the "traumatic event," and by recurrent dreams of that event. I came upon remnants of such patterns in one man who described the urge "to throw myself on the ground" whenever a flashbulb would go off in his presence; and in a second-hand account of another *hibakusha* who,

---

* This suspicion is consistent with a ten-year interest among psychosomatic researchers in psychological factors in cancer. William A. Greene, a leading worker in this field (and one trained in both psychiatry and medicine), has claimed that the evidence so far justifies "the working assumption that there *is* a significant relationship between the manifest development of neaplasia [cancer], as represented by the leukemias and lymphomas, at least, and the psychological reaction of the individual to various life events."[8] While recognizing the obscurity of the mechanisms involved, he stresses the significance of psychological patterns of separation and loss.

having tried unsuccessfully at the time of the bomb to pull a girl out by her legs from the debris of a collapsed building, experienced phobic reactions to shoes and to the legs of mannequins in store windows.

But the most generalized pattern of this kind that I encountered occurred in a Nagasaki physician. Exposed to the bomb at fifteen hundred meters while a medical student, for some time afterward he experienced fear of crowds and of noise, and had this recurrent dream:

> I am walking along in a place that is like a desert. There is absolutely no shelter anywhere. Then I see a plane flying above, which I know is carrying a nuclear weapon. I am terrified, because I realize that when the bomb falls, I will have no protection. At that moment I wake up.

The dream recreated the sense of absolute helplessness and vulnerability experienced at the time of the bomb. Its psychological function, like that of the phobias, was to master the "traumatic event"—and particularly the residual death anxiety and death guilt—by psychologically reliving it.

Had I done the study years earlier, I would undoubtedly have encountered many more clear-cut examples of traumatic neurosis. In any case much of what we have observed in relationship to bodily fear surrounding "A-bomb disease" and "A-bomb neurosis" may be looked upon as psychological equivalents of traumatic neurosis, as may much of the general psychohistorical residuum we shall discuss in subsequent chapters. But the concept of traumatic neurosis does not in itself adequately encompass the dimensions of psychological experience imposed by an event such as the atomic bomb.

It is difficult to say much about the general incidence of discrete or incapacitating neurotic patterns in *hibakusha* because of the paucity of statistical information. There are comparative statistics for psychosomatic entities, such as peptic ulcer and ulcerative colitis, often placed under the category of neurosis, which show no discernible increase among *hibakusha*[9]—suggesting perhaps the fundamental importance of early psychological and physical predisposition to these conditions rather than a stressful experience in itself.

In the case of the psychoses, the major mental illnesses, the situation is even more difficult to evaluate. These too are sometimes loosely referred to as "A-bomb neurosis," though the term "A-bomb psychosis" has also been used. The latter term is no more precise but conveys an interesting difference in emotional tone. While "A-bomb neurosis" suggests a "weak" and "inappropriate" reaction to the bomb in a person who doesn't, so to speak, have organic justification for behaving that way, "A-bomb psychosis" suggests a more direct relationship between the A-bomb and the mental condition, an imposed form of insanity in a person who can't help behaving as he does because of what the bomb did to him. The difference is related not only to attitudes concerning the A-bomb but to those universally held in relationship to neurosis and psychosis as such.

Concerning the actual incidence of psychoses among *hibakusha*, statistics are again lacking. But psychiatrists and other physicians I spoke to were not struck by a marked increase either at the time of the bomb or immediately afterward. What they did describe were frequent psychoses—or other psychological or neurological disturbances—in which either the patient or his family would express the suspicion that the condition was brought about by some kind of emanation from the atomic bomb.

A leading Hiroshima psychiatrist with whom I discussed these problems divided psychiatric conditions he encountered in *hibakusha* into three categories: anxiety neuroses and related psychosomatic complaints (mostly of the nonspecific kind we have discussed), which he considered to be reactions to the atomic bomb experience; psychoses, usually schizophrenia, which he thought to be mostly unrelated to atomic bomb effects; and organic brain damage, particularly to the midbrain (or diencephalon), which he believed caused by radiation effects. But he admitted that these categories were incomplete and not always applicable. He was critical of the tendency of many physicians to apply the term "A-bomb psychosis" to many long-standing schizophrenic patients, and thereby give the false impression that their condition had been caused by the atomic bomb.*[10]

I did not attempt a detailed study of the complicated question of interplay between the atomic bomb experience and schizophrenia. But considering the origins of the condition in pathological family patterns acting upon varying degrees of individual hereditary predisposition,[13] it would be difficult to say that the A-bomb *in itself* could produce

---

* Some investigators report a variety of neurotic symptoms among *hibakusha*, particularly those who experienced symptoms of acute irradiation at the time; but these are attributed, on the basis of electroencephalographic findings, to radiation damage rather than psychogenic factors.[11] Psychological abnormalities have been reported among exposed children, especially among those exposed *in utero*, but the findings are somewhat ambiguous.[12]

schizophrenia. What is quite possible is that the profound original trauma and later conflicts of the atomic bomb experience were significant contributing factors to individual cases, whether symptoms appeared at the time or later on.

There is also the possibility that at the time of the bomb and immediately afterward schizophrenic tendencies in some people diminished, or were at least temporarily suppressed, because the environment itself took so total and so bizarre a hold upon the individual. that the schizophrenic adaptation was no longer necessary—a pattern that has been described in other extreme situations and could well have been particularly true of the atomic bomb environment because of its own external "schizophrenia." The one thing certain in the relationship between schizophrenia (or psychosis in general) and the atomic bomb is the tendency on the part of patients and doctors to blame this condition too upon "invisible contamination," to view it as still another manifestation of "A-bomb disease."

This association was made by the professor of education—the one person among those I interviewed who had experienced a psychotic episode (a few years prior to our meeting)—though denied by his doctor. At that time he apparently had symptoms of depression and emotional withdrawal with some delusional content, and during our interview referred to the episode (as Japanese frequently do) as a "neurotic" one:

I have on the whole been quite well but I have worried about my health. For instance, when I became neurotic, I wondered whether this had any relationship to the bomb. I asked the doctor and he said it had nothing to do with it. . . . Of course, even if there were a relationship, I thought, it can't be helped [*shikataganai*]. . . .

His implication was that the mental illness was not in itself as frightening as the possibility that it might be related to A-bomb effects. But the fact that he went on to express resentment (partly toward me but toward the other doctors as well) of those who "treat me as an A-bomb patient," and insisted that "I have too much strength and energy to be an A-bomb patient," suggested a lingering concern that he was just that, as well as a probable fear that his psychosis might recur.* All this

---

* Another possible interpretation is that his concern about being treated "as an A-bomb patient" was itself part of a lingering paranoid tendency, and that his psychosis was not entirely in remission.

represents the complex interweaving of atomic bomb symbolism with his condition rather than causation per se. Knowing, however, of his unusual difficulty in dealing with conflicts around death and guilt at the time of atomic bomb exposure—his need to "turn away"—it is quite possible that these conflicts contributed significantly to his eventual psychosis. This could remain no more than an impression, as his need to "cover over" his psychotic episode—to "turn away" from it as well— made it inadvisable to question him more closely about its onset.

I was also told that many psychotic patients in Hiroshima incorporated various kinds of imagery about the atomic bomb into their delusions and hallucinations. But this tendency occurs in psychotic patients everywhere, since the extreme grandiosity and end-of-the-world visions of psychosis always draw upon imagery of the most powerful and destructive forces available. We have spoken of the possible suppression of schizophrenic tendencies by the atomic bomb environment, but another question which arises is that of the long-term influence of the "lived-out psychosis" (the "end of the world" and "death in life") upon ordinary *hibakusha* in the sense of whether or not it created an inner "knowledge" of the psychotic state—or even a tendency to resort to psychotic-like behavior under certain forms of stress—without lapsing into full-blown psychosis.

When *hibakusha* did describe others' "going crazy" at the time of the holocaust, their details were often vague and the image seemed to be another manifestation of the aura of absolute power surrounding the weapon—of the feeling that anyone exposed to it *should* have gone crazy, just as anyone exposed to it *should* have died, which in a symbolic sense is saying close to the same thing. Guilt is also of considerable importance here: the feeling that in one's right mind, one would or could not have seen and done the things one did see and do—that without being temporarily "crazy," one would not have committed the ultimate evil of surviving.

There was also imagery of people later dying from mental effects caused by the bomb. One story of this kind told by a woman in Nagasaki illustrates the extension of A-bomb mythology into a confused area encompassing mental and physical contamination:

Mr. A. died of mental confusion. I think it was due to a nervous breakdown from economic and social pressure. . . . The doctor said that the confusion was due to the last stages of A-bomb disease. . . . He had divorced his wife, telling her he was going to die—he was like a crazy man. His diagnosis was leukemia. And according to the doctor at the university hospital, the last stage of leukemia makes the patient confused. . . .

And the same is true of a description by a man in Nagasaki of his wife's death:

> She died in 1957 after complaining of severe fatigue. I think she died of neurosis. The doctor told me she had poison in her blood. I think it was due to radiation, because she went to the bombed area the day after the bomb in order to get our injured son and bring him home. He died two days later, and my wife at that time had severe diarrhea and almost seemed to be in a coma. . . . We were always worried about her symptoms recurring but they never did until she died from a heart attack. . . . I say she died of neurosis because she had been extremely concerned about her condition. . . . She was worried about the flood in her native area in July, 1957, . . . about her brother . . . and refused to eat. And she experienced deep grief during all of these years over our son. . . .

While the mythological tone here is strong and three different reasons are given for the woman's death ("poison," "neurosis," and "heart attack"), we may look upon this unscientific description as an effort to convey the inseparability of physical and psychological factors and the extraordinary impact of their combination—and, in this sense, as still another example of the psychological truth contained in A-bomb mythology.

:

"A-bomb disease" and "A-bomb neurosis" are inseparable. Their loose evocativeness reflects a third level of death encounter in which the original "curse" becomes an enduring taint—a taint of death which attaches itself to one's entire psychobiological organism and, beyond that, to one's posterity as well. *Survivors feel themselves involved in an endless chain of potentially lethal impairment, which, if it does not manifest itself in one year—or in one generation—may well make itself felt in the next.* Earlier imagery related to death and guilt is absorbed into a larger constellation now perceived not as an epidemic-like experience but as a permanent and infinitely transmissible form of impaired mind-body substance.

3) City of Bodily Concern

Anxiety surrounding A-bomb disease cannot be grasped without examining the milieu in which the term flourishes. Any "extreme experience" creates its own special environment, which takes shape from the continuous mutual interplay of individual responses to massive death encounter and group efforts to establish meaningful social forms. The new behavioral patterns which emerge can take on a fierce autonomy which far outlasts the original experience.

The matter becomes clearer when we examine the components and history of the term A-bomb disease. The Japanese word, *genbakushō*, is a vernacular abbreviation of *genshibakudanshō*, the full term for atomic bomb disease. Some Hiroshima doctors trace "*genshibakudanshō*" to the celebrated lecture one month after the bomb, by the radiation expert Masao Tsuzuki, but others had the impression that it had been used by military physicians even before then. In any case, it was a near-immediate officially sponsored term for acute radiation effects. But the *shō* of *genshibakudanshō* can either mean specifically "wound" or "injury" or else, more generally¹, "disease" or "diseased state," according to the written form used. Here doctors again dispute the early usage. Some claim that Tsuzuki, a surgeon, quite naturally stressed the first meaning ("wound") and that the second came into being only much later on; others recall the broader form being used almost from the beginning by military physicians in their need for a term to write on soldiers' death certificates. Both recollections may well be true, but a good deal of additional evidence (including the early diaries of Yōko Ōta) make clear that atomic bomb disease very quickly came to suggest any pathological effects whatsoever brought about by the weapon.

Much less certain is the time when the shorter term, A-bomb disease (*genbakushō*), came into use, though it seems safe to say that it did not achieve wide general currency until some years later. A number of those I interviewed in Hiroshima related its general usage to the "Bikini incident" of 1954, in which a group of Japanese fishermen were exposed to fallout from American hydrogen bomb tests in the Pacific, resulting in the death of one of them, and in an enormous national outcry. One scholar, who had made a special study of Hiroshima's encounter with the bomb, nonetheless used a personal recollection in concurring with this judgment:

> My own older sister died of leukemia in 1954 [just prior to the Bikini incident] and it was simply said that she died of leukemia. . . . In those early days when people died, it was said they died of leukemia or cancer—not of A-bomb disease. . . . I don't know exactly when, but sometime . . . following the Bikini incident the term A-bomb disease began to be used. . . .

But he also stressed the importance of a second event, the construction in 1956 of the Atomic Bomb Hospital as a new unit of the Hiroshima Red Cross Hospital to be devoted entirely to patients with atomic bomb effects:

> After the A-Bomb Hospital was built—since no one was admitted to the hospital unless he had A-bomb disease—well, when they made announcements, they began to mention those who died of A-bomb disease. And also, those who died of it in other hospitals or other places were announced to have died of A-bomb disease. . . .

There is also a definite impression in Hiroshima that accompanying this increased use of the term A-bomb disease was a greater tendency than before to associate virtually any bodily complaint with radiation effects. And hard upon the heels of "A-bomb disease" came not only "A-bomb neurosis" but also "the Hiroshima disease," which has been used as synonymous with either. We shall have occasion later to return to the Bikini incident, but even this schematic account begins to suggest the way in which the general psychohistorical dimension affects individual reactions to the experience. We may consider this dimension by turning our attention first to mass-media treatment of A-bomb disease, and then to the medical and legal structure that has evolved in relationship to the problem.

MASS-MEDIA IMAGES

The entire subject of the atomic bomb and its delayed radiation effects has been front-page news in Hiroshima—first within the restrictions imposed by censorship policies of the American Occupation (1945–1952), and without any such restrictions thereafter. When we discuss Japanese-American interplay around the atomic bomb, we shall see that this censorship was by no means complete or even consistent, but it nonetheless (apart from the question of resentment) intensified the already existing mystery and general emotional impact of all information surrounding the atomic bomb.

Since the end of the Occupation, Hiroshima mass media (and to some extent those throughout Japan)—newspapers, magazines, radio, and television—have dealt with A-bomb problems extensively and dramatically, particularly in relationship to the issue of "A-bomb disease." But in the process these media have been prone to a general moral dilemma: there is on the one hand the urge to give full publicity to the horrors of nuclear weapons through vivid descriptions of effects and ·suspected effects of atomic bomb radiation—thereby serving warning to the world, and also expressing a form of sympathy to survivors through recognition of their plight; and on the other hand the growing awareness that lurid reports of illness and death have a profoundly disturbing effect upon survivors. Responsible media have struggled to reconcile these conflicting moral pressures, and to achieve balanced treatment of an unprecedentedly difficult problem; less responsible media have made no such effort, and have readily succumbed to the commerical temptations of sensationalism. In public discussions journalists have tended to emphasize the moral obligation to disseminate information, and physicians the dangers of increasing anxiety among *hibakusha*. But from all sides opinions have varied, as has the degree of accuracy of information transmitted.

The classic anxiety-producing image (which we have seen to have such overwhelming effect on so many *hibakusha*) is that of patients dying in the "A-Bomb Hospital" of "A-bomb disease"—as depicted in the following article from the *Yomiuri Shimbun* of 1 May 1962:[14]

LIFE CLAIMED BY A-BOMB DISEASE

On 30 April of 0150 hours at the A-Bomb Hospital, Mrs. Hatsue Hamaoka, 61, Principal of the Aloha Sewing School, 661, Shinonome-chō, Hiroshima-shi, died of chronic myelogenous leukemia caused by A-bomb disease. She is the 22nd person to die this year.

She had been exposed at her home in Nishi Kannon-machi, 1.5 kms. [1500 meters] from the hypocenter and sustained bruises when her house collapsed. She developed acute radiation symptoms but recovered. Six years ago she visited the U.S. and extended encouragement to the A-bomb Maidens who were undergoing treatment. She also visited a number of high schools in the U.S. to appeal for the ban of A- and H-bomb tests.

In September last year, she had a recurrence of her disease, and was hospitalized on 25 April, the day when resumption of nuclear tests was announced.

We note the sequence of original exposure, early symptoms, and a later "recurrence of her disease," conveying the sense of continuous invisible contamination leading to eventual death. The mention of resumption of nuclear tests is not only an expression of bitter irony, but also of a tendency to associate nuclear testing, directly or symbolically, with A-bomb disease.

A story in the *Asahi Shimbun*, Japan's leading newspaper, the following year tells of the death, also of leukemia, of an eighteen-year-old girl, who had originally been exposed *in utero*, two days before birth, at twenty-one hundred meters. It ends with the comment: "Dr. Shigeto [director of the Atomic Bomb Hospital] says that this was the first death of a patient who was in the mother's womb at the time of the bomb." Whatever the ambiguity of the sentence itself, or of the part played by the A-bomb in causing the condition, *hibakusha* are left with the imagery of the bomb continuing to snuff out the lives of the youngest among them.

Similar imagery surrounds death from cancer, and we note (in the following article in the *Sanyō Shimbun* of 26 December 1961) its direct equation with "A-bomb disease," despite its somewhat less established relationship to radiation effects and despite the age of the victim:

A-BOMB PATIENT DIES, 37TH VICTIM DURING THIS YEAR

Kina Matsuo, 82, of Itsukaichi-chō, Saeki-gun, Hiroshima-ken, who had been an in-patient of the Hiroshima A-Bomb Hospital, Senda-machi, Hiroshima City, died about 1315 hours on 24 December 1961 with A-bomb disease (pulmonary cancer).

The deceased had been exposed to the A-bombing of 6 August 1945 at Senda-machi at the distance of 1600 meters from the hypocenter. She was admitted to the hospital on 24 August 1961. Thirty-seven A-bomb patients died, including Mrs. Matsuo, during this year.

Other reports describe deaths, in various hospitals, from conditions other than leukemia or cancer, of *hibakusha* who were not in Hiroshima at the time of the bomb but were exposed by coming into the city within the next two weeks. An article in *Asahi* of 4 March 1962, for instance, tells of a fifty-one-year-old police officer who came into the city the day after the bomb, spent a week engaged in rescue work and disposal of dead bodies, and nine months before his death was diagnosed as suffering from "leukopenia [diminished number of white blood cells] due to secondary radiation." And even when qualifying adjectives (like "presumably") are used to suggest doubt about causation (as in an article in the *Chūgoku Shimbun* of 21 January 1962, telling of death from anemia), the headline, general tone, and subsequent content are likely to more than cancel out this qualification:

AN EX-SERVICEMAN WHO ENGAGED IN RESCUE WORK IN POST A-BOMB PERIOD DIES WITH A-BOMB DISEASE AT YOSHIDA HOSPITAL

Kyujiro Yamasaki, 55, a farmer of Saka, Mukaihara-machi, Takata-gun, died at 1130 hours at the Yoshida Welfare Federation Hospital, Yoshida-chō, Takata-gun, of anemia presumably associated with A-bomb disease. He is the first exposed patient who has died at this hospital.

On 8 August 1945, two days after the A-bombing, Mr. Yamasaki entered into Hiroshima City and visited Hakushima, Yokogawa, and Hijiyama in search of his missing younger sister. As a member of [the] Ex-Servicemen's Association, he participated in rescue work in the city from 20 August 1945, and then in Mukaihara-machi he helped with the cremation of those who perished in the A-bombing. Since then he developed A-bomb disease, but on 13 December 1961 he was hospitalized for medical care.

Nor is there any such qualification in an article in the same newspaper (of 26 January 1962) describing the death of a fifty-eight-year-old woman "of liver dysfunction caused by A-bomb disease," though liver dysfunction is considered by many doctors even more dubious an area of atomic bomb aftereffects than anemia and leukopenia. The seemingly definitive attribution of these deaths to "A-bomb disease" often derives from the patient's having been placed in a medico-legal category, which, with considerable latitude, recognizes the *possibility* of radiation effects having played some part in a particular condition.

"A-BOMB DISEASE" AND SUICIDE

A frequent theme is the equation of A-bomb disease and suicide, as in the following *Asahi* article of 19 September 1961:

AN AGED MOTHER COMMITS SUICIDE IN HIROSHIMA UNDER THE STRAIN OF A-BOMB DISEASE

ON SEVENTH DAY AFTER BEING DIAGNOSED

About 2320 hours on 17 September 1961, Mrs. Akino Okino, 64, the mother of Mr. Sekito Okino, a confectioner at 3-chome, Misasa Honmachi, Hiroshima City, hanged herself to death with an electric cord in a two-mat room* of her son's house.

Mrs. Okino had been exposed to the A-bomb at her home. Four years ago she developed heart trouble, and she was receiving treatment at a nearby hospital but her condition did not show any improvement.

On 11 September 1961, she was examined at the Hiroshima A-Bomb Hospital and the diagnosis of A-bomb disease was established. Mrs. Okino was greatly shocked at this.

According to members of her family, Mrs. Okino told them often that she wanted to die, since she was suffering from incurable A-bomb disease. The family members shared the same bedroom with her as a means of preventing any attempt at suicide.

Again there are ambiguities about the kind of disease she suffered from (we do not know whether the diagnosis of "A-bomb disease" refers to the heart condition or to some additional ailment), but the message is nonetheless clear: "A-bomb disease" is diagnosed, is incurable, and therefore leaves one utterly hopeless to the point of suicide. The factors which influence suicide, however, are always complex. Even assuming that the diagnosis of "A-bomb disease" was important as a precipitating cause, several possibilities present themselves. If the diagnosis of "A-bomb disease" referred to newly discovered leukemia or cancer, then the suicide could be said to have been based upon an accurate impression of impending death. But if the designation was made merely for the purpose of placing her in a category that afforded her certain medical and economic benefits, it could be said that she tragically misinterpreted an administrative convenience as a death sentence. And there is always the possibility that the suicide resulted from long-standing emotional conflicts independent of either the recent diagnosis or the atomic bomb experience per se, and that the reconstruction of cause-and-effect was

---

* Each straw (tatami) mat is about three by six feet, which would make the room about six by six feet—the smallest size room in a Japanese house, and apparently not the bedroom referred to later in the article in which several family members slept together.

essentially journalistic. The truth may lie in some combination of these three possibilities, but wherever it does lie, the average *hibakusha*-reader has had impressed upon him a terrifyingly absolute relationship between "A-bomb disease" and suicide.

Even in the absence of "A-bomb disease" the mere fact of being a *hibakusha* can be associated with suicide, as is indirectly implied in an article of 24 December 1961 in the *Yomiuri*, describing a man found in critical condition after having taken sleeping pills in a city several hundred miles from Hiroshima, and including the sentence: "The Atami police revealed that this man had with him an A-bomb survivor's health handbook issued by the Hiroshima City Office, but there was no note to explain the cause of his attempted suicide." The unspoken assumption, which could be true, untrue, or partly true—we have no way of knowing—is that there is a significant (perhaps crucial) connection between his *hibakusha* state and his suicide. In addition to reinforcing the *hibakusha* death taint, there is the suggestion of an existential closeness to suicide which makes the act more or less appropriate for a *hibakusha*.

Suicide can also be associated with the idea of the atomic bomb driving one crazy through fear—as in the following description of a schizophrenic man in the *Sankei Shimbun* of 3 November 1961, included here almost in its entirety despite its length because of the important psychological issues it raises:

"FEAR" CAUSED BY SECONDARY RADIATION DRIVES YOUNG MAN TO DEATH

GREAT SHOCK EXPERIENCED IMMEDIATELY AFTER A-BOMB EXPLOSION REVIVES AFTER 13 YEARS

TURNS PALE AT NEWS OF RESUMPTION OF NUCLEAR TESTS

A young man seized with fear of the A-bomb recently committed suicide by hanging himself. This person was not directly exposed to the A-bomb but received secondary radiation in Hiroshima. This caused him to suffer from a nervous breakdown, and his symptoms became especially aggravated at the news of resumption of nuclear tests. His family refused to comment on his death, but it is felt that this is not a problem which can be treated merely as "a young man with nervous breakdown who committed suicide by hanging himself." (Reporters Tsujigami and Shiba.)

It was from about January 1959 that it was rumored in Kinehara Village, Takaya-chō, Kamo-gun that "Mr. Ichikawa's son appears to have gone mad, probably as a result of exposure to radiation from the A-bomb." This young man is Mr. Morimune Ichikawa, 34, first son of Mr. Tsumoru Ichikawa, 68, a farmer in this village. Many people . . . expressed their sympathy. . . . The family cultivates a farm of about one hundred acres . . . [and] leads a well-to-do middle-class life. Morimune was a very gentle-natured man of introverted temperament. Though he became mad, his actions were not violent. He was seen idling away his time at home and sometimes helping weed the paddy field.

Now let us return to the problem of secondary radiation which is said to have driven him to a nervous breakdown. Before the termination of the war, he graduated from Takaya-chō Primary School and began to work at Saijo Communication Sub-district of the National Railways Corporation at the age of 18 years. When the A-bomb was dropped on Hiroshima, he was stationed here. However, as Hiroshima Station was destroyed, a relief team . . . was organized [which] included Morimune. . . . Hiroshima City immediately after the A-bomb explosion was in a chaotic condition, and he had to dispose of many dead bodies . . . which was a great shock to the youth. In about three months he returned to his sub-district, but subsequently began to feel ill and was often absent from work. For this reason, he was discharged in 1949 when the National Railway Discharge Program was enforced. Since then, he had been helping on the farm and doing repair work on radio and television sets. . . . If he had continued to live in this way, he might have been loved by all as a youth of exemplary behavior, married a beautiful woman and succeeded to his family estate. However, the shadows of tragedy darkened the picture.

"OH, THE A-BOMB IS FALLING"

His symptoms became gradually aggravated. Sometimes he wept, saying, "I am sorry. I am sorry." Sometimes he would cry out, "Oh, the A-bomb is falling." His condition was far from normal. As the family became concerned, he was hospitalized at Seiyoin Mental Hospital, Fuchu-machi, in February 1959. He recovered soon and was discharged in August. However, from the beginning of this year, his symptoms became aggravated again, and he was hospitalized at the Psychiatric Division of Senogawa Hospital. Dr. Kobayashi of this hospital explained his symptoms at that time as follows: "He was a case of severe schizophrenia. Whether this was due to fear caused by the A-bomb or not could not be discerned. However, as there is no family history of mental disease, I feel this case cannot be viewed as being completely unrelated to the A-bomb." Though he did not recover completely, he was discharged on 5 March. Since then he would seldom go out. When he met with a neighbor, he would exchange greetings but then immediately begin to talk about the A-bomb. The village people saw him earnestly offering prayers at the nearby cemetery. It was as if he were praying for the repose of the souls of A-bomb victims.

WEEPS AT NEWS OF RESUMPTION OF NUCLEAR TESTS BY THE U.S.

On 5 September he was hospitalized at Tsuhara Hospital, Takaya-chō, and was discharged on 10 September. In the afternoon of that day, he returned home together with members of his family. When he entered the room, the radio was broadcasting "the resumption of nuclear tests by the United States." At this news, he turned pale. It is said that he was trembling as he cried, "This situation has occurred because I had the United States make the A-bomb. I am sorry." The family felt concerned over his condition and tried to keep him from listening to the radio and reading magazines, but he had already become completely terror-stricken by the A-bomb. During meals, he would suddenly cry out to his family, "Don't you see dead bodies lying over there?" (The impression of Hiroshima after the A-bomb explosion must have weighed heavily on his mind.) He said, "I am responsible for killing a large number of people by the A-bomb. I am very sorry." Whenever funeral services were held in the village, he used to go, clasping his hands in prayer, saying, "This person was killed because I made the A-bomb."

What is the cause for his great A-bomb phobia? He was free of abnormalities at least from immediately after the termination of the war until about 1957. Is it possible that A-bomb phobia suddenly develops after the lapse of 13 years? Summarizing the statements of his family, neighbors and physicians, it appears the great shock he received from seeing the great number of dead bodies in Hiroshima after the A-bomb explosion remained in his subconscious mind. Physically he might have been affected by secondary radiation and [feared that he] might have developed leukemia. It was from about 1958 that the problem of A-bomb medicine for A-bomb survivors in Hiroshima was taken up as an important subject. As this discussion and research started to be actively conducted, Morimune came to fear that he might have been affected by radiation. This gradually developed into a strong fear of the A-bomb. In relation to this point, his father, Tsumoru, said, "Morimune had complained of physical abnormalities since 1949 and 1950. I think this was due to radiation. Something should have been done earlier. . . . Since then the A-bomb must have occupied his mind." It is said that about one half of the twenty National Railway employees who had gone to Hiroshima as members of the relief team have already died, which might have caused him to develop fear of the A-bomb.

STATEMENT BY PROFESSOR YUKIO SAKAI,
SCHOOL OF EDUCATION, HIROSHIMA UNIVERSITY

"It is not strange that the tragedy of the A-bomb explosion should come to the surface after the lapse of more than ten years. Of course, we should oppose nuclear tests, but on the other hand if this fear should be over-exaggerated, we must bear in mind that such effects will occur."

In this extraordinary account we note four dimensions of fear associated with the atomic bomb: first, the image of a normal, likeable, financially comfortable young man being driven crazy by a combination of original psychic trauma (from working among the dead), later fears of secondary radiation effects, and actual physical radiation influences—all resulting in a form of "invisible contamination" which emerges thirteen years later; then the development of "A-bomb phobia" (really a full-blown delusional system); third, intensification of fear to the point of mental breakdown and suicide—because of circulation of medical information about A-bomb disease in Hiroshima, and of news of the deaths of more than half of the people who had entered the city with him on the rescue team at the time of the bomb; and fourth, the implication that the news of American resumption of nuclear testing gave him a decisive setback, just when he was beginning to show some improvement. Generally speaking, the fear of A-bomb disease is the organizing image around which the boy's self-inflicted death is explained.

This kind of imagery misleads in its insistence upon the A-bomb as the specific cause of mental breakdown and suicide, but it nonetheless contains considerable psychological truth. Even if we assume that the boy had abnormal tendencies from very early in life, and might well have become psychotic without being exposed to the bomb—an assumption consistent with our knowledge of schizophrenia and with the description of his "introverted" nature—there remains the considerable likelihood that his overall atomic bomb experience contributed significantly to the psychosis and suicide that did occur. His later delusions that the bomb was still falling, and that he was responsible for the deaths of others and for the bomb itself, may be regarded as extremely pathological forms of patterns with which we are familiar: the continuing encounter with death (and retention of a death taint), identification with the weapon, and, most of all, the burden of retained death guilt. In mental illness in general delusions and hallucinations are attempts at restitution, at recovery of psychic function; thus we may say that within a psychotic idiom his were (unsuccessful) efforts at atomic bomb mastery. And the news of American testing could well have reactivated all of his conflicts, as we shall later observe to be frequently the case with *hibakusha*.

What this account conveys particularly vividly is the way in which *the fearful image of A-bomb disease can embody the entire psychic constellation of atomic bomb exposure in its most disturbed form*. And the uneasy comment by Professor Sakai at the end of the article comes close to expressing the moral dilemma mentioned before, concerning mass-media dissemination of information about atomic bomb effects. For this case itself demonstrates the vicious circle of individual pathology and such mass-media dissemination: an already existing morbid process was probably intensified by mass-media messages about A-bomb disease (though it is often difficult to evaluate the schizophrenic's response to external stress); and the mass-media interpretation of that case undoubtedly contributed in turn to general *hibakusha* anxiety by spreading the simplistic message, " 'Fear' Caused by Secondary Radiation Drives Young Man to Death."*

STATISTICS—USE AND RESPONSE

Beyond these descriptions of fatal illness and suicide, various general statistics quoted in the press can have enormous impact. These statistics are frequently tied in with concerns about nuclear testing, as in the following article in the *Sanyō Shimbun* of 31 October 1961:

LEUKEMIA CONTINUES TO INCREASE

HIROSHIMA CITIZENS HORRIFIED BY NUCLEAR TESTS

It is reported that in spite of the strong protests voiced from Hiroshima, Soviet Russia tested a 60-megaton superbomb in the evening of 29 October. With the nuclear tests carried out in rapid succession, a large amount of radiation has already been detected in

---

* The quotation marks around the word "fear" in the original article probably suggest not so much a questioning of its use as a sense that it conveys something more than ordinary fear, as well as the idea of a reaction shared by a large group of people.

rain and dust in the air, and it is feared that radiation disturbances, such as leukemia, might increase. The A-bombed city of Hiroshima is also a city of cancer. Cancers due to the A-bomb particularly continue to occur, causing anxiety among the citizens in general. At such time, the series of nuclear tests, including this new superbomb, will further increase this anxiety. A study of leukemia in Hiroshima City, which has recently increased remarkably, was undertaken.

65 PER CENT OF DEATHS DUE TO LEUKEMIA ARE EXPOSED PERSONS

CANCER CONTINUES TO OCCUR

A survey by the Prefectural Health Department revealed that 2,484 persons died of cancer in Hiroshima Prefecture last year. This number of deaths has remained almost unchanged for the last several years. The mortality rate is high, 113 per 100,000 population. About one fourth of the above deaths, or 565, died of cancer in Hiroshima City. Of course, the population density of the city proper differs from that of rural areas, and all of such deaths in Hiroshima City cannot be attributed to A-bomb radiation, but the majority of the 44 deaths at the Hiroshima A-Bomb Hospital . . . from January to 30 October 1961 were due to cancer. A survey of the deaths from leukemia in Hiroshima City from 1946 to 1960 conducted by the Research Institute for Nuclear Medicine and Biology of Hiroshima University reveals that during this period 223 persons, or 4.3 per 100,000 population, died of leukemia, and that 65 per cent of them were exposed persons.

Experienced medical researchers and statisticians would be hard put to distinguish what is significant and what is misleading in this imposing array of figures. For ordinary *hibakusha* such statistics frequently take on an aura of scientific sacredness and become a form of incontestable numerical confirmation of their worst atomic bomb fears. In this article, as in many others, there is the definite implication that nuclear testing will render statistics of A-bomb disease even more devastating. The assumption is not without some truth, since nuclear tests do intensify *hibakusha* fears of "A-bomb disease," which in turn increase symptoms; and because, as many international scientific authorities have stated, such testing can increase the general danger of leukemia everywhere. What is misleading and without scientific basis is the suggestion that because of their prior exposure to radiation, *hibakusha* are *particularly* liable to increases in leukemia and cancer resulting from nuclear testing.

*The hibakusha-reader is thus left with an overall message that Hiro-
shima is a city of leukemia and cancer, a doomed city whose death taint
has been statistically confirmed and is ever renewed and intensified by
forces let loose in various parts of the world.* Again, this kind of message
represents both an accurate expression of inner imagery held by *hibakusha,* and an anxiety-stimulating intensification and public formaliza-
tion of that imagery.*

But negative findings can evoke their own kind of anxiety, particularly
when reported by American researchers. A *Chūgoku* article of 3 July
1961 depicts "A Gloomy Controversy" between the ABCC and the
Japan Council Against Atomic and Hydrogen Bombs (*Gensuikyō*).
While the article quotes directives from both groups, it consists mainly
of objections raised by *Gensuikyō* officials to certain scientific conclusions published earlier by an ABCC physician: namely, that the risk of
genetic abnormalities was small, that findings in most controversial areas

---

* While newspaper articles, like the medical evaluations they quote, vary in
accuracy, they are likely in some way to carry messages of doom. For instance, an
article in the *Chūgoku Shimbun* of 17 December 1961, reporting statistics of a prior
five-month period, states that although 200 of 251 patients admitted to the A-Bomb
Hospital were discharged improved or completely recovered, 32 of the 51 who died
had been identified as suffering from atomic bomb sequelae. Similarly, an *Asahi*
article of 13 March 1952 states that a Welfare Ministry survey reveals that "about
40 per cent of A-bomb survivors are suffering from various symptoms," with the
incidence of cancer, cardiac disease, and diseases of the nervous system higher than
in ordinary populations; that from April, 1957, to March, 1961, "857 new cases of A-
bomb disease were found in Hiroshima Prefecture (excluding Hiroshima City)," and
that "of these cases . . . 60 per cent are people suffering from anemia . . . and 11
per cent each from hepatic disturbances and ankylosis following recovery from
keloids." Such statistics mislead by combining part-truths with inaccuracies and
questionable conclusions. Even essentially accurate articles can mislead, as for
example in the *Nagasaki Shimbun* of 22 November 1961, describing an increase in
exposed *hibakusha* (confirmed by several medical studies) of thyroid cancer. A
subheading, "INCIDENCE APPROXIMATELY 40 PER CENT AMONG A-BOMB SURVIVORS,"
could easily be construed to mean that 40 per cent of *hibakusha* suffer from thyroid
cancer, rather than the actual finding that among *hibakusha* undergoing surgery for
thyroid disease, 40 per cent were found to have cancer—by no means a piece of
good news, but hardly the same thing.

Where the article's headline suggests a note of reassurance (as in the *Chūgoku* of
11 July 1962: "CASES OF LEUKEMIA DECREASE"), it is likely to be followed
by an ominous subheading ("NUMBER OF CANCER CASES STILL LARGE"), and an
equally ominous general statement in the article ("The number of certified [as
having A-bomb disease] patients who can be discharged with complete recovery is
diminishing steadily"). Rare indeed is the reassuring article, such as that in the
Sankei Shimbun of 20 November 1961, telling that a four-year ophthalmological
study had led to the conclusion "that there are extremely few A-bomb patients with
cataracts at the present time . . . and that there is no need for these patients to
worry about tendencies toward progression in these cataracts"; the article concluded
by calling this a "valuable report," which "will be appreciated by such patients in
that it removes their anxiety."

of possible radiation effects were negative, and that those exposed beyond two thousand meters did not tend to receive pathologically significant radiation dosage. This last finding was especially resented because survivor groups were involved at that time in a legal effort to change, from two thousand to three thousand meters, the distance from the hypocenter which officially qualified *hibakusha* for various medical and economic benefits. A statement by a pathology professor then active in *Gensuikyō* shows how this concern became intertwined with other issues:

> To underestimate radiation disturbances as the ABCC has done is to expose mankind to the danger of radiation, and to undermine the welfare of A-bomb survivors who desire that the application of the A-bomb survivors' medical treatment law be expanded.

The article also contained scientific objections by physicians and scholars associated with *Gensuikyō*, and an accusation that the ABCC reports had "political intent."

Without taking up now the issue of the complex feelings surrounding the ABCC in Hiroshima, we may say that the newspaper article touches on the *hibakusha*'s great sensitivity to anything perceived as minimizing or negating radiation effects. For apart from the issue of medical and economic benefits, he may feel insulted by such reports, as if accused of inauthentic fears and even of malingering. They stimulate his own inner conflicts over whether his fears and symptoms are justified, whether he should view himself as normally active or abnormally weak, and whether he is worthy of the medical and economic privileges he is given and further seeks. He reacts with anger toward those who seem to him to be questioning his need for special help because his own inner doubts have been aggravated.

He therefore experiences, in relationship to mass media, a corollary of the psychosomatic bind: dramatic dissemination of information about A-bomb disease intensifies his already strong death anxiety, but negation of these dangers intensifies conflicts over dependency and guilt. The media themselves are inevitably affected—though confusedly and in conflicting ways—by pressures emanating from both sides of this dilemma.

Thus, during the late 1950s daily radio broadcasts dramatically reporting deaths from A-bomb disease were so disturbing that following protests from some *hibakusha*, they were modified in the direction of restraint. *Hibakusha* groups have also occasionally initiated campaigns to counteract exaggerated statements in the mass media about A-bomb disease. But other survivor organizations, peace movements, and ideological and political groups publicize the effects of the bomb in ways that intensify anxieties about A-bomb disease—whether on a generally humanistic basis, or in quest of narrower political goals within the unique Hiroshima atmosphere.

None of these groups or media can be said to have created the problem of A-bomb disease; rather they are its public voice. Nor are the public passions I have described simply manufactured ones; they are the inevitable expression of the impact of a disaster of this magnitude upon basic human conflicts and anxieties. Exaggerations and distortions are themselves products of the bomb. They are built upon an underlying lethal reality of acute and delayed radiation effects, and upon the genuine possibility of still undiscovered forms of bodily harm. As they emerge from, and then feed back into, fundamental *hibakusha* conflicts, they become part of the atomic bomb's overall psychohistorical constellation.

REGULATIONS AND POLICIES

A closely related area is that of public policy regarding *hibakusha*, and particularly the elaborate code of medico-legal regulations concerning status and benefits.

To understand these, we must recall that during the years immediately following the bomb, when medical care was most needed, very little was available. The Atomic Bomb Hospital was not opened until late 1956, and the national medical law providing benefits for survivors was not enacted until 1957. There were undoubtedly many different factors involved in this twelve-year delay. On the Japanese side, there was the devastated condition of the country in general, and the impoverished situation of government agencies and private groups; the absence of a strong tradition for social welfare; political conflict at national and local levels, including a good deal of reluctance to make special provisions for one or two Japanese cities in the face of dire national needs, as well as rivalry between Hiroshima and Nagasaki; and resistance among influential Hiroshima physicians to public medical programs that might threaten their sources of income. On the American side, there was a tendency to avoid placing any stress upon atomic bomb aftereffects, and when the problem was attacked, an emphasis upon research rather than treatment, with the reason given that Japanese physicians preferred it this way. (It must be added, of course, that American financial support, official as well as private, did eventually play an important part in the construction of medical and other facilities.)

Since 1957, however, a series of laws and amendments have been passed which provide increasingly comprehensive medical coverage for *hibakusha*.[15] I intend neither to make a complete listing of all these provisions nor to pass judgment upon those responsible for enacting them, but rather to explore their general contours as still another psychological ramification, and a very important one, of atomic bomb consequences.

We have already listed the distinguishing features of the ordinary *hibakusha* as defined by these medical laws (those within Hiroshima city limits at the time of the bomb, who came into the center of the city during the fourteen-day period following it, who handled dead or wounded, or who were *in utero* and whose mothers fit into any of the first three categories). But within this general group "special *hibakusha*" are designated, on the basis either of being nearest the hypocenter at the time of the bomb or of showing evidence of medical conditions considered to have some relationship to atomic bomb effects. Special *hibakusha* receive wider benefits, and the tendency in recent years has been toward enlarging this category. Through two revisions put into effect in 1962, distance from the hypocenter, as a criterion for eligibility, was extended from two thousand to three thousand meters; and qualifying illnesses were also extended to include many which are not considered specifically related to radiation. Not only cancer but heart disease, endocrine and kidney disorders, arteriosclerosis, hypertension, and a number of other conditions were included on the basis that they could have been aggravated by the overall atomic bomb experience.*

In addition to the regular free examinations to which all *hibakusha* are entitled, a special *hibakusha* can have half of his medical expenses taken care of when suffering from almost any general disease, with the exception of such things as dental problems, certain congenital conditions, and mental illness which had existed prior to the bomb.† Moreover, those among special *hibakusha* who become "certified" by official government examiners as having illnesses specifically related to the

---

* In 1963 and again in 1965 additional amendments further extended the category of the "special *hibakusha*."

† Despite the general concern about harmful mental effects, the laws tend to neglect mental disease per se; the absence of any designation of A-bomb-linked mental illness probably reflects the strong organic bias generally prevalent in Japanese psychiatry, and the belief that most mental illness is congenital.

atomic bomb—including leukemia, ophthalmic diseases, various forms of anemia, leukopenia (low white count), leucocytosis (high white count), purpura (bleeding syndrome), or diseases of the liver and lymphatic systems—receive, at government expense, full medical treatment for the "certified" condition, and are also eligible for monthly benefit payments of 3,000 yen, or about $8 (as of 1964—prior to that it was ¥ 2,000, or about $6) in addition to receiving all other privileges of special *hibakusha*.

Physicians have played a prominent part in formulating these regulations, together with city officials and political leaders, but all have been subject to the conflicting pressures which we have described in relationship to A-bomb disease. Thus, while the original regulations of 1957 focused primarily upon conditions believed directly related to the atomic bomb, later amendments have embraced a much broader philosophy to encompass whatever illnesses *might* have been affected by radiation, however indirectly. And city officials responsible for administering the laws were quick to admit to me that these amendments were passed in relationship to strong political pressures from *hibakusha* and groups representing them.

The dilemma of *hibakusha* and lawmakers alike is similar to dilemmas we have observed in other areas: all are caught in a conflict between humanitarian provision for medical need, and the dangers of encouraging in survivors the development of hypochondriasis, general weakness, and psychological dependency to the point of "A-bomb neurosis." Or to put the matter in another way, there are two conflicting images, each with some validity: the first, that of the A-bomb victim who has undergone unprecedented forms of pain and suffering, is still subject to unknown physical dangers, and who deserves every possible advantage that can be made available to him; and the second, that of the survivor who, though essentially healthy and physically normal, if "certified" as an A-bomb patient, can thereby be made into one and rendered sick.

There remains a great deal of controversy about these laws in other ways too. *Hibakusha* criticize them for being still insufficiently comprehensive, resent attempted distinctions between what is, or is not, related to the A-bomb, or complain about their cumbersome categories and subcategories which in the end deny full care for certain conditions. The rationale of the laws, particularly as later amended, has been to give survivors "the benefit of the doubt" about matters not yet scientifically resolved. This "benefit of the doubt," however, can often include not only the right to be treated for illness but the prerogative of illness itself.

Given the atmosphere of Hiroshima, it is difficult indeed for a politician, city official, or physician to express public opposition to the expansion of any medical program. In all these ways—in the anxiety and confusion surrounding the programs and in the medico-legal binds they include—the laws accurately reflect, as well as perpetuate, the city's overwhelming bodily concerns.

4) *Physician and Disease*

The physicians of Hiroshima have inevitably found themselves enmeshed in the problems of A-bomb disease, and their conceptions of it take on considerable importance. For they inevitably convey these conceptions to their patients—sometimes through public pronouncements, more often through the combination of stated medical opinion and unspoken feelings communicated within a private consultation. Moreover, the special aura of magic which surrounds practitioners of the healing arts in any culture is strongly intensified in a disease-conscious atomic-bombed community.

In pursuing these matters with a considerable number of doctors in Hiroshima, I found them to differ strikingly with one another in their outlook. The quality of these differences seemed to me to shed unique light on the dilemma of A-bomb disease, and at the same time to say something about the general psychology of scientific formulation, particularly about the effects of psychic stress upon medical thought.

Based upon attitudes toward "A-bomb disease," the doctors I spoke to could be divided into four general categories, though one must keep in mind the approximate nature of the categories as well as the difficulty of fitting certain individual doctors into any of them. The first category is that of the All-Embracing Concept: here physicians implicate the atomic bomb not only in those conditions where its effects are generally agreed to be present (such as leukemia), or in those where there is controversy (growth and development of children, or certain anemias), but also in virtually every bodily ailment, whether of the heart, kidney, lungs, or any other organ. The second category is that of a Moderately Inclusive Concept: A-bomb disease extends to accepted and controversial areas, but stops short of the more general bodily systems and can include psychological influences. In the third category, that of Skepticism, physicians question the term itself, and while accepting the influence of radiation as definite in leukemia and probable in cancer, and entertaining the possibility of its influence in certain borderline areas, they object to claims of wider A-bomb-induced pathology. The fourth category, that of Outright Rejection, contains physicians who attack the concept of A-bomb disease both because they think its promiscuous use does great harm and because they do not believe in the existence of chronic radiation effects as a genuine clinical entity; they grant radiation influence in leukemia and eye cataracts, and possibly in cancer, but look upon virtually all other complaints as either psychological in origin or due to something else, and stress the need for clear-cut statistical evidence drawn from comparative population groups before coming to any conclusions.

In the absence of anything approaching a systematic survey, I had the distinct impression that generational and national factors were important: that is, while Japanese physicians run the gamut of all four categories, they are much less likely than American physicians to be in the third and fourth; and older Japanese physicians are more likely to be in the first and second groups than are younger ones. An important influence here is the much stronger commitment of American and younger Japanese physicians to the exacting criteria of the scientific tradition, and the greater susceptibility of older Japanese physicians to group pressures within the society, in this case involving strong identification with a victimized group. On the other hand, the judgment of American and younger Japanese physicians could be affected by a form of scientific identity which required them to seek very great psychic distance from the discomfort induced by emotional and physical consequences of the bomb.

Of great importance for every individual doctor is the nature of his particular struggle with guilt. Non*hibakusha* (Japanese) physicians could readily feel guilty over having escaped the bomb, and over various kinds of hostility they have felt toward *hibakusha*, including resentment of them for posing such insoluble medical problems. *Hibakusha* physicians face the potential guilt of "betraying" their fellow survivors should they undermine their claims of organic (that is, A-bomb-caused) pathology, but could also feel guilty toward them for giving their condition the dreaded label of radiation effects—not to mention the *hibakusha* physician's susceptibility to having his own death guilt reactivated. The guilt potential of American physicians has to do with their affiliation with the nation which dropped the bomb, with the complexities of official American governmental connection while carrying out the research, and with their own group pressures and internalized standards relating to scientific research. Indeed, the conflicts engendered by the interplay of science and "human feelings" were present in all physicians I met, whatever their age or background—an area of conflict of considerable intensity in the modern world in general and in

Japan in particular, and one which reaches unprecedented dimensions in relationship to atomic bomb medicine. But we shall soon see that here as elsewhere there is more than one kind of science.

It would be wrong to take any single emotional or intellectual factor as *the* cause for a physician's ultimate medical position. We can only say that a variety of intellectual and emotional forces come together to enter into the formation of that position. We can, with somewhat greater conviction, relate specific emotional factors to the *tone* expressed by physicians toward *hibakusha*, though even here we must look for patterns of influence. We must turn to the words and images of a few individual physicians for a more direct understanding of these problems.

ALL-EMBRACING CONCEPT

A non*hibakusha* medical administrator in his sixties described health problems of *hibakusha* in phrases very similar to those used by ordinary *hibakusha* themselves:

> *Hibakusha* are more sensitive than ordinary people to external stress —for instance they are likely to be more tired in the summer. This is hard to evaluate as a symptom, however. For instance, it is sometimes said—by Americans—that this feeling of being more sensitive to the heat of summer has to do with a psychological reminder of hot weather, and is related to memories of the August sixth dropping of the bomb. But we feel it is a medical problem. They lack vitality, and possibly their adaptational ability is also decreased. They also react more sensitively to coldness. They catch colds more easily. And if they suffer from disease in general, they tend to have a different course of that disease—more severe symptoms, more prolonged effects—than does the ordinary person. Under normal circumstances they are the same as anyone else—but if there is some particular stress or disease . . . they are not the same. . . .

In addition to this stress upon organicity rather than psychological causation, he took the point of view that A-bomb disease could be looked upon as a condition derived from radiation effects in combination with additional influences, so that "it is very difficult to prove statistically the incidence of such a disease, or to prove the specific influence of radiation," And although he admitted it might "sound rather extreme" to claim that "any medical disturbance which manifests itself in exposed persons may be looked upon as A-bomb disease," he thought this position "not too unreasonable—since without A-bomb radiation . . . such a disease might not have appeared." And he used a colloquial metaphor to illustrate this general adaptational principle: "One might say that the A-bomb pushes these patients over the threshold—or, according to the Japanese expression, gives them just that extra burden which makes it difficult for them to keep their heads above the water.*

His discussion of leukemia, cancer, and related problems included a sophisticated and generally accepted point of view—in effect, since leukemia is caused by many factors in addition to radiation, and since many of those in Hiroshima who would have been likely to develop leukemia independently of the bomb have already done so, it is possible that the incidence of leukemia in the near future may dip down below the average rate; and that the same pattern of increase and then decrease below the average could well occur in various forms of cancer. To which he added, "And then other diseases may follow the same pattern, one after the other"—a comment which could be viewed as a logical extension of his thesis, but was put forth in an ominous tone, which again strikingly resembled that of ordinary *hibakusha*.

His subsequent discussion of more questionable areas was characterized by a distrust of present scientific criteria and an inclination to see possible radiation effects everywhere:

> In regard to liver disease, this is very hard to determine, even if we have liver function tests. Because even if the tests don't show anything specific, and do not indicate that there is any difference between *hibakusha* and others, there still might be some impairment. . . . Concerning blood disease—here we can determine specific numbers of red blood cells and white blood cells, so the problem is a little easier than in the case of liver disease. But we are still looking only at the peripheral blood, and from this alone we cannot conclude that there is no disturbance. . . . Anemia is very common, and it often is caused by nutritional factors, so we use the term "social anemia." . . . But there may also be some form of anemia which comes from radiation, although affected by other factors. . . .

In addition he stressed the difficulties in treating those forms of A-bomb disease characterized by a low white blood count, and suggested that *moxa* (a "burning herb") cauterization (or *kyū*), a therapeutic technique derived from ancient Chinese medicine, "may have some

---

* He used the phrase *geta o azukeru*, literally, "to deposit a *geta* [wooden clog]," but having the idiomatic meaning of adding a burden.

beneficial effect on the white blood count." I had the impression that his belief in this method might well have been stronger than these words suggest, but that his concerns about being "modern" and "scientific" (perhaps particularly when talking to an American colleague) led him to express it carefully.

His concluding remarks were something in the spirit of a public pronouncement. They suggested both a utopian vision of preventive care and, once more, a close identification with the aspirations of the *hibakusha* group:

> Our goal is to improve the medical care for the exposed people, to supply them with complete medical care without waiting for actual symptoms to develop in them. When such symptoms develop, we consider this to be too late, and we would rather take measures to prevent these A-bomb effects from manifesting themselves. And this also requires economic betterment and economic help. . . .

The force of this identification with *hibakusha*, along with his relatively tenuous ties to certain aspects of the scientific tradition, led him to publish some highly questionable findings concerning radiation effects. But it must be added that some of his emphasis upon adaptation and general stress comes close to a new scientific spirit being expressed in contemporary theories of disease—a spirit which has some connection with the principles of balance and imbalance contained in the traditional Japanese (and Chinese) thought, medical and otherwise, which he espouses.

VARIETIES OF SKEPTICISM

A *hibakusha*-physician of the same generation, a hospital director, equally traditionalistic in thought (he quickly identified himself to me as a Confucian and a Buddhist), took a very different point of view. A man with a long record of humane dedication to fellow *hibakusha*, he nonetheless spoke critically of the "many *hibakusha* who feel they should have special privileges because they were victims of the bomb." This judgment was in keeping with equally moralistic and conservative attitudes in other areas: condemnations of students who participated in peace demonstrations of any kind, because "the duty of a student is to study," and the opinion that those from poor families should take the "more practical" course of finding jobs after high school rather than attend universities.

On medical questions he identified himself strongly on the one hand with scientific caution in evaluating radiation aftereffects. He favored what was generally regarded as the ABCC American position because "after all, they have such elaborate equipment," and spoke with disdain of other physicians' tendencies to exaggerate A-bomb influences. But on the other hand he seemed to revert to the opposite philosophical perspective, and to a traditional Japanese tone, in emphasizing that the problem of radiation effects is simply unknowable, is one that "man cannot solve"—with the implication that much of the general struggle to grasp and conquer the problem was futile.

When I asked him about general anxieties concerning A-bomb after-effects, he lost his composure and smiled in a manner which (in Japanese culture) suggests both discomfort and irony, giving me the sense that a raw nerve had been exposed:

Yes, of course, people are anxious. Take my own case. If I am shaving in the morning and I should happen to cut myself very slightly, I dab the blood with a piece of paper—and then, when I notice that it has stopped flowing, I think to myself, "Well, I guess I am all right."

It seemed clear that his own *hibakusha* anxieties were involved in his formulation of radiation effects; and that to cope with these anxieties, he called forth patterns of denial and detachment which could draw upon deeply ingrained Buddhist feelings as well as upon a pattern of identification with "Science" (rather frequent among Japanese), based more upon perceptions of its power and beauty than its reasoning processes. Medically speaking, he fits best in the third category, but his inner emotions (usually repressed) could be said to propel him, at least at certain moments, into the second or the first.

:

Very different from the approach of the two older men was that of a younger (fortyish) hematologist, a non*hibakusha*, who had trained in the more scientifically-minded postwar milieu, performed considerable research upon *hibakusha* both independently and in collaboration with American-sponsored groups, and become recognized as a leading Japanese authority in his field. His crisp forthright manner was the antithesis of the traditional allusiveness we observed in both of his senior colleagues, and he differed particularly from the medical administrator in his stress upon the decrease, even disappearance, of radiation effects, and his insistence upon the significance of psychological influences:

Five years ago I began to find that there was no longer any great difference in the incidence of leukemia in *hibakusha* and non*hibakusha*, so I began to speculate that there were no longer any direct effects from radiation occurring. From then I began to think of the psychosomatic problems involved. I began to see many cases with complaints of many different kinds, and they would all say that these were related to the A-bomb. Their complaints were so diversified and so broad and vague that I felt the problem should be clarified, not only from the medical side, but from the psychological side. I felt that because of the mass media, people were hearing so much about A-bomb disease that they began to have great fear, and this fear in turn brought about a kind of illness in them, a feeling that they were sick. . . . I feel that the psychological side becomes added to the physical side. . . . I do not really think it is possible actually to differentiate A-bomb disease, to say that a particular disease is specifically caused by radiation. . . . Of course, leukemia is quite different, but that is the only clear-cut entity.

He was skeptical not only of the general concept of A-bomb disease but also of the role of radiation effects in various controversial areas, and expressed doubt that any form of chronic anemia or liver disease was related to the A-bomb. He felt that any claim of radiation influence was meaningless in the absence of precise scientific evidence, and emphasized the extreme difficulty in obtaining such evidence. He illustrated his position with a vivid personal account of his experiences with blood-count preoccupations among *hibakusha*:

Many patients are brought to me with reports of leukopenia or anemia. They have a report of a white blood cell count of 3,000 [the normal count is between 5,000 and 10,000]. Then I take their white blood count and find it to be 6,000. The next day I take it again and it is 3,500 or 4,000. It is quite variable as I continue to study it, and then I explain to them that it can change from day to day. Then the patient can begin to recognize the situation and get some relief. As long as there are figures involved, the patient can feel that he understands. But if there are no figures involved, this makes it very difficult. . . .

We see here the dual problem of "figures," since he sees them as misleading and yet necessary to *hibakusha*. There was much to suggest that for him, too, as a scientifically-minded physician, the absence of "figures"—of confirmatory statistics—made things "very difficult."

Thus, in discussing the frequent complaint of malaise (*"karada ga darui,"* literally, "the body is weary")—along with headache, lethargy, decreased ability to work, and loss of memory—he wavered between attributing them to a general Japanese physiological tendency to "a rather low and inadequate function of the stomach and intestine," and to psychological fears associated with the A-bomb. He treated these conditions with vitamins and hormonal extracts, added that "I wish I knew more about psychological methods," and made a further comment which suggested that he did indeed possess at least the beginnings of a genuine psychosomatic perspective: "These patients say they lack energy —and it is often a question of activity . . . activity of the gastrointestinal tract, and activity of all kinds—mentally and physically."

But there is nothing equivocal in his stand concerning the abuses of the concept of A-bomb disease—its use as a refuge for ignorance and medico-economic convenience—or in his evocation of the general atmosphere in which Hiroshima doctors work:

> Doctors . . . come to this conclusion too hastily. They try to escape from a situation that is very confusing and very unclear, because they are not able to make a definite diagnosis. The doctor often will take the matter very lightly: "You seem to be tired. This could be an effect from the A-bomb. Let's look at your white blood count—yes, it is rather low—it may be A-bomb disease." But the patient takes this very seriously, and thinks that if his blood count is low, this *must* be A-bomb disease. . . . My thinking is this: one of the main reasons why the term A-bomb disease is widely used is in relationship to arranging treatment for these people. Many of them are very poor, so this becomes an economic factor—and it is from this standpoint that the doctors often use the term A-bomb disease. But from the standpoint of science, it is a very obscure and vague concept. . . . So we doctors must always look at the matter in two ways: in this first more or less economic way; and in the second or scientific way. In my clinic we do not use the term A-bomb disease in treating patients—neither we nor they speak of it. . . . A-bomb disease is not really a diagnosis, but simply a convenient category for a condition that is not understood.

I found no clearer depiction of the actual operation of this web of social, economic, and psychological forces spinning itself about physician and patient alike. And he went on to extend these principles in a provocative comment about the different atmospheres in the two A-bombed cities:

My impression is that at Nagasaki Medical School the doctors tend on the whole to underestimate the effects of the A-bomb in producing disease, while here in Hiroshima there is . . . a tendency to overestimate A-bomb influences upon disease. And because of this, I think, the patients in Hiroshima feel A-bomb disease—or feel that they have A-bomb disease—to a greater extent than do those in Nagasaki.

We shall learn later of the reasons for the differing atmospheres in Hiroshima and Nagasaki; what concerns us here is his perception that these differences influence psychosomatic complaints.

The hematologist's imagery of A-bomb disease places him somewhere between the third and fourth categories. He gives little evidence of the conflict we have noted in the other non*hibakusha* physician, and seems neither to be hostile to, nor to overidentify with, his *hibakusha* patients. But there is the possibility that his strong involvement in scientific tradition and his stress upon the concrete and the numerical (emphasized generally in Japanese culture) are associated with a certain amount of psychic numbing, which could in turn be an influence toward minimization of atomic bomb effects. I would again caution that such elements cannot be said to "explain," negate, or confirm his intellectual position, but only to be part of the overall self-process from which that position emerges.

OUTRIGHT REJECTION

A young staff physician at a Hiroshima hospital was even more adamant in his dismissal of the concept of A-bomb disease. He spoke of its "political tie-up," by which he meant the array of non-medical considerations affecting existing regulations and influencing individual physicians' diagnoses. He was dubious about most areas of alleged radiation effects, thought them certain only in leukemia, and even in relationship to cancer thought that additional information was needed before anything definite could be said. But he was at his most bitterly illuminating when he discussed the ways in which prevailing practices encourage lifelong fixation upon the bodily taint of A-bomb disease:

With these special benefits, the more you receive, the worse the situation becomes. I am very dubious about social welfare programs. . . . The more social welfare made available, the weaker the population becomes. . . . Once these people become A-bomb patients, they will be A-bomb patients the rest of their lives. I can cure an ordinary case of anemia within two weeks. But when I tell a [*hibakusha*] patient that his anemia could easily be cured in two weeks, he insists upon benefits of an A-bomb patient. Then this man will have to carry the burden of the A-bomb all the rest of his life. If he lives to be seventy or eighty years old, he will realize that he has lived a normal life and his condition is not in the A-bomb category. But just from trying to get this 2,000 yen [about $6] benefit [each month], these people shoulder the burden of the A-bomb for the rest of their lives. . . .

In this description, and in his subsequent demand for scientific demonstration, one could feel his frustration and anger:

In many cases I feel that, speaking strictly from my medical viewpoint, a man is cured. But he will still bring up new complaints, and these new complaints are difficult to understand and interpret. I always say it would be very good if there were a scientific way to measure the fatigue they complain of, and the other symptoms, too. . . .

And he ended the interview with a statement of medical belief notable less for its intellectual novelty than its unusually strong tone of skepticism:

I myself don't think those who have anemia, cancer, or even leukemia can, in a strict sense, be said to have an A-bomb disease. . . . Even leukemia patients who die do not, I believe, die from the A-bomb. But when the reports come out in the newspapers, they are described as A-bomb deaths . . . although I myself don't feel these things are directly related to the bomb. . . .

Midst his astute observations and his recoil from loose practices, the staff physician reveals a particularly strong embrace of a precise physicalistic version of medical science. His disdain for weakness and acceptance of help from others, moreover, was not limited to *hibakusha* but extended to ordinary accident patients. While there is no denying the real dangers of perpetuating invalidism in such patients, there is also inevitably involved (as in A-bomb problems) a certain amount of psychological need to be taken care of; and those physicians who react so strongly to this need usually do so out of personal conflict over problems of dependency. Thus, we may suspect that his imagery concerning A-bomb disease is affected by a certain amount of intolerance for emotional needs in general, and for those relating to dependency in particular. There were also indications of the non-*hibakusha* physician's guilt toward, and psychic need to close himself off from, his *hibakusha* patients. In any case, he fits squarely into category four, and went further than any other Japanese physician I interviewed in his skepticism about radiation effects and his rejection of the concept of A-bomb disease.

:

An American research physician associated with ABCC expressed comparable ideas, but in a somewhat different idiom which was not uncommon among his countrymen working in Hiroshima:

It is extremely important to obtain accurate data on a comparative basis, and to have meaningful information, we need enormous samples. Then there is the problem of correlating radiation dosage with medical history in the various studies we are conducting. All this is quite difficult to accomplish. . . . Now, many people who don't feel too kindly toward the United States tend to exaggerate the effects of the bomb—also many well-intentioned people who say that almost any illness which occurs in Hiroshima is due to the effects of the bomb. But except for leukemia and cataracts we have found virtually nothing in the way of significant differences between the exposed and the non-exposed groups. Of course, there have been a lot of genetic abnormalities talked about, but after all, we encounter genetic abnormalities in clinics in Baltimore or San Francisco; the point is, they are not higher in the exposed population than they are in the non-exposed group. One very important thing we do here is to reassure people in the community—the ones who have been exposed, and the children of the exposed—that they can go ahead and marry without fear of producing abnormal offspring. I have seen what this has meant to people. . . . You know, there is so much written about what the bomb has done—but an awful lot of it is just pure propaganda. . . . Someday I would like to see someone write about the way in which people have been able to recover from the bomb, get back on their feet, and continue with their lives. . . .

Beyond the forceful defense of scientific accuracy as opposed to loose claim, and the articulate presentation of a category-four position, the tone of this passage is one of reassurance concerning radiation effects; these are seen as limited, and the emphasis is upon a "positive outlook." A variety of intellectual and psychological influences come together to contribute to this overall imagery, including a reaction against exaggerations and false claims, strong identification with statistical emphases within the scientific tradition, and awareness of (but impatience with) psychological factors. Also important are the American's (suppressed) guilt over the use of the weapon, his need for psychic numbing, and his wish for minimal culpability—tendencies which can be intensified by one's inner awareness of conducting the work under the sponsorship of an official American organization (the Atomic Energy Commission) which is still deeply involved in the making and testing of nuclear weapons.*

THE SPECTRUM OF A-BOMB DISEASE

We have already seen indications that individual physicians can simultaneously embrace seemingly contradictory images of A-bomb disease, and by looking further into this pattern we learn still more about the physician-patient interplay in this condition.

A young *hibakusha* who was both physician and writer, for instance, first described radiation aftereffects with an absolute kind of death-linked imagery that seemed to have little relationship to the scientific approach:

> You may look healthy from the outside but all of a sudden something goes wrong and you are sick fatally. We don't find this in other forms of death. Also, once you fall ill with A-bomb disease it is very difficult to recover—unless the doctor made a mistake in diagnosing the illness as A-bomb disease. . . .

But he then took a seemingly opposite point of view in stressing the need for restraint in diagnosing A-bomb effects, illustrating his opinions with his own experience as a skin specialist:

> There are some doctors who attribute almost everything to the effects of radiation. But I am not so careless. I attempt to encourage my patients by saying to them: "This particular symptom might or might

---

* Any research affiliation enters importantly into one's professional identity and overall self-process. The emotional influence upon research scientists of an official government affiliation can be presumed to be greater in Hiroshima—where, as we shall see, the research organization has also served as a continuous "American presence"—than in, say, Bethesda, Maryland, for those affiliated with the National Institutes of Health. Even if these affiliative emotions do not affect research findings, they influence feelings and attitudes about these findings. These principles apply despite the ABCC's fundamentally scientific identity.

not be related to the A-bomb, so that your having this symptom doesn't mean that you are suffering from A-bomb disease." This attitude is better than the other one because it gives spiritual and moral encouragement to patients. . . . For instance, some ladies come in with red spots on their skin and think they might be suffering from [A-bomb] aftereffects. Some ladies have a rough kind of skin and think this is the result of the A-bomb . . . or elderly people with normal spots think it might be related to cancer, or else to the A-bomb. . . . Any form of cancer or unusual growth can be attributed to A-bomb disease—but no one can be sure that they result from the A-bomb. . . .

However cautious he may consider himself, we sense that he conveys his own *hibakusha* anxieties to his patients ("this particular symptom might or might not be related to the A-bomb"), even as he seeks to reassure them. Here he reminds us of the hospital director, also a *hibakusha*. But as a younger man, less anchored in dogma or tradition, he was much less certain of where he stood and more open to various influences in the city.

One of these influences was a "White Paper" on the subject of A-bomb disease, written by two scientists of some standing in Hiroshima, and strongly critical of the research conducted at the American-sponsored ABCC. The report itself is hostile in tone, and sponsored by an organization (*Gensuikyō*) with considerable bias in these and related matters; nonetheless it raises an important issue concerning the significance of negative results, and the possibility that statistical focus upon specific symptoms or organ systems may overlook various patterns of radiation effects.[16] This problem has been recognized by some within the ABCC itself,* and when the physician-writer spoke of "many doctors" in Hiroshima being influenced by the report, he did so in a way that left his own position not entirely clear ("It is a matter of the relative importance of how much significance you place on radiation effects").

We may thus say that he wavers between categories two and three, but at moments moves further out toward both one and four. Involved in this ambiguity were such factors as his own *hibakusha* anxiety and guilt, a particularly strong quality of receptivity often found in a creative

---

* Lawrence R. Freedman, for instance, has written: "There are a number of problems involved in the evaluation of negative results. Most prominent of these to me stems from the need to analyze so many features of the routine examination. For

artist, a possibly ambivalent relationship to the scientific tradition, and the ambiguity inherent in a situation in which so much is still unknown.

:

Physicians in Hiroshima, then, brought their own complex A-bomb reactions to their *hibakusha* patients. They are called upon to combat an illness whose physical, psychological, and social ramifications exceed their medical knowledge and prior experience. They suffer the frustrations of partly informed experts and of impotent healers confronting therapeutic demands rendered both contradictory and insistent by the pressures of death anxiety. And they do so at a time when scientific medicine itself is undergoing profound changes in its continuing quest for a fundamental understanding of the nature of health and disease.

There is a new point of view which seems to me the only one adequate to a phenomenon like A-bomb disease, but it is still, unfortunately, in its infancy. I refer to the recent stress upon thematic and formative aspects of science in general,[18] and the tendency within medicine to view disease as a "unitary" and "multi-factor" concept which allows for "the many levels of behavior and response characteristic of any disease process." This concept rejects the traditional notion of disease as a "discrete 'thing' inside the body, an entity having an existence of its own, apart from the patient, who is the helpless victim."[19] Every disease is seen as having its own overall symbolism within the mind-body combination (in diabetes mellitus, for instance, one behaves "as if one were starving"), and the focus is upon "man's state of being—his health or illness—as an aspect of his way of life."[20] Decompensation at any level—of the mind-body or the social system— can influence the disease process, and "the presence of a complaint must be regarded as presumptive evidence of disease."* This point of view has enabled investigators to correlate various forms of individual and group stress with increased incidence of illness in general; and even in malignancies such as leukemia and cancer, psychic components have been recognized as interacting with organic and genetic tendencies.[22]

---

mechanical reasons, it has been necessary to lump together many different conditions. As a result, many radiation effects may be masked by dilution with non-radiation affected variables." As one solution he advocates "a closer look at a variety of organ systems."[17]

* Engel emphasizes that "a diagnostic label rarely, if ever, fully defines the illness," and that any complaint "indicates that there is a disturbance in the dynamic steady state and that this disturbance is now being reflected as something unpleasant." He intentionally broadens the concept of disease in order to view it as "a natural phenomenon," in contrast with the physician's role in a society which is "a social and institutional phenomenon": "The fact that a physician arbitrarily excludes

An application of this unitary perspective to atomic bomb problems would invalidate both prescientific intellectual nihilism and one-sided mechanistic or physicalistic emphases within the scientific tradition. For instance, a proper evaluation of leukemia would involve not only the dosage of radiation received but the psychic stresses experienced, particularly in relationship to loss, along with additional information about genetic background and prior physiological functioning. Similarly, the more obscure manifestations of "A-bomb disease" would require investigation of a particular person's experience with his physician and with the mass media, in connection with the general psychological and physical estimate being made. The four categories of physicians would then, at least ideally, disappear, as each would be found wanting, though each would have its contributions to make. The skeptical approach of those in categories three and four would be confirmed by a *rejection of the concept of "A-bomb disease" as an entity caused solely by the atomic bomb.* But in another sense the concept would take on added significance as a *symbolic expression of the malignant influence of the atomic bomb on every level of human experience.* (This would confirm some of the imagery of physicians in the first and second categories, but would give it more valid intellectual form.)

"A-bomb disease," in whatever ephemeral or lethal form, turns out to be a disease after all, in the true sense of the word, an "absence of ease" or "cause for discomfort." It is an A-bomb-related disturbance in the harmony of the individual—within himself, his social milieu, and his historical epoch.

---

certain categories of complaints or signs as not appropriate is a reflection of his concept of his role as a physician and does not necessarily bear any relationship to the scientific question of what is disease."[21]

five

A-BOMB MAN

1) On Being a Hibakusha

Exposure to the atomic bomb changed the survivor's status as a human being, in his own eyes as well as in others'. He became a member of a new group: he assumed the identity of the *hibakusha*. Nor is this identity of significance only for atomic bomb victims.

One of the methods I used to explore the nature of this identity was to encourage survivors to associate freely to the word *hibakusha*. In doing so, they inevitably conveyed to me the sense of having been compelled to take on a special category of existence by which they felt permanently bound, however they might wish to free themselves from it—as in the case of the shopkeeper's assistant:

> Well . . . because I am a *hibakusha* . . . how shall I say it—I wish others would not look at me with special eyes. . . . Perhaps *hibakusha* are mentally—or both physically and mentally—different from others. . . . But I myself do not want to be treated in any special way because I am a *hibakusha*. . . .

He went on to complain that he was frequently asked to appear on television and then interviewed in a way that brought out "the darker side of the problem," which, he felt, created "a burden for me," since "if I am ill in bed I don't want people to know about it." He was thus protesting general imagery of the *hibakusha as victim*, and the internalization of this imagery in a form spoken of as "victim-consciousness." Not only is this kind of self-image humiliating to the *hibakusha*, but it separates him in his own eyes from the rest of mankind.

Some, like the mathematician, associate *hibakusha* with physical vulnerability and poverty, with an overall image of the downtrodden:

> I use the word for those with a hard life—those with financial difficulty—or those people who seem to suffer most from aftereffects. The financially well-to-do can rest if they are tired and can eat nourishing food. The poor people cannot, and they easily become sick. . . .

Others simply make the familiar equation: *hibakusha* equals fatal A-bomb disease—as in the case of one man whose associations went from "people in the hospital who die, even nowadays" to "I might suffer from some form of atomic bomb disease."

But there are also protests against this image of debilitation—such as that put forth articulately by a souvenir vendor:

> When August 6 approaches, all of the newspapers begin to print articles on the atomic bomb. I hate that. . . . If they would write on some of the brighter aspects, that would be all right. But they always write about such dark, melancholy things which I do not like. Up till now journalism has made one specific frame for *hibakusha* and has treated us as if it were most appropriate for *hibakusha* to live within such a frame. The *hibakusha* themselves also believe that this shrunken life inside of this shell is the way of life of a *hibakusha*. I always tell them that they should cast off the shell, that seventeen years have gone by, that a shut-in life within such a shell is not the *hibakusha* way of life . . . that the idea itself of having to live that way makes them unhappy, and they ought to . . . have more fighting spirit toward life. I myself got out of that shell and graduated from that stage a long time ago. . . . I am the kind of *hibakusha* who often goes to see movies, I frequently go to coffee shops when I have the time, I go out to drink saké. But then people ask, "How is it you . . . go out drinking?" I protest to them: "You talk so foolishly— why shouldn't *hibakusha* go out drinking? . . . What does it mean to be like a *hibakusha* or not like a *hibakusha*? I am a *hibakusha*, but at the same time, before being a *hibakusha*, I am a human being."

. . . I joke with girls and tell them, "Even though you are a *hiba-kusha* go ahead and fall in love with a boy." Then these girls say, "Why, I can't do that." I want to tell them there is no reason that they should not. . . .

More than just conversations with other *hibakusha*, his words represent his own interior dialogue between the normally vigorous human being he aspires to be and the devitalized *hibakusha* he still feels himself to be.

Indeed, he was literally protesting against his own impotence, as he had undergone a loss of sexual potency following extensive hospitalization for physical injuries from the bomb—a symptom occasionally mentioned or hinted at by male *hibakusha*, and probably even more frequently experienced. It was invariably thought of as an organic effect of the bomb, but psychogenic influences were probably of great importance in most cases. The symptom can epitomize the dilemma of the *hibakusha* as victim: an expression of powerlessness in the midst of protest against this degrading imagery; along with the constellation of unacceptable dependency, resentment, and guilt that is generally associated with sexual impotence. In the case of the *hibakusha* this constellation is specifically related to residual death taint and death guilt, with the need to suppress joy and vitality as alien and undeserved.

One of the very few affirmative expressions I heard of fellow-feeling around the *hibakusha* identity came from the European priest, and in it we recognize once more his tendency to idealize a group within Japanese society to which he wishes to belong:

If a person says to me that he is weary [*darui*], if it is a *hibakusha* who says it, it gives me a different feeling than if he is an ordinary person. He doesn't have to explain. . . . He knows all of the uneasiness—all of the temptation to lose spirit and be depressed—and of then starting again to see if he can do his job. . . . It is intuition, not logical reasoning—in one flash, one moment—that kind of knowledge. . . . If a Japanese hears the words "*tennō heika*" [His Majesty The Emperor], it is different from a Westerner hearing them—a very different feeling in the foreigner's heart from what is felt in the Japanese person's heart. It is a similar question in the case of one who is a victim and one who is not, when they hear about another victim. . . . I met a man one time . . . [who] said, "I experienced the atomic bomb"—and from then on the conversation changed. We both understood each other's feelings. Nothing had to be said. . . .

Such fellow-feeling and unspoken understanding are, of course, by no means entirely absent among *hibakusha*. But they tend to be out-weighed by the negative elements of the overall identity. For as the same priest goes on to explain, this time with a touch of sardonic humor, being a *hibakusha* is at best a questionable distinction:

> I always say, if anyone looks at me because I received the Nobel Prize, that's okay, but if my only virtue is that I was a thousand meters from the atomic bomb center and I am still alive, I don't want to be famous for that.

An occasional survivor claimed, as did the physicist, that the general antipathy to the word was somewhat overcome by its relationship to nuclear weapons protest movements, that once these had been initiated in Hiroshima "people began to give [the word *hibakusha*] social meaning." But he, too, quickly associated to fear of radiation aftereffects ("If anything happens to me physically . . . even before there are clear manifestations, I try to take care of it"), suggesting that this "social meaning" could not overcome the more fundamental anxiety connected with the word and the identity.

"A-BOMB OUTCASTS"

The *hibakusha*'s sense of low self-esteem has been furthered by experiences of discrimination. Not only have *hibakusha*, as an aging population which does not replenish itself, become literally a minority group in Hiroshima—one fifth of the city's inhabitants—but they are generally considered to be at the lower socioeconomic levels as well.[1] Discrimination against them in both marriage and employment was apparently greatest during the years immediately following the bomb; but it has left its mark, and has by no means entirely disappeared even now. While survivors regularly work and marry, they often do so with a sense, as *hibakusha*, of impaired capacity for both.

In the case of marriage the sense of impairment can include factors with which we are familiar: a general feeling of undesirability as a mate, fears about abnormal children or about the ability to have children at all, and diminished sexual potency.

Concerning work, older survivors often described an overall sense of having been unable to overcome their physical, mental, and economic blows and mobilize sufficient energy to compete with ordinary people. Younger ones who may feel themselves to possess that energy fear that being identified as *hibakusha* could seriously damage their occupational standing. A few told me of being informed on occasions in the past that they were ineligible for particular jobs because they were *hibakusha*; and many had the impression that employers were reluctant to take on survivors because they thought, as one man put it, "although *hibakusha* look perfectly all right from their outward appearance, they are likely to want extra time off and need extra rest." A few were rejected by prospective employers under ambiguous circumstances, leaving them with the suspicion that their *hibakusha* state was the deciding factor. In other words, whether discrimination is present, absent, or an ambiguous possibility, a *hibakusha* can retain the sense of having been rejected because of his own bodily inferiority, because of his impaired substance.

Consequently, *hibakusha* have been noted to make up a disproportionate number of a group known as "day laborers," those employed on a day-to-day basis for the most menial tasks at the lowest wages and who are very close to the bottom of the social scale. The internalization of this low status has been ironically summed up by one commentator as an attitude of "I apologize for having been exposed to the atomic bomb."*

Vicious circles of rejection, anticipated rejection, and self-created rejection can occur, especially in those who, like the shopkeeper's assistant, lost their families and became homeless wanderers:

I switched my job many times . . . not because of the job itself . . . but . . . I was completely alone and I would look into others' faces . . . watching their eyes . . . in order to be able to tell how they felt about me. . . . I think I was much too sensitive, but as soon as I noticed something unpleasant, then things became impossible for me. . . .

All of these tendencies have led to comparisons of *hibakusha* with Japan's outcast or "untouchable" group (the *eta* or *burakumin*)—as described by the physicist:

There is the phrase, "A-bomb outcast community [*genbaku buraku*]. This comes from the inferiority complex—physical, mental, social, economic—which *hibakusha* have, so that when people hear the word

* Unemployment rates in Hiroshima in 1958 were reported to be third highest among all Japanese cities, according to population ratios. Many factors can affect statistics on day laborers and unemployment; they are in any event relative, and should not be understood to suggest that all *hibakusha* are impoverished.[2]

[*hibakusha*], they don't feel very good, but rather feel as though they are looked down upon.

There have even been reports of *hibakusha* who *literally* joined the ranks of the outcasts by moving into the special slum areas where they live and becoming virtually indistinguishable from them, a pattern which can take place with any group tumbling rapidly down the social ladder.

The argument is sometimes made (here by a non*hibakusha* observer) that in contrast to outcasts and other victimized groups, the *hibakusha* encounter a "reasonable" form of discrimination:

> *Hibakusha* are not discriminated against in an unreasonable way as in the case of the outcast communities [*buraku*] in Japan, the Jews in Europe, or the Negroes in America, but rather tend to encounter discrimination on reasonable grounds. Employers may hesitate to employ them, first because no one knows when they might become ill, and second because they tend to need more rest and therefore do request more days off . . . and one must also think of the factor of age, since many have already passed their period of greatest employability. . . .

One may defend or contest this "logic of discrimination," depending upon one's view of the nature and extent of A-bomb aftereffects. (One could also mobilize "logic" of various kinds to explain discrimination against Jews, Negroes, or Tibetans.) But I would claim that underneath this "logic" is the all-important factor of the *hibakusha* death taint, which causes others to turn away and *hibakusha* themselves to withdraw. In perceiving this death taint, outsiders experience a threat to their own sense of human continuity or symbolic immortality, and feel death anxiety and death guilt activated within themselves. I shall in fact argue (in a forthcoming study) that these general patterns—death anxiety, death guilt, and threat to symbolic immortality—are fundamental to the general phenomenon of prejudice or victimization.

Significant here is another bit of A-bomb mythology, the belief expressed to me by a few *hibakusha* that A-bomb exposure made people's skin permanently darker. Again one can find a kernel of "truth" or "logic" in the belief. A White Russian *hibakusha*, for instance, when interviewed shortly after the bomb, described crowds of Japanese she had seen as "Negroes, just Negroes—they weren't Japanese—they were Negroes."[3] The darkening of the skin she refers to was, of course, produced by burns, which were reported by doctors to have actually caused pigmentation resembling "a deep walnut stain over the entire surface of the burn."[4] This pigmentation, moreover, was noted to be greatest in dark-skinned *hibakusha*. But keeping in mind that dark skin has been as much an undesirable trait in Japan as elsewhere—it has been considered to be an identifying characteristic of such victimized groups as *burakumin* and Koreans—the idea that bomb exposure per se darkens the overall skin surface forever is another way of perceiving *hibakusha* as a lowly, stigmatized, death-tainted group.

Hibakusha inevitably internalized this "logic of discrimination," as a young white-collar worker makes clear:

> It can't be helped. From the company's viewpoint, it is only natural for them to wish to employ healthy people rather than those who might have the possibility of dying at any time.

And a Nagasaki engineer revealed how directly children could relate their own discrimination against *hibakusha* (or the children of *hibakusha*) to the theme of death:

> I spent three months in the hospital because of extreme weakness. . . . Everybody in the farming area where we lived knew where I was. . . . My children were treated very unkindly at school. Other children would taunt them and cry out: "Son of a patient of the A-Bomb Hospital." They said these things because they thought I was definitely going to die.

The young are forthright enough to say what many of their elders feel: the death-tainted are a threat, an enemy, and finally, an inferior breed. Thinking back on the advocacy of sterilization on the part of some *hibakusha* themselves, we can now understand it as a wish to excise symbolically not only the death taint as such but the entire *hibakusha* identity in which this taint is enmeshed. But both—as for other victimized groups to whom they may be compared—turn out to be all too enduring.

2) A-Bomb Stigmata

The keloid, or whitish-yellow area of overgrown scar tissue which can disfigure hands and particularly faces, has come to symbolize the *hibakusha* identity. The keloid is by no means specific to atomic bomb exposure. It can be produced by severe burns from any source, particularly when these receive inadequate treatment, are complicated by infection, malnutrition, and general debilitation, and occur in racial groups (such as the Japanese) especially susceptible to keloid formation. Nor can keloids now be found on more than a small minority of survivors. But they have nonetheless come to represent stigmata of *hibakushka*hood, marks of defect, disease, and disgrace.[5]

One must recall that the flash burns from which keloids resulted were the major cause of death and injury at the time of the bomb. And during the following months, as the sociologist tells us, Hiroshima became virtually a city of keloids:

> Right after the war, although not exactly everyone in the city had keloids, very many people did. . . . When I would travel on trains and streetcars then and see people with keloids . . . my immediate thought was a simple feeling of pity for them. . . . But I also felt anger . . . not only because of the material damage but because of the human consequences of the bomb. . . . I believe that a keloid gives a very special feeling to people. . . . As far as the power of destruction of the A-bomb is concerned, the difference between it and other kinds of bombs is only a quantitative one. . . . But there is more than this. . . . When you think of the effects upon people later on . . . you see the qualitative differences . . . and when you see people with keloids, you receive the strongest impression of these qualitative differences. . . .

The "very special feeling" is that of altered body (especially facial) form to the point of dehumanization. The visibility of the stigma, as the sociologist goes on to point out, creates a humiliating sense of having one's *hibakusha* taint "exposed" and stared at—especially when outside of Hiroshima, "so those with keloids, in a psychological way, come to feel that they should confine themselves to the city and not leave Hiroshima."

A married bargirl makes clear (particularly in her first sentence) the keloid's psychological link with A-bomb disease, and with the overall *hibakusha* identity, in a symbolic A-bomb trinity:

> The word *hibakusha* has the sound, not of ordinary people, but of people with diseases caused by the bomb—with keloids—and such things. . . . When I go to the A-Bomb Hospital, even after all these years, I feel sick. . . . I am afraid of disease. . . . And I find myself recalling the past. . . . When I was evacuated at the time of the bomb, people had white medicine on their faces, and these white faces have sometimes appeared in my dreams. . . . The other day my child had a skin rash, so I put white medicine on his face. In the middle of the night I woke up, and seeing his face, I felt frightened. . . . I remembered the white faces I have seen in the dreams. . . .

Her further associations of death and disfigurement are also characteristically associated with the keloid, as the most evident part of the trinity. And a third non-keloid-bearing *hibakusha*, a young tourist agency employee, expresses even more extreme imagery about keloids:

> Of all the things connected with those days, what makes the strongest impression on me is the mark of a burn scar. What is it they are called? . . . Yes, the keloid. This may have something to do with my character but I really hate to see a keloid—though when I walk down the street I often encounter people with a keloid. . . . When I do, rather than sympathy, the strongest feeling I have is to try to avoid seeing it. . . . When I see a keloid on a young girl, she seems to have become a deformed person. . . . And I think that anyone finds it painful to look at a deformed person. . . . If I had such a keloid, I would feel reluctant to be questioned about it or to go to see a doctor. . . . I would probably feel that I did not want to see others. . . . When seeing someone, I would assume that he was looking at me. . . . If he saw one side of my face [without the keloid], I wouldn't mind, but if he looked at the other side [with the keloid], it would give me a very unpleasant feeling. And even if most people had no special desire to see it, still it would grate on my nerves—though this may be a rather warped outlook.

Here the *hibakusha* possessing a keloid is felt to be close to a leper, an untouchable, or an "unseeable"* (even the word keloid cannot be

---

* The term "unseeable" has sometimes actually been used for the Indian outcast group.[8]

remembered). Keloids (especially on young girls) become another form of lasting "ultimate horror"; they evoke near-phobic responses because they reactivate elements of the *hibakusha* identity in the keloid-free survivor which have long been suppressed, as well as guilt over being able to bury his taint, in contrast to his keloid-bearing counterpart. At play is the kind of death anxiety we have mentioned in connection with victimization (prejudice) in general, in this case on the part of one who is himself a "victim" toward a more severely "marked" member of his group.

Similar feelings about the keloid as a perpetual psychological reminder are expressed by a war widow:

> In the city of Hiroshima there are still many people with scars on their faces. . . . And not only their faces, their bodies too,* as I observe when I go to the [public] bath.† I go quite often, so that even if I try to forget about the bomb, I cannot. We see such people here all of the time and unless these people disappear, I will be unable to forget. . . .

The implication is that she would like to "wish away" the keloid-bearers so that she might be rid of visible reminders of her own *hibakusha* state.

"FOR A WOMAN TO LOSE HER BEAUTY"

Those who actually have the keloids experience a particularly pressing kind of *hibakusha* identity. Their impaired body substance is on the surface for all to see; their taint cannot be denied. The psychological consequences of the aesthetic impairment alone are severe enough, all the more so in a culture which places such great stress upon aesthetic presentation and "appearance" in every sense. Beyond that, the disfigurement affects the keloid-bearing *hibakusha*'s image of his entire organism. Indeed, I often found the air to be charged with tension during interviews with such *hibakusha*. The detailed experience of two of them can give us some grasp of the psychological forces involved.

:

The hospital worker, so disfigured as a girl of thirteen that her parents did not recognize her, describes a sequence of emotional reactions

---

* Severe burn scars without actual keloid formation can themselves be disfiguring, though I had the impression that she referred here to keloids.

† A large percentage of the Japanese population still attend public baths regularly— because they are economical and pleasantly social, and because of the general importance of bathing in Japanese culture.

related to the sense of impaired body image. She tells how she first discovered that her face had been mutilated—through comparison with others and through her own touch:

> I had the sensation that my whole body had been split. . . . But I didn't know what had happened, and everything seemed strange. . . . I saw many horrible things . . . and asked my friend whether anything had happened to *my* face. . . . [She] cried out to me and said that I too had been burned and should go home. . . . I touched my face and the skin stuck to my finger. That frightened me. And when I touched my nose, I had no sensation of my nose but my finger felt something swollen and hot. . . . Then my friend asked me about her face, but although it was swollen nothing particularly had happened to her skin. . . .

For the extensive burns on her face, neck, arms, and breasts she received primitive treatment ("They put cooking oil over my body and washed out the burned areas") at a temporary aid center and then at home. She also had radiation symptoms, and she could tell from the tone of the encouragement received from her parents and neighbors ("Mi-chan, no matter what happens, you must live, because . . . you will have some good days ahead, too") that she was close to death. But the encouragement nonetheless helped her: "When I heard these words . . . I felt a little stronger."

After three months, however, when she began to feel stronger and wanted to see what she looked like, she discovered that her parents were trying to prevent her from finding out:

> I thought about getting up and I wanted to see myself in a mirror. But whenever I asked them for a mirror, they would say that they did not have one in the house. . . . Then I got much better and my parents thought it was all right for me to get up. They still insisted there was no mirror around . . . but I knew there was and I was able to find it. The mirror was broken, with only a third of it remaining, but since I was small, the [one] third was enough for me to see myself in. Then for the first time I realized that I was no longer the same me. . . . Up until that time I was determined to go on living. But at that moment I felt that the adults had lied to me. I could not tear myself away from the mirror. It took some time for me to believe that this was now my true self. . . .

The mixture of fascination and repulsion with which she contemplated her new self reflects her struggle to adapt herself to the lasting identity of the "disfigured *hibakusha*."

She went on to equate the deception of adults concerning her disfigurement ("When they said that no matter what happens, I should go on living . . . and I myself determined to live . . . it never occurred to me that I would not return to my . . . previous form") with the earlier adult deceptions of national authorities who instilled a spirit of sacrifice in her and her classmates and were responsible for their being assigned to the work detail near the center of the city where they experienced the bomb ("Believing everything the adults said, I worked hard in the labor service . . . [and] the result was my becoming like this—it was too cruel"). She felt herself no longer able "to believe or trust in any adults," and was left with "anger, hatred, and resentment" —usually of a general kind, though at times specifically directed at her own parents: "I knew they did everything possible for me . . . [but] having lost my [previous] appearance, I even hated them."

She continued to protest against the deformed state the mirror revealed to her ("I had the strong feeling that I wanted to break all things . . . that could reflect one's appearance"), considered herself "dead," and behaved accordingly:

> Rather than the joy of having survived, my regret over having become this way was much more profound. . . . And however much I was encouraged by others, I could not help believing that for a woman to lose her beauty is equivalent to death. All I could do was live in a corner of my house. I didn't even like to ride a streetcar. . . . I wanted to escape from the world . . . and if possible I wished to die. . . .

Suggested here is a form of self-loathing which contains not only overt shame but also hidden guilt.

During the years that followed she underwent repeated surgical operations, mostly upon her face, but always found the results disappointing because "I did not become as I had been before," and was always struck by the discrepancy between what she and the doctors looked upon as a successful result: "From a medical standpoint . . . if a bent arm can be straightened, the outcome is successful, but what I wished to be the meaning of cure was to have my appearance completely restored." What she really wanted restored was her pre-bomb identity; "cure" meant being relieved of the entire burden of her death-tainted keloid-bearing *hibakusha* state.

Only gradually and reluctantly, with the help of parental devotion which she found herself now able to accept, "I grasped the idea that there was a stage at which, no matter how much I sought out medical treatment, it would be of little help." But even then she remained distraught over the limitations of surgery and the continuing psychic conflicts surrounding her keloid and her *hibakusha*hood. Relief came only by discovering a means to put affliction to use; she joined the peace movement, and participated in it mainly through highly emotional public renditions of her personal experience as a form of plea against nuclear weapons:

> I received strong support from a large number of people. . . . For the first time I realized that I was not alone in my suffering and that there were so many people who could understand us. . . . From the deep inspiration coming from those meetings I believe that my present self was born. . . . In crying out to the world that such a tragedy should not be repeated . . . I found a purpose in life. The experience was somehow a form of deliverance for me. . . .

From a "mark of shame," her keloid took on the other meaning of stigma and became a "mark of honor." Her "deliverance" was a release from the burden of guilt and humiliation, and her "new self" was that of a *hibakusha* who had found significance in—who had been able to formulate—her experience. The transformation was far from being as total as she wished to believe, impeded as it was by an array of complex currents surounding the peace movement and affecting all public *hibakusha* actions. But with the conflicts surrounding her keloid so strong, she had no choice but to continue on her course, however incomplete the relief and fulfillment it brought.

:

The grocer's experiences illustrate other ways in which the possession of a keloid can crucially influence a *hibakusha*'s life pattern. He describes his "mark of wounds" as a central theme of his existence, but seems to equate these interchangeably with other stigmata of *hibakusha*-hood which "do not show":

> I have a special feeling that I am different from ordinary people . . . that I have the mark of wounds—as if I were a cripple . . . that I

am inferior to them . . . of course physically, but also mentally. . . . Ordinary people don't have this kind of scar. They don't have to experience the feeling of humiliation that I have had. . . . I imagine a person who has an arm or a leg missing might feel the same way. . . . It is not a matter of lacking something . . . but rather . . . a handicap—something mental which does not show . . . the feeling that I am mentally different . . . and incompatible with ordinary people. . . .

He felt incompatible with others less because of overt unkindness from them than its opposite, a form of special emotional protectiveness, which he found intolerable:

If one has this kind of scar in Hiroshima . . . people know it is from the A-bomb and, of course, they have understanding. . . . But their attitude is often that of pity. . . . They say nice words, but the words are empty. . . .

In order to escape from this humiliating pity, he made plans during his high school days to leave Hiroshima and go to a different city, where "people might look at you curiously and express their feelings frankly, or they might ignore you," and where "I had to do things on my own." His goal was to develop a less sensitive attitude toward others and "gain immunity in regard to the keloid," to "test myself . . . [and] realize myself fully." That is, he wished to bring the fact of his keloid and its full psychic consequences out into the open so that he could confront it and discover in the process where the keloid ended and the rest of him began.

He was able to pursue this psychological quest by attending a university in Kyoto for four years. He thrived on student camaraderie ("They were indifferent . . . and treated me just like everyone else"), and from other people outside the university he encountered the ordeal he sought:

Well, I don't think one can understand it unless one experiences this kind of attitude . . . being looked at with "white eyes." They look at me while pretending not to look. At times I feel that if there were a hole, I would like to jump into it in order to avoid their eyes. . . .

To be looked at with "white eyes," in the Japanese idiom, means coldly, suspiciously, critically, with condemnation. Again, the sense of being scrutinized by others' eyes reflects the *hibakusha*'s own sense of guilt and shame; but here with the added factor of the specific external stigma—the death taint worn on the face—which painfully intrudes upon all dialogues and "confirms" his ultimate isolation.

While he claimed that after four years of this kind of experience he achieved the "immunity" he sought, his words were belied by the anxiety with which he spoke of these matters, by his use of the present tense in describing his suffering, and by his admitted social and sexual inhibitions:

> I felt that [a girl] could take up with anyone she wished and did not have to associate with me. I had a strong sense of being handicapped, and feeling this way, I could make no forthright approach.

But the real crisis in this extra-Hiroshima experiment—its moment of failure—came with job interviews just before graduation. Here the same painful dialogue—with its awkward, guilt-tinged mutual discomfort—had devastating results. He had the impression that the interviewers from the large firm he wanted very much to join "tried to keep their distance from me and not burden themselves with responsibility for me."* It is impossible to say whether, or to what extent, he was turned down because of his keloid; we may suspect that his anticipation of rejection also contributed to the outcome. In any case, we observe the strong psychological influence of his keloid in his sense of being a "burden" for others, in his resentment of the uncomfortable state of dependency imposed upon him. Thoroughly defeated, he was left with "the impression that we are shunned by others"—"we" meaning *hibakusha*, keloid-bearing *hibakusha*, stigmatized human beings.

He settled for an inferior position with a small firm requiring no formal interview, and remained in Kyoto a little longer. But the turning-point had been reached—economically† as well as psychologically. He returned to the protected existence in Hiroshima he had previously rejected, took over his family's small retail store, and accepted a way of life a great deal more limited than that ordinarily available to a graduate of a major university. He also mustered the courage to approach and

---

* Such "responsibility" is greater in Japan than elsewhere, since employment in a large company generally means employment for life; thus a company might have great difficulty if it wished to get rid of a tainted employee. This issue is probably of some importance in *hibakusha* employment problems in general.

† The contrast is extreme in Japanese society between the prestige and financial security within one of the large firms dominating the national economy and the anonymously meager existence in the kind of small company he entered.

marry a local girl, though here too it is possible that his parents were helpful, and that he chose a girl he sensed would offer no great challenge. He has found solace and satisfaction in this domestic life, though we know him to have unusually strong fears about his health and the normality of his children. Generally speaking, however, his return to his biological and larger Hiroshima "family" was also a symbolic return to his keloid-bearing *hibakusha* identity, that is, an acceptance of limitations imposed by permanent physical and mental stigmata:

> I have the feeling that in just about everything, I cannot do as well as others . . . and it is quite natural for me to feel this way. . . . The fact that I am ugly in my external appearance—well, even if I myself ignore this, others feel it . . . which is a big handicap. . . . Well, it is not that I couldn't accomplish what others do if I tried very hard— it is the feeling I have that I cannot, which I think is very bad for me. . . .
> :

We have seen how the special atmosphere created by the keloid dramatizes problems of the overall *hibakusha* identity, problems of being "identified" as a *hibakusha*. The following story, told to me by a survivor sympathetic to the mistreated woman he describes, shows how far this pattern can go:

> This young married girl had a very bad keloid on her face. She was treated very badly by her mother-in-law and taunted because she had no children. Finally she had a child, but the mother-in-law then insisted that because of her keloid, she should not nurse the baby. The mother-in-law felt that if she did, she might transmit something unhealthy to the baby.

Here again the keloid is the mark of the *hibakusha*-as-leper, and we sense the fear of contagion or transmission (via mother's milk) of the dreaded "disease." Also involved, of course, is the rivalry between wife and mother-in-law, and in Japanese tradition the mother-in-law in some ways has greater claim upon the children than the wife since they represent the husband's family line—an issue which can become especially charged when that family line is felt to be threatened by death taint. However exaggerated the story may have been in the retelling, we cannot doubt the emotional truths in conveys.

The actualities of "keloid psychology" could thus blend with mythological elaboration, and even become springboards for creative thought: whether in relationship to "A-bomb literature" (as we shall later observe) or to general thought about the significance of atomic victimization—as the sociologist makes clear:

> The simple feeling of pity I first had when I saw . . . the external ugliness and strangeness . . . of people with keloids . . . became a kind of starting point from which I could develop my feelings about peace. . . .

Here, as in the case of the hospital worker, the stigmata assume affirmative significance—on the order of what Saint Paul called "marks of the Lord Jesus on my body." But more often these ennobling associations are weak or absent. The keloid then comes closer to the pre-Christian meaning of the stigma as a mark or brand for slaves and criminals, and to the related "post-Christian" idea mentioned earlier: "A mark of disgrace or infamy." Most of all, it takes on the recent medically influenced meaning we have also noted—an "indication of disease"—in which the "disease" mars not only the bodily surface but the entire idea of the self.

3) *Denial and Transcendence*

Like any victimized group, *hibakusha* undergo considerable conflict over how much of their victimized identity to retain.[7] The issue is by no means one of a simple conscious decision. At all levels of psychic life patterns of negation, affirmation, and transcendence of *hibakusha*hood constantly take place. Most *hibakusha* experience elements of all three, with their various psychological dangers and possibilities. Thus, negation may be associated with the psychological defense of denial ("Nothing happened to me"), and affirmation with constriction and exclusiveness ("I am *nothing but* a *hibakusha*"). Only transcendence can provide the ideally inclusive identity ("I am a *hibakusha*, but I am much more as well").

The *hibakusha* whose reaction is primarily that of denial tries to "wish away" the experience and live *as if* it had not taken place. He is likely to insist upon a constellation of normalcy: the minimal personal impact of the original encounter, his good health and lack of worry, his general optimism and easygoing nature, and his disapproval of any attempt to attribute special qualities, psychological or otherwise, to the atomic bomb survivor in general. The denial tends to betray itself by the intensity of its reiteration, and even more importantly, by sudden outpourings of anxiety which can no longer be successfully contained—often in the form of terrifying bodily fears, which insist upon reminding him that he is, after all, a *hibakusha*.

The relationship of denial of *hibakusha* identity to the problem of mastery is illustrated by the pattern of the Nagasaki physician whom we remember to have had a severe atomic bomb exposure at fifteen hundred meters. In our first conversations he ridiculed the general concern in Hiroshima about aftereffects, stressed that Nagasaki *hibakusha* had a more healthy attitude about things, and insisted that there was no distinction whatsoever, medical or otherwise, between *hibakusha* and non*hibakusha*. But over a period of time he gradually began to make a series of admissions: he has been troubled by fatigue, especially during the summer, and thought this must be because he was getting older (he was in his early forties); he therefore decided to give up strenuous athletics; and he was concerned about a tendency toward a somewhat low red blood count and anemia, and also about irregularities in his white blood count (which had remained a bit high for some time after the bomb). These were all classical *hibakusha* complaints, albeit in a vague and controversial zone of symptoms, and were his way of revealing inner fears of radiation effects. As a doctor he had always known that aftereffects of some kind were possible for one who had been exposed at fifteen hundred meters, but he had suppressed this knowledge and kept it from his own awareness. Recalling also his dreams of terrifying vulnerability to nuclear weapons which recurred for some years after the bomb, and his various phobias, we further observe the limitations of the mechanism of denial in protecting the *hibakusha* from the anxiety he seeks to avoid. *Indeed, exaggerated denial of hibakushahood always reflects a gross psychological inability to master the atomic bomb experience.*

This is true even where the denial of *hibakusha* identity is only partial and contradictory—as in the case of the shopkeeper's assistant, who would sometimes stress his special problems as a *hibakusha*-orphan (of being unwanted, and of anticipating and encountering discrimination), and at other times would claim that "there is no difference" between a *hibakusha* like himself and other people, and that special attitudes toward *hibakusha* "do not exist."

But it is particularly true where the denial of *hibakusha*hood is more total and consistent—as with the tourist agency employee. Despite the extreme anxiety and near-phobia we noted him to manifest in relationship to keloids, he denied any personal concern about radiation difficulties. He even claimed (like the young housewife) that his health had improved following atomic bomb exposure, and by contrasting his own well-being with others' severe afflictions, he could deny his *hibakusha* identity in unusually literal fashion:

> When I hear the word *hibakusha*, it reminds me of people in a severely burned state. I think only of such people as *hibakusha*, and never think of regarding myself as a *hibakusha*. I have no special symptoms and have never had the idea of looking upon myself as a *hibakusha*. . . . *Hibakusha* seem to be different from me . . . unrelated to me. . . .

Here the inner fantasy is: those deadly and disfiguring experiences happened only to *them*, not to *me*. But during his interviews there was evidence of overwhelming anxiety—retained from his original exposure at the age of five, and now expressed in relationship to later concerns. The problem keloids posed for him was that they reactivated inner imagery ("people in a severely burned state"), which he struggled so desperately to extinguish and which reminded him of his own inseparability from these afflicted people. Each keloid he saw undermined his entire structure of denial.

The same young man illustrated another important manifestation of the pattern of denial: the failure to register as a *hibakusha*. I had come upon his name in my random selections from the list only because his mother had taken it upon herself to register him. But he possessed no *hibakusha* card, and had never gone for the routine physical examination provided for by the medical laws and constantly urged upon *hibakusha* by city authorities. He said he was "too busy," but this was clearly another way of behaving as if he were not a *hibakusha*.

Authorities estimated that at least 10 per cent (and possibly 15 or even 20 per cent) of all *hibakusha* remained unregistered. According to the prominent politician, the cause for this lay in practical considerations about marriage, especially among women:

> Because of marriage problems, the women are the ones who try hardest to conceal it. The men have other chances, so they don't care too much. But the women hide the fact that they are *hibakusha* even though they become excluded from [free] medical treatment. . . . Sometimes after marriage the husband says, "Since you are a *hibakusha*, why not register?" She will then say [at the registration office], "All right, I have come here to register as a *hibakusha* with the permission of my husband."

But we suspect that more is involved than the woman's protection of her marriage opportunities. For one thing, given the thoroughness of investigative procedures engaged in by Japanese families prior to marriage, it would be extremely difficult to conceal the *hibakusha* state— particularly within Hiroshima itself, where there is general awareness of who is a *hibakusha* and who is not. What seems more likely, at least in the kind of example given, is that husband and wife indulge in a shared fiction that the wife is not a *hibakusha* in order to still both their fears about offspring; and that they live out this fiction *as if* it were true, perhaps even half believing it, until either bodily fears or increased awareness of medical advantages induce them to give it up. The wife's announcing that she has her husband's "permission" to register is consistent with the Japanese cultural idiom of the woman's public obeisance to her husband; but it also suggests her calling forth his authority to justify past and present behavior—and, more important, her need to assert his "confirmation" of her right to exist *as a hibakusha*.

While a *hibakusha*'s failure to register could be partly a function of ignorance, cultural deprivation, geographical distribution, or the availability of virtually equivalent medical care under company insurance programs, such was the intensity of the city's registration campaigns that we may assume that more was involved in this form of "action by inaction." The inner fantasy (resembling that we spoke of in those who register but resist medical examination) is: If I do not register as a *hibakusha*, and if in other ways I act as though I were not a *hibakusha*, then I will not *be* a *hibakusha*, and therefore will not be susceptible to all of the terrible things that can happen to *hibakusha*.

The woman with the eye condition, although registered, expressed precisely this inner sequence in a way that was not without insight:

> I have never felt myself to be a *hibakusha* . . . so the word doesn't strike me in a direct way. . . . I think I have a complex about having been exposed to the bomb. . . . There are, of course, survivors of incendiary bombs, but the A-bomb survivors are the most miserable. And since it was the bomb being dropped on Hiroshima that ended the war, this makes *hibakusha* the sacrifices [*giseisha*]. Connected with being sacrifices are many kinds of misery. . . . I refuse to carry on my back all of that misery. . . . So I always have the feeling that I wish to deny [*hitei shiyō*] all of this. And because of this complex, I don't really experience an awareness of being a *hibakusha*. . . .

Her difficulty was that her insight could not make sufficient contact with her deeper symbolic life to alter significantly her feelings or her behavior; her denial of *hibakusha*hood continued to exact its psychological toll in contributing to her eye condition and her semi-invalidism.

For denial is an alternative to the achievement of the kind of symbolic integration that goes with mastery. Under the guise of "moving on" and leaving one's atomic bomb encounter far behind, one is actually held fast, bound to the very experience one wishes to ignore. Since no *hibakusha* is capable of absorbing the experience fully, each must make use of a certain amount of denial. And the distinction between denial and transcendence can be difficult to draw.

Perhaps the best example of this difficulty is the attitude of resignation (*akirame*) and of "it can't be helped" (*shikataganai* or *shōganai*) expressed to me by large numbers of *hibakusha* about A-bomb problems. Generally viewed as "Asian fatalism," this attitude draws deeply upon Japanese tradition and includes strongly Buddhist influences. In psychological terms it has often been thought of as a form of "passivity," in the sense of the inner image: "I am helpless before the great forces of destiny, so why try to influence them?" But I would also emphasize an "active" element that is usually overlooked: "No matter what happens, I carry on." Either of these two sides of the principle of resignation can be associated with denial in the form of the idea that "nothing really happened anyway, so why not just carry on?" But in the more profound individual and cultural expressions of resignation there can be a predominant element of transcendence: of psychologically "taking in" an experience, however extreme, and simultaneously reasserting one's sense of connection with vast human and natural forces which extend beyond that experience and outlast its annihilation; that is, of reasserting one's sense of immortality.*

Another mixture of transcendence and denial was contained in the souvenir vendor's phrase: "I am a *hibakusha*, but at the same time, before being a *hibakusha*, I am a human being." He was on the one hand making a genuine plea for inclusive identity, for being both a *hibakusha* and something more. But on the other hand he was behaving *as if* he had achieved that transcendence, and thereby denying the *hibakusha* conflict that still plagued him and exerted a constricting influence upon his life. We observe here a general pattern which can be called the conflict of transcendence: the wish to be more than merely a weak, impotent *hibakusha*, together with the inner sense of being bound by death guilt to precisely that state. The solution is likely to be the combination of denial and partial transcendence we have noted.

A related emotional combination could be detected in an issue raised by the mathematician concerning the relationship between atomic bomb exposure and choice of professional interest:

> During the years after the war I have had no desire to study about the bomb. . . . I studied relativity and quantum mechanics. My choice of studies was in no way affected by the A-bomb. I feel great resistance toward what some people say about this—that scientists

* There are various modes in which this sense can be experienced: biologically (through family continuity); theologically (through a life after death); through one's enduring works of human influences; and through a tie with the "permanent" natural world. The sense of immortality referred to here probably includes elements of all four.[8]

who experience the A-bomb have the responsibility of studying it, and [I also feel resistance] when scientists in Hiroshima say that as scientists who are themselves victim of the A-bomb, they are against nuclear testing. My feeling is that anyone should be against nuclear testing, whether he is from Hiroshima or not. . . .

Wishing to be simply "a scientist like everyone else" rather than have his intellectual and moral concerns dictated by his *hibakusha* state, he conveys something of the impression that he would like to reject the state altogether. His potential for transcendence, however, as opposed to mere denial, is enhanced by his general intellectual resources and his willingness to confront elements of his *hibakusha* experience in universalistic terms ("My feeling is that anyone should be against nuclear testing, whether he is from Hiroshima or not").

A very different form of transcendence, also incomplete, was that of the bargirl, who told me of a long series of painful experiences of discrimination in employment because of her *hibakusha* state, until finally entering what is known in Japan as the "water world" (*mizu-shōbai*)—that special entertainment subculture including geisha, prostitutes, and bargirls—so named because of the ephemeral ebb and flow of life within it. In the bar where she worked she found that people were insufficiently interested in her as a person to worry about whether she was a *hibakusha* or not. But it turned out that in becoming a bargirl, she was reverting to her mother's profession, of which she had always disapproved; and in seeking to transcend her *hibakusha*hood, she felt herself treated as a "thing" and (at least in this way) divested of all identity.

"IF I HAD A SON OR DAUGHTER"

A major expression of denial-transcendence conflict is the *hibakusha*'s marriage preference, the urge we have noted in some to marry non-*hibakusha*. In general, of course, survivors remain bound to one another, both by painful memories and by geographic and social ties. When they stress the wish to marry an "outsider," the question of children is often uppermost. But rather than merely a fear of increased likelihood of genetic abnormalities, some, like the hospital worker, stress the issue of *psychological* transmission:

I don't mean to say that I am postponing marriage because of this. Even a *hibakusha*, if a really wonderful person . . . might cause me to have a different thought. But the ideal person I would like to marry is a non*hibakusha* . . . because I feel it would be unbearable for both of us to have such pain in our lives. . . . And after marrying, I would like to become a mother as well. And . . . in the course of the child's upbringing, if our agony continued . . . this might have a bad effect upon the child. If one parent is a *hibakusha* and the other is not, I think that to some extent this tendency would be counteracted and diminished. . . .

Keeping in mind her constant reassertion of *hibakusha* identity in her peace activities, these words become all the more striking. The implication is that concerning fears for the next generation, emotional "agony" and physical taint become inseparable. One senses a genuine urge toward a more inclusive life space, along with a hint of guilt over the wish to "betray" the group to which she is so committed.

And there are further difficulties. For she finds that when her parents initiate possible marriage arrangements with non*hibakusha*, her own *hibakusha* status (and, undoubtedly, her keloid as well) makes it necessary for the go-between to "sell" her to the other family:

The go-between would say that I have the disadvantage of being a *hibakusha*—that even though I am a *hibakusha*, I have this good point or that good point . . . and I wonder on what basis the man can evaluate me. . . . I feel the go-between is making up a "good story" about me, and then I feel utterly miserable about my situation.

We suspect she fears that she may indeed possess the *hibakusha* defects the go-between plays down, and is therefore being "oversold," so that the whole procedure becomes doubly inauthentic. She reacts by holding to idealized standards of close mutual understanding,* and goes on refusing arrangements—much to the unhappiness of her parents, who fear she will never marry.

Even the use of the idiom of bodily fears to justify the preference for a non*habakusha*—as in the claim (by a young female office worker) that "If I were to get sick . . . if both were to get sick . . . then there would be great trouble"—is likely to be accompanied (as in her case) by an expression of more generalized emotion: "I prefer one who is not like me." Here we encounter a rather naked expression of the characteristic

---

* Such standards are difficult to achieve anywhere, but perhaps especially in contemporary Japan, where the traditional legacy of relative emotional distance between marital partners comes together with a variety of institutional and personal confusions. The *urge* toward unspoken emotional intimacy, however, has strongly Japanese overtones.

"self-hate" or "intra-group hate" of the victimized; there is a need to deny the taint by which she feels plagued but also perhaps to seek wider horizons than those of bodily fear.

Yōko Ōta addressed the issue with a comment, which, at least within the context of American racial problems, has uncomfortable overtones: "If I had a son or daughter, I wouldn't want him or her to marry a person who had been through the bomb." The parallel here is less the classic question, "Would you want your daughter to marry a Negro?" than the insistence of a Negro mother that her son or daughter not marry another Negro, or at least not a dark Negro. The *hibakusha*'s quest for transcendence becomes bound up with the overall dynamics of the victimized group and of erasing one's taint by means of intimate association with the untainted.

But an alternative form of victimization could help one transcend one's *hibakusha*hood through its own emotional claims. Thus, a young woman leader in the *"Burakumin* [Outcast] Liberation Movement" considered attitudes toward this struggle and toward the principle of feminine equality to be of greater importance in marriage than the issue of whether or not one was a *hibakusha*:

> My mother . . . and many people of the older generation tend to think that marriage is everything and that a girl should get married when she reaches a certain age . . . but I don't want to follow that pattern. . . . I want to marry someone whose thoughts and actions coincide with mine, for instance in this kind of [*Burakumin* Liberation Movement] activity. I oppose the kind of marriage in which I must "shrink myself down in wretchedness" [*chijikomaru mijime ni naru*]. . . . I do not think I will be happy with a person from town [a euphemism for an ordinary non-*burakumin*]. . . . [About the question of marrying a *hibakusha* or a non*hibakusha*] I do not think this should be a consideration. Some people may have special feelings toward those who are physically handicapped, who lost a leg or the like . . . and those handicapped people may have inferiority complexes. . . . But in order to get rid of such feelings—for that purpose, too, I think our protest movement is necessary. . . .

It became clear during interviews that her identity as a *burakumin* leader was the driving force of her life, subsuming other important sub-identities—that of the "new Japanese woman" and the "*hibakusha* peace movement spokeswoman." But she nonetheless is inwardly aware of a double taint, and her reference to "handicapped people" with "inferiority complexes" seems simultaneously to embrace physical cripples, *burakumin*, and *hibakusha*. While protest can have its own elements of denial (she speaks of "*those* handicapped people"), there was little doubt of her general progress toward transcendence—toward becoming a *burakumin-hibakusha* with vitality and pride, active within the wider human arena.

A less successful m :ging of the *burakumin* and *hibakusha* identities took place within the *burakumin* boy. While we know him to have fears of illness as well as other unpleasant associations to *hibakusha*hood, when the subject of his *burakumin* state came up, all else was forgotten. He became extremely tense, and then tearful, as he explained how *burakumin* are exploited and made to work at substandard wages, how he dreaded job interviews because as soon as he gave his address he was identified as a *burakumin*, how he would be turned down without being told anything directly and was left with the strong suspicion that his being a *burakumin* was the cause; he quoted to me the popular Japanese saying: "It takes ten years to gain confidence, but just one day to lose it." As with the young woman leader, his *hibakusha*hood was more or less absorbed by his *burakumin* identity; but his transcendence was much more fragile, containing neither vitality nor pride, and depending almost entirely upon being the lesser of two negative self-images.

A similarly negative form of transcendence was that brought about by a personal tragedy unrelated to the atomic bomb. An elderly housewife expressed relatively little concern about being a *hibakusha* compared to the overwhelmingly painful memory of the death of her only son in a wartime military aviation accident twenty years before. While descriptions of atomic bomb experiences far exceeded her story in horror, none was recounted with a more vivid expression of loss. Indeed, as she told of visiting with her husband the place where her son had crashed, then viewing his body in the coffin and looking into his face, absolutely determined not to cry but rather to be proud that he had died for his country, the tears rolled down not only her cheeks, but those of my assistant as well, and I too was moved by the power of her grief. The whole experience dramatically illustrated the way in which the full recounting of a single death can evoke more direct and empathic response than descriptions of scenes of thousands of deaths.

Another woman I interviewed, a maid in a boarding house, had lost her husband and four brothers in military combat, and then two children in floods and landslides accompanying the severe typhoons which occurred a month after the bomb. So painful were her recollections of all of these deaths and her bitterness toward war and wartime military leaders—she was convinced of their responsibility for the deaths not only of her husband and brothers but her children too, as she claimed that military installations weakened the soil of neighboring hillsides and contributed to the landslides—that it seemed almost a relief for her to turn from them to discussions of the atomic bomb. This was also true of another woman who was totally preoccupied with the overwhelming problems surrounding her husband's drug addiction. In such cases, however, there is always the possibility that atomic bomb conflicts can reassert themselves, since they have not necessarily been overcome.

:

An additional vantage-point for examining the denial-transcendence continuum is the situation of the *hibakusha* living outside of Hiroshima. The estimated total of *hibakusha* in Japan is 290,000, of whom 160,000 were originally exposed in Hiroshima; of the Hiroshima group, 90,000 live in the city itself, 35,000 in the surrounding province, and the remaining 30,000 or so in various places throughout Japan.*

In Tokyo, for instance, there are thought to be at least seven thousand *hibakusha*—some of them longtime Tokyo residents who happened to be in Hiroshima or Nagasaki when the bomb fell, and others who chose to live there for various practical economic and social reasons. But there are undoubtedly a certain number for whom residing in Tokyo or in other large cities presents an opportunity to "pass" into non*hibakusha* society, much in the way many light-skinned Negroes "pass" into white American society. There is evidence of this in the observations by leaders of a *hibakusha* organization in Tokyo that many hide their *hibakusha* identity, either do not possess or else make no use of their *hibakusha* health cards, and have nothing to do with *hibakusha* groups there (it was estimated in 1963 that only one third of Tokyo *hibakusha* belonged to the general *hibakusha* organization).[10] There is said to be less understanding for *hibakusha* in Tokyo than in Hiroshima, more discrimination in marriage and employment, and less knowledge about their medical problems. In other words, when detected, *hiba-*

---

* These statistics vary, and I have given them in round figures. They are based largely upon a 1950 census, but a 1958 Daytime City Population Survey of Hiroshima identified 92,850 *hibakusha* as living in the city; a 1960 survey revealed 171,293 in Hiroshima Prefecture. While the overall number of *hibakusha* must diminish over the years, statistics may be confused by increasingly effective registration procedures.[9]

kusha are perceived as more specifically alien and tainted. But *hibakusha* status can be hidden more readily and there is much less *hibakusha* anxiety in the general atmosphere (when new reports of dangers of A-bomb aftereffects are broadcast or printed, it is said that friends and family members often take it upon themselves to prevent *hibakusha* from learning about them). Weighing all of these factors, one is left with the general impression that many *hibakusha* living outside of the Hiroshima area attempt to conduct their lives as if they had never been through the bomb—to live out a pattern of denial. But transcendence plays a part here too, as some, without particularly hiding their *hibakusha* state, find a move to Tokyo or other cities necessary for breaking out of suffocating A-bomb preoccupations and seeking greater general fulfillment.

:

Nor are the patterns of transcendence described in this chapter the only ones possible. Indeed, every functioning aspect of oneself—whether as a student, businessman, worker, wife, father, or even dreamer—is a potential avenue of transcendence, as is one's general relationship to Japanese cultural tradition, to contemporary historical forces, and to the psychobiological universals of human experience. The difficulty lies in the constellation of emotions around guilt and death which impede transcendence, and which tie the members of any victimized group to self-defeating patterns of denial and psychic numbing. The *hibakusha*-victim, then, is a man on a treadmill who presses constantly toward a psychic state he can never quite reach, and who often seeks to separate himself from others on the treadmill in order to create the inner illusion that he is not really on it.

4) Counterfeit Nurturance

Among the various conflicts over dependency there is one general tendency which dominates the *hibakusha* experience and affects all human relationships—a pattern we may term *suspicion of counterfeit nurturance*. Contributing to this "tainted dependency" are special features of atomic bomb exposure, general aspects of the psychology of oppression, and certain Japanese cultural emphases.

Suspicion of counterfeit nurturance includes two seemingly contradictory attitudes, which we may observe in the hospital worker. The first is one of antagonism toward any kind of "special attention":

> I don't like people to use that word [*hibakusha*]. . . . Of course, there are some who, through being considered *hibakusha*, want to receive special coddling [*amaeru*] . . . but I like to stand up as an individual. When I was younger they used to call us "atomic bomb maidens." . . . More recently they call us *hibakusha*. . . . I don't like this special view of us. . . . Usually when people refer to young girls, they will say girls or daughters, or some person's daughter . . . but to refer to us as atomic bomb maidens is a way of discrimination. . . . It is a way of abandoning us. . . .

She is saying that special nurturance given *hibakusha* imposes upon them so constricted an identity that the experience becomes the person, and the *hibakusha* is made to stand alone as a *hibakusha* and nothing more. But on the other hand, she craves something very close to the same "special coddling" (*amaeru**) which she finds so objectionable:

> When I sense unkind attitudes—how shall I put it—although I still feel I would like to go on living, a very sad feeling comes over me

* The word *amaeru* refers particularly to the child's expectation of love and care from a parent. "*Amaeru*" (or *amae*, the noun form—both words derive from *amai*, meaning sweet) is itself basic to Japanese psychology, and to the very strong cultural stress upon dependency. Takeo Doi argues that the pattern of *amaeru*—of expecting, presuming upon, and soliciting another's love—takes its model from child-parent relationships, but comes to dominate all later relationships as well. Dr. Doi emphasizes, correctly I believe, that the emotions surrounding *amaeru* are by no means unique to Japanese but are particularly intense in them. Similarly, Japanese, and especially victimized Japanese, bring great intensity to universal conflicts over dependency, such as the suspicion of counterfeit nurturance. Masao Maruyama, a leading political scientist and intellectual historian, has criticized his countrymen for what he considers an inclination toward "victim consciousness."[11]

from the depths of my being. . . . We underwent such a terrible ordeal in which we experienced a state between death and life . . . so I wish others to have a more sympathetic understanding of us. . . .

The *hibakusha*, then, both craves and resents special nurturance, and is threatened either way by abandonment. Should his craving be denied, he is left with the sense that his unique death encounter is being ignored, and he feels abandoned—that is, rejected and misunderstood. But should his special need be responded to, he views the nurturance offered him as inauthentic because it seems to confirm his weakness, humiliation, and death taint; he feels "abandoned" to these hated manifestations of *hibakusha* identity.

The problem is intrinsic to any form of victimization. The victim inevitably feels himself in need of special sustenance, which, when received, intensifies his "victim-consciousness" and thereby perpetuates a vicious circle of counterfeit nurturance and abandonment. Nurturing offered threatens to isolate the victim and further undermines his self-esteem, but the humiliating temptation to accept it is always there. Hence the victimized group's hatred for its toadies, real or suspected, its "Uncle Toms" who succumb to this temptation; and for its would-be benefactors, the "white liberals" who continue to offer nurturance.

But every victim, certainly every *hibakusha*, succumbs in some degree. For instance, we may look upon the grocer's "Kyoto experiment" as an effort to discover whether he could survive psychologically in the absence of the counterfeit nurturance he felt himself to receive in Hiroshima because of his keloid. But his conclusion was that however counterfeit, this nurturance was necessary to him. Another form of suspicion of counterfeit nurturance was the same man's accusation that doctors were "irresponsible" in being unable to cure A-bomb disease. And still another manifestation was the European priest's ironic contrast between the authentic distinction of winning a Nobel Prize with the counterfeit one of being a *hibakusha*.

For any identity based upon victimization is perceived as counterfeit, and the survivor's lifelong struggle against being *nothing but a hibakusha* is a struggle against counterfeit existence. One may use as a psychological model, though not as an exact analogy, "Momism": the child deeply resents the nurturance he receives, feels suffocated and imprisoned by it, but cannot do without it.

Of course, the attitude of those offering nurturance is of great importance, but what I wish to stress here is the *hibakusha's* general sensitivity in this psychological sphere—as revealed in an incident described by the writer-physician:

> Some time ago the labor unions called a meeting in Hiroshima having as its theme: "We should do our best to help the *hibakusha*." When I saw this motto—"Help the *hibakusha*"—I felt resentful. I didn't see why they should do this, especially here in Hiroshima. . . . I felt resentful because I thought they were using the A-bomb for their own purposes. But maybe the fact that I had this kind of reaction means that I am a *hibakusha*.

His last sentence suggests that not only are *hibakusha* sensitive about such matters but that to a significant extent their group identity is built around this sensitivity—around feelings (often largely unconscious) of sharing a special need which is virtually impossible to fulfill, and being perpetually subject to inauthentic "offerings" from others.

These feelings strongly color *hibakusha*'s attitudes toward "outsiders" in general. The downtrodden woman laborer, for instance, complained to me about outsiders' lack of concern about *hibakusha*, their feeling that "It's someone else's affair, not ours"; she expressed the wish that they would "have more conscience" (*ryōshinteki*) about the matter, and went on to condemn them for speaking ill of people behind their backs:

> In the case of a burned person with an ugly face, they will tell him sympathetically how sorry for him they feel, but then later [when he is gone] they will say, "What a wretched face he has."

While Japanese culture in many ways encourages this discrepancy between publicly expressed and privately held feelings (one, we might add, hardly unknown in other cultures), *hibakusha* sensitivities bring to the problem the intensified emotions of tainted victims toward intact people around them. An illustration of this kind of sensitivity is the reaction described by the *burakumin* woman leader while observing a group of Western visitors taking pictures during the performance of a play which re-enacted the atomic bomb experience:

> With camera in hand, they chased after the actors portraying A-bomb victims . . . but although I understood their intention, their doing such a thing gave me a miserable feeling. . . . I don't know exactly why . . . but I wanted them to really comprehend not just the external shape of things but the true feeling, inwardly, from the heart [*kokoro de*]. . . .

Again a Japanese cultural stress, this time upon intense "heartfelt" identification, is magnified by the *hibakusha* experience. Outsiders' attempts at empathy, however well-meant, are bound to be looked upon as superficial and counterfeit, the problem in this case complicated by the synthetic nature of the situation (a play *about* the bomb).

What becomes clear is that the *hibakusha* himself has a considerable need to maintain this separation from the "outsider." He divides the world into those who are like him—who have been through the entire ordeal—and those who are not. The apocalyptic nature of the experience, along with the taint of its resulting identity, create a semi-mystical quality which the uninitiated cannot be expected to grasp. Hence I encountered such comments as: "We have a different feeling from other people who have not experienced the A-bomb"; "If you haven't seen it with your own eyes, you can't understand it"; and the observation that when with non*hibakusha*, "I find it difficult to explain the experience to them." This exclusiveness serves the further psychological function of lending some value to the *hibakusha* status, whatever its taint; and of creating a group posture from which the sense of special need can be expressed, whatever its ambivalence.

Thus, the professor of English told me that when an English writer emphasized to *hibakusha* the necessity for their recognizing the sufferings of others, such as those who had been in Nazi concentration camps, this caused resentment among some because "they tend to live in just their own world." Unable to find a path of autonomy and transcendence, the victim clings to his own group and resents outside rivals for precisely the nurturance he looks upon as counterfeit.

Contributing to these problems around dependency are various kinds of guilt, including guilt over survival priority and over the things one did to survive. The elderly domestic worker describes the struggle over food in a way that suggests an early paradigm of later counterfeit nurturance:

> When we evacuated to Jigozen [a suburban area], we had absolutely no food to eat. I went to buy some potatoes with money I had at the time but the farmers said they wouldn't sell anything to those who were bombed in Hiroshima—not even vegetables. . . . This gave me a wretched feeling—that such a thing could happen between Japanese, between town people and country people. . . . Even though we offered them money they would not sell us anything . . . so we stole things and ate them. . . . Although I am ashamed to tell you this . . . the memory of these events lingers in my mind. . . .

This kind of hostility between bombed, hungry city people and relatively unscathed, well-supplied country people took place all over Japan (and in Europe) during the period after the war. But for many *hibakusha* it signified the beginning of a post-bomb pattern of discrimination coming from "outsiders." Whether or not farmers actually said that they "wouldn't sell anything to those who were bombed in Hiroshima," the use of the phrase, particularly in relationship to food, suggests this early sense of being denied the authentic nurturance one craved—just as the recollection of stealing suggests the need to resort to illegitimate (inauthentic) measures in order to survive at all. It is then not a difficult step, psychologically speaking, to suspect all outsiders of withholding that which is authentically needed and providing (or causing one to seek) only that which is counterfeit.

Because of this conflict around counterfeit nurturance the outsider often perceives *hibakusha* as hungry for attention, perpetually demanding something from others. And in relationship to this image non-*hibakusha* and *hibakusha* alike have used "A-bomb beggars" to describe the kind of *hibakusha* who has surrendered all autonomy in favor of a continuous plea for help. Implicit in the term is the counterfeit nature of anything the "begger" may receive, the demeaning nature of his stance, and its negative impact upon others. All this is suggested by a young Hiroshima-born writer, not himself a *hibakusha* but deeply and thoughtfully involved in *hibakusha* problems:

Many of the *hibakusha* have a special kind of group sense that makes me feel very uncomfortable. *Hibakusha* come up to me and say, "Write about our experience"—and this makes me very uneasy. It is an unfortunate psychological climate—since this kind of thing shows that people have stopped living, and instead have been relying upon others for comfort and coddling [*amaeru*]. . . . Of course, *hibakusha* vary a great deal, but if you meet one person of this kind, you have met them all. . . . It is hard to say whether they existed in people before and were simply brought out by the experience—but the feelings are there.

Suggested here is an atmosphere of demand and suspicion so great as to constitute a symbolic death ("people have stopped living, and instead have been relying upon others for comfort and coddling"). Prior conflicts over dependency are magnified to the point of dominating one's existence.

We may thus say that the atomic bomb, like all disasters but to an unprecedented degree, disrupts the balance between autonomy and nurturance within individuals and groups; and that once the disruption has been initiated, it tends to be self-perpetuating.

"MY NEIGHBORS' EYES WERE FIERCE"

This disruption can also be observed in conflicts among *hibakusha* themselves. No one acquainted with Hiroshima life can fail to note the intensity of jealousies and resentments felt by *hibakusha* toward one another, especially toward those who step forward and take some kind of initiative. Here we may partly implicate a pervasive Japanese cultural emphasis of the universal intolerance for unconventional behavior, as expressed in the popular saying, "A nail which sticks out will be hammered down." But the tendency is aggravated by the competitive aspects of the quest for nurturance, with the individual *hibakusha* often fearful that others in his group will have greater success in achieving that (counterfeit) goal.

Envy was perhaps most frequently expressed in relationship to medical benefits. It was fed by the obscurity of the psychosomatic issues involved and by the inevitable misrepresentation by some *hibakusha* of factors affecting their eligibility (original distance from the hypocenter, shielding, symptoms, etc.). The technician, for instance, suggests the extraordinary atmosphere surrounding the medical and economic benefits he received while suffering from a protracted series of ailments which were organically debilitating but ambiguous in their relationship to the atomic bomb:

When people knew that I was in the hospital, their attitude was not so bad. But when I came home, and received treatment in my house . . . they would say I was receiving good things while doing nothing. . . . My neighbors' eyes were fierce, and they would say bad things about me . . . their attitude was cold . . . and this affected me very strongly. . . . They were people who had themselves been through the bomb but were not suffering from any illness. . . . They would write or talk to welfare officials in the City Office about what I had or did not have . . . and when the officials came to our house to ask questions, they would not tell us which people had been talking to them about me. . . . Once, having heard rumors . . . I went to the welfare office myself and suggested they talk directly to my doctor. . . .

It is quite possible that his own inner conflicts over whether he was entitled to this nurturance led him to do things that antagonized his neighbors or to exaggerate their behavior. But there is no doubt that such jealousies have existed. Indeed, much of the dilemma over medical and economic benefits described in Chapter IV can be viewed, from a psychological standpoint, as the expression of citywide conflict over suspicion of counterfeit nurturance in which *hibakusha* suffer in relationship to three perceived possibilities: they will not receive help they need, they will receive help but it will be counterfeit, others less deserving will receive more help than they. This last fear is expressed by the electrician (speaking on behalf of his son) in a way that raises the question of "cheating" within the competition for nurturance:

> All you needed in order to obtain a card as a special *hibakusha* were the signatures of certain people such as the head of the neighborhood organization or two or three people who were working at the same place. . . . Rather than honesty it was sometimes a matter of skill as a talker and cleverness in arranging this testimony. . . . Yet my oldest boy . . . came into the city later that day . . . walked through the center of the bomb area, and can certainly be looked upon as a person exposed to its effects. . . . But since he was outside of the city when the bomb fell . . . he is not eligible for the special *hibakusha* card. . . . If we were to say that he was with the other children [who were within three kilometers] he could receive one . . . but we don't want to say anything that is not true. . . .

Involved in this bitterness toward those who cheat (and thereby obtain nurturance that is the most counterfeit of all) is the temptation he so clearly felt—but resisted—to do the same.

Similarly, those who have suffered from the bomb but who are not quite eligible for *hibakusha* status greatly resent *hibakusha* privileges—as was the case with a civil service employee, who lost a brother and underwent, with his *hibakusha*-parents, great economic hardship. He complained of people who "lean on" their *hibakusha* cards and use them in a way that is "slipshod" and "objectionable"—that is, for conditions having no relationship to the bomb. Much involved in this kind of criticism were various kinds of guilt—toward his dead brother for having himself survived, and toward his other family members (and all other *hibakusha*) for not having himself been exposed to the bomb.

Among *hibakusha* themselves the loss of close family members—

sources of authentic nurturance—also greatly aggravates the problem of counterfeit nurturance. Combinations of guilt and anticipated envy lead *hibakusha* who have not experienced such losses to hesitate to discuss family matters with those who have. For instance, one would particularly avoid talking about one's mother in the presence of a person who has lost his mother, and the same applies for parents' discussion of children. For the nurturance received from either side of the parent-child relationship is probably, in various psychological ways, felt to be the most authentic of all. In comparison, all other relationships run the risk of seeming counterfeit.

On the other hand, should families who have lost children gain particular recognition in relationship to their loss, they in turn become objects of envy and resentment. Thus it was reported that following the death of Sadako Sasaki (the girl who died of leukemia and who became the "Anne Frank of Hiroshima"), the national journalistic and cinematic treatment of the event made neighbors extremely jealous and highly critical of the ostensible fortune the family was thought to have received. The family apparently was given virtually nothing, and was said to have been forced to leave the city because of the intensity of emotions and general pressures surrounding these events, including pressures of creditors.

Hibakusha who have participated in international events relating to their atomic bomb experience have met similar resentments, particularly when they have received some benefit from such participation. Thus, the "Hiroshima Maidens"—a group of young women with keloids or severe burn scars sent to America for plastic surgery—met with severe criticism upon their return to Hiroshima; they were accused of such things as having received too much personal attention in America, become too "Americanized" in their dress and manner, too much changed in general by the experience, etc. The girls themselves, as we shall observe, actually underwent a difficult inner psychological sequence in both countries, but the point here is the degree to which other *hibakusha* were agitated by the apparent nurturance received. In such cases ordinary *hibakusha* may feel "betrayed" by those who have moved beyond the conventional quietude of the victimized state.

In other words, the *hibakusha*-victim, hating yet clinging to his imposed identity, is threatened by another's being helped to transcend *hibakusha* exclusiveness. And in this perpetual rivalry for nurturance, and constant anticipation of the counterfeit, a psychological state is reached in which the more one wins, the more one loses.

5) *Identity of the Dead*

The ultimate counterfeit element for *hibakusha* is life itself. An extraordinarily persistent identification with the dead underlies the problems of dependency we have been discussing and extends into all areas of existence. For *hibakusha* seem not only to have experienced the atomic disaster, but to have imbibed and incorporated it into their beings, including all of its elements of horror, evil, and particularly of death. They feel compelled to virtually merge with those who died, not only with close family members but with a more anonymous group of "the dead."

We encounter concrete expressions of this identification in A-bomb orphans' continuing sense of intimacy with dead parents—as conveyed in the twice-daily reports by the shopkeeper's assistant made before the family altar containing the memorial tablets of his father, mother, and younger brother:

> Even though they are dead now, every day in the morning and in the evening I still give a kind of report to my father, mother, and younger brother . . . as if talking to my parents. . . . I tell them, with a feeling of gratitude, that I have been able to spend another day safely. . . . Although they are actually dead I feel as though they are watching over us . . . with the feeling that in my heart they are still alive . . . which . . . helps me a great deal. . . .

Although only nominally a Shin Buddhist, he reflects the general emphasis of Japanese popular religion upon continuity with the dead, and upon one's responsibility for placating the souls of the dead in order to insure that they are content. He told me that he had carried the memorial tablets about from place to place until finding a permanent home, and "Now that I have been able to become settled, they must be settled too, and I feel that in whatever I do they give me spiritual support." But the other side of this belief is the fear that should such souls be uncared for, they will become restless, agitated, and may bring harm to those of the living who have neglected them. Here too the atomic bomb in various ways upsets the balance: the obeisance never seems adequate; the ordinary mourning process never seems to be completed.

Yet the effort continues to be made. The bargirl, also an A-bomb orphan, told me that "I think more and more about my mother," that (regarding difficulties with her husband and her child) "I can tell her things I have on my mind that I cannot tell others," and that "just imagining my mother makes me happy." She also described "reporting" regularly to her mother; and on the day she turned eighteen, she did so in the form of a prose poem, which she wrote in her diary:

I am eighteen. I have experienced many hardships and much sadness but have now become a young woman. Putting a little powder on my cheek, a bit of rouge on my lips, wearing a flower-patterned dress, I take a romantic walk in the park. Can you see me now, Mother, as I grow? I cannot remember your face. But in front of your picture I make a new dress, I comb my hair, each time to show you. Can you see me, Mother, from such a far place?

Publicly, too, the dead must be continually placated. At memorial ceremonies in both Hiroshima and Nagasaki, I observed A-bomb orphans express similar sentiments toward their parents and all dead parents. At the ceremony in Nagasaki the mayor stated directly, "The city has been rebuilt under the protection of the souls of the dead." And in a widely distributed film, during a sequence about atomic bomb orphans in which the children were told (in the midst of a fire drill) that they should take with them only their most valuable possessions, they were shown rushing inside to rescue pictures of their dead parents.

We find similar patterns in parents of dead children. The emotions contained in the phrase (quoted before in reference to parents collecting the remains of their dead sons) "My son, I am taking you home" become permanent ones, and by no means limited to the uneducated. I was told of a distinguished educator whose daughter was thought to have died near the university grounds (no one knew exactly where since no remains were found), who, each August 6th, "made his way silently to a place where he believes his daughter might have been killed, digs up a bit of dirt and says a prayer for her soul, in order to feel close to her."

The symbolism of water withheld from the dying also has lasting effects. It reappeared in an account, "Rivers of Hiroshima," published in a national magazine in 1964,[12] in which the writer described seeing a woman—"a strange person"—among the many visitors to the A-Bomb Memorial Monument one summer, carrying beer bottles wrapped in a *furoshiki*; she knelt before the monument, poured water from the bottles into her hand, and sprinkled it over the flower offerings lying there—then repeated the process before each of several monuments. She turned out to be a kindergarten teacher who told the writer of the article that at the time of the bomb she had encountered many pleas for water from dying people, had denied it to them in accordance with instructions received, but "even so, one by one, after much suffering, they became cold corpses." As a form of "asking their apologies" many years later, she had gone the night before to a shrine which contained a waterfall and performed a ritual of purification there; the next morning she drew water from it to offer to the dead. The article refers to both the beauty of the rivers and to their having "swallowed up many souls" at the time of the bomb. Also mentioned is that "it never rains on August 6th in Hiroshima." Water, in other words, is seen as an essentially life-giving force, but one which can also dissolve life. The little ceremony performed by this anonymous lady epitomizes the psychological struggle of the living to "make it up" to the dead, to return symbolically to the dead the lives which they, the living, feel that they "stole" from them. This guilt over survival priority is the source of the continuing citywide preoccupation with the dead.

Less verbalized but of equal importance is the fearful wish to separate oneself from the dead, the inevitable ambivalence that lies behind the stress upon continuity and merging. The young office worker, for instance, in discussing the possibility of future nuclear wars, thinks of the A-bomb dead with great fear, associating them with the possibility of her dying in that same gruesome fashion:

> If I were to die the next time, I would then come to know all about the painful experiences of those who died before. . . . If I were to die in the same way they did . . . it would be wretched. . . . I think they died in great pain . . . from dreadful diseases. . . .

It is not quite clear whether she was suggesting a fantasy of reunion with the dead, though in any case her identification with them is strong. At the same time they remain deeply threatening to her, and her stress upon the way they died—their "dreadful diseases"—is in keeping with another Japanese folk belief to the effect that the souls of those who die in such violent or premature ways are particularly restless, unhappy, and dangerous to the living. This continuing fear of the dead is the perpetuation of the urge we noted in many *hibakusha* at the time of the bomb to rid themselves quickly of the corpses of their relatives; retained images of grotesque external and internal impairment aggravate what is in any case a universal form of anxiety.

In his exaggerated obeisance to the dead, then, the *hibakusha* is atoning not only for his own survival but for his unacceptable wish to sever his connection from those who did not. Some such combined urge for continuity and separation is again universal to the human condition, and fear of the dead is as strong in Japanese culture as in most others. But the disruptions and contaminations of the atomic bomb, physical and symbolic, intensify the need for continuity even as they heighten the urge toward separation.

One of the resulting patterns is a particularly strong emphasis upon the dead as spiritual arbiters—as the source of moral standards for the living. Sometimes, in response to questions about the bomb, I would get such answers as: "Those who could tell you about it best are now dead" or "Those who died are unfortunately voiceless." And some in Hiroshima quote a popular saying, "The dead have no mouth." Behind such expressions lies not only the feeling that the dead "know best" about the horrors of the A-bomb, but also that only they, and not survivors, are entitled to make ultimate judgments in relationship to it.

The professor of English expresses this sentiment, again with the aid of a literary allusion, this time a line from T. S. Eliot:

It seems to me that those who are alive are quite fortunate. . . . They have their voices to express themselves, and you have of course been talking to them. But what about the voices of those who died? I am thinking of T. S. Eliot's poem . . . [in] *Four Quartets*, a line which, as far as I can remember it, says: "There are some people whose voices were never heard during their lives, and after they die . . . finally have their chance to speak within the fire." When I read these words, I felt very moved. . . . I thought of the fires of Hiroshima. . . . These days . . . we are losing our faith in language . . . but when I read these lines in T. S. Eliot, I returned to my former naïve faith in language—in its ability to express what we feel. . . . The voices of those who died—that is the important question. I hope after you have finished your research you will ponder this question. . . .*

---

* I did ponder the question, even while doing the research. What particularly struck me about his associations was his need to find a connection with the moral authority of the dead as a means of restoring his personal faith in language, which is virtually to say, his faith in life. The lines he referred to actually read: "They can tell you, being dead: the communication of the dead is tongued with fire beyond the language of the living."[13] They suggest even more strongly the fierceness of this

This need for moral obeisance to the dead has profound influence upon the inner question of what is permissible in the *hibakusha* identity, or more accurately, what is not permissible. *Hibakusha* constantly judge, and indeed judge harshly, their own behavior and that of other survivors on the basis of the degree of respect and awe this behavior seems to demonstrate toward the dead. They are, for instance, exceedingly suspicious of any individual or group attempts at social action in relationship to the atomic bomb experience. If anything, they are more critical of a *hibakusha* prominent in such programs than they are of outsiders, constantly accusing such a person of "selling his name," "selling the bomb," "selling Hiroshima," or seeking to become an "A-bomb star." The Japanese nail-hammering cultural ethos as well as the overall struggle with counterfeit nurturance mentioned before are important here, as are survivors' bitter experiences of being manipulated by ambitious leaders. But more fundamental is the inner feeling that such actions, in their very vitality, are "impure" and an "insult to the dead."

These feelings are internalized by those *hibakusha* involved in social action, and become forms of self-accusation. The prominent politician, whose controversial career has combined old-style political methods with passionate promotion of *hibakusha* programs of medical and economic assistance, spoke defensively, as if anticipating criticism:

Perhaps you have met many victims, and some may have complained about certain situations. . . . I have not tried to sell my name—that is not true. My concern has been only to help these people—my whole life is dedicated to this. . . .

Apart from responding to actual accusations of "selling his name," his words revealed his unacceptable realization that entering into his activities were motivations of personal ambition and self-seeking—precisely what are most impure and most an "insult to the dead"—rather than their being purely altruistic service on behalf of *hibakusha*. Since all actions (particularly political ones) contain elements of personal ambition and self-seeking, he found himself subject to an impossibly purist form of judgment and self-judgment (though I might add that he nonetheless appeared to carry on quite effectively in his public activities and private life).

---

moral power of the dead; or, in psychological terms, the inner force upon the living of images of the dead, associated as these are with a sense of guilt-saturated human continuity. Recalling and reciting lines of poetry in a language other than his own, the professor had retained Eliot's psychological message if not his exact words.

The history professor described a related personal struggle around the idea of "selling the bomb" in connection with a book he wrote about his atomic bomb experience, dedicated to his dead wife, and entitled (in a rough English translation) *My Wife's Corpse in My Arms*. An introduction by a friend states that "It is far from my intention, and of course that of Mr. H. [the history professor] to 'sell Hiroshima,'" but rather "our sole purpose is to express our pure and sincere wish that there will be 'no more Hiroshimas' on this earth, anywhere, for the rest of time." Then the author himself, in a long introductory poem, explains how he had at first looked forward to using the royalties from the book for buying much needed clothes for his children and building a home "in a corner of Kyoto" in his wife's memory. But as the poem goes on to explain, the matter of royalties troubled him deeply:

When the publisher sent his confirmatory letter / it made me feel timid and suddenly nervous / and the proposed royalty frightened me. / I became sleepless at night / and restless during the day, / for before my eyes there appeared / hundreds of thousands of pitiful ghosts— / the dead who departed with you on that day / and those still missing after these three years. . . .

The idea of making money from writings on the bomb evokes imagery of the dead, pathetic but also threatening, and this imagery is the essence of all self-accusations of "selling the bomb." After two days and nights of these thoughts and visions, he decided to turn over all royalties to impoverished survivors. He felt greatly relieved, and (at least momentarily) free of the intrusive ghosts: "The sun brought in a bright new day / and my heart grew light." Again we observe the tyrannical moral injunction to act solely on behalf of the dead, to reduce personal needs to the point of selflessness in order to do what one can to right the impaired organic balance of death and life.

Nor is the outsider who investigates atomic bomb problems free of these pressures. Several *hibakusha* asked what I planned to do with my material when I had completed my study—and one, an elderly country-woman, more naïve and bold than most, went on to raise the question of my "selling the bomb":

Well, on a radio program which I heard yesterday . . . a young woman described how she was asked about different things to help . . . collect materials on the A-bomb. But she said she did not want to . . . since the kind of study that was being made would end up by selling the materials. . . . This reminded me of having talked with you last time, and I wondered if you were making a study in a similar direction in which you were collecting materials on the A-bomb in order—though it is improper for me to say this—to sell them. . . .

Here I was made to feel personally the stringent moral requirements emanating from the A-bomb dead—as formalized (and perpetuated by mass media) in imagery of "selling the bomb." Nor have I been unaffected by these currents, or free from self-accusation concerning the interplay of personal gain and larger responsibility in carrying out the work.

:

Hibakusha thus live under the perpetual burden of their survival. The emotion that the Buddhist priest described in them at the time of survival—"All of these people felt the miracle, the special mercy, the destiny which enabled them to live . . . [they] felt blessed [*arigatai*] . . . grateful to have missed death"—becomes a permanent psychic state, in which one is never permitted to forget that others received no such blessing. It is as if they have made an unspoken pact with the dead which specifies that the latter, in return for having died and permitting the survivors to live, are entitled to an aura of moral perfection, in contrast to the survivors' own pledge of self-condemnation and attenuated life. The statement we quoted by the Nagasaki educator—"Those who die are dead and must bear their fate, but the living must live with this dark feeling"—can be understood as an expression of the survivor's bondage to the dead. Are we then justified in saying about Hiroshima what has been so often said, by heads of state and participants in the general nuclear debate, about future wars: "the survivors envy the dead"? There are undoubtedly moments when they do, but I would stress, rather than envy, the *hibakusha*'s identification with the dead to the point of feeling *as if* dead himself.

The *hibakusha* identity, then, in a significant symbolic sense, becomes an *identity of the dead*—taking the following inner sequence: *I almost died; I should have died; I did die, or at least I am not really alive; or if I am alive, it is impure of me to be so; anything I do which affirms life is also impure and an insult to the dead, who alone are pure; and by living as if dead, I take the place of the dead and give them life.*

Can it then be said that this identity of the dead, with its condemnation of vitality per se, propels the *hibakusha* along a straight path to suicide? I do not think so. During the period of near total disintegration immediately after the bomb, many undoubtedly did cease to struggle to live and thereby hastened their deaths. And we have observed, in our discussion of mass media, the widespread imagery of the A-bomb "driving people crazy" and causing them to kill themselves—imagery which always oversimplifies and frequently distorts, but can nonetheless contain elements of truth. Yet while there were no conclusive statistics available on suicide among *hibakusha*, my general impression was that they did not, as a group, demonstrate particularly strong suicidal tendencies[14]; that on the contrary, at all stages of their experience, they clung tenaciously to life. Although they entertained imagery of exchanging their lives for those of one of the dead—as we know to be true of the writer-manufacturer—they tended, like him, to reject literal self-destruction on this basis:

> Though I said I would sacrifice my life for that of my daughter [who had died of A-bomb disease] this doesn't mean that I don't value my own life. There were people who committed suicide after the war, but I have no respect for them because they had no respect for their own lives. I don't think you can solve anything by just dying.

In this man, as in other *hibakusha*, the whole constellation of inwardly experienced death symbolism—the embrace of the identity of the dead—may, paradoxically enough, serve as a means of maintaining life. For in the face of the burden of guilt the survivor carries with him, particularly the guilt of survival priority, his obeisance before the dead is his best means of justifying and maintaining his own existence. But it remains an existence with a large shadow cast across it, a life which, in a powerful symbolic sense, the survivor does not feel to be his own.

ATOMIC BOMB LEADERS

A few in Hiroshima could seize upon their *hibakusha* identity and put it to public use. They became the kind of leaders who emerge from any disaster, or general historical crisis, to help ordinary people cope with extraordinary circumstances.

While it would be difficult to say that any of them belongs to the select category of the "great man," each has aspired to exert upon his contemporaries the kind of influence characteristic of the great man: to combine personality and idea in a way that made contact with what Freud called the "wishes" of the rank and file, either by reviving "an old group of wishes" or providing "a new aim for their wishes";[1] and (in Erikson's phrase) to "increase the margin of man's inner freedom by introspective means applied to the very center of his conflicts."[2] For *hibakusha* these conflicts were concerned mainly with retained death imagery, and the inner freedom sought was release from death anxiety and death guilt. The unifying theme of *hibakusha* leaders, therefore, has been the idea of "conquering death"—of demonstrating ways of comprehending a profound upheaval in patterns of life and death, and ultimately of comprehending the fact of human mortality itself. This theme, I would submit, is the primary function of all leaders and all great men, though strangely neglected in our explanations of leadership and greatness.

Great men are, of course, rare, and by no means always immediately recognizable. Their exceptional qualities, moreover, usually manifest themselves in relationship to a gradually evolving crisis, and are themselves products of generations—even centuries—of psychohistorical struggle. The split-second annihilation of nuclear weapons allows for no such nurturing time sequence. Greatness in response to Hiroshima, if there is to be such, may well come later, and possibly from places far removed from the city itself.

But the "emergent leaders"[3] who have appeared in Hiroshima are nonetheless a notable group. What they have been, done, and symbolized have had great significance for atomic bomb survivors, and are also of unique importance in illuminating certain aspects of the atomic bomb experience. Given the special ordeal they confronted, and its various binds and vicious circles, we shall hardly be surprised to discover that they met with considerable frustration and failure. Yet such were the special dimensions of their task that, even in failure, they teach us much about the overall problem of the great man and of the less-than-great man who becomes a leader.

I shall summarize seven different life patterns, the first six as brief vignettes and the last in more detail, in order to suggest styles of leadership which have developed from atomic bomb exposure. My list is by no means complete, nor are the styles depicted always absolutely distinguishable from one another. But they do suggest the various ways in which leaders have been able to live out inner imagery of death and rebirth, and to do so in a manner that could be imparted, however imperfectly, to followers.

1) *The Heroic Response*

Of enormous importance to victims of a large catastrophe is the kind of leader who, immediately and totally, applies himself to the task of combating the assaults upon the environment and sustaining life. This style of leadership was epitomized by a Hiroshima city official, at the time of the bomb in his late thirties and serving in a section concerned with wartime distribution of food and other goods. Hiroshima-born, he had, despite a family background of no special distinction, achieved elite status through Japan's competitive educational channels, obtaining a degree from a department within Tokyo University that has trained generations of national leaders. This elite sense, along with a quality of physical and mental discipline that had made him an outstanding athlete in his youth, may have influenced his sudden mobilization of energy in the face of the radical disorganization and demoralization surrounding him. In any case, he became the city's great post-bomb provider—of food, clothing, and whatever could be made available to keep people alive.

Finding the City Office in flames when he arrived there immediately after the bomb fell (he had been at his home three thousand meters from the hypocenter), he quickly set up a temporary headquarters in a building still standing. There he worked and slept, and from his makeshift office he went everywhere in the city, walking and riding among the dead, and encouraging the living. Learning that the mayor was dead and observing that many older officials were incapable of effective action, he simply—without thought or hesitation—took over:

> They say I shouted at and directed the deputy mayor and other officials who were my superiors. I did not know I was doing this, as I was working like a man in a dream.

He demonstrated great ingenuity in locating goods and getting them to people who needed them, along with unusual human skills in exhorting and shaming apathetic and even resistive people (city employees and soldiers) to help in his crusade—again with that special intensity of total absorption:

I cannot say how much I devoted myself to the work, but I do know that for the year I was doing it, I simply was not aware of whether I was living or not.

Intrinsic to his leadership was his personal experience of the kinds of psychological suffering characteristic for survivors in general. While carrying out his herculean task and living at his office, he had little contact with his immediate family other than briefly checking to make sure they were all right. But a few days after the bomb an urgent note summoned him to the bedside of his dying father-in-law, abruptly reminding him of family responsibilities ("Strange to say, until that incident I had no thought of my relatives"). He made the painful decision of remaining at his work, and did not reach his father-in-law's house until after the latter's death, though he did take a few hours off to attend an improvised funeral service. He was left with strong feelings of guilt ("I still feel miserable about it"), and in a later memoir referred to neglect of family duties as "my great blind spot" and described lifelong "confusion" over conflicting demands of family life and public service—a classic individual conflict within East Asian tradition.

Also in the manner of other survivors, he became "terrified" about his own bodily state when his white blood count, taken because of the persistence of suspicious symptoms, was reported to be markedly low; but instead of submitting to the complete rest in the country that was recommended, he found a compromise solution in continuing to direct distribution procedures while confining himself to the City Office. He was also capable of considerable despair—first at the news of Japan's surrender ("I envied those of my fellow officials who were dead"), and then at the combined assaults let loose upon Hiroshima ("When I looked at the burned ruins, and then the flood, I simply did not know what to do").

He was, however, unusually sensitive to suggestions of rebirth—whether in the form of flower buds of the first post-bomb spring ("these had special meaning for us"); visits from members of the Royal Family, particularly the Emperor ("It is something like a child who, having a hard time in a stranger's country, craves to see his parents. . . . I was completely moved"); or simply evidence of the most modest reassertion of life in the city. And like a number of other Japanese leaders, he was also responsive to international programs of spiritual rebirth, particularly the Moral Rearmament Movement, with its combined stress upon individual guilt and public attainment.

Repeatedly elected to high city office during the postwar period, he was able to apply his energies to the more methodical tasks connected with rebuilding Hiroshima. He combined his determination to "turn calamity into good fortune" (as a popular Japanese saying he was fond of quoting puts it) with skills in negotiation and compromise necessary for dealings with the Japanese national government, the American Occupation authorities, and various survivor groups. Withal, he retained fierce local loyalties not only to the people but the geographical site of the city; and when some suggested that rather than building on such a scorched and devastated area, it would be better to "leave this place as it is and obtain an entirely different and more adequate spot on which to reconstruct a completely new city," he commented with some pride that people were making their own decision on the matter by rebuilding their homes and putting up new shacks on that very scorched and devastated area. Nor did the people of Hiroshima fail to notice that he and his family were forced to undergo considerable personal deprivation when Occupation authorities required him to set a personal example by prohibiting his wife from purchasing food at the black market, then used by almost everyone in the struggle to get enough to eat.

Over the years he applied his talent for what might be called psychohistorical mediation to the painful decisions Hiroshima was required to make about the problem of memorializing the bomb. He responded simultaneously to the international interest in the city's unique experience, the complex feelings of *hibakusha* about any form of ceremony, and the civic and economic pressures upon the city to put its past behind it. Thus, discussing Hiroshima's larger responsibilities, he told me:

> This experience should not be just confined to us. It is a great and significant experience—it should be shared with the world.

But a little later his emphasis was somewhat different:

> My real feeling about Hiroshima is to make it a city of brightness. In terms of geography and climate it has many advantages. It has beautiful surroundings, and we are very fortunate in this. Now I would like to emphasize the inner lives of citizens—to develop a bright and forward-looking city population.

Throughout he demonstrated a flexibly autonomous political talent (at one point he left his party and broadened his support by becoming an independent); a capacity to blend effectively postwar principles of democratic government (with which he was strongly identified) and traditional Japanese stress upon personal ties of obligation and dependency; and a continuingly passionate commitment to small and large *hibakusha* problems.

This city official has been able to lead by living out the classical pattern of the hero: first the "call" or "summons"—the atomic bomb itself—which is at the same time an immediate "awakening of the self"; then the "road of trials," in which terrible obstacles, especially that of death, are met and overcome; there was even, in the death of his father-in-law, a symbolic "atonement with the father," in which the hero reasserts his paternal bond even as he transcends it; and finally, his achievement for himself and particularly for his people of "the freedom to live."[4] His initial heroism was that of "action response," a capacity, in relationship to crisis, to convert inner interpretation into active confrontation so quickly that there is not even time to formulate conscious convictions. This quality was reflected by his tendency, during our talks together, to punctuate his words with facial and bodily movements in a manner (unusual for Japanese) that suggested impatience with any gap between thought and action.

But also significant was his protean style of self-process,[5] an inner fluidity which permitted him to draw upon old strengths and old identity components (related to Japanese and Hiroshima tradition) while at the same time embracing new currents and bold innovations. In addition, it permitted him to experience, inwardly and publicly, the entire gamut of survivor conflicts, so that all *hibakusha* could share in his individual death-and-rebirth symbolism and in some measure identify with his heroic exploits. The same protean style contributed to his mediating skills by enabling him to touch and feel all of the complex convolutions of atomic bomb controversy, and then make compromises in the service of renewed community life.

In all these ways he has helped *hibakusha* to move beyond preoccupation with misery, to enlarge their identity without denying it. But he, too, faces the inevitable burden of guilt: over survival priority, as epitomized in the episode of his father-in-law's death; and later over "selling his name" or "selling the bomb." These latter accusations were made readily by his political opponents as the luster of his early heroism dimmed before the moral compromise inherent in everyday politics; they were believed by some of his fellow *hibakusha*, and inevitably struck raw nerves in their target. But if these currents of guilt sometimes weakened his heroic pattern, they did not prevent him from achieving what has been perhaps the most prolonged and successful pattern of individual leadership that has yet occurred among those exposed to the atomic bomb.

2) *The Mystical Healer*

A very different style of life-sustaining leadership was exemplified by an elderly married lady who has achieved notable distinction in Hiroshima through organizing a *hibakusha* group dedicated solely to excursions to the hot springs resorts in the area. What appeared to be a matter of simple physical and spiritual balm turned out to be much more. Lame from an old A-bomb injury, large in her dimensions, and outspoken in her opinions, she created an imposing figure as she described the development of her group.

Her first version was a more or less "logical" one. Having sustained multiple bodily injuries and bone fractures from the bomb, she emerged from twenty months of hospitalization with one leg considerably shortened. Three years later she began to suffer continuously from what she looked upon as "A-bomb disease": mainly a severely eczematous skin condition, but also persistent upper-respiratory and recurrent gastrointestinal symptoms, and general aches and pains. After she had experienced these symptoms for about six years, her husband convinced her to try hot springs bathing, recalling his own remarkable benefits from the baths years before when afflicted with a chronic illness. She had never cared for the baths and agreed to try them only out of desperation, but was profoundly impressed by the improvement they brought about in her condition. After three weeks she felt completely well, and then began to return to the hot springs resort regularly, noting that her symptoms tended to recur if she stayed away too long. She began to recommend the "treatment" to friends and acquaintances suffering from what were thought to be A-bomb effects, soon found herself arranging informal group trips, and finally, with the help of her husband and partly through their own financial contributions, set up a structured organization which eventually came to include several thousand *hibakusha*.

But there was a second version I was to hear in subsequent interviews which, while in no way contradicting the first, revealed the much less rational and more fundamental psychological processes involved. This version centered upon death and survival ("There were at least ten times when I thought it was all over with me, that I would not live"), upon supernatural intervention ("a path God has given me"), and upon a vision of an "enormous black Buddha" which she experienced when hospitalized and close to death:

> . . . it [the Buddha] was . . . in a *zazen* position.* . . . The more I looked at it, the bigger it seemed to get—and the strange thing was that it was absolutely black. I thought . . . I was about to die, so I said: "It is all over with me. I am now praying before a black Buddha."

Upon arriving at the hot springs resort some time later, she learned that there was a shrine nearby for a Buddha who was said to have come out of the hot springs about two thousand years ago, containing a statue of him that could be seen and worshiped only once in thirty years. She then inquired as to whether it was black and covered with dust, as had been the one in her vision, and was told, "Yes, it is buried in dust, since it is exhibited only once in thirty years." Further information she obtained about its facial and bodily features convinced her that it was "exactly like the Buddha I had seen" and that "this is really the guidance of God."

Similarly, the "logical" group benefits she spoke of earlier—fatigue replaced by a sense of well-being, opportunities for elderly *hibakusha* to relax, do traditional dances together, and unburden themselves to one another—give way to accounts of miraculous cures: a woman whose face had been so distorted by keloids that her mouth was twisted out of shape and she could not open her eyes had her mouth restored to its normal position so that she could open and close her eyes without difficulty; *hibakusha* had very low white blood counts dramatically return to normal; others who had been unable to breathe because of severe respiratory ailments suddenly breathed easily; and so on.

She summarized what she had accomplished with a combination of awe ("All this is a great source of wonder to me . . . a country woman with no education and no special abilities") and a pride that was by no means modest ("I am the first person in the world to advocate hot springs bathing for *hibakusha*"). She stressed her precedence over orthodox medical circles in creating the program, and was resentful of doctors' initial skepticism toward it; but she was visibly pleased by the

---

* Classical sitting position for Buddhist meditation, with legs and thighs interwound, sometimes called "Lotus position."

grudging approval eventually given her program by some medical and welfare circles because of its observable benefits.

Turning to her past life, she described the kind of childhood one is likely to encounter in female saints and shamans, including the female shamans who abound in traditional Japanese folk religion: great loneliness and unhappiness (she was brought up in an isolated farming area, her mother died when she was a very young child, and she was burdened early with unpleasant responsibilities); emotional distance from others, thought to be related to the possession of some special quality (she was looked upon as being "different" and unusually "sensitive"); and exposure to an early emphasis upon spiritual purity by a meaningful person (her father was an unusually devout Buddhist who exhorted her to "always live wholeheartedly," a characteristic Japanese plea for sincerity and dedication). But not everyone with that kind of background becomes a saint, shaman, or healer, and her childhood and adult married life had been quite unremarkable until encountering the atomic bomb. She thought of this encounter as "the greatest event in my life," the stimulus for her religious immersion ("I thought I had come to the extreme point—the very end—and there was absolutely nothing to depend upon but religion").

She came to look upon herself as a mystical healer who had been put through what was "not a common human experience," which invested her with supernatural qualities ("My coming across this would not have been possible through ordinary human power"), and she implied that her very presence caused others to derive healing benefits. But underneath these convictions there was a suggestion of defensiveness and uncertainty—in phrases that she used such as "this may sound strange," "some people may not believe me," and "this seems odd to say in an age when men are flying off into space," as well as in her apparent conflict about how much of her supernatural identification to reveal to her friends and followers.

Hence we may say that she emerged as a leader through an ordeal of illness in which she seemed to enter the realm of the dead and return from it, and to do so in a way that made contact with widely shared themes within her cultural tradition. This is the classical mode of the shaman and of the mystical healer. And it is likely that these shamanistic qualities are unconsciously conveyed even to those in her group who know nothing about her religious vision.[6] Also involved is imagery of "therapeutic waters"—particularly strong in Japan but found everywhere—which once more reverts to the idea of water as a life-giving, death-defeating substance; and to related mythological beliefs of gods or heroes who emerge from a particular body of water (in this case the Buddha who came out of the hot springs) to magically work their cures.

She has thus made the hot springs resorts her group frequents into healing shrines, something on the order of the Catholic shrine at Lourdes, at which the themes of magic, faith, and group intimacy in varying proportions operate with considerable force. But the tone of defensiveness mentioned before suggests that her own belief in her personal myth is far from complete, and that she is troubled by an incomplete "fit" between this personal myth and the social field in which it is expressed. That is, her own relationships to rationality and science on the one hand, and to the supernatural and the miraculous on the other, are deeply ambivalent. Her resulting reluctance to reveal the full content of her emotional experience may be in some ways prudent, but it inevitably places strong limits on her power as a mystical healer and as a leader in general. Also contributing to this limitation is the general suspiciousness in Hiroshima (which she herself shares) that any such "cure" is likely to be counterfeit.

3) *The Spiritual Authority*

A third type of leader is a more conventional interpreter of spiritual matters. The Buddhist priest whom we have referred to before, for instance, has called upon existing theological principles in his emergence as a prominent spokesman on matters concerning the bomb. I found him to be a tall, erect man in his sixties who, despite a definite air of authority, immediately adopted a tense and surprisingly personal tone in discussing all atomic bomb issues. For his own exposure, and the impressive circumstances surrounding it, became the source of whatever power his leadership contained.

At the time of the bomb he had been kneeling in prayer at his temple seventeen hundred meters from the hypocenter, so that he could maintain his religious imagery even as "everything crumbled around me," and had the immediate thought: "Now I am going to undergo an ordeal." While at first "this feeling made me calm," he was frank to admit that he could not maintain his calm in relationship to what he witnessed immediately afterward—"members of my own family dying, and many others dying also"—so that "although I thought I had strong faith . . . when confronted with the reality of all of this death . . . I became uneasy, filled with worry, and with a sense of emptiness." And during those post-bomb days he found himself in the predicament of a spiritual authority who was himself deeply confused:

> I had to say something to encourage people . . . but I myself didn't really have confidence in the encouragement I was giving them . . . because I didn't know anything about the A-bomb. . . . Although I encouraged them, I really didn't know when many of them might die. . . .

His solution was to tell them that "If we die, we die together." But he knew this to be inadequate, and his statement about people's capacity for belief at the time—"If it had been possible for a person to have faith, he would have wished to have such faith"—suggested the extreme difficulty all faced in maintaining a prescribed religious interpretation of what they were experiencing. But although his own confusion and inner terror were no less than the next person's, he found the strength to feel that "in one way or another we simply had to live." When conventional theology failed, he resorted to more simple and direct forms of human encouragement ("Don't be like that—you shouldn't be defeated by a little thing like the A-bomb"); and he set a personal example of effort and ingenuity in foraging for food, growing it himself, and in obtaining the "things" he emphasized as necessary for life.

Behind this strength lay a beginning formulation of his survival which channeled his guilt and put it to psychological use:

I asked myself the question, "Why was I saved?" Thinking of my situation—the bomb falling while I was in the midst of prayer in the main temple, and the enormous pillars in this large building which collapsed almost completely—I had to conclude that it would have been quite natural for me to have died. It was strange that I still lived. And when these huge pillars fell and the ceiling collapsed on top of me, there was an opening above me . . . if something had come through that opening it would have hit my head and killed me. But nothing did. I found that I could stand up so that half of my body came out through the opening; this was because a roof-tile had been blasted away to create it. I simply pulled myself out through the opening and was saved. When I thought about this, I could only feel that it was a miracle. I felt that someone who should have died had been saved. I was living, though I did not know why. I thought that my having survived was not through my own efforts, but that an outside force had brought it about, and allowed me to live. This gave me a feeling of mission. I thought there must be some mission for which I had survived. . . .

This sense of a special "mission" made possible by a "miracle" was widespread among *hibakusha*, but his position and theological background led him to carry it further than most. Regarding himself as one "obliged to serve . . . in a higher cause," he described feeling a "new source of light, which allowed me to recover myself and surge back . . . a call to keep on living." He attributed to this "call" the energy he brought to the difficult task of rebuilding his own temple, which he looked upon as a "spiritual pillar" to sustain the people of Hiroshima.

Over the years he felt the need to carry his formulation further into Buddhist thought, and came to relate the atomic bomb to the concept of *mayoi*, of being lost or straying. He thought of the bomb as "an expression of the fact that human beings were in the dark, unable to find the light of truth . . . the extreme indication of how strong this

mayoi had become." Referring to Buddhist conceptions of "evil elements"—hell, hunger, beastliness, and strife—he concluded that "The
A-bomb came at a time when the world was furthest from Buddha, and
had absorbed these four evil elements as the maximum expression of
mayoi." And his prescription similarly followed traditional Buddhist
doctrine: "Man must come back to the posture of truth" as the only
way of attaining real peace, and "Man's basic task is to rid himself of
evil attachments." He favored the erection of a *bussharito*, or tower for
the ashes of Buddha (the ashes to be sent from India), and emphasized
that "We should not be overly concerned about Hiroshima" because
"the main point is to overcome within ourselves this attachment to
evil." Although he himself had participated quite actively in peace
movements, he criticized these because "they do not confront the real
mayoi—man's lost state," and stressed that "individual reawakening to
truth is essential for any peace movement." While it is difficult to
evaluate the general impact of his ideas, my impression was that they
were not widely understood or embraced, and that he was considerably
less successful as a long-term conventional spiritual authority than he
had been during his more informal leadership immediately after the
bomb.

:

We may thus say that his greatest effectiveness as a leader derived
from his early capacity to mobilize his guilt into a Buddhist-derived
sense of special "mission," and then experience and communicate to
others a "call to life" in a way that emphasized the *hibakusha*'s right and
even duty to remain alive. But once this spontaneous early formulation
hardened into the contours of classical religious theory, his leadership
became much less impelling—particularly so during a historical period
in which Japanese in general find most conventional Buddhist practice
to be stagnant and ritualistic. Indeed, these abstract theological principles cannot contain his own still powerful feelings of guilt and despair
which clearly emerge in his emotionally charged recollections. He
undoubtedly maintains considerable sway over his followers, but his
"ordinary" spiritual interpretation of the bomb cannot adequately deal
with its extraordinary impact.

4) *The Scientific Authority*

Interpretation through scientific rather than theological authority creates another form of leadership particularly important in dealing with the effects of a "scientific product" such as the atomic bomb. The physicist we have quoted before has been prominent in Hiroshima not only for his academic position but for his active involvement in atomic bomb social questions and peace movements. A middle-aged man who was at first somewhat reserved with me and possibly a little suspicious about the nature of my work, he became increasingly responsive and outspoken during two lengthy interviews. Even when assuming an attitude of scientific detachment, his own passionate involvement in atomic bomb problems broke through.

Three guilt-laden features of his experience greatly affected his later behavior and style of leadership. The first was his intimate relationship with the pre-bomb militaristic regime as a consultant and enthusiastic supporter, a relationship to which he constantly referred. The second was the intensity of his death anxiety (we remember his feeling that "the world is ending") and his guilt in relationship to the death of two colleagues: one whom he later thought he should have attempted to help, and the other, his senior professor, whom he did help—carrying him to a hospital, unsuccessfully trying artificial respiration, spending a night with the body in the open before it was cremated, and then remaining with the dead professor's family for an entire week, all the time behaving and feeling much as a son does in relationship to his father. The third, and unique, feature of his experience was his professional error in asserting that an atomic bomb had not fallen on Hiroshima when military authorities sought his opinion concerning the short-wave radio announcement (from America) that one had. Although he soon reversed himself, and although aware that the general confusion was a mitigating factor (he told me that even a much more famous physicist sent from Tokyo a day later made more erroneous scientific statements), he nonetheless retained the inner burden of a man who, when thrust into a position of sudden responsibility during his early thirties, made an incorrect judgment with perhaps damaging consequences. We are not surprised that following all this the surrender message had an overwhelming impact upon him:

> I felt the entire structure of my life crumble. I decided to quit the university . . . because I felt that my work and everything else was meaningless. Physically, the structure of the school was destroyed, so it seemed meaningless to stay at the university . . . but this collapse of the foundation of my life was much more a psychological sentiment than anything else. Many said they felt a sense of relief with the end of the war. I did not have this feeling myself. During wartime . . . I just simply and naïvely went along with the military leaders and went on with my work. . . . This loss of a sense of meaning in my life was a very personal feeling, a loss of a sense of anything I could rely on . . . a kind of despair. Before this I had hope and felt it in the significance of the work I was doing. Now, my work was terminated and I felt a complete loss of hope. . . .

He grieved, in other words, for the symbolic integrity of his life, as well as for his dead colleagues. But he did not leave the university. The professional challenge of rebuilding his department, both its physical plant and its personnel, served as a stimulus to his individual rebirth. Once more he was thrust into a position of formidable responsibility ("At the age of thirty-four or thirty-five I was at the very center of this rebuilding program"), but this time he discharged it with considerable success and in a way that reasserted his sense of dignity as a scientist.

Yet his capacity to integrate atomic bomb problems with his scientific identity came slowly. He had a simultaneous feeling of having been "defeated in the scientific field" by American superiority and of being implicated in what might be called "scientific guilt" ("I felt that science had a lot to do with this enormous destruction"), suggesting that even one on the receiving end of the atomic bomb can *as a physicist* (in Oppenheimer's phrase) "know sin." His difficulties were compounded by his own bodily fears. Since he found that these fears were intensified by his scientific knowledge of the bomb, it is possible that they in turn blocked further knowledge ("I had no true feeling of the reality [of the bomb] in relationship to radiation until two or three years later")— though one must also keep in mind the general ignorance concerning this issue during early post-bomb years. In any case, science provided him with a sense of survival-justifying mission, not unlike that of the Buddhist priest:

I feel a special obligation, a kind of mission, both in relationship to my own experience and because of being a physicist. My point is not simply to stress the greatness or largeness of the effects of the weapon, but rather its special quality, the ways in which it differs so much from other weapons, and in this sense I feel an urge to tell people about it, especially as a physicist.

This mission required that he expand his scientific identity and become, as he put it, "knowledgeable in social science as well"—which for a Japanese intellectual at that time meant a study of Marxism and affiliation with various leftist groups, in his case those concerned most directly with the peace movement. His sense of being a scientist was still crucial to him, but he now concluded that "science sometimes had a very good influence, sometimes not, depending upon its sponsorship," and he became concerned with the need to bridge "the enormous gap between the masses and the intellectuals." His embrace of Marxism followed what was again for Japanese intellectuals a fairly characteristic shift from a "restorationist" (in political terms, rightist) to a "transformationist" (leftist) stance; and although important emotional patterns remained unchanged, the shift helped him restore his sense of integrity.[7] He eventually came into conflict, however, with not only communist dogma but competing communisms, and he eventually came to a somewhat disillusioned, slightly more eclectic position. Yet he retained throughout a science-related emphasis upon the unique significance of Hiroshima, a belief that "there is a special historic destiny which Hiroshima had been given in relationship to atomic energy, and that atomic energy has a special role to play in changing or converting mankind and influencing human culture."

And it was as a scientist that he came to his general conclusions about nuclear weapons—about their destructiveness ("I know that the weapon itself changed the nature of war . . . not just in quantity but in quality as well"); about their use ("We scientists don't ordinarily use the word 'absolute,' but in this case I feel we have the right to do so, and to say that nuclear weapons should *absolutely* never be used under any circumstances whatsoever"); and in comparison with other man-made death immersions ("Auschwitz shows us how cruel man can be to man, an example of extreme human cruelty—but Hiroshima shows us how cruel man can be through science, a new dimension of cruelty"). His continuous dual emphasis upon *hibakusha* and scientific identities was contained in his assertion that he feels it necessary for him to take the initiative in nuclear problems "because I experienced the bomb myself, and because I am a scientist and know about these weapons."

:

In general, he remained a highly respected scientific spokesman on A-bomb problems, but a much more controversial figure concerning his political involvements. As in the case of the Buddhist priest, there were suggestions of residual fear, guilt, and despair which undoubtedly interfered with his leadership. But his status as a scientific interpreter exposed him, in addition, to the god-devil emotions which surround science and scientists, a polarity universally experienced in our contemporary world but especially strong in Hiroshima. There the tendency is to place those scientists who have in any way contributed to the construction and use of nuclear weapons among the devils, and those who have used their knowledge to do battle with these weapons among the gods. But it is always possible for some of the "devil imagery" to spill over onto even those scientists who fit into the "god group," so that a physicist among *hibakusha* can both exert particularly strong influence and arouse considerable ambivalence and doubt. In this case, moreover, we suspect that being thrust into a god role creates special problems for one still struggling with painful memories of having been all too fallible and "human" in his judgment and his behavior both at the time of the bomb and before that. Overriding everything is the sense, in the physicist himself as well as in his followers, that science—physical or social—is incapable of supplying a precise formula for mastering the atomic bomb experience or its related international dilemmas.

5) *The Moralist*

Moral protest itself can become the philosophical center of interpretation and action, as was true of the leadership style of a *hibakusha* philosopher-activist also prominent on the Hiroshima academic and political scene. Elderly but vigorous, his rather "soft" manner was accompanied by a straight-backed posture of determination, and at the beginning of our talk he struck a somewhat unexpected note of self-questioning: "The more I look into the A-bomb problem, the more I realize how much I do not know about it." He also spoke of the humanitarian concerns which motivated his early involvement in the problem (he originally worked with A-bomb orphans) and have remained at the center of his thought: "Just talking with one girl [who lost both parents and was left with a keloid scar]—only with her—you feel that . . . we should stop the bomb."

He too had been closely associated with the military regime prior to the bomb, as a professor of ethics who indoctrinated students with "love of nation" and with "dedication to victory." More than anyone else I interviewed, he directly emphasized his residual sense of guilt over this association as a stimulus for later peace activities:

> Ever since the defeat . . . I have had in my mind the idea of atoning for my mistakes . . . and during all the time that I have worked for peace, this idea has been prominent within me.

He could nonetheless make use of a portion of his earlier restorationist ideology ("We used to stress the feeling of living together in a community—of family or clan or race or nation—which shared the same destiny in life and death") to derive a more inclusive world view and sense of shared human identity ("but with the atomic age, past conceptions of the world are inadequate, and I now look upon all of mankind as a community sharing this same destiny of life and death").

In his immersion in the struggles and conflicts of the peace movement, his particularly severe stands against American actions were influenced by both organizational policy (domination of the movement by groups hostile to the United States), and by personal memories (he had been seriously injured by the bomb and had lost the function of one eye). But he eventually took a strong position against any "double standard" concerning Soviet or American (and later Chinese) nuclear testing, stressing that "I feel rage in both cases—there is not so much difference." To be sure, his use of "so much" suggests that he does inwardly feel *some* difference; in any case, his integrity in such matters was recognized even by his political opponents.

Over the years he engaged in virtually every form of protest—mass meetings, marches, petitions, and manifestoes—but shortly before I met him he had adopted a new technique to express his opposition to a series of American nuclear tests: that of simply sitting before the Cenotaph in the Peace Park and encouraging others to sit with him. In doing so, he followed classical Zen practice, holding a Buddhist rosary and sitting in the *zazen* position, quite fatiguing for the uninitiated, though not so for him because "I have been used to [sitting this way] since my student days." Although a number did join him, particularly among the devout, he later thought that "if I had held on to my knees in a more relaxed way [that is, in a way that did not suggest a religious mode] many laborers might have come, so I don't know if I did the right thing or not."

But his sitting in that manner was connected with traditional Japanese feelings to which he also gave expression: the philosophical doctrine of spirit over matter. He thus told how, during the third day of his protest, a little girl approached him and asked, "Can you stop it by sitting?" Struck by the profundity of the question, he evolved and publicly proclaimed that "A chain reaction of spiritual atoms must defeat the chain reaction of material atoms." He went on to equate the splitting of the nucleus of matter with the much more difficult task of "splitting the nucleus of the human—the ego," the latter also a Zen principle. And he emphasized that "once you sit for ten minutes, not for yourself but for others, as an instrument of human help, then you lose ego." He was not above a little self-mockery concerning his own moral earnestness, and was quite proud of having been labeled (by an American writer) "a human reactor." But he was profoundly serious in his conviction that there was no alternative to spiritual protest, since "If it cannot stop war, mankind will be destroyed—so we must go on doing it." Underlying these philosophical assumptions was his sense of serving, and drawing support from, the A-bomb dead:

There is something special about sitting in Hiroshima in front of this cenotaph—I sat there on behalf of the dead, two hundred thousand people, on behalf of the "voiceless voices."*

* The phrase "voiceless voices" (*koe ga nai no koe*) has been popularly used for any group not readily heard. It gained great national currency during the mass

He went on to emphasize the special significance of the *hibakusha* experience per se, and at the time we talked was engaged in compiling a large number of recollections of it for publication three years later on the twentieth anniversary of the dropping of the A-bomb. He would sometimes idealize *hibakusha* emotions in such claims as "Every *hibakusha* deep in his heart has the sincere desire that this should not happen to anyone else" and "The ultimately reliable people in the peace movement are the *hibakusha* themselves." Yet he also recognized impediments in *hibakusha* participation in peace activities—"they don't want to remember . . . and what they went through is inexpressible"— and he knew that the "spreading fire" (he used the Buddhist term *tobihi*) of his form of protest had not spread very far. He closed our talk, much as he had opened it, with a combined tone of determination and confusion, emphasizing that he still felt "a very strong urge" to work for his humanitarian goals, but was completely at a loss as to what kind of new projects might be most effective in confronting the "really extremely difficult problem" of actualizing Hiroshima's special potential for contributing to world peace.

:

We may thus say that as a moralist and a philosopher of protest, he had come to an impasse involving personal as well as historical dimensions. While his strong reassertion of classical forms of Japanese identity and ideology was a great source of strength to him, and undoubtedly saved him from the psychological limbo in which many rebellious Japanese intellectuals have found themselves, it also created profound problems in leadership. For not only did it cause conflict (within himself as well as his followers) with prevailing currents strongly opposed to these very traditional forms, but it left him with a philosophical idiom (spirit over matter) hardly adequate to the task he set for himself, and with a dichotomy between the two which both contemporary physics and philosophy increasingly look upon as false. A man who seems never free from despair, he finds psychic replenishment in his commitment to genuinely felt universalism, his concrete focus upon alleviation of individual suffering, and perhaps most of all in his sense of continuity with atomic bomb dead. But these cannot free him from inner feelings of death guilt or from his own and others' suspicion

---

demonstrations of 1960, when Prime Minister Kishi employed it to characterize his allegedly silent supporters. After that it was used mockingly by his opponents, and here the moralist reclaims the phrase for what he considers a properly serious meaning.

of counterfeit nurturance, nor can they overcome larger historical patterns of moral contradiction and ideological narrowness within the peace movement in general. He thus remains a highly revered figure in Hiroshima whom not too many follow, a man whose integrity and determination are of great symbolic importance to *hibakusha* but not to the extent of convincing them that mastery of the atomic bomb experience lies in the direction of protest.

6) "A-Bomb Victim Number One"

Leadership may also take a form we may term "bodily protest," as in the case of the souvenir vendor we have already referred to, known widely in Hiroshima as "A-Bomb Victim Number One." His small shop was located next to the shack in which he lived, very close to the Dome, and many of the post cards and souvenirs he sold had A-bomb themes. Further, he was known to enter readily into discussions about the atomic bomb with Japanese and American visitors, and on occasion to take off his shirt and demonstrate the extensive keloids on his chest. These activities have led many to point to him as the arch example of "selling the bomb"; and he has received additional public attention from his active participation in protest meetings and in a grass-roots *hibakusha* organization he helped to found.

Tall, heavy-set, robust-looking, with long unruly hair, his flamboyant manner and relaxed movements made one unaware of the claw-like deformity of one of his hands and the general keloid formation on the other as well. He was at first slightly wary of my possible political connections, but when informed of the purposes of my work, he spoke freely, indeed volubly, with the articulate skills of a raconteur. In describing his background, he told how his father, despite being an eldest son, had been denied the family inheritance in a rural area near Hiroshima because of being judged "financially incompetent"—a label the father proceeded to live out as he drifted from one small business venture to another ("whatever enterprise he tried to start would fail") until finally achieving a certain amount of prestige as a rightist-adventurer in Manchuria, a kind of minor administrator of the plans and plots of the military clique there. While the vendor remembered having little respect for his chronically absent father, he did recall a certain amount of affection for him and spoke of him as having been "large-bellied" (*futoppara*), that is, bold and magnanimous. It was his "good mother," however, a strict and orderly woman and a devout Christian, who took almost full responsibility for his upbringing, and who arranged for him to be baptized and trained in Christian principles.

He had limited schooling, and after a certain amount of technical training he made his way (partly following in his father's footsteps) into the more or less floating element of the Japanese working-class culture in Tokyo, moving easily from place to place and job to job, embracing the Marxism then being widely disseminated in these groups. Despite having known a certain amount of economic hardship, he could later look back on that decade of his young adult life with considerable nostalgia. Returning to Hiroshima for military service and civilian technical work supporting the war effort, his leftist ideology dissolved under the strong group pressures of coercion and enthusiasm mounted by the military regime, and he experienced what was known as *tenkō*, a form of *volte-face* or political conversion (really closer to "backsliding") common among Japanese intellectuals and workers at the time.

Running throughout his early life was a pattern of rebelliousness toward all agencies of authority, but a rebelliousness that was constantly thwarted: when in conflict with his father, he withdrew, and then eventually adopted many of his father's ways; originally opposed to rightist thought, he later embraced it; when doing his military service, he was appalled by the gratuitous brutality he observed, but adapted himself to it without protest; and when he objected to hypocritical behavior on the part of Christian authorities, he simply drifted away from Christianity. He was unable to commit himself to any authority sufficiently to find personal stability within the balance of obligation and dependency required by his culture. The easygoing pattern of self-indulgence which he adopted, however, was to become modified by pre-bomb fears, and the attitude which resulted was expressed in a motto he and his friends adopted: "We might as well die with a healthy color."

He admitted that "I trembled with fear," and the contours of the severe burns sustained on his hands were related to his having, at the moment the bomb fell, "instinctively" squatted and thrown his hands protectively around the back of his head. Exposed at fifteen hundred meters, he was able to dig himself and his wife out of the debris in which they had been buried, but he experienced a painful ordeal, with extreme residual guilt, in relationship to the death of his father. For during this initial period "I did not think of my father"; and when he found him nearby, naked, bleeding, almost unrecognizable, he was unable (injured as he was himself) to support both his wife and the older man in crossing a nearby river to flee the city. He therefore left his father by the river bank, and heard from a neighbor who brought his remains ("These are your father's bones") that he had died shortly thereafter at an aid station to which he had been taken.

The vendor himself spent more than five years in hospitals, mostly because of his severe burns and external injuries, though he also remembers being told that both his red and white blood counts were at first very low and that he was considered on several occasions to be close to death. Because of the severity and prototypical nature of his injuries, he was frequently singled out for demonstration to visiting Japanese and American medical dignitaries, to which he seemed to react with mixed feelings of resentment and pride. And he himself initiated a series of struggles with hospital authorities over the way in which his case was handled. He raised particularly strong objection to discriminatory practices because he was a public charge rather than a paying patient, and insisted that doctors perform operation after operation to restore maximum function of his hands because "in order to work as a man in society . . . I wanted to leave the hospital only after being completely cured." Significantly, his protests did seem to improve the care he received, both in the form of new drugs, from which he recalls striking benefits, and in the innumerable surgical procedures performed on his hands. He also formed a small patient organization, which voiced collective concerns about inadequate food and sanitation, and exposed various kinds of petty corruption within the hospital. Looked upon by hospital officials as impertinent and demanding, he was finally more or less forced to leave by the cutting off of his welfare privileges.

According to his account, the idea for his souvenir stand came from an American officer with whom he had cooperated in submitting to demonstrations of his bodily injuries; the same officer helped obtain approval for the stand to be set up in an area close to the hypocenter. He also describes American complicity in his being unofficially designated "A-Bomb Victim Number One," smilingly referring to a group of American journalists who interviewed him in the hospital as "godparents" in the christening, and specifically attributing the term to one of the American group. Again his attitude about being singled out for this kind of distinction was ambivalent ("I didn't know whether I should feel grateful or not"). He claimed that he disliked the name and found it "embarrassing," but added: "I can do nothing about it . . . and it somehow has become part of my being."

His organizing a *hibakusha* group was partly a result of the response to a diary he published concerning his A-bomb experiences. The book had significance for him not only in successfully reawakening a long-forgotten literary interest, but also in the pride he took in having been able to complete its actual writing by an idiosyncratic way of manipulating his pen with his injured hand (he had dictated the first portion of it) and in the development of a rather distinctive handwriting in the process. In any event, the letters and personal visits he received encouraged him, together with others, to create this organization of people who, he felt, shared "a common destiny" of suffering, and could now "encourage and console each other." He and his fellow leaders first turned for help to Christian groups in Hiroshima, Japanese and American, because these groups were particularly active in welfare programs and because they had material resources made possible by American contributions. But he rejected this affiliation, as he had once before in the past, and became highly critical of Japanese who became what he called "instant Christians" on the basis of "chocolate and clothes" they received, and who overcame their "strong inferiority complex" by "being able to speak with Americans in broken English . . . or by just walking with an American in the town." He was equally critical of Christian churchmen for imposing their own beliefs upon *hibakusha*, and utilizing them for their own purposes. But he nonetheless specifically compared his own activities in visiting fellow *hibakusha* and encouraging them to "unburden their hearts of their worries" to the work of Christian ministers.

He and his group sought to promote *hibakusha* interests by obtaining further medical treatment and wider economic benefits, and also allied themselves with militant forces within the peace movement in order to protest nuclear weapons testing. He emphasized to me that *hibakusha* had a special stake in nuclear problems because "we who have already been affected by radioactivity . . . are in more danger of our lives than are non*hibakusha*," and because "we *hibakusha* know what A- and H-bomb war really is and what would happen to mankind if there were a new war in the future." Concerning the power of these weapons, he echoed popular sentiment in insisting that "We *hibakusha* don't need the scientists to tell us this."

One group of scientists he attacked with particular fervor was the American-sponsored Atomic Bomb Casualty Commission. He demanded that the program be turned over to Japanese scientists, that *hibakusha* receive medical treatment instead of being examined only for research purposes, and that they receive financial remuneration for the time devoted to being examined. Whether or not he was the first to use the term "guinea pigs" in reference to the American group's treatment of *hibakusha*, as some believe, it became for him a clarion call, and (as we shall see later) took on enormous importance for overall Japanese-

American atomic bomb relations. He told of speaking to the head of the ABCC in the following terms:

> Most *hibakusha* have to work very hard to earn their daily living and support their families. When they come to your place, they spend half or even a whole day. In doing any research, even guinea pigs are fed, but you are treating us worse than guinea pigs—which means you are not treating us *hibakusha* as human beings. Since your research is made possible by *hibakusha* alone, since your guinea pigs are living, and since we are human beings, it should not be too much to ask you for some compensation.

Yet he favors more, rather than less, American involvement in *hibakusha* problems, urging that Americans who come to Hiroshima, instead of simply saying "I am sorry" or "Please forgive us," find a more useful "form of atonement and restitution for their sin" and "make reparations toward *hibakusha*" by creating a special center which would both provide jobs and arrange other employment for them.

As might be expected, his effectiveness as a leader has fluctuated greatly. Over a period of time he has become a convincing public speaker, and many have responded favorably to his hearty, often witty, workingman's style. Others have found him erratic, exhibitionistic, and self-promoting. One observer commented that "The great burden [of burns and injuries] he carries gives him the feeling that he is justified in making others yield to his opinions"—suggesting some of the difficulty he has had working with others.

When things were not going well with his leadership, as was true at the time of our interviews, he would experience periods of negativistic despair, lash out at rival peace movement leaders, and express a general sense of futility in everything he was doing. He described feeling personally abandoned because, concerning a threat of dispossession from his shack (in accordance with a city plan to turn the area into a park), "no one has seriously worried about me," and contrasted this neglect with his own spiritual and physical assistance to other *hibakusha* in the past. He directed much of his bitterness toward the two great nuclear powers for their continued testing (in 1962) and even gave voice to a version of the ultimate expression of retaliatory *hibakusha* hostility— "Perhaps America and Russia don't really know how terrible the A-bomb is, so if we dropped a bomb on, say, Red Square in Russia, and made them become victims for once, then they might understand a little better"—adding that he had often heard such things said by *hibakusha* but now for the first time found himself sympathetic to them. He went even further and spoke (with more anger than humor) of the idea of starting a "despair movement," in which *hibakusha* would cease their protests and tell the world: "You can go on making your nuclear tests, and if you are not satisfied with tests alone, you can go ahead and drop A-bombs and H-bombs."

:

While no single psychological cause can explain this despair, it can be looked upon as a generalized expression of the impotence we have noted in him before. For just as his exhortation of *hibakusha* to be vital and sensual was veiled by his own sexual "death," so may we say that his many forms of insistence upon *hibakusha* "rights" veiled an inner suspicion that both the goals and the quest were counterfeit. Thus, when accused of "selling the bomb," he would angrily point out that he was a poor man just managing to live and ask, "Why don't you try having burns as bad as mine, having your life hang by a thread, and then living through the painful conditions I have for the past seventeen years?" But he did so in a way that made clear that considerable guilt had been aroused. For in a man so much in need of recognition, being criticized and particularly being ignored (he had also undergone a loss of personal status in *hibakusha* organizations) can strongly exacerbate every form of prior potential for self-condemnation.

What strikes us about his leadership in general was that it revolved totally around the problem of counterfeit nurturance. From his first being selected as a "classic example" of atomic bomb injuries, he became something like the hypothetical man mentioned before who received the Nobel Prize for experiencing the atomic bomb: his prestige and power came to depend upon his having been victimized. Paradoxically, his severe atomic bomb exposure and prolonged hospitalization taught him a new way to deal with old conflicts over dependency, a way of giving in to a previously suppressed urge to be cared for and of mobilizing his antagonism to authority accompanying that urge. That is, with the atomic bomb, he found his métier, a means of expressing his previously thwarted rebelliousness in a manner both useful to himself (improving his medical treatment, etc.) and meaningful to a larger group. But in the process he came to symbolize the painful *hibakusha* · conflict over continuing demand and unrelenting suspiciousness toward that which is offered, precisely the problem of counterfeit nurturance.

His combination of injuries and psychic inclination toward exhibitionism enabled him to make his body almost literally speak for him. But while this could be done with some force, and he could relate his pleas to larger human problems of peace, the use of a damaged body in this way is ultimately profoundly humiliating—so that his leadership through bodily protest is still another symbolic expression of his struggle with impotence. Also deeply enmeshed in problems of counterfeit nurturance is his profoundly ambivalent relationship to America and Americans, his combination of closeness to and resentment of those who did so much to create his special "image" and his way of life, and from whom he continues to demand help. He even came to suspect as counterfeit his entire involvement with the militant peace movement (a suspicion, to be sure, encouraged by much of the dogmatism and ritual within that movement).

His strength as a leader lay in his capacity to use his own "big belly" —his largesse and general human skills—to live out every *hibakusha*'s problem over counterfeit nurturance. And there is no doubt that he has had considerable success in doing so; or that he has in the process achieved, and helped others to achieve, a considerable measure of autonomy, however compensatory his quest. But leadership so bound up with the negative equation of counterfeit nurturance (the more one wins, the more one loses) is bound to bog down in guilt and despair.

7) A-Bomb Zealot-Saint

A final style of leadership is that based upon absolute individual dedication to counteracting the "devilish" influences of the atomic bomb, as was true of another "common man," a thirty-four-year-old "day laborer" whom some in Hiroshima thought a fanatic, others a saint. He was known mostly as a leader of a children's group called the Folded Crane Club, which has carried on a broad range of activities—visiting hospitals to help A-bomb patients and to serve as a "family" for *hibakusha* dying of "A-bomb disease," providing various services (setting up chairs, sweeping halls, etc.) for peace meetings as well as participating in them, disseminating additional pleas for peace printed on a crude hand-operated mimeograph machine, conducting correspondences with children and peace spokesmen throughout the world, and greeting international visitors to Hiroshima with leis of folded paper cranes—with the day laborer himself always actively encouraging, instructing, and shepherding his flock.

The one-room shack which he and his wife occupied near the A-Bomb Dome also served as a clubhouse for the group. It was virtually devoid of furnishings or personal possessions but full of scrapbooks, mementos, and pictures, particularly of children who had died of A-bomb after-effects. Small and frail, looking considerably younger than his thirty-four years, he would sometimes (during a series of interviews) seem quiet and passive or smile in a childlike fashion. More often he was extraordinarily alert and intense as he generated the soft-voiced emotional electricity of his concerns and convictions about the atomic bomb, in relationship to which he never smiled.

A background of a special kind of deprivation had much to do with making him into the unique man he became. He spent his early childhood in a Japanese community in Peru. His father died when he was two years old, leaving him with a mixture of guilt ("I was born and he died") and of mythologized imagery of a near-martyr, who in serving as an assistant to a Catholic priest, "spent his last penny on the poor" and drove himself so hard that "he gave his life for his work." His being denied access to pictures or possessions of his father seemed to intensify his identification with him, and he told of later comments of his family friends to the effect that "my father's blood was running through my veins," and warnings that he "take care not to repeat my father's folly."

The special quality of this imagery was revealed in a strangely vivid memory of being taken, at the age of ten (just before leaving Peru for Japan), to his father's grave, where he was first shown "a large building in which the coffins were kept," where "I saw my father who had become a skeleton . . . and the clothes he had been wearing which had turned brown." The memory (which was probably a mixture of confabulation and actual experience) also included the recollection that "the cemetery was filled with wreaths of flowers"; it conveyed awe, dread, and festive beauty, along with the indelible impression "that my father must be someone with a very deep relationship to me."

Other legacies from his father were a Catholic baptism and the name "Angel" (or rather the Japonized version of the Spanish word) by which he was known through his early childhood.

His mother, a stern, hard-working woman whose life was a constant struggle against poverty, conveyed to him what might be termed a philosophy of emotional withholding, emphasizing that a child permitted too much *"amaeru"* (love, affection, dependency, or spoiling) becomes insensitive to others' needs. She also practiced this philosophy, and he still recalls with pain a general sense of love denied, as exemplified by his mother's failure to attend school meetings for parents, by her "not having the time" to prepare *sushi** for school outings "as other children's mothers did," and by residual bumps on his head which he equated with her having neglected to care for him properly (turn him over when necessary) as a baby. Though at times he justified her behavior ("I know what a severe life she had"), he was left with an impression of "what a terrible mother she was . . . because even toward a cat we feel protective and affectionate." She ignored her husband's Catholicism and brought the child up under the sway of a strict, fundamentalist Buddhism: on the one hand showing him ghastly pictures of emaciated people undergoing extreme suffering midst the horrors of Buddhist Hell, emphasizing that "if you do not do good things, this will happen to you"; and on the other, opposing the taking of life of any kind because "Buddha has mercy upon all creatures."

Gradually becoming aware of the "mothering" and "fathering" he was missing, and later of the antagonism toward his mother and himself

---

* Pats of raw fish (or vegetable) with rice, flavored with vinegar and spices, an indispensable element of children's (and adults') excursions.

emanating from his father's family, he came to feel himself, in a basic emotional sense, an abandoned child. He referred to himself, in retrospect, as "like a Korean boy in Japan" (a strong statement when one considers the discrimination and hatred the Japanese have directed at Koreans), and still experiences sadness and envy when observing babies receiving loving care from their mothers. He was also a "hungry child" (who, when scolded by his mother, would rush to a nearby banana field and "fill my stomach by eating bananas") as well as a "hoarding child" (who, rather than play with the few toys he received, would hide them in obscure places to make sure that no one stole them from him). These early tendencies take on particular significance in the light of his later reversal of them and his emergence as a "man without appetites." But even as a young child he had an urge to nurture others, as expressed in an ambition to become a department store manager who could set very low prices and "supply things of good quality" to all.

He developed two other characteristics probably necessary to leaders, though insufficiently studied as such. One was a quality of flexibility in sexual identity which cannot be dismissed as mere confusion. In addition to associating the name "Angel" with a feminine inclination, he enjoyed "playing girls' games with girls" and abhorred the fighting and violence of boys' games. These tendencies contributed both to later nurturing capacities and to a quality of psychobiological neutrality which made it possible to negate personal interests and enlarge his sphere of social response.

The second characteristic, probably closely related to the first, was a particular sensitivity to the problem of death. His father's early death as well as the various forms of supernatural Catholic and Buddhist imagery he was exposed to undoubtedly contributed to this sensitivity, but perhaps of equal importance was his experience of prolonged feelings of abandonment so profound as to constitute a symbolic death. In any case, early death anxiety was prominent, as expressed, for instance, in an intolerance for the scenes of bloodshed and death which occurred so prominently in Japanese period films. But accompanying this anxiety was a sense of himself as a savior.

He thus recalls an episode in which, at the age of nine or ten, he suddenly interrupted the play of a group of children in a closed-off room because he remembered a lesson from science class to the effect that without air, men die. He announced to the others that "we would die soon," and having initiated a general rush to open windows and doors, "I felt I had saved the lives of many children." This image of himself as one who could rescue others from death—who could provide life—contributed greatly to his lifelong inclination toward pity and nurturance for all those he felt to be oppressed—for the giant turtles in Peru he tried to protect from children's teasing, the Indian children he slipped free candies to when they came into his mother's store, the Koreans he befriended in Japan, and the hospitalized soldiers he voluntarily nursed at the age of eleven or twelve. But his attempts to do the same with his own mother when she became critically ill—to tend (as a boy of twelve) to her needs, to keep the family store (now in Japan) going in order to be able to pay for a doctor and at the same time continue to attend school—ended with the "failure" of her death and his resulting sense of guilt.

He then literally became a homeless waif ("From that time on I was alone in the world"). He worked sporadically at odd jobs, was unable to remain in school, often went hungry, and was once picked up by a policeman and sent to his father's relatives. But he was unable to remain there long both because he was badly treated and because of the tendency of these relatives to speak ill of his dead parents (which his suppressed resentment toward his parents for "abandoning" him and his guilt would not permit). In other words, he became an "A-bomb orphan" long before the A-bomb. But he did eventually manage to find semi-skilled work in a factory outside of Hiroshima, and with the help of the moral indoctrination he received at a youth school, managed to work there continuously for several years until the age of seventeen, when the bomb fell.

He was then called upon to join a rescue team which entered the city by truck. He found himself immediately overwhelmed by the things he saw and particularly sensitive to the issue of survival priority which confronted him at every turn. He recalled one body, piled among those about to be cremated, which began to blink its eyelids and move its eyes, felt enraged by the refusal of the others on the truck to heed his pleas and stop, and was left with the self-accusation that "I had committed a kind of crime." His "ultimate horror," however, was the image of a policeman trying to force open the mouth of an injured three- or four-year-old boy to feed him some moistened biscuit; of the policeman pointing to a dead woman covered with blood and explaining, "This little boy was clinging to his mother and crying, 'I'm hungry! I'm hungry, Mother! Mother, wake up!'"; of the boy finally himself becoming still in the policeman's arms. He was so absorbed by the scene at the time that he did not notice his truck drive away without him, and he choked up with sobs when telling me the story seventeen years later. He remembered feeling fierce hatred toward America at that moment, wishing to be called up quickly into military service (he had volunteered for the Navy shortly before) so that he could do his part in retaliating and "not let them get away with this."

Affected by general fears of invisible contamination, he felt guilty over "cowardly thoughts" about his own death. Indeed he seemed, more than anyone else I interviewed, to take inner responsibility for all of the death and symbolic social death around him. He found it "really unbearable" that people stole wristwatches from the dead and the dying, experienced "grief over the wretchedness of human nature," and then in the days that followed felt "very much disheartened" by "the kind of situation in which people had to live by deceiving others," particularly since he himself could not be immune from such "deceit" and went furtively every day to a special place in the surrounding mountains where he could find wild grass to eat, and which he did not want others to learn about.

Groping about in despair, repelled by the gruff attitudes of fellow workers at the factory ("Some were proud of saying that they lost their eyesight from atomic bomb cataracts but the truth was that it came from drinking [wood] alcohol"), feeling weak and ashamed of the fact that his hair seemed to be falling out, disappointed in his attempts to find guidance (his old youth-school teacher told him to write the old Imperial Rescript on education ten times every day, which he did try for a while, until he discovered that it "did no good at all"), still only seventeen years old and totally adrift, he began to become preoccupied with how he could best kill himself. In that state he performed an act of extreme desperation which was at the same time a form of symbolic death and rebirth. After severe taunting from other workers over his skinny physique and general weakness, he suddenly exploded with hatred toward his mother and father for bringing him into the world in such an inferior state and thereby exposing him to such ridicule, grabbed his parents' mortuary tablet, which he had formerly revered ("I myself made it and kept it carefully as a precious thing"), flung it violently against the wall, and ignoring warnings from observers that he would invoke divine retribution, pounded it into small pieces.

Even more strongly than most he was struck by the easygoing American troops, decided that these men were not really responsible for what happened since "they didn't actually see the bomb being dropped

. . . didn't see the dead bodies with their own eyes," and that "I no longer felt any desire for revenge." He concluded that the superior behavior of American troops, as contrasted with cruelties perpetrated by Japanese and other soldiers, was possible "because they were controlled . . . by Christianity"; and hearing of the economic opportunities in America, he thought seriously of emigrating. While he was not entirely uncritical of Americans, his identification with them and ethical flexibility were such that he even found virtue in the sexual liaisons between American soldiers and Japanese "pompom" girls which others so bitterly condemned: "These girls' deeds enabled their families to eat delicious foods and then sell the surplus on the black market as a way of sustaining themselves." He admired certain Occupation policies, such as the breaking up of *zaibatsu* (the mammoth business enterprises), and responded warmly to the American film *The Gold Rush*, finding "something in common" with Charlie Chaplin's portrayal of a little man struggling against large annihilating forces (and perhaps also in the "frontier atmosphere" shared by turn-of-the-century Alaska and postwar Hiroshima). Where he came into conflict with America and Americans was in his embrace of postwar Japanese pacifism during the late forties and early fifties, particularly in his positive response to militant leftist demonstrations against American-sponsored military, political, and economic programs ("I experienced a great shock, was deeply stirred . . . had goose pimples and an unforgettable feeling"). These emotions were dramatically intensified by the sudden, and in Hiroshima, deeply shocking, outbreak of the Korean War in June of 1950, by the scenes of American military activity that could be observed all around, and by the feeling that "World War III was creeping up on us."

Only in Christianity did he find a means of coming to terms with these conflicting attitudes toward America, and with other inner emotions that otherwise threatened to tear him apart. Feeling that "I would eventually collapse if things kept going on as they were," he gravitated toward English-language classes sponsored by Protestant groups in Hiroshima and also began to attend their church services (he said that he preferred the "democratic atmosphere" he found there to the more distant solemnity of Catholic ritual). He was troubled, however, by the thought that "they might be trying to smooth over the problem of the A-bomb by talking a lot about Christ." This suspicion was furthered by a communist slogan that "Christians are traitors," particularly since he had been deeply impressed by the dedication of communists to social action "on the side of those who were suffering," and had in fact resisted joining them only because of their tendency "always to express hatred toward those who criticized them."

He solved these dilemmas by attaching himself to a small group of people who combined intense Christianity with equally intense pacifism and sympathy for the downtrodden. The group was centered around the Hiroshima chapter of the Fellowship of Reconciliation, and the affiliation provided him with what the name suggests: "fellowship" in the sense of belonging to a "new family"; and "reconciliation" with America and Americans (who were prominent in the group), with conflicting attractions to Christianity and communism, and with seething inner hatred and death guilt which could now be mobilized on behalf of peace by means of protest activities carried out within a creed of militant Gandhian nonviolence. Indeed, he found that the group helped him forge a sense of identity that was universalistic as well as personal and idiosyncratic; and on one occasion, when picked up by police after being knocked temporarily unconscious by a rock thrown during a demonstration, he could say to them: "I am a member of the Fellowship of Reconciliation and therefore behaved according to my conscience."

In eventually seeking Protestant baptism, he emphasized that he was attracted not by dogma ("It was not from any belief . . . or thought of miracles") but by the nurturing and stabilizing bond it represented, and particularly by the personal example of Christ. He was deeply moved by stories of Christ washing the feet of his disciples and distributing bread among the hungry so that "all the people knew they would receive a fair amount"—always interpreting such stories in a way that de-emphasized the miraculous and stressed Christ's impressive personal qualities, especially his capacity to remain humble and yet be a savior and a cosmic nurturer. This identification with Christ, a "day laborer" in his time, gave form and forceful expression to inner imagery long held in relationship to himself.

He once had the thought that "if I become a member of a church I can avoid becoming a delinquent," and the psychological, if not literal, truth of this thought was affirmed by a strange sequence of events surrounding an actual murder. A few years after the war he came across a newspaper account of a murder committed by a man who had exactly the same name as himself—both family and given names were rendered in the same Japanese characters—and was just one or two years younger. A number of people, when reading the story, apparently thought that he had committed the murder, and one friend, with uncomfortably intuitive psychological insight, remarked: "With exactly the same name, one man is a murderer who killed someone, and the other is a peace-fanatic who runs around telling about people who are killed . . . so with your not working, and being so close in age to the man described, I really did worry." And even his wife (better described as his closest companion) told him that the incident reminded her of the British novel by Robert Louis Stevenson, *Dr. Jekyll and Mr. Hyde,* which she had read in translation and which suggested to her that it was possible for "a very mild and modest day laborer to turn into a wild and mad one." He became agitated, and in his sense of close identification with his namesake seemed almost to wonder whether he himself really was the murderer: "If it were true that I was the killer, then what would I do?" What he did do was go directly to the police station to try to make contact with the other man. Denied a personal meeting, he left a letter of encouragement ("from D. to another D.") and a Bible, because

> I thought I should do something to compensate for the crime that another D. had committed . . . and that inside the conscience of the murderer D., there must be a small something that is good which could be directed toward opposing war and opposing A- and H-bombs, which are the real mass killers of men.

We may thus say that he, and others close to him, sensed the relationship between the death-obsessed pacifist and the killer, between the would-be saint and the murderous emotions he must conquer. The namesake became for him a representation of his "old self," before it had been "tamed" by Christian pacifist discipline, and before its well of hatred had been channeled into protest against nuclear weapons. At the same time it was an "opposing self" or "double," which reminded him that his own transformation was still by no means complete.

He had, from the beginning, befriended and helped A-bomb orphans, but his Christian affiliations gave him more structured opportunities to develop his special talent for working with children. He constantly related this work to his own background ("I had experienced cruel treatment and I knew that there were people who had experienced even more cruel treatment than I"), and in a way that made clear his unconscious imagery of the young as symbols of rebirth ("When I began to spend time with children who had almost died or who had become cripples . . . it was partly because I myself was feeling very lonely, and also because I was concerned with what kind of thoughts these children would develop toward their own future lives"); so that in "saving" children, he was saving himself. Nor would he fail to instill his young followers with related principles of pity and compassion:

> I don't simply say, "Let us have a good time," but rather I say, "We are now going to sing songs, but remember that there are people who are deaf or dumb and cannot speak or hear or sing, and there are others who live in out-of-the-way places in the mountains where they can rarely have a chance to sing—so as we sing our songs we must think about those people even while we feel our own happiness . . . and think about what we can do to help such people."

He was the main behind-the-scenes figure in the creation of the Children's Monument, as Sadako Sasaki, the girl whose death inspired it, had been one of three children he knew who died of leukemia within one year. The original idea of the monument seems to have been his (though he had a group statue in mind, including all stages of childhood from infancy to the late teens), and he pursued the project with characteristic zeal as he moved back and forth among school officials, teachers, peace groups, parents, and (most of all) the children themselves. Especially effective was a pamphlet crudely mimeographed by the children which explained the purpose of the campaign, circulated at a conference of educators which happened to be convening in Hiroshima at the time, and was widely publicized by mass media throughout the country. Although the appeal succeeded brilliantly, the day laborer remained bitterly critical of the hypocrisy of the school principal who at first opposed the idea and then, when it gained momentum, virtually claimed full credit for it; and of other officials who tried to dominate the unveiling ceremony with pompous, self-dramatizing speeches, which all but ignored the children themselves and the larger purposes and actual human efforts originally associated with the monument. Concluding that "the reason that [peace] movements invariably become torn apart by antagonisms is that they cease to represent the feelings of the people who died . . . and become utilized for other purposes," he attempted to evolve an approach which remained true to the dead and was animated by a spirit of "childlike purity," which he considered a precious entity to be protected from adult manipulation.

Inevitably, he has been criticized for everything from "selling the bomb" to consorting with communists, but the criticism most difficult for him to counter is that he himself manipulates the children by using them to reflect his own views. For while he does encourage initiative, there is little doubt of his and his wife's influence upon their eleven- to fifteen-year-old followers, and his close identification with the children may well cause *him* to become confused over who initiates what. Some had the impression that he was saddened by seeing the children "outgrow" his group during their late high school years and gradually break their ties with it.

Whatever the case, he demonstrated extraordinary flexibility in his work, mastering storytelling techniques in order to entertain young children and camping methods for trips taken with older children, though having had no previous experience with either. And while he cared for others, he responded strongly to being himself cared for by people in Christian circles who "are kind to me and worry about me just as though I were their child," thereby symbolically functioning as father and mother to the children and as son to the other adults. The latter was particularly true in his relationship with a distinguished woman missionary and teacher who has been model, mentor, and "mother" to him. And his sense of responsibility for any suffering or errant "child" knew no limits. He once insisted upon taking into his home a twenty-year-old A-bomb orphan who had no place to stay after being released from juvenile prison, and then persisted in his unsuccessful efforts at rehabilitation until his wife rebelled at this invasion of her privacy (not to mention the young man's enuresis, slothfulness, and stealing) and moved out until the boy left—the day laborer himself retaining feelings of guilt over "throwing him out into the dark world."

He brought similar principles to his work with adult groups, and in a variety of ways demonstrated a consistent "instinct for the universal." He emphasized the need to transcend differences in thought and race since "the reason for the making of A- and H-bombs was the confrontation of ideologies between nations"; answered complaints that communists take over peace movements with pleas to others of varying views to participate more actively and "promote the movement in the right direction"; and while appealing to the consciences of Americans still engaged in making atomic and hydrogen bombs, expressed sympathy toward them concerning the risks they take and even added, "We must not forget to love them." Together with his children he conducted an impartial international correspondence, now encouraging a youth group in China or a peace group in India, now asking Philadelphia city officials to express themselves concerning the atomic bomb on the occasion of their celebration of Independence Day, now chastising Russian groups for their failure to apply the same critical standards to their own nuclear behavior that they applied to others'.

At the same time he was wary of any form of ideological totalism, criticized those leaders who "require their followers to look up to them and pay no attention to anything else," and emphasized his policy of "following a path in which I am exposed to the ways of thinking of all kinds of people and then figure out what is behind the opinions which people state." While some of these actions were not devoid of a suggestion of gentle grandiosity, no one had more intimate contact with needy *hibakusha* or greater capability of transcending petty prejudices in helping them. For these reasons he was often selected by people of wider experience and education to supervise distribution of gifts or mediate among contending factions.

This mediating talent did not lessen his demand for continuing militancy in opposing the ultimate evil, nuclear weapons. He complained of the tendency of *hibakusha* to expend their hostility on doctors or on each other rather than upon the atomic bomb, which they tended to look upon as "like a natural calamity," and of the fact that "Many die in great pain but only a few die protesting A- and H-bombs." His willingness to do anything whatsoever to further this protest—to demonstrate suffering *hibakusha* to foreign visitors, or to obtain "extras" (himself included) for films about the atomic bomb and then supervise makeup, costumes, and acting approaches—led one Hiroshima observer to speak of him as a "producer for the A-bomb victim show." But another, noting his "inability to stop thinking of those who are dying in hospitals" and his "moving about everywhere because he feels it his personal responsibility to know of, seek out, and take care of all A-bomb patients," concluded that "if we can speak of such a thing, he is an A-bomb mental doctor."

He was surely both. Indeed his virtuosity made him "all things to all *hibakusha*." He attributed his energies to his two ultimate sources of strength. The first source is suggested in the Japanese saying he quoted, "A child one carries on his back gives him a direction," that is, the capacity to experience a continuous sense of renewed life through contact with children.* In this light he was also aware of the special capacity of children to melt the selfish ambitions of adults (for instance, among competing "patient bosses" on various floors of the A-Bomb

---

* The Western counterpart ("A dwarf standing on the shoulders of a giant may see further than the giant himself") is often associated with Isaac Newton but actually goes back to Didacus Stella in the first century A.D.; it seems to convey a reverse emphasis of reliance upon the wisdom of ancestors, but the two sayings are by no means unrelated, and together stress the profound mutual need of older and younger generations.[8]

Hospital). His second source of strength lay in what he referred to as an emphasis upon "internal" rather than "external" matters, which in actuality meant a focus upon the dead. And even in a city so generally preoccupied with its dead, and in a culture which encourages this preoccupation, his insistent stress upon remembering, recounting, and displaying every conceivable detail of A-bomb horror led many to accuse him of promoting an unhealthy "death cult."

His private life, if one can speak of his having one, is dominated by an all-prevading asceticism. No sooner is something given to him—money, clothing, food, possessions of any kind—than he turns it over to others he considers in greater need. He has refused regular employment because of his belief that it would interfere with his peace activities, and turned down paid positions in peace organizations because these would take away his independence. Instead he has worked sporadically as a day laborer or a night watchman to earn enough to keep going, eating minimally and sleeping irregularly, his only form of relaxation an occasional movie he may go to with his wife, usually one with a serious message. He never misses a film about the atomic bomb itself, and his idea of "entertaining" a patient in the A-Bomb Hospital, at least on one occasion, was to take him to see *On the Beach*.

He and his wife have what could well be called an "A-bomb marriage." Their relationship initiated and nurtured through Christian and A-bomb concerns, he was drawn to her originally partly out of pity because of a bodily deformity exacerbated by atomic bomb exposure. Virtually everyone who attended their wedding was actively engaged in A-bomb problems, and right after the ceremony and reception he and his wife went directly to the Cenotaph in the Peace Park, where "with flowers in our hands we made our report of our marriage and pledged . . . to those who have been sacrificed . . . to dedicate ourselves to peace." This paralleled the traditional Japanese custom of reporting to ancestors on ceremonial occasions, suggesting that the A-bomb monument had become the day laborer's family monument, and that through their marriage he and his wife were entering the family of the atomic bomb dead and pledging eternal loyalty to it. And they have since lived out the pledge through the teamwork in A-bomb activities which dominates their relationship.

He and his wife have frequently been mistaken for brother and sister, and having lived together more or less as such for some time, their decision to marry was influenced by a combination of encouragement and pressure from Christian associates. They engage in no physical relations, and whatever the part played in this decision by a general disinclination toward heterosexuality, it too becomes related to the A-bomb. Thus he attributes his restraint to "my wish to express my sense of apology toward an A-bombed woman," and to their inability to seek sensual pleasure after their daily rounds of assisting sick and needy *hibakusha.* Their decision to have no children was not only a consequence of this policy of sexual abstinence, but also of a fear of producing malformed infants "which would make me a kind of assailant toward future generations"—a fear intensified by the experience of his wife's sister who, following A-bomb exposure, was reported to have given birth to two abnormal children. But he also mentioned additional considerations: the difficulty his wife would have, because of her injury, in giving birth to and caring for a child; and his doubts that he could do all for a child that it required. He related this last reason to his own sense of having been so deprived as a child, and it reflects his resulting tendency to idealize the child as one for whom no parent is good enough. He and his wife have experienced conflict at times when she has not been up to the totality of his demands for self-sacrifice, when he has felt unable to receive from her the nurturance he seeks, and more recently in relationship to her own increasing prominence in peace activities.

The driven quality of his life—he is a man who is never still—is related to a precarious balance between two inner images of himself. One of these is a heroic image, suggested in the expansiveness of his activities and in his references not only to Christ and Gandhi but also to Napoleon and Hideyoshi, the great sixteenth-century general who unified Japan and then became its ruler. But the other image is the opposite one of a childlike, weak, totally dependent creature who is incapable of taking care of the simplest personal need. Both of these images are intimately bound up with emotions related to guilt and death. His exquisite sensitivity to guilt is expressed in his very frequent use of the expression "How pitiful!" (*Kawaiso*), in his compassion for weak-looking birds and even for mosquitoes and flies (which goes beyond his mother's Buddhism), and in his refusal to eat fish with their heads intact (although this is done routinely in Japan). Such lifelong inclinations to guilt, as well as to death, have made possible his unparalleled identification with A-bomb dead and maimed. This identification was responsible for his reluctance to leave his shack near the A-Bomb Dome, though it did not fundamentally change when he was finally forced to do so. It has been accompanied by thoughts about his own death and about the idea of suicide, but at such times he immediately becomes concerned about "how dead my body would be, and how I would not be able to make use of myself." He has been thinking recently about arranging to have his eyes donated to an eye bank upon his death. For giving of himself to others has become his way of dealing with both life and death, of achieving a sense of immortality.

:

His style of leadership is based upon having been, almost from the beginning of life, a guilt-prone "survivor"—of many symbolic deaths as well as of the biological deaths of each of his parents—and upon his capacity to convert this guilt into the compassionate energies of a "savior." He found the model of a saint in the idealized memory of his father and of a zealot in his mother. But to make inner use of these models, he has had to maintain a constant process of transformation of diffuse and potentially debilitating guilt and rage into disciplined weapons in a crusade against evil, against the A-bomb. But how are we to account for his reversal of the most extreme kind of "unsocialized" attitudes into his peculiar ascetic dynamism: of an abandoned child's bitterness into the perpetual nurturing of others, of exaggerated "hunger" and retention into total generosity, of murderous hatreds into dedication to peace and nonviolence? Such reversals are characterized, in classical psychoanalytic terminology, as "reaction-formations," meaning the mobilization of the antitheses of early impulses as a compensatory means of character formation. But what also needs to be stressed once more is the inner symbolism of "touching death" and then transcending it as the source of the power to "save" others.

Hence his inner fusion of allegiance to the dead with such rebirth-promoting forces as the militant-nonviolent Christianity modeled upon Christ himself, and with the purity and perpetual renewal of children. This fusion afforded him a means of countering and in a sense "undoing" the abuse of the atomic bomb while simultaneously countering and undoing the abuse of his own childhood. His special sensitivities to guilt and death, so vital to this process, were the source of both his pain and his power. He made use of them with an emotional fluidity characteristic of both the artist and the leader—quick shifts between love and hate and between controlled wisdom and passionate one-sidedness, along with continuous ingenuity (often unconscious) in rechanneling fundamental emotions (such as those related to sex and death) for use in a larger crusade. This capacity, though sometimes referred to as "regression in the service of the ego," is actually less a form of regression than it is a quality of access to primitive feelings, along with the ability to give these form which has significance for others. It is the "pan-emotionality" (including "pan-sexuality") which the leader or artist calls forth in his special quest for symbolic immortality, in his neglect of ordinary patterns of sexual reproduction and biological continuity in favor of near-cosmic identifications meant to revitalize the entire human species. And the day laborer's destruction of his ancestral tablet symbolized, among other things, his break with the "ordinary" biological mode as a necessary preliminary to the larger vistas of his leadership.

But when the guilt and the death imagery which underlie the quest come to dominate it, as they do in his case, the resulting zealousness may be difficult for all to live with. This domination made it impossible for him to develop the true saint's cohesiveness of life-style and steadiness of inner transformation—for him to evolve the disciplined leader's reliable method of demonstrating to followers a special form of mastery over death (as was found, for instance, in the public fasts of Gandhi, a leader whom the day laborer in some ways resembled).* In contrast, both his life-style and his efforts at transformation have been erratic, and his insatiable hunger for nurturance has rendered him as much a follower as a leader. Moreover, his chosen antagonist, the A-bomb, has been too strong for him to vanquish. The convoluted death imagery it inspires constantly heightens his own emotional imbalance.

What he had done is to live out a special form of the heroic myth—a one-sided emphasis of its element of the "orphan" or "abandoned child" (the hero, generally considered to be of supernatural origin, is usually brought up by parents other than his own). But he has far from achieved the hero's redemption of his people. Rather, his combination of unceasing effort and unattainable goals exemplifies the Sisyphian dilemma of every A-bomb leader, the dilemma of a task whose accomplishment is beyond human capacity. And in his death-obsessed struggle against death, he expresses in peculiarly exaggerated form the dilemma of human existence itself.

---

* These resemblances went beyond Gandhian influences which the day laborer absorbed in his leadership. Through various discussions with Erik Erikson concerning his work in progress on Gandhi, I have been struck by the basic psychological similarities of the two men, as well as the difference which made one a "great man" on a universal scale and the other a controversial local figure with heroic but also self-defeating qualities. I shall discuss some of these issues further in section 5 of Chapter XII.

seven

RESIDUAL STRUGGLES:
TRUST, PEACE, AND MASTERY

1) Contending Symbols

The limited attainments of A-bomb leaders suggest the depth of residual conflict. The conflict has existed within individual *hibakusha*, in the general Hiroshima community, and, in fact, throughout all of post-bomb society. *Hibakusha* struggles to absorb their experience are therefore problems of psychohistorical mastery. The contending symbols within and around *hibakusha* are those which affirm life and those which subvert it; the polarity is that of *reintegration versus residual distrust*.

For individual *hibakusha* the experience of being loved and cared for could, gradually and against obstacles, re-create life-affirming imagery and re-establish the capacity to live.

In the case of the shopkeeper's assistant, for instance, the pattern of suspiciousness and homeless wandering we noted before was interrupted by four human relationships sufficiently profound to be experienced as an A-bomb orphan's re-establishment of "family": with a welfare official, who took responsibility for the boy's life to the point of taking him into his own home and "treating me like a younger brother"; with a university professor and his wife (introduced by the welfare official), who became "parents" for a whole group of A-bomb orphans and with

whom he could "feel at ease . . . because of the warm and homey
atmosphere—as if I were in my own family"; and with an employer
(introduced by the university professor), who he felt also treated him as
a younger brother. The academic couple also did much to encourage his
marriage to a girl from the same group of A-bomb orphans, and became,
in effect, "grandparents" to the two children resulting from the marriage. Finding himself stabilized, he felt that his dead parents and
younger brother—or their souls—"could also settle down." Involved in
his reconstituted family viability was inner imagery of being reintegrated
into the continuity of human existence via the biological mode of
symbolic immortality so emphasized in East Asian culture.

But his reintegrative process, despite the remarkable help he received,
has been tenuous, accompanied by a persistent sense of deprivation ("I
have cried often since the bomb was dropped because of having no
parents") and anger ("I don't know how to put into words the rage I
still feel about the bomb"). Moreover, the quality of his references to
his early life—including the pre-bomb family utopia he describes—
conveys the sense that he still struggles against a tendency to view all of
his post-A-bomb care as counterfeit. This tendency does not result from
any absence of either sincerity or generosity on the part of those who
offered the care, but simply from the fact that it came from people
other than his real parents, and was a consequence of his parents'
deaths. Part of the function of his continuing emphasis upon the
emotional support still received from his dead parents is that of keeping
vivid his momory of his last and only experience of totally authentic—
that is, actual parental—nurturance. And retained death guilt throws a
shadow even upon that.

Sensitivities about counterfeit nurturance were extremely strong in all
children forced to depend upon special care, particularly care coming
from city or government agencies. One close observer commented that
such children

> always feel backward and cannot see the bright side of things as other
> children do but . . . seem to be sitting on the sidelines and crouch-
> ing to make themselves small . . . trying to hide the fact that they
> are being publicly cared for, and that they have no parents.

Diffuse residual bitterness can be felt toward Hiroshima itself and the
people in it, as expressed by the bargirl, whose loss of her mother made

her an A-bomb orphan at the age of four, in a poem written during her teens:

I Hate Hiroshima

Hiroshima, where my grandfather and my mother were
killed by the A-bomb.

Hiroshima, where my surviving grandmother and I are
living as beggars.

Those who look at us in this state with cold eyes are
the people of Hiroshima.

I hate, hate, hate the town of Hiroshima and the people
of Hiroshima.

When I talked with her, I found her to be an unhappy-looking girl of twenty-one who was clearly having difficulty fulfilling the requirements of marriage and motherhood, difficulty which she attributed entirely to the bomb's having deprived her of nurturance: "After all . . . because of it I had no parents . . . and if I had parents, they would have taught me about these things." Actually, her father had left the family some years before the A-bomb and her mother had led an irregular life in the "water world," so that we have reason to believe that much of her emotional conflict could have developed independently of the atomic bomb. Her simple view of the bomb as the *source of all evil* nonetheless contains considerable psychological truth: because the bomb probably did have crucial influence upon her emotional life by depriving her of a mother she so desperately needed, and because the interpretation itself expresses her *sense* of the bomb's profound disruption of her life and of the insolubility of her resulting conflicts. But in its very absoluteness this interpretation further binds her to the A-bomb experience and to its death imagery, and thereby militates against adaptation and mastery.

A much more successful pattern of reintegration was achieved by the social worker. Not only did his death guilt influence his career in ways we have observed, but so strong was his urge to dedicate himself to helping A-bomb orphans that he defied his father's absolute opposition to this financially insecure low-status work and went on to become head of one of Hiroshima's major orphanages. Some of the first residents of his institution were the stray children he picked up in front of Hiroshima Station during the early post-bomb months and gently but forcibly conducted to the home. Having faced unusual difficulties, he was proud of the fact that among all of its kind in Japan, his institution sent the greatest number of children to high school and college—and honest enough to add, with a smile and a touch of irony, that it also sent the greatest number to jail. He emphasized how frequently an individual youngster would embrace and defend an exclusive concern with immediate pleasure on the basis of having "in a single instant—while enjoying his breakfast together with his family . . . lost both of his parents and his home," how they "cannot believe in tomorrow" and "can have no adequate philosophy or disciplined point of view about life." What became clear, however, in his associations was that in rescuing these youngsters from atomic bomb disintegration and from resulting antisocial behavior, he was reasserting not only *their* imagery of life but his own. He was "rescuing" himself from severe death guilt and struggling against the sense of sudden and total annihilation he too had experienced. For the antisocial behavior which may occur in an atomic bomb orphan is merely one extreme expression of the general experience of all who are exposed to the bomb: of *a vast breakdown of faith in the larger human matrix supporting each individual life, and therefore a loss of faith (or trust) in the structure of human existence.*

"IF MY FATHER WERE ALIVE . . ."

The complicated ways in which atomic bomb exposure contributes to this pattern of residual distrust are illustrated in the experience of the woman with the ophthalmic condition. Somewhat confused, as we noted before, in how much of her general difficulty to attribute to the A-bomb, she definitely implicated it—through having caused the death of her father—in a profound attraction she described to a life of *decadence* (she used the Japonized version of the French word, and meant, essentially, sexual promiscuity).

Just thirteen at the time of the bomb, she told of having been prematurely exposed to adult sexual interests, first by her mother's confidences and then by men who came to the home to see her mother but became involved with the daughter instead. These encounters—particularly an early one in which an older man attempted to force himself upon her—left her feeling "dirty" but at the same time strongly aroused. She in fact associated the onset of her eye condition with a temporary interruption in a prolonged affair with the man she later married. Despite finding sexual fulfillment in the relationship, severe quarreling led to a separation. Then, finding herself unable to work because of her eye condition, and left alone with her young child and her own erotic inclinations, she came to look upon herself as "good for nothing." Critical of her mother's "carelessness" in this sequence of events, while recalling her father as a man with exemplary character, she came to the conclusion that "without a father—the main pillar of a family—I became spiritually loose." She attributed her early interest in older men to "a strong wish to have a father," and emphasized that "It is a question of my mind rather than a question of my eyes," since "a child brought up by only one parent is likely to become one-sided and abnormal."

While we know little about her actual relationship to her father while he was alive, we may say that his death, and particularly her (and perhaps her mother's) guilt over his death, disrupted the family's sexual balance: rather than having an opportunity to resolve the attraction every young girl feels toward her father, she found herself, as an adolescent, simultaneously at the mercy of aroused sexual feelings and a great need for fathering. The resulting pattern of promiscuity (or of wished-for promiscuity) undoubtedly exacerbated various forms of guilt, including death guilt toward the father.

Of particular significance was her inner association of sexual "*decadence*" with the *hibakusha's* ultimate form of hostility and cosmic retaliation:

> My luck [in being exposed to the A-bomb] was bad, and I feel very angry about my unlucky fate. Being angry about it, I sometimes wish that all of the earth would be annihilated. . . . I am attracted to both destructive and constructive sides of things. That is the state of my mind. . . . For instance, rather than have pain that is not understood . . . I have the desire to forget about my conscience and indulge in the decadent life. This is the destructive side of my desire. On the other hand, the constructive side is to apply great effort toward leading a very orderly life—and working toward a goal that might take even ten years to achieve, but doing so without going astray. . . .

More than just family sexual balance, the A-bomb disrupted the larger moral universe she had previously known, so that neither sexual nor aggressive impulses could any longer find patterned or controlled expression; chaotic and guilt-ridden perceptions of both then became inwardly associated with the end-of-the-world wish or total nuclear destruction.

:

A similarly fundamental loss of paternal protection was involved in the experience of another divorced woman (whom we have previously referred to as the divorced housewife). Also thirteen years old when her father was killed by the bomb under strongly guilt-stimulating circumstances, she too found herself rendered extremely vulnerable. She felt subsequently "deceived"—by her husband, who turned out to have been living with another woman at the time her marriage with him was arranged; by the go-between, who had managed to allay her family's suspicions; and by her mother, who had initiated the marriage despite the girl's preference for further study. She was convinced that

> if my father had been alive . . . our lives would have been different . . . and I would not have had this kind of failure in my married life because he would have given me various kinds of advice from a man's point of view.

The complex three-way family ambivalences which enter into her difficulties were suggested by a vision experienced by her mother when desperately ill, in which the father appeared and called the mother to join him in death, was then "scolded" by the daughter who insisted the mother stay with her, and as a result benignly withdrew. Mother and daughter interpreted the vision as indicative of the dead father's considerateness and continuing protection, and it is undoubtedly true that their continuing identification with him provides important emotional sustenance. But also involved in both the vision and the general pattern described is a re-enactment of family conflicts—including mother-daughter rivalry for the father and the daughter's intensified need for her mother. Both the mother's sense of added burden following the father's death and the daughter's sense of loss increased tensions between them. Again, the atomic bomb was both the cause of these exacerbations of family conflict, and the symbol of absolute evil from which, it was believed, all conflict emanated.

:

These examples demonstrate differing patterns derived from loss in the A-bomb of one's mother, father, or both parents.[1] Resulting conflicts included those which occur with the early loss of parents from any cause, as well as those specific to the A-bomb constellation. Thus, the loss of one's father led to a sense of extreme vulnerability in which *hibakusha* status itself combined with a general loss of family prestige and with severe intra-family emotional disruptions to create a strong expectation of being further victimized, which was all too frequently fulfilled. Loss of one's mother resulted in a more basic deprivation of nurturance and profound mistrust of subsequent relationships. Sexual differences are apparently of great importance: losing a parent of the same sex deprives one of a model for adult identity (there was some evidence that it predisposed boys toward patterns of delinquency), while losing a parent of the opposite sex distorts and impairs sexual and other forms of maturation in ways we have noted.

Death of both parents was likely to produce a severe combination of vulnerability and impaired nurturance, and a lifelong struggle against total incapacitation. Brothers in such cases have been noted to show unusually great hostility toward each other, sometimes associated with antisocial behavior. And Japanese sociologists have described a profoundly disaffected prototype of the A-bomb orphan as a young adult: working irregularly at low-status jobs, moving about frequently and having no permanent address, diffusely anxious and in poor health, and living generally on the fringe of society where he is hard to locate for census-taking and is sometimes in difficulty with the law. Even when a "new family" provides a measure of stability, A-bomb orphans have been observed to be looked down upon and further victimized by certain pressures of Japanese family life. A girl who marries into a farming family, for instance, may be treated harshly because of her ostensible inability to carry the working load for which the family "acquired" her. In all these ways the A-bomb's original disruption of psychological and social bonds becomes perpetuated, and inextricably bound up with the general dislocations of postwar Japanese experience.*

Hibakusha can also retain residual distrust of their own capacity to nurture others. Thus, the abandoned mother continued over the years to feel anxious about the problem of caring for her children. Her way of dealing with this anxiety was to emphasize to them what might be called a principle of absolute mutual dependence in relationship to survival. She would tell them:

> Without you children having survived, I would not have either; but if I had not survived, then you children would not have been able to.

This emphasis did not save her from enormous emotional and financial difficulty, or from her continuous sense of abandonment. But it did

---

* The extreme importance which East Asian culture places upon the intact biological family unit tended to increase the psychological impact of these dislocations. Other factors which did the same were the difficulties of remarriage (especially for women) in Japan, the very limited tradition for social welfare and for adoption procedures for orphans, and various forms of institutional dislocation accompanying social change.

suggest her ability to draw upon a family pool of emotional sustenance as a way of ameliorating everyone's general mistrust. This capacity to make use of her children's strength was expressed in her admiration for qualities of directness and autonomy she observed in their generation, an attitude in sharp contrast with the more usual middle-aged parent's despair at the younger generation's lack of the old virtues. And she was sufficiently proud of the little home she eventually managed to create for herself and her children to welcome the idea of holding one of our interviews there. But her post-bomb experience seemed to revolve about the inner question: "Feeling myself so deprived of support, how much authentic nurturance am I capable of providing for others?"

There were some *hibakusha* who stressed the tendency toward re-integration in their psychological lives, toward what the writer-physician described as "revival—becoming human again." He spoke of a special interest in "the process by which people who have been demolished . . . fight against various forces around them, and finally either succeed or fail." While aware of the importance of economic factors, he emphasized that something more was involved:

I have been observing a number of people suffering from fatal diseases who first lose hope entirely and then, after a certain time, regain their spiritual strength.

His choice of example suggests a half-awareness that the mastering of death anxiety is crucial for recovery, along with an unconscious sugges-tion that whatever their spiritual rebirth, *hibakusha* are essentially doomed.

Many expressed the idea that the price of individual reintegration was a lower level of psychic and socioeconomic existence than one would have settled for had one not been exposed to the bomb. The electrician, for instance, whose dedicated post-bomb vigil at the railway station had left him with such a feeling of futility, subsequently underwent years of difficult economic struggle and severe physical illness. He then decided against acting upon promising opportunities to start his own business, and instead requested transfer to a quiet and comfortable unit of an affiliate of his large company. Forty-three at the time of the bomb, in his late forties at the time of the transfer, and sixty at the time of our interviews, he found that "the experience of being exposed to the bomb can make one grow senile," and told how many men he knew of about the same age had reactions similar to his own:

We have no inclination to lead others or do anything of that sort. All of us are old people, and we do not take interest in things other than concentrating closely on our own individual work in the sections we are assigned to.

He conveys an overall sense of psychic numbing, and what might be called premature retirement. In contrast to traditional East Asian patterns of retirement, in which, at an *appropriate* time, one shifts from a life of activity to one of contemplation and spiritual authority, we are here confronted with restrictions in living arbitrarily imposed. Rather than the image of a mature and contemplative wisdom, he describes a man whose recognition of his own early "senility" (old age, uselessness, perhaps even foolishness) causes him to make minimal requirements upon himself, seek out what feels safe, and avoid challenge.

This psychological issue is bound up with the controversial physiological one surrounding "premature aging" of atomic bomb victims. Whether or not such a physiological trend is actually present is difficult to say; this may well be another area in which a clear distinction between the psychological and the physiological is almost impossible.* But the *hibakusha*'s inner *sense* of premature senility occurs independently of any such distinction and is still another form of residual distrust.

A strikingly different point of view about the residual struggles of *hibakusha* was expressed by the young Hiroshima-born writer. Rather than distrust or weakness, he spoke of a special kind of strength he thought them to possess:

> It is usually said that those who went through the bomb have a kind of despair . . . but I think that they may have another quality too, a kind of toughness. For instance, in the case of those who return from war, they may of course be . . . disturbed in various ways—but there is another side as well. During peacetime, in ordinary life, men are restricted by social codes and tradition, but in war they are freed from such restrictions. So that those who experience war know what man really is and what he can do. They may return with a realization that man can do almost anything—whether in a constructive or destructive sense.

He went on, however, to qualify his assertion almost to the point of negation ("But the A-bomb experience is different, so what I have said

---

* Medical reports on the subject are contradictory and inconclusive.

is not necessarily true for it"); and, it must be added, he himself is not a *hibakusha*.

He nonetheless raises the important issue of the potentially strengthening effects of the survival of a death encounter. For the kind of symbolic conquest of death described before among A-bomb leaders was to some extent experienced by all *hibakusha*. The difficulty with such a "conquest" in relationship to the atomic bomb is its constant undermining by the various kinds of death guilt and death anxiety we have observed, and by the retained aura of counterfeit nurturance. We shall discuss later this duality of survival potential, but we may note now that it is evident in the opposing metaphors applied to Hiroshima itself. Thus, the city has been publicly characterized as "a Phoenix arising from the ashes," and described to me privately by one observer as "a crippled child trying to conceal its handicap."

THE NEW HIROSHIMA: VITALITY OR SHAM

These conflicting images bring us to the larger symbols of reintegration and residual distrust surrounding the rebuilding of Hiroshima as a city. For *hibakusha* were profoundly affected by the dramatic appearance, within less than ten years, of a much larger and in many ways more impressive city than the one which had existed prior to the bomb.

Many said such things as "I didn't think it possible that the city could be rebuilt so quickly," and even a man as skeptical as the history professor could not help but view this resurrection as a form of life-affirmation:

> I never imagined that I would see Hiroshima reconstructed as it is now. This makes me think of the extent of human vitality—of the urge of the people to live—which is stronger than one can imagine.

But for many the sense of affirmation is once more undermined by suspicion of the very symbols which suggest it. To Miss Ōta the new Hiroshima was all sham—because (she told me) it was so different from the old one:

> People say that Hiroshima has been rebuilt. I don't think that Hiroshima has really been rebuilt. Another Hiroshima has appeared and I am not pleased by this. . . . I think back to the old Hiroshima . . . which was not really beautiful, but still a very nice small place in its own way. I say, give us back the old Hiroshima. . . .

Because "to rebuild anything means recovery, and I don't feel that Hiroshima has really recovered"; and because the elegant new façade serves only to hide the real atomic bomb horrors:

> The new Hiroshima is a city for sightseeing . . . made to be shown to visitors. . . . The people who are really suffering are hidden— people living in small shacks—they are not shown. They are less than people. . . . The city planning is not useful. The Hundred-Meter Road [a large highway running through the center of the city] was built by order of MacArthur, and such a wide road is not needed. Fifty per cent of the space of the city has been taken up by these wide roads but little space has been used for living areas. . . .

And because a horde of immoral outsiders "create bars, cabarets, and strip shows," and "pay the city and government people for the right to put up their shops along the wide roads, make big profits," and thereby turn Hiroshima into a "national colony," while the "true survivors" experience a life of poverty. To Miss Ōta the "real characteristics of Hiroshima"—that is, its only authentic symbols—are the impoverished day laborers: "deformed women . . . and men who have lost interest in life."

However overdrawn her picture may be, all of its individual images were expressed to me by other survivors as well. Such themes of inauthenticity as the glossing over of real horror, and the obliteration of the past, must accompany the rebuilding of any large environment that has been so totally annihilated. For the survivor feels the need to keep around him some evidence of **his** pre-disaster life and even (however ambivalently) of his death encounter. The new attractiveness is associated with "selling the bomb," gaiety and sensuality with forbidden pleasure; and all such vitality becomes an insult to the dead. Moreover, there remains the suspicion that however restored the physical contours may be, death lurks beneath them—as epitomized by a news story which appeared in Hiroshima fourteen years after the bomb, with the headline "PERHAPS THE BONES OF ATOMIC BOMB VICTIMS?", and which told of two deformed skulls found on a river bank.*

Less controversial to *hibakusha* was natural symbolism of rebirth. We

---

* In the Hiroshima edition of *Asahi Shimbun*, January 26, 1959, the river bank was identified as a place where many corpses were cremated at the time of the bomb. The skulls were found by laborers reinforcing the river bank, and the article went on to say that "as the work advances, similar discoveries may be made in greater numbers."

have already noted the response to the first post-A-bomb spring, and even fourteen years after the bomb a commentator spoke of the city's "nostalgia for greenery" and longing for the "forest city" of the past (though when postwar allocations have been carried out, there will be a much higher percentage of land used for parks than there was in the prewar city).[2] For while nature can be perceived to exist in a counterfeit setting, nature itself is never counterfeit, and the hunger for it is a hunger for authentic symbolism of life.

Economic symbols have had great importance too, and Hiroshima's economic boom was described as representing the city's emergence "from nil to something." By the late 1950s Hiroshima was said to have a higher percentage of households with washing machines and television sets than any other city in Japan—a statistic related to the city's generally impressive financial recovery, but which might also suggest (since Hiroshima apparently does not have the highest per capita income of all Japanese cities) another form of post-A-bomb hunger for symbols of rebirth, this time in the form of electronic manifestations of "the good life."* Inevitably, however, mention of the city's prosperity or of its other accomplishments brings an immediate cautionary statistic about unemployment and economic hardship among day laborers, and about the high percentage of *hibakusha* in this group: "Hiroshima is well known as the 'Peace City,' but that Hiroshima is also the 'unemployed city' is not well known."[3] And with a similar sense of contrasting imagery, it is pointed out that people with keloids are no longer frequently observed because "they seem to feel hesitant to go out and be seen on the clean and bright-looking streets of the city."[4]

GANGS AND PROSTITUTES

Also contrasted are the peace ethos and the widespread civic violence, particularly in the form of the notorious gang wars of the postwar period—or what one observer termed "the bloody affairs of the Peace City of Hiroshima." For early black-market activities eventually gave way to more varied operations of organized criminal gangs. I have been unable to uncover adequate statistical evidence to determine whether there has actually been a greater long-range incidence of crime in Hiroshima than in other cities; but there probably has been, and if not,

---

* Here, too, many other elements can enter into these statistics, and it is quite possible that there is no causative relationship between the atomic bomb experience and later hunger for household applicances and television sets. Even so, the contrast is striking to *hibakusha* themselves.

it has certainly seemed that way.* Ironically, this crime has emanated mostly from areas which were *not* destroyed by the bomb, from sections of the city which, just peripheral to the zone of total destruction and thus not included in building programs, rapidly turned into slums that became known as "Gangland Area."

Gang activities, while involving such minority groups as Koreans and Chinese, emerged from specifically Japanese criminal tradition. But whereas prior to the bomb members of such gangs, like everyone else, had their definite relationship to Japanese society—distinct from legitimate social groups yet maintaining tight intra-gang discipline based upon feudal ethics—during the postwar period they, also like everyone else, experienced a loosening of order and discipline and became chaotically intertwined with the rest of society. In place of their onetime romantic aura postwar gangsters came to be called by the contemptuous term "*gurentai*"—"stupid ones."

These gangs had national connections, but Hiroshima's "frontier atmosphere" gave them extraordinary opportunity to flourish. Some gangs simply transferred themselves to the city from other areas en masse, while others combined outside and local membership. In addition to preying upon ordinary people through various kinds of racketeering, violence, or threatened violence, they also engaged in murderous feuds with one another. One particularly notorious feud, between the Murakami and Ōka gangs, began with a killing in 1946, and led to at least fifteen cases of murder and homicide during the late forties and fifties, to be replaced by new rivalries which, in one form or another, probably persist even today.

There has been a continuum from such violent criminal gangs to borderline racketeers to merely uncouth entrepreneurs. And the resulting symbolism has also inevitably been mixed, including: a heightened sense of energy and life force, like that we observed in relationship to early black-market activities, and possibly also including an identification on the part of some *hibakusha* with *active* violence in contrast to their own passive exposure to death at the time of the bomb; a general sense of robustness and spontaneity (in relationship to milder borderline activities) with James Cagney- or Humphrey Bogart-like overtones

---

* I was advised by city officials as well as by sociologists that accurate comparative statistics were especially lacking during the early postwar years. In Hiroshima crime was virtually uncontrolled immediately after the bomb. With order established, the crime rate apparently remained high, reaching a peak around 1950 and 1951, diminishing somewhat after that.[5]

(or their Japanese equivalents), and a liberation from traditional decorum; but also the sense of further disintegration and intensified death anxiety, inevitably linked in people's minds with the atomic bomb, and with further reason for viewing Hiroshima as a blighted city whose life-sustaining capacity could not be trusted.

Similar mixed symbolism, humorous in retrospect but seriously felt at the time, occurred in relationship to post-bomb prostitution. As an active military city Hiroshima had long possessed a celebrated red-light district; and its officials sought to maintain this pattern in relationship to Occupation troops through an officially endorsed program. Since it was felt that such a program would minimize potential violence or abuse on the part of the Occupiers, and would in any case be necessary, girls were recruited with the same organizing slogans that had been used in relationship to the Japanese war effort—"Working for the Nation" and "Loyalty to the Nation."[6] Here too the "energy"—the girls themselves —came from the outside, both because, as one observer put it, "In the very early days the girls victimized by the blast could not, physically or mentally, engage in such activities"; and because there is a tradition in Japan for importing girls from outlying rural areas for work in the "water world" of large cities. But before long there came an order from MacArthur's headquarters prohibiting organized prostitution and "emancipating" all prostitutes; this did not, of course, end prostitution but made it more chaotic, disorganized, and linked with crime—often with the wandering orphans or *furō-ji* around Hiroshima Station serving as pimps. Japanese authorities kept insisting that their plan was more sensible, but they were met with traditional Anglo-Saxon (in this case British and Australian, as well as American) resistance toward any form of "institutionalization of evil." Various compromise arrangements, official and otherwise, were worked out—until eventually, after the end of the Occupation, the Japanese themselves decided to outlaw prostitution.

More specifically related to atomic bomb imagery was a group known as the "Widows' Club," formed in about 1951 and made up mostly of Hiroshima women, a large number of them *hibakusha*. Many in the group were apparently part-time prostitutes, and a number turned out to have husbands who were very much alive and who even endorsed their wives' activities. Women with keloids were noted to be prominent among them; and one suspects that the group in general, identified as it was with Hiroshima and the bomb, had a somewhat exotic aura for outsiders (including a suggestion of linking sex with pain and victimization, or with sadomasochism), and perhaps for local clients an aura of familiarity. Economic factors were undoubtedly of great importance, but it is also possible that both the "widows" and their customers felt themselves to be countering atomic bomb death imagery through sexual reassertion of life.* Undoubtedly equally prominent, however, were feelings of guilt toward the dead, feelings made all the more intense by the socially unacceptable nature of this expression of vitality—and by the literal implications of "selling the bomb." For *hibakusha* as a group we may suspect that all post-bomb prostitution in Hiroshima, and the Widows' Club in particular, symbolized an eroticization of their taint (and therefore a tainted eroticism), a further humiliation of the deformed and an extension of residual distrust into the sexual area.

ILLUSORY REPOSSESSION, OUTCASTS, AND TAINTED PRIDE

Population trends in Hiroshima also convey a duality of imagery. On the one hand, the return of *hibakusha* to their city, following the initial post-bomb flight, has been impressive. By 1950, for instance, of 157,575 known Hiroshima *hibakusha* throughout Japan, 98,102 (a little less than two thirds) were living in Hiroshima City and 26,864 more were living in other parts of Hiroshima Prefecture. Since many who were in the city at the time of the bomb had permanent homes elsewhere (the military population, estimated at 90,000, came from all over Japan, and large numbers of civilians who worked in the city lived in outlying places in Hiroshima Prefecture), these figures attest to an impressive trend toward repossession rather than exile.

The other side of the picture is the much more extensive influx of outsiders into the city and the increasing disparity between the expanding group of outsiders and the diminishing number of *hibakusha*. Thus, by 1950 *hibakusha* made up one third of the city population of 285,712, but by 1964 the 93,608 *hibakusha* constituted less than 20 per cent of the city's overall population of 506,949, according to the Hiroshima City Office. Hence the paradox that over the years, as *hibakusha* have made their general recovery, a sense of genuine repossession of Hiroshima has been increasingly impossible—and the individual *hibakusha*'s sense that, on every level, he belongs to a "dying" group.

:

We have noted that *hibakusha* have sometimes been identified as "A-bomb outcasts," but the post-bomb experience of actual outcasts (*bura-*

---

* There is a certain tradition for the "sexy widow" in Japanese folklore and literature, which still finds echoes in contemporary life.

kumin) in Hiroshima is also worth noting, and has important bearing on long-range symbolism. With the destruction by the bomb of many *burakumin* areas, Japanese social commentators saw a historical opportunity to eliminate centuries-old patterns of discrimination and ghetto practice—through the simple expedient of dispersing the *burakumin* among the rest of the population.* But the *burakumin* ghettos somehow gradually re-formed themselves until, within a few years, things were pretty much the way they always had been. Most observers attributed the failure of the experiment to the tenacity of prejudice, the feeling that "even the A-bomb could not blast away this wall of discrimination."[7] One cannot contest this assertion, and the enduring nature of this "wall of discrimination" becomes the more impressive when one considers that *burakumin* are not physically distinguishable from ordinary people, so that they have to be continually identified through close observation and reporting techniques characteristic of Japanese culture. Moreover, it is quite possible that their own experience of being victimized made *hibakusha* even more prone to prejudice than before, more in need of another group to victimize, a pattern that would be consistent with the general psychology of victimization. But also important in the restoration of *burakumin* ghettos is a factor generally ignored—the continuing psychological need of *burakumin* for one another, and for the security of living among their own group. We have observed such needs in *hibakusha* themselves, as well as in those who are both *burakumin* and *hibakusha*, which are consistent with the well-known tendency for ghettos of all kinds to re-form themselves.[8] But from the standpoint of symbolic impact upon *hibakusha*, we may say that the re-establishment of *burakumin* ghettos represents a "return to normalcy," which could suggest a kind of social reintegration, but also conveys a reminder that base human qualities survive everything—a reminder which becomes particularly disturbing in relationship to the puristic moral demands perceived as emanating from the dead.

:

Finally, we can observe contending symbolism in the uneasy distinction Hiroshima has achieved as a city. A number of *hibakusha* I interviewed were impressed that an American such as myself would come to their city and seek them out, and made such comments as "this [atomic bomb] experience we have had has made the name of Hiroshima known all over the world—made the world aware that there is a place

---

* Some of the *buraku* areas were left relatively intact because of being located outside of the central area of the city.

called Hiroshima." But such statements, never free of irony or ambivalence, once more conveyed the sense of dubious distinction suggested by the man who contrasted *hibakusha* fame with winning a Nobel Prize. A few expressed such sentiments as "I know things that others don't know" or else referred somewhat nostalgically to the grim trials of the immediate bomb experience and its aftermath; but again these expressions of pride were accompanied by indications of strong fear, humiliation, and guilt. Still others, without becoming leaders, related themselves to their *hibakusha*hood in ways that made them individual symbols of atomic bomb destruction. Such was the case with one young woman who, six years after the bomb, developed a severe and persistent skin condition whose relationship to the atomic bomb doctors found difficult to evaluate; she then demonstrated her infirmity at various atomic bomb protest meetings, earned her living through performing needlework in association with a *hibakusha* organization, and during an interview manifested an extremely aggressive form of self-display which was part of a life-pattern built around anger, distrust, and conflict over the authenticity of the nurturance she demanded and received.

:

Although these polar themes of reintegration and residual distrust everywhere confront *hibakusha*, there is great variation in responses to them and in their weighting within individual psychological life. Differences depend upon such factors as severity of original death encounter, prior socioeconomic position, professional and educational skills which can be called upon, and those elusive but important capacities suggested by the terms "strength of identity" and "ego strength." Of particular importance have been capacities to absorb death imagery, to maintain flexible patterns of dependency, and to relate individual life experience to larger symbols or ideologies of reintegration. But these individual variations, as important as they are for the post-bomb life of the *hibakusha*, could not exempt any from a permanent struggle with contending symbols of life and death.

2) Commemoration

It was perhaps predictable that Hiroshima, after experiencing the world's first atomic bomb, would call upon the peace symbol as its rallying point for commemoration and rehabilitation, and that this symbol would become a psychic motif of great significance for individual *hibakusha*. What was less predictable was the psychological complexity of the need, response, and disillusionment surrounding the symbol.

The place to be converted into a "City of Peace" had possessed, almost from its beginnings, an unusually strong military identity. Originally a "castle town" (the center of a feudal fiefdom) with considerable economic importance for its area, during the early years of the Meiji Restoration Hiroshima was able to be readily transformed into a modern city, and by the outbreak of the Sino-Japanese War in 1894 it was the main military base for operations on the Asian mainland. It was to maintain this function for the next half-century, taking on added luster with Japan's victory in the Russo-Japanese War of 1905 and with her resounding successes in South Asia during the early phases of World War II. True, Hiroshima also had a "softer" side—as a cultural and educational center and the home of one of Japan's leading institutions for the training of teachers (later to become Hiroshima University), and as an easygoing provincial capital small enough for people to know one another and observe pleasant amenities. But the undeniable significance of warmaking in the city's background lent a note of retribution to the atomic bomb experience. As a local newspaper put it at the time of the city's seventieth anniversary in 1959: "The accelerated tempo in Hiroshima's development as a military city eventually prepared it for its ultimate tragedy."[9]

The principle that Hiroshima should be reconstituted as a peace city apparently found unanimous agreement from the beginning—consistent as it was with the wishes of ordinary *hibakusha*, city officials, and Occupation authorities; with Japan's general postwar mood of pacifism; and with the universal reaction of horror at the first use of nuclear weapons.

The necessary political steps were more difficult to bring about. But in 1949 a law passed by the Japanese Diet (with Occupation approval) conferred upon Hiroshima the title "International City of Peace" and granted a financial subsidy with which it could give material shape to this new identity. The Peace Park was built near the center of the city, close to the bomb's hypocenter, containing the official Atomic Bomb Monument or Cenotaph (completed in 1953), the Peace Memorial Hall (1955), the Peace Memorial Museum or Atomic Bomb Memorial Exhibition Hall (1955), and the Children's Atomic Bomb Monument (1958), as well as various other smaller monuments and designations. Constructed nearby were the Peace Bridge and the Peace Road (or, because of its width, "Hundred-Meter Road"). The rebuilt university was envisioned as an intellectual center for peace. And the general tendency to use "Atomic Bomb" and "Peace" almost interchangeably in naming these monuments suggests the psychological effort to equate the two in the sense of the latter springing from the ashes of the former.

There is no denying either the reintegrative symbolism of these physical expressions of the city's peace identity or the conflict and bitterness that have been associated with them. In the case of the construction of the museum, after much disagreement with the central government and among Hiroshima leaders themselves, a decision was made to proceed on a scale greater than that provided for by the Ministry of Construction in Tokyo. But lack of funds resulted in a prolonged interruption of work which left only the façade standing, causing people to be fearful that even that would collapse, and making a caricature of the intended symbolism of the building. More significant was the resentment aroused by the decision to place a large hotel adjacent to the monuments at the edge of the Peace Park, in anticipation of an influx of foreign visitors and in response to pressures from various commercial groups in the city. The distinguished architect originally selected to design both the Peace Museum and the Memorial Hall objected vehemently to the hotel, and was quoted as saying that, from it, visitors "would be looking down on the dead." Whatever the accuracy of the quotation, its sentiment was consistent with the emotionally-charged accusations of commercial desecration and of "selling the bomb" expressed to me by many individual *hibakusha*.

They also raised objections about the other monuments. The Peace Bridge, a striking contemporary structure designed by Isamu Noguchi, was frequently described to me as "strange" and "alien" to Hiroshima; one Buddhist group publicly called it a "Christian view of designing" rather than a truly "Oriental form"; and there has been the further complaint that Noguchi was not even Japanese (he is a Nisei, that is, a second-generation American of Japanese extraction), but was asked to design the bridge because he "just happened to be in Japan." The Hundred-Meter Road has also been termed inappropriate and, more pointedly, referred to as "the Royal Road to the ABCC." Running through these criticisms is a basic suspicion of counterfeit nurturance and a related fear of American influence—that is, of the city's being recast in the image of the nation that dropped the bomb. But also involved are the difficulties, architectural and psychohistorical, associated with reconstructing the city's form and identity within a *contemporary international idiom*.

Concerning the university, although a respectable academic institution it has had neither the intellectual nor material resources nor the unity of outlook necessary to become the "mecca of peace" which some envisioned. The Children's Monument is perhaps the most generally accepted of the commemorative structures, but it is something of an accessory to the main monuments, and we are already familiar with some of the controversy which surrounded its creation.

:

In their symbolic importance two among the completed monuments, the Peace Museum and the Cenotaph, have aroused particularly intense responses among *hibakusha*.

The museum was largely the creation of one man, a geologist who at the time of the bomb noted that rocks had melted, and began to make careful observations and collect a great variety of specimens (mostly the rocks themselves), which he chose for the shapes they had assumed and the shadows which had been imprinted on them. These early activities, carried out with great energy, were both a professional-technical form of psychic closing-off and a creative response to death guilt ("With so many people dying, I thought that something must be done," he told me). Despite disruptive jealousies among colleagues, his collection eventually became the nucleus for the museum's exhibits and he became its first curator.

Under his leadership the museum expanded its collection of specimens and also came to display such things as a matter-of-fact bilingual description of the dropping of the atomic bomb (much of it from *Life*), and of the weapon's destructive features; a group of mannequins representing actual people injured or killed, showing the clothing they had been wearing and indicating to what degree it had protected them from radiation effects at the particular distance each was from the hypocenter; and an extensive series of photographs of the dead and injured, and of the city's general devastation, taken during the days immediately following the bomb, the exhibit which has undoubtedly made the strongest impression upon visitors.

But the longer-range development of the museum inevitably gave rise to controversy. The curator wished to enlarge its exhibits and make them into what he considered a popular, but completely scientific, display of the "true nature" or "essence" of the atomic bomb experience. The city, however, moved cautiously, because of its own reluctance to provide additional funds and because of increasing pressures from various parts of the Hiroshima community to avoid placing too much stress upon the horrors of the bomb—pressures originating not only in commerical groups but in genuine emotional ambivalence within ordinary *hibakusha*. The result was a compromise in which existing displays were retained but expansion was limited, and an exhibit of the "peaceful uses of atomic energy" was added (though later discontinued).

Most *hibakusha* who discussed the museum with me shared the curator's wish that it convey the "true nature" or full horror of what they had been through. But they thought this impossible, and were convinced that its beautiful modern exterior and orderly exhibits fell far short of genuine representation.

:

Even more emotionally charged was the controversy surrounding the actual A-Bomb Monument, the Cenotaph. The monument was preceded by a "Soul-Reposing Tower," hastily constructed the first spring after the A-bomb; however crude, it seemed to be a meaningful part of the city's early rebirth, and probably conveyed for many a greater sense of authenticity than did its more elaborate successor. In the case of the Cenotaph, conflict springs not so much from the design itself—which is abstract, simple, and strong—as from its public function and significance. Difficulties began when Hiroshima officials' plan to make it large enough to include actual remains was overruled by the Ministry of Construction in Tokyo, which insisted that this was not economically feasible and that the monument need contain only the names of the dead. The decision did not violate traditional practice and was in fact satisfactory to many *hibakusha*: as one told me, "My son's name included on the very first memorial list gives me a strong sense of his soul being there in repose." But it undoubtedly left some with the feeling that the extraordinary quality of Hiroshima's experience was not being taken into account. Or, at a psychological level, we may say that *hibakusha* were not being permitted the added obeisance to the dead which they sought in order to relieve their extraordinary guilt.

Much more resented was the inscription on the Cenotaph which in translation reads:

Rest in peace.
The mistake shall not be repeated.[10]

Here the controversy revolves around the question of *whose* "mistake" the A-bomb was, with the problem compounded by the vagueness of the Japanese language, particularly concerning the subject of a clause or sentence. Many *hibakusha* thought the inscription implied that they, the victims of the A-bomb, were being blamed instead of those who used the weapon. But some saw virtue precisely in this vagueness (apparently intentional on the part of the university professor who wrote the inscription) because of its suggestion of universal blame. Mayor Hamai, for instance, spoke of the "mistake" as "the use of the fruits of science for killing, maiming, and destroying," and emphasized that although in relationship to atomic weapons it was America who first did this, "all belligerents had a desire to possess such formidable weapons," so that "everyone, as part of mankind, must bear his portion of the responsibility." He added that the phrase about the mistake not being repeated "means not only that we ourselves will not repeat it but that we will try to prevent any other people from doing so."[11]

The real difficulty with the inscription, however, is that it made public and permanent the *hibakusha*'s own unconscious self-accusation, his conviction that his "mistake" in remaining alive was the cause of atomic bomb deaths. This pattern was clarified, and also intensified, by an angry comment of a visiting Indian jurist, comparing what he saw as a Japanese tendency to look upon the disaster as their own fault to a similar tendency of Indians to hold themselves responsible ("because they are bad") for oppression at the hands of the British. The astuteness of his comparison lies in its suggestion of the universal guilt of the victim. And when he went on to claim that both cases illustrated the tendency of the white race to encourage such self-condemnation by its victims as a means of covering up its own sins, he raised the uncomfortable issue (which we shall later discuss) of the association of the atomic bomb experience with racial emotions.

Underneath these city struggles over memorialization was a nostalgic tone of a municipal paradise lost. Like Miss Ōta, *hibakusha* longed for what one described as "that special intimacy found in a castle town," and another as "the feeling of brotherhood for which Hiroshima people were famous . . . the Hiroshima mentality which, since the atomic bomb, has been lost." The same man went on to state that as yet "no new Hiroshima mentality has been born,"[12] again suggesting that the synthesized identity of the "City of Peace" falls short of satisfying emotional needs, and that the combination of instant devastation and post-bomb confusion has intensified universal longings for childhood innocence—for a state without knowledge of guilt or death, one which no monument can restore.

A-BOMB DOME: RECEPTACLE FOR AMBIVALENCE

A monument left by the atomic bomb itself, in the form of a ruin, has taken on the greatest symbolic significance of all. The Atomic Bomb Dome (or Peace Dome) consists of the remains of what was formerly an industrial exhibition hall located close to the hypocenter. One of the few reinforced concrete buildings in Hiroshima, its dome-shaped outline stayed intact midst the total rubble around it, and was then permitted to stand as a reminder of the atomic bomb experience. Over the years its aura of desolation has contrasted increasingly with the glistening new city growing up around it. And its picture has been featured in so many stories and books dealing with the atomic bomb that it has probably become the dominant visual image of Hiroshima's exposure to that weapon.

It has been an equally dominant center of conflict: publicly, between commercial and civic groups which insist it be torn down, and peace movement groups which demand it be retained; and privately, in the psychological lives of individual *hibakusha*. This conflict was revealed in three different attitudes about the Dome expressed to me.

One group of *hibakusha* favored keeping the Dome as a permanent reminder of the atomic bomb experience. The shopkeeper's assistant, for instance, looked upon it as "a kind of warning, the only thing that remains [to suggest] that such a thing once happened [and make clear] in people's minds that if another war occurs, the same thing would happen again." Others stressed that it is needed mostly for American visitors, that it should be kept "so that when people come from America, they can understand, by seeing it, what a terrible thing the A-bomb in Hiroshima was."

But ambivalence was the keynote—the idea that the Dome's retention was necessary but painful—as expressed by the white-collar worker:

> I would rather see it preserved. Without it, we would tend to forget the event completely and simply be easygoing. But whenever I see it, I feel my nerves becoming taut . . . not so much pain as a kind of tension and a sense of responsibility. . . . Despite having been in the midst of so many people being killed, I am now living. . . . Yes, it is a responsibility coming from my being alive.

Here the tone is that of "lest we forget": clearly he would *like* to forget, but he does not feel he has the right to. The Dome both reminds him of his guilt over survival priority (which he makes explicit) and becomes a constructive channel for the guilt (the "responsibility coming from my being alive").

Similarly, the physicist, although publicly committed to the principle of retaining the Dome, admitted that this was "a rather cruel thing" to ask of *hibakusha*. He thought they should bear the pain because of the larger good the Dome might do for peace, but concluded that

> If I could really feel at some future time that the people of the world understood the enormity of the bomb to the extent that I do, then I would say that the Dome should be torn down.

To grasp the full force of emotions which surround the problem, we must turn to the second group of *hibakusha*, those who advocate that the Dome be immediately removed. The tourist agency employee, for instance, related a series of associations to illustrate his strong conviction that the Dome is worthless because it makes an intolerable emotional impact upon *hibakusha* and leaves everyone else unaffected:

> On the way here [to your office] I saw children swimming in the river. Those who went through the bomb would never swim there. . . . I remember passing that spot and seeing dead bodies floating on the water—burnt and black dead bodies. . . . Whenever I see the river there, and when I see the Dome at the same time, I recall that scene. . . . But present-day children are indifferent to such things and simply enjoy themselves. So even if the Dome is kept, to those who have not experienced the bomb it will appear to be simply an object. . . . I think it would be better to tear the Dome down without hesitation, rather than increase this grief. . . .

He went on to say that the Dome might have some value if visitors "could see the burned bodies of actual people just as they were at the time," but since this is impossible, "the best thing would be to make it into something like an amusement center—a place for family outings." His requirements, in other words, are uncompromising: either absolute fidelity to the experience (meaning the experience itself), or else absolute obliteration of reminders of that experience.

The abandoned mother was also reminded of the appearance of people at the time of the bomb, and expressed the same sentiments more simply:

> As I walked along the street by the Dome [on the way to your office] I felt frightened, afraid. . . . I had a sense of dread, and that building [the Dome] itself seemed dark, gloomy, and horrible.

Others emphasized how the Dome "works on people's emotions" and "spoils the beauty of the city," and suggested that it be removed so that they could "feel refreshed"—or else expressed the related idea that the Dome had to be removed for *hibakusha* to overcome hostility to America, since "even though people speak of having a friendly relationship between Japan and America, its being there reminds us that America dropped the bomb."

There was also the persistent theme of inauthenticity, of the Dome having "value for tourists but no value for those who live in Hiroshima," and of its becoming associated with "selling the bomb"—or as the grocer puts it, "selling the Dome":

> Well, I don't mind leaving it as a memorial, but selling the Dome as a sightseeing object or—well, I can't stand people's impure motives becoming mixed in with it. Since such impure motives are unavoidable—and since we have the Memorial Hall and the Cenotaph —well, I think we better simply remove it. If I were in charge, I would have it taken away right now.

Suggestions were offered concerning a more authentic structure: The Buddhist priest's idea (mentioned before) of a *bussharito* or tower for the ashes of Buddha, "So that we can forget, not remember such things, and attain true peace." And the history professor's more original opinion to the effect that since the Dome "is not the true hypocenter" (it is thought to be about a hundred meters from it) and is "misleading," as it could have been produced by an ordinary bomb, then authenticity should be sought in "nothingness":

> We should figure out the exact hypocenter—and possibly put some small artistic monument on it—or better still, leave it devoid of anything at all ˙. . . in order to symbolize nothingness at the hypo-center—because that is what there was. . . . Such a weapon has the power to make everything into nothing, and I think this should be symbolized.

The third group of *hibakusha* favor an ingenious compromise solu-tion, which has actually been proposed as policy by the city administra-tion: neither tear the Dome down nor permit it to stand indefinitely—but instead wait until it begins to crumble of its own in a way that could be dangerous to people near it, and then simply remove it. This solution makes use of a traditional East Asian pattern of action through inaction, of depending upon the passage of time to contribute to the solution of a problem that might be made worse by immediate intervention. It also responds to the excruciating ambivalence of *hibakusha* without resorting to either of the disturbing alternatives.

Indeed, this "third way" fuses those alternatives. Thus, the heroic city official told me that he was "very much in favor of retaining evidence of this enormous experience—of letting everyone know about it," but of doing so without exposing survivors to further pain because "they are precisely the ones who already know about the experience"—and he illustrated his point with a conjugal example:

> My wife lost her parents and her uncle and many other relatives, and she simply cannot tolerate seeing the Dome—or even relics of the experience—she just can't look at these things.

Similarly, the philosopher carefully weighed these painful *hibakusha* associations against the recognition that tearing down the Dome im-mediately might "hurt many people's feelings" and "dilute or weaken anti-A-bomb sentiments," and concluded that the compromise solution was best. The "third way," in other words, is the way of harmony, of reconciling contending forces within the individual and within the city at large, and in this way also makes contact with Japanese tradition.

But it is also an attitude behind which one can hide. Thus, the elderly widow accepted the compromise because "I guess those people [in authority] are better equipped to take care of the matter," and the female poet because "I feel both ways and I don't know which is right."

Some, like the writer-physician, reject the Dome as a symbolic object around which to deal with A-bomb concerns: "I myself have little interest in it. I don't care if it is preserved as a monument or if it is cleared away." Or, like Miss Ōta, in more forceful terms: "I don't care. It doesn't symbolize anything. It is simply dirty." The writer-physician and Miss Ōta are people who care about symbols; and although they may be suppressing certain emotions about the Dome, they are telling us that midst the great public furor, the Dome has lost its power as an *authentic* symbol and has become (in Miss Ōta's words) "a stereotype."*

The involvement of visitors in this balancing effort was suggested by some wry comments of a minor city official:

> Some of the foreigners who come to Hiroshima are disappointed at seeing how beautifully the city has reconstructed itself . . . and would like to leave the Dome there as a symbol of this extraordinary manmade atomic bomb. . . . But half of the Hiroshima people . . . [including] actual victims . . . who don't want to remind themselves . . . really want it torn down.

He concluded with the practical observation that the issue has come up only because the city owns the property on which the Dome stands, and that if it were privately owned, "the building would have been torn down, and the land used for another business project." This last opinion was more or less confirmed by the construction right next to the Dome in 1965 (three years after my study, and after this section had been written) of a nine-story office building (in the words of an American commentator) "dominating it, belittling it, making it nearly invisible from some directions."†[13]

But whatever is done to the Hiroshima landscape, the psychological issues surrounding the Dome remain important clues to *hibakusha* emotions. Slightly fewer than one third of those I interviewed expressed

---

* She used the word "*manneriszumu*," which is the Japonized version of "mannerism," but in ordinary usage has come to mean "roteness" and "stereotypy" more than "mannerism" as such.

† One year later, as if out of contrition, the Hiroshima City Council voted to preserve the remains of the Dome permanently. A campaign to raise ¥ 40,000,000 ($110,000) for that purpose through popular subscription, inaugurated in November, 1966, at first fared badly. But renewed efforts by Hiroshima officials and various kinds of national publicity accelerated the response, and on March 14, 1967, Mayor Hamai announced its successful completion and said that reinforcement work would soon be undertaken for the purpose of "eternal preservation."

themselves as being in favor of retaining the Dome, one third favored tearing it down, and slightly more than one third either favored the "third way" or else refused to express any definite opinion. There was only a slightly greater tendency in the special group of *hibakusha*—those most publicly concerned with the A-bomb problem—toward retaining the Dome. And although all three groups were characterized by great ambivalence, the desire to get rid of the Dome seemed to reflect much more powerful inner emotions than did the wish to retain it.

In general, we may characterize the Dome's psychohistorical function as that of providing a focus for the expression of struggles for mastery. It is an external receptacle for, as well as a reflector and intensifier of, A-bomb emotions. It has brought about a measure of release from conflicts over guilt by means of "taking on" some of the responsibility to the dead, including that of the survivor's mission of alerting the rest of the world to nuclear danger. But this positive function has been more than canceled out by its exacerbation of conflicts, by its seeming demand that the individual *hibakusha* not only stay guilty, but be dominated by guilt at the center of his being, just as the city at its center has been dominated by the Dome. The psychological quest in keeping the Dome, then, is to maintain a receptacle for guilt; that of tearing it down is to hack away guilt; and that of the "third way" is, so to speak, to resolve guilt without resolution. Ambivalence pervading the Dome issue therefore extends over such fundamental dimensions as the idea, both embraced and rejected, of serving as human symbols of A-bomb death; feelings of love and hate toward the dead, and the wish to remember and forget them; and the question of the authenticity of any external object in representing the dead, and of the survivor's right to allow such an object to assume his responsibility.

AUGUST 6: CEREMONY, FESTIVAL, BATTLEGROUND

The yearly commemoration of the bomb heightens struggles over mastery by epitomizing the *hibakusha*'s relationship to the dead, and by serving as the *annual moment in time around which the entire hibakusha identity revolves*. It too has inevitably become enmeshed in conflict.

The first August 6 commemoration, during the still desperate post-bomb days of 1946, was perhaps the most generally satisfactory one. There was a simple ceremony held in front of the Soul-Reposing Tower, mostly religious (Buddhist, Shinto, and Christian) in nature, with mourners of all kinds observed in quiet prayer—"bereaved families . . . repatriated soldiers praying for their lost wives, an old lady placing prayer beads around the hands of her grandson, victims with keloids presenting flowers to the dead."[14]

But the subdued atmosphere did not last. By the following year city authorities had decided to conduct a larger ceremony modeled upon the traditional *Shōkon-sai* (ceremony for the invocation of the spirits of the dead), Japan's national equivalent of Memorial Day. *Shōkon-sai* was customarily a joyous occasion, and Hiroshima had long been known for the elaborateness and gaiety of its version of it—including dancing, carnival acts, horse races, and what might be viewed as the Japanese version of a Mardi gras spirit. During the three-day period of the second commemoration the old *Shōkon-sai* spirit prevailed, along with a few postwar and post-bomb touches: jazz music over loudspeakers, flashing neon signs, songs about the "brilliant flash" of the "atomic sphere" and the "upward flight of the doves of peace," beautiful girls from the "water world" wearing elaborate kimono and flowers in their hair dancing to this music, and "atomic" shops of every kind featuring "big peace sales." Although there was also a dignified memorial ceremony, including sober messages from General MacArthur and the mayor of the city about the need for mankind to learn the lesson of Hiroshima, most people seemed to recall mainly the festival atmosphere. The shocked reaction of foreign visitors also made considerable impact upon the city.

In subsequent years these activities were greatly modified, and emphasis was increasingly placed upon declarations of peace. But the problem of tone and atmosphere of the August 6 commemoration has never been solved and probably never can be. For it would seem that however much *hibakusha* have resented "impure" patterns of commercial activity and general gaiety, they have also sought them. They have connected these patterns with their cultural traditions, and have lacked any alternative principles on how to behave when commemorating an atomic bomb.

Additional problems also came to affect the ceremonies: the deteriorating international situation, and a new American stress upon military vigilance and upon the rearming of Japan, brought about a change in emphasis in General MacArthur's yearly messages, with less said about peace and more about reconstruction. And there developed in Japan a militantly leftist political movement which embraced the peace symbol in its own fashion and came to play an increasingly important role in August 6 ceremonies.

The result was that in 1950, with the anniversary coming up just after the outbreak of the Korean War, Occupation authorities decided to cancel most August 6 activities. But a certain amount of violence did occur between demonstrating laborers and Hiroshima police; and *hibakusha* began to register resentment both toward Japanese political groups recognized as manipulators of peace protests and toward Occupation authorities at whose command such protests were suppressed. Witnessing these disturbing public clashes, as well as later ones revolving around the better organized and more aggressively dogmatic activities of *Gensuikyō* (Japanese Council Against A- and H-Bombs), could only cause most *hibakusha* to recoil in anger and confusion. Their yearly atomic bomb commemoration had taken on the contours of a political battleground.

"ANNIVERSARY REACTIONS": * AUGUST 6, 1962

During the ceremony I attended on August 6, 1962, such political antagonisms were much in evidence, side by side with a more restrained commemorative spirit.

On the afternoon of August 5 there was a large demonstration and march to the Peace Park made up mostly of labor groups and sponsored by *Gensuikyō*. The children of the Folded Crane Club joined the march, starting out from the A-Bomb Hospital; and I was later told that when patients waved at the children from their balconies, there were tears in the eyes of everyone present, including those of an American television cameraman sent to cover the event. The demonstrators assembled in the Peace Park, where they were addressed not only by their own leaders but by the mayor and other city officials, since this kind of event had become part of the city's overall program, despite its controversial nature and despite the mayor's known disapproval of the movement's one-sidedness. Much less polite were a group of student hecklers from the *Zengakuren* (All-Japan Federation of Student Self-Governing Societies) who made use of small portable loudspeakers to denounce *Gensuikyō* in the strongest terms, and to demand that it condemn Russian as well as American nuclear testing.† Feelings were

---

* The term has been used in psychiatric research to describe a somewhat different but related phenomenon: the tendency of patients to re-enact—in symbolic and often pathological form—disturbing childhood events, particularly loss of a parent. The "anniversary reaction" occurs either when the patient reaches the age at which the parent died, or when the patient's child reaches the age the patient was when the parent died.[15]

† The *Zengakuren* is itself a radical organization which has on many occasions protested against American actions. But it (or its dominant faction) has frequently

particularly strong on that August 5 about *Gensuikyō's* nuclear double standard (condemning American testing while defending as necessary testing by "peace-loving nations") because it had been learned just the night before that the Russians had begun a new series of atmospheric tests by exploding a thirty-megaton bomb.

A final touch to the scene were the dedicated efforts of two members of an American pacifist family living in Hiroshima—world-famous for its protest voyages into American and Soviet nuclear test zones—a mother and her teen-age daughter, attempting to mediate across language barriers between demonstrators and hecklers, pointing out to the latter that many of the groups taking part were opposed to the one-sided policies dictated within *Gensuikyō* from above, and were themselves working hard to promote a more balanced position on nuclear testing. But these "peace negotiations" were of little avail, and mutual recriminations continued.

The atmosphere in the Peace Park early the next morning was very different. From 7 A.M. people began to gather near the Cenotaph, several thousand in number, although one did not get the sense of a city turning out en masse. Standing under the extremely hot morning sun (they say in Hiroshima that August 6 is always clear and hot, and coming as it does during the summer dry season, it usually is) while waiting for the ceremony to begin, one could understand the *hibakusha* tendency to associate both the heat and the occasion with the original day of the bomb. The program consisted mostly of brief speeches by city officials—notably a peace message from the mayor—and of the laying of wreaths in front of the Cenotaph by representatives of various city, national, and international organizations concerned with *hibakusha* and with peace. A children's choir and orchestra and a mothers' choral group provided musical interludes. Also part of the ceremony was the adding of 125 new names to the Cenotaph, 42 of whom died from illnesses believed related to A-bomb effects and the remainder newly discovered victims of the original disaster. At exactly 8:15 A.M. a thousand peace doves were released from cages kept at the side of the monument, and an A-bomb orphan rang the bell of peace by striking a large gong several times. Shortly afterward the ceremony ended. My general reaction to this brief official commemoration was that although public and therefore "staged"—that is, planned by its organizers as an expression of

---

been at odds with *Gensuikyō* and with other organizations controlled by the Communist hierarchy (from which many of its own leaders originally split off), and it has taken a universalistic position in its opposition to nuclear weapons.

Hiroshima's symbolic role as the first A-bombed city—it was nonetheless dignified and impressive.

Even more impressive were scenes that took place immediately afterward, as people—many of them very old—made their way to the Cenotaph and burned incense to the souls of dead relatives. As they wiped their faces with handkerchiefs in the extreme heat, it was difficult to distinguish perspiration from tears. Throughout the rest of the day, in various locations in the Peace Park, there were smaller religious ceremonies conducted by Buddhist, Shinto, Christian, and other religious groups (including postwar sects), all paying tribute to the dead and stressing themes of peace. Many *hibakusha*, I was told, found these smaller ceremonies more congenial than the larger ones.

But that same afternoon political strife returned to the Peace Park with *Gensuikyō*'s international conference in the adjoining Peace Memorial Hall. The atmosphere was less that of a peace meeting than an armed camp, as tough-looking *Gensuikyō* guards wearing identifying armbands held themselves alert at the entrance to the hall, anticipating further difficulty from the *Zengakuren*. The *Zengakuren* pickets did appear but were few in number, and the protests they shouted into their hand megaphones were drowned out by shrill *Gensuikyō* speeches from within the hall which were piped out through larger amplifiers attached to the outside of the building, causing them to reverberate throughout the entire surrounding area. On the floor of the meeting too there was bitter ideological struggle, along with suggestions of physical combat. With the passage of a resolution condemning all nuclear testing, whether Russian or American (in a brief reversal of the national *Gensuikyō* position brought about by the Hiroshima prefectural branch of the organization), the entire Chinese and Russian delegations and two members of the North Korean delegation dramatically walked out of the meeting. And a few *Zengakuren* students, who had somehow made their way into the hall, were forcibly ejected from it. (There was also, a little later on, a more quiet peace meeting held in the same hall by a rival peace organization known popularly as the "Second *Gensuikyō*," but it attracted relatively little attention or support.)

That evening there again occurred the type of sudden change of atmosphere one had by this time become accustomed to. A festival spirit came over the city, though one of a very special kind. People walked actively about dressed in *yukata* (summer kimono), making purchases from small booths selling either materials for mourning (incense sticks, paper lanterns, etc.) or else food, souvenirs, and knickknacks of every variety. Magnificent fireworks were set off in front of the Peace Park. All this was in preparation for the main activity of the evening, the floating of paper lanterns along the rivers, each lantern bearing the name of a person killed in the atomic bomb and usually a prayer for peace as well. This custom, now a regular feature of August 6 commemorative activities, was derived from the traditional summer festivals for the dead, held annually throughout Japan, whose name, *bon*, is often translated as "festival of lanterns." The scene was extraordinarily beautiful, and one had the impression that the emotional pain of individual *hibakusha* was tempered by their immersion in the aesthetics of the experience.

I also watched the Folded Crane Club conduct its own special lantern ceremony. Led by the day laborer ("zealot-saint"), a group of about twenty children marched solemnly through the Hiroshima streets, chanting simple anti-A-bomb slogans and reciting what are probably (at least in Japan) the most famous words written about the atomic bomb, the first lines of a poem by the now dead Hiroshima poet Sankichi Tōge: "Give back my father, give back my mother/Give grandpa back, grandma back/Give our sons and daughters back. . . ." The lanterns the children had prepared bore the names of other children who had died from the A-bomb, except for one with the name of a seventy-three-year-old man included because he had no other family. They also floated, from the secluded river bank they had chosen, a little paper barge bearing a replica of the Children's Monument in the Peace Park, along with a protest against Russian resumption of testing and a demand for an end to all nuclear testing. As the children marched away from the river bank, again chanting their slogans and the lines from Tōge's poem, a teen-age girl among them suddenly broke down and began to sob uncontrollably—it turned out that her brother, a *hibakusha*, had died of leukemia four years before. The day laborer rushed over to comfort her, but he too soon became very excited and began to shout words to the effect that the world must stop this kind of barbarism and put an end to weapons that cause so much human misery. Spotting me just a few yards away, he ran toward me and shouted, "Please let them know about these things in America."

These two emotional outbreaks were not isolated events but part of the general intensification of A-bomb feelings in relationship to the August 6 ceremony. At just about this time, for instance, one of my assistants, not a *hibakusha* but Hiroshima-born and close to the general problem, told me that the strain of our interviews was becoming a burden for him; and a young woman *hibakusha* who had been assisting my wife with literary research expressed the same feeling to her.

This kind of "anniversary reaction" both stimulates and is stimulated by a monthlong buildup in the mass media prior to August 6—interviews with prominent survivors, poignant descriptions of continuing suffering, and discussions of peace movement issues, international nuclear dangers, and of Hiroshima's special responsibilities. All emotions seem to be intensified by the summer sun, until on August 6 itself a citywide crescendo is reached; the events of that day permit discharge and decrescendo; and the cycle begins again the following July—the general pattern consistent with psychological inclinations of the Japanese toward atmospheric rhythms of this kind.

I felt that these events of August 6 combined elements of sad conflict, lightness, fantasy, beauty, protest, commercial concern, and reportorial awareness. Sad conflict was evident in various kinds of mourning behavior, including tears shed. The lightness had to do with the general festival atmosphere—by no means wild or abandoned, but rather one of easygoing activity, of effortless flow with the tide, of enjoying the pleasures life holds out, of moving away from pain. Fantasy was expressed in the childlike aura surrounding all Japanese festivals, a sense of make-believe which here included a magic plea for the calm of the dead and for peace among the living; the implicit belief, "If I float this lantern, his or her soul will be taken care of, and I will be protected," was accompanied by the realization, at another level, that all of this really was make-believe. The beauty pervaded virtually all events (with the notable exception of the political ones) in their grace of ceremony, and in a tone of aesthetic sensitivity associated with sadness and impermanence which dominates much of Japanese literature and emotional life. Known as *mono no aware* (the "suchness of things" or the "sad beauty of existence"), this quality is strongly related to the capacity to transcend death. Protest included a wide range of expressions, from hard-core ideological manipulations to the most spontaneous of individual outpourings, but was for most muted by the other demands of commemoration. Commercial concerns were clear enough in the visible buying and selling, and were undoubtedly even more formidable in behind-the-scenes arrangements; although considerably less glaring than reputed to have been in the past, they were still a problem to individual *hibakusha*. The reportorial focus was evident in the ubiquitousness of cameras and journalists, and undoubtedly contributed to a strong (and ambivalent) sense on the part of many *hibakusha* of sharing their event with the outside world and having to behave accordingly. In response to these various currents I made a four-word note to characterize the ceremonies: incense, fantasy, politics, cameras.

THE DEAD REVISITED: INDIVIDUAL REACTIONS

Can individual *hibakusha* be anything but confused by this array of forces?

Some, despite everything, speak with affirmation of the events of August 6—as was true of the shopkeeper's assistant:

> When the day comes around . . . the memory of the bomb comes back to me . . . and I have a feeling I cannot describe. . . . I feel that up to now . . . with all of the hardship, I have somehow managed to come through. . . . I have the feeling that I must go there [to the Peace Park]—I just can't help going. . . . Well, there are the souls of the people killed by the bomb and I can pray to them. If I don't go, I have the feeling something is wrong—I go there because . . . I want to sleep peacefully.

We may say he feels called by the dead; but although his participation has the compulsion of guilt, it nonetheless symbolizes for him another step toward mastery and toward the right to mastery.

The *burakumin* boy described similar feelings. After first attempting to stay away and "as much as possible not think about it," he somehow found himself in the Peace Park, virtually in the midst of the dead, where he experienced

> a kind of loneliness . . . [which] came from the people who died— from those who were sacrificed—it was their influence.

The electrician also spoke of August 6 as "for the most part a lonely day," but upon lighting incense for his son and "seeing all of the incense burning there—all of the flowers and all of the people, including foreigners"—he found himself "feeling very happy." Loneliness, in other words, was appropriate; and his happiness consisted of a sense of satisfaction at fulfilling his obligations toward the dead, sharing his sentiments with other *hibakusha*, and having his actions approvingly "confirmed" by outsiders.

But there are others who experience maximum psychological pain—a direct revival of death guilt and of ultimate horror—as revealed in the civil service employee's immediate associations to August 6 commemoration:

Well, the color of my brother's keloid—the color of his burns—mix together with my feeling . . . what I saw directly—that is, the manner in which he died, that's what I remember. . . . The color was similar to that of a dried squid when broiled—so that I think of it whenever I see dried squid. . . . I have the feeling that the A-bomb was so terrible . . . a very lonely feeling.

Emotions like these cause many to avoid the Peace Park and to commemorate the occasion in private. A number of *hibakusha* emphasized their need for simplicity and purity of experience—"I place a candle on the family altar, and worship alone by reciting a sutra"*—and their wariness of public observances in which "People gather together for all sorts of purposes that I can't approve of."

There were some, however, who objected not to the violation of the commemorative spirit but to that commemorative spirit itself, which they saw as stifling necessary protest. The *burakumin* woman leader, for instance, with characteristic militancy, emphasized that it is not enough for people merely to "gather before the Monument and clasp their hands":

They ought to go further than simply feeling individual sorrow . . . and express their feelings by taking action. . . . Praying for the repose of the souls of the dead may be necessary, but we should make efforts, as is written on the Monument, to make sure it won't be repeated . . . and then the sacrifices will not have been for nothing.

Protest becomes her means of achieving reconciliation with the dead, the psychological equivalent of commemoration; and she also expresses the rebel's demand to be active rather than acted upon. Her *burakumin* identity, as well as her having been just an infant at the time of the bomb—and therefore less burdened by subsequent death guilt than others with clearer memories of it—are undoubtedly important factors in her attitude.

But perhaps the most characteristic *hibakusha* reaction was resentment of political and commercial activities surrounding the August 6 ceremony. A typical comment was that of the abandoned mother: "I somehow feel animosity toward people who made a noisy clamor at those mass meetings." The grocer went further in describing the event as "utterly empty, no more than a festival—a festival that gives people a

---

* A Buddhist prayer, or sermon of Buddha.

chance to be noisy," accusing city leaders of "selling the fact that the A-bomb was dropped." And the history professor described such "great resentment" toward the "big festivals" on August 6 that

> I used to have to get out of the city because I found it unbearable.
> . . . There was something about them which almost drove me crazy.
> . . . Sometimes shops would have special sales. I felt like slapping people for doing this, for making such a thing of this day. Now it is changing somewhat, and I noticed that this time things were quieter.
> . . . But I don't take much part in it. . . . I have always felt that this should be a silent occasion—expressing a form of warning.

Behind these negative reactions is a deeply disturbing sense of desecration of the dead, and of violated responsibility of the living to the dead, causing *hibakusha* guilt to be magnified to an intolerable level. Much of the anger has to do with the fact that these "violations"—whether commercial, ideological, or in the form of festival gaiety—activate latent urges of *hibakusha* themselves either to ignore the dead, to combine ritual attention to them with joyousness, or even to take part in the economic or political activities they so bitterly condemn. The problem is complicated by patterns of historical change which render increasingly less acceptable the old ethos of festival gaiety in relationship to the spirits of the dead, and at the same time give rise to many of the resented financial practices and ideological passions.

The *hibakusha's* struggle over commemoration, then, is a search for a mode of involvement with the dead which stresses his continuity with them, absorbs his guilt, and reasserts his own right to live. Public behavior which flaunts vitality, particularly vitality associated with personal aggrandizement, maximizes guilt. In contrast, behavior which stresses quietude is more likely to minimize guilt by symbolizing a kind of "leveling off" with the dead. But the *hibakusha* requires something more than merely the opportunity for subdued individual worship. To deal with the enormity of his experience, he requires some form of group symbolism of rebirth so that he can associate himself with Hiroshima's living out its difficult historical task as the first atomic bombed city. Since this task requires a certain amount of manipulation, vitality, and general public "noise," his struggles over commemoration take on the quality of walking a psychological tightrope between angry sensitivity to all that seems to desecrate the dead, and participation in that same desecration.

3) Dimensions of Peace

Beyond monuments and commemoration, questions of organized peace movements, nuclear testing, and Japanese rearmament have important bearing upon residual *hibakusha* conflicts and upon struggles for mastery.

Hibakusha, as usual, find themselves in a confusing position. Their A-bomb exposure has made them the symbolic core of Japan's powerful postwar peace sentiment, and has contributed greatly toward making their country the most peace-minded nation in the world. But because of having been for some time rendered inarticulate by the physical and emotional impact of that exposure, and because of lacking a geographic tradition for intellectual leadership, most of their ideas about organized peace efforts have had to originate from the outside. While they themselves have in no way lacked strong feelings about war and peace, these feelings have had to relate themselves to systems of thought quite removed from their own experience.

Some have placed the entire blame for this *hibakusha* inarticulateness upon Occupation censorship of writings about the atomic bomb. But this claim ignores not only the conflicts over vitality and protest we have been discussing, but also the initial American encouragement of an attitude of pacifism. What can be said is that early censorship contributed to a "delayed explosion" of atomic bomb emotions, both among *hibakusha* themselves and Japanese in general.

It was only after the Bikini incident of 1954 that Japanese peace sentiment was shaped into a mass movement. At that time a group of Japanese fishermen were exposed to fallout from American hydrogen bomb testing in the Pacific, resulting in the death of one of them. The movement then originated in a ban-the-bomb signature campaign conducted by a housewives' reading club in Tokyo under the leadership of a former university professor who had lost his position because of wartime military involvements (reminding us, in this personal shift, of two of the Hiroshima A-bomb leaders we have described). The movement spread with such rapidity that within two years forty million signatures were said to have been collected, more than a million of these in Hiroshima Prefecture alone. The effort culminated in the formation of

Gensuikyō and in the First International Conference Against A- and H-bombs held in Hiroshima on August 6, 1955, the tenth anniversary of the dropping of the bomb. This was the honeymoon period of the Japanese peace movement, with *Gensuikyō* generally thought of as a loose non-partisan confederation of representative groups from within Japanese society, a means of calling forth the nation's vast reservoir of peace sentiment. *Hibakusha* were called upon to epitomize this sentiment, and were said to have been invited to visit all parts of Japan to share their experiences with eager audiences.[16]

Even so, conflicts existed from the beginning. A number of survivors, for instance, expressed resentment to me over sudden attention given Bikini fallout victims when *hibakusha* had so long been neglected. They used such phrases as "We suffered also," and the metaphorical Japanese saying, "The crow behind came out in front." One man contrasted the way in which the fisherman died—his family receiving sympathy from all over the country as well as financial compensation from the American government—with the totally unnoticed death the day before (from suspected radiation effects) of a *hibakusha* who had received inadequate medical care and "not one sen of compensation."

Political leaders were quick to recognize the enormous potential of the mass emotions that went into the formation of *Gensuikyō*, and they turned its theme of peace into a fulcrum for partisan ideological passions. The organization became the center of a series of bitter struggles, all of them highly visible in Hiroshima since it has been the site of annual international meetings from 1955 on. There was first an uneasy Communist-Socialist coalition, followed by the withdrawal from the organization of more moderate Democratic Socialist elements who formed their own peace group, *Kakkin* (often referred to as "Second *Gensuikyō*"). Increasing Communist domination of central policy led to the double standard on nuclear testing mentioned before, and to a particularly embarrassing impasse concerning Russia's resumption of testing in 1961; *Gensuikyō* leaders had previously declared publicly that whoever broke the official moratorium would be considered "an enemy of the peace," and their hedging when confronted with their previous words greatly accelerated the organization's precipitous drop in national influence. Still later, there took place an equally bitter struggle between "Chinese" and "Russian" Communist factions, and when the former won out, *Gensuikyō* found itself in the strange position (for a peace organization) of condemning the partial nuclear test ban treaty of 1963 (which China opposed). This led to another split and the formation of a third peace organization, *Gensuikin*, consisting of socialists, radical pacifists, and various groups oriented toward Russian and Eastern European communism. Nor is there much to suggest that any of the three groups has transcended political affiliations sufficiently to become an independent and universalistic rallying point for antiwar emotions of *hibakusha* and others.

Most survivors have, in fact, viewed the entire proceedings with a mixture of amazement and contempt. An elderly poet, for instance, contrasted the "genuine desire for peace" of *hibakusha* with the "impure" machinations of outsiders, and summarized Hiroshima's peace movement experience in characteristic metaphor:

> The young tree, with its few buds and leaves, had begun to grow bigger and to sprout branches—and then the worms began to feed on it.

Others, like the writer-physician, emphasized the initial helpfulness of outsiders in "teaching *hibakusha* how to use their voices . . . when they did not know how to express themselves," until the latter became blind followers of these outside leaders who used them "for their own purposes," so that "gradually it became impossible to express the true message of the *hibakusha*."

We note the consistent image of *hibakusha* as a core of authenticity within the peace movement, taken advantage of by self-seeking and parasitic forces, which prevent them from expressing their special truth. The image neglects emotional conflict within *hibakusha* themselves, conflict intensified by such complex historical events as the Cold War, the spread of nuclear weapons, the Korean War, patterns of militant Marxism, Japanese remilitarization, and the war in Vietnam—in the face of which the stance of simple pacifism many *hibakusha* wished to assume came to feel increasingly inadequate. Moreover, as many have noted, the emotional intensity of Japanese peace movements has not been matched by programmatic depth: as one *hibakusha*-commentator put it, "Japanese love tears, but foreigners esteem facts."[17] Still another problem, though until recently one rarely raised by the Japanese themselves, has been the emergence of an aggressive nationalism in association with the peace movement. For Japan's unique atomic victimization made this movement an important channel for reassertions of pride and identity, and for dramatic switches from "restorationism" to "transformationism" in which the potential for new forms of chauvinism and for "ideological totalism"[18] has been strong.

Confronted with these cosmic "impurities," individual *hibakusha* have frequently expressed visions of reassertion of purity through more direct ties between themselves and the rest of mankind. As the same *hibakusha*-commentator observed:

> Hiroshima now possesses an international character whether we like it or not—and its participants in the anti-A- and H-bomb movement must realize that each one is connected with the whole world.[19]

But these aspirations were constantly undermined by new home-grown impurities, by constant bickering and envies among *hibakusha*, frequently over precisely this issue of international connection—in the sense that many who went abroad were accused of having become "haughty" when they returned, and some did indeed find themselves less satisfied with life in their provincial city.

" . . . WHAT IS PEACE?"

In discussions of peace movements during individual interviews, I was not surprised to find that distrust came easily, or that it was compounded of witnessed external manipulations and internal sensitivities toward counterfeit nurturance. *Hibakusha* accused the peace movement of "selling the disaster," "using the A-bomb as their flag," and "including the problem of nuclear weapons simply to attract us and win us over . . . and then using us as sacrifices to their movement." This last accusation was made by a skilled worker, and the word he used for "sacrifices" (*gisei*) also means scapegoat and victim, precisely the word *hibakusha* frequently employ in relationship to their having been the ones chosen to experience the bomb. He made an exception for survivors themselves appearing at peace meetings ("because when the person on the platform is one who actually had the experience, he has natural power in his speech"), but toward the end of our talk launched into a remarkable soliloquy on the meaning of peace which was somewhat reminiscent of Orwell's "newspeak":

> I would like to ask, What is peace? What is the meaning of peace? What does peace consist of? I am doubtful about the word peace and don't know what it is. Politicians use it all the time, but what is it really? What do they mean? I have been wondering about that since I was sixteen years old. . . . When I think about peace, I connect it with war—because in wartime they always talked about peace in the

Far East and throughout the world. At that time, when I asked about the meaning of peace, I was told that I better be careful or I would be arrested by the military police. After the war I began to wonder, is this really peace? I don't know what peace is—whether this is peace or not. . . . If the day comes when the world can forget about war and simply live at peace, would that make people happy or unhappy? . . .

This poignant combination of confusion and psychological insight is perhaps appropriate to anyone who came to adult life during World War II, especially in Japan, and most especially for a *hibakusha* and a somewhat suspicious and misanthropic one at that. His difficulty is not only that of profound symbolic confusion ("when I think about peace, I connect it with war"), but his viewing as counterfeit the entire spectrum of war, peace, and hypocritical in-between states.

His stress upon the value of direct *hibakusha* expression, however, found many echoes. The shopkeeper's assistant, for instance, urged that instead of "staging big parades demanding peace . . . we should start from something near to ourselves . . . directly from our lives"; he advocated various forms of open discussion and mutual help, within the *hibakusha* community and reaching outward to people of other countries. A few among *hibakusha* activists wavered between what might be called "*hibakusha* purity" and the "political necessity" of their organizations. But even among them there was a tendency to see inauthenticity in various practices initiated by outsiders which, they claimed, turned the peace movement into a "big show" with "too many stars." Most characteristically, *hibakusha* viewed all political influences within peace movements as contaminations unworthy of the A-bomb dead, and stressed idealistic programs, such as that of the philosopher, in which

peace [would be seen as] no single country's problem [but] a matter of life and death for mankind [requiring] a movement which could be said to be spiritual . . . not tied to politics . . . [but] connected only with humanism. . . .

We sense here that the *hibakusha* experience on the one hand confers upon peace activities a special emotional power and a universalizing influence; but that on the other it demands a purity so stringent as to lead to immobilization.

NUCLEAR TESTING: ''. . . THEY MUST BE MAD''

In relationship to nuclear testing, *hibakusha* emotions were much more simple: anxiety to the point of terror. To some extent one may say the same of all their countrymen, for particularly since the Bikini incident of 1954, nuclear testing anywhere has brought to all Japanese lips the term "ashes of death" (*shi no hai*): large numbers of Japanese scientists and technicians bring their Geiger counters into operation, and mass media dramatically disseminate reports of radioactivity while emphasizing Japan's geographic susceptibility to fallout.[20] I could observe this pervasive sense of fallout danger in Tokyo and Kyoto during periods of American and Russian testing, before going to Hiroshima, and it seemed evident that much of Japanese anxiety about nuclear death in general had been channeled into this invisible but measurable symbol of it. For instance, an article published in the *Chūgoku Shimbun* in August, 1958, began as follows:

RECORD-BREAKING LEVEL OF RADIOACTIVITY CONTAINED IN HIROSHIMA RAINFALL LAST MONTH EVEN DETECTED IN LARGE AMOUNTS IN WATER SUPPLY

This last July there was a greater quantity of radioactivity-containing rainfall than has ever before been experienced in the Hiroshima area. In the dust in the air, in the swimming pools at schools, and in drinking water and the water supply system, an extraordinary level of radioactivity was present. Measurements . . . made it clear that it was greatly affected by the nuclear explosions conducted by the Americans at the Bikini and Eniwetok Atolls. As long as such tests continue, their radioactive rainfall will fall on Japan, and if this abnormal condition should continue, it is clear that it would become fatal to life.

I observed similar reactions following Russia's explosion of a fifty-megaton bomb in 1962. At such times, there was the constant assertion, publicly and privately, of the belief that fallout endangers *hibakusha* more than other people because of their previous exposure to radiation. The assertion is, as we know, related to an overall sense of *hibakusha* vulnerability, and therefore prevails over repeated denials by Hiroshima medical authorities. (None of this discussion is meant to imply that fallout is not dangerous, or that it is "irrational" to be afraid of its harmful effects. Rather, I am stressing the special emotional intensity of reactions to fallout in Hiroshima and throughout Japan.)

Thus, the electrician emphasized that "People like ourselves . . . the only ones to have gone through an attack by a weapon such as the A-bomb, should have some form of protection . . . in case such a bomb is ever dropped again." Like many *hibakusha*, he associated testing with the thought of nuclear war, and this thought was so disturbing that he imagined himself, should he again survive, clearly envying the dead:

> It terrifies me. Whether it is America or Russia it makes me tremble. . . . If you are killed by the bomb, well, that's that. But if you survive, that would be horrible—the fear—well, I would rather not survive. The suffering for those who do—well, it's impossible to describe to anyone who hasn't been through it.

Others experienced bodily anxieties ("When I hear about nuclear testing on television, I feel my blood suddenly go thin"); or recalled their original exposure and had their death guilt revived ("I think of the people who were burned to death right in front of our eyes—I think how much luckier we were than they"); or else felt the significance of their experience to be negated ("I then think that despite all of my own injuries and all that I saw that day—especially the children—nothing can be done"). And *hibakusha* very commonly associate testing with end-of-the-world imagery, as did the elderly widow:

> I know the scale of the Hiroshima bomb but those recent tests were bombs of a much larger scale. How much larger? Tens or even hundreds of times. . . . With such bombs . . . there might not be anybody left in the world in the future. . . . I wish them to stop it.

Such imagery expresses a combination of actual memory, realistic appraisal, and retaliatory hostility, emotions which could be expressed indirectly—as in the case of the high school student who told me that he found the thought that another war might eliminate all human beings from the world to be "sickening," and the statement of the writer-manufacturer that "I don't think anyone will ever drop another A-bomb on Japan, but they shouldn't drop an A-bomb on America or Russia either."

Hibakusha also related nuclear testing to issues of reality and sanity. Typical were the shopkeeper's assistant's comment that "the thought occurs to me that they must be mad"; the history professor's agitated insistence that testing "is utterly absurd" and that "both countries seem to be playing a sort of game . . . because they don't really grasp its terror"; and the middle-aged businessman's claim that "the people of America and the Soviet Union don't have a true sense of the suffering caused by the bomb . . . of its realities . . . because they didn't see them with their own eyes," that they "know about such things as the amount of damage, but think that this damage won't affect them."

The leftist woman writer combines this theme of reality with remembered imagery of world destruction in an expression of cautionary anger:

> I know that the American people feel they can survive if hit by bombs one hundred thousand times more powerful than those used in the past. But we who have seen the end of the world know how wrong this kind of American thinking is.

Miss Ōta addressed herself in a different way to the issue of reality. Noting that some considered the national Japanese reaction to the Bikini incident to be exaggeratedly emotional, she insisted: "We were not really hysterical—we simply knew what it was." Another Hiroshima writer, after the Bikini incident, was quoted as having said, "Now we are relieved," a remark which conveys—in addition to its hostility, satisfaction in shared misery, and rivalry for counterfeit nurturance—the *hibakusha*'s realization that his particular anxieties had now become national, had finally become accepted as legitimate and appropriate.[21]

An elderly Catholic nun in Nagasaki expressed her sense of the absurdity of nuclear testing through an angry-humorous demand for a change in the ground rules:

> I don't want to have this kind of war—with nuclear weapons. Maybe they should fight . . . the way old samurai used to fight, one man against one other man. Maybe there should be a fight between Khrushchev and Kennedy, with their fists—that would be enough.

This concern about appropriateness and reality is the *hibakusha*'s way of asserting his special *organic knowledge* of nuclear weapons, a form of knowledge which is bound up with severe conflict, but is nonetheless, in its perceived value to the world, of great importance in the struggle for mastery.*

This "knowledge" was not necessarily reassuring. Most *hibakusha* demanded that testing cease and nuclear bombs be outlawed as weapons of war, often pointing to the example of poison gas. But their own experience with the bomb, along with the fact of continuing testing,

---

* I refer here to the kind of knowledge in which bodily and mental "information" are fused. Strictly speaking, only a *hibakusha* can have such knowledge of the atomic bomb, but a non*hibakusha* can approach it through imagination and empathy.

often produced a tone of bitter skepticism—as in the case of the female poet:

> Some say that the leaders of the world are not stupid enough to drop A- and H-bombs all over the world. But I can't be so optimistic about this. Once the A-bomb has been dropped, this means it might be dropped again. I have this feeling all of the time. . . . It used to seem unbelievable that such a weapon as the A-bomb could exist, and now Russia and America are testing these weapons. This seems to me just as stupid.

In other words, the rest of the world may indulge in its psychic numbing, but *hibakusha* know better. Nor is this skepticism entirely free of retaliatory resentment.

While most of the *hibakusha* anxiety we have been discussing arose in response to nuclear testing per se, there were occasional responses to the particular country doing the testing. These mostly concerned America and Russia (at the time I was in Hiroshima, England had ceased testing, France had done relatively little, and China none). Reactions to American testing had to do both with the fact that America was the country which dropped the bomb on Hiroshima, and with the greater expectations of America created by her postwar relationship with Japan. Thus, the technician strikingly combined in a single sentence themes of retaliatory anger and dependent expectation:

> If the bomb had been dropped not on Japan but on America, so that Americans knew how terrible it was, and how many people were killed, then President Kennedy would take the lead in opposing nuclear testing . . . and being the kind of leader he is—and because America is a great country—this would enable the anti-nuclear testing movement to be much stronger than it is now throughout the whole world.

Similarly, the abandoned mother shrugged off Russia's testing as no more than what one could expect ("Well, she is an Iron Curtain country"), but toward American testing took the attitude of incredulous annoyance with an erring family member ("I wonder why America tests—America is a country with greater understanding . . . a kind country—so why does she have to do it?"). Her conclusion ("I think that if America stopped, Russia would, too") again suggests a kind of expected leadership, but also, perhaps, a primary blame.

The grocer, despite his bitter condemnation of America for her "irresponsibility" in dropping the bomb without being able to cure its effects, was relatively sympathetic toward American testing, which he considered "more reasonable" because "they don't stress the size of it any more than necessary, and aren't too proud about their country's power," than he was to Russia's, which "is not done openly but something like the manner of a thief—without good reasons and secretively—and in a way that tries to frighten the world." He is partly reacting here to Russian boasts of nuclear bombs of superior dimensions, which made him "very angry," because, we may assume, of the intense death anxiety they stimulated.

But only one *hibakusha* expressed to me an absolute distinction between nuclear testing by the two countries, unqualifiedly supporting one and condemning the other. The European priest insisted that America had no alternative ("In the concrete circumstances of the present, there is no other way"), and that the Russians and the Japanese leftists exaggerated fallout dangers from American testing and are generally hypocritical ("The Russians don't believe that their own fallout is doing any harm"). But his conclusion, that political questions in general involve double-dealing ("It is all the same—a very dirty business"), suggested that despite the conventionally "Western" ideological views he expressed, his *hibakusha* experience led him to feel inwardly that all nuclear testing was intrinsically "dirty" or evil.

The sense of resignation was considerably less prominent—and if present, less convincing—toward nuclear testing than toward other aspects of the atomic bomb experience. Thus the comment by the *burakumin* boy that "as long as America and the Soviet Union exist, it [testing] just can't be helped" could be viewed as a form of resignation, but could also be interpreted as a by no means innocuous suggestion that if America and Russia did *not* exist, the problem would be solved. The hostility accompanying apparent resignation can be even more direct, as in the case of the bargirl's observation that "all the protests of the anti-nuclear weapons movements have no more effect than chanting sutras into a horse's ear," and her further comment, "This makes me very mad." The tone is more that of futility and rage than of simple resignation.

A more ambivalently sophisticated form of "contaminated resignation" was that expressed by the history professor in relationship to the Bikini incident:

I would not say that what happened was natural—but since Russia was competing with America, it just couldn't be helped. . . . We should of course have some form of movement to stop them [from testing]. But just how much we can do, this I don't know. I feel very doubtful. . . . I also think it very strange to use what I would call primitive techniques—as when people get together to protest and then shove and strike others—to stop scientific techniques.

Here elements of resignation, resentment of and sympathy toward America, and aversion to peace movement "violence" all merge. But his way of contrasting "primitive" and "scientific" techniques also suggests a certain amount of identification with the technological and scientific power of nuclear weapons.

REARMING JAPAN: "IF WE DON'T HAVE ARMS, WE CAN'T FIGHT AT ALL"

I also questioned *hibakusha* about their feelings concerning Japanese rearmament, particularly about the much discussed national issue of whether or not to change the clause in the Japanese Constitution prohibiting rearmament. Since rearmament had long been taking place under other names, Japanese in general have been torn between the "logic" of making legal that which already exists and at the same time possibly paving the way for further military expansion, and the moral appeal of the Constitution along with its possible advantages in restraining the extent of rearmament.

Hibakusha share the general Japanese ambivalence, but perhaps with particular intensity. Extremely characteristic was the shopkeeper's assistant's wavering back and forth between the wish that no country in the world required armaments and the realization that this was far from the actual situation, his initial insistence that "I just can't come to any definite conclusion" and his coming to one despite himself:

. . . Still, if I am to speak honestly, I am against rearmament. After all, if we have arms, and if anything happens to cause us to fight, then we would fight. If we don't have arms, we can't fight at all, so I think it is better not to have arms.

His *hibakusha* conflicts actually provided him with a stronger position than he thought he possessed, namely, that anything is preferable to nuclear war. But we also suspect that he might experience a certain amount of anxiety related to the helplessness of being so totally without arms that "we can't fight at all."

Others, like the mathematician, put the matter in more immediate and personal terms—"I am against changing it [the constitution], strongly against it. After all, I have children in the age group eligible for military service"—but one suspected here too that A-bomb exposure influenced his vision of what his children might experience should there be rearmament and war.

The A-bomb experience even intruded itself upon the ideas of those who expressed themselves as favoring rearmament. The technician, for instance, represented what may be termed an older-generation point of view associated with general political conservatism, which emphasized that "there is no country in the world without arms" and that arms were needed "to defend our own country"—particularly, as it turned out, in relationship to such controversies as those surrounding Korea's self-proclaimed "Rhee Line" and her actions against Japanese fishing boats found inside of that line. Yet after saying these things, he suddenly qualified his position so drastically as almost to reverse it:

> From the financial point of view, however . . . I don't think Japan could manage to maintain many airplanes, as jet planes are very expensive—so I think it may be a little too soon for us to build up our arms. . . . And even if we had all that money, we should use it to help out some of the most miserable *hibakusha*.

His conventional patriotism had been undermined by identification with fellow survivors and specifically by death guilt; the "most miserable" *hibakusha* are those symbolically closest to the dead. And although what are perceived to be the moral commands of the dead can be highly inflammable in military matters, *hibakusha* would sometimes understand these as a matter of simple resistance to rearmament—as in the case of one A-bomb orphan: "Opposing Japan's military expansion is the best way I know to console the souls of my dead parents and sister."

If the position taken was that of limited rearmament, the limitation insisted upon was likely to be that of nuclear weapons. The history professor thus insisted that "as long as conflicts between countries exist there is no sense, if Japan is to be an independent country, in saying that she cannot have armaments," but added that "I think it would be terrible if the budget for education, welfare, and other constructive things were to be spent for nuclear weapons." The purely economic reasoning of several of these points of view suggests the *hibakusha*'s difficulty in coming to grips with the intensity and complexity of his feelings on the subject. In this case, for instance, it is possible that the history professor is partly drawn to the idea of nuclear weapons (both because of their enormous symbolic importance for any nation's sense of national power and because of the element of identification with them we know to be present in him), but that his A-bomb-related death guilt makes it impossible for him to sanction these weapons.

The writer-manufacturer directed his attention to outer space rather than to either nuclear weapons or rearmament, and expressed a point of view which combined political pragmatism with a classical East Asian stress upon harmony and balance:

> I would like to say something about the Cold War. I feel anxious every time I hear about Russian space ships, because of Russia's having taken the lead in this area. I hope that the Americans will catch up quickly, because with the world in its present condition, I believe that world peace depends upon a balance of strength between the two.

Here he addresses himself to matters outside of *hibakusha* or even Japanese influence, but is in effect pleading for an environment within which he can feel reasonably comfortable, safe, and free from both predatory external dangers and from the lingering internal *hibakusha* conflicts we know him to have.

BEARING WITNESS

Hibakusha have strong feelings about conveying their experience to others—about the question of whether they must take on a special mission to make known to the world the true nature of nuclear warfare.

As is true for survivors of any extreme experience, *hibakusha* strongly doubt the possibility of communicating what they have actually been through to anyone who has not himself undergone the ordeal. Exquisitely sensitive to its misrepresentation, but at the same time convinced of its relevance to world problems, they return constantly to the principle of direct personal reconstruction of the event in a way that virtually puts others through it. The tourist agency employee, for instance, says of those producing and testing nuclear bombs: "I want them to think about it more from the inside, because if they did, they would feel differently." And the history professor expresses the same principle in terms both more general and more specific:

I would like to tell the facts of the experience in a way that people will know about it, not only with their minds but will feel it with their skin. . . . I believe that if Kennedy and Khrushchev could have seen those people [at the time of the bomb] even once, they would feel that they should throw all their nuclear weapons to the bottom of the sea . . . and that is why the first thing to do is to help people understand the actual situation of human beings that day.

Intellectual knowledge, in other words, is not enough. *The demand is that the outsider immerse himself in atomic bomb exposure, feel it with his body and his mind, and thereby come to possess the survivor's own organic knowledge of it.*

Impressed with the difficulties of imparting this kind of knowledge, the grocer suggested using tape recordings of the day of the bomb—"maybe of one person's suffering, or even of moaning voices." He knew it unlikely that such recordings were available but thought that if they were, hearing the voices of those actually going through the experience would, to some extent, "help people to be able to imagine it."

Others, like the war widow, advocated displaying people with keloids to world leaders:

This would be a more direct way than peace parades. . . . They would see how terrible war is even seventeen years later. It is impossible to look at those *hibakusha* with keloids—even a person like me, who went through the experience, still can't look at them—and if leaders of the world were to see them, they would imagine how they would feel when their own families got to be like that.

Again the demand, by no means without hostility, that the outsider acquire organic knowledge to the point of becoming a "survivor" surrounded by atomic bomb stigmata. And she went on to make programmatic suggestions: "Young girls would be better than older people . . . however painful for those girls . . . [and] if the leaders could meet and talk with them, say two or three times a year, I think it would be effective."

The physicist went further in shaping this programmatic approach to organic knowledge into a general theoretical orientation:

In Hiroshima we have the fact of the A-bomb, and therefore we must stress the full horror of the A-bomb. Here is our responsibility and our emphasis. . . . I think we can say that . . . in both Hiroshima and

Japan in general the peace movement is based upon the fact of the A-
bomb. . . . I think that the destruction of Hiroshima has important
connection to the whole problem of human survival. . . .

Organic knowledge of atomic bomb exposure, in other words, is Hiroshima's precious contribution to the world, an organizing principle for
mankind's peace struggles. More indirectly suggested by his words is the
related principle that the *hibakusha*'s efforts in contributing to this
wider organic knowledge can be of help to him in mastering his own
experience.

But to move toward such mastery, the *hibakusha* must traverse the
path of his own guilt. The same death guilt which in large part
stimulates his sense of mission in disseminating A-bomb knowledge also
leads him to question his style of dissemination. He has constant
difficulty separating "exportable" aspects of that knowledge from his
own harsh self-judgments. He constantly asks himself, however unconsciously, "Was it really as bad for *me* as I say it was? Do I have the
right to be saying these things at all?" Only the dead, he inwardly
believes, possess genuine organic knowledge, and his efforts to represent
them make him feel something of an impostor. Neither by speaking out
nor by refusing to can he fully assuage his guilt.

Thus, the Hiroshima A-bomb authority described a "double feeling"
in *hibakusha:* "They want to forget the past and they also want to make
their plea to the world." As a peace movement activist himself, he felt
that they had to speak up because "they can't escape from reality
however much they wish to, [and] I think the direction of history is
being influenced by their feelings." But other commentators contested
this opinion, particularly one journalist who wrote sympathetically of
"atomic bomb nihilism,"[22] criticized peace movement leaders as "at-
torneys for the voiceless," and contrasted their demand for "moralistic rage" with the "coolness" and "inner toughness" of ordinary
hibakusha. Moreover he insisted that this detached form of "Japanese
nihilism" was a genuine response to overwhelming violence and should
even be valued as a possible source of peace sentiment in the future. We
recognize in what he describes various forms of guilt-induced silence,
psychic numbing, resignation, and simple adaptation—but what he is
really getting at is the need for authenticity of feelings, whatever they
may be, rather than wishful or manipulated attitudes.

This last sentiment was echoed by many individual *hibakusha* in their
insistence upon silence as the only form of authenticity, though the

silence they kept was uneasy and ambivalent. The abandoned mother, for instance, told me that "I am ashamed to say that even though I am a *hibakusha* . . . I feel no urge to make people understand," and that "I feel it is useless to go into crowds and make a fuss." But she admitted that "If people have a special interest and ask about the situation, then I do have the desire to tell them"; and her introductory phrase, "I am ashamed to say," suggested that she had by no means reconciled her silence with her residual guilt.

Similarly, the sociologist justified his silence on pragmatic grounds:

> Of course I want peace. I need peace if I am to realize even my own small desires. But while I am able to make a realistic effort for the small desires, for the larger issues of war and peace I feel that there is no realistic effort at all that I can make.

Yet gradually, during the course of our talks, he began to express passionate concerns about his own atomic bomb experience and about nuclear issues in general. It became clear that these concerns had been covered over, not only by individual psychological tendencies toward denial, but also by his determination not to participate in what he viewed as inauthentic representations of the atomic bomb being made everywhere around him.

Related sensitivities were involved in the white-collar worker's statement that he didn't mind discussing the A-bomb "in a serious way" but greatly resented "people who boast about having been in the bomb— not exactly boast, but are pleased with themselves, as if they had some special merit for having gone through such a rare experience." He is troubled by *hibakusha* tendencies, including those within himself, to see themselves as a "chosen people"—tendencies which may be perceived as profoundly inauthentic despite their frequency among survivors and their derivation from the sense of having conquered death.

Ultimately, the ineffability of atomic bomb exposure—its relationship to cosmic mysteries that one can neither grasp nor explain—gives *hibakusha* an inner sense that *all* talk about it is inauthentic. In this sense the moralist's sitting silently in *zazen* position before the Cenotaph was unique in its bringing to *hibakusha* expression a combination of silence, sense of mission, and obeisance to the dead. But we also recall that it was isolated, slightly anachronistic, and of little effect.

4) *Hiroshima and Nagasaki: "Proper" Post-A-Bomb Behavior*

When discussing Hiroshima, the question always arises, "What about Nagasaki?" "Why," people ask, "is it always ignored?" I spent just one week in this second A-bombed city, and my knowledge of it is limited. But by making certain comparisons between Hiroshima and Nagasaki— between observable patterns within the two cities as well as imagery about them—we learn a little more about atomic disaster.

A useful beginning point for comparison is the unprecedented problem of how much to emphasize *as a city* a nuclear weapons exposure: how, and in what ways, to permit a city's development and identity to become related to that experience; and to what extent to ignore, compensate for, move beyond, or in any way de-emphasize, the original holocaust.

An article comparing Hiroshima and Nagasaki in this regard (captioned "Tale of Two Cities"), which appeared in *Time*[23] while I was conducting my research, held up Hiroshima, in effect, as a bad example: a city which refuses to forget the A-bomb and remains "grimly obsessed by that long-ago mushroom cloud," "the only city in the world that advertises its past misery," and one which "has made an industry of its fate." In contrast, Nagasaki was seen as the good example: a "monument to forgiveness," "a tranquil, beautiful seaport" with "no bitterness," which "has never been invaded by anti-nuclear demonstrators," but has itself forgotten the A-bomb experience, which "the world has seemingly forgotten" too. The comparison is a particularly crude example of the kind of imagery frequently held about the two cities, by Japanese as well as Americans.

In evaluating this alleged polarity, I would first emphasize my impression of the *essential similarity in conflicts of individual hibakusha in both cities*, so that what I have written about responses in Hiroshima would, in general terms, apply to those in Nagasaki also. But if this is true, it becomes all the more important to understand just what is actually different about the two cities.

FIRST AND LAST

Here the most important single point to grasp is that *Hiroshima has become the world's symbol of the consequences of nuclear weapons—a geographical representation of universal fear and guilt in relationship to man's capacity to destroy himself—and that Nagasaki has not become such a symbol.* (This difference was officially recognized when Hiroshima was designated by the Japanese national government as the International City of Peace and Nagasaki as the International City of Culture, the first a title consistent with a specific symbolic function, the second quite nebulous.) There are, I believe, several reasons why, of the two, Hiroshima has assumed this role.

Probably of greatest importance is Hiroshima's having been the first of the world's cities to encounter the bomb. As such, it was the city whose experience immediately evoked in everyone the contrast between the pre-bomb world that was forever lost and the post-bomb world which so suddenly and horrifyingly came into being. The Nagasaki educator commented to me on this point with some irony:

> It is like giving out prizes in any contest—first prize gets a gold medal and second a silver medal. Hiroshima received the gold medal and Nagasaki the silver medal.

Similarly, a Nagasaki doctor quoted in the *Time* article looks upon his city as "like the man who flew the Atlantic after Lindbergh." There is a quality of atomic bomb gallows humor in this kind of ironic "competition." And although it causes many outsiders to react with uneasy sarcasm, it contains important psychological currents related to such things as ambivalent pride over dubious distinction, and rivalry for counterfeit nurturance, both mentioned earlier in relationship to individual and group *hibakusha* identity.

Nagasaki has, in at least one sense, attempted to take on its own time-bound distinction. At its memorial ceremony in 1962 the prefectural governor said: "The bomb fell first on Hiroshima, then on Nagasaki. Let Nagasaki be the *last* place it falls." But while this distinction certainly evokes less ambivalence than Hiroshima's, it is also much less capable of capturing the world's imagination.

A second factor in Hiroshima's symbolic distinction was its near-total annihilation. The bomb exploded almost directly over its center—over flimsy wooden structures on flat terrain—and literally left no city standing. Nagasaki's bomb fell on a suburb located in a hilly area so that although of greater explosive power than the Hiroshima bomb, it left about two thirds of the city (including a somewhat larger number of concrete structures) still standing—in addition to the fact that its casualties were not as extensive.

A third factor is Hiroshima's relative accessibility to Tokyo: it is about five hundred miles away, and also on the main island of Honshū, while Nagasaki is almost twice that distance from Tokyo and located on an outer point of Kyūshū, the southernmost of the major Japanese islands. Hiroshima is therefore more sensitive to intellectual and ideological currents (national and international) stemming from Japan's dominant city which encourage atomic bomb symbolism.

The fourth issue is that of pre-atomic bomb identity: Hiroshima, despite its military importance, was virtually unknown internationally, while Nagasaki had an illustrious cosmopolitan tradition. Nagasaki had been a major locus of Japanese Catholicism from the time of the arrival of Francis Xavier, the first Western missionary to visit Japan, in the sixteenth century; a longstanding center for trade between Japan and the outside world; Japan's main point of contact with the West during a major part of her two hundred years of self-imposed isolation, from the late seventeenth to the late nineteenth centuries; and even had a special place in the Western imagination as the locale of the Madame Butterfly story. I was frequently told that because of their special historical experience, the people of Nagasaki were "more gentle in attitude," and that this characteristic has influenced their post-A-bomb behavior—a claim that is difficult to evaluate. What can be said is that Nagasaki had a strong historical identity to call forth and build upon in its post-bomb reconstruction, an identity made accessible by the physical existence of two thirds of the city. Hiroshima, in contrast, had no such physical or historical resources—little identity to draw upon other than that of an A-bombed city.

Having dominated the world's symbolic imagery surrounding the atomic bomb for all of these reasons, Hiroshima has inevitably spawned more protest than Nagasaki and more conflict surrounding this protest. But even here the attempt to impose absolutely antithetical images on the two cities is seriously misleading. For it is simply not true that Nagasaki "has never been invaded by anti-nuclear demonstrators" (as the *Time* article asserted); it has, in fact, along with Tokyo and Hiroshima, been one of the three Japanese centers for international peace meetings since these began in 1955.

Indeed, Nagasaki has given rise to some of the most eloquent (and psychologically astute) words of protest ever written about the atomic bomb:

Today, we of Nagasaki, living on in the atomic wasteland, apply our energies to reconstruction. . . . Does it seem, then, that the deadly work of an atom bomb can be repaired?

Moreover, we know that, in the nations of the world since that time, scientists have studied the effects and the aftereffects of the atom bomb. . . . What they have learned they have passed on to the councils of the generals and statesmen.

And by this, the conferences to free the world of atomic menace succeed or fail, and I understand they have failed; by this, the decision to use or not to use the bomb is made, and I hear they do not regard it as so fearful, so unusable. . . . "A city cannot be obliterated wholly. . . . Not everyone dies. . . . Radioactivity in time is dissipated. . . . It is just another weapon, with greater physical effects than those which preceded it."

Greater physical effects! . . . Do they understand, have they investigated what it does to the heart and conscience and mind of those who survive? Do they have any knowledge of our society of spiritual bankrupts, now striving lamely to function as a community?

We of Nagasaki, who survive, cannot escape the heartrending, remorseful memories.

We carry deep in our hearts, every one of us, stubborn, unhealing wounds. When we are alone we brood upon them, and when we see our neighbors we are again reminded of them; their as well as ours.

It is this spiritual wreckage, which the visitor to Nagasaki's wastes does not see, that is indeed beyond repair.

This plea comes from the concluding portion of Dr. Takashi Nagai's *We of Nagasaki*,[24] a book whose protest included evocation of general emotional disruption (its Japanese title, *Genshi Senjō Shinri*, means "Atomic Battlefield Psychology," and in the passage quoted we note the stress upon emotions related to residual guilt).

A Catholic convert who died of leukemia in 1951, Dr. Nagai, perhaps more than any other A-bomb victim, lived out the pattern of a martyr. His leukemia resulted from longstanding exposure to x-rays (he was a specialist in radiology) and predated the atomic bomb, but was of course symbolically associated with it. Moreover, his exposure to the bomb at eight hundred meters, including severe injuries and loss of blood, could well have aggravated his condition and hastened his death.* In any case, he totally dedicated his waning energies to combat-

---

* It is also possible that the bomb exposure contributed to a temporary remission in his leukemia, as irradiation is one of the forms of medical treatment ordinarily used for the condition.

ing the bomb's disruptive human influences. He did extensive medical work at the time of the bomb, later gave various forms of help to other *hibakusha*, and wrote continuously about the problem from a one-room shack which he built on the site of his former house, where his wife had been killed and which he called *Nyokodō*, or (as sometimes rendered in English) "Love-Thy-Neighbor-As-Thyself House." The Catholic-humanist form of protest he embodied was more characteristic for Nagasaki than Hiroshima, not only because of Nagasaki's strong Catholic influence but because its bomb fell in a predominantly Catholic area of the city, destroying the two great cathedrals and killing an inordinately large number of Catholics. Some, in fact, have attributed Nagasaki's relative lack of militant protest to a quality of resignation which combines original Buddhist influence with later Christian stress upon forgiveness and sacrifice in the face of persecution. But Dr. Nagai's life and writings make clear that the most profound aspects of *hibakusha* psychology—including death guilt and the impulse toward a post-bomb mission warning the world about nuclear weapons—have existed in Nagasaki survivors as well as those of Hiroshima.

FATE, MONEY, AND PURITY

The claim that Hiroshima, not Nagasaki, "make[s] an industry of its fate" strikes us as a first cousin to the accusation of "selling the bomb," and we sense that it represents psychological conflicts in the accuser as well as actions by the accused. Here we may say first that given man's extraordinary capacity for adaptation to adversity, every city (as every individual) "makes an industry of its fate." The unique fate of nuclear disaster shared by Hiroshima and Nagasaki can hardly be separated from their subsequent commercial rehabilitation. But in commercial as well as in other areas, Hiroshima has been particularly plagued with the problem of carving out a new city identity while trying to avoid becoming *nothing but* an A-bombed city. For worldwide fears and moral concerns about nuclear weapons spill readily over into tourist money, and Hiroshima's sense of its responsibility to these world needs spills equally readily over into commercial opportunity.

At the same time both *hibakusha* and morally concerned outsiders demand from an A-bombed city that its behavior manifest a degree of purity commensurate with its tragedy, since only in such purity can lie the seeds of restitution for the healing of the "wound in the order of being" which such a city represents. To the *hibakusha*'s inner insistence that city behavior be appropriate to the sacrifice of the dead is thus added the outsider's need that good be born of evil, perhaps particularly so in the case of the American outsider because his sense of contribution to evil has been greatest. One observer commented that "it is the foreigners who made Hiroshima famous." And the same minor city official who told of foreigners' need to have the Dome standing claimed that while "We in Hiroshima tend to forget about the bomb . . . outsiders keep bringing it up," keep writing to the city "requesting pictures and exhibits and information about survivors' lives," keep sending donations, and generally "turn toward Hiroshima" in their peace movement activities.

His picture may be somewhat oversimplified, but the point here is that outsiders, like *hibakusha* themselves, bring to Hiroshima demands for purity that cannot be met. The alternating stance toward Hiroshima as either a city of noble victims or crass opportunists represents the continuing pressure of these demands, together with their continuing disappointment. The fact is that victims of an atomic disaster are neither more nor less virtuous than anyone else. And the A-bomb-related commercial energies which are found to be so distasteful represent the usual human combinations of vitality, adaptability, ingenuity, and greed, in this case called forth as part of the city's reassertion of life.

Again, who is to set the standards for how an A-bombed city should behave? *Time* implies that the normal or healthy thing to do would be to forget about the experience and move ahead; for militant peace groups health lies in the opposite direction, in aggressively revived memories; some commercial entrepreneurs see health in the unrestricted admixture of A-bomb residua and tourism; many *hibakusha* view anything related to tourism or commerce as a desecration of the city and its experience. But all of these standards crumble before the complexities of human behavior as the two cities struggle with their historical and commercial fate—differing from each other mainly in the intensity of the struggle.

PAIN AND PLEASURE

This difference in intensity can become important, however, perhaps even in the medical area. We recall the hematologist's impression that doctors in Nagasaki tend on the whole to underestimate the effects of the A-bomb while those in Hiroshima overestimate them, and that patients in Hiroshima are more likely to feel that they have "A-bomb disease." Many physicians I spoke to in both cities tended to agree, and to confirm *Time*'s statement that "Nagasaki's citizens seem to be less fearful of 'atom sickness' than their fellow survivors in Hiroshima." Doctors' attitudes in Nagasaki would seem to be part of a general psychohistorical tendency: relatively less focus by mass media on A-bomb disease, less anxiety-stimulating protest against nuclear weapons, and therefore less social exacerbation of bodily anxieties of individual *hibakusha*. But before coming to any definitive conclusions, one would have to study the entire psychosomatic issue more thoroughly. One would have to explore the possibility, for instance, that while Hiroshima exaggerations of A-bomb disease increase anxieties, these can often be brought out into the open; but that Nagasaki restraint (what the hematologist called medical underestimation of A-bomb disease) may be associated with tendencies of denial, shared by physician and patient, which cause anxieties to remain buried, and possibly contribute to other impairments not yet clearly recognized. In any case, all this is again a matter of degree.

Nagasaki *hibakusha* have been subject to the same rate of increase in leukemia, the same findings concerning cancer and other physical influences. They cannot be free of the sense of bodily taint and related death anxiety we have observed in Hiroshima. What can be said is that Hiroshima's symbolic A-bomb role has significant repercussions in the realm of bodily concerns; and that, more generally, the experiences of both cities suggest the important impact of psychohistorical process upon disease patterns.

Hiroshima and Nagasaki survivors also differ in their relationship to outsiders. Everyone in Hiroshima at the time of the bomb felt exposed to it, and was later designated as a *hibakusha*. Each then encountered two types of "outsiders": returning Hiroshima residents who happened to be elsewhere when the bomb fell, outsiders only in the sense of being non*hibakusha*; and those with no previous connection to the city who decided to move there from former overseas possessions or from other parts of Japan. Nagasaki *hibakusha*, in contrast, were from the beginning a minority in relationship to non*hibakusha* residents of their city. Since there was no comparable influx of people from the outside—with more of the city standing and fewer deaths, there was less of a void to fill in a city that was in any case more geographically isolated—they have tended to be absorbed by the original non*hibakusha* population. They have therefore never experienced the Hiroshima *hibakusha*'s sense of being dispossessed by an amorphous mass of outsiders who without having suffered reaped later rewards. This threat to identity could well have been a further stimulus for Hiroshima survivors to reiterate the importance of their A-bomb exposure, since the focus upon it, however painful, was a way of avoiding a sense of being snuffed out entirely.

:

Two additional features of postwar Hiroshima do not have equivalents in Nagasaki. One is the unusually lively, and in places strikingly attractive, entertainment district. Made up of both old "water world" elements and newer forms of pleasure, it consists of bars, restaurants, hotels, tea (geisha) houses, *pachinko*** parlors, dance halls, coffee shops, and transient quarters for various kinds of illicit sex. To be sure, its four famous commodities—beautiful girls, superior *sake*, excellent fish, and delicious pickles—were found in prewar and wartime Hiroshima (lavish entertainment districts are always a necessity in military cities). But its reappearance and expansion during the postwar period have made it one of the most outstanding entertainment districts in all of Japan, and have created the most extreme kind of contrast to the city's grim web of A-bomb emotions.

An observer I have frequently quoted told me that people visiting Hiroshima, foreigners and Japanese, fall into two categories: "those who are interested in the bomb and those who want to amuse themselves in the well-known entertainment district." While a demand for purity can cause people in the first category to be appalled by those in the second, there is no doubt that many deeply concerned with the bomb, whether visiting or living in Hiroshima, find much needed relief in the city's sensual delights. Moreover, the two interests can unexpectedly converge through the sudden intrusion of the A-bomb into a conversation with a waitress or bargirl who turns out to have been exposed to it, an intrusion all the more poignant because of the surroundings and because of the light touch with which the matter is treated.

One frequently hears it said in Hiroshima that outsiders—especially businessmen—are the main frequenters of the entertainment district; and that *hibakusha*, if involved at all, do the menial jobs within it, or else, as hostesses or bargirls, lead outwardly glamorous but inwardly painful lives. We have observed much to confirm this assumption, notably the *hibakusha*'s guilt-saturated antipathy to pleasure. Yet there is no doubt that *hibakusha* too indulge, and find amusements—from

---

* A pinball game extraordinary both in its utter simplicity and in the fascination (often addiction) it has held for large numbers of people in postwar Japan. Part of the attraction is auditory—the lively atmosphere created by the continuous clinks of small metal balls and the loud background music played in the *pachinko* parlors.

pachinko to geisha parties—commensurate with their socioeconomic level. The absoluteness of the distinction, therefore, is related to a general need for a polarized image of the rich, greedy, and "loose" outsider versus the poor, downtrodden *hibakusha*.

For one must keep in mind the universal human tendency to move away from pain and toward pleasure, as well as the significance of pleasure in any form of individual or group rebirth. Several important questions therefore present themselves in relationship to Hiroshima's amusement section: How much has it to do with movement away from A-bomb pain? Is it an extension of the "loose" frontier atmosphere of earlier post-bomb Hiroshima? Or is it merely the re-establishment of one of Hiroshima's traditional features midst the widespread postwar Japanese stress upon concrete forms of pleasure seeking? Or perhaps, in its elements of compulsive search for pleasure, a manifestation of A-bomb and other despair? It is surely all of these things. But in the end it can neither be entirely separated from the A-bomb experience in general, nor—since Nagasaki lacks anything comparable—from Hiroshima's particular exposure and later symbolism. Nothing, it seems, in Hiroshima can.

The second special Hiroshima feature, which involves practically everyone in the city—"from the governor down to the ragpickers," as one man put it—is the baseball team, the Hiroshima Carp. Hiroshima fans are known for their fanaticism, despite the fact that (or because) their team seems to be perpetually in last place. It appears to possess that special charisma of certain losing baseball teams, such as the New York Mets of the mid-1960s and the Brooklyn Dodgers of the past. Again, one simply cannot say to what extent the atomic bomb experience might have contributed to the town's fanaticism about the team (or how much significance one should attribute to the absence of a baseball team in Nagasaki). What one can say is that once the fanaticism appeared, it became inseparable from atomic bomb issues. My observer on these matters commented, "It gives us something quite the opposite of the solemn and tragic thoughts about the atomic bomb—only intellectuals and social workers criticize it." While he probably underestimates intellectuals and social workers, some peace movement activists (the day laborer, for instance) have criticized the attention given to the team and to the building of its stadium, and demanded that these energies be used instead for helping atomic bomb victims. But the more widespread feeling in Hiroshima is that the city has a right to—indeed strongly needs—this outlet for enthusiasm.

Both the baseball team and the entertainment district raise A-bomb-related questions about guilt ("Do I have a right to pleasure?") and vitality ("Am I entitled to share in affirmations of life?"). Perhaps equally important, they symbolize a return to "ordinary pleasures" in the constant struggle against death-linked pain. It may be that baseball is a less controversial "return to pleasure" for guilt-ridden people than is indulgence in food, drink, gambling, and sex—even in a society which has not traditionally associated these pleasures with guilt per se. Again comparing Hiroshima and Nagasaki, we may say that there is no lack of opportunity for pleasure in either city, but that Hiroshima approaches its pleasures with a greater mass intensity—just as it does its A-bomb message.

But neither city has found, or can expect to find, a precise answer to the question of how to deal honorably with, and at the same time master, an atomic bomb experience. Both feel themselves under the watchful eyes of the dead in their continuing struggles with contending inner and outer symbols, in their ambivalent commemoration and troubled peace imagery, and in their quest for the right and ability to rediscover pleasure.

1) *The Bomb and After*

Since conducting the study, I have been constantly asked how survivors feel about America. The question is usually raised by other Americans, and behind it there is often either the fearful expectation of seething and unremitting hostility, or else the wishful one of no hostility at all. Even knowledge of man's generally ambivalent nature, or of his complex response to catastrophe, does not necessarily alter these either-or anticipations. For an event of this magnitude creates in everyone, and particularly in victims and "instigators," a strong need to believe in certain clear-cut responses to it.* Determining survivors' actual emotions about America, therefore, takes on much more importance than simply satisfying Americans' anxious curiosity. It raises general issues of anger, resentment, and hate (issues sometimes blurred by the use of the attentuated psychological term "hostility"), and of the relationship of these feelings, or their absence, to mastery of an extreme experience. Still more generally, it confronts us with questions of the "appropriateness" of such negative emotions, of man's capacity for sustaining them, and of their own psychological toll.

However muffled or suppressed during the early stages, emotions of

* I use "instigators" to represent the wide spectrum of Japanese and American feelings concerning individual Americans' relationship to, or responsibility for, use of the bomb.

anger and resentment have been an integral part of the symbolic death-and-rebirth process. Thus, immediate anger ("The bastards!" or "Damn *them!*" or "Damn *it!*") expressed the sense of being suddenly jolted from a safe, predictable, and functional world, and thrust into one of chaos and annihilation. In contrast, the joyous "rising of the dead" described by Dr. Hachiya in response to the rumor of Japan's having dropped atomic bombs on American cities, suggests (in addition to identification with the weapon and retaliation in kind) the restoration of an orderly symbolic world in which old authorities were still in control, enemies could be dealt with, and structure and meaning still existed. But these early epithets and wishful rumors of retaliation were only preliminary responses. More specific focus of hate required time, along with strength to formulate an object of hatred and a style of hating. Resentment and hate, moreover, varied in their psychological function: they could greatly enhance mastery by bringing together emotion and idea in a way that passed judgment on the experience; or in their static persistence they could be a formidable barrier to mastery.

Descriptions of past resentments had a great deal to do with the way in which a *hibakusha* felt *at the time of the interview* toward America and Americans, and toward me as an American investigator. I generally avoided questions about resentment until I felt that a particular *hibakusha* had become sufficiently relaxed with me to answer them freely. In some cases, however, such feelings emerged quickly and spontaneously, whether in the form of direct statement or general emotional tone. Nor were resentful feelings by any means the only emotions important to examine. Recognizing that any emotions expressed related to everything a particular *hibakusha* had felt from the moment of the bomb (and before that) to the time of our talks in the spring and summer of 1962, I nevertheless found it useful to divide reactions to America into five general categories of relationship: between victims and instigators of a nuclear disaster; between the militarily defeated and occupied and the victorious occupiers; between early nuclear victims of, and later spokesmen for, a dominant nuclear power; between those who had become objects of medical investigation as nuclear victims and those who came to study them as representatives of the country which used the weapon; and between the specific people I interviewed and myself.

VICTIMS AND INSTIGATORS

These categories could, of course, greatly overlap, and resentments associated with original exposure to the bomb could become inseparable from those stimulated by later forms of bomb-related victimization—as the bargirl reveals:

> After all, what good could have come from killing so many people? . . . And those who gave the order to drop the bomb, I wonder what kind of feeling they had at that time. I also wonder what feeling those who dropped the bomb had as they did it. . . . I think they must have been crazy. . . . [Toward them I feel] nothing but hatred. . . . Until recently . . . I didn't like Americans in general. . . . I got over this feeling, but when a company refused to employ me because I had been exposed to the bomb . . . I felt that hatred again. . . .

Having lost her mother in the bomb and been forced to grow up under borderline conditions, often missing school because of having to care for a sick grandmother, the themes of deprivation, disruption, and humiliation become the basis for her hatred. The hatred itself is needed to restore an overall sense of moral order within which she can recover her own self-esteem and integrity. Thus her concern with "those who gave the order to drop the bomb" is an effort to establish responsibility; and her labeling "crazy" those who dropped it is her way of asserting standards of rational and irrational behavior. *Hatred is her only means of bridging the technological distance between instigators and victims.* But the moral order she constructs around it is tenuous; she would readily give up the hatred were it not for the continuing frustrations which cause her to fall back upon it.

Others, like the middle-aged businessman (whose young son was killed by the bomb) must retain their hatred because of a sense of irreparable loss, of unresolved and unresolvable mourning:

> My wife still talks about the boy now. I tell her not to, because this makes me remember also, but she does anyway. I think she just can't forget. . . . Perhaps we still have a strong impression of the boy during his first year of middle school, when we didn't have enough food and couldn't feed him enough. . . . It was to me a matter of principle for my family not to buy things on the black market . . . and now I feel great pity toward the boy and I also feel I treated him badly—so I tell her not to talk about him. . . . Everyone says that . . . America has done many good things to make our society better. But although my children's generation may feel differently, I have always said that no matter what wonderful things America has

done for us, until the moment I die I will feel resentment toward America. . . .

He went on to relate this unresolved mourning to the persistence within him of a terrible image of ultimate horror— ". . . having an A-bomb dropped, with so many children killed—that's what I can't forget"—and we are left with the impression that *the continuing intensity of his guilt makes it impossible for him either to reconcile himself to his loss or to surrender his hatred.*

The generational difference mentioned by the businessman is confirmed by a recollection of the young Hiroshima-born writer:

My grandmother lost a son and a daughter-in-law in the A-bomb. She used to say, and in fact did not stop saying until the moment she died, "Don't talk to Americans."

Contributing to this implacable antagonism is profound guilt over the death of children one could not protect; as well as the general inability of a generation brought up on hatred for America, and already in middle age when experiencing its hate-producing losses, to reconstruct its symbolic world sufficiently to be able to surrender its hatred.

The writer-manufacturer, for instance, in his sixties when I spoke to him, contrasted the "unfair" A-bomb deaths ("people died without having a chance to resist") with the ritualized equality between opponents in traditional Japanese sumo wrestling and Bushidō (or samurai code), and went on to express angry imagery of retribution which seemed to combine Buddhist principles of karma with Judeo-Christian Biblical injunction:

I feel that those who dropped the bomb—and especially President Truman, who ordered that it be dropped—will be punished in the future. I have a strong hatred for Mr. Truman. I think he is a cold-blooded animal, and I am quite sure he will be punished—if not he himself, his children, or their children. . . . This is something beyond science, so I cannot tell you in what way Mr. Truman or his offspring will be punished. But you know that man consists of both his body and his spirit, and the body consists of various elements. If a man has done something wicked, I am not sure he will be punished physically but I believe he is destined to be punished spiritually. . . . Truman knew very well the enormity of a disaster that would be created by the bomb and yet he ordered it to be dropped. I think this is the most wicked act I have ever known . . . If the A-bomb is dropped either in America or in Russia, we would have to feel extreme sorrow for those who suffer from its effects, and this would be almost unbearable for us because of our own experience with the A-bomb. . . .

His anger was also related to unresolvable mourning, in his case over the death of his daughter from early radiation effects. But his focus upon the bomb's "unfairness," President Truman's "wickedness," and the idea of the bomb falling on America or Russia (the two countries at that time engaged in nuclear testing) was his way of seeking moral order and symbolic cohesion. Having done so, he was able to carry on effectively in his life and to have friendly feelings toward America and Americans.

A sequence more typical for the younger generation is reflected by the civil service employee, who first felt "rage toward America" when his brother was killed by the bomb, and then found that "gradually my feelings toward America changed" so that "the anger faded—perhaps faded away." Significantly, however, he added, "I myself feel rather strange about this." That is, his continuing guilt toward his brother makes him question his right to surrender his hatred of America.

In general, feelings toward America tend to be associated much more with ambivalence than pure hatred—as we can observe in a series of contradictory emotions expressed by the technician. He condemned the bomb as "a murderous weapon" and recalled having thought in the past "how cruel America is," but came to be impressed with the argument that "because of the A-bomb we could more quickly have peace." At first bitterly angry at "the people who came flying into Hiroshima on their B-29s and dropped the bomb" and convinced (with many others) that "these pilots [should] be executed in accordance with international law," he later adopted the position that "they acted on the order of their superiors, and in the reverse situation, Japanese also would have acted according to the orders of their superiors." This ambivalence concerning responsibility has important bearing upon issues of revenge, as he reveals by bringing up the Eichmann question, which had aroused some interest in Hiroshima:

Recently when a Japanese from Hiroshima went to Israel, the people there asked him why the Japanese don't hate the people who dropped the A-bomb as they, for all of their lives, have hated Eichmann. . . . Seventeen years after the end of the war the Jewish people maintained that hatred, and the wish to get the enemy in their hands and achieve their revenge. Now they tell the people of Hiroshima that we should have the same feeling. . . . But my view is, as I said before [in relationship to the A-bomb] that because he [Eichmann] did these things on orders from superiors, they couldn't be avoided. What do you think?

Here he was in effect asking such personal psychological questions as: "Do I have a right [duty?] to hold on to my hatred?" "Should I cultivate it or should I surrender it?" Nor could any question be more calculated to arouse conflict in an American Jewish investigator (though I do not know whether he was aware that I am Jewish), so that it was a means of expressing resentment toward me while at the same time exploring his own conflicts. For whatever the differences between Eichmann's actions and those of American pilots in Hiroshima—and we discussed these differences in relationship to his question—his embrace of the thesis of non-responsibility served an inner need to convince himself of his own "non-responsibility" in failing to help others at the time of the bomb, of his also having been (as a member of an erratically functioning rescue team) "on orders from superiors." Again, continuing hatred for America was tied up with unresolved death guilt, in this case death guilt of a generalized kind. But it turned out that he required still another outlet for his hatred, that it was more comfortable for him to shift from victim to victimizer by reasserting an old Japanese national prejudice:

The Koreans are an aggressive people. . . . This is their national characteristic. . . . I myself have some Korean friends, and during the war, we got along very well and there was no discrimination shown them. . . . But Rhee, after causing an anti-Japanese riot [he refers here to the prewar period during which Korea was a Japanese colony], escaped to America where he received some education . . . and where he was greatly spoiled by Americans. . . . And during the postwar years, if there were American or Australian soldiers on a train, a Korean would get up and declare he was a Korean. . . . But during wartime the situation was the reverse, and he would declare that he was a Japanese. . . . There is a Japanese proverb about a wolf borrowing the authority of a tiger. That is the kind of national characteristic they have. At the end of the war, Americans occupied Korea below the 38th Parallel and General MacArthur went there also—well, through this backing of America, Korea got to feel itself bigger.

In addition to the chilling sense his words convey of the universal similarity of images of prejudice, his implication of America as the party responsible for "feeding" Korean duplicity is significant. Characteristically, he attributes to the group he victimizes elements of his own "negative identity":* tendencies toward rapid shifts in identification and toward leaning heavily upon others (particularly Americans) for nurturance, both traits generally observable in Japanese during the postwar period and particularly strong in the technician as an individual. He and others of his generation thus made use of this longstanding prejudice, both to express diffuse feelings of resentment and to deflect hatred felt toward America which they were loath to recognize. Either way, it is a means of recapturing familiar psychological ground on an otherwise badly shattered terrain.

"THE RESPONSIBLE PERSON"

The tendency for many *hibakusha* to direct anger at President Truman can be a means of avoiding wider and more malignant forms of hatred. One young working wife, for instance, conveyed a sense of diffuse resentment as she asked me a pointed question: "How do you, and also the American people, feel about having dropped the bomb?" But although she went on to speak of the weapon itself as "cruel and terrible," it became clear that she was involved in an inner struggle to find an object upon which to settle her entire inner constellation of angry conflict:

> . . . About the responsible person—well, it may be difficult to say who is the responsible person, but, after all, my anger was directed at the President. . . . It may sound exaggerated to say this but it was toward one specific person, not toward all Americans. . . .

She seeks a manageable moral universe in which ultimate evil, together with her own residual hate, can be focused upon "one specific person."

Such a focus could also be a means of dealing with death anxiety, as was true of the young company executive. He described what amounted to three emotional stages: first, resentment "toward America in general"

---

* Erikson speaks of negative identity as being made up of the "evil prototypes" presented to the growing human being.[1] I consider the issue of prejudice or victimization to be more fundamentally related to conflicts over death imagery mentioned before. These will be discussed again in the last chapter as well as in my later volume.

with the feeling that "to massacre countless people by dropping such a bomb on ordinary civilians is really contrary to all humanity"; then, six months after the bomb, following his discovery of Truman's involvement, "I felt strongest resentment . . . toward the ultimately responsible person, President Truman," so that more generalized anger toward America "decreased as the years went by"; but still later, as a direct consequence of American nuclear testing, this anger "has come back again." Nuclear testing reactivated generalized anger by reactivating death anxiety; focused anger is a means of containing that anxiety.

Also important was the issue of Americans' prior knowledge of what their bomb would do. The female poet, for instance, both assumed such knowledge and concluded that its existence rendered those involved particularly evil:

> I am quite certain that the people who made the bomb knew when they used it what it would do to people. And when I think of the fact that they did know, then I think of what terrible creatures human beings are. In comparison to dogs and cats, man is much worse, since dogs and cats have never made such a thing as the A-bomb.

We know that her anger was also related to various forms of unhappiness and inner conflict. But her suggestion that human beings were more "inhuman" than animals suggests that this anger was also related to a breakdown of moral order so extreme that alternative emotions were difficult to muster.

To others, like the grocer, America was "irresponsible" precisely because it did *not* understand what it was doing in dropping the A-bomb, and did not know how to cure its own victims—all of which he thought "a kind of sin." So much so that as a high school boy during the early postwar years,

> I thought that although I did not want to go to war against any of the countries of the world, if a war began between Japan and America, I would join the fight.

His anger resulted from a sense that America was being doubly sinful: first, by brutally "experimenting" upon Hiroshima people; and then, by failing to provide, despite being all-powerful, the authentic (curative) nurturance required by victims of that experiment. The mathematician expressed a similar sentiment when he said "To drop a bomb causing those terrible and prolonged effects without knowing about them is really an evil thing to do."*

But in both the grocer and the mathematician there is an additional unspoken source of anger: their own sense of having participated in the "sin"—by simply being victimized and thereby becoming part of the A-bomb's evil, and by having survived. Further, there was the universal "sin,"—everyone's willingness to kill and destroy in the most "in-human" way, as expressed in the mathematician's additional comment in relationship to the atomic bomb: "Germany tried. Japan had the idea too." *Hibakusha* (and of course not only *hibakusha*) are angry and frightened because at some level of psychic life they have been made aware that the world is a place in which man cannot be counted upon to control these terrifying impulses.

A few *hibakusha* expressed less resentment toward America than toward Japanese military leaders.† This was true of the leftist woman writer in her recollection that "The anger we felt at the end of the war was not toward the bomb but toward the Japanese militarists"; but her later change of heart, which she attributed to feeling "deceived" by American-sponsored Japanese rearmament, might also have been influenced by previously suppressed resentment related to the original use of the A-bomb. Others chose militarists in general as targets for anger (notably one woman whose former husband came from a military family), or else scientists of any nationality who worked on nuclear weapons.

Some, like Miss Ōta (in a passage written a few months after the bomb), directed resentment at several of these targets simultaneously. Concerning her country's leaders, she said: "The bomb was dropped upon us by America but at the same time it was also dropped by Japanese military politics." She condemned both the weapon itself ("As long as A-bombs are used in any of mankind's fights, they are flowers of evil") and war in general because it led to the use of such a weapon:

* It is difficult to give a simple answer to the question of whether Americans really did know what the bomb would do. Some of its destructive potential was, of course, understood, though estimates of its explosive power and of its radius of general devastation tended to be too low. Concerning its radiation effects, these were known only theoretically, from laboratory work and from observations on disease patterns in radiologists. The actual acute and chronic medical impact of the bomb's irradiation would seem to have been neither understood nor thought about too extensively.[2] In addition to actual scientific ignorance, one must consider the influence of psychic numbing upon any group involved in the preparation of deadly weapons.

† It is likely that additional resentments felt by many toward Japanese military leaders were not articulated during my interviews, focused as they were mainly upon the atomic bomb, and coming so long after the war.

"In fighting, no one can say what part of a person's body should not be hit, and no one can prevent any kind of weapon from being used." She nonetheless felt specific anger toward America—toward "the will to use the A-bomb"—and declared that "Even if there had been no poison gas in the bomb, the wounds we have received in our hearts were nothing but wounds of poison gas." The very diffuseness of her targets, along with her later comment—"We have even forgotten to resent the A-bomb"[3]—suggest the difficulty she and other *hibakusha* have had in relating their hatred to enduring convictions or using it in a way that enhances mastery.

There were some, like the sociologist, who stressed immediate transformation of anger into universal moral principles, while almost justifying the use of the bomb.* And the woman we have referred to as the mystical healer described America's original use of the bomb as "like a parent striking his own child." But these "justifications" were undoubtedly influenced by subsequent contacts with America and, for that matter, by my own presence. In addition they covered over strong emotions concerning the bomb which we know both people to possess— the sociologist in his preoccupation with its "inhumanity," and the mystical healer in her mobilization of spiritual and therapeutic energy against its effects. In both cases transformation of hatred into purposeful ideas and programs was of great significance, but was accompanied by an element of psychic numbing which required that residual anger be denied.

It seems that *hibakusha* must retain some resentment, however amorphous, as a psychological link between the original A-bomb experience and life afterwards, just as they need some transformation of anger to prevent that link from becoming an immobilizing shackle.

DEFEAT AND OCCUPATION

We have already observed the difficulty *hibakusha* had in connecting the apparently good-natured and (at least at first) well-disciplined American troops with the bestial rapers and looters wartime propaganda had led them to expect. All over Japan women had been instructed to remain in their homes, lock their doors, and avoid wearing any clothing that might be provocative; and people in general had been told not to

---

* We recall his statement that "The anger we felt was directed not toward the country which dropped the bomb but toward war itself," and his belief that in addition to being "bad fortune," the experience was "understandable punishment." To which he added: "Their anger was directed toward Japanese military leaders."

carry wristwatches or any articles that might tempt the Occupiers. But in Hiroshima the actual encounter took place against a background of both sides' uneasy awareness of the city's special experience with an American-induced holocaust. Hence the Allied policy of leaving most of the occupation of the city to Commonwealth Forces, largely Australians and New Zealanders. Yet the fact that Americans too were in evidence —in the initial takeover, and in other ways—subsequently forced *hiba-kusha* to confront the difficult paradox of perfectly human (even likeable) people from a country which had, in their eyes, behaved so "inhumanly."

The great curiosity toward Americans, and the quick acceptance of American authority, have caused some observers to overlook the mixture of anger and humiliation many *hibakusha* actually experienced. In the case of the social worker, for instance, these feelings were associated with spotting a crumpled-up cigarette wrapper ("I can't remember whether it was Camels or Chesterfields") near the entrance of a shrine on about August 20th. Looking around and actually seeing a few Americans,

> I thought, "They have already come." . . . I was stunned, and at that moment, for the first time, I felt indescribable hatred . . . toward them . . . not so much the desire to fight those men who were standing right before my eyes as a strong feeling that we were defeated.

His first awareness of hatred, in other words, was associated with a "moment of truth," a confrontation with the special combination of physical and symbolic annihilation he had witnessed.

Beyond these early impressions, long contact with American authority (which everyone knew to dominate the Occupation), at a time when American influence was at its zenith throughout the world, inevitably affected atomic bomb reactions.

An early issue of contention was the Occupation policy limiting the dissemination of information about the A-bomb. This censorship originated largely from fear that writings about the weapon could become a stimulus for some form of Japanese retaliation. But one cannot escape the impression that American embarrassment, guilt, and even horror at the effects of the bomb also played a part; or that over a period of time censorship became tied in with wider American political concerns. Implementation of this policy was apparently by no means consistent. Japanese and American writings on the A-bomb did appear in Japan during the postwar years, though they were sometimes required to be modified and their publication was often delayed. And restrictions greatly diminished during the last few years of the Occupation.

But the policy fed bitterness, especially over medical questions. It became known, for instance, that Dr. Masao Tsuzuki, the radiation expert sent from Tokyo immediately after the bomb fell, came into severe conflict with American officials over this problem just as he had earlier with Japanese officials.*

The Hiroshima A-bomb authority made clear to me the way in which resentments became entwined with other A-bomb psychological themes:

> Survivors in Hiroshima died without proper treatment. Many of us feel that the use of the bomb itself was, after all, an act of war, and not too much can be said about it. But when it came to the matter of Americans refusing to give proper treatment to survivors, we feel that this is really an inexcusable thing. We think it is clear that they did this in order to keep all information about the A-bomb from being known, so that the Russians would not find out anything about these weapons. So I feel that this opposition between America and Russia—the Cold War—killed many people among the Hiroshima survivors.

While few *hibakusha* put the matter so strongly (the statement itself reflected a specific ideological position), his words nonetheless convey widely held feelings that A-bomb victims had been "sacrificed" to America's international ambitions.

One must keep in mind that much was expected of America—as we learn from the leftist woman writer in her reaction to the experience of her husband (also a writer) in being called to Occupation Headquarters regarding a violation of the "Press Code":

> Talking about the meaning of the A-bomb disaster was supposed to be against Occupation policy and was not permitted. We felt that this was not very democratic, and that although Americans claimed to be democratic, they were taking away our freedom. . . . They would

---

* Dr. Tsuzuki was eventually placed on the Occupation's "purge list" and thereby prevented from resuming academic or other public positions. Many Japanese had the impression that this was done because of his opposition to Occupation medical censorship rather than his prior association (which had indeed been intimate) with the military. Others attributed it to harmful information spread about him by jealous Japanese colleagues. Whatever the reason, various accounts testify to his close cooperation with American physicians during the early post-bomb period.[4]

point out that certain things said were not favorable. Even though there was strict censorship, they told us never to let it be known that we were cutting anything out . . . no use of black ink or anything like that. They always pretended that there was perfect freedom of speech.

For this was the time in which the "democracy boom" was sweeping Japan, and the general benevolence of the Occupation made these inconsistencies all the more disillusioning.

An ironic case in point was the censorship of A-bomb issues during the Hiroshima mayoralty election of 1947, including the cutting off of one candidate in the middle of a radio speech because of something he said about the atomic bomb, since this was the first local election to be held under the nationally sponsored democratization program.

Another incident gives us an idea of the part played by American feelings of guilt in at least some of the censorship decisions. When Takashi Nagai completed his book *Nagasaki no Kane* (*The Bells of Nagasaki*), he and his publisher were told that it would be permitted to appear only if a description of Japanese military atrocities were added to the volume. But what the particular American, or group of Americans, who made this decision did not realize was that the equation of the two was a tacit admission that the dropping of the atomic bomb was also an "atrocity"—not to mention the extent of general uneasiness revealed in this pained effort at keeping things "balanced."

Moreover, it is quite possible that American guilt made contact with *hibakusha* guilt in relationship to censorship policies—that is, that some survivors unconsciously welcomed the restrictions because of the guilt aroused in them by any public discussion of the A-bomb. Insofar as such a "conspiracy of silence" between instigators and victims did exist, we may suspect that, in the long run, it increased or at least did nothing to alleviate the guilt of both groups.

Apart from such direct atomic bomb issues, more general impressions of Americans were also important. Exemplary conduct on the part of American troops could last just so long, and there soon appeared the inevitable collusion between groups of occupiers and occupied in prostitution, narcotics, and petty crime—all of which could appear to many *hibakusha* (as to Japanese in general) as *nothing but* the corruption of "Americanization." And this view could be seemingly confirmed by a wide gamut of GI abuse of Japanese, from humiliating shows of prejudice or contempt to physical violence and murder.

Under such conditions resentment on the part of any defeated group becomes associated with the despoiling of the purity of its culture in general, and of its women in particular. In discussing these matters with me, *hibakusha* would mention other forms of American influence—particularly from films and popular culture—as contributing to the breakdown of Japanese morals, especially among the young.

The technician, for instance, recalled proudly his own strict upbringing, his mother's impressive personal discipline and virtue, and the restrained and platonic relationships he and his friends, as young men, conducted with the opposite sex. In contrast he spoke bitterly of the sensuality of youth today, condemned particularly their dancing, which he thought appropriate only to strip-tease girls or the like, and insisted that for ordinary girls to "twist their waists like that" was "out of keeping with our national characteristics." As was true of many *hibakusha*, his overall imagery suggested the sense that from the time of the dropping of the bomb through the present, America had "raped" his entire nation and its cultural heritage—especially the feminine-maternal substrate of that heritage. In his case the perverse sexual tendencies which we noted before caused him to be attracted to the entire process, and therefore intensified his resentment. But even survivors relatively free of such tendencies were attracted to various American influences, coming as these did at a time of considerable disillusionment with their own cultural tradition and their recent past. They would then feel themselves to be identified with the "plunderers" of their individual and cultural "essence" as well as with the victims of this "plundering"—and the ambivalence itself could be channeled into A-bomb resentments.

A considerable sense of intimacy has accompanied this ambivalence. The professor of education, for example, speaking for himself and "many others," stressed a difference between people's feelings toward America and Russia:

> Even if they seem to respect Russia, and talk about America in a very critical way, they still feel friendly toward America and feel both respect and a sense of threat in relationship to Russia.

Here we recognize the "family feeling" we spoke about when discussing nuclear testing.

But while there is little doubt that this intimacy has existed, and that Japanese have often had feelings toward America similar to those of children to their parents, it is seriously misleading to view the entire

Japanese-American interplay solely in terms of a "family model." Rather, I would stress the special psychological use Japanese have made of their relationship to America and Americans in their struggles for self-definition and autonomy; their need to absorb what they perceive to be "American" as a means of re-creating themselves. More than simply a mentor, America became a kind of psychohistorical "double" or alter ego. The process involved did not begin in 1945, but has evolved over more than a hundred years of being culturally and psychologically overwhelmed by the West (after having been originally "opened" to the outside world by American military power). What did happen in 1945—particularly for *hibakusha* but in some measure for all Japanese—was the actual experience of previously feared annihilation at the hands of the West, followed by an extraordinarily intense period of Western cultural influence. And since America has been the main Western representative on both scores, the annihilating force was immediately thrust into the position of the mentor-double. Or to put the matter another way, Japanese have felt the need to become like their annihilators in order to discover their postwar selves.

Some of the complexities this pattern poses for *hibakusha* are illustrated by the professor of English. Having experienced as a young man a sense of personal emancipation in the discovery of Western literature and political liberalism, there was some basis for suspicions on the part of Japanese wartime leaders that he and others like him could not be fully trusted. His way of dealing with fear and conflict at the time was by added conscientiousness in carrying out his wartime responsibilities (conscientiousness which, we remember, might well have saved his life). But with the defeat his longstanding Western identification was reawakened in connection with atomic bomb problems. He thus played an important part in introducing John Hersey's *Hiroshima* into Japan, told me "how deeply moved" he was by the humanism inspiring the book, and gave me the impression that *he* had learned much from *it* concerning how one should feel and think about the A-bomb experience.

His Western-American identification was further evident in his stress upon what he called "the spiritual power behind American materialism." But in discussing the atomic bomb in general, he also made such comments as "No such disaster has ever been experienced by Americans," and asked the rhetorical question, "Do you think that American women could have stood it?" His tone was gentle throughout; together with this kind of retaliatory hostility, directed primarily at American women, was an unusually strong identification with me and with my task as an American investigator studying the effects of the bomb. To some extent I became for him the "psychohistorical double" he had always sought from the West. His earlier struggles with Western identification, as well as his A-bomb experience, contributed to his considerable ambivalence toward me and America. But he put the ambivalence to use, both in his own public actions and in conveying to me the complexity of his and others' responses while constantly raising important psychological and moral issues.

In drawing upon the American conscience—notably Hersey's but mine as well—he was seeking a model of individual commitment to universal principles, a model which has not been particularly developed in the group-dominated Japanese cultural tradition. We also observed this process in the day laborer (the "A-bomb zealot-saint"), and I suspect that it has had considerable significance for most A-bomb leaders and for not a few ordinary survivors. Victorious American Occupiers, then, psychologically speaking, have been agents of both annihilation and benevolence, truly demonic in their power for both good and ill—people to be hated, admired, identified with, and pushed away so that one could discover oneself.

2) *Later American Spokesmen*

No wonder, then, that *hibakusha* have had extremely sensitive antennae for later American attitudes about the A-bomb. This is especially true for Americans involved in the original decision to use it, and the obvious case in point is that of former President Truman. While Mr. Truman has emphasized the revolutionary nature of nuclear weapons and the importance of bringing them under international control, he has, over the years, made repeated statements to the effect that the bomb's use was necessary, that it saved lives all around, and that he has had no regrets—no disturbances of conscience—over his decision. The impact of these statements in Hiroshima has been considerable. For instance, a segment from a television interview broadcast on February 2, 1958, was reproduced in *The New York Times* the next day as follows:

"Any regrets?" Mr. Murrow asked.

"Not the slightest—not the slightest in the world," Mr. Truman responded.

As for the earlier decision to use the atomic bomb against Japan, the former President recalled that the alternative would have been an invasion in which casualties probably would have run to a half million.

"And when we had this powerful new weapon," he said, "I had no qualms about using it because a weapon of war is a destructive weapon. That's the reason none of us want war and all of us are against war, but when you have the weapon that will win the war, you'd be foolish if you didn't use it."

Under questioning, he expressed the hope that the "new and terrible hydrogen weapon" would never be used.

"If the world gets into turmoil, however," he said, "it will be used. You can be sure of that."

For *The New York Times* these comments on the atomic bomb were not even the most important part of the broadcast (it contained a more newsworthy dispute with President Eisenhower on unrelated matters); and Mr. Truman himself, when asked about his "most difficult decision" as President, mentioned the Korean War and not the atomic bomb. But perspectives in Hiroshima were very different. Within a few days Truman's statements about the bomb had been featured, and bitterly condemned, in all mass media; and letters of protest had been sent to him by the mayor of the city and the governor of the prefecture. Moreover, the comment that "if the world gets into turmoil . . . it will be used" was at times interpreted as suggesting that under such conditions he would *favor* using the hydrogen bomb. But what people seemed to react to more than anything specific in the content of the statement was its tone of unqualified justification, its absence of regret. As the heroic city official put it to me four years later, in a way that represented both official and unofficial opinion in Hiroshima:

> I think the atomic bomb was an inhuman weapon and should never have been used. But the bomb was dropped during wartime, and of course such things can happen in war, so I can understand how America came to use it. But what I cannot understand—and what we in Hiroshima greatly resent—is Truman's claim that he did the right thing in dropping the bomb and that he has no regrets.

Contained in this point of view is a Japanese cultural stress upon reconciliation between contending groups through some form of apology which demonstrates concern for those one has injured, makes retaliation unnecessary, and permits re-establishment of harmony.

But involved in the matter are problems of mastery that would affect any group so victimized. For Truman's uncompromising defense of his action, and his unwillingness to deal with the issue of its human cost, suggested to *hibakusha* that *the man who bears the greatest individual responsibility for dropping the bomb remains psychically numbed to what it did to them, that the way toward resolving burdensome resentments still felt toward America had been barred because of the impossibility of achieving a shared formulation of the original event— one in which each side would recognize the difficulties of the other.*

What is not taken into account, of course, is the degree to which a man in Truman's position might psychologically require vociferous denial of regret as a means of quieting his own conscience and protecting himself against feelings of guilt. The vociferousness of *hibakusha* reactions in turn has to do with *their* guilt, with *their* lack of "regret" about having survived "instead" of those who did not. Also involved is a reawakening in them of death anxiety and general vulnerability—fear that the demonic power responsible for their ordeal is capable of creating, and unwilling to avoid, a repetition of that ordeal. One is reminded of a comment by an American observer at the time of the Bikini incident concerning generalized Japanese sensitivities, the feeling that "whenever America lifts an atom, some Japanese gets hurt."[5] In *hibakusha* this sense of heightened vulnerability is inseparable from guilt over survival priority.

The writer-physician makes clear how, with threats to peace of any kind, *hibakusha* vulnerability and death guilt come together in anger:

> After the war the Japanese were given a new constitution, and we were very optimistic in thinking that the world would be peaceful and that the souls of the dead would be able to rest in peace. But this optimistic outlook has been mercilessly destroyed by what followed— the Korean War, and the fact that Japan had to join one of the two power blocs of the world. As a *hibakusha* I feel I have to say something about this situation. I can't help feeling indignation . . . and an aroused feeling. . . .

Whatever, in other words, aggravates the constellation of atomic bomb conflict leads to some form of resentment.

For this reason a good deal of bitterness followed upon Eleanor Roosevelt's visit to Hiroshima in 1953 because of statements she made defending President Truman's decision to use the bomb. When asked if she agreed that the weapon should never be used again under any circumstances, she was quoted as saying that should war break out, "no one can be sure that the atomic bomb, or an even greater weapon, would not be used," and that "In order to defend peace, it may be necessary to use the atomic bomb." While there could well have been misunderstandings and altered meanings in translation, the anger her statements aroused was again related to their impact upon *hibakusha* conflicts—as one account makes clear:

> If she had at this point [when the question was asked] just said "Yes" [meaning she agreed that the weapon should never be used again], it would have been worldwide news, and concerning the feelings of the people of Hiroshima, the deaths caused by the atomic bomb would not have been meaningless. . . . But in her words there was no consideration of the Japanese internal problem.*

---

* "Internal" refers more to the national (or "domestic") level than the individual one, but the reference to psychological conflict is nonetheless present.[6]

Much more favorably received was her reaction to a meeting with a small group of "Atomic Bomb Maidens." She was reported to have been visibly moved by the experience, to have expressed indignation at the girls' not receiving medical treatment for their keloids, and to have later commented that "My heart ached from what I saw and heard." Apart from *hibakusha* reactions, Mrs. Roosevelt's behavior strikingly demonstrates the contrast between the direct emotional impact of visible atomic bomb effects (in this case keloids) and the psychic numbing which can be imposed upon anyone by general ideological commitments.

THE PERILS OF GOOD WILL

Even personal sympathy, however, has its pitfalls—as suggested by a caustic commentary on a visit to Hiroshima by Father Flanagan, the well-known American director of Boys' Town, during which he met with and said Mass before large numbers of A-bomb orphans:

> He reported on his return that they said, "Father, thank you," and that he was deeply moved. This Father was satisfied that the atomic desert could serve as a background for his admirable deed, and as for the problem of the whole world confronted with the possibility of becoming such a desert, or of how these children came to be atomic bomb orphans—these problems may be left to God to solve. These attitudes are nothing more than sympathy toward the poor Japanese from the grand Americans, and their intention is to educate the Japanese in the American way (that is, to become human beings capable of dropping the atomic bomb), so that there is nothing else to say but, "Thank you." I can understand these people's "good will" and "generosity"; but they have left out the main problem of the responsibility for the atomic bomb. Therefore, their good will comes close to self-satisfaction, their kindness to hypocrisy, and their deeds become offensive.[7]

While the harsh tone is partly a function of a leftist political stance (there were undoubtedly many in Hiroshima who responded warmly to Father Flanagan's visit), the passage suggests another important manifestation of suspicion of counterfeit nurturance: the potential humiliation and anger stemming from perceptions of "charity" in which the weak must remain weak and accept the benevolence of the strong. The problem is in many ways at the heart of Japanese-American personal and political relations, and one to which we know *hibakusha* to be exquisitely sensitive.

Where Americans have combined humanitarian concerns about *hibakusha* with strong convictions concerning the control or elimination of nuclear weapons—as have John Hersey and Norman Cousins—they evoke less ambivalence, because *hibakusha* can make common cause with them in a way that renders the atomic bomb experience meaningful, and therefore diminishes anxiety and resentment. Even they, however, have not escaped criticism for what the same Japanese commentator calls "the American approach to peace." By this he meant a stress upon good will rather than upon specific measures to strengthen the world anti-nuclear weapons movement; and while he grossly underestimated the activities of both men in precisely that area, the atmosphere in Hiroshima has been such that strictures of this kind have gained a hearing.

Reactions to one of Mr. Cousins' projects, that of the "Hiroshima Maidens," illustrate the psychological complexities of any philanthropic effort. In collaboration with the Japanese minister who had originally organized the group, Mr. Cousins and others working with him arranged for a group of American surgeons to undertake the repair of the girls' burn scars in New York. But resentments quickly arose: jealousies among the girls themselves, particularly among those in the group who were not chosen to go to America for surgery; indignant questions by *hibakusha* and others as to why such surgery could not be done in Japan by Japanese physicians; a few angry accusations by Japanese when one of the girls died unexpectedly under surgery (of causes apparently unrelated to radiation effects); disappointment among some of the girls at the limited improvement in their appearance; criticism among the more militant *hibakusha* for focusing only on surgical treatment, for "too much politeness" on both sides in avoiding "really difficult problems" about the atomic bomb, and for relying "simply on the conscience of the American people" rather than embarking upon a more independent crusade against nuclear weapons; and, upon the group's return to Hiroshima, severe antagonisms between the girls and other *hibakusha*, the latter accusing them of having become "haughty," "Americanized," and "spoiled," and the girls in turn looking upon their critics as narrow-minded and provincial. Nor were these the only resentments. For the project lent itself particularly strongly to certain kinds of imagery of counterfeit nurturance among *hibakusha*: not only in the sense of being confirmed in their victimization, but in the bitter irony of submitting to repair of A-bomb stigmata at the hands of the nation which inflicted them. Yet in an overall sense a considerable amount of "repair" was accomplished—not only of the burn scars themselves but of guilt and resentment within the Japanese-American atomic bomb interplay. For one significant hostility-dissolving message —*Americans care!*—did get through to the Hiroshima community, and to many individual *hibakusha* I spoke to.

Both the power of this message, and the inevitable difficulties which accompany it in Hiroshima, were exemplified by Floyd Schmoe, an elderly Quaker university professor who organized a program of construction of new homes for *hibakusha*, known as the "Hiroshima House Movement" (or Peace Houses), as an expression of American "regret and repentance" over the atomic bomb. With extraordinary dedication he and his wife overcame severe financial and physical obstacles to make their way to Hiroshima for several stays during the late forties and early fifties, worked on the houses with their own hands, and enlisted others of various nationalities to help them. His efforts greatly moved the Japanese, and he was even granted an audience with the Crown Prince. But the project was bedeviled by a series of misfortunes: fraud was discovered in the handling of applications for occupancy; a sexual liaison caused a minor scandal and the breakup of one of the first families to move in; several A-bomb orphans and *hibakusha* children had to be sent away because of tuberculosis and severe emotional disturbance; and a Korean occupant, whom Schmoe had insisted upon bringing in as an effort at improving Japanese-Korean relations, used his dwelling to brew illegal whiskey, and in the process started a fire which burned the house down. Yet once more *hibakusha* responded to an American who converted his "apology" into action on their behalf, in this case one who identified with their plight sufficiently to become virtually a *hibakusha* himself, thereby re-establishing human connection between victimizer and victim in a way that almost eliminated these disturbing categories. But the bedevilments associated with his efforts are probably more than coincidental. They suggest that atomic bomb dislocations were so vast that they engulfed the attempts of a single man to combat them; that individual demonstrations of repentance and self-sacrifice, in their very "purity," court disillusionment because they neglect considerations of human frailty; and that the best-meant outside effort cannot eliminate—and indeed inevitably stimulates—intramural jealousies and undertones of counterfeit nurturance.[8]

There have been a number of other Americans whose actions have contributed to the resolution of *hibakusha* resentment. Linus Pauling's ceaseless agitation against nuclear weapons and emphasis upon their consequences made some *hibakusha* feel that he has grasped something of their condition. The same has been true of Earl and Barbara Reynolds, who lived in Hiroshima for some time with their children (the American pacifist family mentioned earlier) and were admired for their wide range of peace activities, though they have been rendered somewhat more controversial by their involvement in the antagonisms of the Japanese peace movement and by their own marital breakup. Perhaps most strongly admired in a direct human fashion has been Mary McMillan, the Methodist missionary and educator long resident in Hiroshima, whose Christian pacifist activities we have noted before in their influence upon the day laborer, and whose railroad-station speech upon returning to the city after the war, in which she condemned and apologized for American use of the atomic bomb, has become something of a legend in Hiroshima.

A number of Americans in official positions, either with the American Cultural Center in Hiroshima or the Atomic Bomb Casualty Commission, have also evoked warm response by their sympathetic interest in *hibakusha* problems and general participation in Japanese life. There is one story—also part-legend—of a director of the American Cultural Center who, when he arrived in 1953 with his family, was said to be greeted with such suspicion that his seven-year-old daughter was taunted by Japanese children: "American, your nose is too high! *Baka!* [Stupid!]. You dropped the atomic bomb on us." But by offering, without a suggestion of condescension, what was most needed—exchange scholarships, library facilities, English lessons, lectures at the university—and by active involvement in the life of the city (he and his wife took part in a public concert prior to their departure), he became so admired that people from all levels of society petitioned the American government to permit him to remain beyond his four-year stay.[9] This and other experiences suggest a hunger on both sides for an intimacy that would dissolve persisting psychological discomforts surrounding the bomb.

INDIVIDUAL RESPONSES: RECONCILIATION AND RETRIBUTION

Involved in this hunger is a need for symbolic reconciliation, for the resolution of mutual guilt and anger. Over the years such reconciliation has been taking place, so that Americans and Japanese in Hiroshima have been increasingly able to come together in various forms of friendship which shunt the A-bomb problem to the background. But the experience can lead both to the wishful conclusion that the problem does not exist. During individual interviews *hibakusha* (many from segments of Japanese society with which Americans do not ordinarily come into contact) made clear to me that they tend to draw a distinction between "repentant" or at least "concerned" Americans who enhance symbolic reconciliation, and "unrepentant" and "unconcerned" Americans who do not.

But the first requirement for any kind of symbolic reconciliation was a sense of *hibakusha* autonomy—as the writer-manufacturer emphasizes:

> I hope you won't be misled into believing that the citizens of Hiroshima are appealing to America for help, or that we are raising up pitiful cries. As you know Hiroshima has had a remarkable reconstruction, so that we have confidence in ourselves to some degree. I want to say that we need little sympathy from America in this respect.

A man who is on the whole well disposed toward America and who is knowledgeable about financial matters, he was undoubtedly aware that American funds of various kinds made this reconstruction possible. Indeed, it may be just this knowledge, as well as a lingering inner sense of special need (we note his phrase about "confidence in ourselves *to some degree*") which makes him so "touchy" about the issue.

The sense of autonomy sought by him and other *hibakusha* requires an inner conviction that recovery has been achieved through their own efforts. Without this conviction, there can be neither symbolic reconciliation nor mastery. It is thus quite possible that the *failure* of a fund-raising trip by the Mayor of Hiroshima to the United States in 1954 enhanced *hibakusha* mastery. There was a certain amount of bitterness at the time, including the mayor's own frustration in dealings with American corporations, foundations, and public relations firms which seemed to fluctuate according to their estimation of public sympathy for Hiroshima, and his somewhat acid conclusion that "for Americans, business is business and sympathy is sympathy."[10] But by later obtaining the needed funds from the Japanese central government (even if American aid helped to make the funds available), *hibakusha* were given a better chance to develop inner imagery to the effect that "We have not needed your help. We have done it ourselves"—even if few would defend the imagery as true in an absolute sense.

The issue of symbolic reconciliation (or of its failure) was very much involved in the reactions to President Truman's remarks, and equally so in perceptions of American pilots involved in the atomic bombing. The reporting in Hiroshima of an expression of repentance ("What have I done?") by one of them, Robert Lewis, after meeting the Hiroshima Maidens, had considerable meaning for some *hibakusha*.[11] But of much greater impact has been the mental illness of Claude Eatherly, the world-famous "Hiroshima Pilot"—as we note in a rather typical reaction by the war widow:

> Let me ask you this. Sometime during the past year . . . I read in a weekly magazine that the man who dropped the atomic bomb had become insane. Is that true? . . . He felt responsibility . . . it was written that he felt great responsibility—but not right after that time, nor even four or five years later—in fact after ten years. . . . According to his words, he saw the faces of over two hundred thousand Hiroshima people. Well, he said something like that. But in any case, what I thought was that this was brought about by the souls of the dead which caused him this fate—this is what we say in our religion. And I believe that these souls, which have been said from ancient times to be eternal, led something to pile up in his conscience and caused him to become insane. . . .

The experience is turned into a simple myth of retribution, expressed here in Buddhist terminology but related to universal psychological and moral needs. For not only is the same theme present in the Judeo-Christian tradition ("He that smiteth a man, so that he die, shall surely be put to death" and "Eye for eye, tooth for tooth, hand for hand, foot for foot"), but this particular myth about Eatherly was, in fact, entirely evolved in America. I shall have more to say about its evolution and general significance in a later volume, but we may note here that Eatherly did not drop the bomb (he piloted a weather plane which flew into Hiroshima a few minutes ahead of the plane carrying the bomb), and that his Hiroshima experience has highly questionable causal relationship to his later mental illness.[12] But the myth, for the war widow and for many other *hibakusha*, puts things in order and re-establishes an acceptable moral and symbolic universe. She went on to explain that upon reading about Eatherly,

> I felt that we should not have war any more—that this kind of history has repeated itself too many times . . . that to retain bitter feelings

and to pass along bitter feelings toward others in life is the greatest tragedy of all.

With her ideological world thus reconstructed, she sees a path toward relief from her burden of "bitter feelings," but she is far from able either to believe fully in the myth or follow the path.

3) *Guinea Pigs*

A special dimension of feeling revolves around American-sponsored medical research into radiation effects, and the resulting complaint of *hibakusha* that they are being made into "guinea pigs." Behind this accusation is an array of inner conflicts and resentments concerned with being "experimented upon," denied needed care, and historically victimized on a racial basis.

Perhaps the root problem has been the Kafkaesque psychohistorical situation (similar to that I mentioned in relationship to my own research) of the nation which dropped the atomic bombs sending its teams of physicians to make objective studies of the weapon's initial and delayed medical effects. Such a situation renders the results somewhat suspect in the eyes of many *hibakusha*—not so much false as potentially biased, tainted, or simply unpleasant. Suspicions were increased by various American pronouncements (sometimes made by non-physicians and unrelated to scientific study) which have seemed to underestimate or unduly minimize long-term radiation influences: a statement quoted from an American official in Tokyo shortly after the bomb to the effect that "All of those who are to die from the atomic bomb have already died"; a similar claim by another American spokesman five years later that survivors had by then "recovered completely from whatever aftereffects they experienced, and no noticeable aftereffects remain"; and a statement made in Hiroshima by an American physicist in 1959 emphasizing that radiation dangers from nuclear testing were insignificant, and that casualties from nuclear research were much lower than those caused by automobile accidents.* While it is true that these pronouncements could have been distorted in translation or in being quoted out of context, they all seemed, at least to *hibakusha*, to be spoken by a single "American voice" saying, in effect: "What we have done in dropping the bomb on Hiroshima—or in testing nuclear weapons—is really not so bad." The tone of minimization which *hibakusha* perceive both re-

---

* The first two statements, if accurately quoted, are clearly misleading; the third combines a controversial impression with a true but perhaps irrelevant comparison.[13] They are, unfortunately, reminiscent of certain statements that have been made in America by official agencies concerning the negligibility of nuclear weapons fallout and related dangers.

awakens their own fears of inauthenticity ("Maybe they are right, and I am an impostor for complaining or being fearful"), and gives them a sense of being trifled with.

Medical antagonisms probably began with the arrival of the first American physicians in Hiroshima about a month after the bomb fell. There was, it must be said, impressive early cooperation between American and Japanese physicians, and the resulting investigative accomplishments and personal friendships formed in association with the Joint Commission for the Investigation of the Effects of the Atomic Bomb in Japan have been ably recorded.[14] But it was inevitable that some Japanese physicians would later complain that Americans monopolized atomic bomb research materials and took credit for work done originally by Japanese—just as others would still later stress Japanese priority in discovering increased incidence of leukemia and cancer. There were also fierce professional jealousies among Japanese doctors themselves prior to the arrival of Americans: one practitioner recalls how, during Dr. Tsuzuki's early trips to Hiroshima to gather material for his investigations, many of the physicians in the city would try to avoid him, or else remain silent in his presence, because "he might try to get something important out of their mouths."[15] But the medical involvement of Americans was to bring, over the years, problems with more sinister overtones. Again I would emphasize that these overtones were psychohistorical in origin—stemming from the sequence of the use of the weapon and the study of its effects—and occurred despite the dedicated, sometimes even heroic work of individual Japanese and American researchers. The combination of scientific ethos and conventional victor's investigative rights was simply inadequate to the extraordinary emotional and physical impact of the new weapon. Perhaps no medical approach could have been adequate, but what might have come closest, had it been possible, would have been an international medical team combining research with therapy, and explicitly committed to the universal sharing of medical data on nuclear weapons on behalf of world peace.

Even then, *hibakusha* would not have been without their suspicions. But confronted as they were with a program initiated by the American military and later sponsored by other government agencies—the Atomic Bomb Casualty Commission, which succeeded the Joint Commission, was established by Presidential order, under the direction of the National Academy of Sciences, with general support of the Armed Forces and funds from the Atomic Energy Commission—*habakusha* found it all too easy to look upon the entire effort as having the dual purpose of "keeping secret" the nefarious things America had done while learning everything possible about the effects of atomic bombs in order to prepare for future nuclear warfare.[16] Such accusations could be neither proven nor entirely disproven: they were often politically motivated, and they ignored the careful investigative efforts undertaken; but even where medical knowledge is the general aim, a sponsoring governmental agency such as the Atomic Energy Commission is bound to be interested in the political and military significance of this knowledge. Nor did the later co-sponsorship of the ABCC by the Japanese National Institute of Health entirely eliminate its "official American" aura.

The basic arrangement having been established, other conflicts inevitably followed. One of these was associated with the site chosen for the permanent location of the ABCC. The "logic" of the selection of a hill overlooking the city could not be denied, given the susceptibility of lower areas to floods which could damage the complex equipment needed and thereby endanger the whole effort. But that same hill happened to have once been the location of the Emperor Meiji's Hiroshima headquarters, and still contained an old military cemetery. The *hibakusha* resentment at moving the cemetery had been predicted by city officials (who had unsuccessfully urged the Americans not to choose the site), and centered not only around the general theme of desecration, but also around that of Americans "looking down" on the inhabitants of the city. (We recall the complaint that one of the broad new highways was built as "the royal road to the ABCC.") This imagery concerning the site closely followed upon *hibakusha*'s sense of America's demonic power, and of her having, through the bomb, already "desecrated" life and death.

A more persistent focus of resentment, bearing directly upon guinea pig imagery, has been the ABCC's policy of research without treatment. Here too the matter is complicated. Many Japanese physicians in Hiroshima, wary of professional competition, strongly opposed the idea of the Americans' providing treatment. City officials urged that the research program be closely affiliated with a Japanese treatment center, a proposal not without its problems but in any case never attempted.*

* American authorities must bear responsibility for the ultimate decision. There were a number of Americans who questioned it and who, at various times, urged that treatment be instituted. But one cannot help suspecting that the policy followed, consistent as it was with general efforts to avoid any special emphasis upon the atomic bomb, was influenced by the same pattern of psychic numbing we spoke of when discussing early American censorship. One may also add that the larger issues

The result was that *hibakusha*, extremely fearful of lingering radiation effects and lacking adequate treatment for whatever effects might be present, were subjected to "pure research" by the country which had set the process in motion by dropping the bomb. It was a situation which lent itself readily to imagery of Svengali-like scientists, who first tried out their diabolical weapon upon unsuspecting people, and then coldly and methodically studied its effects upon those people, both in order to satisfy their curiosity and to gather information necessary for even more diabolical schemes in the future. This extreme picture could be accompanied by a much more favorable one, even within the same *hibakusha* mind; but it has been hard to eradicate entirely. For it gives expression to universal fears of being manipulated, attacked, or annihilated by all-powerful forces, along with a certain amount of attraction to such abuse.

The sexual component of this Svengali imagery has been manifest in the frequent complaints of young women being examined, or kept waiting for long periods of time, in an entirely nude state. Whatever actual tactlessness was involved in early examining procedures, the emotional symbolism is that of being raped by a powerful alien force. Similarly, *hibakusha* have been constantly alert for harm or mistreatment of any kind during ABCC visits. But the ultimate theme of the Svengali imagery has been that of tampering with the dead—a theme evoked in relationship to requests by the ABCC for permission to perform post-mortem examinations on *hibakusha* as part of its research program. The day laborer's wife revealed the intensity of feeling which this request could call forth:

On the day of the funeral . . . a jeep from ABCC came and asked us if they could dissect the body. They said it would be for the good of society as a whole, and that surely Father would not have been opposed to it. Now what are they trying to take from the corpse of my father? They have dropped the atomic bomb which filled my father's later life with agony and caused him to work until his body was completely ruined—still what have they come here for, and what do they expect from my father's body? Even if my father's body might help the work of ABCC by adding a small line on a graph, what good would that do society? Based upon my father's body, would they make further discoveries for bigger atomic and hydrogen bombs? I can't just hand over my father's body for that. Not being content

---

involved in such a decision are more readily grasped in retrospect than they could be under the early post-bomb pressures experienced by both nations.

with the great sacrifice my father had to bear, they tried to cast the shadow of their war-smelling hands into eternity. Father, who had become a small parcel of bones, kept calling to my soul: "Stand up strongly!"[17]

Here she accuses the American agency of something very close to a morbid lust for corpses, of necromanic violation. She sees it as a kind of corporate Svengali, extending its "experiments" into the mysterious realms of death and eternity, thus committing an ultimate form of desecration. Her remarks about lines on graphs suggest that living as she does in a scientific age, some part of her may also believe that there is merit in gaining information through autopsies; but death guilt (in her case toward her father) causes her to suppress this alternative belief.* Even those who accede to autopsy requests are likely to be severely troubled by such guilt.

Additional psychological and political influences have combined to reinforce the theme of ABCC lust for corpses. At the May Day celebration of 1956, for instance, placards bore two particularly prominent slogans: "Peaceful Use of Atomic Power" and "Don't Sell to the ABCC the Corpses of Those Who Have Been Sacrificed." The metaphor of "selling the bomb" or "selling one's name" had now been extended to the idea of "selling corpses"; for a *hibakusha* to agree to do so meant being implicated in this necromanic evil; the *hibakusha* (or a *hibakusha*'s family member) was being warned to resist the pressure and the temptation, and to stand fast as one who protects the dead.

What all this suggests is that the ABCC has become symbolic of the American presence in Hiroshima, and that the guinea pig imagery directed at it has come to reflect every kind of anxious and hostile image held by *hibakusha* (and to some extent Japanese in general) of America: A-bomb-wielding annihilator, causer of social and economic suffering, destroyer of the Japanese essence, dispenser of counterfeit nurturance, and Svengali-like experimenter, rapist, and desecrator of the dead. Yet paradoxically, these resentful images have resulted partly from *hibakusha*'s sense of intimacy with America; associated with the guinea pig constellation are psychological themes of manipulating parents and historical mentors who may be demonic in power but are also, or should be made to be, benevolent and loving.

---

* Also involved are old cultural taboos concerning the disfiguring of corpses. Only recently, partly through the influence of the ABCC, have post-mortem examinations been done in Hiroshima with any regularity.

"THERE'S SOMETHING UNNATURAL ABOUT THEM"

These varying emotions emerged during individual interviews with *hibakusha*. Many immediately raised the question, to me or to one of my assistants, of whether I was in any way affiliated with the ABCC, and made it clear that had I been, they would not have wished to talk to me. A typical comment was that of the Protestant minister:

> It is a good thing you are not associated with the ABCC because Japanese don't have a good feeling toward them—there is something unnatural about them which puts us in a difficult position. But in your case you will be able to talk freely with *hibakusha*, and they with you.

His word "unnatural" refers inclusively to the array of negative images we have discussed, and to the general sense of disharmony perceived by the *hibakusha* in his relationship to the ABCC.*

Some of the complaints expressed to me, moreover, had a ritualistic quality which suggested that *hibakusha* were reacting as much to a kind of shared public agreement about how one was supposed to feel as to his actual experience at the ABCC. Thus, the female poet combined themes of sexual assault and absence of therapeutic care in her complaint that "they simply asked us to take off our clothes and examined us—but gave us no advice, no medicines, no treatment at all," and then added: "I felt angry—everyone feels this way about the ABCC." She also brought up the frequently mentioned issue of salary discrimination there—"They give less to Japanese than to Americans"—discrimination which actually existed because of the great differences in the two economies, but which conveyed deeper connotations of prejudice. Then she made a final revelation which threw further light on *hibakusha* feelings about the ABCC, claiming that it was their doctors who, nine years before, "sent me a long report which said I had . . . signs of cancer of the uterus." Since no such malignancy turned out to be present, we suspect that her image of the ABCC as a death-tainted organization (because of the nature of its work, the Svengali imagery surrounding it, and its general association with American use of the

---

* It is possible that some who made such statements would have spoken with me even if I had been affiliated with the ABCC, just as (for reasons we shall soon discuss) many with very mixed feelings about the ABCC have cooperated in its research program. But as the minister suggests, they would probably have lacked the spontaneity of expression so crucial for psychological investigation.

bomb) led her to misrepresent what the report actually said—and that the anxiety surrounding such imagery in *hibakusha* in general is a major source of their anger.

Concerning the issue of the ABCC's failure to provide medical treatment, however, the professor of English took a very different view:

> . . . there is another opinion about this too. The Japanese are a very proud people, and many would not wish to have such treatment—especially from America—and would feel that we must stand on our own feet.

He is of course raising issues of autonomy and, indirectly, of counterfeit nurturance. Moreover, although he did not mention it, American treatment would have posed, at moments of failure, the same problem we observed in connection with the Hiroshima Maiden who died under American surgery: the specter of *hibakusha* still dying at the hands of American scientists.*

But much more characteristic was the view that a powerful nation with "specialized knowledge" was withholding something from a group in desperate need—here expressed by the technician as he recalls thoughts he had while "lying in bed" following an operation for a condition he attributed to radiation effects:

> I thought that the Japanese government should hold out a helping hand to those of us suffering from illnesses caused by the bomb . . . but it didn't seem to have the ability to do this. . . . So, I thought, well, since the American government too knows very well about this terrible event—I thought that they should surely help us.

It was this frustrated need, rather than any specific discourtesy encountered during an examination; which led him and many others to cling to the guinea pig imagery. While he himself had had no experience with the ABCC, he observed that two friends were dealt with politely there and "don't seem to feel that they were treated as guinea pigs"; yet in a way that did not entirely commit him but implied that he by no means fully rejected the accusation, he concluded that "in general

---

* In general, there is little specific therapy available for conditions caused by radiation aftereffects, and it could therefore be argued that America's decision not to offer treatment created no great deprivation. But such an argument ignores the symbolic significance of "care" as opposed to mere investigation, whatever the limitations of a nonspecific, mainly supportive, treatment program—not to mention the potential medical significance of treatment for burns and injuries.

people say that they do treat us like guinea pigs because their main purpose is not treatment, but research."

There were some, however, like the shopkeeper's assistant, who were willing to use their own experience to counteract this imagery:

Many years ago I heard from people that the ABCC treats people as guinea pigs. But some time later, when I went there for the first time, I didn't find that to be particularly true and didn't feel any pressure at all. And now I am not too much impressed by what is said about the ABCC.

But even though such affirmative experience with the ABCC, as well as the simple passage of time, have caused guinea pig imagery to diminish, *hibakusha* tend to retain it as a lasting A-bomb theme— sometimes vivid, sometimes muted.

Two writers who have used the ABCC as subjects for novels (which we shall discuss in Chapter X) suggested further sources of resentment. One stressed the great contrast during the early post-bomb days between the general atmosphere of disintegration and the elegance of American equipment, particularly the new automobiles sent to pick up *hibakusha* and bring them for examinations. His comment to me, "When I would see the ABCC station wagon, I would have a very rebellious and negative feeling," reflected anger not only at this contrast, but at his own temptation to ride in the car and share the power and affluence it represented.

The other used an analogy with reversed victimizer-victim roles in order to illustrate what I have called the Kafkaesque psychohistorical situation:

Hiroshima is of course different from Pearl Harbor—but let me use the comparison here. If, after Pearl Harbor, Japan took the island over and called people in for diagnosis without therapy—what kind of feeling would that have caused among the people?

Whatever the limitations of comparing Hiroshima to Pearl Harbor, we get a sense of the sequence of being victimized by an annihilating blow and then made the object of scientific study. The same writer went on to make a more sweeping observation:

I don't know whether the ABCC is a form of good will or not—but in general American expressions of good will are misunderstood everywhere, including in Hiroshima.

He is telling us, in other words, that problems surrounding suspicion of counterfeit nurturance bedevil American "aid" throughout the world; that, as in Hiroshima, the recipients of whatever America offers tend to equate it with weakness and impaired autonomy.

:

One might well wonder why *hibakusha* cooperate at all with ABCC research. Yet there has been no doubt of this cooperation, particularly in recent years, and ABCC spokesmen point out that the rate of return visits would be more than respectable in an ordinary clinic in, say, Boston or New York. The coexistence of this pattern of cooperation with guinea pig imagery requires some explanation.

An important consideration, as I have already suggested, has been the simple passage of time, and the increasing ability of *hibakusha* and Americans in Hiroshima to adapt to one another. For in the past cooperation with ABCC research was by no means as impressive, and at one point an unsatisfactory rate of return visits led to an overhauling of administrative procedures in which more careful attention was paid to *hibakusha* sensitivities.* The ABCC has, moreover, extended its services to the community in various ways, including programs of free consultation and even treatment for certain kinds of cases. Antagonisms over the years have also been diminished by such developments as the availability of medical treatment in Japanese facilities, a general decline in public expression of atomic bomb conflicts, a loss of influence of groups using the peace movement for purposes tied up with militant anti-Americanism, and a general increase in Japanese-American intimacy on both national and individual levels.

In addition, whatever resentment *hibakusha* may feel toward the ABCC, their bodily anxieties often led them to place great value on the thorough examination they knew to be available to them there. And the general Japanese pattern of compliance to authority—strikingly demonstrated throughout the American Occupation but not necessarily limited to that period of time—has made it difficult for many, whatever their feelings, to refuse to agree to an appointment or enter a car when it appeared.

But the most important explanation of the coexistence between guinea pig antagonisms and active cooperation in the research lies in the general human capacity for complex and contradictory inner imagery,

---

* Research methods have also been altered and improved in recent years, with elimination of many loose practices said to have existed during the early days of the organization.

that is for ambivalence. We may go so far as to say that the constellation of guinea pig imagery has had a certain psychological usefulness in enabling *hibakusha* to express their ambivalence.* In this sense the ABCC, as the most prominent American presence in Hiroshima during the postwar years, has provided *hibakusha* with an emotional sounding-board for their conflicts in relationship to the country which dropped the bomb, and to some extent to the entire A-bomb experience. Put another way, guinea pig imagery has been a way of dealing with sensitivities to counterfeit nurturance while at the same time grasping at the benefits of whatever nurturance was available.

"THE WHITE RACES AND THE COLORED RACES"

But guinea pig imagery does express a lingering hurt. *For, I would hold, it derives ultimately from the experience of having been made "historical guinea pigs" when victimized by a weapon so new, powerful, and mysterious that its effects could not be known until it had been "tried" on a particular city.* And while this imagery was magnified and made concrete by later American-sponsored medical study of the effects of this "experiment," it is possible that equivalent emotions would have arisen even if such research had not been conducted.

Feeling themselves victims of a terrible historical experiment, *hibakusha* find themselves asking a disturbing inner question: "Why were we chosen?" One answer is that their victimization was racially based—and we are not surprised that this kind of suspicion is particularly strong in a "double victim" (that is, an "outcast" as well as a *hibakusha*) such as the *burakumin* boy:

> Some people bring up the question of the colored races—that the white race regards the colored races as inferior. Well, for some time I think I have had such a feeling. And there is also the problem of the [American] Negroes. . . . Well, it may be that the A-bomb was dropped here entirely by accidental choice of a place . . . but still, I can't help feeling it has some connection between the Caucasian and the Negro, that is, the relationship between the white races and the colored races. . . . That is, that America had been specifically planning to drop it on Japan. . . . Well, I am not at all definite about

---

* The Japanese psychological tendency toward syncretism, and toward compartmentalizing divergent elements in a way that they are acted upon more or less independently, could also be important here. These tendencies might at times even permit resentful *hibakusha* to cooperate with the ABCC without experiencing a very strong sense of ambivalence.

this, but somehow I have this feeling . . . although I think it is much better for me not to think in this way. . . .

The suspicion is filled with such bitterness that a *hibakusha* who holds it, as in this case, is likely to struggle against it. But his awareness of America's victimization of her own "colored race" makes it difficult for him to dismiss the thought entirely.

Others, such as the war widow, made similar inferences in associating America's hypocrisy in race relations with her nuclear weapons policies:

> Well, this may not be true only of America but in other countries too—but while mouthing words of justice, they do things which are the very opposite. They claim to be peaceful, but they conduct nuclear testing, and about their treatment of the Negroes—well, I disapprove of such things.

Also involved is an awareness of longstanding American prejudices against Japanese, particularly on the West Coast, including the decision to place American citizens of Japanese extraction in internment camps during the war. That the Japanese themselves have been prejudiced against Nisei, that they have in their own country victimized groups such as *burakumin* and Koreans, whom they look upon as "dark," and are in general a people with considerable race consciousness—all this undoubtedly tends to increase, rather than diminish, the tendency to bring in the issue of race. *For the awareness, at whatever level of consciousness, that racialism could enter into anyone's choice of victims inevitably feeds suspicion that the nuclear "experiment" was based upon racial considerations.*

Because of the deep mutual shame which surrounds the entire racial issue, it has become a more or less unmentionable one between Japanese and Americans—something of a later expression of the "conspiracy of silence" which followed immediately upon the use of the bomb. Even now it lies behind a more general difficulty Japanese and Americans have in discussing atomic bomb issues with one another. One friend, for instance, told me he found it virtually impossible to talk about the subject with most Americans, seemed to hint at a racial consideration but quickly denied it, and then belied his denial by immediately bringing up the acute discomfort he experienced at a recent academic seminar when an American political commentator spoke of "the dangers of the yellow and black races of the world gaining the ascendancy."

From the American side, discomfort about racial considerations tends to take one of two polar forms: angry dismissal of the entire issue as nothing but communist propaganda; or, more rarely, the accusation that racial prejudice was without doubt *the* reason for the decision to use the bomb on Japan. Various interlacings of guilt and ideology are of course related to both American responses. But what is so painful for all concerned is that although the general history of the making of the atomic bomb speaks against racial considerations (the original stimulus was provided by the fear of German scientific progress in the same area), no one could be entirely certain that these considerations were entirely absent from the psychic processes of some of the people involved in the decision to use the weapon.

Returning to *hibakusha* themselves, we may say that simply the idea of a historical "experiment"—that is, of selective use of the weapon under a specific set of conditions—tends to make people wonder about the possibility of racially based victimization. Thus, the divorced house-wife, whose sense of the experimental nature of the weapon we remember to be related to her feelings about chance survival (". . . if work on the bomb had been finished before it was used, none of us would have been able to survive"), went on to speculate:

Well, the bomb was not dropped on Germany . . . and I wondered why. But regarding its being dropped on Japan, well, I imagine they dropped it as an experiment. They didn't know what would result—and in half-believing and half-doubting, they dropped it as an experiment. They chose Hiroshima as a good place in Japan for the experiment.

Ultimately, then, guinea pig imagery is inseparable from the sense of racial victimization in the original exposure, and therefore also inseparable from the death anxiety and death guilt associated with that exposure. These psychological relationships were expressed years later in a memoir by a *hibakusha*, through a statement referring to those killed by the bomb: "There exist no words in any human language which can comfort guinea pigs who do not know the cause of their death."[18] To be made into a guinea pig, in other words, is to be snuffed out prematurely and in total ignorance of the agent of one's death—imagery held by survivors not only about the A-bomb dead but, in a somewhat different way, about their own possible post-A-bomb fate. This lingering sense of having been historically rendered into expendable laboratory animals has kept alive resentment toward America and at the same time posed a formidable barrier to mastery.

4) American Interloper

Nor could these feelings about America fail to influence reactions to me and to the new form of "American intrusion" I represented. This sense of intrusion was, I believe, minimized by my way of approaching *hibakusha*—through introductions by people of considerable local standing, and as an independent academic investigator who knew something about their country and whose work was associated with concerns about war and peace. The tone of my questions as the work proceeded—my interest in their ideas and feelings—further helped dispel suspicions that I might have some hidden ideological ax to grind. But *hibakusha* also became aware of an invasion of an emotional area which had previously been accessible only to their own group, or else sanctified by silence.

The professor of English summed up various sources of ambivalence to me and my work:

> Your work in Hiroshima will be very delicate . . . there will be difficulties . . . because people often feel that no one can understand their experience unless they have been through it themselves . . . and because you are an American, from the country which dropped the bomb . . . and what is most important, because you are from a wealthy country and people may think of you as looking down upon them.

His sense of what was "delicate" and "difficult" stemmed from his own inner reservations—about an "outsider" from the country which initiated the "experiment," and about perceptions of American power and superiority (he used "wealth" as a euphemism) with which I would be associated. Essentially sympathetic to me and my work, he seemed to group me with certain Americans and other Westerners whose "immediate and profound understanding" of the atomic bomb issue had deeply affected him. We in fact know his identification with the West to have impelled him toward furthering such understanding—as he did by introducing Hersey's book and by his talks with me. I was therefore both a source of some uneasiness to him and a welcome agent of symbolic reconciliation. Others, such as the mathematician, raised indirect suspicions about the possibility of my work being used for "military purposes," rather than for the more desirable one of "helping America to avoid using weapons of this kind"—though I felt that his mention of the issue was a way of "clearing the air" and inwardly justifying his own, as it turned out, enthusiastic participation. For where such suspicions are strong, any cooperation with Americans could create a disturbing sense of betrayal of the dead and of self-betrayal.

The *burakumin* woman leader expressed a very different concern—that I not fall into a pattern of "tragic sentiment" she noted in many writings about the A-bomb, adding that, after two interviews, she was convinced that my work "will probably not turn out to be like that." The "probably" meant that she was still uncertain; for, as in her criticism of fellow *hibakusha* for merely "clasping their hands" before the Cenotaph, she generally found that people did not live up to her militant standards of Marxist "objectivity."

Only once did I encounter direct and intense anger expressed by a *hibakusha* toward me and my research effort. At the beginning of my second interview with the skilled worker (the man who expressed bitter confusion over the meaning of "peace"), I asked, as was my custom, whether there was anything he wished to bring up. Rather belligerently he said that there was, asked a series of pointed questions about my work, my way of going about it, and its purpose—and then made clear that he was by no means satisfied with my answers:

> I understand . . . but during the course of the last interview I wondered about this. . . . I had a somewhat unpleasant feeling. . . . It's difficult to express—but somehow though I have talked about the A-bomb on many occasions, I felt that this case was very different. . . . I never put my feelings in words like this before, so it was a new experience for me. . . .

He went on to suggest that my being an American was part of the trouble, as was the problem of "having another person [my research assistant] come between us," and also that a non*hibakusha* "can't really understand." But what seemed to trouble him most was something else:

> This interview is rather late, and in some ways beside the point. It is too late, I feel. Now it is more important to think about actual living rather than about that [the A-bomb]. . . . Well, I don't mean anything profound—just living in the present—well, there are many electrical appliances these days, and we are able to buy almost anything—to have a comfortable life is our present wish. . . .

I felt that he was trying to tell me that Americans like myself had not been around to help when help was most needed, and that all I was doing now was reopening old emotional wounds (and one must remember that he had a physical one too, a severe keloid). And also that, after much suffering, he had come to terms with his experience—had achieved a precarious equilibrium of bitterness, psychic numbing, and focus upon immediate comforts—and then along came an A-bomb "experimenter" to stir everything up again. At the same time there was a suggestion (in his resentment of "having another person come between us") that he craved a close understanding with me, but felt the need to retreat from it both because it was "too late" and because it too would have threatened the emotional equilibrium he had achieved. Thus, although I contested nothing that he said, when I asked him at the end of our talk whether he would like to come to see me on a third occasion to discuss these matters further, he replied: "If I come to see you, we would only have an argument, so I better not."*

Very different was the attitude of the psychologist, for whom my alien origins were an advantage:

> The situation in Japan is such that most professors feel very reluctant to discuss the atomic bomb very frankly. . . . Political pressures and various kinds of special sentiment have prevented any balanced evaluation of any kind from being made. So it is very good that you are undertaking such objective research.

It turned out that in a personal sense "objective research" meant an atmosphere sufficiently without bias to permit him to discuss his feelings freely and at length, especially those revolving around still severe guilt over survival priority. He thus sought out our meetings eagerly, and the relief he obtained from them was related not only to guilt but to the resolution of resentments that lay beneath his enthusiasm.

This kind of quest for a therapeutic experience with me as a means of achieving symbolic reconciliation could be expressed more indirectly. When the day laborer made his comment that Americans and Japanese tended to be "too polite with one another" about the atomic bomb, for instance, one of his points of reference was our interview, as he

---

* Strong residual guilt could influence patterns of communication even more than hostility. It could cause some *hibakusha* to be defensive and monosyllabic in their responses, while insisting that nothing very much had happened to them; and others to be verbose in justifications of their A-bomb behavior, or to embellish their recollections with protective distortions.

proceeded to demonstrate by pouring out his story without restraint. Or the therapeutic experience could reveal itself in a specific change in behavior during the course of two or three interviews, as in the case of the seamstress. Having undergone complicated emotional experiences with both Americans and Japanese as a returned A-Bomb Maiden she was still extremely sensitive about her keloid, and was at first apprehensive and somewhat resistive. But during the latter part of our first meeting she seemed to relax, and at our next one expressed herself with unusual warmth and appreciation as she explained that

> The way I feel when I talk about the past with someone like you is different from when I talk about it with my mother. I wanted to forget the past—and tried very hard to—but now I feel I should make some use of it.

In addition to suggesting "transference" in the sense of my temporarily becoming like a parent, she was also referring to a renewed sense of personal value in relationship to her experience. For she was exploring that experience more deeply than she ever had before, making it known to another in a way that might help many; and she was at the same time integrating it into her general life pattern and thereby moving closer toward mastery.

What became clear was that *hibakusha*, and those closely associated with them, had great difficulty discussing the subject in a completely open way with one another. The young Hiroshima-born writer, for instance, spoke of the rarity of someone "thinking with me while asking questions" in the form of a "true conversation." He told me then of his grandmother who, "until the moment she died," insisted to him, "don't talk to Americans," and went on to say that

> I am very glad we have been able to talk so frankly—without façade [*tatemae*]. There are many leaders of the peace movement who cannot do this, and who are unable to admit, for instance, that there are *hibakusha* who would like to see the whole world blown up.

He was, so to speak, wallowing in forbidden ideas as his way of celebrating the breakthrough he felt that he and I had achieved in the Japanese-American "conspiracy of silence" about unpleasant A-bomb truths.

Not that all hostility toward America, or toward me, was dissolved during these interviews with him and others. But even where a *hibakusha* insisted upon his lingering resentment—as in the case of the middle-aged businessman over the loss of his son—the articulation of that resentment to an American contributed, however slightly, to a diminished burden of hatred, and to the general process of symbolic reconciliation. *Vital to this process was the hibakusha's overcoming crippling imagery of victimization—of hatred and self-hatred—and thereby enlarging his "life space" in a way that both liberated the self and transcended it in connection and purpose.* Precisely this process, I came to suspect, could well be the essence of all psychotherapeutic accomplishment.

This kind of therapeutic pattern was evident in my sessions with the history professor. He seemed to welcome the most probing questions, and we recall his extreme self-accusation in relationship to his behavior at the time of the bomb and to his "hypocrisy" before that. But rather than simply indulging in a neurotic form of self-flagellation, he was struggling to articulate a sense of personal transformation which was intricately bound up with the general Japanese encounter with America and Americans:

> The Japanese are a kind people who blindly follow those in power. The Americans came in and needed help, so the Japanese suddenly shifted their loyalty. I thought it was sad to see this sudden shift in loyalty. But as a historian I knew that the Japanese had never experienced a Renaissance. There had never in Japan been a liberation of the individual. Then the end of the war brought about this liberation of the individual. . . . If you have never had experience with the Japanese military, this might be difficult to understand—but the limits were external, not internal. If there was a man with a high rank present, one worked hard; if not, people did not do their duties. . . . When I was in the military, I felt the weakness of these vertical relationships—which have existed also historically in relationship to the Shogun and the Emperor. People never had a chance to be individuals, but were beaten down by power from above. . . . Americans have their weak points, but what impressed me was their sense of responsibility for their own individual duties. . . . Now I always tell my students that they should be good individualists. . . .

Contact with Americans, he is saying, made possible his release from authoritarian bonds, and our interviews crystallized what was generally favorable in this larger encounter. But there was also the implication that he feared that his apparent personal transformation might turn out to be merely a new version of the old "hypocrisy"—a "shift in loyalty" toward Americans (and toward me) of the type he so deplored.

His conflict was further revealed in two comments which followed immediately upon one another. The first was a justification of the bomb's use of a kind I did not encounter with any other *hibakusha*, and which I found particularly striking coming from a man who had suffered so greatly and expressed himself so strongly in other ways:

> Of course, war itself is immoral . . . but it inevitably includes the all-out effort to win, with no limit on weapons used. . . . So I don't agree with those who criticize the use of the bomb. . . . If it had not been used, we would have had even greater destruction.

And the second, a caustic comment on racism:

> I spoke once with a reporter from Australia. I told him that it was very illogical that a big country like his does not permit others to come in. Our country is small and full of people. It would be wonderful if human beings didn't think in terms of racial rivalries. This is the essence of human stupidity.

On the one hand we note an identification with America which encompasses not only its use of the bomb but the bomb itself, but on the other hand an inner suspicion, suggested by his sequence of unconscious associations, that the use of the bomb was related to racial antagonisms. Had the interviews continued beyond three sessions, it is quite possible that this "unmentionable" subject could have been examined, and that a considerable amount of unexpressed anger would have been found to exist side by side with more positive feelings about his American-induced transformation. Even lacking this further exploration, however, I felt that our meetings had helped him considerably in his efforts to integrate both his atomic bomb experience and his complex relationship to America, and to overcome anger and move toward formulation and mastery.

I do not mean to imply that I saw my function in Hiroshima as one of diminishing *hibakusha* resentments, or for that matter of bringing to bear any particular influence upon *hibakusha*. But interviews are, or should be, dialogue. Although on the whole I attempted to avoid imposing my personal opinions upon *hibakusha* (unless asked, at which time I tried to be candid), I have no doubt that many of my attitudes got through to them, and in some cases had considerable impact upon them. Among these attitudes I would include my sympathy for self-knowledge and for the kind of broadening of imagery we spoke of before as transcending crippling hatred. And the fact that this attitude came from an American, and one with strong concerns about nuclear weapons in general, could not help but suggest at least the possibility of symbolic reconciliation. But by the same token, it is also possible that *hibakusha* were adversely affected by whatever conflicts might have been engendered in me by the work.

CONTRADICTIONS, "MISUNDERSTANDING," AND PARTNERSHIP

There were *hibakusha* who, because of unresolved emotional struggles, reacted to me in confused and contradictory fashion. The female poet, for instance, very quickly—perhaps too quickly—expressed enthusiasm for my work: "I am very pleased to hear that you are studying the spiritual effects rather than just the physical effects, as these are very important." But before long she adopted a tone of thinly veiled retaliatory resentment, as revealed in a series of comparisons aimed (at least unconsciously) at stimulating my own guilt. She abruptly asked, "Dr. Lifton, do you have any children?" and when I told her I had a fourteen-month-old son, she immediately replied:

> One of my cousins had a baby just that age who was killed, along with his mother. She was one of twins, both of whom died. . . . The father was all right, and even took care of arrangements and attended the funeral. Then suddenly he died too on August fifteenth, from aftereffects of the bomb.

In a similar vein was her pointed observation about me, "I am glad to see that you are so young and healthy," together with the question quoted before, "Can you tell me how it is possible to put my body into good health?"; and still another question (when talking about religion and human conflict): "Do you, Dr. Lifton, feel that your heart is completely pure?" Through the remainder of our two interviews she alternated between ingratiating and accusatory approaches to me. These fluctuations were made necessary by the demands of her anxiety and her inner doubt (noted before) about the genuineness of her physical debility, that is, by her overall confusion in formulating her A-bomb experience and her relationship to Americans.

An even more striking series of fluctuations in attitude occurred during my contacts with the war widow. When my social worker-assistant and I first called upon her, we found no one home and left our cards with a neighbor, along with a note from the social worker that he would return in a few days to arrange for an interview. But the next day she abruptly appeared at my office, and declared with some feeling, having apparently "misunderstood" my message, that it would be "impossible" for me to come to her home:

> My husband, who was killed by the Americans, is enshrined there . . . and he would not want you there. . . . My own life has been ruined by the Americans. They killed my husband and they dropped the atomic bomb which destroyed everything I owned. . . . My life has been very hard. It might be better for you to talk to other people instead of me because my experience has been the very worst one. If ever there was a sacrifice, I am it.

Despite the things she said, her tone seemed more that of petulant instability than profound anger. This impression was confirmed when, after a few words of reassurance and a brief explanation of the nature of my work, she accepted an invitation to sit down and discuss her experiences with me right then and there. What is more, she suddenly assumed an attitude of submissiveness and flattery, and told me how, from the beginning of the war, "I knew that we would lose because America was too strong," and how from what she saw of the Occupation, "I found much to admire in America." What became clear was that part of her "misunderstanding" of our arrangements had to do with her urge to talk with an American like me—both because of a desire to partake of American power, and a need for relief from what she referred to as "the tragedy of having to live with bitter feelings," that is, because of a need for symbolic reconciliation.

But toward the end of this first interview, she reverted equally abruptly to her earlier tone of condemnation. She insisted that "A-bombs and Americans are inseparable," asked me whether I had undergone personal suffering in the war, and then contrasted my good fortune with her own extreme hardship in having lost her husband and been forced to struggle alone for her own and her daughter's livelihood. Once more recollections of pain and loss had made their way into our interview, as had a mixture of death guilt toward her husband and anger at him for "abandoning" her by being killed in battle. Yet she readily agreed to a second interview, and at that time I noticed that she was more relaxed and steady in her manner, and had neither the need to make accusations nor to be unduly submissive. Two factors seemed to contribute to her ease. She had just obtained a new job as a school librarian, and could herself recognize that this security enabled her to experience much less "envy and bitterness" than she did before. And she had, in her early histrionic behavior, satisfied herself that the interview situation with me was "safe" and could even afford her emotional benefits. Indeed, while her fluctuations in mood were related to an individual tendency toward hysterical character structure, they are also part of a Japanese cultural emphasis upon relatively abrupt shifts in mood, and of the "protean" explorations in emotions and ideas mentioned before as characteristic of contemporary psychological experience. In work with her and with a number of other *hibakusha* (as in observations on much of present-day existence), I have been struck by the precarious but functional marriage between instability and adaptability, and by its blurring of distinctions between emotional strengths and weaknesses.

I occasionally encountered requests for a kind of direct advice or spiritual guidance I did not feel I could provide. In at least one such situation, toward the end of my second interview with the woman with the eye condition, I felt that my reluctance to make more than general comments led to disappointment tinged with resentment, on the order of guinea pig imagery: the impression that here was another American who made use of *hibakusha* suffering in the name of "research." Behind such a request there was likely to be particularly severe inner conflict (and in this case physical debility as well) on the part of the individual, along with a cultural tradition for spiritual unburdening to any authority to be accompanied by highly directive advice from that authority.

But more frequent was the opposite experience of therapeutic benefits to *hibakusha* where they had not consciously been sought—as in the writer-physician's sudden realization, in the midst of an interview, that our discussion had released him from a literary block (as we shall discuss in Chapter X); and in a somewhat vague but significant feeling expressed to me by a few other *hibakusha* that they had benefited from our talks for reasons they did not understand.

I have suggested that a number of *hibakusha*, especially among academic and medical colleagues, expressed a sense of partnership with me in my work. But this could involve an urge to influence the outcome of the work, as well as sympathy for it and curiosity about it. The Hiroshima A-bomb authority, for instance, advised me to "always keep in mind what the survivors might feel and think, and place this at the center of your work." While he was raising an important question about the very real responsibility any investigator has concerning the impact of his findings upon his research subjects, I felt that he was going further and virtually suggesting that I reach conclusions which are "favorable" to *hibakusha*. His advice was partly stimulated by the *Time* article, which he spoke of in terms of a "bad example" of a calloused American approach. But it was also related to the Japanese (and generally non-Western) cultural stress upon community harmony, as opposed to the Western emphasis upon objective truth.

Similar advice was offered me by the non*hibakusha* social scientist who earlier expressed the idea of "logical discrimination":

> Just demonstrating pity for *hibakusha* over their experience does little good, and is hardly appreciated by them, especially when this pity comes from other Japanese. On the other hand, when it comes from Americans in the form of true sympathy, particularly when the sympathy is accompanied by a strong stand on the issue of preventing war, this profoundly moves the individual *hibakusha* and is both effective and appreciated. I mention this to you because you are an American.

We have already observed, in the phenomenon of symbolic reconciliation, the psychological truth of much of what he says. But the question again arises as to whose "strong stand" on preventing war one adopts, and the advice offered was colored by his own militant involvement in a movement which sought to attract international support but foundered on its own ideological bias.

The kind of advice given by both the social scientist and the Hiroshima A-bomb authority, moreover, tended to become associated with the promulgation of a public image of *hibakusha* as people who, having suffered grievously, were now totally dedicated to an altruistic mission of saving the rest of the world from similar suffering—an image which, at least in its pure form, we have seen to be simply not in accord with the complexities of human behavior. It was in fact precisely this image that the young Hiroshima-born writer attacked with his focus upon such "unmentionable" A-bomb emotions as the wish of some *hibakusha* that the whole world be blown up, because he felt that only by doing so could more truthful dialogue be established.

The physicist sought partnership through intellectual exchange, and made a point of engaging me in discussions about such difficult issues as that of the Dome, the Cenotaph, and more broadly, the relationship of the A-bomb experience to general psychological principles:

I gather it is your intention to see how humans experience such a disaster. . . . But I would like to ask the question of whether or not there is a difference between this disaster and what you have previously studied psychologically . . . whether you find important differences between the Japanese people you have studied in Tokyo, Kyoto, and Hiroshima, and the Americans you have studied before.

But I felt that he was combining genuine intellectual interest with his own concerns about my findings, particularly about whether I recognized the special nature of the A-bomb. Moreover, his questions about reactions in other cities, and about cultural differences, could well have been his way of dealing with resentment related to the combined issue of "historical experiment" and racial victimization. Nonetheless, his stress upon dialogue was his way, as an intellectual, of approaching symbolic reconciliation.

Others sought partnership by soliciting my advice on their own specific programs, as did the moralist concerning the peace movement:

Is it possible for someone like you, who comes to Hiroshima from the outside and lives here for five months, to make any suggestion about how we should proceed?

Or by emphasizing their wish to share with me what they perceived to be a compelling moral purpose, as in the case of the philosopher:

I heard . . . that you were making an academic study for the sake of a higher cause, and I wanted to participate—not for myself, but for this higher cause . . .

Although the sense of partnership was most likely to occur with survivors whose backgrounds included personal and professional concerns similar to my own, the principles involved applied to all. For the individual *hibakusha* sensed that in coming together with an American in common concern, he was at least moving in the general direction of healing the A-bomb-inflicted "wound in the order of being." But although the death-linked resentments which *hibakusha* brought to the encounter could be directly or indirectly aired, modified, or lessened, they could hardly be eliminated—involved as they were with lifelong struggles to absorb and master, by giving inner form to, the entire atomic bomb experience.

FORMULATION:
SELF AND WORLD

The path beyond anger is formulation. By formulation I do not mean detached theories about the atomic bomb, but rather the process by which the *hibakusha* re-creates himself—establishes those inner forms which can serve as a bridge between self and world. Ideology and "world view"—often in their unconscious components—are central to the process, and by studying their relationship to A-bomb mastery, we gain a sense of their significance for mental life in general. Formulation includes efforts to re-establish three essential elements of psychic function: the *sense of connection*, of organic relationship to the people as well as non-human elements in one's life space, whether immediate or distant and imagined; the *sense of symbolic integrity*, of the cohesion and significance of one's life, here including some form of transcendence of the A-bomb experience; and the *sense of movement*, of development and change, in the continuous struggle between fixed identity and individuation.[1] Conflicts we have discussed over issues of trust and peace, as well as struggles with residual anger, are part of the "psychological work" involved. And the internal "A-bomb philosophy" which results—the imagery of formulation—not only enhances mastery but, in an important sense, contains the mental representation of mastery or its absence.

In this larger sense all *hibakusha* live on the basis of *some* formulation of their experience, whether complete or fragmentary, overt or implicit. My experience was that an unusual degree of inarticulateness (I refer not to intellectual level but to the general incapacity to convey feelings or ideas) was likely to be associated with particularly strong residual anxiety, whatever the part played by prior emotional traits or by reservations about the interview situation. For example, the young office worker gave repeated answers of "I don't know at all" or "I don't know what to say" to most questions about her experience, then came to reveal unusually strong fear about physical aftereffects leading to a strong preference for marrying a non*hibakusha*, as well as a fantasy of dying in another nuclear war and thereby being reunited with the A-bomb dead. Both the general fear and the anxious fantasy were elements of her unspoken A-bomb formulation.

On the whole I found that women had less capacity than men for expressing their formulations with coherence or completeness. Further exploration could sometimes reveal, rather than total inarticulateness, an implicit formulation containing a strong feminine commitment to the perpetuation of organic life and a related propensity for "organic knowledge." In contrast, men made greater demands upon themselves for overt formulation, and anxiously struggled with suggestions of inarticulateness. Thus, it was with fear and anger that the white-collar worker told me: "I just can't put these feelings into words"; and with a sense of impairment and lingering guilt that the grocer concluded: "I just don't want this to happen to my child—that's all I can say about it." Both, moreover, were annoyed with themselves because of their verbal limitations. The psychobiological differences between the sexes that play a part here are given particularly strong emphasis in Japanese cultural tradition.*

---

* Japanese culture has placed general emphasis upon aesthetic expression and nuance of feeling at the expense of abstract, interpretive thought. For women the pattern has been intensified by a rather narrow definition of acceptable "feminine" behavior. Even more than in most cultures, a Japanese woman demonstrating incisive theoretical gifts runs the risk of being considered (by herself as well as others) "unfeminine." These attitudes have contributed to longstanding discrimination in educational opportunity, and to stress upon woman as nurturer and seductress, while woman as "knower" has been restricted to personal and informal areas.[2]

1) *Two Modes: Non-Resistance and Special Mission*

The two predominant patterns of formulation may be termed psychological non-resistance and the survivor's sense of mission.

The first of these suggests ultimate mystery. The ways of the A-bomb were unknowable, as implied in a comment by the elderly Nagasaki official: "One of my nieces . . . vomited extensively but is healthy now. A sister of mine also vomited but died a week later." Or else they are ineffable, as the downtrodden woman laborer tells us: "It was beyond words." In both cases, the quality of the experience which ostensibly prevents formulation is itself part of formulation—the sense of one's continuing involvement in a mysterious, and, by implication, more than natural encounter.

Another aspect of the formulation of the same woman laborer was that most characteristic for all *hibakusha*, the sense of resignation, which in her case had sustained her through early injuries and feelings of abandonment as well as through later fears:

> Well, I am not too anxious about things. I do brood sometimes but not to the extent of severe worry because I soon come to a feeling of resignation [*akirame*]. . . . This helps me . . . and seeing that I have been getting along all right so far, I feel that it will be so in the future also. Of course, if I had a serious disease, I might not be able to hold this kind of idea, but because that hasn't happened to me, I continue to think this way. . . .

One submits without resistance to the most extreme blows because one views oneself as caught up in larger forces one can in no way influence. The "psychological non-resistance" involved is in the service of a greater harmony and can, as we noted earlier, represent a good deal more than mere passivity. (We recall the coexistence of the inner principles: "I am helpless before the great forces of destiny, so why try to influence them?" and "No matter what happens, I carry on.") The implicit formulation accompanying psychological non-resistance, in other words, includes a vision of ultimately indestructible human continuity, a vision which enables one to look beyond immediate upheaval while psychologically "rolling with a punch," and to reassert inner imagery of connection, integrity, and movement.

But although made necessary by the scope of the experience, psychological non-resistance may itself be incomplete, as the *burakumin* boy makes clear:

> As for me, I have a feeling of resignation—but no feeling of anger. After all—well, I can't put it very well—but because the whole thing was so huge in scale. . . . Though I cannot say I was exactly happy to have been exposed . . . and in fact I have a rather unpleasant feeling about it.

As we already know, his "unpleasant feeling" includes thoughts of racial victimization in connection with the use of the bomb, and also becomes tied in with rage at his *burakumin* status.

I suggested in an earlier chapter that resignation (or psychological non-resistance) can be associated with denial. But it can also have the opposite function and permit painful reality to penetrate the inner life—as the elderly *hibakusha*-poet suggests in describing his reaction to the death of his wife and children:

> For about a year I could not stop believing that they were still living somewhere—I have never located their bodies or their bones—but gradually I began to feel that not only my family but many other people as well had died, and this feeling began to foster something like a sense of resignation in my mind.

We observe here what Freud called the "work of mourning,"[3] the surrender of the initial denial of loss—and in our terminology the overcoming of the psychic numbing associated with that denial. The poet implies that a sense of resignation was the outcome of this psychic work, but we may also say that resignation was the formulative stance which made the process possible: the loss could not have been absorbed without his embrace of the imagery of larger human continuity contained within his psychological non-resistance.

And as the same man goes on to reveal, such a stance can include strongly active and highly critical feelings:

> People involved in the A-bomb never anticipated their own death. They were killed all of a sudden by something which had nothing to do with them, so in a way we can say that their deaths were more cruel than are deaths in actual warfare. . . .

This kind of anguished philosophical speculation can exist in tenuous equilibrium with acceptance of the irrevocability of what has taken place. And here it is significant to note that the Japanese word for resignation (*akirame*) is derived from a verb (*akiramu*), one of whose early meanings is "to probe or illuminate," and conveys the idea of *active* confrontation of powerful forces, rather than the more or less passive submission now generally associated with the concept of resignation.* The "illumination" of events stressed in the early meaning of the verb is probably still a major function of resignation—illumination in the sense not of gaining purely intellectual knowledge about these events but of giving them *significant inner form*. The poet's interpretive comments were an effort to do this, and their tone of anguish, or even despair, had to do with aspects of the experience he is still unable to "illuminate."

This inability, in his and other cases, had to do with the special features of A-bomb death. Thus, the writer-physician first emphasized his sense of resignation—"I felt that this was our fate, that Japan lost the war and it was just unfortunate that we were hit so hard"—but then made clear just what being "hit so hard" meant:

> The kind of death . . . faced by atomic bomb victims was different from natural death—something unprecedented in history—a total annihilation of human beings. . . .

The words and the tone resemble those of the *habakusha*-poet. For both men still felt the effects of having been overwhelmed by the suddenness, brutality, and grotesqueness of A-bomb death. This unmastered, and to some extent unmasterable, death encounter prevents *hibakusha* from grasping or "knowing" what they have been through. It prevents them from making the experience part of their ongoing self-process.

Still another form of resignation relied extremely heavily upon psychic numbing, as here described by a Hiroshima observer we have previously quoted:

> Basically, it is losing hope, but there is something different in it from defeatism. There is a long tradition [in Japan] that a human being cannot do everything, that there is some leeway for the intangible.

---

* There are actually two different written forms of the verb *akiramu*. The earliest one 明 suggests the idea of clarification, while a later version 諦 includes both the sense of active probing and more passive "resignation."[4]

. . . There is the Japanese saying, "Good and bad fortune are like intertwined coils of rope." . . . It is being utterly in a nil position.

The implicit message of this form of "nihilistic resignation" is: "The experience is unknowable and makes no sense; I can best deal with its formlessness by remaining insensible to it; then I, and life in general, can carry on." In this process imagery of connection, integrity, and movement are suspended—either as a protective device in the service of their later recovery, or in a more or less permanent way that borders on despair.

RELIGIOUS FORMULATION

Virtually every form of resignation and psychological non-resistance has been cultivated by Japanese Buddhism. Buddhism did not, of course, create this universal psychic pattern. But it has so embraced it that even when the idea of resignation was expressed in secular terms, the words used were likely to have had long Buddhist associations. And some *hibakusha* directly equated their resignation with their Buddhist belief —as did the elderly widow:

> About what has happened, well, it can't be helped [*shikataganai*], and it is best not to think about it too much. . . . My faith [*shinkō*] is the basis of my life. . . . And even when I find very wrong things in the world, I try to think of Buddha's teaching—"Do this. Don't do that." . . . I am the kind of person who has never thought very deeply. But well, when I experienced such a dreadful event . . . and saw actual hell in this world . . . since then I have felt that I should be more dedicated in my religious worship. . . .

We have the distinct impression that she is talking about a program she seeks to follow, rather than fully achieved psychic states, both regarding her religious convictions ("I *try* to think of Buddha's teaching"; "I *should* be more dedicated") and her resignation itself (". . . it is *best* not to think about it too much").

Religious imagery tended to relate itself to the issue of survival itself, as in the case of the psychologist's vague but strongly felt conviction that "something more" than rational effort was involved:

> When I really think about it, I believe that my actually getting out [from the debris in which he had been trapped] was a matter of destiny. Whatever my own careful efforts, I feel that there is a limit

to what human beings themselves can do, and in regard to this moment I have the deepest respect for religion. . . .

The sense of awe at the "miraculousness" of survival is, as we have observed, associated with persistent death anxiety and death guilt.

What must also be kept in mind is the Japanese cultural tendency to require of its religions and philosophies relatively little in the way of clear-cut dogma, and to emphasize instead a general emotional atmosphere. Thus, *hibakusha* often expressed nonspecific "religious feeling," usually tied in with their association with the Jōdo Shin (or True Pure Land)* Sect of Buddhism, which dominates the Hiroshima area, rather than a structured religious formulation. But we have seen that even vaguely expressed sentiments can have implicit imagery of considerable interpretive significance, and the failure of *hibakusha* to achieve psychologically adequate formulations had less to do with this cultural emphasis than with qualities of the A-bomb psychic constellation that no thought system could totally absorb. Buddhist influence could help a *hibakusha* to attenuate, rather than resolve, residual emotional struggles; to approach, rather than fully achieve, formulation and mastery.

Religious imagery could also fluctuate, even for the individual survivor, as is evident from the reactions of the elderly countrywoman. A member of the Konkō Sect (one of Japan's older "new religions" which combines traditional Shintoism with elements of Buddhism and Christianity), she was one of the few people I encountered who described the kind of sudden loss of faith at the time of the bomb which one might expect to occur more frequently in the West (and which, it is said, occurred in considerable numbers among Japanese Catholics in Nagasaki):

At that moment we all became completely separate human beings. Seeing those wretched figures of people, I felt great pity. And having experienced such a terrible state of living hell, I thought, "There is no God, no Buddha. . . . There is no God, no help."

She was reacting to a sudden sense of total abandonment, and rejecting a deity who could protect her neither from anticipated annihilation nor

---

* The Pure Land, "Amida's [Buddha's] Western Paradise," is a vision of heaven in which "all enjoy wonderful powers of body and mind," sometimes an eternal dwelling-place, though originally a place of "peaceful and blissful sojourn on the way toward the attainment of nirvāna or even Buddhahood." In Pure Land Buddhism there is also a purgatory, images of which we have already heard expressed.[5]

from profound death guilt. But when her fortunes improved, and various family members who had been either missing or injured began to reappear and recover, she found that "my feelings began to change" —so much so that she reversed herself completely:

> Even though, in the middle of the painful experience . . . with no house and everything burned down, I couldn't believe in the existence of God or Buddha . . . as time passed and the world became peaceful . . . I began to feel that we owe everything to God. . . .

She then applied her recovered religious belief retroactively to her original escape from death, and did so with considerable specificity:

> I cannot attribute the fact that I was not killed to my own power. . . . I believe that God ordered me to put on a pair of sandals [zōri] which just happened to be there. With all of the glass scattered about, it was impossible for anyone to walk with bare feet—I would not have been able to have walked at all if it hadn't been for the sandals. . . . And I attribute all of this to Konkō-sama [the Deity of her religious sect]. . . .

In other words, once she could re-establish connection and meaning within her religious imagery, she was eager to restore to her deity full power over life and death. But we have previously observed the intensity of her retained death guilt (over the dying child she did not help and her brother who "preceded me in death"), and this guilt tends to undermine her religious formulation. Thus, in speaking of her dead brother, she suddenly dispensed with her Konkō theological idiom and referred to "Nature" as the ultimate arbiter of individual destiny—a momentary reversion to the ancient natural theology which still has considerable power over the Japanese mind. And her self-deprecatory conclusion was: "I belong to the Konkō Sect, but my faith is not very deep."*

Similarly tenuous were those Buddhist formulations taken directly from conventional dogma, as we have already observed in the case of the Buddhist priest's interpretation of the entire A-bomb experience as *mayoi* or man's "lost state." On a more simple plane the boarding-house maid described her determination to be true to a promise she had made to her dead husband when he left for the battlefield that should he die,

---

* Her stress upon belief and unbelief is probably related to a similar emphasis within Konkō itself, to its exhortations to "believe in God."[6]

she would see to it that proper religious rituals were performed in his name. She therefore took to chanting *"Namuamidabutsu,"* an incantation of the Buddha for the purpose of being reborn—or enabling someone else to be reborn—into the "Pure Land" of Buddhist heaven. And she sought to grasp the significance of her extraordinary series of losses (deaths of her husband and four brothers in the war, and then of her two small children in post-A-bomb floods and landslides) within a classical Buddhist idiom of cyclic retribution and harmony:

> At first I wondered why I had all of these misfortunes, and I felt resentful about things in this life. But having been given a life as a human being, I concluded that I must have sown bad seeds in a previous life . . . and was now being punished for them. . . . This gave me peace of mind. . . .

There is no denying that she derived solace from this formulation, which provided her with a certain emotional distance from her own guilt (the "bad seeds" of a prior existence) and, more important, with significant form for that guilt within a structured cosmic order. Yet in this bitter woman ("People were not cooperative . . . they were cold . . . people enjoy others' suffering") one could observe very little of the "peace of mind" she mentioned.

Even where the immersion into Buddhism was more thoughtful, consistent, and complex, as in the case of the writer-manufacturer, the formulation derived could accomplish just so much. Few called upon their religion so quickly, and in such direct relationship to death guilt:

> In the midst of the disaster I tried to read Buddhist scriptures continuously for about one week, hoping that my effort could contribute something to the happiness of the dead. . . . It was not exactly a sense of responsibility or anything as clear as that. It was a vague feeling—I felt sorry for the dead because they died and I survived. I wanted to pacify the spirits of the dead. . . . In Buddhism we say that the souls wander about in anxiety, and if we read the scriptures to them, they lose their anxiety and start to become easy and settle down. So I felt that if I read the scriptures, I could give some comfort to the souls of those who had departed. . . .

His continuing involvement in this Buddhist imagery did contribute greatly to his, on the whole, impressive mastery of the A-bomb experience. But it could not rid him of his sense of unresolvable guilt and loss over the death of his daughter. Nor could it reconstruct his shattered symbolic universe—as revealed by his condemnation of President Truman as a "cold-blooded animal"—though he maintained a similar Buddhist formulation in his prediction of eventual retribution for Truman. The continuing strain of his formulative struggles was further revealed in a seemingly irrelevant discourse on Christianity, in which he stressed the alien nature of that religion to the Japanese, and concluded that

> Both before and after the A-bomb very few common people of Japan appealed to Christianity for salvation or consolation. Many tried to pray to Buddha, but not to Christ. . . .

Partly at issue here was his classification of American-sponsored Christianity as counterfeit nurturance (and we recall his sensitivity to this general problem in his stress that Hiroshima did not need American "sympathy" or material help). But more fundamental, I thought, was his inner fear that Buddhism, or at least *his* Buddhism, was faltering; that Christianity might in some way loom as a more attractive or more powerful force (it had made considerable gains in Hiroshima, and throughout Japan, during the postwar period); and, most of all, that the Buddhist formulation upon which he had staked so much might lack truth or relevance.

VARIETIES OF "RESIGNATION"

Christianity too encourages psychological non-resistance, and the pattern, moreover, can be observed in a Western *hibakusha*. The European priest evolved a formulation that could well be described as a "Westerner's *akirame*," which he attributed both to his prior "temperament" ("I am not the kind who becomes depressed or worried") and to his "Japaneseness":

> I easily accustom myself to a new place, and I like the Japanese way of expressing themselves. . . . When [the bomb fell] I thought, "Well, this is war." . . . I was already Japanese. . . .

Actually his psychological non-resistance was related to a malleability of identity in which adaptive skills and denial were both prominent—as was a sense of connection with a force larger than individual human life expressed in a conventional Catholic formulation:

As a good Jesuit, I am bound to find God in all things. . . . I am not a good theologian, but I look at it as God's providence. . . .

Yet here too both his words ("I am *bound* to find God in all things") and the despair we have observed in him suggest that the religious formulation is an ideal vision which he holds out to himself—one which is constantly eroded by A-bomb-linked death fears:

If a man doesn't believe in another life, then there is only death, and death is the most terrifying thing that can happen—all is finished. . . . But if there is another life, death is not the worst thing. . . . I know that many people will not agree with me . . . but really convinced Catholics . . . in the depths of their souls are not uneasy. Of course, there is physical fear—if there is a large cancer operation, they are not glad about it—but if you believe in another life, you are not uneasy, not frightened. . . . The uneasiness does not go to the depth of the soul—if anything, it is personal fear—but the depths of the soul are quiet. . . . From our standpoint there is no difference if you leave this world at forty or eighty—that is, no difference in principle; of course, there is some difference.

We note his exaggerated need to deny his fears, along with confusion over how much uneasiness to admit—how much "difference" it makes at what age one dies. He went on to relate his way of thinking to the Japanese forms of resignation, but also insisted that it contained something more:

This kind of thinking is positive, not only *akirame* or *shikataganai*, but positive: If God wills it, I am ready.

He reveals here a Western theological (and psychological) stress upon "active submission" to the deity which moves to the outer border of psychological nonviolence as the principle of "will" (of both supplicant and deity) replaces that of effortless harmony. His own problem was not so much that of submission per se as an inability to achieve through submission a formulation sufficiently powerful to still death anxiety. He first tried to deny what he called "special feeling" about atomic bomb exposure by placing *hibakusha* in the category of people with "ordinary" illnesses:

If you have a family with TB or leprosy—then it is the same as that of a victim [of the A-bomb]. . . . If one has TB . . . one also thinks,

"How will it be next year?" . . . I feel we must not be hypocrites
because we are victims of the bomb. . . .

But even this equation with impairment turned out to be inadequate
for grasping the *manmade* origins of A-bomb suffering:

They [other patients in the hospital] said, "Father, the difference
is—with leprosy and TB—these are natural illnesses—but the A-
bomb, it is artificial, caused by man, and done with the intention of
damaging man." I thought there was something in this. It was man
who initiated it. This is difficult to express, but there is something in
it—a difference in the kind of *kimochi* [here he used the Japanese
word for feeling, or quality of feeling] you have—you have it, but it is
hard to explain.

This perception of the experience as initiated by other human beings
has bearing on the theme of the "historical experiment" (and its related
guinea pig imagery) as well as that of a loss of faith in human existence
in general. Not only did these disturbing feelings resist his Catholic
explanations, but at one point he jettisoned the Catholic idiom entirely
(much as the elderly countrywoman had her Konkō terminology) and
insisted upon using a Japanese word to characterize the A-bomb—
atsukamashii, meaning shameless, audacious, brazen, and suggesting a
form of hubris more vague but also more inclusive than that conveyed
by most theological judgment. For although Catholic theology could
supply him with a rather complete system of thought for interpreting A-
bomb emotions, it could not provide him with a sense of trust or faith
superior in strength to the symbolic blows he had received.

:

There were additional sources of religious formulation available from
Japan's polyglot postwar spiritual offerings. The woman with the ophthalmic condition, for instance, told of her conversion to Sōka Gakkai, a
militant contemporary version of Nichiren Buddhism, at a time when
she was deeply troubled by her bodily and marital difficulties and was
feeling "very much alone." One would not ordinarily associate the term
psychological non-resistance with the aggressively proselytizing representatives of the sect who called upon her and applied their well-known
"*shakubuku*."* Yet the religion did offer her its own form of resignation,

* The term literally means "to break and subdue," and refers ostensibly to evil
spirits,[7] but in practice *shakubuku* becomes a severe emotional assault upon the
personal impurities of the prospective convert and upon the hypocrisies of all rival
religions, including other forms of Buddhism.

a combination of rules to live by, channels for expression of guilt, and renewed connection—achieved mostly through a process which can be viewed as a theological version of group therapy:

> I don't do anything very formal . . . but I do say prayers and chant a sutra in the morning and the evening. . . . [And at meetings] we can say exactly what we feel—talk about dissatisfaction, suffering, and pain—tell everything to what we call the "principle image" [*go-honzon*]. . . . I can see images of many different people and ask them about ways to improve myself . . . try to become like them. . . . In my present life I had many complaints and I think my mind is very ugly. I feel impeded† by this ugliness within me, and I try to reflect upon myself. . . .

It turned out that her father, whose death in the bomb had caused her such extreme guilt, regularly appeared among her spiritual "images":

> Well, as he does not exist in the world now, his image is in ideal form. I am very glad to see my father in this way . . . and I strongly feel him to possess this ideal form. . . .

This "reunion" with her father both relieved guilt and helped maintain a nurturing sense of continuity with him. It thus became a partial formulation of both A-bomb issues and immediate life problems. We have had ample evidence of the limitations of this formulation in her guilty struggles between sexual "*decadence*" and a "constructive life," her occasional wish that "all of the earth . . . be annihilated," and the general contribution of her conflict and despair to her eye condition. Yet it may well be the ordering principle which keeps her from even more serious emotional or physical disintegration.

The resemblance between her experiences and those of the divorced housewife (both lost their fathers in the bomb, had considerable conflict with their mothers, and then had failures in marriage) extended even into this area of religious formulation. In the case of the divorced housewife contact with a local religious sect (primarily Shinto) was initiated by her mother, partly as a means of relieving family tensions ("She had no place to go, and thought that if prayer could bring peace to our family life, that would be a good thing"); and she herself took it up after her divorce because her mother "thought it would be good for

---

† She used the word *sumanai,* which is a rough Japanese equivalent of a sense of guilt.

me." Her religious experience, as compared to that of the woman with the eye condition, placed greater emphasis upon a mentor with supernatural powers:

> We worship the usual gods—the *Ujigami* and the Miyajima gods*— various Japanese Gods—all kinds of gods. . . . There is a teacher and we talk to him about many things . . . and I think that something like a divine spirit—coming from God—enters this teacher's mind. There are about two hundred believers, and we have the feeling that whatever the teacher suggests is always right . . . that he does not make mistakes . . . so we consult him about everything . . . since things I cannot understand—which we cannot see with our eyes . . . seem to emanate from this teacher. . . . I go there first thing in the morning when I finish breakfast if I don't have any very important business. And if I don't go—such as on Sundays when it is closed— then I have a gloomy feeling that whole day. So I feel that I am strengthened in many ways by being able to depend upon the gods. . . .

But she too had the experience of her father's entry into her religious worship—not in the regularized manner described by the other woman, but in much more dramatic fashion, following a series of personal austerities connected with purification:

> At that time, just at the end of the ceremony while we were praying, my father appeared among the gods. . . . It was the teacher who told me that my father's vision had appeared. And he said that this kind of occurrence was very rare and meant that my father had achieved a very elevated state and that he was very concerned about me . . . and also that the fact that he had appeared among the gods meant that he was very strongly protecting me. Since then . . . I have had the very strong feeling that my father is always present as my ally [*mikata*].

Here the father is idealized to the point of appearing "among the gods," in an idiosyncratic version of traditional Japanese ancestor worship. While it can be said that her feelings toward her father and toward the religious mentor are similar, the first symbolized direct personal protec-

---

* *Ujigami* is a general term for the "guardian gods" or "ancestor gods" of any particular area which are made up of the collective souls of generations of former inhabitants and are locally enshrined. Miyajima, the small island just off Hiroshima, has long-standing sacred associations as a "home of the gods" and is the site of a large Shinto shrine.

tion and relief of guilt, the second an emissary from a larger world of meaning. Compared to the woman with the eye condition, she gave an impression of having integrated her formulation more successfully into her general emotional life—even if she could not avoid retaining a sense of "the bitter feelings in everyone's heart."

SACRIFICE AND MISSION

Christian formulations of ordinary survivors did not achieve any greater psychological success than those of Buddhism or other religions. There was one, however, of a Korean woman *hibakusha* which I found quite remarkable. About fifty years old and looking older, her face, neck, shoulders, and hands covered with keloid scars and residual swellings, she had lost five of her six children in the bomb. She lived on a borderline economic level in an outcast community (as Koreans often do in Japan). Yet she told her story without self-pity, and in fact with considerable vitality and even humor. Having been befriended by an elderly American woman missionary who had lived in Korea in the past, she had become a Fundamentalist Christian. She thereby found a way to give retrospective form to what was undoubtedly a staggering burden of death guilt and loss—both in a general sense ("Everybody died, and when I was sleeping among worms, everybody gave up on me—but I survived—I think God saved me") and in specific relationship to her children:

> I said that I could not go into the presence of God because of my guilt—that I had killed my children. . . . I had not given them enough to eat during the food shortage. . . . But she told me that God had sent his only child for the sake of all guilty people in the world, and that everyone's sins would be redeemed by Jesus Christ . . . and that He would pray for me too. . . . So I went there . . . and although the world was cold to me, still God loved the world. . . . People were pleased to welcome me with warm hearts and love me. . . .

Her formulation, moreover, could encompass (as that of the Western priest could not) the human origins of the atomic bomb—because everything ultimately derives from "God's power":

> Hiroshima was reduced to ashes by the power of human beings, by the A-bomb which was dropped. But still I came to believe in God's power—to believe that the world was made by God . . . and I had a

strange feeling of becoming stronger. . . . Even though people say that we should do this or that, if it is not done by God's power, peace will never come. . . . Even though we build big buildings, when the A-bomb is dropped, everything will be in ashes. . . . Well, in the Bible—in the Old Testament—when I read that, I thought that everything in the world is exactly that way—so everyone has to have faith.

The A-bomb is not only manmade, but represents, as do nuclear weapons in general, punishment for man's guilt. We suspect that in her literal Biblical imagery she views Hiroshima's experience as analogous to Sodom and Gomorrah; and she surely envisions all nuclear destruction, including that of Hiroshima, as apocalyptic expressions of God's will. Indeed, the capacity of her formulation to absorb her extraordinary losses teaches one something about the power Christianity has possessed (but rarely possesses today) in helping man to confront his most extreme kinds of fear and guilt:

When I was about to leave the hospital, my son [her last living child] suddenly became ill. All of the fingernails on his hands were a strange color—there were spots—and he would faint, so I thought he had trouble with his brain. I took him to the hospital, but they couldn't tell the cause of his illness, and there was no medicine to use. . . . His hair came out, and he would fall down from the bed, and he couldn't urinate. . . . At first I prayed to God for help . . . and then thinking about Abraham and his son Isaac . . . I thought that if God wanted this last child—having already lost five children—I would give him this one too. I can't describe how I felt then, but I prayed . . . and that night he suddenly got better. I felt very strange, but I thought it was God who helped us. . . . I used to be greedy— but now I realize that the short period of life we have—of about fifty or sixty years—is just like the morning mist—and that it is eternal life we should seek. . . . I would say that I was reborn.

More than merely an ideal vision of how she *should* feel, her formulation, to a degree unusual among *hibakusha* I interviewed, had taken full command of her psychic life, enabled her to absorb extreme adversity, and propelled her toward mastery. Yet even in her case basic A-bomb conflicts remained. Two final comments she made, one after the other— "If I don't forgive others' guilt, then nobody will forgive my guilt" and "When I think about my children, there is no end to my feeling"—

suggested the persistence of the most ineradicable of A-bomb legacies, that of death guilt.

Her attitude reminds us of the Protestant minister's similar sense of "sacrificing" his daughter to God when performing the ritual of the Lord's Supper just prior to her death. We recall also his sense of being himself ordered by God to die, and his feeling that "this is the time to die, and I should have died." His eventual formulation of the awesome fact of his survival, like that of the Buddhist priest mentioned earlier, took the shape of a powerfully experienced sense of mission:

> It means there is something that in living I have to do—these words outlast words of death.

He therefore threw himself, with great energy, into various peace and welfare activities, and saw as "the task of my life" that of a Christian-oriented study of those human problems that lead to war. The extent of his agitation during our interview suggested that his formulation fell short of providing a sense of spiritual harmony; but it did express, via Christian dedication, the general theme of "special mission" as the price of survival.

Indeed, the survivor's sense of himself as a "missionary on behalf of the dead" can make contact with the Christian tradition of spreading the gospel—as was true of a young hospital patient in Nagasaki who, following recurrent illnesses believed related to the atomic bomb, underwent a conversion experience:

> I want to help others and to be a servant of God. I want to do what I can to stop atomic bomb tests and even the existence of these weapons. . . . People have to walk together hand in hand, and this can be accomplished through religion. . . . I would like to do missionary work, as I have had great spiritual anxiety and then found God. I needed something I could trust, and I want to help others to find Him too.

But the apprehensive and slightly depressed tone in which he told me these things suggested that residual guilt and fear accompanied his sense of mission.

The elderly Catholic nun poignantly conveyed a sense of the limitations of Christian principles of "sacrifice" and "mission." As head of a girl's parochial school in Nagasaki in which the majority of students were killed, she explained these deaths—to the girls' parents and to herself—as gently as she could, with the help of conventional Catholic doctrine:

> I was in bed [with injuries] and mothers kept coming to me, looking for their daughters. I told them that their daughters made a peaceful exit from the world—that it was a good ending. . . . [I myself believe] those girls were a sacrifice. They were sacrificed for human sins; for the sake of others they had to die. They took others' places. It was a time of Redemption—and their deaths were for the sake of other Catholics and of all of the Japanese people. . . .

Yet she could not help immediately adding:

> But it should be the last sacrifice of that kind—this is enough—this should be enough.

"Enough," of course, meant "too much." Her dutifully expressed formulation simply could not absorb her still powerful feelings of guilt and loss, could not enable her to accept the deaths of those young girls.

Certain public formulations, particularly when offered in unthinking ritualistic fashion, could cause resentment. The day laborer tells of the reaction of a woman whose child was killed by the bomb to a minister's statement made at a Christian prayer meeting to the effect that "Those who had committed sins in this world have been called by God." The mother responded heatedly:

> No! No! In a militaristic society which disliked Bibles and hymns my little daughter read her Bible and sang hymns. How can you speak of sins committed by my daughter?

To which the day laborer's own comment was: "Such abstract sermons disgrace God's name and hurt all souls"—by which he meant that rote formulations of this kind are insulting because they treat the A-bomb experience as "routine" rather than extraordinary, and because they impugn the purity of the dead.

:

In summing up the *hibakusha*'s use of religious formulation, we may say that while it sometimes contributed to mastery, most found it lacking in various ways. This was so partly because of the limited influence of contemporary Japanese religious thought in general, but largely because of the enormity of symbolic breakdown involved and the persistence of peculiarly unabsorbable death anxiety and death guilt. Religion made its greatest contribution to *hibakusha* formulations in giving shape to the two universal survivor needs, those of psychological non-resistance and special mission. While these two tendencies may appear to be contradictory, they are related expressions of human adaptation to the most extreme kind of experience. The first gives silent form to an ultimate reassertion of human continuity while permitting a protective blunting of emotions. The second gives form to death guilt, and enables the survivor to make use of this guilt and at the same time go beyond it. Without psychological non-resistance, the survivor would be unable to absorb his losses. Without a sense of special mission, he would be unable to justify his continuing life.

:

An occasional *hibakusha* formulated the disaster through what might be called imagery of historical intervention—that is, through a version of Marxist ideology in which all large events are seen as caused by an inexorable History, and by the class structure it creates. The *burakumin* woman leader, in discussing matters of A-bomb responsibility, disagreed with those who singled out the pilot of the plane, and blamed instead the "privileged classes" of all countries and their concentrations of capitalist power:

> I know that within a large system the individual becomes very weak, and in Japan's case everything was done in the name of the Emperor. So my anger is directed not toward the individual person but toward the existence of this enormous power that makes all individual struggles futile. . . . And against . . . Japanese capitalists—probably not only capitalists but against all privileged classes [throughout the world] whose war it was. . . .

The Hiroshima A-bomb authority took a similar perspective toward *hibakusha* problems:

> We must think about feudalistic practices and contradictions in present-day Japanese society . . . which combine to oppress survivors.

For both the *burakumin* woman leader and the Hiroshima A-bomb authority these views were part of a comprehensive set of images which could be applied to virtually every aspect of individual and group life, including holocaust. In terms of the formulative modes we have been discussing, this kind of Marxist ideology tends to de-emphasize and denounce psychological non-resistance, and to stress strongly the sense of mission. And the "mission," as defined, could provide a vivid sense of connection with all "mankind," along with an elaborate structure of meaning and a lively sense of movement. But very few *hibakusha* could find in it the philosophical and experiential relevance—particularly the emotional immediacy—which effective formulation required.

At the other end of the ideological spectrum were efforts, like those of the technician, to call forth very old Japanese moral principles to combat A-bomb effects and achieve personal rebirth:

> I improved bit by bit so that even a doctor told me that my condition today is due to my practicing *budō* [samurai code]. I myself believe this. . . . In *kyūdō* [a form of archery associated with *budō*] one must concentrate one's strength in order to forget about oneself—this is the main idea. Then one is not easily beaten by anything. "Enduring and not permitting defeat"—this was the idea I was taught. I think this was a big advantage for me. . . . I realized that I should not depend upon others, however physically weak I might be—and that I myself had to do things. . . .

But he admitted that his approach did not come easily ("At times I forced myself to go along with this [*budō*] conviction"). And knowing of his unusually strong conflicts over dependency and counterfeit nurturance, we may say that his formulation had something of the quality of whistling in the dark. It did provide meaning, but its restorationist embrace of past symbols, themselves partly dishonored in a postwar society, was hardly a match for A-bomb conflicts.

2) *Negativity, Nothingness, and Beyond*

Where neither psychological non-resistance nor a sense of mission were present, whatever formulation existed was likely to be negative and dominated by imagery of breakdown. The female poet, for instance, expresses such imagery in a way that combines her own feelings with those of a young cousin who had experienced extreme loss, deprivation, and a sense of abandonment:

> Her mother and father and all of her close relatives were killed by the A-bomb. She became very upset . . . and having lost everything, had to go from the house of one relative to another. . . . During her days of wandering . . . she said that she wished others would be made to go through such an experience so they would understand what she had gone through. . . . She had a "crooked heart" at that time, so her relatives didn't like her very much. . . . When she expressed such feelings . . . her relatives repeated them to others because they were scared and thought she was an awful girl. . . .

Here we encounter that ultimate "negative formulation" that has become a kind of underground theme in Hiroshima—expressed openly by a child and by adults in whispers—a formulation which says, in effect: "I can accept having been singled out for this special degree of suffering only if everybody else is put through it; I can accept the A-bomb only if the world is engulfed in nuclear disaster."

With most *hibakusha* negative imagery is of a less total quality, and formulations are used in ways which make it difficult to tell where adaptability ends and negativistic cynicism begins. Even in the case described above it was said that the girl, after marrying and getting a job, expressed her underground theme much less frequently, though she did not give it up entirely. Such imagery of bitterness has its function—either in the cathartic sense that the Chinese call "vomiting bitter water," or in supplying a more psychologically disabling compromise in which one carries on while acknowledging the permanent breakdown of the symbolic world one inhabits.

The elderly housewife, for instance, never recovered from her son's death in a military plane crash, and never forgave either the Japanese authorities for their negligence or the larger forces of destiny for their cruelty. When describing to me the general selfishness and callousness she and her husband observed during the post-bomb period, she declared that "We could depend upon nothing but our bank account." My impression was that for them life as an affirmative experience had ended with the death of their son. Their family line, or biological mode of immortality, had been destroyed, and in an immediate sense there was no one to care for them in their old age. Indeed, when I met them, they were considering two solutions to their problem: "adopting" a son-in-law into the family to take the place of the dead son (and carry out the symbolic and practical functions); or else selling their house to get enough money to enter a comfortable old-age home—a course which, especially in Japan, carries an aura of abandonment.

In her efforts to comprehend her loss she thought back on the events that led eventually to her son's death. Her account conveys both a vivid picture of the family dramas which could take place in the midst of the Japanese totalism of the thirties and forties, along with her personal sense of having been victimized by male stubbornness and stupidity:

From the beginning I thought the Japanese people wrong to make war with America because Japan is a poor country and I always wondered why we started a war with such a big nation. . . . And when our son began to wish to go to military school, I strongly opposed this. But he was a worshipper of [General] Nogi.* His character was a little strange and he always expressed his wish to be like Nogi. . . . I told him, "If you enter the military, since you are our only son—we had a girl but he was the only boy—I will kill myself." But he said, "Even if Mother commits suicide, I still wish to be a soldier." I told him that since his determination was that strong, he could become a soldier—but from the beginning I hated very much to see him become one. And even when our country was involved in the war, I used to say that we would be defeated and that I couldn't see why people continued with the war. . . . But at that time people like me who said such things were looked upon as traitors . . . so I couldn't express my ideas and had to go along with the current. Even at home, when I mentioned my beliefs, my husband would tell me not to say such a thing. He said we wouldn't be beaten because Japan is a divine country, but I said that this isn't the kind of thing that being a divine country can guarantee.

* The military hero who committed ceremonial suicide in 1912 at the time of the death of the Emperor Meiji, and has come to symbolize pure dedication to Japan's tradition of self-sacrifice, particularly in martial form.

A little later in the same interview, as if to confirm her opinions on male obtuseness, her husband chimed in to suggest a strange regret in relationship to the A-bomb:

> As our son was in the Air Force, we had a special Japanese sword made for him, and we now greatly regret that it was lost in the fire. I don't know why it was burned—there was another sword that belonged to a family we knew [which was not destroyed] but we couldn't find our sword anywhere, and when we fled, we had to leave it behind.

In the wake of unprecedented devastation and death, this intense concern over a lost military weapon is somewhat jarring. But it once more attests to the fundamentally symbolic quality of human emotional response. For such swords were more than mere military weapons; they have had a mystical significance in Japanese tradition as physical embodiments of immortal power—and whether because of this or simply as military weapons, the Occupation required that they be turned over to American authorities. Since in this case the sword was also a physical extension of the dead son, its loss symbolized the loss of the boy, and the father's special concern over it was related to guilt over having failed to "protect" either the sword or his son. His "regret," then, had to do with symbolic impairments he experienced in relationship to Japan's defeat and to his son's death.*

The wife, therefore, was probably speaking for both herself and her husband in uttering a final statement of despair:

> If it [a nuclear war] should ever happen again . . . I would die at once—at that very moment. This is all that a person like me can feel. Being already an old woman, if it should be used again, whatever may happen, I would rather die.

What she meant, I thought, was not only that at her age she lacked the strength to deal with future holocausts, but that the psychic blows sustained from the combination of her son's death and the atomic bomb experience had so shattered her life space that only a part of her—and that tenuously—had remained alive.

---

* Considering the centrality of money, psychologically and otherwise, in the lives of this couple (and of everyone else), the husband's concern about the sword might also have been connected with the great economic value such weapons had for those who chose to violate the Occupation decree and either retain or sell them.

EXPANSION OF IMAGERY

Occasionally, with considerable difficulty, *hibakusha* did seem to arrive at formulations which contributed impressively to personal mastery through *expansion of imagery*. Sometimes in such imagery psychological non-resistance would appear to prevail, at other times the sense of survivor mission; but usually the two were in a workable equilibrium.

Thus, the sociologist first placed great emphasis upon resignation:

> Something beyond the personal effort we make—maybe not the influence of God, maybe a kind of personal destiny—controls individual existence. I don't mean to say there is no room for effort. . . . But I believe that even individual destiny is controlled by a larger destiny. . . . The fate of the world may depend upon whether or not Khrushchev presses the button. . . .

But his sense of survivor mission was evident not only in comments quoted earlier about the impact of keloids upon evolving peace attitudes, but also in his qualification of his resignation:

> Since public opinion can have a significant influence . . . in the long run, we cannot really say exactly to what degree fate is determined for us . . . and within limits I try to make an effort . . . through my research [on various contemporary Japanese social issues] . . . to make a contribution toward a better public opinion which could have an effect on the direction of the world. . . .

One could sense an inner dialogue between classical Buddhist acceptance of the world and modern man's determination to influence his own destiny. There seemed little doubt that in a psychological sense the older tendency toward acceptance and harmony was by far the stronger. But it was the interplay of the two that gave qualities of relevance and active tension to his efforts at mastery.

The expansion of imagery achieved by the moralist, conversely, placed heavy stress upon survivor mission, which in his case included "the idea of repenting for my mistakes" in having been so actively associated with the military regime. But as we noted before, his stress upon applying old principles of "family, nation, and race" to the wider arena of "the whole of mankind"—and even his method of protest through sitting—suggested elements of traditional psychological non-resistance. The result was a genuinely inclusive formulation, as stated in in his writings:

Never until now has the concept of man in the highest context of genus, namely the world of human totality, been an actuality. . . . We have . . . come to the knowledge that we, as [a] unity, live and die in a common fate. The world, we now realize, is the ship we sail in together. . . .

The virtual impossibility of achieving this idea contributed to the confusion and despair we also noted in him previously, as did the uneasiness of his inner equilibrium between survivor mission and psychological non-resistance. But there is no denying the significance for him (and for many Japanese intellectuals) of both the accomplishments and pitfalls of his formulative shift from rightist mysticism to leftist humanism.

A related kind of expanded imagery, also associated with A-bomb involvement, was expressed to me by Hiroyuki Agawa, a prominent Japanese (non*hibakusha*) writer originally from Hiroshima:

I have been traveling widely, and I feel strongly that there should be no separate nations—no demarcation of borders between countries. I felt, while traveling in Europe, that in many places these barriers became very low—very small—and this is one way to peace. . . .

Nowadays people begin to talk again of patriotism. Let patriotism be tied up with love for a particular place. Those who come from Texas can love Texas. Those in Hiroshima can love the Inland Sea. If one loves Texas, one can also love California—there is no war between Texas and California—or between Hiroshima and Shiga Prefecture. This is what I mean when I say that patriotism should be love for one's native place. . . .

I don't know too much about world history but I think the fact that there have been fewer wars recently in the world may be due to the development of both weapons and communications. . . . Maybe to the fact that we have these A- and H-bombs, and that we can get from Tokyo to New York so easily—maybe I emphasize these things because of the A-bomb experience. . . .

It isn't just my opinion—but also of men like Russell and Schweitzer—that the solution to the A- and H-bomb problem must come before any other question—and this opinion is widely shared. . . .

He also repeated to me a "joke" he had read in a popular Japanese magazine:

QUESTION: What would you buy to have ready in case of another war?
ANSWER: Poison.

His conclusion and his death anxiety resemble those of many *hibakusha* (the elderly housewife, for instance), but he is freer than they in bringing humor and speculation to his formulative efforts. His entire statement, in fact, suggests the influence of the atomic bomb upon Japanese intellectuals in their search for inclusive—even protean—formulations. The problems involved are also protean, but again this does not lessen the significance of the vision.

''I GO THE WAY OF NOTHINGNESS''

Another theme, often profound if with mixed effect, was an East Asian stress upon "nothingness." Related to the A-bomb "nihilism" we spoke of before, this kind of formulation could envision the atomic bomb as a "clearing away" of past impediments, so that the symbolic tabula rasa created became a prelude to psychological and moral rebirth.

Miss Ōta suggests this cycle in her phrase, "the destruction returned everything to nothingness," after which she went on (as quoted before) to call for "a revolution against mankind's tragic tendency to be unable to make any progress without being destroyed," and expressed the hope that "this defeat can be the thing that makes Japan truly peaceful" as "the meaning of my writing this book in the midst of pain."[8]

The history professor used the theme of nothingness for a strangely imaginative set of ruminations, which began with the Old Testament:

> The story of Noah's Ark is more than a myth to me. Except for a few humans and animals, it is a story of everything becoming nothing. Maybe this will happen again—everything disappearing and becoming nothing except for a very few. . . . If we continue to make and use more powerful bombs, there may be only a few people left . . . chosen by chance. . . . As for myself, I go the way of nothingness. I don't have a strong desire to go about telling people about these things, or to talk in a loud voice about my A-bomb experience. But if I am able to be useful, I like to do what I can. . . .

Although we know him to have expressed a particularly strong sense of survivor mission, the "way of nothingness" turns out to be associated with a special version of psychological non-resistance which he relates to Oriental psychology:

> I feel that once people have invented the A-bomb, they will not give it up. They will want to keep it and use it. . . . I feel they will go their own way. . . . So when I think about it, I feel that people are

not making progress, but are on the way to nothingness—on the way to destruction. . . . Maybe this is a negative attitude of *akirame*—but the feeling is very strong in me. Maybe I am far from being progressive. . . . But although I have not studied this carefully, I subjectively think that Orientals tend to adapt themselves to their own environment—which is a form of *akirame*—while Westerners try to conquer their environment. . . . When we think about these things, we feel they are just. something we can't do anything about. . . .

We note that his main meaning for "nothingness" is adaptive resignation, but that he also uses it to suggest annihilation. He went on to suggest a "far out" solution to the world's (and his) dilemma—a science fiction fantasy of the kind we have learned, in our contemporary world, to examine carefully lest it turn out to be not quite so far out as it appears to be:

What I am going to describe now is almost like a dream, but because of the progress of science it may not be simply a dream. My thoughts about the future of the world, though they may be unrealistic, are these. As long as we people on earth live without contact with an outside planet, we will go on having wars. But if we have contact with other planets—and I read of space ships these days which venture out beyond our own planet—we may be able to live in peace. . . . I don't usually talk about these things . . . but because you ask, I will try to explain. . . . The human animal is such that the strong win the victory, the weak are defeated. It is a question of power. . . . Only when beings from earth have to face beings from another planet will they be able to unite to defend themselves. . . . This may seem pessimistic . . . but [is in keeping with my idea] that human beings have made very little progress since Christ and Buddha. . . . Of course, there will be wars and atomic bombs will be used [by the united earth beings against the beings from outer space]. . . . There are many satellites around the sun—and because there are so many planets, the process is endless. . . . I know this is really too strange a dream to have . . . quite vague . . . and too cynical . . . but it is my own hypothesis . . . and cannot be said to be either optimistic or pessimistic. . . .

Here perhaps we approach the central meaning of the formulation of "nothingness': Rather than "progress" or genuine change, a vision of infinite strife which is at the same time not without harmony; a self-world relationship in which one must blend with and be acted upon by events surrounding this strife and harmony; and a view of man's survival as being made possible only by enlarging the dimensions of the physical and psychic arena. The formulation maintains the principle of psychological non-resistance in the midst of the violence contemplated, and reaches outward beyond our own planet in the effort (in this case only partly successful) to master not only anxiety and guilt but to cope with end-of-the-world imagery.

The young Hiroshima-born writer also raised the issue of nothingness in discussing differences between Western and Oriental attitudes:

> At the center of Western civilization is the idea of man. Man is less important in the Oriental way of thinking. So in the Pacific war, for instance, we had the feeling of fighting against great amounts of material. The Allied Forces, I think, had the feeling of fighting against men. I think that Europeans in particular have a different feeling when they see destruction in front of them. Their landscape is human—so that if this landscape is destroyed, they feel despair. . . .

He sees this distinction as affecting images of nuclear annihilation:

> In Western peace movements leaders keep saying that if the A-bomb continues to be produced and is dropped all over the world, then all of humanity will be annihilated. That is characteristic of the Western way of thinking. But if you follow the Oriental thinking about this, we feel that no matter what the degree of annihilation, something will be left.

When I asked him whether this "something" included man, his answer was: "Perhaps not. Perhaps it will be a scene from which man is absent. . . ." What he is saying here is that the Oriental view of man as being, so to speak, just a speck in nature, can provide a sense of symbolic immortality even in the face of total human annihilation—again the feeling that "the mountains and rivers remain." He went on to claim that the Western mode of thought was dangerous, as it caused men to feel that "Since we are to be annihilated, why not annihilate our enemies first"—while from the Oriental standpoint, "No such thinking develops." It follows that with their symbolic immortality thus intact, Oriental resignation (or psychological non-resistance) provides formulative strength not readily available to Westerners:

> Oriental people have less fear about the future than Westerners. We feel that whether we are killed first or whether it is our enemies, we

all return to our natural state in the end. And the other side of *shikataganai* [it can't be helped] is *nanatokanaru* [there is some way out]. I think I myself have this kind of toughness, and others do too—but Westerners may not have it. It is possible to call it a kind of optimism—though it is a mixture of pessimism and optimism. . . .

Returning to the subject of the A-bomb and comparing it with Pearl Harbor, he sees it as a perverse expression of the Western tradition of human-centeredness:

The Japanese Air Force attacked Pearl Harbor because they were interested in exhibiting their power by destroying the enemy's military forces. But when the Americans dropped the A-bomb, they were interested in exhibiting their military power through the number of people killed. At Pearl Harbor man remained man; at Hiroshima man was reduced to numbers. . . .

He is therefore led to conclude that "the A-bomb represents the termination of Western thought."

But he then added, with characteristic unorthodoxy, an image resembling his earlier one of "*hibakusha* toughness" in which he saw the A-bomb as an energizing force:

For instance, as soon as I am confronted with a decision, I think about the A-bomb. And then I jump into the decision. The only way I can explain this is by using a metaphor: radiation goes into one's marrow, and one has to blow out this radiation—get rid of it—to make the decision. The A-bomb as such is extremely bad and immoral. But if you take nuclear fission as such, it is something highly admirable, because in a sense man has created a second sun. So when I blow the radiation out from my bones, I make use of this constructive form of energy . . . the radiation is then like a vital force I emit as I go along—neither good nor bad in itself—but a vital force.

This image too was related to the idea of having conquered death. But no one else in Hiroshima mentioned such a formulation to me. It seemed to require for its expression a person who was, like him, articulate, psychologically perceptive, young—and not a *hibakusha*. Nor did most survivors have his confidence in Oriental thought and feeling as a means of dealing with the A-bomb. Their experience had rendered them more deeply aware of symbolic breakdown, and their formulations could not be free of profound doubts about the continuity of life.

ten

CREATIVE RESPONSE:
1) "A-BOMB LITERATURE"

Artistic re-creation of an overwhelming historical experience has much to do with the question of mastery. Artists can apply to that experience their particular aesthetic traditions and individual talents to evolve new ways of "seeing" it and giving it form. In Hiroshima or elsewhere the relationship between the quality or popularity of artistic works and the degree of collective mastery is imprecise and difficult to evaluate. But an important relationship does exist. For these works are special distillations of group psychic response, and in their accomplishments and failures can both reflect that response and profoundly influence it.

I therefore tried to learn what I could about artistic reactions of every kind to the A-bomb, particularly in Hiroshima itself, and to a lesser extent in other parts of Japan and the rest of the world. Since the most significant efforts—in quality, number, and general influence—have been made in literature and film, all of this chapter deals with the former, and most of the next chapter with the latter. Stage, radio, and television drama, as well as painting and music, are treated more briefly. In no case shall I attempt to be all-inclusive. Rather, I shall focus upon what I consider to be the most important general themes, paying special attention to the artist's individual psychic struggles and their relationship to his creative work, particularly in the case of those artists (mostly writers) with whom I was able to explore such issues directly. We shall note important differences between *hibakusha* and non*hibakusha* artists, but also strikingly consistent patterns having to do with the nature of the A-bomb experience and the formidable barriers it poses to all re-creation.

1) Problematic Genre

Turning first to writing, the dilemma which immediately presents itself is whether or not there is such a thing as "A-bomb literature"—a term that has been used to include just about everything written which mentions the atomic bomb. Like "A-bomb disease," it illuminates important problems by its very ambiguity, as well as by the contention it inspires.

We have, in earlier chapters, quoted from one kind of A-bomb literature, the personal diary or memoir—most frequently from Yōko Ōta's *Town of Corpses* and Dr. Michihiko Hachiya's *Hiroshima Diary*. Memoirs, of course, never merely record events, but re-create them through the author's personal formulation of them, however hidden this formulation may be. In Miss Ōta's case, we have observed the blending of exquisite psychological sensibilities with an angry anti-militarism; and in Dr. Hachiya's, a combination of medical commitment and non-judgmental detachment (not to mention the further distillation of his *Hiroshima Diary*, and in a sense reformulation of it, by Warner Wells, the articulate and morally responsive American physician who rendered the book into English).

Such memoirs derive, at least in part, from two longstanding Japanese literary conventions: the use of the personal diary; and the related "I-novel," a form of first-person narrative which all but obliterates the boundaries between autobiography and fiction. We are therefore hardly surprised that many A-bomb memoirs, including Miss Ōta's, have been labeled novels.

But the distinction between memoir and fictional transformation is of considerable importance. Indeed, the difficulty in taking the imaginative leap from the one to the other was a preoccupation of just about every writer I spoke to who was concerned with A-bomb literature. A Hiroshima literary critic conversant with these matters told me that there have been three sequential stages of writing about the A-bomb: first, that of "reportage" (or what we have called the "personal memoir"), beginning at the time of the bomb and extending until about the mid-1950s; then, that of a "novel" so autobiographical that it differs only slightly from reportage (and perhaps is best termed the "memoir-novel"), lasting roughly until 1955; and a subsequent "stage of confusion" in which writers have attempted, with relatively little success, to convert the A-bomb experience into a genuinely fictional idiom. The critic's conviction was that writers "have already exhausted the resources of the immediate experience," and that they must now deal with it as "something of a more symbolic nature" by portraying "ordinary people and ordinary circumstances while having the A-bomb unmistakably present in the background." He went on to describe a pattern of moral and literary compulsion among Hiroshima writers which we can immediately recognize to be a product of the A-bomb's circle of guilt:

> The fact that they are in Hiroshima . . . makes many feel that they must write about this special experience of the A-bomb . . . and those who don't want to write about the A-bomb . . . feel that they have to try to work out reasons for not writing about it. . . .

He stressed the literary problem presented by the A-bomb as "an alien object removed from human beings"—that is, by its technologically induced distance. And like many other Hiroshima writers I spoke to, he insisted that "past literary methods . . . are inadequate for dealing with the A-bomb," but could say little about what new approaches might suffice. He thought too superficial the "shifting of literary focus from the A-bomb itself to more political elements . . . and peace movements," and also raised the dilemma of how to evoke the bomb's unprecedented dimensions:

> . . . If you describe the A-bomb in an ordinary way, from a standpoint of personal relationships, your description differs very little from that of other disasters—such as ordinary bombings or earthquakes. But writers feel that the A-bomb has special significance . . . and is different from these other disasters. Yet they are unable to find a way to bring out this special significance. . . .

Finally, he raised the issue of the *hibakusha*-writer's particular inclination toward silence:

> Those who have been through the experience are hesitant about writing about it—and therefore seem, at least outwardly, to be more passive in their attitudes.

But this silence is acceptable neither to *hibakusha*-writers themselves, as we already know, nor to their critics—notably those from the highly centralized Tokyo "literary establishment," perceived by Hiroshima writers as a kind of Big Brother, now chastising provincial colleagues for failing to speak up about the A-bomb in their work, now ridiculing the entire genre of "A-bomb literature" with the disdainful challenge, "What is A-bomb literature anyway?"[1] And of course there is the very real question of how many gifted writers could be expected to appear in a particular provincial area, whatever its special historical experience.

No wonder, then, that some wished to abandon the whole concept of A-bomb literature, and indeed the A-bomb itself as a literary subject—as did one provocative woman writer in a somewhat sensational proposal put forth in an article in a Hiroshima newspaper in early 1953:

> The A-bomb is not a special genre of literature. So-called A-bomb literature was written mostly from immediate feelings of indignation, anger, hatred, and repentance. But now that seven years have passed, isn't it about time to stop writing in this fashion and instead to deal with the more essential things of life? . . . What is important to us is not death but love, romance, peace, happiness. . . . It is important for writers to think seriously about love and romance . . . in order to try to understand the essential meaning of life. Literature should not be used for special purposes, whether political or scientific, and A-bomb literature has been used for such purposes. . . .[2]

This plea for a "cheerful" literature of individual sensual experience was partly a reaction to the self-consciously "purposeful," even manipulative, tendency of much that had previously been written. The trouble, of course, was that her proposal came close to advocating that Hiroshima's unique history be totally ignored. In the lively debate that followed, some writers angrily denounced her "escapist attitude," while others, in more measured tones, granted the weaknesses of existing A-bomb literature but insisted upon its general significance. One observer wryly summed up the debate: "Just about everything that could be said about A-bomb literature was said . . . but this did not necessarily produce any A-bomb literature."

As a way out of this literary and psychological bind, some, like the literary critic, suggested that Hiroshima writers turn away from preoccupation with victims alone and "write about the A-bomb from the other side"—that is, from the standpoint of those who dropped the bomb and possibly deal with "the story of the pilot who went insane," keeping in mind that "it is quite possible that if the Japanese had the A-bomb, they would have used it." It turned out that his plea was answered, though not in Hiroshima itself. But to understand these various dilemmas, we must turn to the actual efforts of individual writers.

2) "Town of Corpses": Literary Entrapment

Until her death in December, 1963, Miss Yōko Ōta was probably Japan's best-known producer of A-bomb literature. She had been writing about the bomb more or less continuously since her original exposure to it. Her books include *Town of Corpses*, which we have so frequently quoted, *Human Rags* (*Ningen Ranru*), and *The Town and People of the Evening Calm* (*Yūnagi no Machi to Hito*)—all essentially memoirs. Not only did she win several literary prizes for these books, but she was constantly called upon to discuss A-bomb problems on the mass media, in keeping with the Japanese tendency to lionize and make pundits of successful writers.

During an extensive interview fifteen months before her death I was impressed by her articulateness on the general subject of the A-bomb, but I was also struck by the severity of her conflicts. Despite my introduction from a prominent Hiroshima friend and colleague of hers, she was touchy and ambivalent about our meeting—stressing to my assistant (who visited her to make arrangements) how busy she was and how bad she felt, and yet never actually refusing to see me. When we did meet, I found her to be a woman in her late fifties who seemed to be harassed and restless. Surrounding her sense of being a leading *hibakusha*-writer was a fragile aura of pride, anxiety, vanity, and suspiciousness. Thus, she quickly told me that she had just had a tooth pulled and "since I experienced the atomic bomb, there is always a danger that the bleeding will not stop and that leukemia might develop"; and upon learning that I had been talking to a number of writers concerned with the bomb, she commented sharply: "I am the only A-bomb writer. Who else could you find?"

But during the course of our talk she softened considerably. She spoke easily and sensitively about her A-bomb reactions, as well as her literary life before and during the war. For by the time of the bomb she had achieved considerable standing as a "woman writer" (a category which in those days conveyed a sense of rebellious feminism), and had long since left her native Hiroshima for the professional opportunities of Tokyo. Ironically, she had returned to Hiroshima, as did many others, because of its seeming wartime safety in comparison with the devastating bombings Tokyo was then undergoing. Once the atomic bomb fell, however, it came to dominate her literary imagination. Carried from her house unconscious by her mother and sister with severe injuries to her head and neck ("My face was like a pumpkin"), then overwhelmed by what she saw and for some time considered close to death herself, she began to write as a form of survivor's mission and a means of staying alive:

> I asked myself what I had been writing for the past twenty years. I couldn't answer, and this gave me a terrible feeling. I began to feel that it was not just a matter of this disaster, but something that leads toward the end of the earth, and that if I lived, I should write about what had happened. I had to write as soon as possible—because I thought I might die at any time. I wanted to write objectively. And I thought that if I could show some endurance, I could live, as I had heard that if one lived until December, then one would not die. And also that when the time came for considering the problem of reparations with America, all of this would be written down. I wrote exactly what I saw—not fiction . . . and I wrote it in great haste. . . .

Thus, *Town of Corpses*, despite having its publication delayed by Occupation censorship, emerged as one of the first detailed descriptions of the atomic bomb experience.

Miss Ōta emphasized that her bomb exposure called forth old emotional and literary inclinations: "When there's a real change in a person's writing, it means that the new elements were spiritually present within him even before." She had been influenced by the "proletarian literature" of the thirties, and even when writing in a romantic vein, dealt critically with Japanese constraints upon the individual, particularly upon the individual woman. But like most writers, she had expressed no direct protest against the militaristic regime ("I didn't want to go to prison"). It is quite likely that guilt over not having done so also contributed to the power of her post-bomb writing, and to its repeated denunciations of Japanese militarism. In any case, as one friend put it, "She wrote with great intensity, in a way she had never written in the past."[3]

For in restoring her sense of authenticity as a writer, we may say that the A-bomb had a liberating effect upon her. We recall how three months after the bomb she was "happy to begin to feel the flame of the writer's spirit within myself," along with her remarkable admission of having been "angrier at the ignorant imperialism which attempted to destroy my writer's life than with the fact that Hiroshima was destroyed." One is angered most by that which creates inner conflicts and self-contempt, and while the A-bomb did this too, it also provided her with a means of emotional and literary purification. That is, it both caused her to suffer and released her from humiliating earlier constraints, so that this purification (as she also told us before) could help dissolve her grief.

Her compulsion to write about the A-bomb was intensified by the later deaths of other prominent A-bomb writers, by the sense that "I was the only one left," so that "When I wrote about anything else but the A-bomb, the image of Hiroshima would come back to me. I could not set it aside." These deaths, in effect, created repetitions of her A-bomb survival. Continued "survival priority," along with whatever satisfaction she derived from becoming the uncontested dean of A-bomb writers, gave further impetus to her guilt and to her sense of mission.

But she was also aware that "to use the A-bomb exclusively in writing is not very skillful," and wished to be more than *merely* an A-bomb writer. She was thus caught in a characteristic A-bomb writer's bind, which we recognize as a corollary of the identity struggle of the *hibakusha* in general. Her dilemma was made worse by what she viewed as the impossible demands of the subject matter:

> It is outside the category of literature. . . . With ordinary fiction, there are patterns and categories—children's literature, romantic stories, and so on. But there is no pattern and no category for the atomic bomb experience. The experience was so strong, so great, so powerful, that one can find no words to describe it. . . .

She developed what we may call a survivor's sense of "sacred historical truth" which made it impossible for her to make use of the fictional mode:

> As a subject for fiction it is very difficult. . . . I don't want to write fictitious things—I just want to write the truth—to describe it as it was without exaggeration. . . . Fiction is usually a mixture of truth and lies. But I don't want to write lies about the A-bomb the way some others have. . . .

In other words, the imprisoning actuality of the A-bomb experience prevented her from entering upon its imaginative re-creation. The psychic truth of fiction then became "lies"; only literal historical truth could be free of desecration. Her further comment that "fiction about the A-bomb is not interesting" would probably be supported by most critics and readers—at least concerning most fiction written *up to then*. But when she quickly added a self-deprecatory comment—"I don't have the strength. . . . Maybe I just don't have the gift for it"—one could feel once more the intervention of her literary judgment, its telling her that the fictional approach to the A-bomb could not be dismissed, however difficult it seemed to her. She went on to reveal an awareness that still unresolved A-bomb emotions interfere with her capacity to write:

> Most people seem to look upon me as an interesting person, and it is often said that I am one of the best women writers—but when talk of the A-bomb comes up, I find myself in a very bad mood. . . . I think I am still very angry at the A-bomb. . . . Maybe I need more time— more distance—before I can write further about the A-bomb. I would like to write about things that have nothing to do with the A-bomb. Because when I write about the A-bomb, I feel physically ill and I have to rest.

We sense the kind of entrapment which she mentioned some years earlier in an introduction to one of the editions of *Town of Corpses*:

> At times I have had my doubts about whether writers must write objectively. And feeling myself entangled by the town of corpses, I have not been able to move an inch.[4]

She is, in other words, entrapped by the identity of the dead, by its disturbing inner questions, which in her case are asked in literary terms: "Do I have the right to imagination? Can what I say about the dead ever be authentic?" Her increasing dissatisfaction with the memoir approach to A-bomb literature, and her inability to evolve an alternative one, undoubtedly contributed to her "anger" at the A-bomb.

Her conflicts also found expression in bodily terms. She suffered from chronic debilitation, which was sometimes diagnosed as "nervous weakness" and at other times was associated with such specific physical conditions as gall bladder and heart disease. Her strong fear of aftereffects was also commented upon, along with her frequent insistence that "my sickness is not A-bomb disease." One friend described her as a "beautiful woman writer who, with much anguish, carried the experience of the atomic bomb on her shoulders, and lived with courage, constantly fighting her fear." Also mentioned were her strong demands upon friends ("like a spoiled child"), her need for others' demonstrations of love, and despite being warm and hospitable, a tendency to lose her composure whenever the subject of the A-bomb came up: "Her speech became strong and violent."[5] We may thus say that early sensitivities concerning love and dependency were exacerbated by her A-bomb experience and her subsequent literary struggles. And in what she told me there were implications that over the years she felt further "abandoned" by publishers and editors who showed less interest in her as a general writer (she had done some work not related to the atomic bomb) than as an "A-bomb writer," and, moreover, showed signs of losing interest in A-bomb problems as well.

She mentioned these matters in association with her sense of the movement of time, and, ultimately, of the meaning of life:

> Whether it seems to be there or not—the past is always with us. We can't forget the past. On August sixth people [publishers and editors] who otherwise forget me come here and ask my opinions. I hate August sixth, and often I go on a trip somewhere in order to avoid them. . . . But the words written [about the A-bomb] will last forever. . . .

She thus felt partly sustained by having made use of the past to carry out her literary mission in a way that promised her a form of creative immortality. But the tenuousness of this formulation of her relationship to the A-bomb was revealed in what she said immediately afterward. She claimed that she suffered from "a kind of neurosis," which caused her general physical condition to "get better when the world seems headed for peace," so that "If there had been no Korean War, I would be better than I am now." While it is certainly true that the inner conflicts engendered by threats of war could worsen her condition, we suspect that she was also struggling with "unmentionable" retaliatory wishes and inner themes of violence.

She went on to describe a typical *hibakusha* sense of weakness ("I feel I am half-sick—my bed is always ready"), along with a premonition of dying: "I have always been a passionate, active person, but now I feel the power of life dwindling." Such premonitions can derive from accurate perceptions of declining bodily and mental function, and while we cannot know exactly how much A-bomb influences contributed to Miss Ōta's death, we may assume that her fatal (apparently coronary) illness was a psychosomatic process in which the kinds of conflict we have been discussing played a significant part. Whatever the case, others inevitably associated her death, as they had her life, with the atomic bomb experience. As one friend wrote:

> Of course, this kind of sudden death is by no means rare. But we cannot think of her death without relating it to the fact that a writer by the name of Yōko Ōta experienced the atomic bomb in Hiroshima.[6]

Beyond the question of medical aftereffects, the association is psychologically and historically understandable. Her literary response to atomic bomb exposure had become, for many, a primary source of information and formulation. Her achievements were rendered all the more impressive by the conflicts surrounding them.

3) "Chinkon"

The writer-physician we have referred to has undergone similar *hiba-kusha* literary and psychological struggles. But unlike Miss Ōta, he had been unable to write about the atomic bomb.

He too had a severe A-bomb exposure (though without the serious injuries and radiation effects experienced by Miss Ōta); included in his retained imprint were the deaths of a family friend in his home, of his wife's mother elsewhere, and of so many neighbors that his family was the only one in his area left intact. His resulting death guilt profoundly affected his approach to A-bomb literature.

Mostly it made him extremely critical. He denounced writers who dealt with the problem "from a political point of view," or from the standpoint of any "cause," even the cause of peace—since such writings, he felt, treated the A-bomb "only externally." When he himself thought of writing about it, he found that as with others, "the images that came into my mind were impressions of the scene itself." But he specifically rejected these as "not enough" and already too familiar. (He was then in his mid-thirties, and much on this order had been written before his own literary career began). To illustrate his point he mentioned the kinds of things he had in mind—

> . . . images of dead bodies immediately after the bomb, of the smell which filled the air, of the fire which crept up the hills, of the unusually clear blue sky a few days later, looking so peaceful that one had the impression that nothing had happened.

—but insisted that "there is no use in repeating them." I had the impression that he was still moved by these images, but at the same time considered them literary clichés.

He looked toward a novel in which he would write about the A-bomb "not for any causes, but for myself." He wished to do exactly what Miss Ōta shied away from, to bring his fictional imagination to the whole issue. He too, however, was blocked by a sense of the experience as sacred: he did not, like Miss Ōta, demand literal historical truth, but he did require near-perfection in re-creating history.

I feel one shouldn't write about the A-bomb unless he is first certain he can write well about other subjects. If you cannot do this and are immature as a writer, and you write about the A-bomb—then you are abusing the souls of the dead. . . .

To avoid "abusing the souls of the dead," he wished to "reserve the subject for such time that I can be sure that I will be able to deal with the very heart of it." Anything less, he implied, would fail to fulfill his survivor's mission and would aggravate his death guilt. He was partly aware (but only partly) that these exacting standards could result in an indefinitely prolonged literary silence about the A-bomb.

In the meantime he continued to confront the problem, but did so indirectly by concerning himself with the larger general issue of the relationship of the living to the dead. Coming upon a collection of verse by a Tokyo poet who had lost one of his sons in the Pacific war, he was struck by its title, *Chinkon*, meaning Requiem, or Consolation of Souls:

I found that the idea of *Chinkon* had a special meaning for me—first, in the sense that I should write in order to console the souls of the [A-bomb] dead, and second, that I should write in order to console or pacify something troubled in my own mind. And this is what I mean by writing about the A-bomb for myself, rather than for the sake of causes.

Derived from ancient Shinto religious practice native to Japan, the word *chinkon* predates Buddhist influence, and originally referred to the ceremony for enabling the soul of a person hovering between life and death to achieve repose—either through urging it not to leave the body, or to return to the body if it had already left.[7] As with the custom of offering water to the dying (which was sometimes part of *chinkon*), the significance was that of maintaining life, either in actuality or in symbolic continuity. In subsequent usage the word also came to signify the pacification or even restraint of souls which had become restless, wayward, and dangerous to the living—whether because of being neglected or because their owners had died unnatural or violent deaths. *Chinkon* suggests a gentle atmosphere of respect and love, and above all *a combination of continued connection with the dead and peaceful separation from them.*

The writer-physician realized that these concerns grew out of his A-bomb exposure ("Because of the experience, I can't help thinking about the problem of death") but dealt with them in essays about the lives and deaths of other writers and held back from what he knew to be his ultimate subject:

> I cannot plunge into writing about the A-bomb experience without first wondering whether the souls of all those who died have really been consoled or not. And by writing, which is a form of *chinkon*, I feel I am doing something for them. I have a kind of ideal, a sense of responsibility and of special mission toward those who died in the bomb—because I might have died myself. I don't know whether it was by the grace of God or not, but the fact that I survived while so many died means that I have to do something about it. . . . This sense of responsibility to the dead is my tie to them. . . .

The idea of *chinkon*, then, becomes for him a path to literary authenticity, a means of both carrying out his survivor's mission and maintaining an appropriate tone of psychological non-resistance. Through an awareness of continuing responsibility to the dead, he can carry out the psychological "work of mourning"; he can gradually separate himself from the dead by means of constant emphasis upon his larger continuity with them. But he finds that there are barriers to achieving this resolution:

> There is something which cannot be consoled or reconciled within myself. That is, I feel two parts of myself to be always at war with one another—that which can be pacified and that which cannot.

He related this "unpacified" part of himself first to a physician's struggle against death itself: "As a doctor, I am aware that whatever threatens human life, whether it is a disease or an A-bomb, causes an aroused feeling in me." But more pressing was "another kind of anger" which occurred in response to all forms of hypocrisy or deception concerning the A-bomb—exaggerations or distortions of any kind, even by those who "cry out for world peace," and military threats everywhere, preventing the souls of the A-bomb dead from resting in peace. His "unpacified" side, then, had to do with anything that undermined a formulation of significant death for A-bomb victims, and thereby reactivated his guilt.

In contrast, he described the pacified side of his mind as "wishing simply to gradually forget the A-bomb experience as the years go by." He admitted that "I don't experience indignation at every moment," that even the A-bomb must be written about "from a humorous and witty approach," and that "there are aspects of my life [such as the publication of his literary group's magazine] which I enjoy thoroughly." But one suspected that this "pacification" or psychological non-resistance—whether achieved through forgetting, through gradual psychological absorption, or through reassertion of vitality and pleasure—became in itself a stimulus to death guilt, which in turn further inhibited his efforts at A-bomb writing.

He therefore felt impelled to apply his medical identity, as he did his literary one, to further study of the general significance of death and dying. He observed that "every human being has his own way of dying, just as each has his way of living," and espoused a psychosomatic approach to death as a "symbol" of life ("For instance, if you die of cancer . . . perhaps it is because you ate too much rice or smoked too much"). He made it clear that these speculations emerged directly from continuing contemplation of A-bomb deaths—and that these deaths continued to disturb him because "One was not allowed to have his own way of dying but was simply annihilated with everyone else," and because of what we recall to be his inability to formulate this "total annihilation of human beings." What he could not emotionally absorb, or creatively transform, was the massive anonymity and the *irrelevance* of A-bomb deaths. Unable to relate these deaths to any cosmology or vision of human continuity, he (and A-bomb writers in general) could not render them either dramatic or tragic. Thus lacking the materials and capacity for narrative, the *hibakusha*-writer finds himself thrown back upon his own self-enclosed death guilt.

Yet in the midst of my second talk with the writer-physician, he suddenly surprised me by saying, "While talking to you just now, I thought of a new theme for a novel." He was referring to an image which he thought could be the beginning of a creative breakthrough, a memory of the dilemma he experienced at the time of the bomb about whether and how to tell a very close friend, then outside of the city, about the death of that friend's mother. The story he had in mind would include details of his relationship to the friend, to the mother (who had been something of a substitute mother for him during a period of study away from home), and between the two families—all against the A-bomb background. But once more the entire vision depended upon the principle of *chinkon*:

> If I were to write a story about this subject, it would be not only from the point of view of my suffering, but also from the point of view of my friend, and of his dead mother—in order to console her spirit.

Consoling the spirit of a particular person provides him with the necessary sense of significance, and of larger symbolic structure, within which to formulate life and death. His explorations with me of his personal and creative difficulties had released him sufficiently from death guilt to allow him to apply to this formulation a slightly greater radius of literary imagination. He could then take what was for him the logical next step: the *direct* creative application of his principle of *chinkon* to A-bomb experience. The episode made me wonder whether much of what we call "writer's block" might not be related to various forms of death guilt.*

In any case, he quickly qualified even this modest bit of serendipity, by adding, "If I ever write this story, I will explain in it just how difficult it is to write about the A-bomb." He seemed to realize (at some psychic level) that his theme was no more than a limited advance and held no certainty of doing justice to the special dimensions of the A-bomb. He then reverted to another concern he wished to write about, "the story of human revival, how people regain their strength after a disaster," but again revealed uncertainty about his capacity to do so:

> . . . the process is so complicated that I have not been able to form a clear image of how this occurs. So all I can do now is to write about things I know from the small limits of my own personal experience. . . .

In this way he reasserted his commitment to authenticity—to what is direct, personal, and accurate—while again expressing reticence in the face of the demands of the A-bomb. We sense that his grasp of his own exacting standards—and his commitment to *chinkon*—make genuine fictional transformation a possibility. But as to whether it can be more than that, the many imponderables involved, including the mysteries of talent, render any prediction hazardous.

---

* What I am suggesting is that the writer, even under ordinary circumstances, may experience guilt associated with various symbolic forms of death, which can cause his literary imagination to cease functioning. (See the last part of Chapter XI.)

4) Experimental City

Non*hibakusha* writers have also contributed much to A-bomb literature, but usually with a different relationship to it from that of *hibakusha* writers. Characteristically, they have deep roots in Hiroshima, were outside of the city at the time of the bomb because of a personal or family wartime assignment, returned shortly afterward to be shocked and awed by the devastation, and took on an identification with survivors which was strongly infused with guilt over not having themselves been through the A-bomb experience. But although this identification included the equivalent of a sense of survivor's mission in producing A-bomb literature, they were not likely to be as overwhelmed as actual survivors by A-bomb demands in carrying out the mission. Neither their inner pressure to write nor their self-critical attitudes toward their own writing tended to be quite as agonizing. They have therefore retained greater freedom to experiment with various symbols of the A-bomb experience, to switch back and forth between A-bomb literature and other forms of writing, or even to abandon A-bomb literature altogether. But being once removed from the A-bomb experience has created its own special problem of authenticity, and its own combination of survivor-like conflicts.

Such has been the case of a Hiroshima-born writer, Toshiyuki Kajiyama, who wrote a particularly controversial short novel entitled *Experimental City (Jikken Toshi)*[8] prior to moving to Tokyo and achieving considerable success with other forms of writing. He received me in his comfortable but modest new house in the Tokyo suburbs, a man in his mid-thirties whose casual dress (he wore informal kimono), easygoing manner, and facile responsiveness all suggested an atmosphere very different from that which I had become accustomed to in talks with people in Hiroshima, and with *hibakusha* anywhere.

Kajiyama returned to Hiroshima during the early post-bomb period at the age of eighteen. Because of the food shortage he had to work as a farmer for two years before completing his education at what is now Hiroshima University. In his dual struggle to cope with the A-bombed environment and establish himself as a young writer, he began to gather information about survivors in association with various literary groups which sprang up in Hiroshima during those years. The names of these groups—"Hiroshima Literature" (Hiroshima *Bungaku*), *Amanojaku* (a Japanese folk-creature whose tendency to do precisely the opposite of what he is asked has made him a humorous symbol of perverseness), and *L'Ami* (the French word for friend)—suggest some of the disparate currents which prevailed. Equally varied were the positions taken in the groups during their protracted discussions of A-bomb literature:

One idea was that of making A-bomb literature "devilish" . . . so that the A-bomb was synonymous with evil . . . and people thought they should try to determine who was responsible—politicians, the American President, the scientists. But it was an endless debate. . . . Sometimes we considered writing with a strong victim-consciousness, sometimes with a humanistic approach, sometimes the political approach. . . . One TV producer said that . . . A-bomb literature is meaningless. . . .

Kajiyama went on to describe additional difficulties faced by groups attempting to produce A-bomb literature: severe economic problems and unfulfilled promises of financial help, a combination of disdainful treatment from Tokyo literary lights and generational conflicts among Hiroshima writers themselves, a tendency among older rural *hibakusha* to look upon the experience as a mysterious natural calamity ("like an earthquake or a great thunder") and to resist having anything stirred up by questions, and a lack of sympathetic understanding on the part of Hiroshima journalists and professors (about whom he commented: "Some of them had never gone through it themselves—for that matter, neither had I").

He spoke about these difficulties with detachment, and conveyed the impression of one who could adapt himself readily to shifting literary tides. But as he went on to explain his decision to leave Hiroshima, he vividly evoked the negative forces at play in the city, particularly as they affected a non*hibakusha* writer like himself:

I wonder if you noticed the strange kind of atmosphere that exists in Hiroshima—the unique situation around the A-bomb. . . . I can understand the tendency of *hibakusha* to want to forget their agonies . . . and the other two thirds of the population who have not gone through the experience also object to writing done about the A-bomb. So I felt that Hiroshima was a kind of closed society. . . . Then some *hibakusha* feel that since they do not know when they might die of leukemia, they are unable to work. We could say that this is a result of the A-bomb, but I feel that if people think their life may not last long, they should concentrate upon living it fruitfully. Of course, I am not sure I can say that about myself because I drink quite heavily, though I am not a *hibakusha*. But as long as *hibakusha* have these feelings, and look upon Hiroshima as a special city, then people there will not really develop. . . . After a while I did not want to stay there, and decided that I would no longer write with a group but would write by myself, and came to Tokyo. . . . I left Hiroshima for many reasons. But if I were to sum it up in a word, I would say I got sick of Hiroshima. . . .

He refers, of course, to the general constellation of counterfeit nurturance, as well as to the array of intra-*hibakusha* and *hibakusha*-non*hibakusha* antagonisms with which we are familiar. In evaluating his decision, one must take into account the general cultural and financial advantages Tokyo offers any writer, as well as his increasing sense that the pressures of the Hiroshima atmosphere were creatively intolerable. His choice of subject matter for his major A-bomb novel was, then, both a solution to a dilemma and an angry farewell to the city:

Many people feel that simply writing about the A-bomb is selling the A-bomb or selling Hiroshima. This feeling people have makes it difficult for us to write. So I thought that rather than writing about the A-bomb, I would write about people and their attitudes toward the city.

His way of avoiding the often paralyzing accusation of "selling the bomb" was to shift the area of literary formulation to that of the Japanese-American interplay, and as the title suggests, to the guinea pig theme. The importance of *Experimental City* (published in 1954) probably lies less in its literary virtues than its representation, however simplistic, of very real emotional issues in Hiroshima, particularly the racial issue.

The novel takes place almost entirely within the confines of the Atomic Bomb Casualty Commission compound at a moment of crisis produced by a strike of Japanese employees. There are five prototypical characters: the cold-blooded American scientist; the calculating, toadying Nisei; the corrupted (Americanized) young Japanese girl; the morally sensitive Japanese physician; and the sincere, psychologically affected *hibakusha*-reporter. The first four are employed by the ABCC, and the last comes into contact with them when sent there to cover the strike.

The tone of the book is established immediately by a stark contrast: on the one hand there is the ABCC's alien American elegance—the strange but "smart-looking" building standing at the top of the hill, its beautiful lobby showing "careful attention to lighting," the well-polished floors, comfortable sofas, and "foreign-made toys for children to play with," all of which is "dreamlike, not really a part of Hiroshima"; and on the other, there is the absolute misery of Japanese victims thrust into this alien conclave:

> Look at the Japanese who come to be examined, with their confused and timid expression, holding their babies or exposing their ugly keloids. They seem to be foreigners here. . . . This place might well be a foreign country.[9]

The author goes on to suggest that the fundamental reason for the strike is not economic (the six hundred Japanese employees, fifty of them physicians, receive better salaries than do other Japanese), and that the public explanation given (discrimination shown in the firing of Japanese employees) was "not quite convincing." Rather, the strikers felt compelled to "take a firm attitude" because of "some hidden element"—that is, the basic conflict surrounding the post-A-bomb American presence in Hiroshima.

The individual embodiment of that presence, the cigar-smoking director of the ABCC, is not so much evil as crudely insensitive and blindly exploitative. He arranges for Japanese doctors working under him to devote themselves to fragmentary and demeaning tasks—examining feces, urine specimens, etc., so that they can "only partially know the terrible effects of the bomb" while "all of the results of these studies are accessible to the director." And the director epitomizes an anti-human embrace of "pure science" characteristic of all American ABCC physicians:

> Humanism. Such a concept is excluded from American doctors' concerns. What are the effects? This is all they are interested in knowing as scientists. We have in our hands a new field of medicine, and we will cultivate this field. Our task is great. At home our people are trying to produce new medicines for treatment, by making use of guinea pigs. And that is being done upon the basis of my findings. Our materials. Other than these, there are no effective weapons. No

strike can stop us from getting these materials. This research of ours
will enhance the life of mankind in the future. We are right. What
else could this be if not humanism? The injured are injured. A
historical necessity. No one can change that. Neither Stalin nor
Christ nor even Hirohito can change that. Tomorrow is what matters.
We are making a contribution to mankind for tomorrow. We are
right.[10]

This scientific fanaticism, in other words, equates actual guinea pigs
used in America with *hibakusha* used for similar purposes in Hiroshima.
The word "weapons" (in Japanese, *buki*), moreover, suggests a military
aura by conveying, in both languages, the double meaning of "war
instrument" and "research tool."

The Nisei, George Matsuda, has a personal identity and a professional
position (liaison division chief) consistent in their amorphousness. Only
thirty-one, he maintains considerable power in the organization through
"cringing before both the [American] director and the Japanese," just
as in his life in general he relies upon a series of false roles. He defends
the American position and explains to the Japanese reporter that "the
whites here are not really bad people" but merely "peaceful scientists,"
becomes a fellow-Japanese suffering under the American yoke (". . .
we Japanese who work here are all robots"), and also speaks of himself
as a "miserable Nisei." But his effect upon the reporter, a bona fide
Japanese, is one of "distaste" and of ill-defined hostility:

His nasal Japanese struck the ears with a strange intonation. The
words sounded like a translation of an amateur play. . . . Somehow
[Kaji] . . . suddenly felt hatred for George Matsuda. And he could
not immediately tell what the nature of this hatred was. This man, he
thought, is a Japanese but he is on a parallel line which never
intersects with the Japanese. In the same way, this man is an
American who shall never intersect with Americans either. Even
when Japanese and Americans come together [to associate] with each
other, this man will still be on that parallel line [never coming
together with either]. Such a man is the Nisei.[11]

The author told me that he wished in the novel to "portray the
particular suffering of the Nisei" who "belonged to the Japanese race
but in a way [as an American] helped cause the disaster." But although
there is a faint suggestion of sympathy in the last part of the above-

quoted passage, the overall tone of the book is one of contempt. The Nisei flatters, deceives, and is in every way inauthentic.

George Matsuda's fiancee and secretary, Aki Kawai, has also, "sold out" to American counterfeit nurturance, on a number of levels. But she at least has a "good reason" for doing so. When she finds herself attracted to the reporter, she reminds herself of George's higher salary, and what it means to her:

> Aki thought of the joints of her mother's knotty fingers. I don't want to have such fingers. [I want] a life with an electric refrigerator and cocktail parties. . . .[12]

More ominous than these aspirations for the American-style Good Life was her association (here through the eyes of the journalist) with the atomic bomb itself:

> The thin and transparent nylon hose shone coolly over the legs of the woman going up the stairway in front of him. Looking at her legs absent-mindedly, Kaji somehow thought of the method of identifying virgins which he and fellow workers had talked about . . . by looking at the woman's ankles. And according to that method, this woman was probably not a virgin. He felt a strange impulse to grab the woman's ankles and drag her down to the floor. Nylon. A distasteful color and feeling, he thought. The company making nylons is said to make atomic bombs also. Nylon and atomic bombs. . . . Forcing a smile, Kaji thought seriously about the relationship between these two things.[13]

American influence not only corrupts the Japanese woman and makes her sexually provocative and dangerous, but also coats her body with a material somehow related to the atomic bomb. The Americanized woman becomes both a betrayer of her race and a "wearer" of the bomb.

"A RACIAL FEELING"

The sensitive Japanese physician, Dr. Tokumitsu, takes the reverse course. "A medical doctor and a gentleman," he has come to the conclusion that he and fellow Japanese physicians working for the ABCC "are purchased very much like courtesans." Now that he plans to resign and return to more honorable medical work in his native village, he literally asks the classical Faustian question: "Having sold one's soul, can one get it back?" And in the midst of his talk with the reporter, Dr.

Tokumitsu has the disturbing fantasy that the other has become a totally dehumanized ABCC patient who has neither lungs nor blood but consists only of a series of index cards listing numbers of white blood cells, red blood cells, and the like. The guilt with which he is assailed has to do with making "guinea pigs" of his countrymen:

> Guinea pigs . . . used for experiments . . . have germs implanted in them, their various reactions recorded, and then their ultimate fate . . . is to be anatomically dissected. These white animals are dissected for the valuable purpose of "making a contribution to mankind." If that is so, then what is the purpose of examining and dissecting [post-mortem] men and women with their faces twisted by keloids, babies who keep having strange bleeding, diarrhea, or fever, girls who have no menstruation, or wives who are sterile? Is the purpose that of making a contribution to mankind? As [Japanese] doctors, their conscience is sometimes troubled. The agony of treating their own people as guinea pigs. The eyes of A-bomb victims who come with earnest pleas for effective medicines first showed supplication, but, as days and months went by, began to flash with anger. It began to seem as though the doctor's only job was that of escaping from these eyes. Ryokichi Tokumitsu has been troubled by those distressed, burning eyes.[14]

Again, the accusing eyes which we have learned to associate with A-bomb-linked death guilt—and indeed Dr. Tokumitsu's spiritual crisis takes place during the dissection of the body of a baby which had died of liver disease. The "white doctor" doing the dissection suddenly becomes exhilarated by an unexpected scientific discovery, emits a low whistle, and whispers excitedly: "I've got it! This is what I have been waiting for!" Tokumitsu feels overwhelmed with anger, and comes to the sudden bitter realization that

> the purpose of the ABCC's work was not to make a contribution to mankind, that it was only for a part of mankind, for those who have skin of a different color from the Japanese. Those words [of the American doctor] could never be said over [corpses of] people who had the same skin as one's own. . . . Tokumitsu realized that the strike might have originated in such a racial feeling.[15]

Contained in this extreme imagery is the accusation of a racial basis for all American "experimentation" upon Japanese—for treating *hibakusha* "like guinea pigs," for vampire-like desecration of corpses, and by implication, for victimization of Japanese by the bomb in the first place.

Kaji, the reporter, is the novel's protagonist, and seems clearly to represent the author's voice (he in fact bears one of the author's pen names). But his *hibakusha* conflicts render him something of an antihero. His vulnerability to guilt is revealed immediately when even before arriving at the ABCC, he has the uncomfortable recollection that his own advancement was made possible by the dismissal of a number of senior people following an earlier strike in his newspaper company (one might claim a parallel here with the *hibakusha's* survival at the expense of those "dismissed" from life). Then, when first approached by George Matsuda, he has a fantasy of a court procedure in which ordinary positions are reversed, so that "a criminal [Matsuda] is questioning a victim [himself]" and "before I knew it, I was put in irons at the dock."

He also retains phobias to flashbulbs (which he associates with the great original "flash"), and to such sharp objects as the celluloid triangle Dr. Tokumitsu holds in his hand (which reminds him of the broken glass at the time of the bomb). He is, moreover, prone to a general sense of weakness and confusion throughout his visit to the ABCC, related to various additional reminders of his A-bomb exposure.

But it is made clear to us that his quest for understanding, like Dr. Tokumitsu's, is genuine (among the various characters of the novel, only these two seem to possess the capacity for introspection). And when he traces the source of his uneasiness—of his immediate impulse "to hate George Matsuda and the ABCC"—he arrives at the same answer that Tokumitsu did: racial victimization. At first he resists this answer:

Race. The word shocked him. A word which he had forgotten. A terrible word. . . . Is it race consciousness which makes him antagonistic toward the ABCC? Partiality toward one's blood kin? . . . He closed his eyes in the manner of one confused. Has his discomfort been race consciousness?[16]

But then he embraces the idea of race as fundamental both to the strike itself and to the general problems of mankind:

This is a human strike between one race and another. . . . Kaji stopped and looked at his wrist. The yellow skin. He thought about the skin of a white who came into the library while he was talking to

George Matsuda. A big hand with brown hairs which reached easily toward a bookshelf. There must be a secret which cannot be revealed concerning the matter of race. Everyone is human but there is an enormous chasm which cannot be filled, a high wall which cannot be climbed. There is no doubt about it. Blood. Language. Nations. Races. There undoubtedly is something which keeps one from accepting another.[17]

These two passages suggest the book's outermost reach toward universal dilemmas. But the expectations they arouse that the author will finally examine his protagonist's inner conflicts to illuminate the complexities of Japanese emotions (toward the ABCC and the A-bomb in general) are not realized. Kaji never surrenders his simple belief that *hibakusha* are "disguised guinea pigs for ABCC," an organization which adheres to its "original [by implication, military] mission" of "studying the effects of A-bombs on people accurately and scientifically."

The novel ends with a characteristically Japanese evocation of death and beauty—though the aura of the A-bomb lends uncharacteristic bitterness to the scene. As Kaji walks down the hill from the ABCC, he sees a lovely elm tree which he thinks would make a good site for a monument for a *hibakusha*-poet who recently committed suicide. His melancholy mood and the beauty of the scene are interrupted by an American going by in a "new car." All seems dark, and he experiences a montage of virtually all of the A-bomb images around which the novel has revolved:

But why this darkness, darkness which looks distorted. It seems to be carrying the shadow of death. It is a dark surface of the river. The river seems to be frightened and sobbing. The gray river which has nothing but darkness. Gazing absent-mindedly at the river, he feels himself empty. . . . He feels himself lost. . . . The city was beginning to be wrapped in an evening haze. . . . The strike. DuPont. Humanity. Nylon. The words came to the surface in a painful way which seemed to attack him and singe his nerve-endings. Guinea Pigs. America. . . . Strike. Kaji moved his hand from the trunk of the pine tree. . . . A celluloid triangle. A piece of broken glass. What an enormous illusion. I must be quite tired after all. It was simply revived pain. He had an unpleasant premonition that the pain deep down in his eye-sockets was returning. . . . There is an unbearable weight on his shoulders. Why must he feel so anxious? What is this heaviness? . . . It occurred to Kaji that he was walking down the mountain road simply from force of habit.[18]

Death, pain, and meaninglessness are, in other words, the American legacies in Hiroshima.

:

Experimental City is a curious piece of A-bomb literature, one not easy to evaluate. A version of the memoir-novel (Kajiyama told me that he came upon much of his subject matter during his A-bomb investigations), its characterizations are largely one-dimensional. Yet the psychological currents which Kajiyama so exaggeratedly depicts have existed in Hiroshima, and have undoubtedly been importantly related to strikes that have occurred at the ABCC (there was one during the summer of 1962 which for a while threatened the future of the organization). More than this the book touches upon some of the major themes of contemporary literature and upon the psychic experience of contemporary man.

The ABCC's director, for instance, combines three important images: the "devil scientist," who uses human beings as pawns (guinea pigs) in the service of experiments and discoveries which ultimately destroy man; the "quiet" or "ugly" American, whose aggressive idealism takes on a sinister dimension; and the "white imperialist" (or "neo-colonialist"), who feeds upon the work and suffering of non-white races while insisting that his superior knowledge is necessary to them in their inferior, backward state. The three images serve both to formulate ongoing history, and to give expression to characteristic contemporary anxieties over dependency and annihilation.

The faceless Nisei, the "man without qualities," epitomizes another contemporary dilemma to which the Japanese are particularly sensitive. Japanese antagonism toward Nisei is related to feelings that the latter are cultural renegades who have betrayed a mystical Japanese racial essence. The intensity of these feelings derives partly from unconscious tendencies among Japanese to be attracted to precisely this kind of "betrayal"—not necessarily specific wishes to emigrate from Japan or cease to be Japanese so much as profound urges to partake of what is felt to be the superior existential state of other races, whether Caucasian or (in a different sense) Chinese. But beyond the issue of race and of Japanese sensitivities thereto, the Nisei can also be seen as present-day protean man in his rootless extreme—a creature who can be everything and is therefore nothing, who must make his way in the world through talents for identification and manipulation.

The Americanized Japanese secretary is the prototype of the seductive, devouring woman. All cultures give form to this universal male fantasy, but here the woman in question becomes associated with the ultimate weapon of destruction. So strongly called forth by various emotional currents in our present world, the devouring woman also takes on unprecedented technological dimensions.

Similarly, the character of the journalist becomes an ultimate version of the contemporary anti-hero. Beyond the confusions of historical velocity in general, his sense of impaired connection and loss of significant relationship to life and death has to do with his being victimized by the most annihilating and dislocating of man's weapons. He ends up, as he began, confused.

Experimental City holds a special place in A-bomb literature because of its explorations of guinea pig imagery and problems of counterfeit nurturance—perhaps all the more so since Kajiyama has in recent years achieved that maximum state of A-bomb writer's adaptibility by ceasing to be an A-bomb writer at all* He has instead devoted himself to a variety of popular themes and is much sought after by the mass media.

* But before doing so, he wrote, from Tokyo, a notorious exposé, "Three Who Sell Peace," which accused a minister, a writer, and a *hibakusha* organization officer of profiting from their peace activities.[19] Most people I spoke to in Hiroshima considered the article to be an unfair attack upon the three men. It was admittedly opportunistic, as Kajiyama told me he had written it in response to an editor's request for "something different" on the A-bomb problem around the time of August 6; and we note his reversal of his earlier critical attitude toward those who made ready accusations of "selling the bomb." He also wrote an interesting radio drama about Hiroshima, which we shall discuss in Chapter XI.

5) Devil's Heritage

Devil's Heritage (*Ma no Isan*)[20] also focuses upon the ABCC, but it is much more ambitious in scope, and is in fact one of the very few fictional works to attempt a more or less comprehensive formulation of the A-bomb experience. Its author, Hiroyuki Agawa, has achieved a high literary reputation through a series of novels dealing not only with the A-bomb but with young men confronting war and death.*

He told me during an interview in Tokyo of the "great shock" he experienced upon returning to Hiroshima from military service in China seven months after the bomb ("My parents went through it, and many of my friends were killed"), and of his feeling at the time that "I should write." Similarly, he spoke of writing *Devil's Heritage* (originally published in 1953) "in order to express specific emotions I felt within myself."

Again, a writer-hero (Noguchi) sets out to investigate the Hiroshima situation, but this time he is, like his creator, a non*hibakusha* returning to his native city on an assignment Agawa himself was given: to prepare a general literary report to be entitled "Hiroshima Eight Years After the Atomic Bomb." From the moment of Noguchi's arrival the author makes clear his concern with such things as hidden residua and impaired purpose—or what we have called struggles over formulation and mastery:

> . . . the appearance of the streets, so compactly built up that it was difficult to catch sight of even the burned-out areas, reminded him of a smashed nest that busy ants, silently and without thinking, were diligently rebuilding without pause. Now, even if you walked around

---

* He wrote an earlier memoir-novel about the Atomic Bomb, *August 6* (*Hachigatsu Muika*), originally published in 1947, when he was twenty-seven years old, consisting of descriptions of the bomb by four members of a family. And his first major novel, *Spring Castle* (*Haru no Shiro*), includes atomic bomb scenes and reactions, but is mainly a part-autobiographical exploration of the struggles of a student-intellectual-turned-naval officer with issues of love and death. A later novel, *Monument in the Clouds* (*Kumo no Bohyō*), published in 1956, leaves the bomb as a subject altogether, and is made up of a series of diary entries of young men "volunteering" to become kamikaze pilots which convey a combination of dedication and disillusionment, a sense of tragic loss of young lives and "sad beauty" in these deaths. Agawa's literary standing is based more upon the latter two novels than upon *Devil's Heritage*, as they are generally considered to be of greater imaginative scope.[21]

Hiroshima with a Geiger counter in hand, the radioactivity left by the atomic bomb was entirely gone and probably the counter would no longer sound its warning click, but for himself when he went about in this rebuilt ant's nest, how would the counter inside his head really react?[22]

His psychic Geiger counter gives him grim answers to his question, right in the home where he is staying. Tsuneko, his young aunt, having lost two children in the bomb and experienced radiation symptoms, still has sudden dizzy spells in which her face becomes swollen and discolored "like an exceedingly pale ghost's." And her eight-year-old son, Ken, exposed to the bomb as a baby, develops an abscess near the anus which fails to heal and turns out to be caused by leukemia. A series of painful hospital scenes depict the sufferings of the helpless child and the futile efforts of Noguchi and the boy's father to hide the truth from Tsuneko.

Noguchi's impressions of ABCC remind us very much of Kaji's in *Experimental City*—so much so that one wonders whether the latter book, appearing one year after *Devil's Heritage*, might not have been strongly influenced by it, or whether both books emerged from some common body of literary and other materials.* In addition to themes of Nisei cultural betrayal and of callous American scientism and racism, there is a grotesque accusation (on the part of a *hibakusha* suffering from leukemia) which may be viewed as the ultimate form of guinea pig imagery:

> . . . the ABCC not only doesn't treat people but feels that for the purposes of its own research it is best to keep people just as they are because after they're healed the work can't be continued.[23]

There are moderating voices too, as the author explores a variety of attitudes. But even a sympathetically portrayed doctor-friend of Noguchi's stingingly denounces the use of the American automobile as a guinea pig lure ("They say that after the war in Europe you could buy a woman for a pair of stockings. Over here things were even cheaper. For a gallon of gasoline you could get about twenty human guinea pigs"), and goes on to say that politeness on the part of the ABCC "somehow . . . makes me feel like swearing." Noguchi himself concludes

---

* Agawa acknowledges two literary sources of some of the scenes in *Devil's Heritage*: the original Japanese version of Hachiya's *Hiroshima Diary*, and Y. Hayashi's *Ichiro* (a boy's name given to a first son, in this case the author's son who died of leukemia).

that, "as far as I can see, this ABCC is skillfully collecting data from the Japanese in order to establish a scientific defensive policy in the event that America undergoes an atomic bomb attack in World War III." Whatever this American group provides, in other words, is deceptive and counterfeit.

Beyond the ABCC itself, the author suggests the counterfeit nature of Hiroshima's general rebirth. Noguchi feels "a strong resistance or even an aversion" to making "the so-called 'pilgrimage to the famous places of the atomic bomb.'" He is "upset" by seeing "carefree, young American soldiers, cameras dangling from their necks," and Japanese officials, "perhaps on business trips, perhaps newly arrived at their posts, pulling up in front of some famous spot in shiny official Buicks," and cannot take seriously the "excuse" that all this "was for the sake of world peace." He is offended by the sign "Atomic Bomb Pinball," on which there was "a bad sketch of the atomic cloud boiling upward"; by the Peace Bridge, which seemed "modernistic," "extremely odd," unrelated to people crossing it on bicycles or in "three-wheeled trucks loaded with radishes," and reminded him of "a collar-bone"; and by another nearby monument, the Western Peace Bridge, more like a "rib-cage." Most of all, he resented the inscription—"Rest in peace/For the mistake shall not be repeated"—on the "saddle-shaped" monument to the A-bomb dead:

> Far from being calm and quiet, as they were apparently intended to be, they seemed to him to be utterly grotesque phrases. Who, in God's name, had made the mistake? Who would not repeat the mistake? This, with the Peace Bridges, would probably go down in history as something that the people of Hiroshima had selected to commemorate the atomic bomb. Inside his head the story that the people of Hiroshima had been extremely cooperative with the ABCC dully repeated itself.[24]

He finds the ubiquitous desecration to be "forbidding and uncanny," as if implying that the living will meet with punishment for these insults to the dead. And he equates the hated inscription with hibakusha cooperation with the ABCC because both denote "grotesque" sub-servience to America as part of the larger counterfeit pattern.

THE AUTHENTIC HIROSHIMA

Authenticity can seemingly be found only in death and suffering, and Noguchi encounters numerous individuals and families enmeshed in leukemic or other forms of doom. But he obtains particularly detailed documentation of this "authentic Hiroshima" from members of the Willow Society, a small group of *hibakusha* who had originally been hospitalized together shortly after the bomb. Although the group took its name from a Chinese poem describing how "a foreign willow will put forth new shoots," its members think of themselves more in terms of a name that had been considered but found "a little extreme": Monsters Club. For most of its members are visibly deformed. one with an "ugly keloid stretching from his left wrist to his upper arm," and with three of his fingers "drawn back into a stiff unnatural position"; another with "hands swelled all out of shape"; and a third, the "Veil Lady," so called because of "a lot of indelible blue spots on her face." Noguchi is invited to join the group in one of its social excursions, a boat trip to a restaurant on the sea. Once more the sensual beauty of the ship's motion against the background of Hiroshima's magnificent waterways becomes the setting for grim details of atomic bomb exposure, as members of the group recount their individual stories for Noguchi's benefit. These tales, often told with savage humor, stress the totality of confusion, of psychological and moral disintegration accompanying that of bodies. In connection with economic recovery, for instance, we hear how "one of the most prominent and wealthy men in Hiroshima" got his start stealing valuable objects from corpses:

> He was pretty badly injured himself, but they say he went around stripping the watches off the dead and dying. They also say that he cut the fingers off the dead to steal their rings. By contrast were the quiet little people who went around sifting through the ashes for metal objects in order to obtain some pocket money. This was called "working in the city mines."[25]

The clear implication is that psychic disintegration has not been eliminated, only covered over.

Members of the Willow Society also render more general opinions about America's atomic bombings. Use of the weapon in Nagasaki is denounced as "completely superfluous mass murder," and the necessity of its use in Hiroshima is also questioned: "If they wanted to show their power, they could have dropped it over the sea or in the mountains." Without specifically embracing any of these positions, the author strongly suggests a general tone of residual bitterness. There is, however, one searching speculation which warns against Japanese self-righteousness:

I wonder if Japan really would have refrained from using the bomb if we had perfected it before America did. We all condemn America for dropping the atomic bomb, but if Japan had used it against America first and if thousands of American civilians had been killed, I wonder if we wouldn't have shouted, "Banzai! Banzai!" and held our victory parades. When I think that, then I don't feel resentful toward America, even though my face is like this now. . . .

But it meets with an ingenious rejoinder which insists upon American guilt:

Well, now . . . you wouldn't say that all murderers should be pardoned even though you might conceivably commit a murder yourself under certain conditions, would you?[26]

And there is a pointed contrast made between America's insistence upon war crimes trials for Japanese leaders and upon Japanese perfidy at Pearl Harbor and Bataan on the one hand, and its willingness to "dispose of" its own use of the atomic bomb as a means of "shorten[ing] the war and . . . save[ing] the lives of many . . . young people" on the other.

Members of the Willow Society do mention individual Americans whose actions have impressed and moved them: the Army colonel, whose tears upon first viewing hospitalized A-bomb patients were followed by generous shipments of desperately needed beds, food, and penicillin; and the Quaker humanitarian who, appalled by his country's action in dropping the bomb, came to Hiroshima to build houses for the dispossessed with his own hands. But, inevitably, there is the return to the "resentment deep down in the hearts [of *hibakusha*] toward that terrible thing," and rejection of the claim that no such grudge exists as having been made "by somebody trying to get on the good side of the Americans."

Perhaps the closest to a sustained universalistic formulation occurs in an interesting sequence on the problem of devouring and being devoured. Noguchi finally sits down with the group to a succulent lunch of red snapper, and as he dips the flesh of the fish, "almost too fresh," into the soy sauce and notes "how really delicious" it is he begins to wonder "how this might appear from the standpoint of the red snapper." He is aghast at

the people sitting there, calmly eating the red snapper that had been so cold-bloodedly killed, and praising its flavor with the same mouths that a little earlier had been arguing the cruelty of the atomic bomb.[27]

He begins to indulge in a fantasy (much like that of the Czech writer Karel Čapek in his book *At War With the Newts*) in which snappers, "victims of Japanese cruelty for so many generation," rise and take their revenge. They master man's speech as well as his weapons and march as an army—"like the warriors in the old romance, the *Tale[s] of the Heike*"—to make war on "the world of men." But despite his being so struck by the hypocrisy of the members of his luncheon party who victimize the red snappers "with such relish" despite being "victims of human cruelty themselves," he is not above doing the same:

> When he saw the head of the big red snapper, its teeth bared, floating in his soup bowl, his appetite was aroused by its big, sleepy eyes in spite of the idle fancies that had just passed through his head.

Man is, in other words, a devourer, not only alive to the sweet taste of his victim, but spurred on—"aroused"—by that victim's very helplessness.

As the fantasy proceeds it becomes associated with racial thoughts—still on a more or less universalistic plane, but no less malignant for that. Since principles of peace and benevolence apply "only to the affairs of men" (and not to snappers), Noguchi wonders whether they apply "only . . . to certain races or peoples." He recalls that until about a century ago Western European racial groups considered such principles applicable only to themselves, and now asks whether these same groups still regarded Japanese, Chinese, Indians, and Negroes as "not much different from pigs and crabs and whales." As he goes on to think about American hypocrisy concerning "human rights," the popularity of "Indian chases" in Western movies, and more generally the "feeling that allowed men to eat beef, pork, and fish without a doubt in the world," he cannot refrain from raising the ultimate racial question:

> It might be an eternal and unsolved riddle, but he wondered whether or not the fact that the Japanese were a colored people was an element in the decision to use the atomic bomb against Japan.

He ends by reasserting the vegetarian principle, prominent throughout his ruminations, that man should refrain from devouring "all living things":

If ever peace were to be realized on the earth—still idle fantasies were going through his head—then it wouldn't merely be a question of men not killing or persecuting those of another race, but it would be because the lives of all living things would be respected and a way would have been discovered to maintain life by eating and drinking only milk and fruit, things that nature had produced as natural foods.

We need not dwell upon the general issues raised in this sequence about the relationship of death anxiety and psychic numbing to victimization, as well as to sadism, aggression, and violence; or about the embrace of vegetarianism as a means of coping with these emotions. What most concerns us is the strong suggestion that *man's deepest inner conflicts— those related to primal emotions about annihilating and being annihilated—become readily attached to the issue of race, particularly in response to a death-saturated event like the atomic bomb.**

:

During the course of the book we become increasingly aware of Noguchi's emotional discomfort and wish to return to Tokyo, until "This desire to leave Hiroshima was felt as a natural physiological craving." For his own survivor-like conflicts—his death anxiety and guilt—begin to overwhelm him:

> . . . an unpleasant, depressed feeling, like that after one has seen a gloomy, completely unrelieved movie, weighed heavily on his heart and would not leave him . . . he felt that if he remained long in Hiroshima his marrow and hair follicles also would be affected by the radioactivity remaining in the earth. . . . So he was seriously aware of this somewhat neurotic fear from time to time.[28]

I have occasionally observed this "somewhat neurotic fear" in Japanese and American non*hibakusha* who have involved themselves strongly with Hiroshima and its atomic bomb problems. It represents a particularly anguished form of identification with atomic bomb victimization, a guilt-laden inability to remain an "outsider" and a need to live and feel *as if* one were a *hibakusha* and were susceptible to all *hibakusha* consequences, including radiation effects. Guilt is further fed by the

---

* I am not here passing judgment upon how much the racial issue entered into the actual use of the bomb, but rather suggesting that with any large holocaust primal emotions of both victims and victimizers can attach themselves to the *idea* of race.

opposite desire (which we also observe in Noguchi) to flee forever from all atomic bomb concerns, and to derive satisfaction from the contrast between *hibakusha* misery and one's own good fortune.

So intense is Noguchi's urge to leave that he refuses his grief-stricken aunt's request to remain to attend the memorial service for her little boy who has just died from leukemia in psychotic agony. He feels the need to visit Kyoto on the way back to Tokyo in order to "refresh his spirit" by wandering through old gardens and temples there, or in other words to reawaken his sense of continuing life in both nature and human culture. The book ends with his feeling of "calm composure" as the train pulls away from the station and he becomes aware of having separated himself from the self-enclosed atomic bomb milieu and re-entered the "outside world":

> The soft, pale-pink interior of the special express already seemed like another world, far from Hiroshima.[29]

In *Devil's Heritage*, a memoir-novel, Agawa makes use of the American presence and the attitudes around it to record a wide variety of A-bomb formulations—some enduring, some ephemeral—which have existed in Hiroshima over the years. But we are left with the impression that the imaginative powers of a talented writer have been blunted by a need to bear literal witness to all aspects of the cataclysm. As rich as the novel is in psychic elements of rage, guilt, and tortured identification, these are not transmuted into the artist's realm of "illusion" or "virtual" (psychic) truth achieved in some of his other works. The book thus falls far short of the sense of mastery conveyed either by genuinely realized fiction or wisely interpretive non-fiction. It therefore readily lends itself to the charges of imbalance it has in fact received from both Japanese and American readers, while at the same time remaining a valuable A-bomb document.

:

Significantly, Agawa himself came to have some understanding of the impulsive quality of his novel. He told me during our interview that after writing it, he spent some time in America, and "when I read it over upon returning, I regretted some of the feelings expressed in it." His regret seemed to embrace not only a more sympathetic view of Americans, but a certain disenchantment with the genre of A-bomb literature:

I really question whether there can exist such a thing as A-bomb literature. I myself spoke from experience. . . . I wrote . . . because I felt strongly I had to write about it. . . . I don't want to write about it any more—unless the world uses these weapons again . . . or if I have specific emotions . . . and I feel that the Hiroshima A-bomb begins to have special meaning for me. . . . People have different missions in life—and perhaps I am lazy.

He wishes to break away from A-bomb writing, both because it is associated with anxiety and because he cannot envision it as lending itself to genuine creative transformation. But he remains ambivalent: like Miss Ōta, he is unable to state his position without raising the possibility of its being due to a personal shortcoming. Similarly, when he discussed the issue of living in Tokyo or Hiroshima, one could not question his stress upon the writer's difficulty in working outside of the capital, or his contention that "if one stays in the country, one remains a 'country gentleman' and cannot get a proper sense of present-day Japan." But as he said these things I could not help thinking of Noguchi sinking contentedly into the plush interior of the express train taking him from the A-bombed city and feeling himself in "another world, far from Hiroshima."

6) *Underground Themes*

Kin Kokubo, another non*hibakusha* writer (whom we already know as "the young Hiroshima-born writer"), differs from the other two in three important ways: he is younger (thirty-two in 1962) and indeed seems a representative of a "new generation," he has remained in Hiroshima, and he has been less exclusively concerned with protest and more with complexity and contradiction. He was indeed the first A-bomb writer I had come across who seemed willing to explore less attractive aspects of *hibakusha* psychology in quest of that elusive goal of artistic truth. An unusually responsive young man with a mobile face, he quickly challenged my motives and methods, and then, following my brief explanation, proceeded to identify himself with them:

> I am interested in something very similar to you—in the differences between those who went through this historical experience and those who did not.

We recall his quest for genuine dialogue about the bomb, as well as his self-scrutiny in admitting that upon returning to Hiroshima twenty-five days after the bomb at the age of fifteen, he was not only amazed at the destruction but also experienced a shock of beauty and the by no means unpleasant sense that "What man has added to nature now has been destroyed." And his later observations on such things as "a kind of toughness" derived from extreme experience, the "unfortunate psychological climate" of *hibakusha* demands, and the "unmentionable" wish of some of them that the entire world be blown up—all these were further evidence of his impulse toward truth, however complex and unpalatable that truth might be. The same impulse had been increasingly apparent in his writings. An early story, "The Midwife" (Sanba),[30] published in 1950, dealt with the theme, already used by a number of Hiroshima writers, of a heroic, severely injured midwife helping a woman give birth in the midst of A-bomb disintegration. But a second story, "Fire Dance" (Hi no Odori), published ten years later,[31] suggests his progress toward paradox.

The *hibakusha*-hero of "Fire Dance" (referred to simply as "He") is neither pure in heart nor particularly pitiable, but primarily a man in conflict. The story begins (something in the fashion of Camus' *The Stranger*) with his seeing a woman killed right in front of him by a truck, and remaining unaffected ("A person died but he felt no agitation"). Kokubo's hero, like Camus', has led a life devoid of feeling —in his case a form of psychic numbing related to all that he went through in the A-bomb, including the death of his mother. His total inability to formulate his experience leads him to feel that "something seems to be lacking . . . the world seems empty." He fights off death anxiety on several levels: in the sense that "he cannot feel sure of his existence"; and in his refusal to seek medical care despite feeling frequently ill, because "if [his suspicion of A-bomb disease] should become a reality, he would surely die, and if not, he would not die for some time." He is caught between this empty form of psychological non-resistance and an equally uncomfortable impulse toward carrying out the mission of retaliation contained in the words of a little boy he encountered at the time of the A-bomb who, before dying, urged him to "take revenge, take revenge." He also reveals, in a childhood memory, a fiercely critical view of what he considered to be a fundamental form of hypocrisy on the part of older-generation survivors—and here the author begins to demonstrate his proclivity for underground themes:

> Are not the adults who now moan over the dead, so ready to show their tears, the very people who so actively supported the war? Is not the purpose of war to kill one another? Having started the war themselves, why do they grieve? . . . Are they simply finding special pleasure in holding a requiem for the dead?[32]

But mostly the hero is preoccupied with his sense of himself as "a person who is dying." This makes him feel unworthy of his girlfriend Eiko's love:

> Who loves a person who is dying? A person about to die is in no way a proper object of love. Love is a possession of living people.[33]

Behaving (in *hibakusha* fashion) as if dead, troubled by physical fatigue, his sexual relationship with her unsatisfactory, he deeply resents her contrasting vitality:

> Her legs and arms are surprisingly plump. She puts her hot, smooth arms around his neck. A cry full of hate begins to well up in him. Damn your white skin, warm body, plump flesh! Damn your eyes,

heart, hands, and feet! How much will you see with those eyes? How much will you feel with your heart? How much will you grasp with those hands? How far will you walk with those feet?[34]

His diffuse impotence and rage lead him not only to emit the *hibakusha's* cry of ultimate retaliation—"I wish atomic bombs would fall all over the world"—but to imagine this cry reverberating throughout the city in underground whispers:

Bathed in the light of the setting sun . . . the city of Hiroshima now lies in long shadows . . . houses . . . people . . . cars. . . . To him it seems that these words are being whispered, from one person to another, secretly, in every corner of the city. "I wish atomic bombs would fall all over the world."[35]

And he remembers hearing the same cry from a girl, disfigured with keloids and close to death, to friends gathered around her:

I will die in the near future. But you people will . . . continue to live. Your faces hang over me like apostles of peace. I don't like them. I don't like them. Let atomic bombs fall all over the world and let everybody become like me. You are all people who have nothing to do with me, outsiders, strangers. . . . Everything that is happening takes place in a world far, far away from me. Only I, who am dying, only this "I" exists here now.[36]

The underground cry becomes associated with an absolute focus upon the self. From this focus the survivor who feels himself dead or dying requires of others that they share his experience and become like him if they are to cease being "strangers" and be accepted by him. Indeed, there is the implication that *the survivor's imagination of others' deaths is his only relief from his own death anxiety.*

In addition to this remarkable exploration of unmentionable themes, the novella addresses itself to the larger "death" of Hiroshima itself—to survivors' sense of losing their history. The hero tells us how "The true Hiroshima died on that day," how it has been "invaded" and "occupied" by "people of other countries" (meaning primarily other parts of Japan), all of which can be understood by means of an ancient historical parallel:

Babylonia was destroyed by Assyria [when] she no longer possessed the strength to overthrow the dynasty that conquered her or to re-establish her own nation. The remnants are, day by day, dying, and Assyria's rule is perfect.[37]

His point is that the claimed rebirth is really total replacement. He goes on to denounce the alien influence increasingly dominating every aspect of the life of the city—from the original confirmation by outsiders that an atomic bomb had fallen on Hiroshima, to later commemorative activities and peace movements, and even in the rendering of the city's name. He then arrives at a terrible vision of historical extinction:

> We were pressed under by alien merchants, alien officials, alien scholars, alien cultures, and alien isms which enveloped us. . . . The original people of Hiroshima, whose numbers are few, are resisting quietly. But what obscure resistance. . . . Is it not the same as that of a dead dog, which I saw some time ago, which was trying to discover who it was by growing completely rotten in the bright sunshine? Someone even this . . . resistance will completely disappear. Motomachi [an area near the hypocenter] will become a nice residential area and the caves in Hijiyama [an area a bit removed from the hypocenter to which many people fled] will be filled up. The site of the castle will become a lovely park. And those who actually experienced that day will be stricken by leukemia and will die one after the other. The original Hiroshima people will become extinct like the Cro-Magnon man. And as a memorial to extinction, that disgraceful [A-Bomb] Dome, which looks like a penis, will be preserved forever. Years ago a thing called an atomic bomb fell on the city, I hear. That's what I hear, too. They say it was very fearful. So I heard. Walking along the green belts by the rivers, they will talk in voices like musical instruments. Their language will no longer be the Hiroshima dialect but will be an unknown tongue. . . .[38]

We are reminded here of Miss Ōta's plea for "the old Hiroshima" and her view of the new one as "a national colony." But Kokubo's imagery of extinction goes further in suggesting an absolute severance of the bonds of human connection and continuity.

The story then ends melodramatically, but its resolution suggests important questions about potential avenues for renewed human continuity. We are told that the hero, during his student days, had been profoundly interested in *hibakusha* problems and had envisioned a vast peace movement that would "tie in the many thoughts of . . . poor survivors to some great system," and help make Hiroshima into a "Mecca for peace and for all that is honest and sincere in humankind."

The implication is that he betrayed these youthful ideals and took the path of least resistance by becoming a "salaried man" in a company— the ambivalent postwar Japanese symbol of all that is safe, comfortable, rote, uninspired, materially desirable, and spiritually impoverished. An ordinary worker in the same company, Nomura, tries to prod him from his lethargy, and tells him to "stand up firmly" on behalf of the leftist labor movement and become "angry as fire." When refused, Nomura denounces his friend's despairing ideas about A-bombs falling all over as "death thoughts . . . a will to destruction," and tells him angrily: "It would be a good thing for a man like you to die just as quickly as possible." Only after the hero learns that not he but his girlfriend, Eiko, is dying of leukemia (she had become pregnant, and the discovery of her illness was made at the time she sought an abortion) does he emerge from his despair and belatedly take on an angry survivor's mission: active participation in the labor union's strike, including breaking the company rules by distributing leaflets. Of particular significance for us is the relationship between his spiritual recovery and his regained sense of immortality:

The thought of life after death is clearly false, but the thought that death is the end of everything is also false, he thought. He opened the package and took out piles of leaflets. When I die, I will dissolve into many kinds of elements, and these elements will be absorbed into the great earth. After a certain period of time these elements will again become something. Perhaps trees, stones, rats, men . . . [which] will again contribute to some scene. He waves a pile of leaflets over his head. . . . He throws [from the roof upon which he is standing] out the leaflets . . . [they] spread out and float down to the ground. In the windless heat of high noon, these leaflets dance up and down. . . . As many billions of people have done in the past, and as many will do in the future, so too will I. . . . When the leaflets had almost reached the ground, the people were beginning to stretch out their arms and cry out for them, he heard the sound of footsteps violently approaching him. Both of his hands were cruelly twisted and the scene [before him] lurched sideways [as he was pulled to the ground].[39]

His affirmation lies in rendering both death and life meaningful. His actions re-establish human and natural connection beyond biological death. We suspect that the story's title, "Fire Dance," refers not only to the "dancing leaflets," but to the ecstatic sense of renewed life and mastery associated with them, as well as to the original holocaust. The story makes contact with struggles for self-definition amidst absurdity and nihilism which are endemic to the postwar young, in Japan and elsewhere. Most of all it takes the risk of exploring emotions *hibakusha* are not supposed to feel, and relates these to struggles with death symbolism universal to our nuclear world. But its melodramatic short-cuts suggest once more the writer's difficulty in finding convincing literary approaches to the atomic bomb.

:

Kokubo himself was keenly aware of this difficulty, as he told me of his continuing creative struggles:

> None of my work goes deep enough. I have been thinking about these problems continuously for a long time—and my thought often wavers, first this way, then that way. Sometimes I don't know exactly where I am going. At the beginning I tried to give an objective presentation of misery. Then I realized that I couldn't just dwell on the past, but had to connect the past with the future. Then, as a means of dealing with the future, I became interested in communism, and began to use the techniques of proletarian literature—though I was also writing about the tragedy of circumstances. And then I realized that social situations were not everything, and that we must consider what goes on in individual human lives. . . .

He was unusual in speaking of the atomic bomb as "a kind of springboard for my writing." He referred here not only to the two stories he had written about the bomb, but to its influence upon his twenty or so additional stories. We are reminded of his earlier image of the metaphorical radiation from the bomb as a "vital force I emit as I go along." And although he is clearly ambivalent about this force—he said earlier it did *not* apply to his writing—he returns to the image in discussing the overall atomic bomb environment as a reservoir of strength and relevance:

> The A-bomb is completely modern, up to date. So to be modern, you don't have to go to New York or Tokyo, but you can simply stay right here. . . . Though perhaps one could not tell this from my writing, I feel that the fact that I am in Hiroshima does contribute to this vital force. If I go to Tokyo, people ask, "What is the situation in Hiroshima?" When I am asked this way, the result of the question is bound to be insincere. But if they leave me alone and I am back in Hiroshima, I feel this force build up in myself.

But he was nonetheless deeply immersed in the classic conflicts of the A-bomb writer—conflicts fed by critical voices from among the living:

> When we publish magazines in Hiroshima, people from Tokyo and other places critize us whether we write about the A-bomb or not. If we write about the A-bomb, they say, "You write about nothing but the A-bomb"; and if we don't, they say, "You neglect the A-bomb." This sort of thing is very harmful to young writers like myself. Suppose someone lived near Auschwitz and had seen the slaughter there. You wouldn't necessarily ask them to write about it. In the same way, even though we live in Hiroshima, it is not just *our* obligation to write about it—*everyone* should write about it.

And from the dead:

> If you write about the A-bomb without serious reflection, it is an insult to its victims.

Both make contact with his own inner voices, reflecting struggles around identification and guilt: voices which sometimes insist that he *must* create from the atomic bomb and sometimes that he has no right to do so; which sometimes suggest that the death-saturated Hiroshima environment confers special power upon him and sometimes that it inflicts him with a debilitating curse. Among non*hibakusha* writers I found him to be most closely identified with the survivor experience and most strongly committed to A-bomb writing. His intensity of involvement both strengthened his vision and accentuated his difficulties. In his talent for probing the psychological "underground," there is at least the promise of artistic transformation.

7) A-Bomb Poets

The closely related genre of A-bomb poetry has faced similar problems, but as an essentially condensed medium is even less suitable to literal re-enactment. A leading Hiroshima anthologist told me of two general stages A-bomb poetry has been through: there was first a "poetry of curse" during the early post-bomb years which emphasized details of suffering and denounced those thought responsible. (Some of the most unembellished examples of this category were poems written by children, such as one entitled "Bad America" ["Warui Amerika yo"] and another, "Why Was It Dropped on Hiroshima?" ["Naze Hiroshima ni Otosunda?"].)[40] There followed a "poetry of calm anger," in which the emphasis shifted "from Hiroshima itself to the entire world," and from the evil of those responsible to "the essential wickedness of human nature."

Although all of the poetry we shall examine will by no means confine itself to these two categories, the anthologist's stress upon a common factor of resentment suggests that even gentle poems may have their origins in such anger, which becomes muted and transmuted by the poet's art. And indeed, at one point he compared early poetic emotions to "the curse of Job in the Old Testament," and predicted that "poets will emerge from Hiroshima like prophets"—thereby suggesting that emotional power and wisdom are contained in their anger. Influenced here by his general readings in Western thought, he was making a plea for the universal task of the poet-artist as seer and spiritual guide. In this vein he took the stand that poetry "must be first a literary work," that "there is no specific entity of A-bomb poetry," but that "as long as the human spirit can express criticism or resistance toward the reality that surrounds that spirit . . . A-bomb poetry must be possible." We begin to recognize the same ambivalence about the existence of the genre that we found in relationship to A-bomb literature in general. But although poets face many of these same pitfalls as writers of prose in transforming their A-bomb experience into their creative medium, it is probably fair to say that they have been less incapacitated by them. One must add, however, that the examples we shall examine probably suffer even more in translation than do excerpts from stories and novels.

POET-HERO

The most celebrated A-bomb poet—and in fact the only Hiroshima writer to become a popular hero—was Sankichi Tōge, a *hibakusha* who died in 1953 at the age of thirty-six. The epitome of the poet of protest, his poem "Give Back My Father" (which we quoted from earlier) has become a rallying cry for peace movements throughout Japan:

> Give back my father, give back my mother,
> Give grandpa back, grandma back,
> Give our sons and daughters back!
> Give me back myself, give mankind back,
> Give each back to each other!
>
> So long as this life lasts,
> Give peace back to us,
> Peace that will never end!

The plea is not only for the return of the dead but for the restoration of pre-A-bomb human connection—or failing these, for a world sufficiently peaceful to permit survivors a purposeful formulation of A-bomb sacrifices.

An earlier poem, "August Sixth," is less gentle in its protest, depicting in unsparing detail the force of survivor memories—as a few excerpts reveal:

> How could I ever forget that flash of light!
> In an instant thirty thousand people disappeared from the streets;
> The cries of fifty thousand more
> Crushed beneath the darkness.
>
> Yellow whirling smoke became light,
> Buildings split, bridges collapsed;
> Crowded trams burned just as they were—
> Endless trash and heaps of embers,
> Hiroshima.
>
> Then, skin hanging like rags,
> Hands on breasts;
> Treading upon shattered human brains. . . .
> Crowds piled on the river bank, and on rafts fastened to the shore,
> Turned gradually into corpses under the scorching sun. . . .
>
> The conflagration shifts . . .
> Onto heaps of schoolgirls lying like refuse
> So that God alone knew who they were. . . .

How could I forget that quiet
Which descended over a city of three hundred thousand?
The calm
How could I forget those pleas
Of a dying wife and child
Emitted through the whiteness of their eyes,
Piercing our minds and souls!

A third poem, "Morning," is considered by many to be Tōge's master-piece. It contains the blend of fierce protest and romantic vision of social deliverance that characterized much of his life.

They dream:
A workman dreams, lowering his pickax, his sweat turned into scars
by the flash.
A wife dreams, bending over her sewing machine, midst the diseased
odor of her parted skin.
A box-office girl dreams, her hidden scars like crab's claws, on both
arms.
A match-seller dreams, with pieces of shattered glass sticking in his
neck.

They dream:
That through an element made from pitchblende and carnotite
By means of an endless chain of energy,
Famished deserts are changed into fertile fields;
Bright canals run round the base of crumbling mountains,
Under artificial suns, in the wastelands of the Arctic.
Cities and towns are built of pure gold.

They dream:
That festival flags wave in the shade of trees where working people
take their rest, and legends of Hiroshima are told by tender lips.

They dream:
That those swine in man's shape
Who do not know how to use the power from the earth's center ex-
cept for slaughter
Survive only in illustrated books for the little ones.
That the energy of ten million horsepower per gram, one thousand
times as strong as high explosive,
Be delivered, out of the atom into the hands of the people.
That the rich harvest of science
Be conveyed, in peace, to the people
Like bunches of succulent grapes

Wet with dew
Gathered in
At dawn.

To these polar images of nuclear power—images of noble possibility
and destructive evil—Tōge brings a lyric imagination which transforms
literal detail into "virtual experience": into the "formulated feeling" (in
Susanne Langer's phrase) that moves beyond the historical event into
the realm of art.[41] One has the impression that this transformation is at
times inhibited by the demands of the A-bomb for "sacred historical
truth" and by the idiom of "socialist realism" Tōge tends to employ.
But even when emitting an ideological rallying-cry—as in the following
poem describing police suppression of leftist demonstrations in 1950—
he manages to convey the reader beyond immediate events into larger
psychic dimensions:

They drive at us,
From here,
From there,
Pistol on hip,
The police drive at us:
August the sixth, nineteen fifty

At the Deadmen's Tower on the bald-burned spot
The outflood of the citizens,
The flowers which they brought
Torn headless in the milling whirlpool,
When those with sweat-stained chinstraps
Let fly into the crowd. . . .

Let the doves fly high,
Let the peace bell ring
And the mayor's peace messages
Twisted in the wind,
The feast of freedom,
Blown to naught
Like fireworks. . . .[42]

A poet of the streets and militant spokesman for the young and
disaffected, Tōge's work could be viewed as a Hiroshima version of the
lyrical-revolutionary tradition of Mayakovsky and Yevtushenko. A combination of poetic talent and personal charisma, together with his early
death, have made him into a legendary figure and an A-bomb martyr.

We must concern ourselves with the impact of his life as such, beyond that of his verses alone.

We are told that his childhood was "very happy" until the age of ten when his mother died; that two older brothers were persecuted because of participation in the labor movement of the 1920s and early 1930s; that Tōge himself, shortly after finishing high school and beginning work, was discovered to have tuberculosis (which was to make him a partial invalid for the rest of his life and eventually result in his death); and that because of his personal suffering, he was drawn to Christianity and was baptized in 1943 at the age of twenty-six. Beginning from the time of his encounter with the atomic bomb, interpretations of his life take on a canonizing tone. Exposed at three thousand meters and receiving relatively minor wounds, it is said that by "persisting in efforts to help relatives and friends," he exposed himself to secondary radiation and had to be hospitalized for severe early symptoms of A-bomb disease; and that the combination of this immediate death immersion, and its later consequences, resulted in a survivor mission of heroic dimensions:

> But the atomic bomb gave a positive direction to the life of Sankichi. After the experience, he suffered physically from the recurrence of tuberculosis, and every two years would vomit great amounts of blood. Yet the soul of Sankichi, confronted with death, threw itself fervently into the movement to stop atomic bombs.[43]

The account goes on to tell of the diverse flow of his interests—from his protest poems to the various leftist and literary and cultural movements he formed, to his love for classical music, flowers, and books. (He was said to have opened not only the first postwar book shop in Hiroshima, later to become an important literary and political gathering place, but also its first flower shop.) All this took place in association with a grim struggle with tuberculosis, lengthy stays in a sanitorium, and the ominous physical and psychic effects of recurrent massive hemorrhage.

The veneration he received from young laborers and political activists is spoken of as having sustained his life: in a literal physical sense, through their constant donating of blood he needed for transfusions; and in a psychological sense, through the fervent, often tearful, response to his poetry which once caused him to write in his diary: "It was a good thing for me to have lived until today." By the same token, suggestions of war are said to have worked against his survival: with the outbreak of the Korean conflict, and the "noise of the cannons and machine guns from the American Army practice grounds" which he could hear from his sanitorium bed, he experienced great "spiritual oppression," so that "As a result of the poet's deep agony, he vomited large amounts of blood."

He is recalled as a warm and loyal man, his marriage as one (especially rare in Japan) of enduring love, and as having held strongly to the principle of "the fundamental freedom of human beings."* He eventually joined the Communist Party, but with some reluctance (as his diary also reveals) because of his concern for individual expression. Significantly, he took the step after a bout of hemorrhage. What he wrote at the time—"This culture movement is the most important goal of my life. Why should the life of an individual be so important?"— suggested that his decision might have been related to a desperate attempt to keep alive, at least symbolically, through this larger connection.

But he had difficulty stifling his broadly humanistic impulses in the service of Party demands, for which he came under considerable organizational criticism. He had better success in working creatively with various groups, and inaugurated a program of "Poems in Life" through which ordinary people could express themselves—especially their A-bomb experiences—in more or less poetic style. But he constantly turned back to his own poetry, to render emotions of parents and children as well as bitter ones of protest. And he expressed in his diary the wish "to live and die as a poet."

The canonizing imagery again emerges strongly in relationship to the end of his life: of herculean activity in editing books about the bomb, continuing work on his own poems and essays, helpful collaboration in the making of the film *Hiroshima*, active participation in peace conferences—all "like a runner nearing the final goal"; of his decision to undergo major surgery for his tuberculosis because "although he was aware of the danger to his life" presented by this surgery, he preferred the risk to the chronic state of illness which prevented him from "fulfilling his duty to the people of the nation"; and finally, of the actual scene of his death—ordinarily detached medical professionals weeping

* More than ten years after his own death Tōge's wife committed suicide. She was said to have been distraught over many things, including fear of A-bomb aftereffects, and the destruction by vandals of a monument to her husband. Whatever the additional personal reasons for her act, it inevitably became part of Tōge's own tragic life-legend.

and taking extraordinary measures on his behalf, so that "when there was no more to be done, the nurses broke the rule of the sanitorium and transfused their own blood into Sankichi. But his eyes were staring at the ceiling."

Taking canonizing needs into account, there is little doubt that Tōge possessed a remarkable capacity to combine moving poetic protest with an emanation of personal purity. He gave others the unusual feeling that both he and they were ennobled by this protest. Whatever his inner conflicts concerning death guilt, he managed to go further than virtually any other poet or novelist in suggesting the outlines of a formulation which included both an examination of the dehumanizing force of the A-bomb, and a general vision of individual and social transformation. The image of A-bomb martyrdom emanating from his suffering and his struggles (with tuberculosis as well as A-bomb exposure) could make contact with the general romantic image of the poet who lives intensely and dies young. While both his politics and his poetry can and have been criticized, the way in which he wrote, lived, and died contributed greatly to others' ability to cope with and rebound from their A-bomb death encounter.

"MY EYES AND THEIR EYES"

Eisaku Yoneda, whom we have previously spoken of as the elderly *hibakusha*-poet, was, at the time I conducted the study, considered by many to be Hiroshima's outstanding A-bomb poet. A forceful, graying man in his sixties, he wrote and spoke—in contrast to Tōge—with a tone of elegy. He told me how his feelings of "sorrow and indignation" at the death of his wife and children were "somehow absorbed by the beauty of nature"—and expressed similar sentiments in his poem "Standing in the Ruins":

Going along the dirt road,
I see the winter sun shine brightly;
The young shoots are through already,
Steadily pushing between the ashes.

And yet I look in vain for my young one,
Hearing only the far sound of a cold wind.

I stand on the Aioi Bridge, sick at heart.
In the deep waters something flashes!
Ah! It is but an image,
An image of his childhood.

He went on to describe to me how the typhoons following the bomb "washed away all the debris," so that "when everything was destroyed, we could pay attention to the beauty of nature." Here Yoneda suggests a theme which finds frequent expression in Japanese literature, that of beauty in destruction.[44] And in another poem he tells how "The river burns on in red flames, forever." He implies that the river has absorbed the A-bomb in a way that creates a new dimension of natural immortality, as also suggested more indirectly in the poem describing the "image" in the river of the dead boy's "childhood."

Yoneda specifically emphasized to me this principle of "new beauty" of feeling and form:

> In this beauty I have seen not only the re-creation of old beauty, but also the creation of new beauty. Not looking backward but looking forward.

Another poem, "The Sand on August Sixth," carries these themes still further in an East Asian expression of the principle of "Earth to earth, ashes to ashes, dust to dust":

> I wonder if each and every grain of sand calms down.
> I wonder if each and every grain of sand still twinkles.
> One and all the grains embrace in deep shadow,
> And they are all on tiptoe when the bell begins to tell. . . .
>
> The blood of men and women has soaked into everything, into every grain,
> And the grains are their very bones ground into atoms. . . .
> They are fanned to fire, like so many sparks,
> Or are they stirring,
> Are they starting to revive?
>
> I wonder if each and every grain will prove a dead man's eye; . . .
> Gazing into the scorching heavens, when the bell begins to toll.
>
> When the stone burns clear like flame
> And the verdure of the springing weed
> Casts its shadow on the sand;
> Till the time when the bell of peace rings out
> All over the world, echoing on the sand,
>
> The wax of the sun itself will not cease to drop,
> As the light of the earth is strengthened by each and every grain of sand.

The most extreme form of human annihilation, that is, can be comprehended and mastered by viewing it as part of the great bio-spiritual continuum; and those who are annihilated remain viable in that continuity, and even energize it.

In discussing with me his feelings about his A-bomb poetry, Yoneda emphasized the fundamental difference in comprehension between *hibakusha* and non*hibakusha* poets ("I don't think that those who have not been through the A-bomb can reach the same depth of understanding"), and therefore in responsibility ("So the writers who have actually been through it must try to express in their poems . . . and make known just what happened"). But to carry out this poetic responsibility, he believed, one should "go beyond the level of simple description," and (in effect) recast the A-bomb into virtual experience through a process of "purification":

> Human nature is very complex. Some good elements are there, but bad elements too. . . . Sometimes I would begin to despair—but then I would think, This is no time for despair, and only by countering the bad elements in ourselves can we bring forth the good elements. This I wanted to do by writing poems. For my poems are in a way my own purification. . . . It is our own responsibility to eliminate these poisons. . . . As my poems find more readers, more and more people will be able to conquer the bad elements in themselves. . . .

These "poisons" are, of course, residual hatreds, but they are also elements of death guilt and of ignoble self-interest. He thus went on to tell of a silent visual dialogue with the dead—terrible in its demands, but also a profound source of poetic inspiration:

> I have always had a kind of burden on my mind as I write. . . . I think the burden comes mainly from the fact that in writing poems, I have had to observe myself with absolute honesty—and this self-discipline is extremely difficult to bear. . . . When I wrote about trees and grass growing, I always saw in front of me the eyes of my child and the eyes of other people I knew who died in the bomb. . . . I thought these eyes were looking into my mind, and felt that if there were anything dishonest there, these eyes would surely reveal it. . . . They were very penetrating . . . and always urged me to write. . . . When I write my poetry, I find that my eyes and their eyes exchange glances. . . .

He derived these images from his search for family members: "I was looking for recognizable eyes . . . that's why I came to notice eyes more than anyone else." And while by no means unaware of resorting to metaphor, he carried the metaphor still further in speaking of the stages of his approach to A-bomb poetry as reflections of these eyes—at first "tearful . . . with only vague, sentimental vision . . . sorrow and perhaps indignation," after which they became "forgiving eyes . . . and that is why . . . I began to write about . . . reconstruction." He continues with this theme as the basis for his literary mission:

> I just wanted to portray whatever [those eyes] had in their expression. . . . I don't know exactly the source of my energy or what sustains me in my creative work. But I feel a strong responsibility to speak about this situation for the sake of the dead . . . perhaps the hope we have for the future . . . or maybe the desire for peace. . . . Every victim has this feeling even though the majority cannot express themselves in any form. I write my poetry to give expression to what is in the heart of the dead, and what is in the heart of victims.

Here Yoneda suggests that he derives the perpetual self-transformation necessary for his poetry from a sense of fusing with the dead and giving expression to their and his combined "vision." His individual emotions of death and rebirth become inseparable from his art, as does his death guilt. All come together in language of virtual experience, and to the extent that his readers (particularly *hibakusha* but also non*hibakusha*) can share this experience—can relate themselves to its symbolism—they can enhance their own mastery of their A-bomb encounters.

:

Yoneda's elegiac verse, like Tōge's protest poetry, thus emerges from a profoundly felt sense of survivor mission. But rather than cry out against the violent intrusion upon ordinary patterns of life and death, it adopts a tone of psychological non-resistance to reaffirm man's sense of immortality in his own and nature's continuity. Where protest poetry runs the risk of literalness (and ceasing to be poetry), elegiac poetry runs the risk of lapsing into cosmic generalities and losing contact with its original inspiration (ceasing to be A-bomb poetry). Both, of course, are exposed to the dangers of "censorship" by the dead—that is, to unmastered death guilt, which results in blunting of imagery, in a general imaginative lapse precluding artistic transformation. Both seek a formulation which overcomes these difficulties by revivifying the sense of immortality.

Ultimately, the two modes are by no means absolutely distinct—there are elegiac moments in Tōge, indirect expressions of protest in Yoneda. Indeed, no A-bomb poem is entirely free of protest, and the basic process in which emotions are transmuted into poetry is related to elegy.

These mixed tones of elegy and protest can be stark in their simultaneity—as in Kishiro Tanaka's "The Setting Sun":

> The child is no more.
> On the barracks
> Of the primary school
> Lingers the glow of the setting sun,
> And here and there the skulls are found.
> My A-bombed Hiroshima.

And in Tamiki Hara's "That Demonic Moment":

> The white ghost of pampas grass
> The hanging mist
> Is ready to drop.
> Cold tears well up in my eyes, well up!

> That demonic moment!
> Trudging down the slope,
> I find the world is lowering its voice;

> A well, wavering and glittering;
> Fair faces, laughing and weeping.

The phrase "I find the world is lowering its voice" takes on particular poignancy in view of the poet's later suicide. One of the best known of the early A-bomb writers, and author of one of the first memoir-novels written about the bomb—*Summer Flowers* (*Natsu no Hana*)—we recall that his suicide was attributed both to the outbreak of the Korean War and to his loneliness for his wife, who had died in the bomb. But whatever the reasons, the poem tells us that he was experiencing something close to what mystics have called "losing the world": that he felt himself unable to "hear" his fellow human beings or to formulate his psychic universe in a way that would have made it more "audible."

When compared to other forms of literature and art, poetry may be said to come closest to maintaining its general standards of symbolic transformation in its confrontation with the A-bomb. But this transformation is only sporadic, and always tenuous. And the problems faced by all literature can be further illuminated by responses in other creative media.

CREATIVE RESPONSE:
2) ARTISTIC DILEMMAS

eleven

1) Dramatic Arts: A-Bomb on Film

The dramatic arts in many ways lend themselves particularly to the re-creation of great historical events. As "performed literature," drama can, at least ideally, supply vivid renditions of these events and at the same time build emotions around them that transform them into works of art. In relationship to the A-bomb experience we shall see there to be a great gap between this potential and what has actually been achieved. But at least two efforts, both of them on film, have made unique use of their medium in approach and impact. And other films, though less successful artistically, also teach us much.

Concerning other forms of drama,[1] Kajiyama, the author of *Experimental City*, achieved the unusual distinction of bringing humor to the A-bomb problem in a radio play entitled "The Mist of Hiroshima" (Hiroshima no Kiri), broadcast in March, 1958, in which ghosts of A-bomb victims hold a convention for the purpose of deciding whom to haunt—the American President, the scientist "Poustein" (Einstein), the Japanese leader Hideki Nenjo (Tōjō), or someone else—but they cannot agree, and end up in a state of poltergeistic confusion. Most radio, TV, and stage plays have been more conventional in depicting general *hibakusha* suffering, fear of aftereffects, shame over deformities, and efforts to avoid discrimination by hiding *hibakusha* identity. Usually written by non*hibakusha* with an interest in the A-bomb problem, these plays have varied in quality from soap-opera level to vehicles of considerable dramatic force. Their elegiac quality is suggested by the names of two of the more notable among them—"Look at the Flower" (Kono Hana o Miyo), a radio play, and "Opening in the Cloud" (Kumo no Sakeme), a television drama based upon poems by Tamiki Hara, the *hibakusha*-writer who committed suicide.

Perhaps the most original has been a stage play by Chikao Tanaka entitled *The Head of Mary* (*Maria no Kubi*),[2] which is set in Nagasaki and revolves around the efforts of a keloid-bearing nurse-prostitute to steal the statue of the Virgin Mary, piece by piece, from among the ruins.* After raising various Catholic issues of sin and responsibility, it moves to a provocative dénouement in which Mary herself, when told she is being called upon to bear witness to the events of August 9, cooperates in the theft and tells those *hibakusha* involved that she wishes to be with them and watch over them. Performed with some success by a contemporary drama group in Tokyo, the play hints at a formulation in which conventional morality is inverted so that *hibakusha* can gain access to divine (authentic) nurturance to help them cope with the anger and confused search for meaning which dominate their continuing A-bomb confrontation.

More characteristic was a play by Kiyomi Hotta entitled *Island* (*Shima*),[3] performed in 1957 first by a stage group and later on a radio network, which depicted *hibakusha* physical fears and other conflicts with a combination of sensitivity and emotional power. Its tone of unremitting hopelessness, however, led to the cancellation of a plan to stage it in Hiroshima, because of concern about the disturbing effects it would have upon actual *hibakusha*. This kind of concern has accompanied most efforts at dramatic re-creation. While it grows out of an accurate evaluation of *hibakusha* vulnerabilities, it also reflects a limitation in most of the dramas themselves—a semi-documentary style which does not achieve sufficient artistic transcendence to lift its level of creative discourse beyond that of immediate *hibakusha* feelings.

:

The characteristics of film which make it, unlike other forms of drama, "the dream mode . . . [in which] the camera is in the place of

---

* The same theme has been used by other writers and is said to have been based upon actual occurrence.

the dreamer"[4] hold out special possibilities for A-bomb re-creation. But most attempts have stuck to the other side of the film equation, the apparent literality of the photographic image, without realizing that this is a "dreamed reality," and that "the closer a movie seems to stick to conventions and reality, the more freely it circulates in the fantasy world."* Overwhelmed by this subject and possessing limited grasp of their medium, film-makers have often tried to reproduce the atomic bomb experience exactly as it happened—efforts which are bound to emerge as inauthentic, particularly to *hibakusha* themselves, as the elderly widow tells us:

> Later, when I saw movies which showed these scenes—and in some cases the scenes were artificially constructed for the movies—they simply could not portray what I had seen with my own eyes.

"A-BOMB RONIN"

There does exist, however, extensive documentary film of the actual event. This film has importance, not only as a record of what took place, but in relationship to one of the more interesting stories of quasi-legendary heroism to emerge from the A-bomb experience.

One month after the bomb the first part of a thirty-man documentary film team was sent to Hiroshima by Nichiei Productions, then Japan's major newsreel company. A later account describes the fears and courage of the men on the team and their close collaboration with Japanese scientists, as well as their determined confrontation with American authorities who, in December, abruptly ordered them to cease shooting in Nagasaki, where they had gone the previous month. They were finally permitted to complete a nineteen-reel (eleven-thousand-foot) film in an English version entitled *Effects of the Atomic Bomb*, on the condition that it be turned over in its entirety to the American Army. But four of the men decided to violate this order and prepare secretly an additional print of more than half of the original film, which they hid away in a photographic laboratory in a Tokyo suburb.

One commentator paid the group the ultimate compliment of comparing them to Japan's great traditional (and also part-legendary) heroes and exemplars of loyalty, the Forty-Seven Ronin. The latter also

---

* The dreamlike character of the film medium suggested by both A. Alvarez and Susanne Langer is, of course, its extraordinary capacity to bring free imagination to its apparent literality. And precisely this combination may be responsible for the emergence of film as the most contemporary of arts—that is, as the art form most attuned to the quality of present-day experience.[5]

formed a secret pact (at the beginning of the eighteenth century), in their case to avenge the death of the lord; went to extreme lengths to disguise their intentions (several divorced their wives, one killed his father-in-law, another sold his sister into concubinage, and many engaged in gaudily dissolute behavior); two years later carried out their mission by surprising their adversary and killing him; and were then accorded by the authorities the privilege of honorable deaths by ritual suicide.

While the comparison is a somewhat romantic one,* the "A-bomb Ronin" did play an important part in the national awakening to the atomic bomb experience. For in July, 1952, just after the Occupation ended, portions of the hidden documentary were shown "with great excitement" at movie houses throughout Japan. Shortly afterwards, on August 6, an issue of the *Asahi Graphic*, devoted entirely to still photographs of Hiroshima and Nagasaki taken shortly after their atomic bombings, also caused an immediate sensation. It was erroneously thought by many that these photographs were taken from the original documentary film. But it turns out that the *Asahi* had a few "A-bomb Ronin" of its own, three or four reporters and photographers who were either in Hiroshima at the time of the bomb or else went there shortly afterwards, and who, also in violation of Occupation orders, retained negatives or positives of the pictures they took.

From the newsreel, and particularly from the issue of the *Graphic*, most Japanese obtained their first real psychic immersion into the horrors of the nuclear weapons experience. As the editorial comment accompanying the pictures pointed out, although Japanese had been "the first victims of the atomic bomb in world history," few knew the "cruel facts." But the "overwhelming power [of these 'facts'] compelled recognition," so that, concerning the decision to devote a special issue to Hiroshima and Nagasaki, "It is history that commands us to do so."

The impact of these photographs was attested to by Japanese I interviewed in Tokyo and Kyoto in connection with another study. They

---

* It is from *Gensuibaku Jidai*, and its exaggerations perhaps reflect not only ideological perspectives of the author but the general hunger for A-bomb heroism of any kind. I was able to obtain first-hand descriptions from some of the men involved in the original episode, and from two books describing it and other photographic exploits at the time.[6] Although the event has been described in various later writings, it does not seem to have strongly captured the Japanese imagination— partly because of resistance to the entire subject of the atomic bomb. But its significance may nonetheless be greater than generally realized and may increase with time.

became, in fact, a pictorial consolidation of postwar Japanese pacifist sentiment, as again suggested by the editorial comment accompanying them: "Those who talk about future wars should look at this special section and be prepared for such a disaster, or for one even more horrible, to occur to themselves." In this sense they were a landmark in national efforts at mastering victimization by atomic weapons. And *hibakusha* themselves in turn, though unable to be free of ambivalence about any such issue, had their own formulations enhanced by the significance their experience came to assume for all Japanese. Of considerable psychological significance for *hibakusha* and non*hibakusha* alike was the fact that the entire sequence of actions, the making of the film and its secret preservation, was accomplished by Japanese—thus making it a powerful expression of autonomy, the very antithesis of counterfeit nurturance.

More important, what the "A-bomb Ronin" achieved was not the vengeance of the original Forty-Seven, but what might be termed a "moral equivalent of vengeance." Their act did express defiance, a sense of "righting the wrong" of American suppression of A-bomb information, and of exposing to the world America's overall culpability in originally dropping the bomb. But stress was upon recording the events in the service of emphasizing the new importance for all to transcend old patterns of vengeance and war. They restored significance to deaths that had taken place, not by producing more of them but by demonstrating the folly of contemporary killing. In this way their actions took on the significance of silent beginnings of an A-bomb formulation.

But the world's difficulties in following through on this idealistic formulation are illustrated by the subsequent fate of the film. Portions of the original have been used in a number of motion pictures about the bomb, documentary and otherwise.* But its use has frequently been associated with ideological purposes much narrower than that involved in its preservation, and the film now sits in a Tokyo warehouse as an incomplete and not very accessible historical record. The presumably complete American copies, according to American journalists who have tried to track them down, have dissolved into the far reaches of military

---

* There was another newsreel, also made by a Nichiei cameraman at the time, which came to be known as *Nippon News No. 257* and was said to have been shown as early as September 22, 1945. But its creator is unknown and it has not achieved the importance of the more extensive ten-reel documentary materials. In addition, photographers were sent with the Nichiei team to take only still pictures, which were later to be reproduced in various books.[7]

bureaucracy, and are known in Japan as the "phantom film" (*maboroshi no firumu*).*

DOCUMENTARIES [8]

Seen in 1962, ten years after its post-Occupation release, these original film clippings by no means lose their effectiveness. The documentary which first made use of them, *Asahi News No. 363*, moves methodically from scenes of wounded and moribund adults, and of partly incinerated children identified as homeless and "waiting to die," to wide-angle shots of the leveled area identified as a "city of death" in which "no trees or grass can be found." But although the whole film lasts less than a half hour, it devotes the last few minutes to themes of rebirth: a charming little pool, which presumably once contained dead bodies, sprouting beautiful water lilies; and scenes of rebuilding whose vitality contrasts sharply with the lifelessness at the time of the bomb. One gains the impression that the film's major concern is to *show exactly how things were*, but to do so in the service of reawakened human continuity.

Yet there is an inherent contradiction: "how things were" is inseparable from the viewpoint of the film-maker, from the implicit formulation contained in the most literal-appearing photographic material. In documentary films this formulation is expressed in such things as the sequences chosen and their relationship to one another, the spoken commentary, background music, additional photographic images added for purposes of contrast, and so on. In the *Asahi* newsreel, for instance, these elements come together to create a controlling image which propels the viewer to a grotesque immersion in death and an elegiac rebirth. Subsequent films of various kinds have resembled A-bomb poetry in their stress upon either elegy or protest, or the two in combination—seeming to confirm the assertion made by some that poetry is the art medium closest to that of film.

Protest films, many of them made under the auspices of such groups as *Gensuikyō* or the Teacher's Union, have tended to contain structured ideological formulations beneath the surface objectivity of the documentary form. Such films can nonetheless make contact both with

---

* On May 18, 1957, it was reported in the *New York Times* that American authorities had acknowledged possession of the film and that a further request by the Japanese government for making it available would probably meet with favorable action, although requests had been refused in the past. Following this report various individuals and groups in Hiroshima spoke out, demanding the film's return; and on June 14 the Japanese Education Minister announced that he would press negotiations on the matter with the American government.

specific *hibakusha* conflicts and general fears about nuclear weapons, as does one of the most influential of them, *The World Is in Dread* (*Sekai wa Kyōfu Suru*, 1957). Subtitled "A True Picture of the Ashes of Death," it brings together Hiroshima, the H-bomb, and America in bitterly accusatory fashion. Described by Richie as "deliberately sensational, a scare-message film, using all sorts of rhetorical shock-devices,"[9] it acts upon the viewer to produce a predominant emotion of fear.

Opening with a scene of ominous clouds, with equally ominous background music and a narrative warning of "invisible danger," it consists mainly of a series of deadly images concerning radiation dangers: birds in a special experimental chamber dying, within minutes, of radiation exposure; scientists extracting strontium 90 from the rainwater collected after American hydrogen bomb tests at Bikini, then demonstrating its presence in soil, its impairment of the growth of rice plants (here, as in many scenes, the viewer can readily confuse experimental possibility with actual occurrence), its being ingested by cows in grass and by babies (shown in nurseries) with their milk. There is a series of quick shifts from scientific laboratories to Hiroshima and Nagasaki: white mice developing cancer after injections of strontium 90, followed immediately by a woman bedridden with cancer in the Atomic Bomb Hospital twelve years after her original exposure; genetic impairments in fruit flies (some born with one eye several generations after initial irradiation) and in fish (some with two heads) and other animals following various kinds of radiation exposure—then a two-headed baby born to a *hibakusha* in 1950, another born without a brain in 1951, a picture of a one-eyed baby said to have been taken by a doctor, and grotesque shots of children, living and dead, who had been born with tiny heads, without hearts or other organs, and with other kinds of malformation. Distinctions are made between genetic impairments and exposure *in utero*, but these are easily lost in the rapid scene-shifting. Shots of scientists confirming radiation dangers and issuing warnings about the future add to the general impact.

Interspersed are "positive" scenes—fish copulating, lovers in Paris, children doing deep-breathing exercises at school—but these, if anything, intensify the horror by suggesting the life force that is threatened (and in the case of the deep-breathing children, suggesting the possibility of inhaling strontium 90). Toward the end of the film there is a demonstration of a solitary mouse dying from radiation effects, with the comment that despite these dangers, despite the rain filled with death ash, despite what happened in Hiroshima, and despite the pleas of

Hiroshima victims, America continues to test her nuclear weapons. Then a final exhortation: "We hope that the mouse's death doesn't reflect the fate of man. The danger of ashes of death is different from that of floods or earthquakes—it is something we ourselves have made— and if man so wills, he can cause it to cease."

The "dream-language" of the film is that of perpetual nightmare; its overall effect is terrifying. Its blurred juxtaposition of real events, dangers, possibilities, exaggerations, and questionable cause-and-effect assumptions evokes an indiscriminate image of nuclear dread, of diffuse death anxiety. And its implicit formulation associates this dread more or less exclusively with America (Soviet testing is not mentioned). This death-saturated formulation of nuclear dangers, including the one-sided accusation of America, could be said to reflect feelings held by some *hibakusha* and by various groups throughout the world. But the film's shrilly didactic tone and absence of artistic transcendence suggest that its director, Fumio Kamei, was partly overwhelmed by his subject matter and partly compelled by political convictions to treat it as he did.

The result is that the film tends to stimulate in the viewer the most primitive kind of emotion related to annihilation. While some may respond with a constructive sense of survivor-like mission, more are likely to experience confusing combinations of fear, psychic numbing, and angrily simplistic (even paranoid) impulses toward extirpating evil, possibly by means of further violence. Moreover, its general tone, as well as the director's background (he studied in Moscow and has expressed communist formulations in a number of his films), encourage many Japanese, whether or not *hibakusha*, to dismiss it and *all* A-bomb films as communist-linked, thereby providing a convenient reinforcement of psychic numbing and undermining the demand so fiercely made in the film that everyone confront the full nuclear threat. In sum, *The World Is in Dread* has considerable impact of a mixed kind, and demonstrates the vicissitudes—artistic, as well as psychological and moral—of filmic A-bomb formulations which, made under the cloak of documentary objectivity, turn out to be considerably less than universalistic.

The same director, in *Still, It's Good to Be Alive* (*Ikite Ite Yokatta*, 1956), was able to convey a related message but with considerably greater sensitivity and emotional scope. The film wavers between a broadly humanistic approach to individual post-A-bomb struggles and a certain degree of propagandistic emphasis upon the role played by *Gensuikyō* (which sponsored it) in rallying *hibakusha* around its program. The tenuousness of the blend again reflects the difficult demands of the subject matter.

SAD BEAUTY

When we turn from documentaries to full-length films, we again enter into the elegiac realm, as illustrated by two prominent examples. The first, A *Thousand Cranes* (*Senbazuru*), was made in 1958 as the motion-picture version of the Sadako Sasaki legend. In recording the story of the fourteen-year-old girl's death from leukemia ten years after the bomb, it presents a characteristically Japanese sentimental evocation of childhood, and then records the cruel annihilation of a particular child.

There are first scenes of children at school and on gay excursions: all is gentle, loving, energetic, and pure. Then the intrusion of illness, the shocking revelation of "A-bomb disease," and the long, losing struggle with leukemia portrayed mostly in Sadako's hospital room. In scenes of infinite sadness her classmates gather at her bedside and hold a private graduation ceremony for her at which they render a Japanese version of "Auld Lang Syne"; and then her father, his eyes tearful, attends the real ceremony in her place in order to pick up her diploma. The children work feverishly to produce the thousand paper cranes thought necessary to make her well, with Sadako herself demonstrating great courage in the face of her physical deterioration.

As the film depicts the children's passionate response to Sadako's death, and their successful national campaign to raise a large amount of money for a memorial statue, we witness the special power of children, when confronted with the world's evil, to accomplish the impossible and move everyone's heart in the direction of good. But in maintaining a one-dimensional view of (childhood) good and (adult) evil, the film avoids all emotional complexity (including the conflicts and hypocrisies we know to have surrounded the actual event) and relies entirely upon elegy and upon *mono no aware*, the "sad beauty" or "suchness" of existence. Its artistic possibilities thus limited, it nonetheless makes contact with the universal myth of childhood purity which is, in turn, integral to imagery of death and rebirth. The film, then, has a double message: the atomic bomb destroys children and childhood; but the world's best hope in confronting the nuclear evil lies in precisely the strength, wisdom, and purity of the young.

:

The other film of this genre, *Children of the A-Bomb* (*Genbaku no Ko*, 1952), was based on a best-selling novel by Arato Osada, a well-known *hibakusha*-educator. It too emphasizes sentiment more than subtlety, but it takes the theme of annihilation of childhood into more ambitious emotional dimensions to suggest the destruction of all that is pure in human existence.

The mood from the beginning is of nostalgic melancholy. A young woman, a kindergarten teacher at the time of the bombing, returns to her native Hiroshima from a nearby island—and although she finds the rivers and the clouds and the sky still beautiful, all else is pain and chaos. An old man in rags, blind from the bomb and living hermitlike in a miserable shack, turns out to be a former family servant; he has reluctantly placed his seven-year-old grandson in an orphanage, but when the young woman offers to take the child, he refuses because "he is the hope of my life." And when he says, "If only I weren't blind. If only there hadn't been a *pikadon* ['flash-boom,' or an A-bomb]," his tone is more of resignation than protest.

An old friend the young woman visits who used to teach with her, now unable to have children because of the bomb, explains that she had first felt great despair, but "I thought of those who died, and then became content." Much of the film centers on the woman's search (begun after she and her friend have looked at old photographs of their kindergarten class) for three children said to have survived the bomb. Flashbacks of nostalgic kindergarten scenes alternate with the dreadful post-bomb situations she encounters in the course of her search. At the first child's home she finds not only terrible poverty but the neighborhood's sudden shock and grief as the boy's father is struck down with A-bomb disease. The second child is herself close to death from A-bomb aftereffects. The third child lives alone with his sister, their parents having been killed, their childhood devoured by their struggle for existence; the boy, about to be further abandoned because of his sister's imminent marriage, tells his former teacher that her visit is "the first happy event since the war."

The film returns to the old man. When he agrees to let his grandson go with the teacher, the youngster refuses to unless his grandfather comes too. The old man decides to clear the boy's path by taking poison; as he loses consciousness he asks that his body be given to a hospital, and then utters his last words: "War, stupid, *pikadon*." The film ends, as it began, with a mood of *mono no aware* surrounding the boat trip between Hiroshima and the island. The young woman and the boy take a last look at the A-Bomb Dome, and we see that the boy is carrying his grandfather's ashes.

Children of the A-Bomb demonstrates both the strengths and the limitations of the more or less totally elegiac film. Highly sentimentalized and containing little rendition of inner conflict, the mood seems to subordinate the plot. Rather than probing individual character as such, it evokes the rhythms of the life cycle—childhood, marriage, the bearing of children, old age, and death—but shows every stage to be profoundly disturbed by the A-bomb. The protest is *sotto voce*, subdued by the psychological non-resistance of *mono no aware*, within which is the formulation that however these rhythms are impaired—whatever the extent of human suffering—life reasserts itself. We recognize a psychological response similar to that of many *hibakusha*, for this kind of formulation is not only the most characteristically Japanese, but also the most universally called upon in response to catastrophe. Yet its capacity to absorb the full impact of nuclear disaster, artistically as well as psychologically, remains questionable.

:

The elegiac mood has been used more complexly—in films which combine it with protest or connect it only tangentially with the A-bomb theme. *The Story of Pure Love* (*Junai Monogatari*, made in 1957 by the leading director Tadashi Imai) does both. It follows the novel from which it was adapted in contrasting the purity of the relationship of two young lovers with the corruption of society. But the girl's tuberculosis is changed to radiation sickness; and her suffering and death—and the accompanying tone of protest—are no longer expressed through the non-specific medical-social symbolism associated with tuberculosis, but rather through a classic constellation of A-bomb themes: ultimate inhumanity, counterfeit nurturance, and American culpability.*

MONSTERS AND MOCKERY

A very different kind of A-bomb theme is expressed in two science-fiction genres which Richie refers to as "the monster-film" and "the

---

* In another film, *Let Us Not Forget the Song of Nagasaki* (*Nagasaki no Uta wa Wasureji*, 1953), an American is sympathetically interwoven with the *mono no aware* theme: through attempting to return a piece of music he had found on the battlefield to its composer's family in Nagasaki, he becomes involved in the suffering of A-bomb victims. This unique depiction of an American occurs in one of the few films whose director, Tomotaka Tasaka, was himself a *hibakusha*. Tasaka, in fact, was thought to be still suffering from physical A-bomb effects while making the film. But although he had in the past been one of Japan's great pioneers among film directors, this was in no way considered a film of distinction. Even his use of an American was partly determined by influences unrelated to the A-bomb—he was connected with a "co-production" project bringing together actors from the two countries. But whatever the influences at play, the sympathetic character created expressed a conciliatory formulative vision.

visitors-from-outer-space picture." Although Japanese versions of these resemble those made in other countries, their number and influence not only in Japan but throughout the world (many of the most successful American monster films have been adaptations of Japanese originals) is probably related, as Richie also suggests, to atomic bomb exposure. (Given Japan's general standing as a market for films depicting cruelty and violence, however, one must also take into account traits of national character acted upon by the A-bomb experience.)

The most famous of the monsters is Godzilla, who appeared in a film of that name in 1954 (the Japonized rendering is *Gojira*), and again the following year in *Godzilla's Counterattack* (*Gojira no Gyakushū*). Godzilla, "a saurian King Kong,"[10] is awakened by the Bikini test explosions, and in his first appearance threatens all of Tokyo until destroyed by a Japanese scientist-hero who must himself be annihilated in the process. We may say that nuclear weapons are symbolized here as catalysts for monstrous devastation, for bizarre and unassimilable death.

In the second genre, visitors or invaders come to Japan from outer space—either out of concern about nuclear tests being conducted on earth (in *Space Men Appear in Tokyo* [*Uchujin Tokyo ni Arawaru*, 1954] they arrive on flying saucers to seek advice from the Japanese); or else as hostile creatures, physically and mentally deranged by radiation effects from these same tests. The deranged state may take the form of the robot, or be directly nuclear (the "H-Man"), or nuclear-charged ("the electric man"). Once more these creatures are defeated, and the universe saved, by Japanese scientists' courage and advanced knowledge.

These films represent efforts at mastery of nuclear problems by first representing them in exaggerated, partly mocking, fantasy, and then calling upon Japan's unique nuclear experience as a source of wisdom. The Japanese scientist-hero's combination of technical competence and dedication, whatever its suggestion of national chauvinism, is a form of "survivor's mission" in which the special power over death associated with nuclear survival is brought forth to "save the universe." Much more than most films dealing with the A-bomb, this "monster" genre makes imaginative use of its medium's dreamlike potential. Moreover, its apocalyptic approach to good and evil is relevant both to dimensions of contemporary holocaust and to the survivor's quest for absolute purity. This approach also gives expression to the attraction (on the part of survivor or viewer) to disaster—the urge to "witness" and emotionally experience either a repetition of what one has been through or an anticipation of what one fears. The monster's (or space visitor's) impersonal, superhuman power suggests, as no other genre can, the radical impairment of life-death balance, a vision of all people on earth becoming helpless guinea pig-victims. The entire experience becomes acceptable to the viewer because of an additional element of implicit formulation to the effect that all of this is make-believe, a satirical exposé of earth's own absurdities.

Apart from these virtues, the films tend to substitute formula for formulation, technological imagination for depth of thought and feeling. They are, as one sympathetic critic has suggested, an "inadequate response" to the general contemporary problem of "the imagination of disaster."[11] But whatever their artistic and intellectual inadequacies, they do, at least for Japanese, encourage a freer flow of extreme psychic elements in creating a workable relationship to the nuclear world. My impression, however, was that a certain detachment was required for this psychic freedom, so that *hibakusha* probably are less able to participate in it than atomic bomb "outsiders."

:

Hibakusha probably find it even more difficult to accept a direct satirical treatment of the atomic bomb, as exemplified by Keisuke Kinoshita's *Carmen's Pure Love* (*Karumen Junjōsu*, 1952). In this film an elderly matriarch who lost a son in the atomic bomb—a "militaristic harridan of a mother"[12]—blames all of life's subsequent vicissitudes on the bomb alone: the appearance of an abandoned baby on her doorstep, the blackmailing of another of her sons, even the defeat of a politician she favored. Kinoshita, a noted comedy director, takes advantage of the idea to poke fun at such postwar Japanese phenomena as the "modern" woman (Carmen is a strip-tease dancer who joins a fellow-stripper to "strike terror into the hearts of the simple country people when they go home to visit the folks"); the "old-fashioned" woman patriot (the matriarch forces her daughter and the daughter's fiancé to submit to a daily singing of the national anthem); and greedy racketeers, politicians, and relatives.

This formulation not only "laughs at the unlaughable," but doubly deflates the A-bomb by mixing it in with the general potpourri of postwar Japanese dislocations. It undoubtedly expresses resentment toward *hibakusha*, partly based upon exaggerations and political manipulations of the A-bomb experience by some of them, partly upon guilt toward them and fear of their death taint. But the approach is liberating because it punctures the image of absolute *hibakusha* virtue and moves toward recognition of paradoxical psychic combinations, much in the fashion of Kokubo's use in fiction of "underground themes." This genre also shares with monster and outer-space films the use of mockery as a release from stereotyped emotions. Were *hibakusha* able to respond to the mockery in either of the categories, one could be sure that they had moved significantly toward mastery. But I have seen little evidence of such response.

NUCLEAR ANXIETY AND A-BOMB LOVE

The most significant Japanese treatment of the Hiroshima-nuclear weapons issue on film—the first moving picture to place the problem at its center and treat it with artistic depth—is Akira Kurosawa's *Record of a Living Being (Ikimono no Kiroku,* 1955), shown abroad as *I Live in Fear.*

The film's protagonist is an elderly man who, as a result of Hiroshima, Bikini, and subsequent bomb tests, becomes obsessed with the dangers of nuclear weapons—and with Japan's special geographic vulnerability to fallout because of its location in a celestial "valley":

> What will happen to those of us who live in this valley? We will lose our hair—and become just bones. I saw the graphic section of the newspaper on Hiroshima. It was dreadful. There was a picture of a little boy like this [he holds his own grandson in his arms]. . . .

He is convinced that safety lies only in taking his family to Brazil (a place of emigration for many Japanese) because of its location in the Southern Hemisphere, where less fallout is likely to be encountered. When a son asks him to look at the matter philosophically ("Well, we all must die someday"), he replies excitedly: "Yes, everyone has to die, but I don't want to be killed, that's all." He is a man whose death anxiety requires that he avoid being *helplessly* annihilated.

The film skillfully blends nuclear themes with ordinary contemporary problems. Hardening family resistance to the old man's plan is associated with various forms of greed and self-seeking, particularly the fear that he will squander his money and leave no inheritance. When he persists in his arrangements without the consent of other family members, they take him to domestic court to have him declared financially incompetent. As all of the family's dirty linen is exposed there, including his longstanding relationships with mistresses, the old man himself can, with some justice, be accused of leading a selfish life. Indeed, when he is finally declared incompetent, only his mistress remains loyal and attempts to help him (later his daughter and his wife also soften, more out of sympathy toward him than out of any convictions about nuclear weapons). Others in his family block him at every turn, and greedily anticipate their inheritances as they observe him to show signs of physical and mental collapse.

In desperation, he burns down his own factory—his logic being: "You said it would be difficult to leave Japan as long as this factory were here, so I burned it down . . . and now we can go to live in Brazil." But as workmen join family members in condemning him ("What about our jobs?"), for the first time he begins to lose his determination and becomes confused; and when his son points out that "Even Brazil is not safe; there is no place that is safe," he looks increasingly distraught and defeated. He is sent to prison, where other inmates make him a laughingstock:

> This man set fire to his own building—he is very strange. . . . You were very foolish to worry about things you should leave to the Prime Minister. If you are so worried about H-bombs, why don't you leave the earth?

He is transferred to an "insane asylum," for by now he *is* insane and thinks himself on a distant planet witnessing nuclear holocaust on Earth:

> This is a safe place. By the way, how is Earth these days? Are there any people there? . . . They should all try to escape. They should come to this planet—this star. . . . [Then, seeing bright sunlight from the window] Ah, Earth is burning, it is burning! At last, Earth is burning!

Between the extremes of the "mad nuclear alarmist" and the "ordinary people," who remain exclusively focused upon matters of immediate self-interest, the film posits a third type, the wise but relatively helpless "mediator"—represented by a dentist and a doctor, who sensitively perceive both sides of the problem, and seem to be spokesmen for Kurosawa's point of view. The dentist (serving on a court panel) holds out for a while against the verdict, on the basis that people are usually declared incompetent because of squandering money, "not because of fear of A- and H-bombs." He insists that "we all share these fears," even if most do nothing, and that "a man who thinks about the matter seriously" can "readily become mentally disturbed." He gets another member of the panel to admit that "it is really a difficult question because he is struggling with a problem too big for one man to solve."

But it is the old man's doctor in the mental hospital who, near the end of the film, articulates what is perhaps its central point:

> Whenever I see this patient, I feel very melancholy. I know that the mentally ill have a sad existence. But when I see this particular patient, I myself—though I am supposedly normal—feel quite uncertain about things, because I feel that maybe we who are able to be normal are really the strange ones.

Kurosawa thus raises the ultimate psychological question in a nuclear world: Who is crazy—the man so sensitive to the threat, so able to envision the "end of the world," and so insistent upon pressing this vision in the face of general resistance that he becomes what is conventionally described as "insane"? or the world's ordinary functional people, who numb themselves to the threat and oppose actions that either remind them of it or affect their material interests? The question is not answered, but the film does emphasize the powerlessness of the individual (and of man in general) to alter the dangerous course of events, as well as the illusory nature of the idea of "safety."

Beyond this, however, the film is confused and melodramatic. There are interminable scenes at the domestic court which do little to further its main themes, and my brief summary suggests a logic of development which it does not really have. Rather, it rambles on in a series of fits, starts, and reversals of attitude by various characters in a way that suggests the director's own irresolution about where he wants to carry his vision. His taking his protagonist across the wide gamut between vigorous family leadership and extreme mental deterioration does dramatize the issue of sanity, but there is little emotional subtlety in the various stages. Richie has attributed some of the film's difficulties to Kurosawa's abrupt decision to divest it of the satirical approach he originally intended to use, following the death (from tuberculosis) of a close friend and collaborator—which, if true, would be another example of the way in which residual guilt from a death immersion, even on this individual scale, can limit psychological and artistic freedom. But we must also take into account the creative refractoriness of the subject itself, even for one of the world's great directors.

Yet these are limitations in a genuine work of artistic transformation. If the impossible demands of the problem lead Kurosawa to resort to melodrama, his characteristic blend of cinematic imagination and realism is by no means absent, and in the end the nuclear issue is brought at least to some degree into the symbolic realm of virtual experience.

Perhaps the film's deepest irony—one which Kurosawa suggests but may not fully control—is the fact that those who most sympathize with the nuclear alarmist's point of view (the dentist and the doctor) end up acting in accord with society's conventional views, and thereby contribute to the evolution and "confirmation" of his insanity. Everyone, in other words, is caught up in a collective destiny, which though unclear in nature (it may or may not include repetition of nuclear disaster), is inexorable to the point that whoever resists it is rendered mad. We seem to encounter here an interesting combination of East Asian resignation and Western tragedy, even if much in the formulation remains obscure. The film's relatively limited success in Japan probably had to do both with its own confusion, and with resistance to and misunderstanding of its universalistic suggestions. Some commentators complained about a treatment of the A-bomb problem which did not condemn America, and some viewers saw it as "simply an indication that one shouldn't worry so much: if you did, you went crazy."[13] In any case, the film succeeds in linking Hiroshima to the world's general nuclear dilemma as well as to everyday life, and does so with unusual sensitivity to paradox. Rather than contributing directly to *hibakusha* mastery, it suggests searching approaches to nuclear dilemmas which are universally applicable.

:

One other film is comparable to *Record of a Living Being* in the scope of its artistic formulation: Alain Resnais' *Hiroshima Mon Amour* (1959). I mention it here because it was made in Hiroshima around the atomic bomb experience and its international success has rendered it the source of many people's imagery about the city and the bomb. Also universalistic in approach, *Hiroshima Mon Amour* seems to succeed where *Record of a Living Being* fails; more important, it fails where Kurosawa's film succeeds.

The idea of the film is strikingly simple: the direct contrast between love's affirmation, however temporary, and the deadly destructiveness contained in the concept of "the enemy." It tells of a love affair between a French girl, who has come to Hiroshima to act in a film, and a Japanese man. The girl is reminded of an earlier wartime encounter, with a German soldier, in Nevers (her home town in France) which ended in his death and her own personal holocaust—public humiliation and temporary madness. Unlike Kurosawa, Resnais seems to know exactly what he is saying as he makes an almost classical Freudian opposition of love and life on the one side and hate and death on the other: authenticity of physical love is pitted against counterfeit situational hatreds.

The love affair has a haunting quality, and the all-pervasive tone is of sad beauty and transience—what Richie calls a French version of *mono no aware*. We are told that not only will the hatreds of Hiroshima and Nevers be forgotten, but so will the love affairs. The sense of man's ultimate separateness—shown in the girl's words ending the film: "See how I am forgetting you, for in this vale of tears there is no meeting"—is thoroughly consistent with traditional Japanese sentiment, but the active insistence upon love's direct antagonism to death is distinctly Western, in this case French, in flavor.

But *Hiroshima Mon Amour* never really achieves an artistic transformation of A-bomb elements. These do appear in the film, in the form of various kinds of A-bomb horrors, scenes from the museum, demonstrations opposing nuclear weapons; and the depth of the city's pain is suggested by the girl's constantly being told by her lover that she knows nothing of Hiroshima, no matter what she is shown or how much understanding she claims. Resnais literally takes the horrors of Hiroshima to the lovers' bed, but they are never brought into convincing confrontation: there is Hiroshima's grotesque death imagery, and there is the intensity of two people coming together in bodily union, but the two themes merely coexist. Indeed, many have asked (like Richie): "Why Hiroshima? Why not *Yokohama Mon Amour?*" The theoretical answer is that Hiroshima represents an ultimate in man's deadly destructiveness which Resnais wished to illuminate against the starkness of physical love. Yet the formulation remains abstract, apart, because the film has recorded but not grasped its environment.

Our conclusion, however, cannot be that Resnais was so little impressed with the atomic bomb that he felt no need to permit it to intrude into his cinematic vision. Rather, because he could not escape the overwhelming impact of the bomb, he dealt with it by attempting to mold it to "ordinary" dimensions in an idiom he understood. The film inevitably aroused opposition in Hiroshima, even while being made, because some *hibakusha* felt that its sensuality was an insult to the A-bomb dead.* Despite this reaction, and despite the film's limited realization of its own visions, we may say that the formulation it suggests has contributed new possibilities to the general artistic approach to the atomic bomb.

* The problem was then magnified by the title given to the Japanese version, *Twenty-four-Hour Love Affair* (*Nijūyojikan no Jōji*), which directs the viewer toward a vulgarized interpretation of the film.

2) "Pictures" and Songs

Painting and music have had much less to express about the atomic bomb than literature and film. But a few efforts, generally significant as A-bomb art and unique to the two media, are worth noting.

The best-known atomic bomb paintings are a series of large murals by a non*hibakusha* husband-and-wife team, Iri Maruki and Toshiko Akamatsu, collectively entitled "Pictures of the Atomic Bomb" ("Genbaku no Zu").[14] They consist mostly of macerated human figures, depicted in a powerful combination of realistic detail and supernatural grotesqueness. Thus, the first five (and most important) are : "Ghosts," in which deathlike figures hold their arms forward, flexed at the elbow, in the traditional manner of Japanese ghosts; "Fire," suggestive of purgatory, with flames consuming their victims; "Water," in which piles of corpses are absorbed by the river; "Rainbow," contrasting the human desolation with the rainbow's beauty; and "Boys and Girls," consisting of particularly explicit detail of dead and maimed children and parents. Five more murals were added later: "The Atomic Desert," "Bamboo Jungle" (or "The Wind"), and "Rescue," about the atomic bomb; "Yaezu," about the death of the fisherman Kuboyama (who came from the town of Yaezu) from hydrogen bomb fallout at Bikini; and "Signatures," about the peace-movement signature campaign.

It is extremely difficult to judge these paintings as art. In reproduction they are primarily a chronicle of horror. Their power lies in their irresistible demand that the viewer enter the scene of the atomic bomb and suffer with its victims—that he experience terror, guilt, revulsion, and fascination. They have undoubtedly had a strong impact upon many Japanese viewers, and upon readers of books in which they have been reproduced and commented upon. They have also been extensively exhibited abroad, mostly in communist countries, where they have won several prizes for their contribution to peace.* Japanese critics have had mixed feelings about their artistic merit. Wary of their ideological content, particularly since both artists have been active in the Japanese

* In March, 1967, work was completed near Tokyo on a "Pictures of the A-Bomb Museum," built under the supervision of the artists for permanent exhibition of murals.

communist movement, they have nevertheless noted their interesting
blending of traditional Japanese and contemporary international techniques (Maruki is known as a *sumie* or black-brush [literally black-ink]
painter; Akamatsu works in oils). Ultimately the viewer is overwhelmed
by the subject matter; or it may be more accurate to say that the subject
matter pre-empts the canvas from both artist and viewer. That is, the A-
bomb experience so takes over the identity of the painting that the
question of artistic transformation is readily cast aside. But when one
does raise the question, one finds that despite the murals' demonic
vision, they do not seem to have rendered the A-bomb experience into
universally significant artistic (or virtual) form.

One suspects that the artists were profoundly moved by the A-bomb
experience and at the same time determined to deal with it in relationship to their ideological convictions. The result is an exaggerated
literality—a modified "socialist realism"—in representing an apocalyptic
vision of an apocalyptic event. The authors' own comments upon their
first mural, "Ghosts," reveal some of these problematic (though also
inspirational) elements in their attitude toward their work:

> It was a procession of ghosts . . . people who had lost completely all
> human thought. . . . There are many ghost stories in . . . Japan
> . . . stories of women ghosts who lift their arms halfway and whose
> hands are burning with anger. . . . Japanese women could not [at
> the time of the A-bomb] express their human anger as anger. They
> could do no more than say in subdued tones, from the other world
> after their death, "I bear a grudge against . . . [*Urameshiya**]. . . .
> But where resentment cannot be expressed for a long, long time,
> malignant and incomprehensible spirits . . . leave their traces.
> Ghosts still live today, calling forth responses hidden by present
> realities. . . . The hearts of those who died were revived within our
> hearts as we painted.

The artists embrace survivors' guilt toward the dead and fear of retribution from the dead. But the combination of their thralldom to the A-
bomb experience and their ideological position, in their comments as in
their painting, renders the ghosts overly concrete and functional, and
also steers them in the direction of vengeance. Thus the survivor's (or
survivor-like artist's) sense of sacred historical truth is reinforced by
ideological need, resulting in the impaired artistic transformation we

---

* The traditional expression of Japanese ghosts when in the midst of haunting.

have spoken of. Despite this, the artists' achievement is by no means negligible. To which one must also add that for any artist to come close to evoking the full psychic dimensions of the atomic bomb would require a major creative breakthrough of a kind that is by no means now clear, and the elaboration of forms which do not as yet exist.

:

In music the "pre-eminently non-representative" art—"no scene, no object, no fact"[15]—the problem of recreating *any* specific event is much greater. There have been a number of serious works composed in relationship to the atomic bomb, but none seems to have emerged as a particularly powerful musical statement. They have frequently been combined with poems—particularly Tōge's, but also Hara's, Yoneda's, and others'—in cantatas bearing such names as "Give Back My Father" (the title of the original Tōge poem), "A Cantata of a Small Picturesque Atomic Bomb," "Oh People!," "Song of Peace," and "Song of the River Bank." Thus, it is the verbal content which concretely relates the fundamentally abstract nature of music to the atomic bomb. Two cantatas composed by Masao Ōki, based upon Tōge's *Collected A-Bomb Poems*, together entitled "Give Back Mankind," have been given particularly frequent performances, and have considerable emotional power. The Tokyo Rō-on (Congress of Workers' Music Councils in Japan) has especially popularized the work in performing it for audiences of laborers. The combination of the subject matter and the recitative choral style employed have rendered it something in the nature of a folk opera, though without any specific dramatic "plot."

Ōki has also written a symphony, entitled "Symphonic Fantasia Hiroshima," first performed in 1954, and derived largely from themes of his earlier cantata. Significantly, this work turned to painting for its content; it was not only inspired by "Pictures of the Atomic Bomb" but its first six movements bear the titles of the individual murals. The symphony takes fifty minutes to perform, and the seventh and last movement is described as simply an elegy. Ōki combined in the work various traditional musical elements from Japanese drama (the Nō), balladry (*jōruri*), epic songs (*nagauta*), and even popular recitation (*naniwabushi*) with the contemporary Western (now international) idiom which dominates Japanese music. He looked upon his symphony as an expression of "the responsibility of the Japanese people" for letting the world know about the A-bomb, but the work does not appear to have been received as one of particular distinction. Much greater musical enthusiasm has been evoked by a work by a young Polish composer, Krzysztof Penderecki, "Threnody for the Victims of Hiroshima" for fifty-two string instruments. When it was performed in Warsaw at a festival of contemporary music in 1962, an American reviewer noted that it "dispenses completely with the concept of exact pitch and intervals as an organizing factor in composition—thus with anything resembling melodic or harmonic relationships," and described it as "one of the most remarkable and certainly the least conventional" of the works presented. Notable here is the suggestion of radical creative innovation as a means of dealing with the radical A-bomb theme.

The musical formulation which has probably had the widest impact has been the semi-popular song, "Let Us Prohibit the Atomic Bomb" (Genbaku Yurusumaji), in which a simple, exhortative poem by Sekiji Asada is set to rather sentimental music. It has been widely sung at different kinds of gatherings, especially those concerned with peace—though it has stopped considerably short of becoming a universal musical rallying call. The first stanza is:

The city of our homes was burned
And on burned earth where bones of our families were buried
White flowers are blooming now.
Oh, we should never permit the atomic bomb
Never permit the atomic bomb, never permit the atomic bomb,
   never permit the atomic bomb
In our city.

In subsequent stanzas it speaks of the sea ("never permit the atomic bomb in our sea"), the sky, and, finally, the world. Despite the banality of the verses, the combination of Japanese musical sensitivities (perhaps the most intense in the world) and A-bomb emotions can render the work a moving experience, particularly when sung by large groups. And whatever its artistic quality, it combines a characteristically Japanese mood of subdued melancholy (or elegy) with its protest, and may be said to have a certain authenticity within its musical limits. Such is the combination of his medium and his creative problem that the composer seeking to achieve adequate musical formulation of the atomic bomb must either collaborate with another, more "representative" art form, or else (as the Polish work suggests) take a bolder path of innovation, the traversing of which requires something close to genius.*

* Another symphony, entitled "Hiroshima," was written by a Finnish composer, Erkki Aaltonen, and performed in that city on August 15, 1955, by the Kansai Philharmonic Orchestra. There have also been an opera and a ballet written and publicly performed with atomic bomb themes.

3) Barriers and Directions

We have noted the intractability of the A-bomb, as an artistic subject, to symbolic transformation via any medium. By exploring some of the facets of this intractability, we may begin to look beyond them toward the creative possibilities which have, in fact, already begun to emerge.

A major impediment is one we may refer to as *creative guilt*. I have so far emphasized questions of survival priority in relationship to guilt, but there is, I would suggest, an added element in all art which can be an extremely formidable barrier. I refer to the guilt over trespassing on the dangerous psychological ground between chaos and form, the retaliation anticipated by any serious artist (or by a creative person in any field) for daring to subvert existing forms and to proclaim new ones previously unrecognized. Creative guilt is related to death symbolism—to the destruction or "killing" of old forms in order to give birth to new, and to the symbolic immortality sought by the artist through the creation of those forms. This kind of guilt is associated with fear of hubris, with the artist's fear of the consequences of his usurping the creative function from higher powers. What happens with the A-bomb is that the event becomes rendered so historically sacred that recreating it in any form can be psychologically perceived as hubris by both artists and their audiences. Any vision which carries the artist beyond the literal into the realm of virtual experience is likely to evoke the kind of retaliatory fear we have repeatedly noted in comments by writers and painters. As a result, creative artists tend to confine themselves to the memoir-novel, the documentary film, the realistic painting, and the structured musical "accompaniment," all of which seem relatively safe because they seek no alteration of the original subject matter. But these literal approaches often turn out to be doubly unsatisfactory, as we have so often observed, because they *must* alter the alleged "literal truth" of the event, and yet do not transform it into the psychic truth of art—or, in Harry Levin's words (in reference to concentration camp writing), they "combine . . . watered-down fact with water-logged fiction."[16]

Also related to the fear of artistic hubris is the *dimension of violence* which the technology of the A-bomb introduces. The artist feels both unable to grasp this dimension imaginatively, and to have no right, as a mortal being, to do so—no right to "cut it down to size" and make it symbolically manageable. Thus Levin further suggests (again referring to concentration camp literature) that "A first-hand reminiscence . . . is bound to be far more impressive than any fictitious approximation." But the key word here is "approximation," for it describes the limiting vision of the creator of the memoir-novel (or its equivalents in the other arts), in contrast to either frank reminiscence or freely exercised artistic imagination.

These technological dimensions lead in turn to a third impediment, the problem of *disconnected death*. The artist is confronted with a form of death so abrupt, total, and above all arbitrary that he has great difficulty relating it to individual lives of victims or executioners, to human relationships in general, or to any form of vitality. He is dealing with violence which (in Simone Weil's phrase) "makes a thing of man in the most literal sense, for it makes him a corpse"[17]—while providing no connection between that corpse and the life symbols an artist must draw upon. The problem exists even in the non-fictional recording of recollections of the event, and one reviewer of John Hersey's *Hiroshima* complained that the author's "antiseptic" naturalism evoked so little pity, horror, or indignation that the victims described "might just as well be white mice"—to which a later commentator replied that those killed in Hiroshima were indeed made into white mice because of the absence of any series of emotional events "leading logically" to their becoming corpses.[18] Here we recognize what we have called the guinea pig theme as an expression of absolute disconnection not only between victim and assailant, but between inert corpse (or corpselike survivor) and previously vital human being. Nor can the artist readily relate that corpse to those expressions of human and natural continuity which provide him with the vision of symbolic immortality so necessary to creative function, as it is to ordinary psychic life. Indeed, I suspect that this threat of disconnected death, and therefore of disconnected life, has had much to do with the prominence of women in certain forms of A-bomb art, particularly in A-bomb literature—whether as practitioners of that literature or as critics of it. In either case, women are expressing their close identification with organic life and its perpetuation as an antidote to nuclear severance.

There is still another possible impediment to A-bomb art, which has to do with psychological characteristics of Japanese culture. Masao Maruyama speaks of a Japanese tendency to distill all experience into "concrete entities," a pre-modern residuum which prevents "a really free flight of the imagination" and results in a general uneasiness toward the essential psychic process of fiction, that of "matter becoming form."[19] What Maruyama is saying is that a certain kind of modern (and Western) capacity for symbolic transformation has been insufficiently developed in the Japanese, so that even their most skillfully rendered fiction remains confused between literal and virtual experience—a confusion perhaps most vividly documented in the specific Japanese genre of the "I-novel." If Maruyama is right, as I believe he is, the capacity for artistic re-creation of the A-bomb becomes further limited.

REASSERTIONS

But art reasserts itself no less insistently than life. And it thrives on complexity. For not only have the Japanese been moving rapidly toward what Maruyama calls a "modern spirit," which "believe[s] in the value and use of fiction," but also toward a post-modern spirit, which, it turns out, has many characteristics very similar to those of the pre-modern residuum he describes—including new ways of merging literal and virtual experience in art. This post-modern or "protean" tendency has created difficult problems, but it has also been associated with innovations appropriate to specific creative tasks of the present.[20] While artists in general have been overwhelmed by twentieth-century violence, they continue to create in its shadow; and those critics who question this creative potential may themselves have been similarly overwhelmed (as what sensitive man has not?), to the extent of underestimating the "survival capacity" of art, even under the most extreme circumstances.

We have been talking mostly about unrealized works, but we have also seen glimmerings—in an occasional A-bomb poem, story, or film— of what art might do. The most successful efforts have drawn upon the qualities of *mono no aware*, the elegiac mood of sad beauty and experiential intensity so integral to Japanese existence, while at the same time transcending it. Artists have gravitated to this quality of feeling, even when consciously aware of its limitations in dealing with the A-bomb and with modern life in general. For when they abandon it entirely, their work tends to fail altogether, just as a Western work would if it sought to cope with a massive death immersion by totally abandoning the emotional and literary heritage of tragedy. While tragedy posits a heroic struggle against death-linked destiny and *mono no aware* a harmonizing acceptance of it, both are means of reasserting the connection, integrity, and movement necessary for symbolic immortality, and they bear greater resemblance to one another than is usually recognized. The difficulty, as we know, is that *mono no aware* lapses readily into shallow sentimentality, and that unless deepened by some contemporary idiom, its approach to nuclear disaster leaves artist and audience profoundly unsatisfied.

Yet if the literature of the concentration camp is any indication (and we shall observe in the next chapter important similarities between the two experiences), there is reason to believe that increasingly significant artistic formulation of the Hiroshima disaster may not be too long in coming. Artists confronting Nazi persecutions have also been dominated by what has been called "factuality," and, at least in earlier efforts, most successful when staying close to recollections of actual experience. But during the late 1950s and early 1960s a number of books have appeared which, according to one observer, have changed the genre from "a specialized subject, a subdivision of the history of an insult to humanity" to a genuinely universal literature, which by "exploring the possibilities of human behavior in inhuman circumstances," becomes "relevant to our own, mercifully more humdrum lives."[21] Thus, in rapid succession, we have had André Schwarz-Bart's *The Last of the Just*,[22] which makes allegorical use of the concentration camp theme to evoke, with extraordinary power, centuries of Jewish martyrdom, along with elemental human truths; Piotr Rawicz' *Blood From the Sky*,[23] a wildly imaginative survivor's tale of the destruction of Eastern European Jewry which resorts to extreme literary experiments with levels of experience and fantasy; and Jorge Semprun's *The Long Voyage*,[24] which, in describing a five-day train trip to a concentration camp, also moves brilliantly across time and consciousness, and does so with masterful integration. As early as 1955 we were given what may still be the most notable of all works of concentration camp art and one of the greatest documentary films ever made about anything, Alain Resnais' *Night and Fog* (*Nuit et Brouillard*). Through its understated narrative and imaginative pictorial alternation (using both stills and motion) between scenes of grotesque death and of magnificent landscape, the film leaves the viewer with a terrifying but profoundly enlarging imprint of the concentration camp experience as it relates to man's general psychic potential. It demonstrates that what we call the documentary form is as capable as any of genuine artistic transformation.

To be sure, the A-bomb experience is even more difficult to deal with artistically than the concentration camps: it is more ahuman, detached, technological. Yet as I was completing this chapter, I came across a rather remarkable expression of A-bomb literature, by a young *hiba-*

kusha-woman writer named Hiroko Takenishi, entitled *Ceremony* (*Gishiki*, published in late 1963).[25] Like *Blood From the Sky* and *The Long Voyage*, the novel moves back and forth through imagination and memory, but it centers its concerns more specifically upon death and upon an A-bomb survivor's preoccupation with the general absence of ritual in association with dying. The author, in fact, sums up the entire death-saturated A-bomb experience as "the omission of various ceremonies." And at the end she raises the question of the survivor's need to master his history, to claim as his own (in a psychological as well as geographical sense) not only the "beautiful land" that existed prior to the bomb but the "land completely changed" by it and its aftermath. While Miss Takenishi's novel does not approach the freedom or brilliance of those by Semprun and Rawicz, it makes clear that A-bomb literature too can be produced which relates itself both specifically to Hiroshima and to universal psychic experience. It also suggests that A-bomb literature is capable of saying important things about the relationship of death to contemporary life, and in a way that no other literary genre can.*

There have also begun to appear a spate of Japanese novels written by non*hibakusha*, taking up various A-bomb issues. *A Group on the Earth* (*Chi no Mure*) by Mitsuharu Inoue† deals with the taint and the suffering of Nagasaki *hibakusha*, their relationship to actual outcast (*burakumin*) communities, including episodes of violence between members of the two groups. Two other novels approach the issue through the mind of an American atomic bomb pilot. One, *Judgment* (*Shimpan*) by Yoshie Hotta,[27] is an ambitious if melodramatic exploration of the question of how, and by whom, the dropping of the A-bomb can be judged. Its hero, an American who participated in both the Hiroshima and Nagasaki bombings, comes to Japan to rediscover and re-evaluate himself; he has a confrontation with a guilty Japanese counterpart who had killed a woman in China, in which the distinctions between their actions are discussed, and then makes his way inevitably to Hiroshima, where he kills himself by jumping off the Peace Bridge.

---

* As if to confirm this judgment, a novel entitled *Kuroi Ame* (*Black Rain*), by Masuji Ibuse, was published serially in Tokyo in 1965–1966; it has been hailed by Japanese literary critics as the first truly distinguished work of fiction to deal with the atomic bomb. A summary of the novel and its psychological relevance has been included in the Appendix.

† This novel also includes the theme of stealing the head of the statue of Mary which its author is said to have been long concerned with and to have written about journalistically in the past.[26]

The other, *American Hero*, or, as the author, Momo Iida,[28] prefers to call it in English, *A Hero of the U.S.A.* (*Amerika no Eiyū*), is a wildly associative and clearly talented evocation of a man modeled closely after Claude Eatherly. It combines mockery, fluidity, and Marxist dogma in its forays through madness and sanity, guilt and retribution, and the varieties of American evil. Though these three novels are of mixed quality, they (especially the last) suggest an expansion of imaginative approach which is part of the process by which A-bomb literature is joining what has been described (in relationship to concentration camp writings) as "our own underliterature," "a perverted, lunatic parody of our own engulfing but otherwise comfortable technological societies" which reveals the "sour destructiveness" beneath the façade of our "well-conditioned domestic psyches." The fascinated horror with which this underliterature is received, as the same critic points out, results from its being viewed as "a small-scale trial run for a nuclear war."[29]

:

A-bomb art thus relates itself to the problem of mastery at several different levels. For the individual survivor and the general community of survivors it importantly contributes to A-bomb formulations. It does this largely indirectly, by entering into a vast pool of ideas and feelings constantly drawn upon and replenished; but sometimes directly as well, as in the case of younger survivors, who frequently described to me how they learned, mostly from films but also from other art forms and mass media, how to imagine a holocaust they knew to be important in their lives but could not remember. For other Japanese it is one of the most important means of coming to terms with a vast historical trauma, which despite being widely repressed and denied, continues to exert far-reaching psychological effects, and to require ever renewed efforts at imaginative interpretation. For the world at large A-bomb creativity becomes part of a wider art and literature of survival which, through directing itself both to holocausts already experienced and those feared in the future, becomes a possible source of wisdom about man's increasingly troubled relationship to the kinds of death which face him. Yet the very limited nature of its contribution to date, and the difficulty with which each small advance in A-bomb art is attained, make mastery almost too strong a word for what we are discussing. We are once more struck by the extent of pain and conflict man has visited upon himself by adding the demands of nuclear weapons to his already troubled imagination.

THE SURVIVOR

I have assumed throughout this book that psychological occurrences in Hiroshima have important bearing upon all of human experience. I have suggested in a variety of ways that we are all survivors of Hiroshima and, in our imaginations, of future nuclear holocaust. The link between Hiroshima and ourselves is not simply metaphorical, but has specific psychological components which can be explored in relationship to the general psychology of the survivor.

We may define the survivor as one who has come into contact with death in some bodily or psychic fashion and has himself remained alive. From this broad perspective we may compare patterns we have observed in Hiroshima to those of other "extreme" historical experiences, particularly the Nazi persecutions, but also the plagues of the Middle Ages; to relevant Japanese cultural practice pertaining to death and survival; and to responses to "ordinary" forms of disaster, as well as to individual survival in association with "the dying patient." I have found it convenient to pursue these comparisons under five general themes—the death imprint, death guilt, psychic numbing, nurturance and contagion, and formulation. As we examine these categories we find ourselves dealing with universal psychological tendencies; the survivor becomes Everyman. But the holocausts of the twentieth century have thrust the survivor ethos into special prominence, and imposed upon us all a series of immersions into death which mark our existence.

1) Death Imprint

The key to the survivor experience, the basis for all survivor themes, is the imprint of death. This imprint occurs whatever one's pre-existing psychological traits, though its quality and force are influenced by contact it makes with "survival" emotions experienced from the beginning of life.

The death imprint of Hiroshima survivors is made unique by three aspects of their ordeal: the suddenness and totality of their death saturation, the permanent taint of death associated with radiation aftereffects, and their continuing group relationship to world fears of nuclear extermination. Nazi concentration camp victims, in contrast, underwent an experience less directly associated with contemporary death anxiety, but involving more prolonged humiliation and terror, and more generalized psychic and bodily assaults—including exposure to starvation, suffocation in crowded boxcars, extreme heat and cold, beatings, forced labor, epidemic diseases, and medical and surgical experimentation. *Concentration camp survivors, therefore, are likely to retain more diffuse and severe psychic impairment, while in hibakusha death imagery tends to be more exclusively predominant.* But various kinds of residual death imagery have also been noted in concentration camp survivors. And I would go further and claim that less intense forms of death imprint are of great importance in all disasters, natural or manmade, and that the tendency to ignore or minimize these has more to do with psychological resistances of investigators than with the experiences being studied.

With both Hiroshima and Nazi concentration camp survivors the *grotesqueness surrounding the death imprint* had additional significance: it conveyed the psychological sense that death was not only everywhere, but was bizarre, unnatural, indecent, absurd. Hiroshima survivors experienced this grotesqueness through a sense of monstrous alteration of the body substance—also resembling feelings suggested by accounts of the "Black Death" or "Great Dying," the plagues which swept Europe during the fourteenth century. These accounts convey not only the grotesque symptoms of the plague (gangrenous inflammations, violent chest pains, vomiting and spitting of blood, and "pestilential odour" from the bodies and breath of the ill), but also a dramatic perception of selective destiny ("From the carbuncles and glandular swellings many recovered; from the blood-spitting none")[1] reminiscent of the *hibakusha*'s sense of supernatural victimization in relationship to the early "epidemic" of A-bomb disease. There was also a very important difference: for those afflicted with the plague recovery from the original attack meant release from the encounter with death ("The few who recovered had no second attack, or at least not of a serious nature"),[2] while for the atomic bomb victim what appeared to be recovery turned out to be the beginning of a lifelong sense of vulnerability to the same grotesque death. After any such exposure the survivor internalizes this grotesqueness as well as the deaths themselves, and feels it to be inseparable from his own body and mind. As Wiesel has written in relationship to the Nazi concentration camp experience: "In every stiffened corpse I saw myself."[3]

Concerning the issue of vulnerability, there is a distinct polarity in the survivor's imagery. One side of that imagery is his sense of heightened vulnerability. This is usually attributed to the shattering of the illusion of personal invulnerability which people tend to hold in both ordinary and dangerous situations. But what needs also to be emphasized is the survivor's having experienced a *jarring awareness of the fact of death*, as well as of its extent and violence. Not only has any pre-existing illusion of invulnerability been shattered, but he has been disturbingly confronted with his own mortality, with his own death anxiety. This sense of heightened vulnerability strongly affects the survivor's overall sense of the world around him. In Hiroshima survivors it was part of the vast breakdown of faith in the larger human matrix, and in the general structure of existence, which we spoke of before. Related symbolic breakdown has been observed in former inmates of Nazi concentration camps; and while most characteristic of massive death immersion, probably occurs in lesser degree in every form of survival.

Yet, as we have also observed, the survivor can retain an opposite image of having met death and conquered it, a sense of *reinforced invulnerability*. He may feel himself to be one of those rare beings who has "crossed over to the other side" and come back—one who has lived out the universal psychic theme of death and rebirth.

Thus *hibakusha* could, in certain activities such as peace movements, assume the aura of a spiritual elite who have "known" death, and then returned to teach others the secret of mastering it. When this happens (as we saw in the case of a few A-bomb leaders) the survivor enters into the myth of the hero; for what is called the hero's "road of trials"[4] is really his death encounter, from which he returns to convey his special "message" of mastery to his people. The partial operation of this pattern could be observed even in ordinary *hibakusha*. One young woman told me how, during years of hospitalization for a severe leg injury prior to the bomb, she was constantly afraid of dying; and then how, after witnessing "on the day of the *pika* . . . the death of so many people taking place right in front of my eyes . . . I no longer feel any fear of death in myself."[5] A similar sentiment was expressed by Rawicz in the phrase "Survival came gushing forth, like a splash,"[6] the feeling experienced by his protagonist in contemplating the annihilation by the Nazis of his own Ukrainian-Jewish community. But Rawicz and his protagonist leave one with the sense of remaining locked in the conflicts of the death immersion, and the woman *hibakusha* quoted was, despite her claim, by no means free of death anxiety. The survivor's reinforced invulnerability, in other words, can be the most fragile of psychic entities. More likely to be pseudo than genuine mastery, it can readily reverse itself and expose the heightened sense of vulnerability that it tends to conceal.

Related to this struggle with vulnerability is what may be called the survivor's "death spell," his thralldom to the death encounter itself. Early in the experience this may take the form of the "spellbound fascination" with scenes of death and devastation which we noted in Hiroshima survivors. Later it is found in an *indelible image* of the death encounter, an image more compelling than any drawn from prior or subsequent life experience. Hence the extraordinary sense of immediacy we observed in the accounts of Hiroshima survivors despite the seventeen-year interval, along with comments such as "the atomic bomb was the most important thing that ever happened to me"; and similar tendencies in concentration camp survivors to, as one psychiatric examiner put it, "communicate . . . an uncanny feeling that nothing of real significance had happened in their lives since their liberation." The force and detail of these memories "almost made the walls of my office disappear, to be replaced by the bleak vistas of Auschwitz or Buchenwald."[7] The same examiner went on to observe that although most survivors wished to drive those vistas from their minds, "there are also a few who seem to derive pleasure from remembering"—such as one woman who would "hurry to get through the affairs of the day so that she could be by herself at night to recall over and over again her own experiences and those of her family." And the survivor-hero in Jorge Semprun's novel *The Long Voyage* describes how, years after the war, when in the midst of a pleasant scene, eating and talking with friends before a wood fire,

> . . . suddenly I had a piece of black bread in my hand, and mechanically I bit into it, meanwhile continuing the conversation. Then, the slightly acid taste of the black bread, the slow mastication of this gritty black bread, brought back, with shocking suddenness, the marvelous moments when, at camp, we used to eat our ration of bread, when, with Indian-like stealth, we used to stretch it out, so that the tiny squares of wet, sandy bread which we cut out of our daily ration would last as long as possible.

Despite the "marvelous" quality of the memories, the narrator feels his heart "pounding like a triphammer," and when his hostess asks him what is the matter, he dismisses the whole thing as "a random thought of no consequence":

> Obviously I couldn't tell her that I was in the throes of dying, dying of hunger, far far from them, far from the wood fire and the words we were saying, in the snow at Thuringia amid the tall beeches through which the gusts of winter wind were blowing.[8]

This sense of having virtually entered the realm of death ("dying, dying of hunger") and yet returned from it, gives the memory its lasting power. The indelible image of the "death spell," then, is the survivor's reminder that he has "touched death." It is therefore a reminder of survival itself. Such memories become repeated re-enactments of that survival. They also reflect a continuous effort to absorb an encounter whose life-and-death absolutes cause it to be perceived as in every way more fundamental—more psychically devastating and illuminating—than any other.

But the death spell, as we have also observed, can be associated with prolonged grief and mourning, with what we may call the survivor's *life of grief*. The early symptoms he experiences have been described as characteristic for "acute grief"; these include preoccupation with the image of the dead, guilt, bodily complaints, various hostile reactions, and disruption of ordinary patterns of conduct.[9] They can, however, become chronic to the point of permanence. We know that the essence of grief is loss. But what is it that the survivor has lost? For what does he mourn?

He mourns, first of all, for family members and for others who had been close to him. And he mourns, as we have repeatedly seen, for the anonymous dead. But he mourns also for inanimate objects and lost symbols—for possessions, houses, streets he had known, beliefs that have been shattered, a way of life that has been "killed."[10] In sum, he mourns for his own former self, for what he was prior to the intrusion upon it of death and death conflicts. For what has been taken from him (and the word "bereavement" suggests being robbed of something)[11] is his innocence of death, and particularly of grotesquely demeaning death. Thus, in relationship to Nazi persecutions, Rawicz' narrator, upon viewing the corpse of a girl he loved, speaks of the need for "fidelity to the selves we were"; and Wiesel tells how a horrified survivor rushes back to warn the rest of his people with the words: "I wanted to come back . . . to tell you the story of my death." For in "dying with"[12] the others, the survivor feels his freedom from death-domination to come to an end. From then on he is bound to the dead—and to his own grief—by his inability to recapture this lost state.

In addition, the survivor of sudden, overwhelming disaster, as in Hiroshima, experiences various kinds of *impaired mourning*—a general inability to accomplish the "work of mourning." He is deprived of opportunity to prepare for his loss, to experience a gradual process of "anticipatory mourning."[13] Nor can he later cope with the totality of loss. Indeed, I had the impression that the grief of atomic survivors was related to a lifelong inability to absorb that initial moment which I spoke of earlier as their sudden and absolute shift from normal existence to overwhelming encounter with death. Examiners of concentration camp victims have stressed the phenomenon of the "missing grave" as an impairment to mourning and a cause of later psychiatric difficulty. But what is really at issue, with both Nazi survivors and *hibakusha*, might more accurately be termed the "missing dead": the survivor's sense that the bodies—the human remains—around which he might ordinarily organize rituals of mourning, abruptly disappeared into smoke or nothingness. In these ways mourning is rendered shallow and unsatisfying, as we frequently observed in Hiroshima, and the reiteration of ties to the dead brings neither relief nor resolution. The survivor then becomes susceptible to the array of mental and physical disturbances that have recently been demonstrated to accompany any form of unresolved grief[14]—and to the other patterns depicted in this chapter. Contemplating such issues, a leading psychosomatic investigator has urged that grief itself be viewed as a disease.[15] But my impression from the Hiroshima work is that the "disease" of the survivor is not grief but its distortion—not mourning but impaired mourning.

REACTIVATION, WORLD-DESTRUCTION, AND PSYCHIC MUTATION

Survivors are also subject to acute episodes of *symbolic reactivation* of their entire constellation of death anxiety and loss. In Hiroshima we saw this reactivation produced by such classic stimuli as mass-media reports of people dying from A-bomb disease, and reports of nuclear weapons testing; as well as by the annual August 6th ceremony, the sight of the A-Bomb Dome, war or warlike behavior anywhere in the world, the onset of hot weather, or simply the sight of another's child when one's own has been killed by the bomb. Similarly, concentration camp survivors experience strong symbolic reactivation of their experience in relationship to such events as the Eichmann trial and the outbreak of anti-Semitism anywhere in the world, as well as to the kind of indirect associative stimulus suggested by Semprun's description of the eating of black bread.

Psychologically speaking, the survivor's actual death immersion is itself a symbolic reactivation of earlier "survivals"—of childhood experiences associated with separation and loss, including the birth process—which serve as "models" for later death anxiety. It has been observed on hospital wards, for instance, that critically ill children, too young to have clear ideas about the nature of death and dying, nonetheless experience heightened anxiety and depression when deaths occur around them. For to the child-survivor these deaths represent not only a painful psychic intrusion of the idea of dying per se, but also the reactivation of earlier separation anxiety.* And even in adult life images of death, loss, and separation remain, to a considerable extent, psychologically interchangeable. A survivor's death encounter, therefore, may be symbolically reactivated by exposure to any of the three, as well as by experiences specifically reminiscent of that encounter.†

* Nattersen and Knudsen[16] have found manifest death anxiety to be present only in older children (from about six to twelve years), while younger children tend to show stronger separation fear, and fear of medical procedures. But they add that "there were indications that anxiety about death may have been present in more subtle form in younger children, even though overshadowed by fear of separation, or fear of the procedures. Such indications were sometimes found in drawings and stories of the children." In both of these groups of children, reactions may be said to have occurred in the absence of "a realistic conception of death as a permanent biologic process," since such a conception does not develop (according to Maria Nagy, whom they follow) until about the ninth year. While I think it likely that children younger than nine possess a more accurate image of death than is generally believed, the principle of their reacting to death prior to clearly understanding it still holds.

† These relationships were pointed out originally by Freud and have been more recently described by John Bowlby and Melanie Klein. But rather than emphasize

Similar principles apply to the survivor's "end-of-the-world" imagery. Particularly in the atomic bomb exposure we may say that the survivor lived out in psychic and bodily actuality an experience ordinarily associated with psychotic delusion. The "world-destruction" fantasies of the psychotic reflect his radically impaired relationship to the world, and his projection upon *it* of his own inner sense of "psychic death." But the survivor of mass death reverses the process so that an overwhelming *external* experience of near-absolute annihilation makes contact with related tendencies of the inner life. That is, it merges with mental images which originally signified the "end of the world" for the young child—threatening images not only of separation and helplessness, but also of stasis and annihilation. *The survivor's imposed picture of world-destruction, therefore, is partly a symbolic reactivation of that sense of psychic death which everyone has always known.* This coming together of inner and outer experience contributes greatly to the indelible quality of the death encounter. It creates, particularly for survivors of such overwhelming events as the atomic bomb, Nazi persecutions, and the plagues of the Middle Ages, an ill-defined but powerfully felt image of "ultimate death" and "ultimate separation."

With such events, so radical is the overturning of the sense of what is "real"—of what must be psychologically absorbed—that the survivor's mental economy undergoes a permanent alteration, a *psychic mutation*. Survivors of the Black Death have left vivid descriptions of the kind of "end-of-the-world" experience, which is associated with this form of psychic mutation:

> How will posterity believe that there has been a time when without the lightings of heaven or the fires of earth, without wars or other visible slaughter, not this or that part of the earth, but well-nigh the whole globe, has remained without inhabitants.
>
> When has any such thing been heard or seen; in what annals has it ever been read that houses were left vacant, cities deserted, the country neglected, the fields too small for the dead, and a fearful and universal solitude over the whole earth? Consult your historians, they are silent; question your doctors, they are dumb; seek an answer from your philosophers, they shrug their shoulders and frown, and with their fingers to their lips bid you be silent.

---

the principle of separation or "separation anxiety" as the basic emotion involved in what we call fear of death, I take the reverse position that these are subsumed by more fundamental imagery around life, death, and survival—imagery unique to man as a symbolizer with knowledge of his own death.

Will posterity ever believe these things when we, who see, can scarcely credit them? We should think we were dreaming if we did not with our eyes, when we walk abroad, see the city in mourning with funerals, and returning to our home, find it empty, and thus know that what we lament is real.[17]

For Nazi concentration camp inmates something in the nature of a psychic mutation was, as one psychiatric examiner has observed, necessary to survival itself: "There is reason to believe that a person who fully adhered to all the ethical and moral standards of conduct of civilian life on entering the camp in the morning, would have been dead by nightfall."[18] And another stressed the extraordinary psychic adjustments necessary "in a world in which cannibalism becomes a reality, in which one is forced at the point of a gun to eat one's own feces." This near-absolute ethical reversal was even more prominent in the concentration camp experience than it was in atomic bomb exposure. But in both cases, the force behind it—the origin of the psychic mutation—is the threat of death.

:

For in all we have been discussing the survivor's fundamental anxiety relates to the issue of his own death. Freud once claimed that only through the death of someone he loved was primitive man "forced to learn that one can die, too, oneself," and that "his whole being revolted against the admission."[19] But I would stress that this death anxiety on the part of the survivor is concerned not just with dying itself but with *premature death and unfulfilled life*. The *hibakusha* and the Nazi concentration camp survivor witnessed mass death that was awesome in its randomness, in its inclusion of small children quite new to life, and young adults at their prime, as well as old people who had in any case not much longer to live. The anxiety-laden imprint retained by both groups of survivors was of death that has *no reasonable relationship to life span or life cycle, of profoundly inappropriate death*.

Physicians have observed similar anxieties among family members who "survive" dying patients. In situations where these patients were very young "the fatal illnesses in the children constituted death threats to the mothers."[20] And with dying adults, relatives' own aggravated death anxiety contributes to the shallow optimism they frequently express to the patient, as well as to their occasional pleas that he be permitted a quick and painless death. The attending physician also shares in these survivor anxieties since, as one investigator put it, "the doctor is called to reflect upon his own death," and "The death of a patient may revive [in him] memories of other deaths and other losses."[21]

In one sense any death a survivor witnesses feels inappropriate, since neither he nor the man who dies can ever be entirely prepared for it. But the shocking inappropriateness of death on a massive scale (as we observed in Hiroshima) causes a more fundamental disruption in the survivor's sense of the general continuity of human existence. Thus, at the time of the plague it was recorded that in the midst of chaos and danger, ordinary citizens vigorously demanded the lifting of Church restrictions on the right to be buried in consecrated ground.[22] These survivors, we may say, were worried not only about being fatally afflicted, but about the immortality they feared would be denied them. Nor has this concern with immortality been limited to the Christian world of the Middle Ages. Whether in a literal-theological idiom or in more symbolic fashion, the survivor of any death immersion feels his relationship to the ultimate forces of death and rebirth to be seriously threatened.

2) Death Guilt

Inseparable from his death imprint is the survivor's struggle with guilt. Since survival, by definition, involves a sequence in which one person dies sooner than another, this struggle in turn concerns issues of *comparative death-timing*. Relevant here is what we have spoken of as guilt over survival priority, along with the survivor's unconscious sense of an organic social balance which makes him feel that his survival was purchased at the cost of another's.

One could claim that under certain hypothetical circumstances, such guilt might be minimal—for instance, in those surviving the death of an elderly head of a thriving and harmonious family who has himself lived fully, within a community where the rhythms of life and death are symbolically viable and given ritual expression. The son (or wife or daughter) surviving such a death could look upon it as appropriate, and could feel himself entitled to the life bequeathed him via the larger organic social balance. But we are speaking of ideal conditions, which, even in the traditional societies where they are said to have existed, were at best imperfectly approximated. In the midst of our present historical velocity the entire image becomes a nostalgic quasi-mythical one. Yet it holds considerable power as a failed ideal, and as such stimulates survivor guilt.*

To be sure, there are differences in degree: we noted in Hiroshima the special intensity of the guilt of parents surviving their children. But even when the young (seemingly appropriately) outlive the old, there are always reasons for them, as survivors, to find fault with the comparative timing, to emphasize the "untimeliness" of death. No survival experience, in other words, can occur without severe guilt.

Freud attributed this guilt primarily to the ambivalent resentments the survivor had experienced toward the dying person in the past. But it may be more correct to say that ambivalence itself, in its most basic

---

* Weisman and Hackett suggest a concept of appropriate death, from the standpoint of the dying person, as having four principal requirements: conflict is reduced; compatibility with the ego ideal is achieved; continuity of important relationships is preserved or restored; and consummation of a wish is brought about. Insofar as survivors can consider such criteria to be applicable to a particular death, their guilt may be minimized. But they are likely to have even more difficulty looking upon that death as "appropriate" than the dying person himself.[23]

sense, reflects contradictory wishes concerning death-timing. For just as a child's early fears of separation are inseparable from death anxiety, so are his retaliatory wishes toward depriving parents (all parents) psychically inseparable from death wishes. And as he gets older, and begins to contemplate his own life span, his wish to outlive his parents is strengthened. He also wants his parents to live indefinitely—because he loves them and because he needs their care. What we speak of as his ambivalence, therefore, permeates every facet of his relationship with them, but has its origins in contradictory feelings which, directly or indirectly, relate to death and survival.

These feelings greatly affect any death encounter and help us to understand the profound guilt over death-timing which we observed in Hiroshima: in relationship to family members (as in the case of the elderly woman who described feeling "very deep emotion" because her brother, after having searched for her in the bombed area, "preceded me in death"); and in relationship to the anonymous dead. The unconscious self-accusation "I am responsible for his death" can easily become "I killed him." In the concentration camp experience, moreover, such self-accusations were sometimes almost literally true. Prisoners concretely asked themselves, as one has subsequently written, "Will you survive, or shall I?"[24] And this *competition for survival* was epitomized by the notorious practice of "selections," in which prisoners were brought before an official, sometimes a physician, who would decide with a point of a finger whether each was to be immediately killed or allowed to go on living. Since decisions were usually based upon the examiner's judgment of whether or not prisoners' physical state permitted them to perform useful work, many sought to influence the choice by such devices as rouging their faces to hide pallor, or stuffing cloth into their clothes or their mouths to disguise their emaciation. Nor was there any doubt about the competition involved: in one case, where girls were periodically "selected" for the gas chambers simply on the basis of odd or even numbers, they "often panicked, pushing each other from their places in line."[25] There were also frequent accounts of prisoners altering lists of people slated for deportation and death by replacing their own names or their friends' with those of other inmates. The guilt which resulted was intolerable, and we can well understand former inmates' tendency to minimize this competitiveness and emphasize the chance element in survival. None, however, could be totally unaffected by a pervasive "either-you-or-me" atmosphere.

The competition could sometimes take grotesquely concrete form: the loading of a hundred people into railroad cars which had room for forty, and even with everyone standing could hold no more than eighty, so that "twenty people in each wagon [car] had to die, and their fellow prisoners, by pushing and stamping on each other, had to kill them"; and another episode in which the Jewish Kapo (or prisoner-official) in the women's camp in Auschwitz "was forced, as a price for her life, to load on the truck going to the gas chamber her mother and her sister." The Kapo was often as dreaded a figure as the SS guards themselves, since, as Bruno Bettelheim has explained, "a prisoner's position of power was always one of being able to protect *and* to kill. . . ."[26]

The survivor of Nazi concentration camps, moreover, like the survivor of Hiroshima, carried the burden of not only what he did but what he *felt*. Thus, Wiesel tells how, as a fifteen-year-old boy, he took tender care of his sick father under the most extreme conditions en route to and within Auschwitz, Buna, and Buchenwald. But when temporarily separated from him, he was suddenly horrified at his wish that he not be able to find him: "If only I could get rid of this dead weight, so that I could use all my strength to struggle for my own survival, and only worry about myself." And when his father died, he perceived "in the recesses of my weakened conscience," a feeling close to "free at last!" He describes feeling both guilty and "ashamed of myself, ashamed forever"; and the indelibility of the imprint of these events is more forcefully conveyed when he recalls how, shortly after being liberated (and following a severe illness of his own), he looked into a mirror and "a corpse gazed back at me. The look in his eyes, as they stared into mine, has never left me."[27]

:

It is precisely this kind of death guilt, rather than external events in themselves, which survivors of Nazi camps and Hiroshima refer to when they speak of their "living hell." And from these extreme experiences we come to realize that no one's emotions about death and survival are *ever* experienced entirely as individual matters; that images of dying are bound up with inner questions about who and what will survive, and images of surviving with who (and what) has died in one's place.

Analogous patterns of guilt over survival priority have been observed in lesser disasters, and in relationship to dying patients. Again, the doctor attending these patients experiences the emotions of a survivor, and "must contend with the guilt evoked by the questioning glance of the dying, with the unspoken question, 'Why should I die while you live?' "[28] Similar feelings of guilt cause mothers of children dying of leukemia to wonder whether some wrong they have committed could have caused the child's illness.

THE HOMELESS DEAD

The grotesque and random patterns of dying we spoke of before have a special relationship to death guilt. Relevant to these absurd and humiliating deaths is the concept of the "homeless dead" found in most primitive and folk cultures.[29] Usually included among the homeless dead are the spirits (or ghosts) of the following: of those who died suddenly, through suicide or violence, while on a journey and far from home, through violating a taboo, lacking biological posterity, or in a specifically unfulfilled state (as in the case of young women between the time of betrothal and marriage); and also of the newly dead, and of those who have been denied proper rituals by their posterity. This last category suggests the responsibility survivors feel for the homeless dead, and the implication that some form of "negligence" has caused these dead to be "homeless"—that is, condemned to a miserable transitional existence in which they are capable neither of rejoining the living nor of settling comfortably among the other dead (they are sometimes also called "living dead"). Homeless dead are considered dangerous to the living, particularly to those who have directly survived them; they may cause them fright, bad fortune, various kinds of physical harm, or even suck their "life blood." They thus include the "wild souls" and "hungry ghosts" of East Asian tradition, as well as the "vampires" of Eastern Europe. Those killed in Hiroshima were thought of as homeless dead: they had died violently, in many cases lacking fulfillment and frequently without posterity, inevitably in the absence of proper death rituals.

In East Asia the idea of the homeless dead is related to ancestor worship and to Confucian stress upon filial piety. Requirements of filial piety include providing parents with a comfortable old age and a proper death and burial, and producing posterity in turn to maintain the family line. The surviving family head in particular becomes the guardian of biological immortality, and of those rituals which emphasize human continuity. Dead become homeless precisely because they signify severance of this continuity, breaks in the immortal chain. Survivors of the atomic bomb (especially if they were family heads) unconsciously condemn themselves for having failed in this most fundamental of responsibilities. And although particularly emphasized in East Asia, these principles are universal, and undoubtedly apply with equal force to former concentration camp inmates.

Further intensifying survivors' guilt is their anxious rejection of the dead. We noted how *hibakusha* sought to rid themselves quickly of corpses of family members, and there were many additional instances of their ignoring and avoiding the dead. Here grotesque patterns of A-bomb dying and fear of physical contamination came together with a more universal survivor's fear of being "contaminated" by death itself. *The survivor is, from the beginning, torn by a fundamental ambivalence: he embraces the dead, pays homage to them, and joins in various rituals to perpetuate his relationship to them; but he also pushes them away, considers them tainted and unclean, dangerous and threatening.*

A universal solution to the dilemma is the survivor's participation in *rites de passage*—funeral ceremonies—which speed the dead on their "journey" to another plane of existence, and "incorporate the deceased into the world of the dead."[30] Japanese Buddhist tradition has stressed "quick separation of souls from physical bodies" so that they "became ancestral souls, gradually became calm, settled in dwellings in high mountains, and came down to their children's homes and rice fields on certain occasions."[31] These calm and appropriately placed ancestral souls are the antithesis of the homeless dead—of the "wild souls" and "hungry ghosts" whose way of dying, or neglect by survivors, caused them to be denied proper separation from, and continuity with, these same survivors. Significantly, at the annual Bon Festival, the time when visits from ancestral souls are expected, special offerings of food are also put out for anonymous "hungry ghosts" who, it is thought, might otherwise have no one to provide for them—another expression of suvivors' sense of responsibility for their "homelessness." The Japanese words used in connection with rituals for the dead (*shizumeru, chinkon,* and *kuyō*) convey the sense of "pacifying," "calming down," or even "subduing" the souls of the dead as well as "consoling" or "making offerings" to them. They suggest the survivor's fear and resentment of the dead; and these unacceptable emotions constantly replenish his sense of guilt.

For the survivor must reject the dead (particularly the newly dead) until he can place them safely within a mode of immortality: in Japanese tradition, permit them to become ancestor souls (or gods); in Christian tradition, immortal souls. Until then (and even afterwards, since the mode is always incompletely realized) they constitute a disturbing suggestion of disconnection and of biological termination.

However contemporary minds may waver in literal belief in souls, they retain the need to visualize the dead as symbolically "living on"—a need which is part of the sense of immortality so integral to psychological existence in general. The survivor's continuing resentment of the dead is therefore fed by whatever difficulty he has in envisioning continuity with them; he resents them for depriving him of his own sense of immortality. The dimensions of "homelessness" imposed by events like the A-bomb and Nazi persecutions lead survivors to spend the rest of their lives struggling to right their relationships to the dead in the face of resentments they can neither express nor recognize.

EXPIATION AND REINFORCEMENT

A question frequently raised is whether A-bomb survivors were able to make psychological use of their ordeal as a means of expiation through suffering—whether it became an outlet for, even a source of relief from, previously existing guilt feelings. The experience certainly made contact with such early guilt feelings, and it probably served an expiatory purpose for some. But my impression was that in the main it activated rather than relieved guilt. This was true partly because of the extraordinary scope of human damage, causing the survivor to be always exposed to someone who had suffered more than he; partly because of his psychological tendency to take on responsibility for everyone's suffering—to feel "I brought on all of this evil," or even "My evil destroyed the world"; and partly because of the general complexity of the experience which made it so difficult for survivor and creative artist alike to absorb it and give it form. Even when certain *hibakusha* adopted a masochistic post-A-bomb life-pattern, through which they derived a certain amount of satisfaction in suffering, death anxiety and death guilt tended to remain prominent, and were often converted into bodily complaints. Concentration camp survivors probably experienced similar limitations in the psychological usefulness of expiation. Only in less extreme death encounters is a pattern of expiation likely to be more effective in restoring psychic function, and even then much depends upon the survivor's prior style of expressing guilt.

A striking feature of the Hiroshima environment is the *communal reinforcement of guilt*—the creation of a "guilty community" in which self-condemnation is "in the air." Indeed, this shared survivor guilt served as an organizing principle around which the *hibakusha* community originally took shape. In this sense the sharing of death guilt can provide a certain amount of emotional support for individual *hibakusha*, and it is possible that the absence of such sharing contributes to the sense of loneliness and lack of understanding experienced by some *hibakusha* living in Tokyo and elsewhere. But we have also seen how this same matrix of death guilt can enmesh and constrict the lives of Hiroshima *hibakusha* and cause some (such as the writers mentioned earlier) to feel that they are unable to remain in the city. And whatever symbolically reactivates the survivor experience in general (nuclear testing, for instance) also restimulates this guilt, and places new stress upon the uneasy bonds of the community. In the case of former concentration camp inmates the absence of a survivor community as discrete as that of *hibakusha* makes these patterns much less evident. But even among them, various forms of communal guilt undoubtedly operate, perhaps particularly in parts of Israel, where large numbers of them live in some contact with one another.

:

The ultimate horror, or epitome of death guilt, which we spoke of among Hiroshima survivors, has general significance for large-scale holocaust. Concentration camp survivors retained similar "ultimate" memories. One example is that of a former inmate of Auschwitz who witnessed the hanging of a fellow prisoner on the night preceding Yom Kippur, or Day of Atonement, the most sacred of Jewish holidays. Not only has the image remained permanently with him, but it is so actively revived every year at the time of the Jewish holidays that "though he knows that this happened many years ago in Europe, he becomes uncertain as to whether it is not also happening at the present time, now, in New York."[32] Here ultimate horror blends with what we spoke of before as the indelible image of death immersion, and brings to that image the full force of self-condemnation. The single memory of a hanged fellow prisoner becomes a distillation of the whole gamut of death guilt associated with the overall survivor experience. We note also the annual pattern of symbolic reactivation (the occasion itself, the Day of Atonement, suggests the communal expression of guilt), as well as a usurping of psychic actuality by the original experience to such a degree that past and present are confused.

IDENTIFICATION GUILT

In studying the Hiroshima experience, I have been impressed by the relationship of death guilt to the process of identification—to the survivor's tendency to incorporate within himself an image of the dead, and then to think, feel, and act as he imagines they did or would. He feels impelled, in other words, to place himself in the position of the person or persons maximally wronged—or else to castigate himself for falling short of such an identification. The same is true of concentration camp survivors. Recalling Wiesel's phrase, "In every stiffened corpse I saw myself," we may say that each survivor simultaneously feels himself to be that "stiffened corpse," condemns himself for not being it, and condemns himself even more for feeling relieved that it is the other person's and not his own. It is this process of identification which creates guilt over what one has done to, or not done for, the dying while oneself surviving, and which leaves every survivor with his own intra-psychic version of "a wound in the order of being."

Such "identification guilt" is based upon the tendency to judge oneself through the eyes of others, as revealed by the great significance the internalized image of the accusing eyes of the dead had for Hiroshima survivors. This pressure of identification with others is stressed in East Asian and other non-Western cultures (where it is frequently referred to as a shame sanction), in contrast to the Western emphasis upon internalized conscience and upon inner evil and sinfulness. But the distinction is far from absolute. For we have seen that identification guilt can become thoroughly internalized and function as conscience. And the Western sense of sin is itself based upon a process of identification, whether with one's parents, with others who mediate society's rules, or with the image of Christ.

Both guilt and shame, in their various forms, are fundamentally related to issues of human connection, and the eye symbolism retained by Hiroshima survivors transcends the somewhat arbitrary distinctions we tend to make between the two. We have already observed that being stared at by the dead signified guilt in the sense of being accused of wrongdoing, and shame in the sense of being "exposed" before others in one's "selfish" efforts to survive. But the basic psychological process taking place is the survivor's identification with the owners of the accusing eyes as human beings like him for whom he is responsible, his internalization of what he imagines to be their judgment of him, which in turn results in his "seeing himself" as one who has "stolen life" from them.

The fact that these eyes frequently belonged to the anonymous dead is of great significance, and suggests that identifications go beyond those emotionally close to one and extend outward to include fellow residents of a city, fellow countrymen, and fellow members of the human species. Indeed, anonymous eyes seemed frequently to have particularly great impact, as though representing, even more than did the eyes of those one knew, the "all-seeing eye" of an unknown deity, or the "evil eye" of an equally obscure malevolent power.[33]

The extreme experience thus demonstrates that guilt is immediately stimulated by participation in the breakdown of the general human order and by separation from it. This is true whether we employ the Western cultural idiom of sin and retribution or the East Asian one of humiliation and abandonment. Death, especially when inappropriate and premature, is the essence of breakdown and separation. In identifying so strongly with the dead—in forming what we have called the identity of the dead—the survivor seeks both to atone for his participation in that breakdown, and to reconstitute a form of order around that atonement.*

We have observed in Hiroshima the extraordinary demands such an identification could make upon *hibakusha*. Similarly, concerning concentration camp survivors, Rawicz has his narrator speak of "the love for these dead that was to swallow me up forever, just as the twilit landscape swallows up the distant shadow of a child"[35]—suggesting a bond no less than devouring in the totality of its inner requirements. The relationship of identification patterns, not only to death but to impaired symbolic immortality, is suggested by another observation among concentration camp survivors: the particularly strong patterns of guilt and depression in those who have lost an only child or all of their children, and who *had no subsequent children*.[36]

Identification also has great bearing upon patterns of guilt and anger. Guilt has often been described as a turning inward of anger. For the survivor this process depends upon a measure of identification with the environment of the death encounter, and even with those persons or forces he perceives as instigators of it. That is, a survivor turns his anger inward precisely because he cannot help but accept and internalize the world in which he has been victimized, including in some degree the motivation and behavior of the victimizer—whether the latter be Nazi officials, the American military (or President Truman), God, or destiny. His quest for adaptation and mastery thus involves him in a limited but

---

* This view of guilt is in some ways consistent with those put forth by a number of recent writers,[34] but I wish to suggest more specifically than they do the fundamental influence of death, and of any form of symbolic breakdown, upon the evolution of guilt.

nonetheless (for him) loathsome "identification with the aggressor,"[37] which in turn contributes to his guilt and confusion.

:

The rhythms of death guilt are also significant. In concentration camp survivors there has been described a "relatively symptom-free interval" during which they could either repress their guilt or otherwise cope with it in a manner permitting them to function fairly well, only to have this guilt reassert itself in severe emotional disorders years later. I encountered some evidence of this among Hiroshima survivors also, though the subclinical nature of their difficulties made the sequence less distinct. And among survivors in both groups there has occurred a related pattern in which early skill in manipulating the devastated world right after the death immersion was followed by an opposite tendency toward guilt-saturated restraint later on.

Thus, there were reports that concentration camp survivors were prominent in black-market operations in various parts of Europe right after World War II. And in Hiroshima, too, survivors were undoubtedly involved in various illegal activities—despite two myths we have already mentioned—the first that *only* outsiders engaged in the black market, and the second that those *hibakusha* who did take part in it later perished from A-bomb disease. These may be regarded as "myths of purification," part of the survivor's effort at managing guilt. The survivor's involvement in amoral or antisocial activity is, in one sense, part of a continuing struggle for life among people whose experience has schooled them to resort to extreme measures when necessary. And we have seen that these activities can be tied in with energies of recovery and rebirth, and with the need to "make up" for "time lost." But also involved is the psychic mutation the survivor has undergone, which includes behavior he would not formerly have indulged in, as well as a general identification with the "world destruction" of the death immersion.

Rhythms of guilt, then, involve the survivor in shifting patterns of troubled identification, from an image of purity modeled upon the dead, to one of destruction and breakdown modeled upon the environment of the death immersion and possibly upon its instigators. These images connect with earlier emotional tendencies, to be internalized and acted upon as part of the continuing struggle with guilt.

:

Identification guilt, moreover, like the bomb's lethal substance itself, radiates outward. In Hiroshima this "radiation" moved from the dead to the survivors to ordinary Japanese to the rest of the world. That is, survivors feel guilty toward the dead; ordinary Japanese feel guilty toward survivors; and the rest of the world (particularly but not exclusively Americans) feels guilty toward the Japanese. Proceeding outward from the core of the death immersion—from the dead themselves—each group internalizes the suffering of that one step closer than itself to the core which it contrasts with its own relative good fortune. Just as identification guilt makes the survivor feel himself "dead," the ordinary Japanese feels himself the "survivor's survivor," and so on. However invisible these patterns may be at the periphery, they can be observed in the behavior of members of one group toward those of another, and they apply for concentration camp survivors as well. Their existence suggests that the guilt associated with identification provides an important basis for the ultimate symbolic connectedness of all human behavior.

We are also struck once more by the inseparability of death and guilt, and of the way in which their mutual effects can spread. Indeed, when we consider the phenomenon of psychological radiation mentioned above, we can begin to grasp some of the legacy of death guilt which events like Hiroshima and Nazi atrocities have bequeathed to the world. The fact that both of these events were manmade greatly aggravates the process because it means that the guilt of the victimizers becomes included in the general "radiation." For all such guilt derives from the temporary annihilation of the bonds of human identification through violently administered premature death on a mass scale.

3) *Psychic Numbing*

The survivor's major defense against death anxiety and death guilt is the cessation of feeling. In our observations on Hiroshima we spoke of this process, in its acute form, as psychic closing-off, and in its more chronic form as psychic numbing. I would suggest now that psychic numbing comes to characterize the entire life style of the survivor. A similar tendency has been observed among concentration camp victims (one observer spoke of "affective anesthesia"),[38] and as a general feature of "the disaster syndrome" (the "inhibition of emotional response" noted to account for the "stunned" and "dazed" behavior of victims of ordinary disasters). But what has been insufficiently noted, and what I wish to emphasize as basic to the process, is its relationship to the death encounter.

We have seen how, at the time of the encounter, psychic closing-off can serve a highly adaptive function. It does so partly through a process of denial ("If I feel nothing, then death is not taking place"), but also through interruption of the identification process, with the additional unconscious equation: "I see you dying, but I am not related to you or to your death." Further, it protects the survivor from a sense of complete helplessness, from feeling himself totally inactivated by the force invading his environment. By closing himself off, he resists being "acted upon" or altered. Concentration camp inmates, according to Bettelheim, sought to resist such alteration by protecting the "inner self": "I became convinced that these dreadful and degrading experiences were somehow not happening to 'me' as a subject, but only to 'me' as an object."[39] And under the combined ideological and physical pressures of Chinese thought reform (or "brainwashing"), participants developed a similar avoidance of emotional participation as a means of resisting fundamental change.[40] In all three cases the survivor was able to attenuate his encounter with (biological or symbolic) death by limiting his psychological investment in that encounter. We may thus say that the survivor initially undergoes a radical but temporary diminution in his sense of actuality[41] in order to avoid losing this sense completely and permanently; *he undergoes a reversible form of symbolic death in order to avoid a permanent physical or psychic death.*

Psychic closing-off also suppresses the survivor's rage, or in a broader sense his resistance, toward the forces manipulating him. In Hiroshima we observed this suppression of anger to have detrimental psychological effects. But it also was adaptive in that hostility or resistance would have meant greater exposure to the psychic assaults of the death encounter, and could have stimulated action interfering with physical survival. Within Nazi concentration camps there has been described a more definite command—sometimes overt, sometimes implicit—"Don't dare to notice!" The message was that inmates had better not "see," that is, recognize and respond to, the vicious killings and other forms of mistreatment taking place around them, since any such recognition suggested a form of resistance and a reassertion of forbidden pre-camp ethical standards. Similarly, all survivors of extreme death immersions experience the inner command "Don't dare to *feel*."

In concentration camps even prolonged forms of psychic numbing (variously called "dehumanization," "depersonalization," and "automatization of the ego") were, as Niederland put it, "highly important . . . [for] the economy of survival."[42] And many camp survivors, when later asked, "How did you manage to survive?" answered simply, "I lost all feeling."[43] This reminds us of similar comments of *hibakusha* ("I became insensitive to human death"), also stressing the survival value of psychic numbing.

But in both Hiroshima and Nazi camps the pattern could drastically overstep itself. The classical example here is the "*Musselmann*" ("*Musselmänner*") or "Moslem," the state in which prisoners became "in a literal sense, walking corpses."[44] The term was coined by inmates themselves to suggest a fatalistic surrender to the environment, under the mistaken notion that this was characteristic of Moslem psychology. But so totally did the *Musselmann* sever his bonds of identification, so extreme was his psychic numbing, that the form of death he underwent was neither symbolic nor reversible—as an Italian survivor vividly suggests:

. . . they, the *Musselmänner*, the drowned, form the backbone of the camp, an anonymous mass, continually renewed and always identical, of non-men who march and labor in silence, the divine spark dead within them, already too empty to really suffer. One hesitates to call them living: one hesitates to call their death death, in the face of which they have no fear, as they are too tired to understand.

They crowd my memory with their faceless presences, and if I could enclose all the evil of our time in one image, I would choose this image which is familiar to me: an emaciated man, with head drooped and shoulders curved, on whose face and in whose eyes not a trace of a thought is to be seen.

Primo Levi's evocation of the *Musselmänner*[45] as a single image of "all the evil of our time" is both a survivor's memory of ultimate horror, and a suggestion of the profound universal danger which surrounds man's tendencies to inflict exaggerated psychic numbing upon himself. Bettelheim speaks of the *Musselmänner* as having "given the environment total power over them," and because of losing their will to live, "permitted their death tendencies to flood them." These "death tendencies," I would hold, have less to do with the unhindered operation of the death instinct (as Bettelheim suggests), than with the total "desymbolization," a breakdown of inner imagery of connection, integrity, and motion, an absolute loss of the sense of human continuity.

From this perspective we can also approach the so frequently raised question of why so many Jews went, without protest, to their deaths at the hands of the Nazis. We may suspect that in response to the threat of death and (in many cases) prolonged brutalization, they experienced various degrees of psychic numbing, sometimes even approaching the *Musselmänner's* inability to think or feel. Such is the conclusion one can draw from a description by Wiesel of a group of Jews who had just arrived the previous day at a concentration camp, but had already witnessed and heard about an interminable series of atrocities:

> Those absent no longer touched even the surface of our memories. We still spoke of them—"Who knows what may have become of them?"—but we had little concern for their fate. We were incapable of thinking of anything at all. Our senses were blunted; everything was blurred as in a fog. It was no longer possible to grasp anything. The instincts of self-preservation, of self-defense, of pride, had all deserted us. In one ultimate moment of lucidity it seemed to me that we were damned souls wandering in the half-world, souls condemned to wander through space till the generations of man came to an end, seeking their redemption, seeking oblivion—without hope of finding it.[46]

In other words, the Jewish survivor's (he was still at that point a survivor) capacity to grasp the deaths of others and the danger to himself was destroyed by the psychic numbing already imposed upon him. In its milder form it consisted of simple denial of the possibility of being killed. But in the extreme form depicted in the above passage, including the reference to "damned souls wandering in the half-world," we have the sense of the state of "death in life" encountered in both Hiroshima survivors and *Musselmänner*, a state of such radically impaired existence that one no longer feels related to the activities and moral standards of the life process.

MISCARRIED REPAIR

In all of these harmful effects, psychic numbing comes to resemble what has been called "miscarried repair."[47] Much like a physical process which originates in the body's efforts to protect itself from noxious stimuli and then itself turns into a deadly pathological force, psychic numbing begins as a defense against exposure to death, but ends up inundating the organism with death imagery. In Hiroshima this miscarried repair took the form of later bodily complaints, of the patterns of fatigue and restricted vitality we so frequently noted. While these are undoubtedly related to radiation fears (if not, as some believe, to physical radiation effects), one encounters very similar complaints in concentration camp survivors. There too organic impairments can be important, particularly those derived from physical injuries or from malnutrition, as can the psychological issue of the exaggerated bodily focus created by Nazi "selection" procedures in which life itself hinged upon the appearance of bodily strength. But in both groups we suspect that generalized psychic numbing is the unifying psychological factor, bound up as it is with death guilt and with the feeling that vitality is immoral.

The expression of death guilt via bodily complaints is in keeping with a recent hypothesis concerning psychosomatic phenomena, namely, that these represent "a final common pathway," a form of "entrapment or immobilization in an interpersonal field which is affectively perceived as threatening to life or [to] biological integrity."[48] The survivor of severe death immersion, in other words, becomes permanently "entrapped" by what he symbolically perceives to be a continuous threat of death, which he is unable either to dispel or to express in any way other than the "language" of his body. In this sense his bodily complaints are a perpetuation of his original "entrapment" at the time of the death immersion. Thus, a Dutch psychiatrist has emphasized the way in which severe war stress, including that of Nazi persecution, "disturbs the existing psychosomatic homeostasis" with a resulting pattern of "pronounced psychosomatic symptoms" and a generally "neurasthenic syndrome."[49]

Neurasthenia literally means nervous debility, and in classical psychiatry has been employed to suggest such symptoms as "weakness" or "exhaustion" of the "nervous system," easy fatigability, various aches and pains, pathological physical sensations, and inadequate functioning of practically any organ or organ system of the body. Many *hibakusha* patterns we have observed could be included under this syndrome, and it has been encountered in even more severe form in concentration camp survivors. One group of examiners, for instance, describes a recognizable pattern of "persistence of symptoms of withdrawal from social life, insomnia, nightmares, chronic depressive and anxiety reactions, and far-reaching somatization";[50] while another group mentions, in addition, fatigue, emotional lability, loss of initiative, and generalized personal, sexual, and social maladaptation.[51] We thus encounter in both Hiroshima and concentration camp survivors, what can be called a pervasive tendency toward *sluggish despair*—a more or less permanent form of psychic numbing which includes diminished vitality, chronic depression, and constricted life space, and which covers over the rage and mistrust that are just beneath the surface.

：

The epitome of the neurasthenic "survivor syndrome," and of psychic numbing in general, is what we have referred to as the identity of the dead. We recall the guilt-saturated inner sequence of this identity (I almost died; I should have died; I did die, or at least I am not really alive; or if I am alive, it is impure of me to be so; and anything I do which affirms life is also impure and an insult to the dead, who alone are pure); and we can see now its suggestion of psychic numbing as itself a form of symbolic death. Hence, when survivors of both Hiroshima and concentration camps use such terms as "walking corpse," "living dead," "walking behind my own corpse," "ghosts," "not really alive," and "as if dead," they do so not only in reference to the original immersion but at least in some degree to the way they still feel themselves to be. We know the identity of the dead to be a treadmill of unresolved grief in which the "work of mourning" is never accomplished. But we also know it to be, in its own way, life-sustaining, a psychic bargain under whose terms the survivor receives (or grants himself) a form of half-life rather than either literal death or full vitality. Indeed, I suspect that some such "bargain" exists in relationship to all neurasthenic symptoms, and that more fundamental than the sexual etiology stressed by Freud is the relationship of the syndrome—in the ordinary neurotic as well as in the survivor—to unmastered death imagery. Further, the neurotic process in general, which has been

historically equated with neurasthenia, may be looked upon as a manifestation of psychic numbing and restricted life space also related to
death anxiety and death guilt.

:

The survivor, both at the time of his death immersion and later on,
requires various combinations of psychic closing-off (or numbing) and
openness to his environment. In Hiroshima, for instance, one could not
afford to feel too much, but one had to feel things sufficiently to
dislodge oneself from debris or flee from the fire. Similarly, in concentration camps one had to avoid both being reactive in a way that
suggested resistance, and becoming numbed to the point of the *Musselmann* state; ideally psychic numbing was combined with an exquisite
alertness to signals from the environment which could enable one to
prepare for the next series of blows. Significantly, the capacity for
cognition may be retained even under conditions of advanced numbing;
what is lost is the symbolic integration which links cognition to feeling
and action.

There were also situations in which doomed concentration camp
prisoners could, through a sudden psychic opening-up, recover that
integration and at least achieve dignity in dying. A story is told of a
young woman who was singled out from among a group of naked
prisoners lined up before the gas chamber they were about to enter and
ordered by the commanding SS officer to dance, as he had just learned
that she had been a dancer in the past. She did so, but in the course of
her dance seized the officer's gun and had the satisfaction of shooting
him before she too was shot to death. Bettelheim suggests that the act
of dancing permitted her to cease being "a nameless, depersonalized
prisoner" and become "the dancer she used to be," so that "she
responded like her old self, destroying the enemy bent on her destruction, even if she had to die in the process."[52]

The survivor may also make efforts to break out of his psychic
numbing years after the actual death immersion. We observed in
Hiroshima the compensatory forms such efforts could take, as in the
case of *hibakusha* who inwardly felt themselves weak and impotent but
stressed the importance of a "fighting spirit" toward life; and in the
urgency with which many Hiroshima and concentration camp survivors
married (or remarried) and had children, seeking not only to replace
the dead but to reassert vitality and biological continuity. These compensatory responses could have important recuperative significance. But
they also could be unfocused and destructive—both at the time of the

death encounter (we have noted the confused activity in the midst of the Hiroshima disaster), and later on in the patterns of agitation and hyperactivity which are prominent in the depressions reported among former concentration camp survivors.[53]

As in the case of guilt there is an outward radiation of psychic closing-off, though in a more selective and complex way. The nearer one has been to the dead (and particularly to mass death), the greater the original need for a global defense mechanism and the more psychic "work" of closing-off required; the greater also the continuing struggle with guilt and the more likelihood of prolonged patterns of psychic numbing spreading to all areas of life. For those at the next remove from the dead (ordinary Japanese, for instance, rather than *hibakusha*), the closing-off process is both more complete and accomplished with a good deal less psychic work. And at still further remove from the experience (for non-Japanese, and particularly for Americans) there may be a near-total emotional separation from the Hiroshima experience through relatively easily accomplished psychic numbing. But we are speaking of a continuum, not of absolutely different reactions, and there remains a fundamental similarity, if very different intensity, in all of these patterns of psychic numbing. At the center as at the periphery there is retained the potential for a reopening of psychic sensitivity to the death immersion.

Strikingly analogous observations have been made on the parents of children dying of leukemia. These parents experience painful inner struggles in which they combine patterns of denial with more forthright "coping behavior" in which they open themselves to the reality of their children's imminent deaths. Whatever their blend of psychic numbing and openness, the death imprint remains strong. In contrast, relatives and friends at one further remove from the experience tend to resort to shallow reassurances and "gross degrees of denial."[54] Numbing for them is effortlessly achieved.

Related forms of psychic numbing occur in people undergoing acute grief reactions as survivors of the deaths of family members—here vividly conveyed in a psychiatric commentary by Eric Lindemann:

A typical report is this, "I go through all the motions of living. I look after my children. I do my errands. I go to social functions, but it is like being in a play; it doesn't really concern me. I can't have any warm feelings. If I would have any feelings at all I would be angry with everybody." . . . The absence of emotional display in this patient's face and actions was quite striking. Her face had a mask-like appearance, her movements were formal, stilted, robot-like, without the fine play of emotional expression.[55]

Lindemann emphasized (as did the woman herself) the importance of underlying hostility in these patients. But I·would stress, as of even greater significance, the identification process and the retained "identity of the dead." This survivor, much like those of Hiroshima and Nazi concentration camps, has made her psychic bargain to live at a devitalized level in return for the right to live at all. Such a "bargain" is always likely to be an angry one, though we suspect that with her the restriction was more temporary, and did not require a "life of grief." In a general sense such pathological grief reactions may well be increasing in contemporary society, as Geoffrey Gorer has suggested, because of the absence of meaningful ritual for mourning.[56] If so, we have a further reason for assuming that tendencies toward psychic numbing abound.

Gabriel Marcel tells us that "what we call 'survival' is in reality an 'under-living' . . . [in] which we advance always more bent, more torn away from ourselves toward the moment in which all will be engulfed in love."[57] He makes clear that "under-living" refers to a loss of a sense of life's significance, and that the latter part of the quotation does not suggest a supernatural reunion but rather an elevated state of feeling in which significance has been recovered and "our existence can take on form." A related concept is a quality of despair which Leslie Farber has called "the life of suicide," by which he means the continuous contemplation of suicide until this contemplation "has a life of its own."[58] As in the case of the Hiroshima survivor's identity of the dead, the life of suicide is a form of psychic numbing in which the thought makes the act unnecessary. Hence the apparent infrequency, or at least lack of unusual frequency, of suicidal attempts among Hiroshima and concentration camp survivors. The suicidal attempt can, in fact, represent a desperate effort to emerge from psychic numbing, to overcome inactivation by the act of killing oneself. He who takes his own life is likely to be a survivor of many "deaths," one who feels bereft of human connection; his suicide can be a way of seeking both to master death and to reassert, however magically, a form of symbolic integrity and a sense of immortality.

I shall discuss these issues as they affect mental illness in my later volume, but I would like to suggest here a view of schizophrenia as a prototype of psychic numbing in the extreme. The various features that have been described in schizophrenia—the "split mind," autism and emotional withdrawal, impaired sense of reality, and tendencies toward concretization of ideas and extreme desymbolization—these can all be understood as a particularly pathological form of identity of the dead. Harold Searles has commented that "In working with schizophrenic patients, one soon comes to realize that many, if not all, of them are unable to experience themselves consistently as being *alive*." He looks upon this pattern as anxiety over the fact of death: "One need not fear death so long as one feels dead anyway; one has, subjectively, nothing to lose through death."[59] Concerning the schizophrenic's frequent fantasies and delusions of omnipotence, he points out that "the companion of omnipotence is immortality." I would suggest further that the schizophrenic requires these primitive fantasies of omnipotence and immortality precisely because of his radically impaired *symbolic* immortality—which in turn is an expression of his impaired relationships in life. For as fundamental as death anxiety is to psychic numbing, it is never death alone that one feels the need to shut out, but rather the relationship of death to one's symbolization of life.

:

Examining some of the larger issues surrounding psychic numbing, we recognize it as an important factor in the general neglect of the human impact of atomic bombing. I mentioned earlier my own need, in attempting to study these effects, for at least that degree of "selective numbing" that could be accomplished through focus upon my scientific task. Such numbing was, as I suggested, essential to carrying out the research, as it is to any work which deals with the problem of death, whether performing surgical operations or serving on a Red Cross rescue team. But here too there is the danger of "miscarried repair," of "professional" and "technical" identifications leading to dangerous degrees of psychic numbing. A grotesque example was provided by the Nazi physicians who conducted brutal medical experiments upon living human subjects, and by those who conducted the "selections" which directly dispensed existence and nonexistence. To the question of how a doctor could lend himself to such activities, Bettelheim replies: "By taking pride in his professional skills, irrespective of what purpose they were used for."[60] The doctors in question *had* to focus upon these professional skills to prevent themselves from feeling. In a more indirect manner patterns of psychic numbing have surrounded the overall creation, testing, and military use (actual or planned) of nuclear weapons: a combination of technical-professional focus and perceived ideological imperative which excludes emotional perceptions of what these weapons do. It is no exaggeration to say that psychic numbing is one of the great problems of our age.

Because it is so pervasive in all of our lives, experiences which help us break out of it are greatly valued. This is another reason for the loving rumination by some Hiroshima and concentration camp survivors on painful details of their death immersions. For these memories are unique in that they enable one to transcend both the psychic numbing of the actual death encounter and the "ordinary numbing" of the moment. Similarly, those who open themselves up, even momentarily and from afar, to the actualities of death encounters, can undergo an intense personal experience which includes elements of catharsis and purification. On several occasions members of audiences I addressed on the Hiroshima experience told me later that their involvement in what they heard was so great that they resented subsequent speakers who dealt with more ordinary concerns. Their participation in the death anxiety and death guilt of those victimized had provided a highly valued moment of breakout from the universal psychic numbing toward death in general and nuclear death in particular.

Many people had similar reactions to the assassination of President Kennedy in 1963. The event made all Americans survivors (as it did practically everyone else in the world), and there were widespread grief reactions of the kind we have discussed.* To accomplish their "work of mourning," many found it necessary to remain glued to their television sets for the details of the assassination itself, the funeral, and the worldwide repercussions. A few days later, when television stations began to return to their routine programs, some felt resentful and let down: the brief interlude of exposure to death, however disturbing, was far preferable to the shallow pattern of psychic numbing encouraged by the ordinary mass-media fare. Psychic opening-up is not only necessary to the resolution of the mourning process but becomes in itself a treasured experience. It is the goal of a great variety of emotional experiments in contemporary life, and is closely related to the "expansion of consciousness" provided by psychedelic drugs.†

Psychic numbing, then, poses constant paradoxes for general issues of

---

* There are many reasons for the intensity of this grief, but I would emphasize the great importance of the sense (among the "survivors" of the world) of Kennedy's premature death and unfulfilled life, and of perceptions of the universal consequences of that denied fulfillment.

† But it would seem that prolonged use of these drugs can result in its own form of psychic numbing.

autonomy and survival. A way of maintaining life when confronted with unmanageable death anxiety, it threatens always to snuff out the vitality being preserved. Our deadly contemporary technologies surround the paradox with ultimate consequences, and make certain that this aspect of the survivor's struggles envelops us all.

4) Nurturance and Contagion

Two themes dominate the survivor's personal relationships and general outlook—his own suspicion of counterfeit nurturance, and his perceptions of others' fear of contagion.

In discussing problems of counterfeit nurturance in *hibakusha*, I have emphasized how feelings of special need combine with great sensitivity to any reminder of weakness and create severe conflicts over autonomy. We can see now that psychic numbing further limits autonomy and cuts off potentially enriching relationships. Help offered threatens to confirm not only weakness but more fundamental devitalization.

Adding to the survivor's anticipation of the counterfeit is what we referred to before as his inevitable identification with the death-dealing force. We have noted tendencies of some *hibakusha* to ally themselves not only with America and Americans, but with the atomic bomb itself. Even more striking was the unconscious identification which led some Jewish concentration camp inmates to take on the ideology and even the mannerisms of individual Nazi guards.* We know that this resort to "identification with the aggressor" is an attempt to share the power by which one feels threatened. For the survivor, this means power over death itself. The near-dead hospital patients whom Dr. Hachiya described as suddenly revitalized by the rumor of Japan's atomic retaliation upon American cities derived their strength from the sense of being part of the force controlling life and death rather than its victims. (I shall argue in my later volume that power in general is, at bottom, power over death, so that here too the survivor is expressing a very general tendency.) Later, the very formation of a survivor identity—a group tie built around common victimization by a deadly force—becomes a more insidious psychic tie to that force. The survivor feels drawn into permanent union with the force that killed so many others around him. His death guilt is intensified, as is his sense that his own life is counterfeit.

* Bettelheim describes how "old political prisoners" (apparently Jews and non-Jews who had been in the camp for some time) went so far as to "arrogate to themselves old pieces of SS uniforms, and when that was not possible they tried to sew and mend their prison garb until it resembled the uniforms"; and to copy such SS "leisure time activities" as "games played by the guards . . . to find out who could stand being hit the longest without uttering a complaint."[61]

We begin to understand the survivor's characteristic "touchiness" toward others, and his susceptibility to more or less permanent "victim consciousness." His suspicion of counterfeit nurturance can cause him to feel abused by everyone, particularly by those most directly involved in helping him. Hence the tendency for survivors of disasters of all kinds to become at some point resentful toward doctors and rescue teams.[62] The furthest extension of this pattern is the guinea pig imagery with which we are so familiar—imagery most characteristic in response to manmade disasters involving new technologies of destruction. Such events, as we observed in Hiroshima, leave the survivor with an especially bitter sense of experimental victimization. He can quite easily see his experience as a "trial run"; his combination of general loss of trust, and angry wish, lead him to anticipate his fate becoming everyone's. Similar feelings contribute to rivalry for counterfeit nurturance, so strikingly illustrated by the resentment of Hiroshima survivors over the attention received by the "newly arrived" (1954) survivors of Bikini H-bomb fallout.

VICTIMIZATION AND PARANOIA

Suspicion of counterfeit nurturance is by no means limited to those exposed to atomic bombs or Nazi persecution. It can be found wherever victimization of any kind has taken place, and in fact in any situation of historically imposed dependency. We can observe it in the intensity and bitterness of emotional reactions in "underdeveloped" countries in relationship to problems surrounding American aid—including "touchy" outbursts on the part of recipients, abrupt reversals of policy, and angry refusals of needed assistance. As with individuals such aid can stimulate intolerable feelings of weakness and inferiority, particularly where accompanied by a historical sense of victimization through some form of earlier colonialism, or where "strings" are attached to the aid in the form of an "understanding" that the recipient will follow political policies favorable to the giver. In this latter case the threat to autonomy becomes extreme, and the recipient experiences bitter confirmation of his suspicions.

Resentments over counterfeit nurturance become especially explosive where racial factors are involved—whether in relationship to an event like the atomic bomb or to more general social phenomena. When a prominent American Negro playwright, LeRoi Jones, speaks of his dramatic group as "a theater of victims" which "hates whites," and when he dismisses two white civil rights workers murdered in the South as mere "artifacts" and "paintings on the wall," he is telling us that *anything* offered by the hated white giver, even his life, must be counterfeit. Also involved is a sense of rivalry with another victimized group for (counterfeit) nurturance. For the two whites killed were Jews, and when this fact, along with the issue of the murder of six million Jews by the Nazis, was mentioned by a Jewish discussant, another Negro present answered: "I'm sick of you cats talking about the six million Jews. I'm talking about the five to eight million Africans killed in the Congo."[63] Here the sense of victim consciousness has become so extreme that the "survivor" of racial abuse takes on a hardened psychic stance in which he no longer is aware of human beings, only victims and victimizers.

:

The next step is that of the most extreme form of victim consciousness, or what may be called survivor paranoia. Some of the reactions we described in *hibakusha* approached this dimension, particularly in the intensity of their guinea pig and world-destruction imagery. And among concentration camp survivors paranoia has been more specifically prominent as a later reaction. This paranoia can be partly looked upon as an imprint of actual brutalization experienced during incarceration, which fuses with earlier images of various kinds of "victimization" retained from childhood. But also of great importance for survivor paranoia is the later struggle with rage over having been rendered so thoroughly helpless and inactivated.* This pattern resembles that of counterfeit nurturance, and the survivor's use of the mechanism of projection—his focus upon "enemies" around him—is his way of expressing the feeling that he is still being victimized. It is at the same time a desperate effort to express vitality. In this sense a paranoid reaction within a Nazi camp could be a superior form of adaptation to that of the *Musselmänner*—though if the paranoia became full-blown and caused a disturbance, one was likely to be quickly killed. In Hiroshima, too, anger bordering on paranoia could sometimes protect one from being totally overwhelmed by death anxiety, and from being totally inactivated by psychic numbing—though such anger, as we have noted, was difficult to sustain and could pose its own dangers.

* Niederland has emphasized both of these points in reference to concentration camp survivors. He has also published a series of papers revealing additional material on the classical "Schreber Case" (the basis for Freud's first extensive study of paranoia) in which he emphasizes the importance of the "kernel of 'historical truth' "—such as data on Schreber's childhood "persecution" by his father—for the paranoid patient's later delusions. He sees this as further evidence for the direct causative influence of severe persecution upon subsequent psychosis.[64]

This view of survivor paranoia is in keeping with a larger tendency in psychiatry to stress, as basic to the paranoid state, severe conflicts of dependency—of being cared for—in contrast to Freud's emphasis upon repressed homosexuality. Harry Stack Sullivan said some time ago that the paranoid's conviction, "*He* does something to me," is a substitute for the profoundly felt but unacceptable inner feeling that "*I* have something wrong with me."[65] And more recently Lionel Ovesey has suggested that "the . . . power (aggression) motivation . . . is the constant feature in paranoid phenomena . . . and . . . the essential related anxiety is, therefore, a survival anxiety." By survival anxiety Ovesey means what we have been calling death anxiety, which he sees as resulting from a sequence of frustrated dependency, extreme aggression, and symbolic distortion, until the feeling "I want to kill him" becomes converted to "He wants to kill me."[66]

In survivor paranoia the same principles apply in a somewhat different sequence: there is first the actual death immersion and the experience of the "end of the world" ('I am being killed by him [them, it]," and "The whole world is dying"); then the extreme inactivation, numbing, and residual death anxiety and death guilt ("I am among the dead"); the sense of impairment and the theme of counterfeit nurturance ("I need help, but everything offered me is counterfeit and poisonous"); the focusing of rage to express simultaneously ultimate retaliation and *active* power over death ("I want to kill him [it, them]—everyone in the world"); and finally, the return, in delusional form, to the death immersion ("He [they, it] wants to kill me").

I would suggest further that survivor paranoia could serve as a model for all paranoia. The paranoid state in general can be understood as a response to a protracted survival-like experience—a symbolic death immersion—during early childhood. Later survivals (particularly of extreme experiences like Hiroshima and Nazi persecution) in themselves contribute to paranoia, but do so always by making contact with earlier prototypes. But all paranoia, I would contend, is related to disturbed death imagery, and represents a struggle to achieve a magical form of vitality and power over death. It is at the same time an extreme form of suspicion of counterfeit nurturance in which the very help needed is perceived as deadly.

:

Suspicion of counterfeit nurturance is also closely related to patterns of depression. Its theme of extreme mistrust, in fact, represents a meeting ground between paranoia and depression. In depression patterns of separation and loss are exaggeratedly *self*-referred, in contrast to the paranoid's projection of his problems of dependency and death anxiety onto others. But there is a prototype of the suspicion of counterfeit nurturance in the "dread of starvation," which exists in severe melancholia, as well as in the refusal of food even in mild depression; in the "furious hostility against specific persons" observed in acute grief reactions, and the mourner's general resentment of those around him who are "busily engaged in renewing old friendships and relationships while he remains inconsolable in his loss." Depression is the closest clinical equivalent of psychic numbing, and the depressed person can become so fixed in his identity of the dead that he, like many Hiroshima survivors we have described, views any affirmation of life to be itself counterfeit. His movement toward suicide is his means of mastering death and breaking out of psychic numbing, in contrast to the paranoid's movement (whether in fantasy or actuality) toward killing others. But many clinicians have stressed the psychological similarities of the two conditions, and have observed that impaired mourning can readily lead to paranoia. One classic existentialist case study[67] demonstrates how impaired mourning can lead to murder, and ends with a quotation from Rilke:

> Killing is one of the forms
> of our wandering mourning. . . .

Behind this poem is a vicious circle of killing and unresolved mourning surrounding the death immersion: the survivor's sense of having "killed" those who died in his place, his subsequent life of grief which can, in turn, lead to a wish to kill. For in both paranoia and depression, as in the survival of any extreme death immersion, suspicion of counterfeit nurturance causes one to question both the right and capacity to exist.

These issues take on special poignancy in relationship to the ordinary process of dying, and to the much debated question of whether the dying patient should be told the truth about his condition and about himself. Recent observations have revealed the inner dissatisfaction of most patients with false or evasive statements—as is illustrated by the following description of an exchange between a physician and a woman dying of breast cancer. It began with her asking him why her headache persisted as it did:

When the doctor said it was probably nerves, she asked why she was nervous. He returned the question. She replied, "I am nervous because I have lost sixty pounds in a year. The priest comes to see me twice a week, which he never did before, and my mother-in-law is nicer to me even though I am meaner to her. Wouldn't this make you nervous?" There was a pause. Then the doctor said, "You mean, you think you're dying." She said, "I do." He said, "You are." Then she smiled and said, "Well, I've finally broken the sound barrier; someone's finally told me the truth."[68]

The "sound barrier" that had been broken through was that of false reassurances which neither doctor nor patient believed, a form of counterfeit nurturance which, at least in this case, was more a product of the former's psychic numbing than the latter's. Even children, when fatally ill, have been observed to have a similar need for authenticity of approach. For in anyone close to death there is a profound urge to reassert the genuineness of one's life and of its larger human connection.

CONTAGION ANXIETY

The fear of "contagion" generated by the survivor, the second great impediment to his relationships with others, is a direct product of the death taint we have spoken of so much. This is particularly true of *hibakusha*, since their exposure to radiation effects gives specific form to their death taint. But it holds for survivors in general. Not only do they tend to be looked upon as "contagious," but they themselves fear the "contagion" of the dead. Recent psychiatric investigators have emphasized "the isolation which the living force upon the dying."[69] This symbolic contagion anxiety has been given literal expression in a tendency found in many cultures for communities to cast out those thought to be near death and leave them in an isolated spot—"in the mountains" or "on the ice"—to die.

We can begin to comprehend the nature of contagion anxiety by examining its literal expressions during the plagues of the Middle Ages—here conveyed by four quotations from survivors and commentators:

The sailors, as if accompanied by evil spirits, as soon as they approached the land, were death to those with whom they mingled.

Seeing what a calamity of sudden death had come to them by the arrival of the Genoese, the people of Messina drove them in all haste from their city and port. . . . The one thought in the mind of all was how to avoid the infection.

Emperors, kings, princes, the clergy, merchants, lawyers, professors, students, judges, and even physicians rushed away, leaving the common people to shift for themselves. . . . In an epidemic in 1563 Queen Elizabeth took refuge in Windsor Castle and had a gallows erected on which to hang anyone who had the temerity to come out to Windsor from plague-ridden London.

The contagion was so great that one sick person, so to speak, would "infect the whole world." "A touch, even a breath, was sufficient to transmit the malady."[70]

These quotations reveal, in sequence, four aspects of contagion anxiety: the image of "carriers of death," who take on a quality of supernatural evil; hostility to the point of armed struggle against such death-carriers; the willingness to judge, condemn, and execute, in the manner of archcriminals or traitors, those who are merely *possible* carriers, if they come too close; and an ultimate form of contagion anxiety in which a single carrier threatens to "infect the whole world."

Other forms of large-scale death immersion give rise to more symbolic expressions of similar attitudes. Concerning the appropriateness of contagion anxiety, we may say that plague survivors could infect others but mainly through intermediate transmission by the flea;* *hibakusha* much less so, but they too were dangerous, particularly if wounded, to those who handled them; and Nazi concentration camp survivors not at all in a direct physical sense, though even they "carried death"—to those who tried to help them at the time of the persecutions and were exposed to great risk, to each other in their competition for life, and if Jews, to non-Jews whom they married or otherwise biologically "contaminated" with "Jewish blood," and thereby made into new victims. We may thus say that contagion anxiety is related to actual physical dangers survivors pose for others. But its symbolic reach goes much further than this "kernel of truth." For just as the individual survivor can become prone to retaliatory wishes that everyone else experience what he did, and that the whole world be destroyed, so are others prone to see him as a "world-destroyer," as one capable of "infecting the whole world." This is partly because they perceive these destructive wishes in him (by imagining the range of their own reactions under the circumstances), and partly because they associate him with the death immer-

---

* Only the pneumonic form of the plague could be transmitted directly, by droplet spray, and this form was almost always fatal. So we cannot speak of those transmitting the malady as survivors.

sion itself. As in the case of "radiation guilt" those at the periphery of the death immersion seek to fend off the chain of fears we have become so familiar with in survivors themselves: fear of death, particularly of violent and premature death, of symbolic world breakdown, and of the loss of human connection and the sense of immortality. The essence of contagion anxiety is "If I touch him, or come too close, I will experience his death and his annihilation."

Hence the universal tendency to honor martyrs and resent survivors.[71] I have heard a number of Japanese express considerable irritation with *hibakusha*—because they "always complain" and are "too conscious of being victims" or "too politically motivated"—only to reveal later profound sympathy for them as atomic bomb victims, as well as other pained feelings about Japan's exposure to the weapon. Involved in such attitudes is the combination of guilt and contagion anxiety characteristic of any community (in this case the Japanese national community) toward those of its members who have undergone a particularly intense form of death immersion.

⠒

I occasionally observed another form of contagion anxiety in Hiroshima, among both Americans and Japanese who, though non*hibakusha*, wondered whether living there for some time might not cause them to experience physical radiation effects of some kind. (We are reminded here of the protagonist of Agawa's novel *Devil's Heritage*.) And although the question was usually raised in a half-joking manner, there was anxiety behind the smile. These were usually people, again like Agawa's hero, who were closely involved with *hibakusha*, so that in the phenomenon we observe the coming together of contagion anxiety with identification guilt. This kind of outsider, as a consequence of his unusually strong death anxiety, is torn by conflicting needs to merge with the survivor in total compassion, and to flee from him in a confused state of guilt and resentment.

Similar problems face medical and psychological examiners of survivors. We have already noted the enormous variation in their approach in Hiroshima. And one can observe among them even more marked tendencies to uneasy resentment and "objectification" of *hibakusha* to the point of dehumanization on the one hand, and equally uneasy identification with loss of professional and scientific judgment on the other. While the former tendency is more frequent in Americans and the latter in Japanese, examiners from both countries are capable of either. These difficulties in perspective have undoubtedly contributed to the extraordinary delay in subjecting the two great holocausts of our time—the nuclear bombings and the Nazi persecutions—to adequate psychological and historical evaluation. When I visited Hiroshima in 1962, I found that psychological studies of atomic bomb exposure had been very few in number and very limited in scope; one could find either technical-statistical summaries in which human experience was absent, or else sympathetic descriptions which made no attempt at interpreting the complexities of human behavior. In the case of concentration camp survivors great numbers of studies have recently been published, but it has taken twenty years for them to appear. As Niederland has commented: "Only with considerable delay and under pressure of mounting clinical evidence have psychiatrists begun to study more closely what has been variously named 'concentration camp pathology,' 'concentration camp syndrome,' 'post-concentration camp syndrome,' or 'persecution-connected personality changes.' "[72] One begins to wonder to what extent our understanding of all of the great holocausts in human history—and much of history itself—has been blunted and distorted by the contagion anxiety of examiners and interpreters.

Contributing to this contagion anxiety and psychic numbing on the part of examiners is the general physicalistic and anti-psychological bias of medical and psychiatric practice in most parts of the world. This bias has been notably strong, at least until recently, in Germany and Japan, but is by no means absent even in places like America, where a more psychological psychiatry thrives, often to the point of creating a bias of its own. The Japanese government, for instance, despite its elaborate programs of medical treatment and financial compensation for *hibakusha*, has made no special provision for dealing with non-organic psychiatric impairment. And while such provision has been made for Nazi concentration camp victims in the restitution laws of West Germany, there have been some strange attitudes about what constitutes psychiatric impairment. Patients manifesting symptoms of mental disturbance, who had experienced the most extreme forms of death immersion and brutalization, have been refused compensation on the grounds, as determined by German psychiatric examiners, that such symptoms were due to "constitutional impairment" or to previously existing (presumably constitutional) tendencies or "*anlage*," or simply because the specific relationship of these symptoms to persecution could not be proven. And when commissioned to make these examinations in the United States, American psychiatrists have sometimes minimized the influence of extreme stress upon later psychiatric impairment—either because they too have clung to a narrowly organic and "constitutional" orientation, or (more rarely) to an equally narrow psychoanalytic one in which all emotional disturbance is attributed to childhood trauma antedating persecution itself.

More recently psychoanalysts and psychiatrists in America, Europe (including Germany), and Israel have given more careful study to the later psychiatric sequelae of concentration camp survivors as part of a general phenomenon of "massive traumatization," and have gradually provided a scientific basis for establishing the causative influence of the persecution itself. These efforts have greatly changed the general climate of opinion. But the physicalistic bias, by no means overcome, can still be observed in the tendency for examining boards to give more favorable consideration to those concentration camp survivors whose claims are based upon organic medical diagnoses rather than psychiatric ones. While granting the existence of genuine differences of scientific opinion, we may say that the contagion anxiety responsible for this physicalistic bias has also contributed to the longstanding tendency toward hostile segregation of the mentally ill. For the physician has long been fearful of being "contaminated" by the "psychic death" of mental illness, and even by the psychosomatic "entrapments" of the physically ill. Contagion anxiety, in other words, has historical bearing of no little significance upon medical and psychiatric practice.

:

Apart from examiners, survivors of various disasters have been targets of more general forms of hostility. In the London blitz, for instance, those who remained and thereby became survivors were frequently resented by those who fled the city. And the question asked of Jewish survivors of Nazi persecutions, "Why didn't you fight?" may unconsciously mean, "Why didn't you die?" (Survivors, of course, ask themselves the same question, either directly in ways that we have seen, or else indirectly when they ask of the dead, "Why didn't you live?") There are multiple psychological dimensions behind such questions, but we may say that contagion anxiety plays an important part in causing outsiders to raise issues which reinforce the survivor's already existing doubts about his right to be alive. For just as the survivor asks this question in relationship to the inner principle of organic social balance, so does the outsider extend this principle to himself. He fears that his own life may have to be sacrificed in order to permit the now-experienced survivor to continue his pattern of surviving others. He may unconsciously view the survivor as a kind of vampire who feeds on death, or even as part of a monstrous force which threatens to destroy all proper relationship between life and death.

THE ETERNAL SURVIVOR

Is there any basis in survivor attitudes themselves for this threatening imagery surrounding them? The question raises the problem of what might be termed *survivor hubris*, by which I mean a tendency to embrace the special "knowledge" of death to a point of rendering it sacred. The effort to reinforce this magical but fragile sense of power over death can result in a "craving" for or "addiction" to the process of survival.

There are suggestions of this pattern in the fascination ordinary people have always felt for death and disaster, in their attraction to executions and their studious attention to the obituary pages of newspapers. Such fascination is usually understood to be a form of denial of one's own death, but this denial includes a fantasy of being what may be called an "eternal survivor." Elias Canetti, one of the few writers to direct himself to this question, refers to survival as "the moment of power," and stresses how it can become, in certain heroes and despots, "a dangerous and insatiable passion." The extreme despot "diverts death onto [others] in order to be spared himself," and "Once he feels himself threatened, his passionate desire to see *everyone* lying dead before him can scarcely be mastered by his reason." This leads to a discussion of paranoia, and to a re-evaluation of the classical Schreber case, which Freud made use of to present his original ideas about the condition: Canetti emphasizes Schreber's wish to be "the only man left alive," and concludes (like Ovesey) that paranoia "is an illness of power in the most literal sense of the words."[73] In our terms, we may say that paranoia is an exaggerated form of addiction to survival, based upon the compelling inner urge to become an eternal survivor.

Only the extreme despot or paranoid leader converts this inner imagery into murderous action. But the fantasy itself is potentially universal, related as it is to death anxiety. During the London blitz, for instance, one woman particularly fearful of air raids alternated (as her analyst tells us) between imagining herself an eternal survivor and the seemingly opposite expectation of being the only one to die.[74] But with *hibakusha* and concentration camp inmates the fantasy was approximated by the experience itself. Wiesel tells us how, as he thought about returning to his native Eastern European town twenty years after his release, he would sometimes imagine finding it "just as I knew it, with its *yeshivot*, its stores, its Talmudists, its merchants, its beggars, and its madmen," and "feel guilty for having dreamed that they were dead." But "At other times," he adds,

> I have the opposite vision: I would be the only one to return, I would walk through the streets, aimless, without seeing a familiar face, an open look. And I would go mad with loneliness.[75]

His terrible vision of being an eternal survivor is by no means the hubris of the despot. The vision was in fact confirmed by what he found when he did return, at least as far as the town's Jewish community was concerned. It is a vision, moreover, of the survivor's eternal wandering through the eerie psychic terrain of death in life.

:

Further evidence of the universality of images of the eternal survivor comes from Japanese cultural tradition. The *Hagakure*, the classical eighteenth-century compilation of principles of *Bushidō*, or *The Way of the Samurai*, points out that "although everyone knows he will die, he feels as if his death will come after everyone else has died, and thinks that it is of no immediate importance," and goes on to condemn this attitude as "an illusion in a dream."[76] We are reminded, of course, of Freud's celebrated dictum that "at bottom no one believes in his own death . . . [and] in the unconscious every one of us is convinced of his own immortality,"[77] but the *Hagakure* more specifically stresses the idea of perpetually surviving others.

A related cultural pattern is that of ritual suicide—*junshi* or self-immolation—which the *samurai* retainer would perform upon the death of his lord as an ultimate act of loyalty. Here the retainer rejects the privilege of survival priority, and suppresses his own wish to be an "eternal survivor"; the lord, although dead, is instead symbolically granted that distinction. But the retainer simultaneously affirms his own sense of immortality, even as he dies, through merging with the "immortal" qualities of his lord.

The retainer's ritual suicide also has the historical function of relating the lord's death to the death of an era, while expressing a refusal to live on in the "new era" that has begun. This principle was dramatically demonstrated in the ritual suicide of General Nogi, a national military hero, immediately following the death of the Emperor Meiji in 1868. This event has already become legendary, a source of inspiration for generations of patriots and writers. Natsume Sōseki, a great novelist of that period, has one of his fictional heroes observe that "the spirit of the Meiji era had begun with the Emperor, and had ended with him"; then find himself "overcome with the feeling that I and the others, who had been brought up in that era, were now left behind to live as anachronisms"; and feel so exhilarated by General Nogi's example that "two or three days later" he too "decided to commit suicide." Through this kind of an "end-of-the-era" suicide the individual converts his sense of being partly dead ("left behind to live as [an] anachronism") into a revitalization of the principles of the past. And behind the entire transformation is imagery of "eternal survival" of the principles and the world they represent.*

But the survivor's quest for symbolic immortality can take the form of impulsive actions which endanger others. In the film *The Americanization of Emily*, for instance (an adaptation of a novel by William Bradford Huie), an American admiral with a long family naval tradition is suddenly made into a survivor by the death of his wife. He becomes psychologically unstable, and with demonic energy pursues a wild scheme for the construction of a "Tomb for the Unknown Sailor," including elaborate arrangements to make certain that a naval man is the first to die on D-Day, and that this death is recorded photographically. The film succeeds in mocking the general idea of the "sacred war dead" by demonstrating the madness of the vision of immortality which can arise from it. But by tying in the admiral's behavior with his personal, nonmilitary death immersion (his wife's dying), the film, in its own fashion, raises the question of survivor hubris. In all of these ways we can see how unconscious fantasies held by survivors and outsiders concerning the death encounter can feed upon one another.

* General Nogi had another reason for his act. Thirty-five years before, during the Satsuma Rebellion of 1877, he had, as a commander, lost his regimental banner to the enemy. And since "the regimental banner was regarded as the incarnation of the Emperor . . . losing the banner to the enemy . . . resulted in extreme shame, which could be redeemed only through death." Nogi's request of his superiors that he be permitted to take his own life was denied, as was the same request twenty-nine years later, this time by the Emperor himself, following heavy losses sustained by the army under Nogi's command during the Russo-Japanese War of 1904–1905, including the death of two of his sons. On that occasion the Emperor was said to have told him: "Now is not the time for you to die. If you so earnestly wish your death, it shall only be after my own death." Sōseki's protagonist also had personal reasons for his act: he had never recovered from the guilt and loneliness he had experienced following an act of deception he had committed many years before which had resulted in the suicide of a close friend. In other words, both "end-of-the-era" suicides were the result of a combination of personal and historical elements; each of the two men was a "survivor" on both levels.[78]

EXCLUSIVENESS, ANTAGONISM, AND COOPERATION

Much more prominent than survivor hubris among Hiroshima and Nazi concentration camp victims has been a pattern of *survivor exclusiveness*. Built around the idea of absolute distinction between "we who have been through it" and "you who have not," the exclusiveness has a paradoxical quality. It is derived on the one hand from a sense of unique possession of man's highest experiential knowledge, the "knowledge of death" to which we have so frequently referred; and on the other from being "untouchable" bearers of death taint and "carriers of death." We may say that the survivor's own contagion anxiety reinforces his exclusiveness.

We are already familiar with patterns of *survivor antagonism*, and with their relationship to rivalry for counterfeit nurturance. Here too contagion anxiety also plays an important part. We recall Hiroshima survivors' fear of being contaminated by other survivors, both at the time of the bomb and later on when encountering those visibly tainted by keloids. The same process occurred among concentration camp inmates, especially when confronted by deteriorated *Musselmänner*. As Bettelheim put it, "One hated them because one feared their example," and we remember also his statement that "not the SS but the prisoner was the prisoner's worst enemy." Fundamental to these antagonisms are first rivalry for life at the time of the death encounter, and later on the complexities of shared death guilt and knowledge of circumstances surrounding that guilt.

The result is a pattern of "antagonistic cooperation"[79] which surrounds the survivor experience—between survivors themselves, survivors and outsiders, and even survivors and instigators of a particular disaster. It is a relationship which combines deep need and equally deep animosity. Again it begins at the time of the death immersion, whether between *hibakusha* who fled together from the flames, or between concentration camp inmates and Nazi jailors who found their ways to collaborate; and can develop into later patterns of collusion, as between "A-Bomb Victim Number One" and his American acquaintances who contributed so much to that identity. Antagonistic cooperation takes place in response to any form of stress, but is most marked in massive death immersion because of the extremities of shared need and fearful distrust evoked. In our disaster-ridden age, with its generally precarious substrate of contagion anxiety and suspicion of counterfeit nurturance, antagonistic cooperation takes on increasing significance as one of the more benign forms of human relationship available to us.

5) Formulation

We have seen that the dropping of the atomic bomb in Hiroshima annihilated a general sense of life's coherence as much as it did human bodies. We have also seen that mastery of the experience depended upon re-establishing form within which not only the death immersion but the survivor's altered identity could be grasped and rendered significant. This quest for formulation turns both *hibakusha* and concentration camp survivors into what has been called "collectors of justice." Beyond medical and economic benefits as such, they seek a sense of world-order in which their suffering has been recognized, in which reparative actions by those responsible for it can be identified.

As part of the "work of mourning" Freud described the survivor's need to come to gradual recognition of the new reality, of the world which no longer contains that which has been lost. He must, as a later psychoanalytic writer on depression put it, "rebuild with anguish the inner world, which is felt to be in danger of deteriorating and collapsing."[80] And an investigator of acute grief reactions speaks specifically of the effort to "find an acceptable formulation of his future relationship to the deceased," which includes "emancipation from bondage to the deceased" and "formation of new relationships."[81] What has not been generally recognized is that this "anguish of formulation" is the basic reparative process following any significant psychic disruption.

The process begins early, even before the actual death encounter. For the "explanations" of Hiroshima people just prior to the disaster as to why their city had not been bombed could be viewed as anticipatory formulations. And the psychic closing-off which occurred when the bomb fell represented another formulation ("If I feel nothing, death is not taking place"), which, however magical and laden with denial, was a functional way of relating self to world under those extreme conditions. To be completely deprived of formulation at any time, even at the moment of the death encounter, is psychically intolerable. As Chaim Kaplan said in a journal he left recording experiences in the Warsaw ghetto: "The worst part of this ugly kind of death is that you don't know the reason for it. . . . The lack of reason for these murders especially troubles the inhabitants of the ghetto." The diary goes on to record that "We feel compelled to find some sort of system to explain these nightmare murders," especially a system which would permit each to imagine his survival:

> If there is a system, every murder must have a cause; if there is a cause, nothing will happen to me since I myself am absolutely guiltless.

Kaplan knows the truth: "The system is a lack of system. . . . The guiding principle is the annihilation of a specific number of Jews every night. . . . Indiscriminately." But this truth is greatly resented because *"People do not want to die without cause."*[82] And years later, in the evaluation of the kinds of stress experienced under Nazi persecution which led to later emotional disturbances, a psychiatric examiner emphasized "the abrogation of causality."[83] What the survivor feels deprived of is not causality in its literal eighteenth-century scientific sense (precisely this cause produces precisely that effect) so much as the existence of an ordered symbolic universe. For any experience of survival—whether of large disaster, intimate personal loss, or (more indirectly) severe mental illness—involves a psychic journey to the edge of the world of the living. The formulative effort is the survivor's means of "return."

Impaired formulation, therefore, becomes a central problem for survivors. In tracing the many impediments faced by *hibakusha*, we noted that a capacity for indignation and anger could, to some degree, enhance the formulative process. We recall the young keloid-bearing hospital worker who channeled her diffuse rage ("a confused mixture of anger, indignation, hatred, and resentment") into active participation in protest movements in a way that gave significance to her experience, purpose to her life, and generally enhanced her self-esteem. But where indignation and rage become fixed and repetitive, there frequently develops what can be termed the *survivor's embittered world-view*. Within this bitterness—or biting anger—is contained the mixture of need and mistrust we have associated with the theme of counterfeit nurturance. It resembles the "embittered vehemence"[84] one psychiatrist has observed in people prone to depression; and I would stress its tendency to dominate the survivor's entire cognitive and emotional life. The embittered world-view becomes his total vision of the way things were and the way things are. Not having been able to "vomit" his "bitter water," such a survivor finds his entire psychic life poisoned by it. The *hibakusha*'s "underground" wish for ultimate retaliation or total nuclear conflagration can be understood as the most extreme expression of the survivor's embittered world-view, and finds its analogy in various emotions of former concentration camp inmates—such as Wiesel's temporary wish "To burn the whole world!"[85] For if he is unable to reconstitute his own psychic world, the survivor finds this sharing of annihilation to be the only kind of relationship with others that he can imagine.

Rawicz suggests the importance of impaired formulation in his protagonist's retrospective realization, concerning the time just prior to his death immersion, "that the moment that lay ahead was to provide me, not only with a lifetime's bitterness, but with an eternal alibi."[86] The "eternal alibi" is the survivor's need to justify his being alive. His "lifetime's bitterness" has to do with the permanent "bad taste" he retains, with his inability to "savor" that which is offered him, and his "biting anger" toward a world he cannot re-enter.

The indelible image we spoke of earlier is also an expression of impaired formulation. The image can include, in addition to the death encounter itself, memories of pre-bomb existence—as in a revealing statement written by a university professor nineteen years after his exposure to the bomb:

> The brightness of the Inland Sea on summer days and the unpleasantly loud noises of a military city. . . . The images of this life of my youth . . . have been fixed in the back of my mind as though held there by the flash of the atomic bomb. The form of that period does not alter. It is the picture of me in my young days, and at the same time is like seeing the picture of a child who died before I did. . . . What would a psychologist call the fixation of memories of individual experience which have resisted every interpretation or solution, and have instead become like a still picture. . . . It is very much like asking the meaning of a picture of one's younger days which is dusted off and hung up, in the midst of a service being held on the twentieth anniversary of one's death. . . .[87]

In one sense these early recollections could be looked upon as "screen memories," which substitute for and shield against the more disturbing memories of the bomb itself. But they are also much more. The writer's equation of an image of himself in his youth with "the picture of a child who died before I did" suggests his inability to overcome either his loss of pre-bomb innocence, or his guilt over survival priority (he makes the latter clear in additional comments as well). The "still picture" of himself conveys a sense of cessation of psychic motion; and the phrase about participation in a service commemorating the twentieth anniversary of one's own death suggests the close relationship between this kind of indelible image and the identity of the dead. He goes on to speak of the bomb as having "fixed everything in one moment," of there being "no words of comfort I could utter to friends who . . . were dying . . ." since (as we quoted him before as saying) "there exist no words in any human language which can comfort guinea pigs who do not know the cause of their death." There can, in other words, be no formulation—the experience must remain an indelible and ineffable image—because no words can convey either its vastness and totality or its suffusion with death and guilt. One remains fixed upon the world that has been annihilated, held motionless because unable to give form to that annihilation and its consequences.

Rawicz tells us of the survivor "living out his memories and the memory of his memories," so that

> The present is present like a lump of dead meat dried up by the malevolent sun. . . . It shortens our lives, and yet remains dead and dumb itself.

Now we can recognize the indelible image as part of still another vicious circle confounding the survivor's psychic life: death anxiety and death guilt confer unique value upon his memories, while at the same time devitalizing all subsequent experience and undermining attempts at formulation; he is thrown back upon these memories (of the event itself and his life preceding it) as his only form of authentic connection; they become all the more indelible, and he is further fixed in unformulatable death imagery, etc. Should he try to forget the memories, he is brought back to them by the call of the survivor mission, by the demand that he (in Rawicz' words) "remember everything" because "The only thing that matters, that *will* matter, is the integrity of witnesses."[88] Hence the sacredness of the literal details of his death encounter we have so often noted, and the worshipful stasis surrounding its image. Indeed we begin to understand why religious and political movements take shape as forms of survival: the significance of the witnessing of the death of Jesus for the emergence of Christianity, and that of the surviving of the Long March for Chinese Communism. The survivor may become a "disciple" not only of a dead leader, or of the collective "dead," but of the death immersion itself. The guilt with which he embraces that event is by no means devoid of love, but should he move toward psychic forms which could free him from its bondage, he risks the disturbing self-accusation of betrayal.

:

The concept of the survivor's impaired formulation is relevant for much recent psychiatric and medical research which has attributed a variety of disorders to problems of grief and mourning. Among widows, for instance, complaints of bodily and mental difficulties have been noted to increase during the period following their husbands' deaths;[89] and the tendency toward delinquency and antisocial behavior has been described as "a manifestation of the mourning process—a substitutive pathologic grief reaction"[90] (reminding us of the case referred to before in which grief stimulated rage to the point of attempted murder). There have also been correlations between childhood bereavement (from the early death of a parent) and adult psychiatric disorder.[91] A distinguished German psychoanalyst has recently gone further and suggested that "repressed mourning" for Hitler and the Nazi movement has interfered with social and political progress in postwar Germany.* We can well understand the insistence that grief itself be considered a disease. I shall explore some of these issues more fully in my later volume, but there are two important principles I would stress concerning these general findings and theories. First, we can better grasp the phenomena involved by a concept of impaired formulation on the part of various kinds of survivors than by focusing upon traditional interpretations of the mourning process per se. And second, the "disease" to be contended with is not grief as such, but a symbolic disruption which can accompany grief or any other form of individual or collective emotional upheaval.

SCAPEGOATING

The survivor's conflicts can readily lead him to a scapegoating formulation. By focusing total blame upon a particular person, symbol, or group of people, he seeks to relieve his own death guilt. When *hibakusha* single out such objects of focused resentment as President Truman, the pilot of the A-bomb plane, Japanese leaders, American scientists, American capitalists, or "Americans," we can observe the process by which the search for responsibility spills over into scapegoating. More specific

---

* In a talk delivered at Yale University in 1964, Dr. Alexander Mitscherlich offered the thesis that Germans have been unable to confront the combination of ambivalent love and residual guilt felt toward their former leader, and have consequently had to rely heavily upon denial.

scapegoating (because its objects are more removed from actual responsibility) can be found in *hibakusha* resentments toward Koreans, Chinese, *burakumin*, foreign residents of Hiroshima at the time of the bomb, outsiders who came in later, the financially successful, and non*hibakusha* in general; as well as toward city officials, welfare administrators, physicians, and research scientists, through the overall constellation of guinea pig imagery and suspicion of counterfeit nurturance. On the whole, however, my impression was that scapegoating in Hiroshima has been fragmentary, and without strong conviction, less part of clearcut formulations than of a generally embittered world-view. The urge toward scapegoating has hardly been absent, but the weapon's impersonality and cosmic destructiveness interfered with scapegoating just as they did with general assigning of responsibility.

In contrast, there is evidence that scapegoating formulations have been much stronger among concentration camp survivors and groups identified with them. These again often enter a borderline area which includes reasonable labeling of responsibility. But we may observe the scapegoating phenomenon where resentments, *instead* of being expressed toward the Nazis, are directed almost exclusively toward groups concerned with restitution payments, outsiders, or other camp survivors; toward the Catholic Church or the Allied powers for their failure to do more for Nazi victims; or toward Jewish leaders thought to have, in their associations with their persecutors, aided the work of extermination. Without arguing the legitimacy of these accusations, I would suggest that the intensity with which they have been expressed has to do with the general issue of death guilt, since all parties involved are survivors (and some are initiators) of the events debated.

The Nazis themselves, coming to power as survivors of Germany's national humiliation during and following World War I, made use of a scapegoating formulation in the extreme: the vision of Jewish responsibility for Germany's various forms of literal and symbolic death immersion, and for all of the world's ills, and the prescription of a "final solution" to the "Jewish problem." That kind of formulation, moreover, had a long history. During the plague of the fourteenth century "many blamed the Jews, accusing them of poisoning the wells or otherwise acting as agents of Satan." But at that time a form of "internal scapegoating" was also prominent, a self-accusatory interpretation of the plague as "a punishment by God for human sins." This interpretation not only gave rise to intensified prayer, but to "half-naked flagellants, members of the century-old cult of flagellantism, march[ing] . . . in procession whipping each other and warning the people to purge themselves of their sins before the coming day of atonement."[92] Very different, but by no means psychologically unrelated, was the behavior of groups of survivors of the Tokyo-Yokohama earthquake of 1923, who simply massacred every Korean in sight in a wild outbreak of murderous scapegoating.

Scapegoating formulations, then, emerge from struggles between internal and external blaming, and create for the survivor an opportunity to cease being a victim and make one of another. But these formulations may not only be dangerous to the newly chosen (or, more frequently, reinstated) victim; they meet with limited success in accomplishing their object, the purging of death guilt. In fact, they add a new psychic burden of guilty anger. They are, moreover, difficult to sustain as coherent entities, and readily disintegrate into amorphous bitterness. The intervention of contemporary technology, as we saw in the case of the A-bomb, further blurs the entire process by creating an adversary whose "magic" is so difficult to grasp, blame, or hate.

Yet a process at least bordering on scapegoating seems necessary to the formulation of any death immersion. It enters into the survivor's theory of causation, and his need to pass judgment on people and forces outside of himself to avoid drowning in his own death guilt and symbolic disorder. The more closely these scapegoating tendencies attach themselves to the actuality of events, the greater their adaptive usefulness, and the better the survivor's chance to transcend them, or at least combine them with more inclusive formulative approaches. What the survivor seeks from his scapegoating formulation is the reassuring unconscious message that "You, and not I, are responsible for the others' deaths and my suffering, so that I have a right to be alive after all." It is a message that he can neither fully believe nor entirely cease to reassert.

In Hiroshima we observed the preponderance of the alternative message: "Having survived at the expense of the dead, I can justify my existence only by emphasizing their virtue and my guilt, and by embracing them to the point of becoming one of them." But this tendency for the survivor to saturate his formulation with self-blame and identification with the dead has its own pitfalls, notably that of lifelong psychic numbing.

:

One can observe the operation of these formulative paradoxes in other situations related to survival—perhaps most strikingly in a group of severely ill people described by two psychiatric investigators as "pre-dilection patients," because prior to undergoing major surgery, they correctly predicted their own deaths. One of them, described as "The Widow Who Could Not Die," had experienced a series of survivals which she found herself increasingly unable to justify. Having under-gone an extensive operation for carcinoma of the rectum at the age of forty-one, she lived as an invalid for the next twenty-eight years, burdened by a colostomy (an opening from the colon through the abdominal wall) and by frequent rectal abscesses. Prior to the operation, she had been pregnant three times, but on each occasion miscarried. Then, over the years, her "favorite brother" died, having also developed carcinoma of the rectum; three sisters died in rapid succession; and finally, her devoted husband died of coronary thrombosis. The psychi-atric examiner observed that she "thought of herself as a plump and sickening slug wallowing and feeding on death," and that she had the feeling "that her survival had been at the expense of other lives, even those of her unborn children." He noted the "solemn immobility" of her face, which "resembled a death mask," and a "sickening atmosphere of death in her room." She expressed to him both her desire to die, and the calm conviction that her death would result from a lung hemorrhage following surgery (she had experienced one after a previous operation, but had been saved by prompt treatment), which it did. Her emotional status "was not that of depression but of flattened affect"—or what we would call psychic numbing—and the investigators' further comments raise a key question about the formulative problem we have been discussing:

> It would be difficult to conceive of a patient who welcomed death as did this woman. She had survived at the cost of every person to whom she was devoted, and managed to live on with a disease of unusually rapid mortality. It was as though something indeed was wrong with her. The persistent sense of being soiled and repulsive clung to her. Her loneliness in the later years and preoccupation with the fate of those she had lost held her encased in the little room, but still she did not die. The important question is not, however, that she wished to die. She had understood for many years that only death could resolve her difficulties. Why had she survived so long?[93]

There is no certain answer to the question. What we can say is that she was an "eternal survivor," but unlike the paranoid despots who seek external solutions for guilt in the form of an unending series of antagonists whom they can survive, she internalized her guilt to create a life of grief. Indeed, I believe that her guilt-ridden formulation of her responsibility for others' deaths was her means of granting herself unconscious permission to go on living—much in the fashion we have described for *hibakusha*. If we accept the likelihood that her psychic state contributed to her death, we may further suspect that her increasing loneliness, together with her mounting guilt, finally negated the adaptational usefulness of her formulation—possibly to the point where it became mobilized to the cause of biological death.

What I am suggesting is that at a certain point the balance can be tipped, so that the survivor's self-accusatory formulation linking him with the dead no longer contributes to his sense of connection and his "right" to life. At that point he becomes overwhelmed by death guilt, experiences a marked diminution of vitality, and embraces a "death-welcoming" formulation, which although not fundamentally different from the one he held before, now accelerates the process of dying. Even this kind of formulation, at least in the "predilection patients" we have been describing, may be said to reflect a kind of mastery. For these "survivors" are neither psychiatrically disturbed nor possessed by the suicidal patient's fantasy of magically conquering death, but achieve a certain degree of integration in which elements of numbing and despair presage the death that is anticipated and inwardly embraced. It is quite possible that such death-welcoming formulations accelerated the process of dying in many Hiroshima and Nazi concentration camp survivors, both during their initial ordeal and later on; and where particularly severe, contributed to the onset of leukemia and other malignancies within the former group.*

:

A key issue in the survivor's capacity to make his self-accusatory formulation adaptive is the retrospective conferring upon the dead of a

---

* William A. Greene, whose work on psychogenic factors in malignancies I have quoted before, relates leukemic symptoms and other forms of physical illness to "disruption . . . of a sense of sequence," of "a feeling of continuity in reference to . . . experiences to date and . . . aspirations for the future"; and "con-sequence in association with another or other persons," which involve "some type of . . . attachment," whether pleasant or unpleasant.[94] Greene's concepts are consistent with what I have called "impaired" and "death-welcoming" formulation. The phenomenon of death-welcoming when in the midst of severe stress is well known, and was observed, for instance, in large numbers of American prisoners of war in North Korea who at a certain point would begin to cease trying to stay alive and would resist whatever help was offered by others. The phenomenon was sometimes called "give-upitis."

quality of glory or of symbolic immortality. Only in this way can the survivor reassert his own sense of immortality. Hence the profound fear of "betraying" the dead which pervades both Hiroshima and concentration camp survivors. For, as Camus tells us in words written in the midst of repeated survivals of comrades in the French anti-Nazi underground in 1943:

> In the period of revolution, it is the best who die. The law of sacrifice brings it about that finally it is always the cowardly and prudent who have the chance to speak since the others have lost it by giving the best of themselves. Speaking always implies a treason.[95]

The "treason" is being alive to have a voice at all. But by recognizing it in one's formulation, as Camus did, one can share in the enduring power of the dead.

"GOLDEN AGE" AND SIGNIFICANT "MESSAGES"

Both Hiroshima and concentration camp survivors, in discussing their early lives, frequently presented images of a "golden age," of "idyllic childhoods, spent in the bosom of close, harmonious families."[96] While expiatory needs to idealize the dead are important here, this kind of image serves another important function: it is the survivor's effort to reactivate within himself old and profound feelings of love, nurturance, and harmony, in order to be able to apply these feelings to his new formulation of life beyond the death immersion. Inevitably these relate to early childhood, a universal "golden age" in which, whatever its pain, one is capable of uncomplicated happiness. Even if drawn from later periods of life, the image is likely to include a childlike sense of the joy of spontaneous play in an ordered world—precisely what the survivor now feels himself most in need of. He must combine these old emotions with a new sense of significant purpose. The Hiroshima survivors' stress upon their "peace city" finds its parallel in concentration camp survivors' actions on behalf of preventing the re-emergence of Nazi or Nazilike movements, and in the participation of many of them in the formation of a "Jewish State" in Israel. This stress upon significant purpose is most vivid where the formulation takes the shape of a specific survivor mission, but it is also quietly present in tendencies toward psychological non-resistance.

In either case, the purpose must in some way derive from a symbolic message from the dead, whether that message emphasizes an enlarged vision or simple revenge. We can look upon the *hibakusha* stress upon the general theme of peace, so prominent in their struggles with their overall experience, as an effort to achieve wisdom and transcend revenge. But the theme of "avenging the dead" is universal. It has been overtly prominent in Japanese tradition, and covertly at issue in postwar controversies over shrines for the war dead and national holidays memorializing them.* Moreover, it is present in diffuse form in *hibakusha* imagery of ultimate retaliation ("Let A-bombs fall all over the world!"). Among concentration camp survivors themes of revenge have been more publicly prominent. But usually associated with them have been efforts to impose responsibility, to punish the guilty, to reassert moral order—all part of the "collection of justice" we spoke of earlier. This dual quest for revenge and moral order has been present in the reaction of concentration camp survivors to later trials of Nazi war criminals, and has contributed to the sense of renewed vitality observed in many following the Eichmann trial and execution.

There is little doubt that a perceived message of wisdom from the dead is, for the survivor, the superior pattern both ethically and psychologically. But emotions surrounding the idea of revenge must be contended with, and in some way expressed, in relationship to any form of death immersion, especially where the sense of being victimized is strong. With atomic bomb survivors the nature of the weapon makes specific revenge—that is revenge "in kind"—virtually "unthinkable," as compared with the accessibility to concentration camp survivors of specific objects for such feelings. This does not mean that retaliatory emotions do not exist among *hibakusha*, but rather that they tend to become more indirect and ambiguous. Yet however vague, they create

---

* The related themes of revenge and military glory became so closely associated with all memorial ceremonies in prewar and wartime Japan that any postwar ceremonial becomes suspect unless clearly associated with an anti-war formulation. Thus, in an exchange published in English translation in the *Japan Times* of June 8, 1963, Tomoji Abe, a university professor and Director of the Association in Memory of Japanese Student War Dead recalls the "grand ceremonies during and before the last war" held in the name of commemorating the dead but "designed to instill the general public with a militaristic spirit" and opposes a government-sponsored plan for a large national ceremony on August 15, the day of surrender. He contrasts the implicit ethos of his own group's program of "lecture meetings, symposiums and . . . homage to tombs of students who were killed in service during the war." His antagonist, Asataro Yamamoto, Director of the Repatriation Bureau of the Health and Welfare Ministry, defends the government plan as responsive to a growing need for "spiritual solace" on the part of bereaved families devoid of "ulterior motives" and dissociated from "revival of militarism in Japan."

extremely strong inner pressure upon the survivor to renounce and overcome them.

:

These general formulative principles can be observed in parents of children dying of leukemia. It has been observed that among such parents the conclusion that the child's fatal condition was caused by something they did, or failed to do, often seemed preferable to "the intolerable conclusion that no one is responsible."[97] Formulated guilt is preferable to meaningless innocence. Beyond this, they often take on a survivor mission of combating the general scourge of leukemia, through first familiarizing themselves with the medical aspects of the problem and then participating in various programs and campaigns aimed at fighting the disease. Some take comfort in the idea that their own child's case contributed to this goal by what it revealed about the condition. Here we may speak of a guinea pig image that is not devoid of honor, the image of an unpreventable death (whatever the parents' feelings of responsibility) made maximum use of for the benefit of mankind—in contrast to the Hiroshima survivor's sense of having been made into a historical victim by a willful human experiment, and then asked to contribute to medical knowledge.

We observed in Hiroshima the tendency for this negative form of guinea pig imagery to be associated with fantasies of retaliation. In a general sense, any survivor's fixed focus upon revenge as the predominant message from the dead may be understood as a profound formulative impairment, in which he is unable to imagine the existence of relevant wisdom emanating from them or any other source.

IMAGES OF SURVIVAL AND MASTERY

We are now in a better position to understand why formulation is so intimately bound up with mastery. For it relates not only to the death immersion itself but to the entire constellation of life-and-death imagery within each individual psyche. This constellation includes three polarities which we have already hinted at: connection-separation, integrity-disintegration, and movement-stasis. To avoid the misleading instinctual language of classical psychoanalysis, and at the same time recognize the presence of the precursors of these polarities at birth, they are best referred to as *innate images*. That is, they form the earliest basis for the individual's world-picture, and for his way of acting upon that world-picture. They are also, inevitably, the prototypes for his later death imagery. And however primitive and unconscious they are during early stages of life, they are from the beginning involved in the creation and re-creation of significant patterns which concern the entire organism.[98]

The first, the connection-separation polarity, has been given considerable stress by psychoanalytic writers, most recently in John Bowlby's elaboration of "attachment behavior" in the very young child. But although much has been written about infantile fears of being devoured or annihilated, and about the young child's terror at being deprived of its mobility, the last two polarities, *as lifelong constellations*, have received relatively little attention. Bowlby and his associates rightly emphasize the significance of very early separation anxiety in the child, and have described a pattern of infantile mourning consisting of three stages—protest, disorganization, and reorganization—which is re-enacted in adult reactions to death and loss. But when they observe that the eighteen- to twenty-four-month-old child, if separated from his mother, behaves "as if his world has been shattered,"[99] we may suspect that the anxiety involved includes primitive images of disintegration and stasis which are inseparable from the sense of separation itself. We of course recognize in this kind of separation the prototype for later survival experiences. But what must also be kept in mind is that the early image formed around it can be reactivated by any subsequent suggestions of disintegration or stasis, as well as separation. The task of formulation is to reassert their polar opposites—connection, symbolic integrity, and movement. Just as one has "known" the experience of survival in every threat to these life-affirming themes, so has one called upon formulation to reconstitute one's inner and outer worlds after each of these "survivals."

This is not to say that childhood experiences "cause" the patterns we have been discussing in this chapter, or that the massive death immersion is "nothing new" and "merely a repetition" of prior psychological tendencies. Rather, we may say that the death immersion reactivates, and at the same time adds new dimensions to, the earlier imagery. Indeed, the emotional power of the death immersion lies precisely in this combination of shock of newness and "shock of recognition."

Of great importance is the age at which the death immersion takes place. In Hiroshima my impression was that the younger a person was, the more fundamental the effect upon his evolving psychic life, but also the greater latitude and flexibility in formulation. The young survivor, therefore, could often achieve considerable mastery over even a severe and indelibly imprinted death immersion. In contrast, older survivors did not "imbibe" the experience in as fundamental a way but retained more incapacitating patterns of despair and psychic numbing. A particularly powerful imprint occurred with those exposed to the bomb during or just prior to adolescence, a period of life when one is extremely sensitive to death imagery, and at the same time old enough for that imagery to take its adult form rather than occur in less specific emotional prototypes. In this group of survivors there tended to occur a formulative struggle of lasting intensity, leading neither to numbed despair nor to mastery. But at whatever age he is exposed, the survivor must call forth life-affirming elements from his own past even as he molds these into a new formulation.

We have noted how formulation enables the survivor to recapture a sense of "active tension"—or of "actuality"—with his environment. All three of the polarities I spoke of are involved in this quest, but particularly those concerned with symbolic integrity and psychic mobility. Yet the seemingly inactive formulative approach of psychological non-resistance, can be, as we have also seen, the most effective one. In a very general sense, psychological non-resistance can be related to an Eastern philosophical emphasis, and the more active idea of "survivor mission" to a Western one. But we have observed the importance of the survivor mission among Japanese in Hiroshima. And Western concentration camp survivors have shown considerable inclination toward psychological non-resistance—as expressed recently in Elie Wiesel's public request for an "accumulation of silence."* Not only has there been so much cultural interchange that philosophical origins have become obscure, but we are in fact dealing with two related aspects of universal psychic forms. Both "non-resistance" and "survivor mission" are means of avoiding a sense of being inactivated or overwhelmed with death to the point of marked psychic numbing. And both provide symbolic integrity, including an active reassertion of the sense of immortality.

To reassert this connection to continuous life, the survivor reverts not only to his personal past but to his historical past as well. We recall the *hibakusha's fear of psychohistorical extinction*, as expressed by some individually and also in Agawa's novel. Wiesel describes similar feelings when he discovers, upon his return to his native town, that all was the

---

* Wiesel was speaking before a dinner marking the twentieth anniversary of the liberation of the Bergen-Belsen camp. Significantly, however, he referred to the silence of Job's comforters, who sat with him for seven days and seven nights without speaking a word, so that the form of psychological non-resistance advocated is mixed with a Biblical sequence notable for its questioning of God's actions, as well as with Wiesel's own continuing survivor mission of bearing witness.

same as before except that "the Jews had disappeared." He is angry with the Gentile townspeople, not for their misbehavior at the time of the persecutions but "for having forgotten them," and "So quickly, so completely."[100] The survivor cannot formulate from a void. He requires the psychological existence of a past as well as a present, of the dead as well as the living. Without these, neither mastery of his death encounter nor a place in human society is possible.

6) A World of Survivors

The atomic survivor, then, is both part of a historical legacy of survivor-hood, and a representative of a new dimension of death immersion. He experiences the same general psychological themes we have enumerated for all survivors of massive death immersion, but the unique features of nuclear weapons and of the world's relationship to them give a special quality to his survivorhood.

His death imprint is complicated by a sense of continuous encounter with death—extending through the initial exposure, the immediate post-bomb impact of "invisible contamination," later involvement with "A-bomb disease," and the imagery surrounding the *hibakusha* identity. Death guilt, stimulated at each of these stages, is reinforced by group patterns within a "guilty community," and further reawakened by every flexing of nuclear muscles—whether in the form of threatening words or weapons testing—anywhere in the world. Psychic closing-off is extraordinarily immediate and massive; and later psychic numbing, inseparable from radiation fears, gives rise to a particularly widespread form of psychosomatic entrapment. Suspicion of counterfeit nurturance is markedly strong, and lends itself readily to guinea pig imagery. Contagion anxiety is similarly great because of the radiation-intensified death taint. Formulation is made profoundly difficult, both by the dimensions of the original experience, and by the complexity and threat surrounding the general nuclear problem. And here we arrive at another quality of atomic survival not unique to it but of unique importance: we all share it.

I say this not only because if Japan or Germany had developed the bomb first, I might have been either among the A-bomb dead or else the American equivalent of a *hibakusha*; just as if my grandparents had not elected to emigrate from Eastern Europe, I might have been a concentration camp victim or survivor. Such accidents of history must be kept in mind. But what I refer to is the universal psychological sharing of any great historical experience, and particularly of this one in this epoch. In a large sense history itself is a series of survivals, but in our century the theme of survival is more immediate and more ominous.

:

We have observed the effects of a relatively localized impact of a "small" nuclear bomb, with the existence of an "outside world" to help.

There is no need to dwell on the magnification and dissemination of destructive power since Hiroshima, or on the uncertainty of there being an "outside world" to help in a future holocaust. We may simply say that Hiroshima gave new meaning to the idea of a "world war," of man making war upon his own species.

Only man, we are often reminded, "knows death," or at least knows that he will die. To which we must add: only man could invent grotesquely absurd death. Only man, through his technology, could render the meaningful totally meaningless. And more, elevate that "invention" to something in the nature of a potential destiny that stalks us all. For, after Hiroshima, we can envisage no war-linked chivalry, certainly no glory. Indeed, we can see no relationship—not even a distinction—between victimizer and victim, only the sharing in species annihilation.

Yet we know that great discoveries have in the past been made by survivors—of dying historical epochs as well as of actual catastrophes. By confronting their predicament, they have been able to break out of the numbing and stasis of unmastered survivorhood and contribute to the enlargement of human consciousness. Our present difficulty is that we can no longer be sure of this opportunity. We can no longer count upon survivor wisdom deriving from weapons which are without limit in what they destroy.

I have tried throughout this book to write with restraint about matters that make their own emotional statements. But behind that restraint has been a conviction that goes quite beyond judgments of individuals or nations, beyond even the experience of Hiroshima itself. I believe that Hiroshima, together with Nagasaki, signifies a "last chance." It is a nuclear catastrophe from which one can still learn, from which one can derive knowledge that could contribute to holding back the even more massive extermination it seems to foreshadow.

Hiroshima was an "end of the world" in all of the ways I have described. And yet the world still exists. Precisely in this end-of-the-world quality lies both its threat and its potential wisdom. In every age man faces a pervasive theme which defies his engagement and yet must be engaged. In Freud's day it was sexuality and moralism. Now it is unlimited technological violence and absurd death. We do well to name the threat and to analyze its components. But our need is to go further, to create new psychic and social forms to enable us to reclaim not only our technologies, but our very imaginations, in the service of the continuity of life.

Black Rain

Kuroi Ame (*Black Rain*)[1] marks a new dimension in "A-bomb literature." A portrayal of the intrusion of the atomic bomb into the ordinary rhythms of a small farming village, its special blend of "the usual" and "the unprecedented" enables it to transmute that experience into significant artistic form. The violence and conflict surrounding the bomb are illuminated by means of a leisurely chronicle of seemingly inconsequential everyday events, in the manner (as one critic put it) of "an old-fashioned family novel."

The story was in fact originally entitled *Marriage of a Niece* (*Mei no Keikon*), and its first three sentences more or less sum up its plot:

> For several years past, Shigematsu Shizuma of the village of Kobatake had been aware of his niece, Yasuko, as a burden on his mind. Especially troubling was his sense that the burden was going to remain with him, unspeakably oppressive, for still more years to come. It was like having a double, or even triple, responsibility for a debt.

Shigematsu's immediate "burden" (or pressing responsibility) is arranging a marriage for his niece, but it is part of the larger—indeed limitless—burden imposed upon both by the atomic bomb. This "limitless burden" is elaborated through an interweaving of present-day occurrences in a village not far from Hiroshima with survivors' diaries describing the time of the bomb—mostly Shigematsu's, but also those of Yasuko, of Shigematsu's wife, Shigeko, and of a doctor who had miraculously recovered from early bomb effects. As a family head and a *hibakusha* Shigematsu is faced with several levels of responsibility, or what might be called the formulation of responsibility: to Yasuko; to himself and his community; to the dead and their other survivors; and to history. These layers of formulative struggle, which we shall consider in turn, comprise what can be viewed as the novel's central psychological theme.

Shigematsu's responsibility to Yasuko is virtually that of a father to his daughter. During the war, when she was still in her teens, he had brought her from the village to Hiroshima (where he was then living), found her work in his factory, and taken her into his home. Shortly after the bomb he wrote in his diary: "So long as I keep Yasuko as my own daughter, if anything were to happen to this child, I would not be able to show my face to Shigeko's parents [Yasuko's grandparents]."

But his efforts to arrange her marriage—the overriding responsibility of a family head to the "daughter" in a Japanese household—are constantly frustrated by Yasuko's ambiguous status in relationship to the bomb, and especially by the false rumor that she had been exposed very near the hypocenter while on labor service. Such is the intensity of Shigematsu's feeling in the matter that for a while he "entertained an idea of hunting down the arch-villain" who had started the rumor. And when an excellent prospective match ("If the truth be told, almost too good for her") presents itself, he decides to "make doubly sure" by obtaining a certificate of health for Yasuko and sending it to the go-between. This, however, only arouses the latter's suspicion and leads to a request for more precise information concerning Yasuko's atomic bomb exposure. Yasuko therefore turns over her A-bomb diary to Shigematsu so he can prepare a copy for the go-between. But although the diary makes clear that Yasuko was fully ten kilometers from the hypocenter, it also reveals her encounter (while returning to Hiroshima after the bomb fell) with the "black rain":

We set out at nine o'clock [on the morning of August sixth]. As we reached the main road there were black clouds rising over the city of Hiroshima. We heard the sound of thunder, and then rain began to fall with drops about the size of soybeans. Although it was the middle of summer I felt so cold that my whole body shivered.

Her face and clothes remain splattered with mud, and the soiled parts of her blouse are worn through. Worst of all, these marks cannot be washed away:

> I went back to the fountain again and again, but the blotches of black rain would not disappear. As a dyeing agent it was quite impressive.

The black rain—that is, the A-bomb itself—is ineradicable.*

When Shigematsu's wife urges him to leave out the part about the black rain because people "might get the wrong idea," he is tempted to do so and is restrained only by his fear of what would happen should the go-between ask to see the original. Partly to resolve the dilemma, he decides to add his own diary as an appendix to Yasuko's in order to demonstrate the contrast between his close exposure (at two kilometers) and her distant one. Noticing Yasuko's eagerness for the match—her "devising every possible way to make herself more attractive without seeming to do so"—he is desperately determined that "this time, no matter what, her marriage must not be canceled." And these emotions spur him on in his diary-copying efforts.

But the marriage is not to be achieved. Yasuko develops symptoms of "A-bomb disease," negotiations are abruptly terminated, and Shigematsu experiences a profound sense of failed responsibility concerning both the marriage and his feeling that he did not take sufficiently good care of Yasuko in the past. As her condition deteriorates he becomes more and more aware of his *oime* or debt—in this case unrepayable—to Yasuko. He feels guilty for having brought her into the orbit of the A-bomb, and for his helplessness before the evil forces assaulting her within that orbit.

Shigematsu's responsibility to self and community†—his sense of harmony with the currents of life within his village—is upset at every

---

* These two passages have been altered in later printings, and do not appear in the same form in the English translation. In early versions of the novel there was some confusion about whether Yasuko experienced the "black rain" upon reaching the highway, as described above, or while on a "black-market boat" which she (and the group with which she was returning to the city) subsequently boarded, or in both situations. The changes made in later printings present this confusion as existing within Yasuko's own mind because of having been "in a state of shock," and establish her exposure to the rain as having occurred only on the boat. But this is at odds with the statement, retained in all printings, that she was exposed at ten kilometers, for the boat would have been closer than that.

† In a certain theoretical sense one could claim that self and community are always psychologically inseparable. But the extraordinary stress in traditional Japanese culture upon the individual's adherence to group standards, which one clearly encounters in this novel, lends itself particularly to considering them together.

turn by lingering A-bomb influences. For he remains under their death-spell, still susceptible to the kind of guilt originally recorded in his diary:

> [The atomic bomb cloud] was an envoy of the devil himself . . . who else in the whole wide universe would have presumed to summon forth such a monstrosity? Would I ever get out alive? Would my family survive? Was I, indeed, on my way home to rescue them? Or was I seeking refuge for myself alone?

Similar death guilt affecting his relationship to the Hiroshima community is revealed in such early incidents (also recorded in his diary) as his turning over to someone else a child he had been helping so that he could make a precarious bridge crossing alone; his feeling impatient at the slow pace of a badly injured neighbor, from whom he also separated, and then hearing of the latter's death shortly afterward; his encounter with a corpse, which seemed to be "puffing out its cheeks . . . taking deep breaths . . . [and] moving its eyelids," but which on closer inspection could be seen to harbor no other life than worms whose movements had created these illusions.

Yasuko's diary reveals her to have been consistently aware of horror and suffering ("Hiroshima is a burnt-out city, a city of ashes, a city of death, a city of destruction, with heaps of corpses a mute protest against the inhumanity of war"), while Shigematsu's records his need (once he and Yasuko were reunited) to insist that they turn away:

> I had to admonish her many times: "This is not an exhibition [*misemono*]. We can't do anything for them, no matter how much we would like to. So walk in silence. Walk looking down."

Confronted by his niece's pure and childlike humanitarianism as well as by his own guilt, he perceives his responsibility to be the counseling of psychic numbing.

But because of his personal injuries (the "strange face I have never seen before" which he finds in the mirror) he experiences a virtual obliteration of self. Overwhelmed to the point of despair, he has momentary thoughts of ceasing the small efforts he has been making toward re-establishing order and throwing his bundle into the river.* A mixture

---

* The load Shigematsu carried consisted of an assortment of primitive food and medicine, old magazines, a small fan, etc.—"things useful to people living in the ruins"—which he intended to bring to officials in the Clothing Division of mili-

of general confusion and bureaucratic rigidity create an image of Shige-matsu as a man caught in a web of circumstances which, whatever his continuing efforts, cannot be unraveled. Such is the cheating and decep-tion around him that he recalls an old saying: "In places exposed to the ravages of war, human depravity does not disappear for one hundred years." His constant self-recriminations—"I felt disgusted with myself" and "It was my responsibility"—suggest the extent to which he has internalized the overall dislocation, assumed its evil and guilt.

And over the years which follow, the pattern is maintained by others' attitudes toward him and two fellow *hibakusha* in the village. On the advice of physicians treating their "A-bomb disease" the three indulge in the leisurely activity of fishing while everyone in the village is "hard at work cutting the wheat and planting the rice fields." The villagers, who had at first revered the three as "precious survivors," came to look upon them as lazy men who "take advantage of" their atomic bomb exposure. To avoid this censure—and "just to be nasty," in the words of one—the three men embark upon a commercial carp-raising enterprise, which enables them to continue to fish but to do so as "a kind of work . . . like running a business," since "so long as one had invested even a little money in the fish one caught, it was not just amusing oneself." Shigematsu also continues to live within the framework of communal custom as ceremonial days mark the passing of time—on one, farmers float lanterns as a form of prayer for the prevention of harm from water (from heavy rain or flood); on another, they hold a kind of memorial service for insects, mostly worms, which they have killed while working in the fields.*

But his most poignant struggles with responsibility occur in relation-ship to the dead and to the impaired life-death balance. His diary tells how, in the early chaos surrounding mass cremations, ordinary amenities must be dispensed with ("There is no one to prepare death certificates when people die . . . [and] even if they could be prepared, there is no place to receive them"). In order to show some respect and maintain a minimum of form, Shigematsu's superior at the factory asks him to

tary headquarters. He wanted both to help them and to influence them toward arranging coal deliveries to his factory so that the making of desperately needed cloth-ing could be resumed.

* The first festival is known as *Onomichi-ko no Sumiyoshi-sai,* and Shigematsu is not described as participating actively in it; but during the second, *Mushi Kuyō,* he presents rice dumplings (*ohagi*) to a friend while returning a metal container, fol-lowing the custom of bringing back borrowed belongings on that day.

chant sutras for employees who die. When Shigematsu insists that he is only an "amateur" (*shirōto*) in Buddhist practice and that he has "no power to guide the dead," he is told that in such matters and under those conditions "there can be no distinction between professionals and amateurs." Earnest if uncertain, he seeks instruction from an old priest, copies passages from Buddhist books, and practices sutra-chanting when alone. But although he gradually acquires some confidence and finds his efforts appreciated, the number of people dying inevitably renders the ceremony increasingly casual, and he reaches the point where "I cannot say that I go to chant sutras with all my heart." One sutra he does chant, "Commentary on White Bones" (Hakkotsu no Gobunshō), sets the tone for most of the book:

> . . . I may be first, others may be first. It may be today or it may be tomorrow. Whether one dies later or earlier, death is unceasing, like the falling of dew on the tip of a leaf. One may be proud of his red cheeks in the morning, and then turn into white bones in the evening. The wind of change has already come; two eyes quickly close, and one's breath is no more. . . .*

But despite this compelling image of resignation, death simply cannot be absorbed or formulated. Riding on a train, Shigematsu brushes up against a woman and through the cloth of her bundle feels the outline of a child's ear. Fearing it will suffocate, he speaks to the woman, only to be told that she is carrying her dead child to her parents' home for burial. He meets an engineer who tells of being "too old" to dig out the bones of his young wife and daughter from the ruins of their house, but also of being worried that the wife's family will insist upon a proper burial. Realizing that the engineer wishes to remember the wife and daughter in their full beauty rather than as mutilated A-bomb corpses, Shigematsu suggests a compromise solution: "How about having some third person dig out the bones?"† He observes two soldiers carrying a

* The Japanese word *mujō*, here translated as "change," is a Buddhist term meaning "mutability," "uncertainty," or "transiency"; its literal meaning, "without permanence," suggests the frailty of human existence. The phrase *mujō kaze*, which I have translated as "wind of change," is often used as a euphemism for death.
† The usual Japanese custom is for the closest relatives to pick out bones from the remains following cremations. This is ordinarily done by two people who co-ordinate two separate chopsticklike instruments, each person manipulating one of them. These bones, together with some of the ashes, are put in a jar which is placed in a plain wooden box and kept in the home of the closest mourner until burial some time later.

corpse on an improvised tin litter, overhears one of them say, "We can hardly manage all these dead bodies"—and notes that the corpse on the litter

> looked like a Pinocchio whose binding nails had all been pulled out. I unconsciously said the sutra "Commentary on White Bones." Hiroshima was no more, but it still seemed unbelievable that the city of Hiroshima could come to an end in such a terrible fashion.

Beyond these general death-distortions, Shigematsu himself (together with his wife and niece) is actually mourned as dead. His mother places pictures of the three before the family altar in her home in the village, along with three teacups with water and a few flowers. She also instructs other relatives to take water and green leaves from the village to the site of Shigematsu's house, and to burn incense there and place next to the incense sticks fruit from his favorite tree, the *kemponashi*,* also brought from the village. Shigeko and Shigematsu later discover these, and when Shigematsu hears the entire story from them, he is "surprised by his mother's thoughtfulness." Shigematsu is thus depicted as a survivor who, from the standpoint of others and to some extent his own, has already "died."

Shigematsu tries throughout to cope with death, as with life, in traditional village ways. His difficulty is that he can find no guidelines for the special quality of "death in life" imprinted by the atomic bomb—no means of guiding either the dead or the living.

All he can do is attempt to record what he has seen and felt, and this *preoccupation with records* becomes his way of expressing his responsibility to history. In addition to his urge to use his diary to influence Yasuko's wedding arrangements favorably, his copying it was associated with a longstanding plan to present the diary—"my history"—to the local primary school's library, where it could be "preserved." So concerned

---

* The *kemponashi* tree, which is related to the jujube and found only in East Asia, takes on particular significance in the novel for both Shigematsu's family and his village. In an old letter, which Shigematsu and his wife dig out from the storage area of their house, an inspector for the then new Meiji government (the letter was written in 1873, five years after the Meiji Restoration, and is referred to in the text below) thanks Shigematsu's great-grandfather for sending *kemponashi* seeds to him via a magistrate from the village of Kobotake who had gone to live in Tokyo. Ibuse describes the *kemponashi* as "a noble tree," and refers to "five great *kemponashi* trees [which] had stood in the garden before Shigematsu's house right up to the time of the Sino-Japanese war," so that it becomes a symbol of his tie to the immortality of nature.

are he and his wife about its possible impact upon posterity that they give considerable attention to the kind of ink that should be used. They examine among old family records a letter written in 1873, one of the first ever received in the area to use Western-style ink; noting it to be "faded to a pathetic light brown color," they decide that traditional brush and Chinese ink would be more enduring.* Shigematsu seeks to apply his personal history to the formulation of a disturbingly confusing chain of events in larger human history. Thus, even after Yasuko's illness has eliminated any possibility that the diary could help bring about her marriage, Shigematsu goes on copying it almost as a man possessed. And he further asserts its wider historical connection by making August sixth his deadline for completing it.

Yasuko's illness is recorded by another diary, this one kept by Shigeko, which serves the dual purpose of a medical record (it is actually presented to a physician) and an additional document of A-bomb suffering.† The same physician in turn produces a diary kept by his brother-in-law (also a doctor) describing a highly unexpected recovery from A-bomb effects, and including a record of treatment as recalled by the man's wife.‡ This too is made medical use of when Shigematsu takes it to the doctor eventually put in charge of Yasuko's case, in the hope it might have relevance for her treatment, and there is even talk of showing the diary to Yasuko for encouragement. Only records, we seem to be told, can enable man to cope with the bomb.

One makes such records so that all can remember. Earlier in the book one of Shigematsu's fellow *hibakusha*-fishermen denounces a woman (who has been taunting the three men) for having forgotten about the bomb, and goes on to declare angrily: "Everybody's forgotten! Forgotten the hellfires we went through that day—forgotten them and everything else, with their damned anti-bomb rallies." Without clear memory of the essence of the experience—without its recordings on the mind—how can one possibly deal with it authentically?

---

* Shigematsu's wife is the one who raises the issue in very specific terms: "You're going to present it to the library for the sake of posterity, aren't you?" But eventually Shigematsu himself becomes convinced of the need to use the older-style—and, one might say, more culturally authentic as well as lasting—form of ink.

† The doctor in turn suggests that Shigeko's diary of Yasuko's illness be given to the ABCC—"a place where they keep survey materials concerning atomic bomb victims and sometimes publish descriptions of patients suffering from atomic bomb disease"—but the suggestion is apparently not acted upon.

‡ The physician-brother-in-law's record is made up of a series of notes and is not an actual diary (which has a somewhat formal quality in Japanese usage), but the general principles we have described concerning recording nonetheless apply.

As a survivor of holocaust Shigematsu does not believe that any record, least of all his diary, can convey what really happened ("Not even a thousandth of what I really saw is described in it"), but he persists in recording small details as well as large scenes. He even asks his wife's help in preparing an additional record of exactly what they had to eat during wartime. However he demeans his own efforts, he sees value in the information as such: "The style of my writing is bad realism. But facts are facts." Carrying out one's responsibility to history is the only way to recover meaning and vitality. As one reviewer said of Shigematsu, "His will to record is his will to live."*

In this sense one can understand the novel as depicting the gradual individual movement, however hesitant and incomplete, toward mastery of the A-bomb experience. Shigematsu's initial psychic stance is that of numbing: at the time of the bomb, as we have observed; and shortly afterward, when people's insistence upon talking to him about bomb horrors results in his being "drawn into those actual feelings" and experiencing "an unpleasant form of fear" which makes him "feel like running away." His later inclination to accept his wife's suggestion that they leave out a portion of Yasuko's diary, apart from its immediate purpose regarding the marriage arrangements, is consistent with his wish to suppress the entire A-bomb experience. Caught in the dilemma of trying to conceal the unconcealable, he can react only by "fuming" (*puripuri*). But as the book proceeds the urge to "run away" is replaced by a determination to stand fast and record everything. Paradoxically, the cancellation of Yasuko's marriage arrangements because of her illness liberates him from the strain of concealment: "I cannot keep on hiding things, and there is now no need to hide them."

Thus released from pressures to deceive others on Yasuko's behalf, he feels less need to deceive himself about the bomb in general. He has moved away from denial toward transcendence. His form of transcendence is a combination of incessant recording and continuing attention to the obligations of a family head in a Japanese village—always against a background of the timelessness of everyday rituals and of nature's perpetual re-creation of life and beauty (his wife refers to his eager inspections of his carp pond as "acts of homage"). And the sense of timelessness is stylistically reinforced by the multiple layers of flashback made possible by the intricate use of diaries.

---

* A culturally emphasized principle is relevant here: the Japanese stress not only upon diaries but also photographs, especially family albums. The preservation of the past, through records that are both concrete and emotionally evocative, has consistently great significance for coping with the present.

Not that the A-bomb is "defeated"—to the contrary, there is no doubt that Yasuko will die from delayed radiation effects, and we suspect that Shigematsu might well meet the same fate. But what has been demonstrated is that one can undergo the survivor's ordeal with honor and dignity; through records one can achieve that most difficult level of expression, authentic protest.

The book's ending is enigmatic. Shigematsu's diary told earlier of a bad omen in the form of a "white rainbow" seen by the factory chief during the worst days of the bomb, just prior to the Emperor's surrender speech.* Instead of listening to the speech, Shigematsu had walked off and found a clear stream in which many small eel were swimming. At the end of the book—after he has finished copying his diary—he again wanders off, this time to his carp pond, where he tries to imagine a happy outcome:

"If a rainbow were to appear now over that mountain, a miracle would take place. Not a white rainbow, but a rainbow of five colors. Should that happen, Yasuko's illness would be cured." He knew such a wish could not be fulfilled, but he still made his prophecy as he looked at the mountain far off.

To expect good fortune, then, is admittedly wishful. But the bad omen has given way to at least *the idea* of a good one—all against a background of fish in water, universal symbolism of life and pointedly so in this novel. Even more important perhaps, Shigematsu has *completed his task*. We are left with the impression that man possesses the possibility, tenuous though it may be, of reordering his psychic world and absorbing the folly of his destructiveness.

:

Ibuse falls into the general category of the deeply concerned and geographically close non*hibakusha* writer on A-bomb themes. Like his protagonist, he is from a small village in Hiroshima Prefecture, and like other non*hibakusha* writers we have encountered, he had intimate contact with actual effects of the bomb. Long recognized as one of Japan's leading older-generation novelists and a member of the Japanese Acad-

* The factory chief had first seen this "bad omen" on the day before the "February 26th Incident" of 1936 in which military extremists assassinated several cabinet members as part of an attempted coup d'état. During the postwar period the incident has exemplified the notoriety of rightist fanaticism, except for a small minority for whom it has remained an example of an admirable Japanese form of absolute dedication to the "higher cause" of national and racial aspirations.

emy of the Arts since 1960, he has written penetratingly about a variety of social themes, including that of military fanatacism. But prior to *Black Rain* he had published only one work on the atomic bomb, a brief memoir-novel (really a short story) entitled *Kakitsubata (An Iris)*,[2] based upon his observations on *hibakusha* who fled to nearby Fukuyama City. His recent novel is said to be a "reworking and reorganizing" of these experiences, accomplished over a period of more than ten years.

It is also said that on the occasion of his being awarded the Order of Cultural Merit (on Culture Day, November 3, 1966) he told friends that *Kuroi Ame* was a failure because it did not capture the *hibakusha*'s special form of silence—reminding us once more of the survivor's tendency to question the authenticity of *anything but* silence, and also of Elie Wiesel's plea (concerning the concentration camp experience) for an "accumulation of silence."

Yet even Ibuse could not escape *hibakusha* sensitivities. A number of survivors have insisted that the book's descriptions fall far short of the full horror of what actually took place. Here we may say that the novel lends itself to this criticism by its very documentary stress, and this may be its major shortcoming. It apparently follows very closely an actual diary kept by a *hibakusha*, and has been characterized by Ibuse himself as less a novel than a document. Though subtle and effective, its diary method cannot be said to be the kind of radical experimentation in style found, for instance, in such concentration camp novels as *The Long Voyage* and *Blood from the Sky:* because it contains no stylistic equivalent of the revolutionary nature of the A-bomb experience, it too readily invites comparisons between what it says and "how things really were." By the same token the book's scientific and medical inaccuracies become both documentary limitations and artistic impediments, although they far from invalidate the book's more fundamental psychic truths.* We know well that no A-bomb novel could avoid negative *hibakusha* responses, based as these are on reactivation of death anxiety and death guilt. But my point here is that even this highly superior novel by a distinguished writer shows a certain amount of imaginative thralldom

---

* The most important inaccuracy surrounds the general idea of the "black rain" as lethal, ostensibly through containing radiation or in this case what is known as "near fallout." Although the general question of fallout from the Hiroshima bomb —that is, of residual rather than immediate radiation—has still not been entirely clarified, most authorities believe that there was no medically significant level, and therefore that the "black rain" was not in itself greatly harmful. According to a personal communication from Dr. Kempo Tsukamoto of the Japanese National Institute of Radiological Sciences, it is possible that the rain, which became black be-

to the A-bomb experience—considerably less than a great majority of works dealing with it, yet enough to demonstrate once more the atomic bomb's severe barriers to creativity.

The rare synthesis the novel does achieve, between the A-bomb experience and life beyond it, has led to such critical accolades as "masterpiece" and "the first genuine work of national literature" to emerge from the atomic bombings, as well as to sales so extraordinary that one must assume that something close to a new A-bomb "exposure" is taking place among the more educated Japanese population. One critic compared the book to Defoe's description of the plague in England, but it probably bears greater resemblance to Camus' novel on the same theme. Like Camus' protagonist, Dr. Rieux, Shigematsu wages a losing battle against superior forces of evil in which the nobility of the struggle serves as an affirmation of symbolic immortality—though Ibuse depicts the struggle (and the evil too) in much more restrained, partly elegiac Japanese tones. Camus' use of the plague as a parable around which to explore the nature of evil is undoubtedly more broadly imaginative than Ibuse's relatively focused confrontation of the A-bomb experience as such. But on the other hand Ibuse manages to inject humor into his

---

cause of dirt blown into it by the blast, could have contained beta radiation sufficient to cause some effects; but these were likely to have been superficial (that is, confined to the skin and scalp) unless a considerable amount of this material was ingested orally or through respiration under some unusual circumstances. It is difficult to come to any definite conclusion because the fission products involved were so short-lived that measurements became virtually impossible within a few hours after the rain fell. (The rain began to fall approximately an hour after the blast, and ceased one or two hours later.) Moreover, the rain fell mainly at the center of the city: it would have been impossible for Yasuko to encounter any ten kilometers away (the distance from the hypocenter of the main highway she speaks of), and highly dubious that she would have been exposed to any on the boat, which, though closer, would also have been well outside of the central area. Also scientifically questionable are descriptions of "A-bomb disease" (Ibuse usually employs the term *genbakubyō* rather than *genbakushō*, slightly closer to ordinary speech but having essentially the same meaning). About Shigematsu and his fellow *hibakusha*: ". . . people like us have only to do a bit of hard work and their limbs start to rot on them." And about one of them in particular: "If he pulled a heavy cart or worked in the fields, he got an ominous rash of small pimples in among the hair of his scalp, but they dried up if he ate nourishing foods, went fishing, or took other exercise." And most important, concerning Yasuko's symptoms: these include fever, diarrhea, loss of hair on her head, swellings on the buttocks, loosening of the teeth, ringing in the ears, loss of appetite, inflammation of her gums, severe general pain, and eventually large numbers of blood cells believed to be white cells but so abnormal as to be almost unidentifiable. This does not add up to any definite syndrome, but seems instead to combine some of the early symptoms of acute irradiation, some of leukemia, and others not really specific to either but often contained in the public image of "A-bomb disease."

account, much more than Camus and from a more difficult vantage-point. That humor is always gentle, but at times gently savage: at precisely the moment when his young pupils "were burned from head to foot," a teacher insists they sing *pianissimo* the patriotic song "Lay Me Beneath the Waves," and then "leads the way in jumping into the river"; a village head making a speech of encouragement to members of the Young Men's Association about to embark for rescue work in Hiroshima urges that they "take care above all not to drop these symbols of your invincible determination to fight on to the bitter end—your bamboo spears," while also adding an apology for addressing them "in this surreptitious manner . . . in the predawn darkness without so much as a light"; a "left-wing scholar" with American connections is so aware of being regarded suspiciously by wartime officials that, to demonstrate his patriotic dedication, he is "always the first to dash outside and rush around calling out 'Air raid! Air raid!' . . . [and has] never been known to take off his puttees [to be in quasi-military readiness] even at home"; and an injured woman with "her arms stretched out toward the [atomic bomb] cloud . . . [who] kept screaming in a shrill voice: 'Hey, you monster of a cloud! Go away! We're non-belligerents! Do you hear—go away!' "

Ibuse is telling us that under conditions of atomic holocaust, what is ordinarily fatuous becomes totally absurd, and that hypocrisies of response are not unrelated to those contributing to cause. Recognition of this dimension of absurd hypocrisy suggests that man possesses the capacity for alternative behavior. The very quality of humor—hardly hilarious, to be sure—is a fundamental component of whatever degree of transcendence author and protagonist achieve. In conveying the sense that A-bomb victims can be more than just that, Ibuse evokes in a very special way the pained wisdom of the twentieth-century survivor.

NOTES

INTRODUCTION (pp. 3-12)

1. Japanese scholars in Tokyo have begun to take cognizance of the situation, and studies of social change in Hiroshima are being initiated by a research team from Keio University. See Keizō Yoneyama, "Hibakuchi Hiroshima ni Miru Shakai Hendō" (Social Change Observable in [Atomic-] Bombed Hiroshima), *Hōgaku Kenkyū* (1964) 37:57–97; and Yoneyama and Kawai, "Genebaku to Shakai Hendō" (The A-Bomb and Social Change), *ibid.* (1965) 38, Nos. 9 and 10. Earlier sociological and psychological research efforts include: S. Nakano, "Genbaku Eikyō no Shakaigakuteki Chōsa" (Sociological Study of Atomic Bomb Effects), *Daigaku-jinkai Kenkyūronshū I* (April, 1954), and "Genbaku to Hiroshima" (The Atomic Bomb and Hiroshima), in *Shinshū Hiroshima-shi-Shi* (Newly Revised History of Hiroshima City) (Hiroshima Shiyakusho, 1951); Y. Kubo, "Data About the Suffering and Opinion of the A-bomb Sufferers," *Psychologia* (1961) 4:56–59 (in English); and "A Study of A-bomb Sufferers' Behavior in Hiroshima: A Socio-psychological Research on A-bomb and A-energy," *Japanese Journal of Psychology* (1952) 22:103–110 (English abstract); T. Misao, "Characteristics in Abnormalities Observed in Atom-bombed Survivors," *Journal of Radiation Research* (1961) 2:85–97 (in English), in which various psychosomatic patterns are described; Irving L. Janis, *Air War and Emotional Stress* (New York: McGraw-Hill, 1951); particularly chapters 1–3; and United States Strategic Bombing Survey Reports, *The Effects of Strategic Bombing on Japanese Morale* (Washington, D.C.: U.S. Government Printing Office, 1947). Additional studies of social aspects of the atomic bomb problem are being conducted under the direction of Kiyoshi Shimizu at the Hiroshima University Research Institute for Nuclear Medicine and Biology; and some of the group's findings are presented in Dr. Shimizu's article "Little-Known Effects of the Bomb," *Japan Quarterly* (1967) 14:93–98 (in English). I have published two essays dealing with aspects of my study: "Psychological Effects of the

Atomic Bomb in Hiroshima," *Daedalus* (1963) 92:462–497; and "On Death and Death Symbolism: The Hiroshima Disaster." *Psychiatry* (1964) 27:191–208.

2. See "Genbaku Iryōhō no Kaisei Jisshi ni tsuite" (Concerning the Enforcement of the Atomic Bomb Medical Treatment Law of August 1, 1960) (published by the Hiroshima City Office).

3. "Reason, Rearmament and Peace: Japan's Struggles with a Universal Dilemma," *Asian Survey* (January, 1962); and in abridged translation, "Risei, Saigunbi, Heiwa: Sekaiteki Jirenma to Torikumu Nippon," *Asahi Jānaru* (July 8, 1962), 14–15.

4. See, for instance: M. Hachiya (Warner Wells, ed. and trans.), *Hiroshima Diary* (Chapel Hill: University of North Carolina Press, 1955); T. Nagai, *We of Nagasaki* (New York: Duell, Sloan and Pearce, 1951); H. Agawa, *Devil's Heritage* (Tokyo: Hokuseidō Press, 1957); A. Osada (compiler), *Children of the A-bomb* (New York: Putnam's, 1963); Robert Jungk, *Children of the Ashes* (New York: Harcourt, Brace & World, 1961); John Hersey, *Hiroshima* (New York: Bantam Books, 1959); Robert Trumbull, *Nine Who Survived Hiroshima and Nagasaki* (Tokyo and Rutland, Vt.: Charles E. Tuttle, 1957); John A. Siemes, S.J., "Hiroshima—August 6, 1945," *Bulletin of the Atomic Scientists* (1946) 1:2–6, and "Hiroshima: Eyewitness," *Saturday Review of Literature* (May 11, 1946), 24–25, 40–45; S. Imahori, *Gensuibaku Jidai* (The Age of the A- and H-Bomb) (2 vols; Tokyo: Sanichi Shobō, 1959–1960); Y. Matsuzaka (ed.), *Hiroshima Genbaku Iryōshi* (Medical History of the Hiroshima A-Bomb) (Hiroshima, 1961); Y. Ōta, *Shikabane no Machi* (*Town of Corpses*) (Tokyo: Kawade Shobō, 1955); Janis; USSBS Reports; and the large number of back issues of the *Chūgoku Shimbun*, Hiroshima's leading newspaper, which include accounts of personal A-bomb experiences.

5. See my essay "Youth and History: Individual Change in Postwar Japan," *Daedalus* (1962) 91:172–197.

CHAPTER II (*pp. 15–56*)

1. Martha Wolfenstein (*Disaster: A Psychological Essay* [Glencoe, Ill.: The Free Press, 1957], p. 26) speaks of anticipation as "a small-scale preliminary exposure on the level of imagination" which "can have an inoculating effect." Such was the situation, for instance, during the London Blitz, where, according to Melitta Schmideberg ("Some Observations on Individual Reactions to Air Raids," *International Journal of Psychoanalysis* [1942] 23:146–175), people became used to bombings and adapted to them by gradual changes in their way of life.

2. Ōta, p. 39. See also Len Giovannitti and Fred Freed, *The Decision to Drop the Bomb* (New York: Coward-McCann, 1965), pp. 40–41, 239.

3. Herbert Feis, *Japan Subdued: The Atomic Bomb and the End of the War in the Pacific* (Princeton, N.J.: Princeton University Press, 1961), p. 183. The classical document with regard to prior warning is the Franck Report of June 11, 1945. See also Alice Kimball Smith, *A Peril and a Hope: The Scientists' Movement in America 1945–47* (Chicago: University of Chicago Press, 1965); Giovannitti and Freed; Gar Alperovitz, *Atomic Diplomacy: Hiroshima and Potsdam* (New York: Simon and Schuster, 1965); and discussions by scientists in William Laurence, "Would You Make the Bomb Again?" *New York Times Magazine* (August 1, 1965), 8–9.

4. I have used the official Hiroshima records, made available at the Peace Museum, for the times of the air-raid warnings and the all-clear. These records list, in addition to the times mentioned, a warning siren at 9:22 P.M. on August 5, an all-clear at

9:30 P.M., another alert at 12:24 A.M. on August 6, an all-clear at 2:09 A.M., and a warning siren at 2:13 A.M. There has been considerable confusion about the exact time of the last all-clear. Ashley W. Oughterson and Shields Warren (*Medical Effects of the Atomic Bomb in Japan* [New York: McGraw-Hill, 1956]) give it as 7:30 A.M.; Fletcher Knebel and Charles W. Bailey (*No High Ground* [New York: Bantam Books, 1961]) as 7:13 A.M.; Janis as "less than half an hour earlier [than the dropping of the bomb]"; and Hersey, quoting a Catholic priest, as 8 A.M. Part of the confusion was between the actual all-clear and the reassuring radio announcement which came about thirty minutes later, just fifteen minutes before the bomb fell. Concerning the broadcast, Hiroshima City records say it declared that there was "No sign of enemy planes in the air" within the general Hiroshima military area; Feis (p. 109) speaks of the spotting of the two B-29s at 8 A.M., and of the broadcast which had a mixed note of warning and reassurance; and Knebel and Bailey (p. 136) report the sightings of the B-29s to have taken place at 8:06 and 8:09 A.M., without reference to a radio announcement. Whatever the discrepancy in details, the recollections of *hibakusha* were consistent in their stress upon a sense of relaxation.

5. The poem is by Jitsuzō Okuda (in Ōta, p. 180), and its Japanese version is *"Shikindan to hitani omoite kashira agureba hibashira agaru gokiro sakinaru."* The concept of the illusion of centrality is discussed in Wolfenstein, pp. 51–56.

6. For estimates of damage, casualties, and mortality, see Oughterson and Warren; W. F. Craven and J. L. Cate (eds.), *The Army Air Forces in World War II* (Vol. V), *The Pacific—Matterhorn to Nagasaki* (Chicago: University of Chicago Press, 1953); USSBS Reports, Nos. 3, 13, and 92; Matsuzaka; M. Ishida and I. Matsubayashi, "An Analysis of Early Mortality Rates Following the Atomic Bomb—Hiroshima," ABCC Technical Report 20–61 (Hiroshima and Nagasaki, 1961); S. Nagaoka, *Hiroshima Under Atomic Bomb Attack* (Peace Memorial Museum, n.d.); and "Hiroshima: Official Brochure Produced by Hiroshima City Hall" (based largely upon previously mentioned sources). Concerning mortality, Oughterson and Warren estimate 64,000, believed to be accurate within ±10 per cent; K. Shimizu (in Matsuzaka) "more than 200,000"; Nagaoka "more than 240,000." The estimate of about 78,000 is given by a large number of American and Japanese sources, but one also frequently sees estimates of "more than 100,000." Much depends upon how long afterward, and in conjunction with which census count, the estimate was made, as well as the manner in which military fatalities are taken into account. Significantly, and perhaps not surprisingly, American estimates tend to be on the whole lower than the Japanese. Casualties among medical personnel are particularly striking: 270 of 298 of the doctors in Hiroshima were killed, as were 1,645 of 1,780 nurses; and 42 of 45 hospitals were destroyed or rendered useless (Craven and Cate, pp. 722–723).

7. Ōta, p. 63.

8. Hachiya, p. 54.

9. *Ibid.*, pp. 4, 5, 37. Only when the hospital went up in flames was "the uncanny stillness broken."

10. Ōta, p. 63.

11. Hachiya, p. 31.

12. See Erik H. Erikson, "The Problem of Ego Identity," *Journal of the American Psychoanalytic Association* (1955) 3:447–466; Martin Grotjahn, "Ego Identity and the Fear of Death and Dying," *Journal of the Hillside Hospital* (1960) 9:147–155; Harold F. Searles, *The Nonhuman Environment* (New York: International Universities Press, 1960); and Rollo May's introduction to the volume he edited with Ernest Angel and Henri F. Ellenberger, *Existence: A New Dimension of Psychiatry and Psychology* (New York: Basic Books, 1958), pp. 55–61.

13. Hachiya, p. 29.

14. Agawa, p. 165.

15. Ōta, pp. 79, 90–91, 153–154.

16. The poem is by Kyoku Kaneyama (in *ibid.*, p. 180), and its Japanese version is "*Asakirō chimata ōishi hirameki wa tada tamayura no yume nimo nitaru.*"

17. Shinoe Shōda, *Mazushiki Gakuto no Haha* (*A Poor Student's Mother*), in *Miminari* (*Ringing in the Ears*) (Tokyo: Heibonsha, 1962), p. 23. It originally appeared in *Sange* (*Confession*) (published privately in Hiroshima, 1947, and said to have been printed at a prison).

18. But Wolfenstein (pp. 57–64) emphasizes that "the feeling of abandonment" is universally characteristic for disaster victims.

19. Ōta, pp. 73, 84–85, 129. Father Siemes ("Hiroshima—August 6, 1945") also comments upon the absence of Japanese initiative in helping victims.

20. Wolfenstein, pp. 189–198.

21. I have discussed these conflicts in Western missionaries to China in *Thought Reform and the Psychology of Totalism: A Study of "Brainwashing" in China* (New York: Norton, 1961). Among them, the urge to gain acceptance within Chinese society—to become "Chinese"—could greatly increase their susceptibility to "thought reform." See especially Chapters 7 and 12.

22. Wolfenstein, p. 189.

23. Ōta, p. 154.

24. Nagai, pp. 180–181. The additional quotations which follow are from pp. 181 and 182.

25. Hachiya, pp. 15–16.

26. Shoji Inoguchi, "Funerals," in Chitomi Ōma *et al.* (eds.), *Nihon Minzo-kugaku Taikei* (An Outline of the Ethnological Study of Japan) (Tokyo: Heibonsha, 1959), Vol. 4.

27. Reported by a White Russian *hibakusha* in an interview conducted by the USSBS (October, 1945) and later made available to me through the courtesy of Mr. S. Paul Johnston, who had been a member of the interviewing unit. Father Siemes corroborates this impression ("Hiroshima—August 6, 1945"), telling how he and his foreign missionary colleagues were reluctant to go into the center of the city "because we thought that the population was greatly perturbed and that it might take revenge upon any foreigners which they might consider spiteful onlookers of their misfortune, or even spies."

28. Anthony F. C. Wallace first expressed this concept in *Tornado in Worcester: An Exploratory Study of Individual and Community Behavior in an Extreme Situation* (Washington, D.C.: Committee on Disaster Studies, Disaster Study No. 3, National Academy of Sciences–National Research Council, Publication No. 392, 1956), pp. 109–141. It is further elaborated in Wolfenstein, pp. 77–84.

29. The comment was made by Rollo May.

30. Ōta, pp. 152, 218.

CHAPTER III (*pp. 57–102*)

1. See Oughterson and Warren; discussion by Stafford L. Warren in *Proceedings of First Conference on Long-Range Biomedical and Psychosocial Effects of Nuclear War*, sponsored by the Interdisciplinary Communications Program of the New York Academy of Sciences (in press); Matsuzaka; Hachiya. Oughterson and Warren and other authors demonstrate statistically that the great majority of cases of radiation effects occurred within the two-thousand-meter radius, depending partly upon degree

of shielding. But this was not understood at the time. Nor has it eliminated subsequent fears of aftereffects in survivors exposed at greater distances.

2. Ōta, p. 210.

3. *Ibid.*, p. 146.

4. *Ibid.*, pp. 37, 144, 152, 195.

5. Hachiya, p. 94.

6. The first two quotations are from interviews with *hibakusha*. The third is from Ōta (p. 150), as is the next passage. Miss Ōta makes clear that this "law of compensation" was supported by medical opinion. She quotes a statement made by Dr. Masao Tsuzuki (Japan's leading authority on radiation at the time, and the man given initial responsibility for investigating the bomb's medical effects) from a newspaper article published in mid-September, and another made to her in person by a physician-friend, to the effect that severe burns helped one get rid of radioactive substance by serving as avenues of exit from the body. But the principle seems highly dubious, and did not find later scientific support.

7. Ōta, p. 196.

8. Wolfenstein, pp. 151–162.

9. *Ibid.*, p. 153.

10. The Atomic Bomb Casualty Commission studies find such residual radiation to have been "negligible" (*ABCC Annual Report* 1957–58, pp. 18–21); while studies conducted at the Research Institute for Nuclear Medicine and Biology at Hiroshima University suggest significant later radiation effects in people who entered the city within the first few days after the bomb fell (*Journal of the Hiroshima Medical Association* [1964] 17 [6]; 566–576). And, as already stated, eligibility for medical and economic benefits is legally granted to those who came into the city within two weeks after the bomb fell, or who came into physical contact with A-bomb victims through rescue work.

11. Hachiya, pp. 65–66.

12. Dr. Tsuzuki was quoted in the *Chūgoku Shimbun*, September 10, 1945; all other quotations are from Chicago newspapers (*Sun, Daily News, Herald-American*) of August, 1945, especially August 7, 8, and 9.

13. Ōta, p. 152. The original passage is not entirely clear, but it does seem to suggest that these pessimistic medical impressions created a psychological state which could itself accelerate the process of dying.

14. Descriptions of these and other features of the early post-bomb environment can be found in Hachiya; Oughterson and Warren; Matsuzaka; Imahori; Jungk.

15. See Hachiya, pp. 21, 36–37, 57, 63, 65–66, 69–70, 97–99, 107–109, 125. Dr. Hachiya also describes (pp. 158–159) the dramatic scene of the lectures: the small audience ("A few had undoubtedly been prevented from coming because of rain, but the poor attendance was really because there were not enough doctors left in Hiroshima to make a showing"); their mutual greetings ("We congratulated each other on being alive"); the impressive figure of Professor Tsuzuki in particular, with his academic and military authority ("He faced us, erect and precise, attired in a neat khaki uniform and leggings"); all taking place within the ruins of a bank ("The scorched, blackened walls made an appropriate background for his discourse on the atom bomb").

16. Ōta, p. 217.

17. See *Chūgoku Shimbun* series (October 6–December 7, 1959) on Hiroshima postwar literary history.

18. Hachiya, p. 48. Psychological currents other than identification were, of course, also at play in this kind of scene, as I shall later suggest.

19. See David Irving, *The Virus House* (London: William Kimber, 1967), pp. 266, 284.

20. Ōta, pp. 136–137.

21. *Ibid.*, pp. 123–124.

22. *Ibid.*, p. 117.

23. See Susanne K. Langer, *Philosophy in a New Key* (New York: Mentor, 1959), pp. 33–54.

24. This is consistent with Janis' opinion (based on USSBS Reports), as well as with many observations made by others during the acute phase of severe disasters.

25. Robert Lifton, "Home by Ship: Reaction Patterns of American Prisoners of War Repatriated from North Korea," *American Journal of Psychiatry* (1954) 110:732–739.

26. Quoted in Jungk, p. 55.

27. From an article in the *Chūgoku Shimbun*, June 27, 1946. For descriptions of the immediate post-bomb period, see Imahori; Jungk; and many additional articles in the *Chūgoku Shimbun*.

28. Ruth Benedict (*The Chrysanthemum and the Sword* [Boston: Houghton Mifflin, 1946]) emphasized the element of obligation, while L. Takeo Doi ("Giri-Ninjō: An Interpretation," *Psychologia* [1966] 9:7–11) has emphasized the underlying element of dependency. Important here, however, is the re-establishment of a sense of inner order encompassing both.

29. Ōta, pp. 154–155, 175, 179.

CHAPTER IV (*pp. 103–163*)

1. The most extensive studies of delayed physical aftereffects of radiation have been made by the Atomic Bomb Casualty Commission, originally an official American institution, but now functioning as a Cooperative Research Agency of the U.S. National Academy of Sciences–National Research Council and the Japanese National Institute of Health of the Ministry of Health and Welfare, with funds provided by the U.S. Atomic Energy Commission, the Japanese National Institute of Health, and the U.S. Public Health Service. The studies are published in "Medical Findings and Methodology of Studies by the Atomic Bomb Casualty Commission on Atomic Bomb Survivors in Hiroshima and Nagasaki," in *The Use of Vital and Health Statistics for Genetic and Radiation Studies, Proceedings* of the Seminar Sponsored by the United Nations and the World Health Organization, held in Geneva, September 5–9, 1960, A/AC.82/Seminar (New York: United Nations, 1962), pp. 77–100. A sizable program also exists at the Hiroshima University Research Institute for Nuclear Medicine and Biology, as reported in the Institute's yearly *Proceedings*, some of them summarized in English. See also J. W. Hollingsworth, "Delayed Radiation Effects in Survivors of the Atomic Bombings," *New England Journal of Medicine* (September 8, 1960) 263:381–487; "Bibliography of Publications Concerning the Effects of Nuclear Explosions," *Journal of the Hiroshima Medical Association*; and Matsuzaka. Concerning the problem of leukemia, see also A. B. Brill, M. Tomonaga, and R. M. Heyssel, "Leukemia in Man Following Exposure to Ionizing Radiation," *Annals of Internal Medicine* (1962) 56:590–609; and S. Watanabe, "On the Incidence of Leukemias in Hiroshima During the Past Fifteen Years From 1946–1960," *Journal of Radiation Research* (1961) 2:131–140 (in English).

2. Betty Jean Lifton, "A Thousand Cranes," *The Horn Book Magazine* (April, 1963); and Jungk.

3. The evidence is especially strong in the case of thyroid cancer. See Edward L. Socolow, "Thyroid Carcinoma in Man after Exposure to Ionizing Radiation: A Summary of the Findings in Hiroshima and Nagasaki," *New England Journal of Medicine* (1963) 268:406–410; and Dorothy W. Hollingsworth, Howard B. Hamilton, H. Tamagaki, and Gilbert W. Beebe, "Thyroid Disease: A Study in Hiroshima, Japan," *Medicine* (1963) 42:47–71. But in a more general statement Zeldis, Jablon, and Ishida conclude that "data thus far analyzed are suggestive that a carcinogenic effect is apparent under the conditions of radiation exposure that occurred in Hiroshima," adding that this effect "is thus far small" ("Current status of ABCC-NIH [Japanese National Institute of Health] studies of carcinogenesis in Hiroshima and Nagasaki," *Annals* of the New York Academy of Sciences [1964] 114:225–240).

4. The most extensive work on these genetic problems has been done by James V. Neel and W. O. Schull. See their "Radiation and Sex Ratio in Man: Sex Ratio among Children of Atomic Bombings Suggests Induced Sex-Linked Lethal Mutations," *Science* (1958), 128:343–348; and *The Effect of Exposure to the Atomic Bomb on Pregnancy Termination in Hiroshima and Nagasaki* (Washington, D.C.: National Academy of Sciences—National Research Council, U.S. Government Printing Office, 1956). See also Schull, Neel, and Hashizume, "Some Further Observations on the Sex Ratio of Infants Born to Survivors of the Atomic Bombs of Hiroshima and Nagasaki," ABCC Technical Report 13–65 (Hiroshima, 1965). Belief in the possibility of an increase in various forms of congenital malformations in offspring of survivors has been stimulated by the work of I. Hayashi at Nagasaki University, as reported in his "Pathological Research on Influences of Atomic Bomb Exposure upon Fetal Development" (English reprint, n.d.); Dr. Hayashi, in summarizing his material, cautions that "one hesitates to give any concrete statement about the effect of the atomic bomb radiation [upon] the growth of fetal life, based on the data available in this paper."

5. J. W. Hollingsworth, former medical director of ABCC, reported this impression at a psychiatric research seminar at Yale University in October, 1962—based upon ABCC Technical Report 11–61: Adult Health Study, Hiroshima, Preliminary Report, 1958–59, p. 15, which he compiled with Paul S. Anderson, Jr.

6. T. Misao (note I, 1, *supra*).

7. George L. Engel, "A United Concept of Health and Disease," *Perspectives in Biology and Medicine* (1960) 3:459–485, 460.

8. Greene. Summary discussion of Conference on Psychophysiological Aspects of Cancer, New York City, April 6, 1965, morning session. See, in addition, his two papers on "Role of a Vicarious Object in the Adaptation to Object Loss," *Psychosomatic Medicine* (1958) 20:344–350, and (1959) 21:438–447.

9. This impression was also expressed by Dr. Hollingsworth at the Yale research seminar mentioned above, though the specific problem has not been systematically studied.

10. See M. Konuma, M. Furutani, and S. Kubo, "On Diencephalic Aftereffects in Atomic Bomb Exposure," *Nihon Iji Shimpō* (Japanese Medical Journal) (1954) 154:5–12; and another study, by the members of the Department of Neuropsychiatry of Hiroshima University Medical School under the direction of Professor Konuma, "Neuropsychiatric Case Studies on Atomic Bomb Victims in Hiroshima," in *Research on the Effects and Influences of the Nuclear Explosions*.

11. See S. Tsuiki, *et al.*, "Psychiatric Investigations on A-bomb Exposed People" and "Electroencephalographic Studies on Neurotic Patients Among A-bomb Exposed People," both in *Nagasaki Igakkai Zasshi*, Special Issue (1958) 33:637–639, 640–646 (English summaries).

12. See S. Tsuiki and A. Ikegami, "Personality Tests on Atomic Bomb Exposed Children" (English reprint, n.d.).

13. See, for instance, Theodore Lidz, Stephen Fleck, and Alice R. Cornelison, *Schizophrenia and the Family* (New York: International Universities Press, 1965); and also the work of Lyman Wynne and his associates at the National Institute of Mental Health.

14. The newspaper articles quoted in this section were all translated by the staff of the ABCC. The only substantial change I have made in the translations is the rendering of *genbakushō* as "A-bomb disease" rather than "A-bomb sickness," though either can be used.

15. The discussion of the question of medical benefits is based upon regulations published by the Hiroshima City Office (especially "Genbaku Iryōhō no Kaisei . . ." (note I, 2, *supra*) as well as upon extensive discussions of the problems involved with officials responsible for administering the law and physicians who deal with its everyday medical and psychological ramifications.

16. Y. Sugisaki and K. Sakuma, "Genbaku Hibakusha no Hōshasenshōsha ni yoru Chihatsusei Eikyō ni tsuite ABCC ni Hanron shi, awasete Genbakushō Taisaku no Kagakuteki Kiso o Kōsatsu suru," *Gensuibaku Higai Hakusho: Kakusareta Shinjitsu* (Objections to the ABCC Concerning Delayed Radiation Effects upon Those Exposed to the Atomic Bomb, and Observations on the Scientific Basis for Measurements in Dealing with A-Bomb Disease), in Technical Committee of the Japan Council Against Atomic and Hydrogen Bombs (eds.), *White Paper on Atomic and Hydrogen Bomb Damage: The Hidden Truth* (Tokyo: Nippon Hyōronshinsha, 1961).

17. "The Status of the Medical Program at ABCC" (January, 1963, mimeographed).

18. See, for instance, Gerald Holton, "Presuppositions in the Constructions of Theories," in Harry Woolf (ed.), *Science as a Cultural Force* (Baltimore: The Johns Hopkins Press, 1964); and Lancelot Law White, *The Next Development in Man* (New York: Mentor, 1950).

19. Engel, pp. 459–460, 462.

20. Stewart Wolf, "Disease as a Way of Life: Neural Integration in Systemic Pathology," *Perspectives in Biology and Medicine* (1961) 4:288–305, 300, 303.

21. Engel, pp. 463, 470, 471–472.

22. Greene (note 8, *supra*).

CHAPTER V (*pp. 165–208*)

1. Nakano (in "Genbaku to Hiroshima") gives evidence for this and discusses various social and psychological problems *hibakusha* face. See also Imahori; Osada.

2. Quotation and statistics from U. Fujishima, K. Maruyama, and H. Murakami, "Hiroshima Sono-go Jūsannen" (Hiroshima: Thirteen Years Later), *Chūō Kōron* (a leading monthly magazine) (August, 1958).

3. USSBS interview protocol (see note II, 27, *supra*).

4. Oughterson and Warren, p. 12.

5. See M. A. Block and M. Tsuzuki, "Observations on Burn Scars Sustained by Atomic Bomb Survivors," *American Journal of Surgery* (1948), 75:417–434; W. Wells and N. Tsukifuji, "Scars Remaining in Atomic Bomb Survivors," *Surgery, Gynecology, and Obstetrics* (1952) 95:129–141; as well as discussions of original burns in Oughterson and Warren.

6. See Harold R. Isaacs, *India's Ex-Untouchables* (New York: John Day, 1965), p. 35.

7. Many parallels can be made with the American Negro. See especially Erik H. Erikson, "The Concept of Identity in Race Relations: Notes and Queries," *Daedalus* (Winter 1966), 145–171. See also the writings of Robert Coles, including "Serpents and Doves: Non-Violent Youth in the South," in Erikson (ed.), *Youth: Change and Challenge* (New York: Basic Books, 1963), pp. 188–216, and "It's the Same, But It's Different," *Daedalus* (Fall 1965), 1107–1132. One is, in fact, struck by the common psychological denominators of all victimization.

8. I have elsewhere discussed the *sense* of immortality as a general psychic need, as a feeling of continuous relationship, over time and space, to the various elements of life ("On Death and Death Symbolism . . ."; note I, 1, *supra*).

9. See "Summary of A-Bomb Casualties and Medical Aid Projects for Bomb Sufferers in Hiroshima" (Hiroshima City Office, August 1, 1962, mimeographed [in English]). City officials gave similar figures in talks I had with them.

10. Interviews with *hibakusha* leaders in Tokyo were conducted on my behalf by Mrs. Kyōko Ishikure.

11. L. Takeo Doi, "Jibun to Amaeru no Seishin Byōri" (The Psychopathology of the Self and Amaeru), *Seishin Shinkei Gaku Zasshi* (Journal of Neuropsychiatry) (1960) 61:149–162; and "Personality Structure," in R. J. Smith and R. K. Beardsley, eds., *Japanese Culture: Its Development and Characteristics* (Chicago: Aldine, 1962). See also Lifton, "Youth and History."

12. N. Konishi, "Hiroshima no Kawa" (Rivers of Hiroshima), *Sekai* (August, 1964).

13. From "Little Gidding," part I, in *Four Quartets* (London: Faber paper-covered editions, 1963), p. 51.

14. This impression tended to be corroborated by statistics on suicide among *hibakusha* between 1950 and 1965, drawing from the ABCC Life Span Study Sample, presented by Y. S. Matsumoto and the First Conference on Long-Range Effects of Nuclear War.

CHAPTER VI (*pp.* 209–252)

1. *Moses and Montheism* (New York: Vintage, 1955), p. 139.

2. *Young Man Luther* (New York: Norton, 1958), p. 252.

3. The term was originated by James S. Tyhurst. See, for instance, "Problems of Leadership: In the Disaster Situation and in the Clinical Team," Walter Reed Army Institute of Research, Symposium on Preventive and Social Psychiatry, April 15–17, 1957 (Washington, D.C.: U.S. Government Printing Office), pp. 329–335.

4. Joseph Campbell, *The Hero With a Thousand Faces* (New York: Meridian, 1956).

5. For a general theory of this protean style in contemporary man, see my essays "Protean Man" (in *Futuribles* series [Paris, January, 1967], and *Partisan Review* [in press]), and "Woman as Knower: Some Psychohistorical Perspectives," in Lifton (ed.), *The Woman in America* (Boston: Houghton Mifflin, 1965), pp. 27–51.

6. See Ichirō Hori, "Penetration of Shamanic Elements into the History of Japanese Folk Religion," in *Festschrift for Adolf Jensen* (Frankfurt: Frobenius Institut, Wolfgang Goethe University), Vol. II, pp. 245–265.

7. For a discussion of these concepts and their interrelationships, as observed in Japanese but also as universal tendencies at times of historical change, see my "Individual Patterns in Historical Change: Imagery of Japanese Youth," *Disorders of Communication* (*Research Publications, Association for Research in Nervous and Mental Disease*) (1964) XLII: 291–306 (reprinted in *Comparative Studies in Society and History* [1964] 6:369–383).

8. See Robert Merton, *On the Shoulders of Giants* (New York: The Free Press, 1965).

CHAPTER VII (*pp. 253–315*)

1. Here, as with many other issues, I base my impressions upon both my own observations and those made by others in Hiroshima. See especially the two previously cited articles by S. Nakano, as well as his "Hiroshima ni Yomigaetta Seishun" (Revived Youth in Hiroshima) *Bungei Shunjū*, September, 1961.

2. From a series of articles entitled "Fushichō Jūyonen" (The Fourteen-Year Phoenix) *Chūgoku Shimbun*, July 22–29, 1959. Economic observations below are from the same newspaper series.

3. Fujishima *et al.*

4. "Fushichō Jūyonen."

5. For general descriptions of these trends, including details of gang warfare, see reports in the *Chūgoku Shimbun* of December 12, 1950, January 14, 1953, and July 30, 1958. An account can also be found in Jungk.

6. For descriptions of prostitution, see Jungk, pp. 57–60, as well as additional anecdotal material in research notes compiled by Kaoru Ogura.

7. "Buraku Mondai" (The Buraku Problem) (*Asahi Shimbun*, August 1, 1958. See also Jungk, pp. 46–47.

8. See, for instance, Nathan Glazer and Daniel P. Moynihan, *Beyond the Melting Pot* (Cambridge: Massachusetts Institute of Technology and Harvard University, 1963). For an extensive discussion of these and other tendencies in *burakumin*, see Hiroshi Wagatsuma and George DeVos, *The Outcast Tradition in Modern Japan: A Problem in Social Self-Identity* (manuscript prepared for the second conference on the Modernization of Japan, January 21–25, 1963); and the same authors' *Japan's Invisible Race* (University of California, in preparation).

9. *Asahi Shimbun* (Hiroshima edition), April 1, 1959.

10. *Yasurakani nemutte kudasai*
    Ayamachi wa kurikaeshimasen kara.

11. From Kaoru Ogura's translations of Hamai's diaries. Many other details of post-bomb Hiroshima experience can be found in these diaries.

12. These last three quotations are from a radio dialogue between M. Niide and S. Nagaoka, as reported in the *Chūgoku Shimbun*, August 2 and 3, 1958.

13. Rafael Steinberg, *Postscript from Hiroshima* (New York: Random House, 1966), p. 22.

14. Imahori, Vol. I, p. 187. Some of the events mentioned below are described in the same book.

15. See Josephine R. Hilgard, "Anniversary Reactions in Parents Precipitated by Children," *Psychiatry* (1953) 16:73–80; and Hilgard and Newman, "Anniversaries in Mental Illness," *Psychiatry* (1959) 22:113–121.

16. Imahori, Vol. II, pp. 144–162. For accounts of the vicissitudes of the Japanese peace movement, see also George O. Totten and T. Kawakami, "*Gensuikyō* and the Peace Movement in Japan," *Asian Survey* (1964) 4:833–841; J. Hidaka, *Nihon no Naka no Ikyō: Hishi Nihon Gensuikyō* (A Foreign Land Within Japan: The Secret History of Japan *Gensuikyō*) (Tokyo: Saikō-sha, 1963); and Lifton, "Reason, Rearmament, and Peace."

17. M. Niide in the Niide-Nagaoka dialogue.

18. See Lifton, *Thought Reform*, and "Individual Patterns in Historical Change."

19. Niide.

20. For a discussion of the Japanese reaction to the Bikini incident itself, see Herbert Passin, "Japan and the H-Bomb," *Bulletin of the Atomic Scientists,* October, 1955, 289–292.

21. Miss Tomoe Yamashiro was quoted as having used the phrase (in "Hiroshima Sono-go Jūsannen").

22. Kiyoteru Hanada, "Genshiryoku Mondai ni Taiketsusuru Nijūsseiki no Geijutsu" (Twentieth-Century Art Confronting the Problem of Atomic Energy), in *Sekai Bunka Nenkan* (Yearbook of World Culture) (Tokyo: Heibonsha, 1955).

23. May 18, 1962, p. 22.

24. Nagai, pp. 188–189. I obtained additional information about Dr. Nagai, and about Nagasaki in general, from the Nagasaki City Office and from Nagasaki *hibakusha* groups in Tokyo.

CHAPTER VIII (*pp. 317–365*)

1. Erikson, "The Concept of Identity in Race Relations."

2. Oughterson and Warren, for instance (p. 6), speak of "problems of a medical nature not hitherto encountered" and of "the then unknown effects of ionizing radiation."

3. Ōta, pp. 38, 154.

4. For other descriptions of Japanese reactions to censorship policies, see the *Chūgoku Shimbun* articles on the history of postwar Hiroshima literature; Imahori; Jungk.

5. Passin, p. 289.

6. Imahori, Vol. I, pp. 181–184.

7. *Ibid.,* p. 168.

8. See Imahori; Jungk.

9. *Chūgoku Shimbun,* May 24, 1957, and *Time,* April 8, 1957.

10. Hamai diaries.

11. This was described by Rev. Kiyoshi Tanimoto (in an article which appeared in English translation in the *Asahi Evening News,* August 19, 1959) as having occurred during an American television program, "This Is Your Life," in which the two men as well as a group of the Hiroshima Maidens appeared.

12. See Claude Eatherly and Gunther Anders, *Burning Conscience* (New York: Monthly Review Press, 1962); and William Bradford Huie, *The Hiroshima Pilot* (New York: Putnam's, 1964). The first book uncritically accepts the myth, while the second too energetically debunks it. Neither deals with the complexities surrounding the whole issue, or with the general psychological significance of the myth.

13. The first statement is quoted in Imahori (Vol. I, p. 148), the second in Fujishima *et al.,* and the third in an article in the *Asahi Shimbun,* March 9, 1959, reporting on the impressions of an American physicist from Oak Ridge during a Hiroshima visit.

14. Averill A. Liebow, "Encounter with Disaster—A Medical Diary of Hiroshima, 1945," *Yale Journal of Biology and Medicine* (1965) 38:61–239.

15. Ogura research notes, from interviews with Hiroshima doctors. Later accusations of American monopolization of medical materials are found in Imahori.

16. For public examples of such accusation, see, for instance, the November 15, 1952, issue of the magazine *Kaizō* in which a group of Japanese physicians and scientists raise direct questions to the Director of the ABCC concerning which of three purposes motivates the group's research: learning better treatment methods for atomic aftereffects, enhancing military preparedness for future atomic warfare, or

interest in pure science. See also a letter written by the Executive Director of the Hiroshima branch of the National Railway Labor Union (reprinted in *Chūgoku Shimbun*, September 22, 1954), also to the Director of ABCC, claiming that the research was being conducted under an assumption "that in the future atomic war will be waged," and that knowledge about treatment would be used "not for atomic bomb victims now in Japan but for Americans [who] might become victims in the future."

17. Ogura research notes.

18. K. Harada, "Genbaku no Kioku" (Memories of the A-Bomb), *Asahi Shimbun*, August 7, 1964.

CHAPTER IX (*pp.* 367–395)

1. Susanne K. Langer equates formulation with the symbolizing process itself, and (paraphrasing Cassirer) with "the natural ordering of our ambient as a 'world'" (*Philosophical Sketches* [New York: Mentor, 1964], p. 59). Here, as in many other concepts I use, my effort is to apply this formative-symbolic perspective within a psychological idiom. See also Lifton, "On Death and Death Symbolism."

2. See my "Woman as Knower."

3. "Mourning and Melancholia," *Standard Edition* (London: The Hogarth Press), Vol. XIV, pp. 243–258.

4. See *Daigenkai, Daijigen,* and *Shinjikan* reference works.

5. See E. Dale Saunders, *Buddhism in Japan* (Philadelphia: University of Pennsylvania Press, 1964), pp. 194–195.

6. See Harry Thomsen, *The New Religions of Japan* (Rutland, Vt., and Tokyo: Charles E. Tuttle, 1963), pp. 69–78, 72.

7. *Ibid.*, p. 101.

8. Ōta, p. 154.

CHAPTER X (*pp.* 397–450)

1. *Chūgoku Shimbun* series on Hiroshima literary history. Much of the background information in this chapter comes from these articles, as do those quotations not otherwise identified. Discussions in this chapter and the next of literary works which have not been rendered previously into English are based upon translations and summaries prepared by Kyōko Ishikure, which I have modified for the sake of clarity and precision.

2. Miyoko Shijō, "Genbaku Bungaku ni tsuite" (About A-Bomb Literature), *Chūgoku Shimbun*, January 25, 1953. This kind of debate finds parallels in controversies over "Negro literature," "proletarian literature," and "socialist realism."

3. Ineko Sada, "Ōta Yōko-san o Shinobu" (Cherishing the Memory of Yōko Ōta), *Yangu Redii* (Young Lady) January 20, 1964.

4. Ōta (1950 edition), p. 8.

5. In addition to Shijō, see Fumiko Enchi, "Ōta Yōko-san no Koto: Shin wa Yasashii Hito Kongo o Kitai Shiteita noni" (About Yōko Ōta: A Sweet-Hearted Person from Whom I Expected Much in the Future), *Asahi Shimbun*, December 12, 1963; and Taiko Hirabayashi, "Genbakushō to Tatakatte: Ōta Yōko-san o Itamu" (Having Fought A-Bomb Disease: Mourning for Yōko Ōta), *Yomiuri Shimbun*, December 12, 1963.

6. Shijō.

7. *Daigenkai*, pp. 1275, 1236, 1239.

8. In *L'Espoir* (a Japanese magazine with a French name), June, 1954.

9. *Ibid.*, pp. 59–60.
10. *Ibid.*, p. 61.
11. *Ibid.*, pp. 64–65.
12. *Ibid.*, p. 62.
13. *Ibid.*, p. 63.
14. *Ibid.*, p. 69.
15. *Ibid.*, pp. 69–70.
16. *Ibid.*, p. 67.
17. *Ibid.*, pp. 70–71.
18. *Ibid.*, p. 71.
19. Heiwaya Sannin Otoko, *Bungei Shunjū*, August 24, 1959.
20. Trans. by John M. Maki (Tokyo: The Hokuseido Press, 1957).
21. *Hachigatsu Muika* was reissued in *Shin Nippon Bungaku Zenshū*, Vol. I (Tokyo: Shūeisha, 1963); *Haru no Shiro* was reissued in 1964 (Tokyo: Shinchō-sha); *Kumo no Bohyō* (published in 1956) was reissued in *Shin Nippon Bungaku Zenshū*, Vol. I.
22. *Devil's Heritage*, pp. 3–4.
23. *Ibid.*, p. 84.
24. *Ibid.*, p. 70.
25. *Ibid.*, p. 187.
26. *Ibid.*, pp. 139–140.
27. *Ibid.*, p. 150. Remaining quotations relating to the red snapper sequence are from pp. 150–152.
28. *Ibid.*, p. 221.
29. *Ibid.*, p. 246.
30. *Sedai*, February, 1950 (issue edited by Hiroshima University Literary Group).
31. *60 + ∞*, No. 1 (May, 1960).
32. "Hi no Odori," p. 107.
33. *Ibid.*, p. 111.
34. *Ibid.*, p. 115.
35. *Ibid.*, p. 119.
36. *Ibid.*, p. 120.
37. *Ibid.*, p. 121.
38. *Ibid.*, pp. 121–122.
39. *Ibid.*, p. 133.
40. M. Ōhara, "Shi ni Arawareta Genbaku Suibaku" (The A- and H-Bomb in Poetry), in E. Yoneda (ed.), *Shishū Hiroshima* (Hiroshima Anthology) (Hiroshima: Kisetsu-sha, August, 1959). I have drawn upon Professor Ōhara's essay for much of the information below. English translations of atomic bomb poetry can be found in the August 6, 1964, and August 6, 1965, editions of *The Songs of Hiroshima: An Anthology* (both published in Hiroshima, the first by the Asano Library, and containing an introduction by Mayor Shinzō Hamai, and the second by the Y.M.C.A. Service Center, with an introduction by D. J. Enright). All poems included in this section, unless otherwise identified, are from this English anthology. In a few cases I have altered the translations slightly in order to give what seemed to be a better rendering.
41. Much of the point of view in this and the next chapter follows Miss Langer's work on symbolic transformation. See her *Philosophy in a New Key; Philosophical Sketches; Problems of Art* (New York: Scribner Library, 1957); and *Feeling and Form* (New York: Scribner's, 1953). See also Ernst Cassirer, *An Essay on Man* (New York: Doubleday Anchor, 1944).

42. The translation is from Jungk, p. 214.
43. Imahori, Vol. II, p. 10. Other quotations concerning Tōge's earlier life are also from this book.
44. A notable recent example is Yukio Mishima's *Temple of the Golden Pavilion* (New York: Alfred A. Knopf, 1959).

CHAPTER XI (*pp. 451–478*)

1. See "Fushichō Jūyonen" for a general description of dramatic (as well as other cultural) responses to the atomic bomb through the first half of 1959. Another television drama, "To Live Today" ("Kyō o Ikiru")—originally entitled "Morning Vacuum" ("Asa no Shinkū")—by Masao Yamakawa, achieved some national response when presented in November, 1959.
2. *Shingeki*, April, 1959.
3. *Ibid.*, October, 1957.
4. Langer, *Feeling and Form*, p. 413.
5. A. Alvarez, "Spellbound," *New York Review*, December 31, 1964, p. 16.
6. Ryuichi Kanō and Hajime Mizuno, *Hiroshima Nijūnen* (Hiroshima's Twenty Years) (Tokyo: Kōbundō, 1965); and Shūzō Niinobe (ed.), *Gurafu Kisha* (Graphic Reporters) (Tokyo: Yūki Shobō, 1959).
7. Notably *Hiroshima, Sensō to Toshi* (Hiroshima: War and Cities) (Tokyo: Iwanami, 1952); and Kanō and Mizuno.
8. For general descriptions of A-bomb responses on film, see particularly Donald Richie, "Mono no Aware—Hiroshima in Film," in Robert Hughes (ed.), *Film: Book Two* (New York: Grove Press, Evergreen Books, 1962), pp. 67–86. See also Anderson and Richie, *The Japanese Film* (Rutland, Vt.: Charles E. Tuttle, 1959); *Chūgoku Shimbun* Staff (eds.), *Hiroshima no Kiroku* (Records of Hiroshima) (Tokyo: Miraisha, 1966), Vol. III; and "Fushichō Jūyonen." I was able to arrange to see most of the films mentioned in this chapter, mainly through special showings, including all of those discussed at any length.
9. Richie, p. 75.
10. *Ibid.*, p. 77.
11. Susan Sontag, "The Imagination of Disaster," *Commentary*, October, 1965, pp. 42–48.
12. Both quotations in this paragraph are from Anderson and Richie, p. 372.
13. Richie, p. 82.
14. Reproduced in book form under the same title (Tokyo: Aoki Bunko, 1953).
15. Langer, *Philosophy in a New Key*, p. 178.
16. *The Gates of Horn* (New York: Oxford University Press, 1963), p. 459, quoted in Frederick J. Hoffman, *The Mortal No* (Princeton: Princeton University Press, 1964), p. 163.
17. *Ibid.*, p. 178.
18. Hersey's critic was Dwight MacDonald, who was in turn quoted and answered by Frederick J. Hoffman (*ibid.*, pp. 174–176).
19. Masao Maruyama (Ivan Morris, ed.), *Thought and Behaviour in Modern Japanese Politics* (London: Oxford University Press, 1963), pp. 251–258.
20. I have suggested some of these artistic directions, particularly that of mockery, in "Protean Man."
21. A. Alvarez, "The Literature of the Holocaust," *Commentary*, November, 1964, pp. 65–69.
22. New York: Atheneum, 1961.
23. Trans. by Peter Wiles (New York: Harcourt, Brace & World, 1964).

24. Trans. by Richard Seaver (New York: Grove Press, 1964).

25. *Bungei*, December, 1963.

26. Kawade Shobō Shinsha, 1963.

27. Tokyo: Iwanami Shoten, 1963.

28. Tokyo: Kawade Shobō, 1965.

29. Alvarez, "The Literature of the Holocaust," pp. 65–66.

CHAPTER XII (*pp. 479–541*)

1. Francis Aidan Gasquet, *The Great Pestilence* (London: Simpkin Marshall, Hamilton, Kent, 1893), pp. 7–8. This and most other passages concerning the plague are quoted from actual witnesses, that is, from survivors of plague deaths.

2. *Ibid.*, p. 11.

3. Elie Wiesel, *Night* (New York: Hill and Wang, 1960), p. 92.

4. Campbell (note VI, 4, *supra*).

5. Ogura research notes.

6. Rawicz, p. 13.

7. Paul Chodoff, "Late Effects of the Concentration Camp Syndrome," *Archives of General Psychiatry* (1963) 8:323–333, 325.

8. Semprun, p. 126.

9. Erich Lindemann, "Symptomatology and Management of Acute Grief," *American Journal of Psychiatry* (1944) 101:141–148.

10. See Searles (note II, 12, *supra*).

11. See George R. Krupp, "The Bereavement Reaction: A Special Case of Separation Anxiety, Sociocultural Considerations," in Warner Muensterberger and Sidney Axelrod (eds.), *The Psychoanalytic Study of Society* (New York: International Universities Press, 1962), Vol. II, pp. 42–74, 45.

12. Karl Stern, "Death Within Life," *Review of Existential Psychology and Psychiatry* (1962) 2:141–144, 142.

13. Lindemann. One can observe particularly strong patterns of anticipatory mourning among such groups as parents of dying children. See, for instance, Bozeman, Orbach, and Sutherland, "Psychological Impact of Cancer and Its Treatment; III The Adaptation of Mothers to the Threatened Loss of Their Children Through Leukemia, *Cancer* (1955) 8:1–33.

14. See, for instance, C. Murray Parkes, "Effects of Bereavement on Physical and Mental Health—A Study of the Medical Records of Widows," *British Medical Journal* (1955) 8:1–33.

15. George Engel, "Is Grief a Disease?", *Psychosomatic Medicine* (1961) 23:18–22.

16. See Joseph M. Natterson and Alfred G. Knudson, "Observations Concerning Fear of Death in Fatally Ill Children and Their Mothers," *ibid.* (1960) 22:456–465.

17. Gasquet, p. 29.

18. William G. Niederland, "Psychiatric Disorders Among Persecution Victims," *Journal of Nervous and Mental Disease* (1964) 139:458–474, 468. The subsequent quotation, from Paul Friedman, is in Niederland, "The Problem of the Survivor," *Journal of the Hillside Hospital* (1961) 10:233–245, 242.

19. "Thoughts for the Times on War and Death," *Standard Edition*, Vol. XIV, p. 293.

20. Natterson and Knudson, p. 465. Other investigators have gone further and stated that "the child's death awakens one of man's deepest fears—death before fulfillment" (Albert J. Solnit and Morris Green, "The Pediatric Management of the Dying Child: Part II. The Child's Reaction to the Fear of Dying," in Albert J.

Solnit and Sally A. Province (eds.), *Modern Perspectives in Child Development* (New York: International Universities Press, 1963), pp. 217–228.

21. Avery D. Weisman and Thomas P. Hackett, "The Dying Patient" (mimeographed).

22. Gasquet, pp. 110–112.

23. "Predilection to Death: Death and Dying as a Psychiatric Problem," *Psychosomatic Medicine* (1961) 23:232–256.

24. Ella Lingens-Reiner, *Prisoners of Fear* (London: Victor Gollancz, 1948), p. 23.

25. Henry Krystal, "The Late Sequelae of Massive Psychic Trauma: The Report of the Workshop" (mimeographed), p. 27. The next two quotations are from pp. 24 and 13. In addition to Dr. Krystal's, contributions to the report were made by William Niederland, Kenneth Pitts, Marvin Hyman, William Grier, and Emanuel Tanay. My own participation in a later workshop on massive traumatization (February, 1965) in this same Wayne State University series—including exchanges with Neiderland, Krystal, Tanay, Martin Wangh, and Ulrich Venzlaff—taught me a great deal about the concentration camp experience, and confirmed my belief in the existence of unifying principles around the constellation of "the survivor."

26. *The Informed Heart* (Glencoe, Ill.: The Free Press, 1960), p. 178.

27. Wiesel, pp. 108, 113, 116.

28. Weisman and Hackett, "The Treatment of the Dying" (published in *Current Psychiatric Therapies*, 1962) (mimeographed, p. 8).

29. Arnold Van Gennep, *The Rites of Passage* (Chicago: University of Chicago Phoenix Books, 1961), pp. 160–161. See also Erwin Panofsky, *Tomb Sculpture* (New York: Abrams, 1964); and Kunio Yanagida, *Shintō to Minzokugaku* (Shinto and Folklore) (Tokyo: Meiseidō, 1943).

30. Van Gennep, p. 146.

31. Taijō Tamamuro, *Sōshiki Bukkyō* (Funeral Buddhism) (Tokyo: Daihōrinkaku, 1963), p. 80.

32. Niederland, "Psychiatric Disorders Among Persecution Victims," p. 460.

33. See Joan M. Erikson, "Eye to Eye," in Gyorgy Kepes (ed.), *The Man-Made Object* (New York: Braziller, 1966).

34. See Helen L. Lynd (*On Shame and the Search for Identity* [New York: Harcourt, Brace, 1958]), Gerhart Piers and Milton B. Singer (*Shame and Guilt* [Springfield, Ill.: Charles C. Thomas, 1953]), and George DeVos ("The Relation of Guilt Toward Parents to Achievement and Arranged Marriage Among Japanese," *Psychiatry* [1960] 23:287–301), as well as certain writings of Martin Buber and Rollo May.

35. Rawicz, p. 9.

36. Krystal and Niederland, "Clinical Observations on the 'Survivor' Syndrome" (mimeographed).

37. Anna Freud, *The Ego and the Mechanisms of Defense* (New York: International Universities Press, 1946).

38. E. Minkowski, quoted in Friedman, "Some Aspects of Concentration Camp Psychology," *American Journal of Psychiatry* (1949), 105:601–605, 602. Friedman himself speaks of the "numbness" he observed in 1947 among former concentration camp inmates held in camps for displaced persons in Cyprus.

39. Bettelheim, pp. 126–127.

40. Lifton, *Thought Reform*, especially pp. 145–151.

41. See Erikson, "Psychological Reality and Historical Actuality," in his *Insight and Responsibility* (New York: Norton, 1964).

42. Niederland, "Psychiatric Disorders," p. 463.

43. Emanuel Tanay, personal communication.

44. Bettelheim, p. 151.

45. *Survival in Auschwitz* (New York: Collier, 1961), p. 82.

46. Wiesel, p. 45.

47. Sandor Rado, "Psychodynamics and Depression from the Etiologic Point of View," in his *Psychoanalysis of Behavior* (New York: Grune and Stratton, 1956), p. 238.

48. Elliot D. Luby, "An Overview of Psychosomatic Disease," *Psychosomatics* (1963) 4:1–8, 7.

49. J. Bastiaans, *Psychosomatische Gevolgen van Onderdrukking en Verzet* (Psychosomatic Aftereffects of Persecution and Incarceration) (Amsterdam: N. V. Noord-Hollandsche Uitgevers Maatschappij, 1957) (mimeographed English summary of pp. 467–472, distributed at Wayne State University Workshop, pp. 2–3).

50. Krystal and Niederland, p. 1.

51. T. S. Nathan, L. Eitinger, and H. Z. Winnik, "A Psychiatric Study of Survivors of the Nazi Holocaust: A Study in Hospitalized Patients," *The Israel Annals of Psychiatry and Related Disciplines* (1964) 2:47–80.

52. Bettelheim, pp. 264–265. He paraphrases the story from Eugen Kogan, *The Theory and Practice of Hell* (New York: Berkeley Medallion, 1958; the original German title was *Der SS Staat*).

53. Krystal and Niederland go so far as to claim that "depression in concentration camp survivors tends to be of an agitated type."

54. Paul Chodoff, Stanford B. Friedman, and David A. Hamburg, "Stress, Defenses and Coping Behavior: Observations in Parents of Children with Malignant Disease," *American Journal of Psychiatry* (1964) 120:743–749.

55. Lindemann, p. 145.

56. *Death, Grief, and Mourning* (New York: Doubleday, 1965).

57. "My Death and Myself," *Review of Existential Psychology and Psychiatry* (1962) 2:105–116, 116.

58. "Despair and the Life of Suicide," *ibid.*, 125–139.

59. "Schizophrenia and the Inevitability of Death," *Psychiatric Quarterly* (1961) 35:631–665, 632. See also discussion of schizophrenia by Silvano Arieti in *The American Handbook of Psychiatry*, which he edited (New York: Basic Books, 1959), Vol. I, pp. 455–484.

60. Bettelheim, p. 261.

61. *Ibid.*, pp. 171–172.

62. For general studies of disaster—in addition to earlier references to Wolfenstein; Janis; and Wallace—see George W. Baker and Dwight W. Chapmen, *Man and Society in Disaster* (New York: Basic Books, 1962); "Human Behavior in Disaster: A New Field of Social Research," *The Journal of Social Issues*, Vol. 10, No. 3 (entire issue); *Field Studies of Disaster Behavior, An Inventory* (Washington, D.C.: Disaster Research Group, National Academy of Sciences–National Research Council, 1961); L. Bates, C. W. Fogleman, and Vernon J. Parenton, *The Social and Psychological Consequences of a National Disaster: A Longitudinal Study of Hurricane Audrey* (Washington, D.C.: National Academy of Sciences–National Research Council, 1963); Stewart E. Perry, Earle Silber, and Donald A. Bloch, "The Child and His Family in Disaster: A Study of the 1953 Vicksburg Tornado" (Washington, D.C.: Committee on Disaster Studies, National Academy of Sciences–National Research Council, 1956), in which the authors give specific attention to anxiety over death as well as to residual family relationships; and George H. Grosser,

Henry Wechsler, and Milton Greenblatt (eds.), *The Threat of Impending Disaster* (Cambridge: The MIT Press, 1964). See also Rue Bucher, "Blame and Hostility in Disaster," *American Journal of Sociology* (1957), 67:467–475, though the "authorities" blamed or held responsible in this article were concerned more with the maintenance of air safety, as the respondents in the investigations were those involved in or affected by plane crashes.

63. Respective references are to Jones himself, Larry Rivers, a Jewish artist and jazz musician, and Archie Shepp, a Negro jazz musician, as reported in *The New York Times*, February 10, 1965.

64. See Niederland, "The 'Miracled-up' World of Schreber's Childhood," in R. S. Eissler *et al.* (eds.), *The Psychoanalytic Study of the Child* (New York: International Universities Press, 1959), XIV, pp. 383–413, 411–412.

65. *Clinical Studies in Psychiatry* (New York: Norton, 1956), p. 146. Sullivan actually described the equation as "It is not that *I* have something wrong with me, but that *he* does something to me," and considered the "essence" of this "paranoid dynamism" to be "the transference of blame."

66. "Pseudo-homosexuality, the Paranoid Mechanism, and Paranoia," *Psychiatry* (1955) 18:163–173, 171–172.

67. Roland Kuhn, "The Attempted Murder of the Prostitute," in Rollo May (ed.), *Existence* (New York: Basic Books, 1958), pp. 365–425.

68. Hackett and Weisman, "Treatment of the Dying," p. 3.

69. Weisman and Hackett, "Predilection to Death." See also K. R. Eissler, *The Psychiatrist and the Dying Patient* (New York: International Universities Press, 1955); and Renee C. Fox, *Experiment Perilous* (Glencoe, Ill.: The Free Press, 1959).

70. The first, second, and fourth quotations are from Gasquet (pp. 12, 13, and 36). The paraphrase in the last quotation is Gasquet's. The third quotation is from William I. Langer, "The Black Death," *Scientific American* (1964) 210:112–122.

71. See Krystal and Niederland.

72. Niederland, "Psychiatric Disorders," p. 458.

73. *Crowds and Power* (New York: Viking, 1962), pp. 227, 230, 443, 448.

74. Schmideberg, p. 166.

75. "The Last Return," *Commentary*, March, 1965, pp. 43–49, 43.

76. This passage was quoted and disseminated by Yoshida Shōin, Japan's great nineteenth-century nationalist. See Bunzō Kaminaga, *Bushidō* (The Way of the Samurai) (Tokyo: Miyakoshitaiyōdō Shobō, 1943).

77. "Thoughts for the Times on War and Death," p. 289.

78. See Jun Etō, "Natsume Sōseki, A Japanese Meiji Intellectual," *American Scholar* (1965) 34:603–619.

79. The term has been used by a number of writers in other contexts. See, for instance, Albert D. Biderman, "Captivity Lore and Behavior in Captivity," in Grosser *et al.*, pp. 223–250, 243–245.

80. Melanie Klein, "Mourning and Its Relation to the Manic-Depressive States," in *Contributions to Psycho-analysis, 1921–1945* (London: The Hogarth Press and the Institute of Psycho-analysis, 1948), pp. 311–338, 321.

81. Lindemann, pp. 143, 147.

82. "A Journal of the Warsaw Ghetto," *Commentary*, November, 1965, pp. 42–58, 52 (italics added).

83. Niederland, "Psychiatric Disorders," p. 466.

84. "The Problem of Melancholia," in Rado, pp. 47–63, 49.

85. Wiesel, p. 110.

86. Rawicz, p. 10.
87. Keisuke Harada, "Genbaku no Kioku."
88. Rawicz, pp. 6, 7, 27.
89. Parkes.
90. Mervyn Shoor and Mary Helen Speed, "Delinquency as a Manifestation of the Mourning Process," *Psychiatric Quarterly* (1963) 37:1–19, 17.
91. See, for instance, Josephine R. Hilgard and Martha F. Newman, "Parental Loss by Death in Childhood as an Etiological Factor Among Schizophrenic and Alcoholic Patients Compared with a Non-patient Community Sample," *Journal of Nervous and Mental Disease* (1953) 137:14–28. See also recent compendia of work in these areas, such as Herman Feifel (ed.), *The Meaning of Death* (New York: McGraw-Hill, 1959); and Robert Fulton (ed.), *Death and Identity* (New York: Wiley, 1965).
92. W. I. Langer.
93. Weisman and Hackett, "Predilection to Death."
94. "Disease Response to Life Stress," *Journal of the American Medical Women's Association* (1965) 20:133–140, 139.
95. "A Writer's Notebook," *Encounter*, March, 1965, pp. 25–35, 29.
96. Chodoff, p. 327.
97. Chodoff, Friedman, and Hamburg, p. 747.
98. I have stated these concepts in preliminary form elsewhere ("On Death and Death Symbolism," pp. 203–210). They are influenced by the work of Joseph Campbell, *The Masks of God: Primitive Mythology* (New York: Viking, 1959), pp. 30–49, 461–472, and Kenneth Boulding, *The Image* (Ann Arbor: University of Michigan Press, 1956). They are part of a theoretical position I hope to develop further in my forthcoming volume.
99. Quoted from James Robertson, in John Bowlby, "Grief and Mourning in Infancy and Early Childhood," in R. S. Eissler *et al.*, Vol. XV, pp. 9–52. I shall not here discuss the far-reaching implications of Bowlby's work or the points of controversy surrounding it, but wish only to emphasize its relevance for earliest formulative efforts. See also by Bowlby: "Processes of Mourning," *International Journal of Psycho-analysis* (1961) 42:317–340, "Separation Anxiety," *ibid.* (1960), 41:1–25, "The Child's Tie to His Mother," *ibid.* (1958), 39:350–363, and "Childhood Mourning and its Implication for Psychiatry" (The Adolf Meyer Lecture), *American Journal of Psychiatry* (1961) 118:481–498.
100. Wiesel, "The Last Return," pp. 46–47.

APPENDIX: *KUROI AME (pp. 543–555)*

1. Japanese serialization appeared in *Shinchō*, January, 1965, through September, 1966, until August, 1965, under the title of *Mei no Kekkon (Marriage of a Niece)*. The first edition of the book *Kuroi Ame (Black Rain)* was published by Shinchō-sha (Tokyo) in 1966. An English translation being prepared by John Bester for Kōdan-sha International (Tokyo) has begun to appear serially in the *Japan Quarterly*. My summary refers mainly to the first printing of the Shinchō-sha hardcover publication, but I have also drawn upon the first installment of Mr. Bester's translation (*Japan Quarterly*, April–June, 1967), which became available to me as I was preparing this appendix, sometimes with slight modification for the purpose of psychological illustration. I am grateful to Mr. Bester and to Jun Etō and Kenzaburō Ōe for discussions of the novel and its author which provided valuable background information about both. The comments by Japanese critics are from a column by Etō in *Asahi Shimbun*, August 25, 1966; an unsigned review in *Asahi*, November 8, 1966; and an article by

Masakazu Yamazaki, "Futatabi Monogatari o Koeru Mono" (Once Again, Something which Is More than a Mere Story), *Chūō Kōron*, April 1967, pp. 280–287.

2. *Kakitsubata* (*An Iris*), in *Ibuse Masuji Zenshū* (Tokyo: Chikuma Shobō, 1965), Vol. V. So personal is this account that even a representative of the publisher, when questioned about it, could not say definitely whether it should be considered a novel or simply a memoir.

LIST OF SURVIVORS QUOTED

Abandoned mother, 42-43, 54, 65, 88, 113, 259-260, 277, 288, 298, 305

Bargirl, 173, 187, 202, 254-255, 299, 319
Boarding-house maid, 190, 374-375
Buddhist priest, 60, 94, 101, 207, 220-222, 226, 277, 383
Burakumin boy, 111, 190, 287, 299, 352, 370
Burakumin woman leader, 189-190, 195, 288, 356, 385

Civil service employee, 199, 321
Cremator, 23, 33, 55, 62, 66, 80, 91

Day laborer ("zealot-saint"), 238-252, 285, 332, 357, 384
Divorced housewife, 40-41, 64-65, 78, 81, 257-259, 354, 379-380
Domestic worker (elderly), 23, 33, 78, 196
Downtrodden woman laborer, 44, 369

Elderly Catholic nun, 297, 383-384
Elderly countrywoman, 40, 206, 373-374, 378, 490
Elderly (leading) hibakusha-poet, 95, 370-372, 446-450
Elderly housewife, 190, 387-390, 392
Elderly widow, 16, 36-37, 278, 372, 453
Electrician, 23-24, 53, 59, 78, 87, 112, 199, 260-261, 287, 295
Engineer, forty-five-year-old, 114
European priest, 16, 46, 120, 122, 166-168, 194, 299, 376-378

Female poet, 63, 122-125, 278, 298, 324, 348, 361

Grocer, 27, 32-33, 80, 87, 93, 107-108, 110, 177-180, 194, 277, 288, 298, 302, 324-325, 368

Heroic city official, 211-215, 278, 334
Hibakusha-physician, hospital director, 153-154, 161

This list is made up only of hibakusha, mainly from the seventy-five interviewed in Hiroshima but including some interviewed in Nagasaki as well.

593